Pro Tools® ALL-IN-ONE FOR DUMMIES® 3RD EDITION

by Jeff Strong

WILEY

John Wiley & Sons, Inc.

Pro Tools® All-in-One For Dummies®, 3rd Edition

Published by
John Wiley & Sons, Inc.
111 River Street
Hoboken, NJ 07030-5774

www.wiley.com

WILEY

About the Author

Jeff Strong, the author of *Home Recording For Musicians For Dummies,* is President of the Strong Institute (www.stronginstitute.com) and founder of Brain Shift Radio (www.brainshiftradio.com). Jeff graduated from the Percussion Institute of Technology at the Musician's Institute in Los Angeles in 1983, and has worked in or owned a recording studio since 1985. He has released over three dozen commercially available CDs and recorded hundreds of tracks for Brain Shift Radio using the techniques found this in book.

Dedication

I am especially grateful for the love and support of my wife Beth and my daughter Tovah, who never cease to amaze me with their capacity to endure non-stop recording talk.

Author's Acknowledgments

This book wouldn't have happened without the inspiration and vision of executive editor Steve Hayes. This is my fifth book with Steve; this one was just as much fun to do as the others.

Books, by nature, are a team effort and this book is the result of an extremely talented and dedicated team of professionals: project editor Blair Pottenger, who kept this book on track with his attention to detail and exceptional editorial skills; copy editor Barry Childs-Helton, who cleaned up my writing and helped me look like I actually know how to write; and technical editor Chris Cosgrove, who offered many excellent insights and ideas to improve this book. I'm indebted to you all.

Publisher's Acknowledgments

We're proud of this book; please send us your comments at `http://dummies.custhelp.com`. For other comments, please contact our Customer Care Department within the U.S. at 877-762-2974, outside the U.S. at 317-572-3993, or fax 317-572-4002.

Some of the people who helped bring this book to market include the following:

Acquisitions and Editorial

Project Editor: Blair J. Pottenger

Executive Editor: Steve Hayes

Senior Copy Editor: Barry Childs-Helton

Technical Editor: Chris Cosgrove

Editorial Manager: Kevin Kirschner

Editorial Assistant: Amanda Graham, Leslie Saxman

Sr. Editorial Assistant: Cherie Case

Cover Photo: © iStockphoto.com / Chris Schmidt

Cartoons: Rich Tennant (`www.the5thwave.com`)

Composition Services

Project Coordinator: Katie Crocker

Layout and Graphics: Jennifer Creasey, Brent Savage, Christin Swinford

Proofreaders: Rebecca Denoncour, Toni Settle

Indexer: BIM Indexing & Proofreading Services

Publishing and Editorial for Technology Dummies

 Richard Swadley, Vice President and Executive Group Publisher

 Andy Cummings, Vice President and Publisher

 Mary Bednarek, Executive Acquisitions Director

 Mary C. Corder, Editorial Director

Publishing for Consumer Dummies

 Kathleen Nebenhaus, Vice President and Executive Publisher

Composition Services

 Debbie Stailey, Director of Composition Services

Table of Contents

Introduction *1*

About This Book 1
Not-So-Foolish Assumptions 2
Conventions Used in This Book.......................................2
How This Book Is Organized 3
   Book I: Home Recording Basics 3
   Book II: Getting Started Using Pro Tools 3
   Book III: Recording Audio 4
   Book IV: Editing Audio 4
   Book V: Managing MIDI 4
   Book VI: Mixing In Pro Tools 5
   Book VII: Mastering with Pro Tools 5
   Book VIII: Getting Your Music to the Masses 5
Icons Used in This Book 6
Where to Go from Here..6

Book 1: Home Recording Basics *7*

Chapter 1: Discovering What You Need.......................9

Eyeing the Big Picture..9
Piping the Music into Pro Tools 10
   Interpreting input devices 10
   Deciphering direct boxes..12
   Perusing the preamp 13
Meeting the Mixer..14
Managing the MIDI Controller.......................................16
Recognizing the Recorder 17
   Digital recorders 17
   The computer...18
Signing On to Signal Processors 23
   Equalizers (EQ) 23
   Dynamic processors...24
   Effects processors 26
Making Sense of Monitors 28
   Headphones..28
   Speakers 29
Mastering Media 30
   CD...31
   Computer files 31

Chapter 2: Getting Connected: Setting Up Your Studio **33**

Understanding Analog Connections 33
The ¼-inch analog plug 34
XLR 36
RCA 37
Delving In to Digital Connections 37
MIDI 38
AES/EBU 38
S/PDIF 39
ADAT Lightpipe 39
TDIF 40
USB 40
FireWire 41
Thunderbolt 41
Working Efficiently in Your Studio 42
Setting up your studio for comfort and efficiency 43
Taming heat and dust 45
Monitoring your monitors 45
Optimizing Your Studio 46
Sound isolation 46
Sound control 48

Chapter 3: Meeting the Mixing Board **57**

Meeting the Many Mixer Types 57
Analog mixer 58
Digital mixer 59
The computer control surface 60
Understanding Mixer Basics 61
Channel strip 61
Input jack 62
Insert jack 62
Trim knob 64
Equalization 64
Channel Auxiliary (Aux) Send knobs 64
Pre/Post switch 66
Pan knob 66
Mute switch 66
Solo switch 67
Assign switches 67
Faders 67
Routing/Busing Signals 67
Master fader 68
Sub (submix) faders 68
Solo/Mute switches 70
Control Room level knob 70
Phones knob 70

Auxiliary (Aux) Send knobs 70
Auxiliary (Aux) Return knobs 70
Aux Assign 70
Master Level meters 71
Deciphering Output Jacks 71
Master Out jack 72
Phones jack...72
Monitors jack 72
Direct Out jacks...72
Aux Return jacks 73
Making Life Easier with a Patch Bay 73

Chapter 4: MIDI and Electronic Instruments 75
Meeting MIDI 76
Perusing MIDI ports 76
Understanding MIDI channels 78
Appreciating MIDI messages 79
Managing modes 80
General MIDI 81
Getting Started with MIDI 82
Sound generators..83
Samplers..86

Chapter 5: Understanding Microphones 91
Meeting the Many Microphone Types 91
Construction types 92
Polarity patterns 98
Buying the Right Microphone for You 102
How many, what kind 103
Detailing applications..104
Partnering with preamps 106
Considering compressors 108
Preamp, compressor, and equalizer combos.......................................109
Analyzing some microphone accessories 109
Caring for Your Microphones 111
Daily care for your mics...111
Storing your mics..112

Book II: Getting Started Using Pro Tools **. 115**

Chapter 1: Configuring Your Computer. 117
Using Pro Tools on a Mac...117
Understanding Mac system requirements 117
Setting system settings 120
Installing the program..122

Using Pro Tools on a PC 122
   Understanding PC system requirements 123
   Preparing to install Pro Tools software 125
   Connecting your hardware 132
   Installing the program 132
Keeping Bugs at Bay: Good Habits to Get Into........................ 133
   Back up your data often... 133
   Back up your system drive 134

Chapter 2: Setting Up Your Hardware **135**
Making Sense of the Mbox Series 137
   Mbox Mini 137
   Mbox... 140
   Mbox Pro... 143
Exploring the Eleven Rack... 148
   Discovering the Eleven Rack input and outputs.............. 148
   Examining Eleven Rack's guitar-processing features 151
M-Audio Interfaces 152

Chapter 3: Examining Software Basics **155**
Keeping Software Straight 155
   Looking at Pro Tools versions 155
   Differences between Macs and PCs.................................. 157
Getting Set Up 157
   Setting hardware settings 157
   Playing with the Playback Engine settings 160
   The ins and outs of inputs and outputs.......................... 162
Dealing with Sessions... 165
   Creating a new session... 165
   Opening sessions 167
   Saving sessions 167
   Creating a session template 170
Getting to Know Audio and MIDI Files 171
   Understanding audio files 171
   Meeting MIDI files... 171
   Finding your session files 172

Chapter 4: Understanding the Pro Tools Windows **173**
Tackling the Transport Window... 173
   Adjusting the Transport window 174
   Basic controls... 174
   Counters.. 176
   Expanded 177
   MIDI controls 179

Examining the Edit Window 181
    Taking a look at track controls 181
    Examining edit modes 184
    Zeroing in on Zoom controls 185
    Elucidating edit tools...186
    Looking at counter displays 187
    Evaluating the Event Edit area 188
    Additional Navigation Controls..189
    Looking at lists 192
    Rulers rule!...193
Managing the Mix Window 196
    Checking out channel strips 197
    Expanding the channel strips view...................................203
    Looking at lists: The Mix Window variant 205
Working with Window Configurations 207
    Creating window configurations.......................................207
    Recalling window configurations......................................209
    Managing window configurations......................................209
    Editing window configurations..212
    Updating window configurations.......................................212
    Deleting window configurations 213

Chapter 5: Importing and Exporting Files. 215
Importing into a Session 215
    Importing audio files...215
    Importing MIDI files 220
    Importing tracks..222
Exporting from a Session..228
    Exporting audio..229
    Exporting MIDI...233
Managing Files..234
    Compacting files..234
    Deleting unwanted files..236
    Backing up data...236

Book III: Recording Audio *239*

Chapter 1: Taking Care of Tracks 241
Understanding Tracks in Pro Tools 241
    Track types 241
    Track formats 242

Setting Up Tracks 242
    Creating new tracks 242
    Duplicating tracks 243
    Naming tracks..243
    Assigning inputs and outputs..244
Altering Your View of Tracks 245
    Showing and hiding tracks..245
    Assigning track color..247
    Changing track size...248
    Moving tracks around 249
    Deleting tracks 250
Grouping Tracks 250
    Keeping track of grouped track parameters 250
    Creating groups...251
    Enabling groups...252
    Editing groups...253
    Linking edit and mix groups 254
Soloing and Muting..255
Managing Track Voices 256
    Assigning voices..257
    Setting voice priority..257
    Freeing up a voice from a track..258

Chapter 2: Miking: Getting a Great Source Sound 259
Tracing Typical Microphone Techniques 259
    Spot miking...260
    Distant miking 261
    Ambient miking 261
    Stereo miking..262
    Mic combinations 265
Taming Transients...266
    Setting your levels properly 267
    Placing mics properly...267
    Compressing carefully..268
Setting Up Your Mics: Some Suggestions 270
    Vocals..270
    Backup vocals 272
    Electric guitar 274
    Electric bass 276
    Acoustic guitars and such 277
    Drum set...279
    Hand drums 286
    Percussion 287

Chapter 3: Preparing to Record 289

Recognizing Record Modes...289
Non-Destructive Record mode....................................290
Destructive Record mode...290
Loop Record mode 290
QuickPunch Record mode..291
Dealing with Disk Allocation 292
Allocating hard drive space...292
Using multiple hard drives for audio 293
Enabling Recording 294
Record-enabling 294
Using Latch Record Enable mode................................295
Running Record Safe mode...296
Setting Levels 297
Setting a Record Range..299
Monitoring Your Tracks 299
Setting up monitoring...300
Choosing a monitor mode 300
Linking and unlinking Record and Playback faders 301
Adjusting monitoring latency.......................................301
Using low-latency monitoring......................................302
Creating a Click Track..304
Getting a click track the easy way 304
Getting a click track the hard way 305
Setting the tempo..307
Choosing the meter 307
Enabling a click track 308
Setting up tempo and meter events 308

Chapter 4: Recording Audio 311

Recording Tracks..311
Recording a single track...311
Managing multiple tracks..313
Using pre- and post-rolls..314
Playing Back Your Tracks...316
Playing recorded tracks 316
Setting scrolling options 317
Listening to playback loops..318
Using the Scrub feature...319
Doing Additional Takes...320
Starting over from scratch..320
Punching in and out...321

Loop recording...324
Using QuickPunch..325
Overdubbing: Recording additional tracks 325
Recording to playlists 326
Auditioning takes 327
Getting Rid of Unwanted Takes 332
Canceling your performance 332
Undoing your take 332
Clearing the file from the Audio Clips list......................332

Book IV: Editing Audio.. 335

Chapter 1: Audio Editing Basics 337

Understanding Pro Tools Editing 337
Nondestructive editing..338
Editing during playback 338
Getting to Know Clip Types...338
Viewing Clips 340
Selecting the track view 340
Adjusting the track height 341
Assigning clip-name and time-location displays...........342
Zooming in and out..344
Understanding Edit Modes 347
Setting grid resolution...349
Displaying grid lines 349
Working (Okay, Playing) with Playlists...................................350
Creating a new playlist 351
Duplicating a playlist 351
Deleting a playlist 351
Renaming playlists 352
Choosing playlists...352
Using the Audio Clips List 352
Selecting clips..353
Using the Audio Clips list drop-down menu...................353
Displaying clip information 355
Managing Undos 355
Setting levels of Undo..355
Performing Undos 356
Knowing when you can no longer Undo 357

Chapter 2: Selecting Material to Edit 359

Selecting Track Material 359
Selecting part of a clip...360
Selecting across multiple tracks 362

Selecting an entire clip..362
Selecting two clips and any space between them 362
Selecting an entire track 363
Selecting all clips in all tracks 363
Selecting on the fly...363
Selecting with the Selection Indicator fields 364
Selecting objects using the Object Grabber tool.........................365
Making a selection with the Tab to Transients function 366
Making Changes to Your Selection...367
Changing a selection's length..367
Nudging selections 367
Extending selection lengths...369
Moving and extending selections between tracks.......................370
Managing Memory Locations...371
Dealing with the New Memory Location dialog box....................371
Creating memory locations 373
Getting to know the Memory Locations window.........................377
Recalling memory locations 379
Editing memory locations 380
Playing Selected Material 383
Playing your selection..383
Using pre- and post-rolls..383
Auditioning start and end points 384
Looping your selection's playback...385

Chapter 3: Getting into Editing **387**

Editing Clips 387
Creating clips..388
Healing clips 390
Placing clips in tracks..392
Using clip synch points 394
Aligning clips 396
Trimming clips 398
Moving clips 402
Locking clips...405
Quantizing clips 406
Muting/unmuting clips 407
Splitting stereo tracks 408
Examining Edit Commands..409
Using the Cut command 409
Using the Copy command 410
Clearing selections..410
Performing a paste..411
Using the Duplicate command 411
Performing a repeat..412

Chapter 4: Adding to Your Editing Palette **413**

Signing On to the Smart Tool 413
   Using the Smart tool in Waveform view 414
   Using the Smart tool in Automation view 416
Perusing the Pencil Tool 418
   Creating a copy of the original file 418
   Using the Pencil tool to redraw a waveform 419
Silencing Selections 420
   Stripping silence 420
   Inserting silence 422
Performing Fades and Crossfades 423
   Dealing with the Fades dialog box 423
   Creating crossfades 426
   Fading in and out 429
   Creating batch fades 431
Cleaning Up Your Session 433
   Consolidating selections 433
   Removing unused clips 433
   Compacting a file 434

Book V: Managing MIDI *437*

Chapter 1: Preparing to Record MIDI **439**

Setting Up Your MIDI Devices 439
   Enabling MIDI devices in Mac OS X 440
   Enabling MIDI devices in Windows 7 442
   Running MIDI Thru 443
   Managing the MIDI Input filter 444
   Quantizing your inputs 445
   Offsetting MIDI tracks 447
Getting Ready to Record 448
   Creating MIDI and instrument tracks 448
   Setting inputs, outputs, and MIDI channels 449
   Creating a click track 451

Chapter 2: Recording MIDI **455**

Recording MIDI Performances 455
   Enabling recording for MIDI and instrument tracks 455
   Setting the Wait for Note option 456
   Monitoring MIDI inputs 457
   Hearing instrument tracks 457
   Recording MIDI and instrument tracks 458

Playing Back Your Tracks 458
    Playing recorded tracks 459
    Setting scrolling options 459
    Changing sounds 459
Getting Rid of Unwanted Takes 461
    Canceling your performance 462
    Undoing your take 462
    Clearing the file from the Clips list 463
Overdubbing MIDI Performances 463
    Using MIDI Merge/Replace 463
    Punching in and out 464
    Punching MIDI on the fly 467
    Loop recording 468
Recording System-Exclusive Data 469

Chapter 3: Editing MIDI Data **473**

Working with MIDI and Instrument Tracks 473
    Taking a look at track views 473
    Selecting track material 476
    Recognizing clips 478
    Setting MIDI patches on tracks 478
Dealing with Note Chasing 479
Editing MIDI in the Edit Window 479
    Perusing the Pencil tools 479
    Custom note duration 482
    Adding MIDI events 482
    Deleting MIDI data 484
    Changing MIDI events 485
    Editing program data 488
    Changing continuous controller data 489
    Using the Smart tool 491
Exploring MIDI Events 492
    Exploring the MIDI Event List window 492
    Editing in the MIDI Event List 496

Chapter 4: Performing MIDI Operations **501**

Getting Used to the MIDI Operations Window 501
Performing MIDI Event Operations 502
    Grid/Groove Quantize 504
    Change Velocity 508
    Change Duration 509
    Transpose 511
    Select/Split Notes 511
    Input Quantize 514

Step Input...515
Restore Performance...516
Flatten Performance 517
Recognizing MIDI Real-Time Properties 518

Book VI: Mixing In Pro Tools.................................. 523

Chapter 1: Mixing Basics 525

Understanding Mixing...525
Managing Levels as You Work...526
Getting Started Mixing Your Song 527
Mixing In Pro Tools 528
    Using a control surface 528
    Using a MIDI controller 528
    Using a digital mixer 529
    Using an analog mixer 530
Using the Stereo Field 531
    Left or right..531
    Front or back...533
Adjusting Levels: Enhancing the Emotion of the Song 534
    Dynamics...535
    The arrangement...536
Tuning Your Ears...536
    Listening critically 536
    Choosing reference CDs 537
    Dealing with ear fatigue..538
    Making several versions..539

Chapter 2: Setting Up Your Mix 541

Revisiting the Mix Window..541
Getting to Know Signal Flow...542
Rounding Out Your Routing 545
    Using a Master fader...545
    Adding auxiliary inputs 546
    Inserting inserts 547
    Setting up sends 548
Accessing Output Windows 552
    Tackling Track Output windows...552
    Setting up the Send Output window......................................554
Playing with Plug-ins 555
    Real Time Plug-ins..556
    Using AudioSuite offline plug-ins 559
    Using AudioSuite plug-ins to process an audio clip 562

Processing with External Effects 562
    Creating a hardware insert 563
    Connecting your external device 563
    Routing your track 564

Chapter 3: Using Equalization 567

Exploring Equalization 567
    Parametric 567
    Low-shelf/high-shelf 568
    Low-pass/high-pass 568
Dialing In EQ 569
    Inserting an EQ plug-in in a track................................ 569
    Perusing Pro Tools EQ options 570
Equalizing Your Tracks 573
    General EQ guidelines 574
    Equalizing vocals 577
    Equalizing guitar 577
    Equalizing bass 578
    Equalizing drums 578
    Equalizing percussion 580
    Equalizing piano... 580

Chapter 4: Digging into Dynamics Processors 581

Connecting Dynamics Processors 581
Introducing Compressors... 582
    Getting to know compressor parameters 582
    Getting started using compression 584
    Using compression 585
Looking into Limiters 589
    Understanding limiter settings..................................... 589
    Setting limits with the BF76 limiter 590
Introducing Gates and Expanders 591
    Getting to know gate parameters................................. 592
    Getting started using gates 593
    Getting started using an expander 594
Detailing the De-Esser 594
Setting Up Side Chains 596
    Setting up a side chain 596
    Using a side chain 597

Chapter 5: Singling Out Signal Processors 599

Routing Your Effects 600
    Inserting effects.. 600
    Sending signals to effects... 601

Rolling Out the Reverb..602
    Seeing reverb settings..602
    Getting started using reverb 604
Detailing Delay 605
    Digging into delay settings..605
    Getting started using delay..606
Creating Chorus Effects 607

Chapter 6: Automating Your Mix **609**

Understanding Automation 609
    Audio tracks 610
    Auxiliary input tracks 610
    Instrument tracks 610
    Master fader tracks...610
    MIDI tracks 611
Accessing Automation Modes...611
Setting Automation Preferences 612
Enabling Automation..614
    Suspending or enabling automation across all tracks 614
    Suspending automation for an individual track.............................615
Writing Automation 616
    Writing automation on a track 616
    Writing plug-in automation..617
    Writing send automation 618
Viewing Automation...619
Drawing Automation 620
Thinning Automation 621
    Automatically thinning data 622
    Using the Thin command..622
Editing Automation Data 622
    Using editing commands...623
    Editing with (surprise!) the edit tools 625

Chapter 7: Making Your Mix **627**

Submixing by Recording to Tracks 627
Mixing in-the-Box...629
    Examining bounce options 629
    Performing the bounce 631
Using an External Master Deck..632

Book VII: Mastering with Pro Tools 635

Chapter 1: Mastering Basics 637

Demystifying Mastering 637
    Processing.. 638
    Sequencing... 638
    Leveling 639
Getting Ready to Master 639
Paying a Pro, or Doing It Yourself 640
Hiring a Professional Mastering Engineer 641

Chapter 2: Mastering Your Music 643

Considering General Guidelines 643
Setting Up a Mastering Session..................................... 644
Optimizing Dynamics 646
Perfecting Tonal Balance.. 648
Balancing Levels 650
Mastering Your Mix.. 651
    Making the most of your bits 651
    Settling on a sample rate..................................... 653
Sequencing Your Songs 654

Book VIII: Getting Your Music to the Masses 657

Chapter 1: Putting Your Music on CD and Vinyl 659

Getting into CD Burning.. 659
Purchasing CD-Rs 660
Recording Your Music to CD-R 661
    Dealing with diversity: Using different CD recorders.................. 661
    Burning for mass production 662
Making Multiple Copies 664
    Making copies yourself 664
    Having someone else making copies........................ 665
Pressing Vinyl 668
Promoting Your Music... 669

Chapter 2: Getting Your Music on the Internet 673

Understanding Downloadable Music Files 673
Bit rate...675
Mode..676
Creating MP3 Files 677
Choosing encoding software 677
Encoding your music 678
Setting Up Your Own Music Website 680
Checking out musician-friendly hosting services 680
Designing your site 681
Putting Your Music on a Music Host Site 682
Engaging in Social Media Networking 683
Offering Free Downloads 684
Selling Downloads 685
Streaming Audio 686
Podcasting 688
Selling Your CDs 689
Promoting Your Music...689
Connecting with an E-Mail Newsletter 690

Index *693*

Introduction

Chances are that after you became interested in recording some music, you started hearing about a great software program — Pro Tools. Maybe you read an article in which an artist said that she records with Pro Tools, or you heard that such-and-such major recording studio uses Pro Tools, or a friend told you that you need Pro Tools to record professional-quality music. Of the many great recording programs that are available, the most popular — and one of the most powerful — is Pro Tools.

Pro Tools is an audio and Musical Instrument Digital Interface (MIDI) recording program. Aside from recording audio and MIDI tracks, Pro Tools offers some of the most powerful editing functions available, allowing you to tweak your recordings to a high level of detail, clarity, and accuracy. You also get excellent mixing abilities that help you mix your tracks together, EQ (equalize) them, and apply effects. Pro Tools is a comprehensive, all-in-one program you can use to control your music from start to finish.

About This Book

Pro Tools All-in-One For Dummies, 3rd Edition, not only introduces you to Pro Tools 10 audio- and MIDI-recording software, but it also presents basic multitrack recording techniques. You find out about the many Pro Tools features and functions and ways to use this program to create the best possible recordings of your music.

This book also acquaints you with the basic audio-engineering skills needed to make high-quality recordings. These skills can save you countless hours of experimenting and give you more time to actually record your music. (What a concept!)

In this book, you can

+ Explore the Pro Tools windows and menus.

+ Get a handle on all the useful functions within Pro Tools.

+ Discover the ins and outs of using the various pieces of equipment in your studio.

+ Explore tried-and-true engineering techniques, such as microphone choice and placement.

+ Find out about multitracking, mixing, and mastering.
+ Get a chance to turn your music into complete songs and also discover how to assemble and release an album.

With this book in hand, you're on the fast track toward creating great-sounding CDs. I cut to the chase, showing you skills you can use right away. I don't bother you with tons of technical jargon or useless facts.

Not-So-Foolish Assumptions

I have to admit that when I wrote this book, I made a couple of assumptions about you, the reader. (And we all know what happens when you ASSume anything.) But what the heck, I did it anyway. First, I assume that you're interested in recording your music (or someone else's) with Pro Tools 10 software.

I also assume that you're relatively new at the recording game and not yet a seasoned professional. Of course, if you are an audio engineer — maybe making the leap from analog to digital — this book offers a great brush-up on many audio-engineering fundamentals and how they apply to the basic functions of Pro Tools. Oh, and I assume that you play a musical instrument or sing — or are at least familiar with how instruments function and how sound is produced, as well as understand some of the basics of music theory such as tempo, meter, measures, and time signature. Finally, I assume that you have some basic computer skills and know how to navigate menus, and work a mouse and qwerty keyboard.

Other than these things, I don't assume that you play a certain type of music or that you ever intend to try to make it in the music business (or even that you want to treat it as a business at all).

Conventions Used in This Book

I use certain conventions in this book to explain how to use the Pro Tools program. For example, when you choose items from the main menu, I indicate this with arrows, as in "Choose Options➪Scrolling➪No Scrolling." This is shorthand for "Click the Options menu on the main menu, mouse over the Scrolling option, and finally, click No Scrolling on the submenu."

When you need to type a number or text, I indicate this with bold: For example, type **Larry** in the Name field. I make web sites stand out a bit from the rest of the text with a monospace font, such as www.dummies.com.

Because Pro Tools is available for both Macs and PCs, I include the commands or shortcut keys for both Mac and PC when they differ. For example, press ⌘+N (Mac) or Ctrl+N (PC).

Finally, the *Windows key* is the key on a PC's keyboard (just outward from each Alt key on the bottom key row) that is labeled only with a Windows logo. This key can activate various Pro Tools features, but some older non-Microsoft keyboards don't have it. If you have a PC without a Microsoft-style keyboard and it doesn't have that pesky Windows key, don't worry: I show you other possible ways to activate the same features.

How This Book Is Organized

This desk reference is organized so that you can find the information you want quickly and easily. Each mini-book contains chapters that cover a specific part of the recording process, and I briefly describe each mini-book in the following sections.

Book 1: Home Recording Basics

Book I introduces you to the basics of home recording. Chapter 1 introduces you to the components of a home studio, explaining what everything is for. Chapter 2 shows you how to make the connections — both analog and digital — that you need when you're trying to get sound from one place to another.

Chapter 3 acquaints you with the mixing board, introducing you to its many functions. Chapter 4 demystifies MIDI and gives you practical advice on how to use this powerful communication tool to enhance your music. Chapter 5 puts you inside the world of microphones. You get a chance to understand what kinds of mics are available, how they work, and which ones work best for different situations.

Book 11: Getting Started Using Pro Tools

Book II leads you into the Pro Tools world, examining the software and the Avid hardware that you need in order to run it. Chapter 1 helps you configure your computer to run Pro Tools and walks you through installing the software on a Mac or a PC. Chapter 2 introduces you to the available Avid hardware options, provides a basic overview of many of the compatible interfaces made by M-Audio (owned by Avid), and shows you where and how to plug in everything.

Chapter 3 helps you make your hardware and software work together and introduces you to *sessions,* which are the standard building blocks of the Pro Tools song-file system. In Chapter 4, you examine the three windows in Pro Tools — Transport, Edit, and Mix — where you do most of your work. Book II finishes off with Chapter 5, which gets you up to speed on file formats and compatibility in Pro Tools. You discover ways to import and export various file types.

Book III: Recording Audio

Book III gets into the meat of actually recording music. Chapter 1 explains tracks in Pro Tools and discusses setting them up properly. Chapter 2 explores the fundamentals of getting a good source sound from microphones. You discover which mics work best for certain instruments and how to place those microphones for the best sound.

Chapter 3 helps you get ready to record your first track. You discover how to set levels, enable recording, and monitor your input signals so that you can hear yourself. This book ends with Chapter 4, in which you begin the process of recording single or multiple tracks in Pro Tools. Chapter 4 also shows you how to listen critically (but practically) to those tracks when you play them back.

Book IV: Editing Audio

Book IV is all about editing the audio tracks that you record. Chapter 1 explains the basics of editing audio in Pro Tools, from knowing which of the four edit modes to use on your music to using the Audio Clip list and playlists to find the material to edit. Chapter 2 gets you comfortable with selecting the material you want to edit. You find out how to change a selection and hear it before you edit it as well as how to use memory locators to move quickly from one part of your session to another.

Chapter 3 gets to the heart of editing in Pro Tools. You get used to working with *clips* (the standard onscreen representations of the music you recorded in Pro Tools), using the editing commands, and using looped material to turn your raw tracks into usable pieces. This book ends with Chapter 4, in which you step up your editing prowess by exploring the Smart tool and other advanced editing features.

Book V: Managing MIDI

Pro Tools offers full-featured MIDI functionality. In this mini-book, you get up to speed on recording and editing MIDI data in your sessions. Chapter 1 helps you set up your MIDI devices. Chapter 2 gets you started capturing

MIDI data by showing you how to create MIDI and instrument tracks and then record your performance. Chapter 3 presents the many Pro Tools editing functions that you can use to improve on your performance. Chapter 4 explores MIDI operations, those specialized commands that you can use to transform your MIDI data in numerous ways.

Book VI: Mixing In Pro Tools

Book VI helps you take your tracks and blend them to create a finished song. Chapter 1 introduces you to the process of multitrack mixing and helps you prepare yourself to mix. Chapter 2 walks you through the process of setting up your Pro Tools session for mixing. Chapter 3 details equalization (EQ) and how you can use it to make all your instruments fit together well.

Chapter 4 examines four types of dynamics processors: compressors, limiters, gates, and expanders. These processors are essential to getting your instruments to *sit in the mix* (sound good together), and this chapter helps you use them properly. Chapter 5 guides you into the world of effect processors, such as reverb and delay. These effects are useful for adding life to your productions, and this chapter shows you some ways to use them effectively.

Chapter 6 covers one of the most useful things about recording with Pro Tools: automating the elements of your mix, such as levels, panning, effects, and so on. Chapter 7 finishes off Book VI by showing you how to mix to a stereo file.

Book VII: Mastering with Pro Tools

Book VII focuses on the often-misunderstood process of mastering music. Chapter 1 details what mastering is and helps you determine whether you want to give it a try or let a professional do it for you. Chapter 2 provides a step-by-step plan to help you in the event that you want to try your hand at the mastering game.

Book VIII: Getting Your Music to the Masses

Book VIII helps you break out of your cocoon so that you can share your finished music with others. Chapter 1 covers how to choose CD-Rs and burn your music to them. You also explore the best ways to make copies of your CDs. If you're looking to cultivate an audience in cyberspace, Chapter 2 helps you make your music available on the Internet. You get a chance to format your music for Internet distribution and discover some ways to promote your band.

Icons Used in This Book

Like all *For Dummies* authors, I use a few icons to help you along your way.

This icon highlights expert advice and ideas that can help you produce better recordings.

Certain techniques are very important and deserve remembering. This icon gives you a gentle nudge to keep you on track.

This icon warns you ahead of time about instances when you could damage your equipment, your ears, or your song.

Throughout the book, this icon shows up in instances where I include technical background on certain subjects. When you see this icon, brace yourself for some dense information. Skip these if you want.

Where to Go from Here

This book is set up so that you can read it cover to cover (and progressively build on your knowledge). Or be a free spirit and jump around to read only those parts that interest you at the time. For instance, if you're getting ready to record a mix of your song and need some ideas on how to use equalization (EQ), go to Book VI, Chapter 3. If you're new to recording with Pro Tools and want to know how to set up a session, check out Book II, Chapter 3. And if you're completely new to the whole concept of home recording, start at the beginning with Book I, Chapter 1.

You know, that's not a bad idea. Starting at the beginning, I mean. That way, you can get yourself up to speed on my way of thinking. Book I, Chapter 1 can also help you understand some of what I discuss in later chapters. Wherever you start and wherever you want to go, you're in for an adventure . . .

Book I

Home Recording Basics

"Aren't you taking this world music thing a bit too far?"

Contents at a Glance

Chapter 1: Discovering What You Need........................9

Eyeing the Big Picture..9
Piping the Music into Pro Tools 10
Meeting the Mixer...14
Managing the MIDI Controller.................................16
Recognizing the Recorder 17
Signing On to Signal Processors 23
Making Sense of Monitors 28
Mastering Media 30

Chapter 2: Getting Connected: Setting Up Your Studio............33

Understanding Analog Connections..........................33
Delving In to Digital Connections 37
Working Efficiently in Your Studio 42
Optimizing Your Studio 46

Chapter 3: Meeting the Mixing Board 57

Meeting the Many Mixer Types 57
Understanding Mixer Basics 61
Routing/Busing Signals 67
Deciphering Output Jacks 71
Making Life Easier with a Patch Bay 73

Chapter 4: MIDI and Electronic Instruments....................75

Meeting MIDI 76
Getting Started with MIDI 82

Chapter 5: Understanding Microphones 91

Meeting the Many Microphone Types 91
Buying the Right Microphone for You......................102
Caring for Your Microphones 111

Chapter 1: Discovering What You Need

In This Chapter

✔ Understanding the components of a home studio

✔ Discovering how each component contributes to the final sound

*W*hether you use a PC- or Mac-based system for your Pro Tools studio, your home recording system of choice employs much of the same basic technology. In fact, your simple Pro Tools studio consists of the same basic components as a typical, million-dollar, professional studio complex.

In this chapter, you discover the purpose of each component of a home recording studio, and you also discover how each of these components relates to the quality of sound you ultimately get from your studio. This knowledge will help you to spend the right amount of money on the right stuff. (See Book II, Chapter 1 for more on purchasing gear.)

Eyeing the Big Picture

In spite of what you may surmise from this chapter — with its long list of equipment — you need only a few things to do multitrack recording with Pro Tools. This simple list comprises instruments and microphones (called *input devices*), a computer, an Avid or M-Audio audio interface or any other compatible, third-party audio interface, Pro Tools software, and monitors (speakers, to you home stereo enthusiasts). No matter how complicated your system becomes and how many pieces of gear you end up accumulating, your studio will still consist of these basic parts.

This chapter breaks down recording systems into the components they have to have, but you may not need to purchase every component separately to get a great-sounding system. Many of these components come bundled together. For example, your Avid hardware will include at least two preamps — or you may find speakers that come with a power amp inside them.

Piping the Music into Pro Tools

As you begin to build your home studio, you'll notice a long list of components — okay, go ahead and call them "extras" — lurking within the Top Five basics of your studio: input devices, computer, interface, software, and monitors. In this section, I focus on these details of input devices so you can understand just what roles they play in your system.

As you get more and more involved in recording, you'll find you can add almost any of these components to your existing system to expand and enhance what you can do.

Interpreting input devices

All your expensive recording gear is useless if you have nothing to plug in to it. This is where the input device comes into play. An *input device* is, simply, any instrument, microphone, or sound module that produces or delivers a sound to the recorder.

Instruments

An electric guitar, a bass, a synthesizer, and drum machines are typical instruments that plug in to the interface and represent most of the input devices that you use in your studio. A synthesizer and drum machine can plug directly into the Line In inputs of your interface, whereas an electric guitar or a bass needs a direct box (or its equivalent) to plug in to first. (In the case of a Avid interface, you need to use one of the inputs that has a preamp.)

A *direct box* is an intermediary device that allows you to plug your guitar directly into a mixer without going through your amp first. (For more on direct boxes, see the upcoming section, "Deciphering direct boxes.") Check out Figure 1-1 for an example of an instrument-input device.

Figure 1-1:
An instrument-input device, which you can plug right into the mixer.

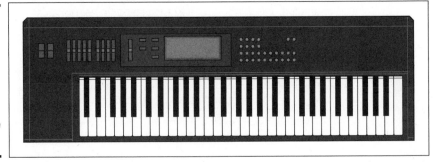

Microphone

You use a microphone (*mic*) to record the sound of a voice or a purely acoustic instrument — sound sources that, last time I checked, couldn't be plugged directly into the interface. A microphone converts sound waves into electrical energy that can be understood by the interface. I detail the several types of microphones in Book I, Chapter 5. Check out Figure 1-2 for a look at a microphone.

Figure 1-2:
Use a microphone when your instrument can't plug in to the mixer directly.

Sound modules

Sound modules are special kinds of synthesizers and/or drum machines. What makes a sound module different from a regular synthesizer or drum machine is that these contain no triggers or keys that you can play. Instead, sound modules are controlled externally by another synthesizer's keyboard or by a *Musical Instrument Digital Interface (MIDI) controller* (a specialized box designed to control MIDI instruments). Sound modules have MIDI ports (MIDI jacks) to enable you to connect them to other equipment.

Often sound modules are *rack-mountable,* meaning they have screw holes and mounting ears so you can put them into an audio component rack. Some controllers, however, are not rack-mountable; Figure 1-3, for example, shows a drum module that rests on a stand or tabletop.

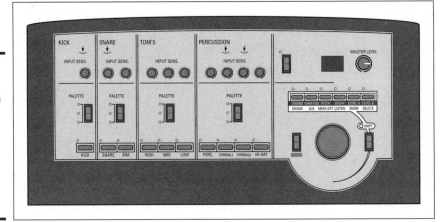

Figure 1-3:
The sound module can be plugged right into the mixer but has to be played by another source.

Deciphering direct boxes

A *direct box* (or DI box, short for Direct Induction) is used to connect a guitar or bass directly into the mixer without having to run it through an amp first. A direct box's purpose is twofold:

✦ **To change the guitar's impedance level** so that the mixer can create the best sound possible

✦ **To change the nature of the connection** from unbalanced (quarter-inch) to balanced (XLR) so that you can use a long cord without creating electrical noise between instrument and mixer

For more on cord types as well as balanced versus unbalanced signals, see Book I, Chapter 2.

For most home recordists, the main purpose of a direct box is to act as an impedance transformer. You're unlikely to need a long run of cords from your guitar to your mixer. Without a direct box changing your impedance levels, your guitar signal may sound thin or have excess noise.

Perusing the preamp

Microphones produce a lower signal level than line-level devices (synthesizers, for example); thus they need to have their signal level increased. For this purpose, you need a *preamp,* a device that boosts a microphone's output. Preamps can be internal or external, meaning they can reside within your mixer or be a separate unit that you plug in between your microphone and mixer.

The preamp is one of the most crucial elements of a recording system because using one can affect your instrument's sound significantly. Most professional recording studios have a variety of preamps to choose from, and engineers use particular preamps depending upon the type of sound they're trying to capture.

The three basic types of preamps available are solid-state, tube, and hybrid. (You can find out more about preamps in Book I, Chapter 5.)

Solid-state

Solid-state preamps use transistors to boost the level of the microphone or instrument. Top-quality (expensive) solid-state preamps are generally designed to produce a sound that's clear and accurate (George Massenburg Labs and Crane Song brands, for instance). Solid-state preamps can also be designed to add a pleasing distortion to the music (Neve and Neve-clone preamps, for example). Many recording professionals prefer the clear and accurate sound of a solid-state preamp for acoustic or classical music or any situation where capturing a very natural sound is important. The preamps in your Avid interface are solid-state. Although not as high in quality as many of the more expensive external preamps, they are certainly serviceable for most purposes and allow you to create top-quality music when you use them correctly. (I show you how to do this in Book I, Chapter 5.)

Tube

Since the beginning of the digital recording revolution, professionals have complained about the harshness of digital recording. As a result, many digital-recording pros prefer classic tube preamps because they can add warmth to the recording. This "warmth" is actually distortion, albeit a pleasing one. All-tube preamps are generally very expensive, but they're highly sought after among digital recording aficionados because of their sound. Tube preamps work well with music when you want to add *color* to the sound (that is, not produce an accurate representation of the original source sound). No wonder they show up a lot in rock and blues — and they're great for recording drums. You can also find tube preamps that are clean and open — much like the high-end solid-state preamps that I describe earlier — such as those made by Manley Labs.

Hybrid

A *hybrid preamp* contains both solid-state and tube components. Most of the inexpensive tube preamps that you find in the marketplace are actually hybrids. (These are also called *starved-plate* designs because the tubes don't run the same level of voltage as the expensive tube designs.) These types of preamps are usually designed to add the classic tube warmth to your instrument's sound. How much the sound is colored by the tubes — and how pleasing that colored sound is to the listener's ears — will depend upon the quality of the preamp. Most hybrid preamps allow you to dial in the amount of *character* (pleasing distortion) that you want.

Your Avid interface will come with one (Mbox 2 Mini), two (Mbox 2 and Mbox 2 Pro), or four (Digi 002, 003, 002 Rack, and 003 Rack) preamps. If you want to plug in more mics than the number of preamps you have — or if you want to be able to produce different sounds from your preamps — you need to buy one or more external preamps, such as the one shown in Figure 1-4.

Figure 1-4: An external preamp.

Meeting the Mixer

A *mixer* is the component you use to bring together and balance what you're recording from all those mics, instruments, effects, and other inputs; it's the heart of any recording system. Take a look at Figure 1-5. Although a mixer may seem daunting with all its knobs, buttons, sliders, and jacks, it's really one of the most interesting and versatile pieces of equipment that you'll have in your studio. With a mixer, you can control the level of the incoming signal, adjust the tonal quality of an instrument, blend the signals of two or more instruments, and do a host of other things. And don't worry; after you read through this book, you'll get the hang of all those knobs in no time.

For the Pro Tools home recordist (that's you), the mixer is usually incorporated into your computer software. (Of course, you can always use an external hardware mixer if you want.) The mixer in Pro Tools does the job well enough that you don't need an external mixer, although some people prefer having physical faders and knobs to mess with.

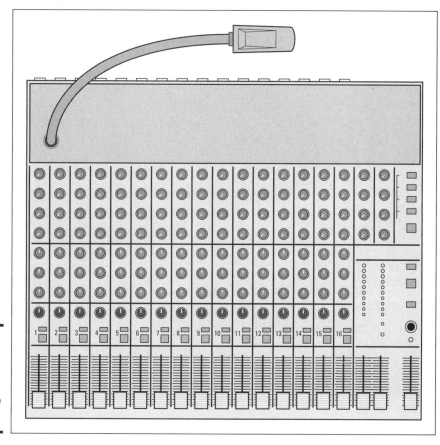

Figure 1-5:
The mixer
is the heart
of your
home studio
system.

If you're a knob-turner and like to physically touch the instrument you're playing (or, for that matter, the gadget you're tweaking), consider choosing the 003 instead of the other Avid interfaces. This unit has physical faders that link perfectly with Pro Tools LE software.

If you already have one of the other Avid interfaces (such as the Mbox or 003 Rack) and you want physical faders, you may want to add a Command|8 (as shown in Figure 1-6) when you have the cash. Third-party control surfaces are available that are compatible with Pro Tools, such as the Mackie Control Universal (by Mackie).

Figure 1-6:
A computer control surface offers you real knobs and faders and still uses the mixer that's part of your Pro Tools software.

Managing the MIDI Controller

If you're like most home recordists, you'll end up using some sort of MIDI controller in your studio. (See Book I, Chapter 4 for more about MIDI.) The purpose of this piece of equipment is to allow the various MIDI instruments to communicate and synchronize with one another.

MIDI is a protocol that musical instrument manufacturers (in a rare moment of cooperation) developed to allow one digital instrument to communicate with another. MIDI uses binary digital data, in the form of 1s and 0s, to tell an instrument to play or release a note, to change sounds, and send a host of other messages. (Discover more about MIDI in Book I, Chapter 4.)

MIDI controllers come in many shapes and sizes. The most common are computer software, keyboard, or standalone controllers. These controllers can reside within the computer (Pro Tools, for example, has MIDI capabilities), a keyboard (synthesizer), or a separate box. They enable you to either play, in real time, another instrument or to trigger another instrument with the *sequencer,* which is a MIDI program that allows you to play an instrument without actually playing (like a player piano). They just need to have MIDI capability and be connected through their MIDI ports (using MIDI cables) or a USB ports if they use one (using as USB cable).

Pro Tools software has fine MIDI capabilities, so you don't need to buy a separate MIDI controller. I recommend that you use the MIDI functions in Pro Tools before deciding to invest in another MIDI controller. I think you'll be pleased with what you can do with Pro Tools.

Recognizing the Recorder

The *recorder* is where your music actually gets, well, recorded. In Pro Tools, your recorder consists of your computer and the software. Sound becomes data and is stored as digital information, as 1s and 0s. Digital recording introduces very little noise into the final sound and can be copied without any loss in that sound quality, depending on the bit depth and sample rate at which you record, of course.

Digital recorders

A digital recorder is included as part of your Pro Tools setup. Digital recorders use two terms to describe the overall quality of the sound that they produce — sampling rate and bit depth.

Sampling rate

Sampling rate refers to the frequency at which the recorder samples the incoming sound source. When a recorder *samples* a sound, it actually takes a small snapshot of the audio signal. Typical sample rates for digital recorders are 44.1 kHz (the sample rate for audio CDs), 48 kHz, 88.2 kHz, 96 kHz (the sampling rate for DVD audio), 176.4 kHz and 192 kHz. The higher the number, the more samples are taken each second, and the closer the recorded sound is to the original.

The more times per second that a digital recorder samples the sound of the incoming signal, the more of the original sound it includes (which results in, among other things, a bigger sound file that takes up more space on your computer). These numbers are described in kHz (kilohertz) — that is, as taking place thousands of times per second. For example, when you record at 48 kHz, the sound is sampled 48,000 times every second. This sounds like an awful lot, but accurate sound requires lots of samples.

Bit depth

When you start looking at digital recorders, you'll hear jargon such as *16-bit* (the bit depth of audio CDs), *20-bit, 24-bit,* and so forth. This is the *bit depth,* which is described in terms of bits. (A *bit,* short for BInary digiT, is the basic unit of information in the binary numbering system used by computers.) The numbers 16, 20, and 24 relate to the amount of digital information that can be contained in each of those sample rates that I describe in the previous section, "Sampling rate." The higher the number, the more accurately the sound is represented; most professional audio gear now records at a 24-bit resolution. With that higher number, however, the sound takes up more of your digital storage space. This usually isn't a big deal, though, considering the low cost of huge hard drives.

Beginning in Pro Tools 10 you can also record in 32-bit floating point mode. This bit depth can be beneficial if you plan on doing a lot of processing with plug-ins (AudioSuite such as effects like reverb and chorus, gain change, and others) because it can help improve quality of this processing (due to the way it does the math). The downside is that working in this mode takes up one-third more space and computer processing power, so you need to have a powerful computer if you want to use this in sessions with a lot of tracks.

A/D and D/A converters

A third variable that affects how good a digital recorder will sound is the type of *analog-to-digital* (A/D) and *digital-to-analog* (D/A) converters that the recorder uses. The A/D and D/A converters are what actually transform the signal from an analog sound source into digital information and back again. They do this by taking small snapshots of the incoming signal (at whatever sampling rate the converter uses) and applying a number to that sample (based upon the bit depth).

For example, suppose you have a 24-bit converter with a 48-kHz sampling rate. When it senses an auditory signal — a vocal perhaps — the A/D converter takes a snapshot (measurement) of that signal 48,000 times per second (48 kHz). Each of these snapshots is given a value between –8,395,008 and +8,395,008 (24-bit resolution has 16,790,016 possible levels), which puts the vocal sound somewhere on a chart corresponding to a waveform shape. The recorder in turn reads these numbers, and the D/A converter translates these numbers back into an analog waveform again. (Pshew!)

Converting an analog signal into digital data and back again is a highly technical process. You can spend days or even weeks reading about the intricacies of audio conversion. (Check out *Principles of Digital Audio* by Ken C. Pohlmann, published by McGraw-Hill Professional; or *The Art of Digital Audio* by John Watkinson, published by Focal Press, if you're into this techy stuff.) The most important thing to remember when considering A/D and D/A converters is how well you like the sound. If the converter sounds good to you, it's a good converter.

You can buy separate A/D and D/A converters that can sound better than the one included in your Avid hardware. Depending on your ears, your engineering skills, and the style of your music, the improvement in sound of external converters can range from barely noticeable to mind-blowing. Before you spend any money on external converters, though, I highly recommend working on your skills as a songwriter, musician, and engineer.

The computer

No matter which platform of computer you choose (Mac or PC), the stuff you find inside your computer plays a major role in determining how smoothly (or how less than smoothly) your Pro Tools system runs. (Book II, Chapter 1 details the best computer setups and needed specs for Pro Tools.)

To set up a Pro Tools computer, you need several things:

+ **A computer (preferably with a speedy processor)**
+ **Bunches (BIG bunches) of memory**
+ **Dual hard drives**
+ **An audio interface**

    If you use Pro Tools 10, you can use any audio interface — but if you use an earlier version, you need Avid or M-Audio hardware.

+ **The software (Pro Tools, of course)**

If you can afford it, get a dedicated computer — one specifically for recording audio — because running other types of applications (home finance, word processors, or video games) can cause problems with your audio applications and reduce the stability of your system.

The following list clues you in on the various pieces of hardware that you find in your computer:

+ **The CPU:** The *CPU* (processor) is the heart of your computer studio. The speed of your CPU ultimately dictates just how well any program runs on it. As a general rule, for audio, get the fastest processor that you can afford. For most audio software, you need *at least* a Pentium IV for the PC or a G4 for Mac.

Because computer hardware is always changing and nearly unlimited options are available for the different components you find on a computer (especially on a PC), I strongly recommend that you consult the Avid compatibility pages at its web site before you buy a computer. Or, if you already have a computer, first check whether it's compatible:

a. *Find compatibility information at*

    ```
    http://avid.custkb.com/avid/app/selfservice/search.
        jsp?DocId=353265Avid
    ```

b. *Choose your version of Pro Tools and hardware or OS type from the drop-down menus.*

If you own a PC and have no idea what's in it, use PC Wizard to find out what you have and compare it against the requirements for running Pro Tools. You can download PC Wizard by going to `www.cpuid.org/pcwizard.php`.

+ **Memory:** Computer-based audio programs and all their associated plug-ins are RAM (random-access memory) hogs. My advice: Get a lot of RAM. Okay, that's not very specific, but how much you really need depends on your recording style. If you do a lot of audio tracks and want reverb or some effect on each track, you need more RAM (and a faster processor).

Pro Tools recommends a minimum of 2GB of RAM for basic operation, but you should really get a lot more, especially if you're using the DV Toolkit or Music Production Toolkit options available for your system. In this case Avid recommends at least 4GB of RAM.

Regardless of the platform you choose (PC or Mac), keep in mind that you can never have too fast a processor or too much memory.

✦ **The hard drives:** To record audio, be sure you get the right types of hard drives. Notice how I said hard *drives* (plural). Yep, you should get more than one if you want to record more than a few tracks of audio. You want one hard drive to hold all the software and the operating system — and the second drive just for audio data. Having two drives greatly increases the likelihood that your system remains stable and doesn't crash on you, especially if you try to run 16 or more tracks.

Choose your hard drives wisely. For the software hard drive, you can get away with a stock drive (usually the one that comes with your computer). For the audio, though, you need a drive that can handle the demands of transferring audio data at high speed. The main things you want to look for are spindle speed, seek time, and buffer size:

- *Spindle speed:* Also called *rotational speed,* this is the rate at which the hard drive spins. For the most part, a 7,200-rpm drive will work well for recording and playing back audio.

- *Seek time:* This is the amount of time the drive takes to find the data stored on it. You want an average seek time under 10 milliseconds (ms).

- *Buffer size:* Often called *cache buffers,* these memory units store data while it's being transferred. You want a buffer size of at least 2MB.

As for the size of the hard drive — again, bigger is better, at least in the audio drive where you store your music. For the core system drive, you can get by with a 60GB drive; for the audio, 120GB is still pretty conservative because audio data can take up a ton of space. For example, a 5-minute song with 16 tracks recorded at a 24-bit resolution and 44.1-kHz bandwidth takes up about 600MB of hard-drive space (about 7.5MB per track minute). Recording at 96-kHz bandwidth takes up about 20MB per track minute.

The track count that your system can handle is directly related to the speed of your hard drive: The faster the drive, the more tracks you can record and play back at once. (Of course, the type of drive you get determines how large a role your processor plays.) My current drives are Seagate Barracuda 7,200 3Gb/s 1.5TB with a 8.5-ms seek time and 32MB cache buffer. (These currently cost about $80.) I've also had good luck with Western Digital drives (such as a 1TB Caviar SATA III; 7,200-rpm drive with 32GB cache, roughly $60).

You may also want to add a third hard drive so you can back up your data. I usually buy a duplicate to my recording drive and transfer my work each day. As computer experts often say, "Your data doesn't exist if it doesn't exist in at least two places." If you prefer not to have a third hard drive, you can burn your data to DVDs or even use an online backup or storage service such as `adrive.com`, `mozy.com`, or `carbonite.com` (you can find more by doing an Internet search for "online data storage").

You can use internal IDE/ATA and SATA drives as well as external FireWire or FireWire 800 drives for recording audio with Pro Tools. However, you cannot use USB 2.0 drives: For some reason, they are slower than FireWire drives in real-world testing.

Getting the sound in and out

After you have a computer with enough speed and muscle (see the previous section), you need the appropriate hardware to get the sound in and out of it. Traditionally (if there can be traditions in such a new technology), you needed a sound card — also called a *PCI card* because it fits in the PCI (Peripheral Component Interface) slot in your computer. You also needed an audio interface, which allowed you to get the sound from your mixer or preamp to the sound card. This is not the case anymore.

Currently, audio can be brought in and out of a computer in several ways:

✦ **Through a PCI card connected to your computer's PCI slot:** No current the Avid interface uses a PCI card. However, several of the M-Audio and third-party interfaces use PCI cards to connect with your computer. These use a sound card that installs in your computer and may or may not have a separate box that houses the converters, inputs, and outputs.

✦ **Through an interface connected to the USB port:** Most of Avid's audio interfaces employ USB connectivity. These include the Mbox 2, Mbox 2 Mini, and all of the newer M-Audio hardware. USB has proven to be a robust format and with the new USB 3 standard, transfer rates are fast enough to handle all the data you need to run multiple inputs and outputs without the latency issues that used to limit the value of the old USB 1.1 standard for recording.

✦ **Through your FireWire port:** The Mbox Pro is the only newer Avid hardware to use FireWire connections, though the older Digi 002 and 003 interfaces are still viable FireWire options. FireWire was preferable to USB because the transfer speed is fast enough to keep *latency* (the delay from the audio going in and coming back out of your computer) to a minimum. FireWire ports are inexpensive and available on laptop computers as well as desktop systems, which makes FireWire interfaces more versatile than PCI-based systems. As you can tell by Avid's newer hardware options, these days FireWire is taking a back seat to USB.

Each of the Avid, M-Audio, and some third-party interfaces are described in detail in Book II, Chapter 2.

Software

Because you're reading this book, I'm going to assume that your main choice in recording software is Pro Tools. Four lines of Pro Tools Software are available:

+ **Pro Tools SE:** This is Avid's entry-level program that offers a limited number of tracks (two simultaneous recording and 16 total audio tracks). This is an inexpensive way to get into Pro Tools; it works well for artists recording their own music.

+ **Pro Tools MP:** This version of Pro tools is created to run only with the M-Audio interfaces. This program offers more functionality than the SE version with up to 18 simultaneous and 32 total audio tracks.

+ **Pro Tools:** Beginning with version 9, Avid dropped the LE from its most common software program. Pro Tools is Avid's most powerful *host-based* program (which means that Pro Tools relies on the power of your computer to run the program as intended), with 32 simultaneous and 96 total audio tracks. This version of Pro Tools is a full-featured program that can do anything you're likely to want to do with your own (or others') music.

+ **Pro Tools|HD:** This is the native solution that requires you to buy an Avid PCI card to provide the processing power to run Pro Tools. This version of the software also offers some extra functionality beyond what you get with the host-based options, which some pros may find useful.

Down the road, you may want to add some other software to your system. You can include (for example) programs such as Acid (for creating loops) or Logic (for more MIDI-intensive work). You can find an online discussion board on the Internet for each of the major audio-recording software programs. Before you buy, go to the sites of the systems that interest you and see what people say about the programs. Ask questions, explore the issues that the people are having with the programs, and look for comments that reflect how well the programs interact with Pro Tools and your Avid hardware. Doing so can save you lots of time dealing with bugs in your system, allowing you to record a lot more music. You can find these sites by using the product name as the keyword in your favorite search engine, or by checking out these Internet forums:

    www.gearslutz.com/board

    www.homerecording.com

    www.prosoundweb.com

    www.recording.org

Signing On to Signal Processors

Part of the recording process involves making adjustments to a sound before or after it's been recorded. This is the job of the *signal processor,* which comes in three varieties — equalizers, dynamic processors, and effects processors. They can be incorporated into the system or be separate, stand-alone units. For most Pro Tools users, the signal processors of choice are integrated into the software as plug-ins, although you can also use external processors by sending the audio out of your computer and back in again.

Equalizers (EQ)

Equalizers enable you to adjust the frequencies of a sound in a variety of ways. In effect, you tell the frequencies to

+ **Go away.** You can get rid of unwanted noise or an annoying ringing by reducing select frequencies.

+ **Come hither.** Add *life* or *presence* to an instrument by bringing the best characteristics of that instrument forward.

+ **Scoot over.** You can make room within the frequency spectrum for each of the instruments in your mix by selectively boosting or cutting certain frequencies.

You can find out more about EQ (and discover some great EQ tips and tricks) in Book VI, Chapter 3. The three main types of EQ are graphic, shelf, and parametric. The following sections give you the rundown.

Graphic EQ

Use *graphic equalizers* to choose a specific frequency to increase or decrease by a certain amount, generally up to 6 or 12 decibels (dB). Doing so enables you to eliminate an offending frequency from the signal or make other adjustments to the tonal quality of the source signal. The graphic EQ has a certain number of frequency bands that you can adjust. You're limited to only those frequency bands that your EQ has available. Figure 1-7 shows a typical graphic EQ.

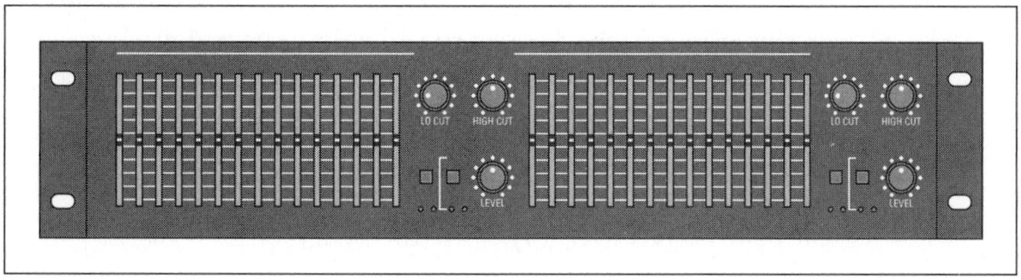

Figure 1-7:
A graphic
equalizer.

Shelf EQ

A *shelf equalizer* affects a range of frequencies above or below the target frequency. Shelf EQs are generally used to roll off the top or bottom end of the frequency spectrum. For example, you can set a shelf EQ to roll off the frequencies below 250 hertz (Hz) in order to reduce the amount of *rumble* (low-frequency noise) in a recording. You can see how this looks in Figure 1-8. Notice how the shelf EQ gradually reduces the amount of energy (sound) below the set point and then levels off — hence the *shelf* in its name.

Figure 1-8:
A shelf equalizer works like this.

Parametric EQ

The *parametric equalizer* enables you to choose the specific frequency that you want to affect as well as the range of frequencies to put around that frequency. With a parametric EQ, you dial in the frequency that you want to change, and then you set the range (referred to as the *Q*) — that is, the number of octaves that the EQ will affect. Check out Figure 1-9: The two diagrams show how the Q relates to the range of frequencies affected. (The higher the Q setting, the narrower the band of frequencies affected.)

The parametric EQ is one of your most useful tools when mixing all your individual tracks into a stereo pair. I describe this tool in detail in Book VI, Chapter 3.

Dynamic processors

Dynamic processors regulate the amount of sound or energy that gets passed through them. This amount is defined as the *dynamic range* — the range between the softest sound and the loudest sound. Dynamic processors come in three varieties: *compressors/limiters, gates,* and *expanders.* I explain each variety in the following sections.

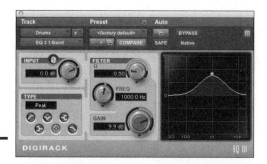

Figure 1-9:
A para-
metric
equalizer
in a digital
system.
Top: Using
a small Q.
Bottom:
Using a
large Q.

Dynamic processors are used in a variety of ways. Use them to

✦ Control the signal going into the mixer and recorder.

✦ Tame the levels and correct the effects of an erratic musical performance when mixing.

✦ Optimize the levels of the finished stereo tracks when mastering.

Dynamic processors are some of the most useful tools that you have in your
home studio. See Book VI, Chapter 4 for more on dynamic processors.

Compressors/limiters

A compressor's job is not only to limit how loud a note can be, but also to
reduce the difference between the loudest and softest note (that is, *compress*
the dynamic range) of the sound being affected. The purpose of the compressor is to eliminate *transients* (unusually loud notes) that can create *clipping* (digital distortion).

Compressors are used extensively on modern recordings; the device keeps
transients at bay by gently reducing the highest level that goes through it.

Compressors are also used in mastering to raise the overall volume of a song without creating distortion. The device does this by reducing the overall dynamic range; as a result, a compressor effectively raises the volume of the softer notes without allowing the louder notes to be too loud and distorted.

A *limiter* works much like the compressor except it severely limits the highest level of a sound source. The limiter is basically a compressor on steroids; it gives you beefed-up control over volume. Any signal above a certain level, called the *threshold,* gets chopped off instead of compressed (as it would be with the compressor). A limiter is a good choice in extreme situations, such as when you want a really in-your-face, snare drum sound. In this instance, the limiter essentially eliminates any dynamic variation from the drummer's snare-drum hits and makes them all as loud as possible.

Gates

A *gate* is basically the opposite of the limiter. Rather than limiting how loud a note can get, the gate limits how soft a note can get. The gate filters out any sound below a certain setting (the threshold) while allowing any note above that threshold to be heard.

Gates are often used on drums to keep unwanted sounds from the cymbals from bleeding through to the tom-tom or snare drum mics, or on guitars by refusing to allow the noise generated by guitar effects to be heard when the instrument isn't playing.

Expander

An *expander* is basically the opposite of a compressor — instead of *attenuating* (reducing the volume of) the loudest notes in a performance, an expander attenuates the softest notes. For example, if you have a singer whose breath you can hear in the mic and you want to get rid of that particular blemish, just set the expander to go on at a level just above the annoying breath sounds to subtly drop the offending noise.

Effects processors

Effects are historically used to mimic real-world situations. As a home recordist, you will likely discover a great affinity toward your effects processors because they enable you to create sonic environments without having to rent some great recording room. For example, imagine dragging your drums and all your recording equipment into a large cathedral, setting them up, and spending several hours getting the mics placed just right. Sounds like a lot of work, right? (I'm tired just thinking about it.) Well, how about recording your drums in your modest home studio and simply choosing the "cathedral hall reverb" patch instead? Now, that's much easier.

I can practically guarantee that you'll use effects processors all the time in your studio. Scope out Book VI, Chapter 5 for how to use them effectively.

In the world of effects processors, you have many choices, and many more show up every year. The most common effects processors are (in no particular order) reverb, delay, chorus, flanger, and pitch correction. Read on for the lowdown on each type.

Reverb

Reverb is undoubtedly the most commonly used effects processor. With reverb, you can make any instrument sound as if it were recorded in almost any environment. Reverb, a natural part of every sound, is the result of the sound bouncing around inside a room. The larger the room, the more pronounced the reverb. The purpose of a reverb in audio production is to make an instrument sound more natural (especially because most instruments are recorded in small, nonreverberant rooms) or to add a special effect. Reverb can make almost any recorded instrument sound better — if used correctly.

Delay

Think of *delays* as a recording studio's version of an echo. The delay can be set to happen immediately after the original sound or be delayed much longer. Delay can sound natural or be used as a spacey special effect. You can have a single echo or multiple delays (very common with the snare drum in reggae music, for instance). Delays are commonly used on vocals and guitar, although you can hear them on just about any instrument, depending on the style of music.

Chorus

A *chorus* effect can make one instrument sound like several. Chorus effects add very slightly off-tune versions of the unaffected sound, which results in a fuller sound. You find chorus effects used on vocals, guitars, and lots of other melodic instruments.

Flanger

A *flanger* (pronounced *flanj*-er) effect is similar to a chorus effect in sound except that the flanger gets its sound from *delaying* part of the affected sound in relation to the original, rather than altering its pitch. Flangers are sometimes used on background vocals and solo instruments to add an interesting texture. This is a unique sound that you recognize almost immediately upon hearing it.

The flanger effect comes from the early days in recording. You can create the flanger effect the old-fashioned way by using a two-track tape recorder to record a duplicate track of the one you want to flange. You then play the two identical parts back at the same time, gently pressing against the edge of the two-track tape (the one with the duplicate part) while it's running. This delays certain parts of the sound slightly and drastically changes the character of the instrument.

Nowadays, you can just choose the flanger patch (sound) on your effects processor to get this sound. Isn't technology great?

Pitch correction

Pitch correction, like its name suggests, is used to correct an out-of-tune note. You can use this effect to help a singer or an instrument player sound better by fixing those notes that are slightly out of tune. Pitch correction (also called *auto-tune*) has gotten a bad rap lately (mainly from its overuse and potential for abuse with a singer who can't sing on-key). When used sparingly and appropriately, pitch correction can make an otherwise-decent vocal performance really shine. Auto-tune can also be used to create some interesting effects, such as that robotic-vocal sound you hear on so many of the pop songs on the radio nowadays. The most easily distinguished example is the lead vocal on Cher's "Believe."

Making Sense of Monitors

To record and mix music, you need to be able to hear it. (Hey, obvious things need love, too.) Monitors make this happen. You can use headphones or speakers as monitors; most home studios use both. Monitors are an essential part of a recording studio because you need to get what you're recording and mixing into your ears before you make sure that it sounds good.

Without good speakers, you won't know what your mixes are going to sound like on other speakers. (Find out more about mixing in Book VI.)

Headphones

Chances are that your first home studio will be in a spare bedroom or a corner of your garage or basement. All your recording, monitoring, and mixing will be done here. If that's the case, a set of headphones is indispensable because then you can turn off your speakers and still hear what's being (or was) recorded. When you go to record a guitar using a microphone in front of the guitar amp, for example, you want to hear only the guitar — not the guitar amp *and* the guitar amp coming back through your monitors. Headphones allow you to do this. (See Figure 1-10.)

Figure 1-10:
Studio head-
phones.

Speakers

For most home recordists, your first set of monitors consists of the home
stereo system. Sooner or later, though, you're gonna want a real set of monitors. Studio monitors come in many varieties, but the home recordist's best
bet is a set of near-field monitors. *Near-field monitors* are designed to be
positioned close to you (which is often the case anyway because most home
recordists have very little room in which to work).

Near-field monitors come with or without an amplifier. The amplified monitors are *active monitors,* and the nonamplified monitors are *passive monitors.*
Which type of monitor you choose depends on your budget and whether
you like the idea of the amp coming with the speakers or you prefer to purchase the amp separately. Figure 1-11 shows an active, near-field monitor.
The amplifier is located inside the speaker cabinet.

Figure 1-11:
An active
near-field
monitor: The
amplifier
is located
inside the
speaker
cabinet.

If you end up getting passive monitors, you need to buy an amplifier to send power to the speakers. The amplifier connects to the outputs of the mixer and boosts the signal to the speakers. A good power amp should be matched in power to work well with whatever speakers you have.

Mastering Media

After you mix your music, you need to save your final music on some kind of medium. The two most common media for Pro Tools users are CD and raw computer files. Which medium you choose depends upon what your goals are. For instance, if you intend to send your finished mix to a mastering house, you're better off saving it as raw audio data in a computer file. On the other hand, if you master your music yourself and just want to have it duplicated (or you want to give copies for your friends to play), you want to use a CD.

CD

With the cost of CD-R (write) and CD-RW (rewrite) drives plummeting, CD mastering is the only choice for most home recordists. With CDs, you can back up large amounts of data at a very low cost, and you can burn audio CDs that can play in any CD player. You can even send out your mastered CD to be duplicated and packaged for retail sale. (Book VIII, Chapter 1 details the process for burning CDs and how to have mass quantities created.)

Computer files

Sometimes you won't want to master your music directly to CD. You may decide to have a professional mastering house do it, or maybe you want to put your music on the Internet. In those situations, store your recordings as computer files. The following sections describe the most commonly used file formats for storing recorded music.

WAV and AIFF

WAV (Microsoft Wave format) and AIFF (Apple; Audio Interchange File Format) files are the formats for audio files found with most professional audio software. The advantage to saving your music to WAV or AIFF is that when you hand over a CD containing your WAV and/or AIFF files to a mastering house, the recorded sound is actually in a higher-quality format than that of the finished CD (provided that your recorder records in 20- or 24-bit, which most do). You can also take your music files to any other studio that supports these file formats and work with them there.

MIDI

A MIDI file is not an audio file; rather, it's a data file that contains MIDI information that can be transferred from one computer to another; it tells the computer how to use a sound module to construct the music. An advantage to MIDI files is that they take up less room than an audio file. The disadvantage is that they contain only the MIDI information and no sound. To play a MIDI file, you have to have a sound module. And the sound you get from the file depends entirely on what sound source you use.

MP3

MP3 is a file format that has become quite popular on the Internet. Its advantage over audio CDs and other computer files is that it takes up less room.

Its disadvantages are that the data is compressed and the sound quality is not nearly that of commercial CDs (contrary to what MP3 proponents claim). You can find out more about MP3s and audio quality in Book VIII, Chapter 2.

AAC

AAC (Advanced Audio Coding) is the file format of choice for iTunes music and some other Internet music sites. This format is said to offer a higher quality of sound than MP3 for its size.

Chapter 2: Getting Connected: Setting Up Your Studio

In This Chapter

✔ **Getting to know the various types of connectors**

✔ **Plugging in your equipment**

✔ **Creating an efficient workstation**

✔ **Making your room sound great (or at least decent)**

*O*kay, so you're ready to turn that spare bedroom or basement into a recording studio. After you unpack all your shiny new gear and get it plugged in properly, you need to get your room to work for you. This involves creating an efficient place to work, but above all, it means getting your room to sound good. This can be tricky; after all, pro studios spend tons of time and money getting the room to sound *great*. You're going to have to do much the same. You may not have to spend a ton of money (as if any of us could), but you will need to spend some time.

After you decide on a space for your home recording system, the next steps involve setting up the system and getting your space to work for you. In this chapter, I help you make sense of all those connectors that you end up using — and help you get them all plugged in properly. I also show you how to find the best way to work in your environment, with a goodly measure of tips and tricks thrown in to make your room sound as good as possible.

Understanding Analog Connections

You've probably had a chance to see and use a variety of analog connectors. If you play a guitar or keyboard (synthesizer), for example, you're familiar with a ¼-inch analog plug. Some microphones use an XLR analog plug. Keeping all these connectors straight can be a little confusing: Why do you have to use one plug for one thing and another for something else? And what's a TRS plug, anyway?

Read on to discover the most common analog connectors: ¼ inch (mono/TS and stereo/TRS), XLR, and RCA.

The ¼-inch analog plug

The ¼-inch plug is the most common audio connector and one of the most versatile. These plugs come in two varieties: mono/TS and stereo/TRS.

Mono/TS

The plug on a cord that you use for your guitar or synthesizer is an example of a mono ¼-inch plug. The *mono* part of the name refers to the fact that you have only one channel through which to send the signal. This type of plug is also referred to as a *TS* plug (short for Tip/Sleeve). The *tip* is the end of the plug, and the *sleeve* is the rest of the metal part. A plastic divider separates these two sections. Check out Figure 2-1 to see this familiar plug.

Figure 2-1:
A typical ¼-inch plug used for guitar and other electric instruments.

TS plugs are used for a variety of purposes — to go from your guitar to your guitar amp, from your synthesizer to your mixer, from your mixer to your power amplifier (amp), and from your power amp to your speakers. You would expect that one cord could work for all these applications. After all, a TS plug is a TS plug, right? Well, not really. The same plug can be wired differently, and it can carry different levels of power. For example, here are the differences between instrument and speaker cords:

✦ **Instrument cord (the one you use for your synthesizer or guitar):** This cord contains one wire and a shield — the wire is connected to the tip, and the shield is connected to the sleeve. You need the instrument cable's shield to minimize noise. If you use a speaker cord (discussed next) for your instrument, you may end up with some noise (that is, you may hear a hiss or a buzz — or even a radio station — coming out of your amp or coming from where you've plugged in your instrument).

Instrument cords are often called *unbalanced lines* because of the way that they're wired. An unbalanced cord has one wire surrounded by a braided shield; the wire is connected to the tip of the TS plug, and the shield is connected to the sleeve. The signal is sent through the wire, and the shield is used for the ground. (It keeps the noise down.) You can also find balanced lines, which I explain in the next section of this chapter.

✦ **A speaker cord:** This cord contains two wires and no shield — one wire is connected to the tip and the other to the sleeve. Because the speaker cord carries a lot more current (power) than the instrument cable, the speaker cord doesn't have a shield. The signal level covers noise that's present in the cord. Because you have much less current present in an instrument, you don't want to use a speaker cord for your instrument.

When buying cords with TS plugs, first be sure to look at (or ask about) what purpose the cord is designed for. Then, when you take the cord home, be sure to note what type it is so that you use it correctly. You can mark your cord in a number of ways: You can put colored tape on it (red for speaker or blue for instrument, for example), put a tag on it, or — gasp — dot it with nail polish (not on the tip or sleeve, of course).

You generally don't need to worry about which end of the cord you plug in to your instrument — the signal can travel equally well in either direction. However, you can buy cords that are designed to send the current in one direction. (This cord has an arrow on it, designating in which direction the signal should flow.) I call these *designer cords,* and two of the most common brands are Monster and Planet Waves. The theory behind these cords is that they do a better job of preserving the sound qualities of the instrument for which they're designed. These cords are specifically designed for almost every instrument and application known to man.

Stereo/TRS

A stereo/TRS (short for Tip/Ring/Sleeve) ¼-inch plug looks like a stereo headphone plug (take a look at Figure 2-2). The tip is the end of the plug, the ring is the small middle section located between the two plastic dividers, and the sleeve is the rest of the metal part of the plug. A TRS plug can be used for the following three types of cords:

✦ **Stereo cord:** A stereo cord is used for signals that contain two separate portions: one for the right channel and the other for the left channel. This type of cord is generally wired with the left-channel signal attached to the tip, the right-channel signal connected to the ring, and the shield wired to the sleeve. This type of cord is typically used for headphones.

Figure 2-2:
Use a
balanced
(TRS) plug
to connect
professional
audio gear.

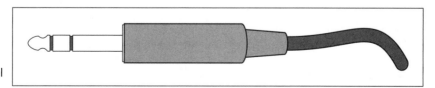

✦ **Balanced cord:** A *balanced cord* is used on professional audio gear to join the various pieces of equipment (to connect the mixer to the recorder, for example). The advantage with a balanced cord is that you can have longer cord runs without creating noise.

Why are balanced cords so conveniently noise free? The balanced cord has two wires and a shield inside and has the same signal running through both wires. One signal is 180 degrees out of phase with the other (that is, their waveforms are opposite one another), and when the signals get to the mixer (or whatever they're plugged in to) one of the signals is flipped and added to the other. When this happens, any noise that built up in the signal is canceled out.

✦ **Y cord:** A *Y cord* consists of a TRS plug on one end and two TS plugs on the other, forming — you guessed it — a nice representation of the letter *Y.* This cord allows you to insert an effect processor — a compressor or equalizer, for example — in the line of a mixer (more specifically, into the insert jack of the mixer). Check out Book I, Chapter 3 for details on mixers. The TRS plug both sends and receives a signal. This cord is wired so that the tip sends the signal and the ring receives it (see Figure 2-3). The sleeve is connected to the shield of each cable.

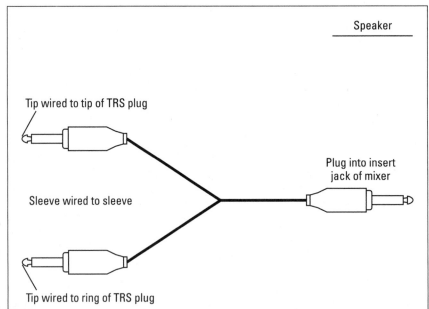

Figure 2-3: Use a Y cord to send and receive a signal.

XLR

The XLR connector is used for microphones and some line connections between professional gear. This cable has a female and a male end (see

Figure 2-4). The cord is wired much like a TRS connector and is balanced to minimize noise. The XLR microphone cable is also called a *low-Z cable* because it carries a low-impedance signal.

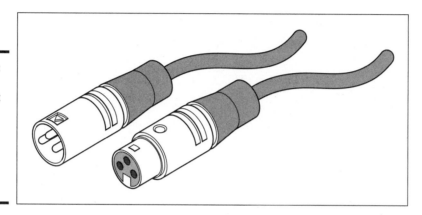

Figure 2-4:
An XLR
connector:
One end
is male
(left), and
the other
is female
(right).

RCA

RCA plugs — named for good old RCA and also called phono plugs — are common on home stereos and on some semipro audio gear (see Figure 2-5). They function much like a TS plug but aren't very common in professional audio equipment. However, you find them on some mixers so that you can connect a tape deck, iPod, or other media device. They are also used for digital S/PDIF signals (see the next section for more details on these babies).

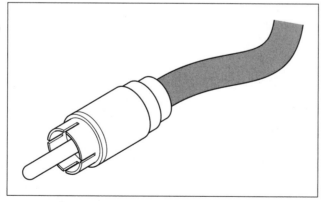

Figure 2-5:
An RCA
plug is used
mainly on
consumer
stereo
and some
semipro
audio
equipment.

Delving In to Digital Connections

If you're going to record using a digital recorder or mixer, you're going to run into digital connectors (plugs and cables/cords). Digital audio equipment is a recent invention, and as such, no one standard has emerged. Because of this lack of standardization, a variety of digital connection methods are on the market, only a few (or one) of which may be on the equipment that you own or intend to purchase. Regardless, knowing about the most common types of connectors and their purposes can help you decide what equipment is right for you.

MIDI

MIDI, short for Musical Instrument Digital Interface, is a handy communication protocol that allows musical information to pass from one device to another. To allow the free passage of such information, MIDI jacks are located on a whole host of electronic instruments. Synthesizers, drum machines, sound modules, and even some guitars have MIDI jacks. And, to connect all these instruments, you need some MIDI cables. The MIDI connector contains five pins (male) that plug in to the female MIDI jack (port) on the instrument or device (see Figure 2-6).

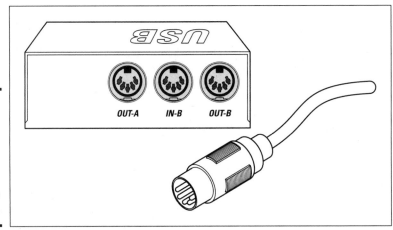

Figure 2-6: MIDI connectors have two male ends. The device contains the female jack.

AES/EBU

AES/EBU (Audio Engineering Society/European Broadcasting Union) cables are much like S/PDIF cables (described in the next section). The AES/EBU standards require these cables to transmit two channels of data at a time. They differ from S/PDIF cables in that they consist of XLR plugs and use balanced cables. (Figure 2-7 shows what the inputs look like on the recording equipment.) AES/EBU was developed to be used with professional audio components, hence the use of balanced cords — the kinds used in professional-level equipment.

Figure 2-7:
S/PDIF and
AES/EBU
connectors
look the
same as
analog RCA
(S/PDIF) and
XLR (AES/
EBU) but
are marked
as digital
on the
machine.

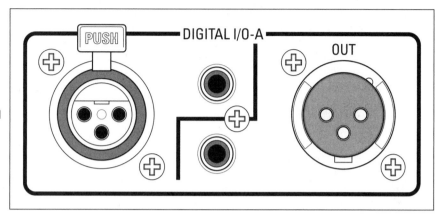

S/PDIF

S/PDIF (short for Sony/Phillips Digital Interface Format) cables consist of
an unbalanced coaxial cable (one wire and a shield) and RCA plugs. (Figure
2-7 shows what the inputs look like on the machine.) These cables can also
be made from fiber-optic cable and a Toslink connector. The S/PDIF format
can transmit two channels of digital data at one time. S/PDIF protocols are
similar to AES/EBU standards, except that S/PDIF was originally designed for
the consumer market — which is why unbalanced cords are used. In spite of
being developed for the consumer market, S/PDIF connectors are found on a
lot of pro recording gear, along with (or instead of) AES/EBU.

If you want to use cords that are longer than 3–4 feet when you're using an
S/PDIF connector — or about 15 feet for AES/EBU connectors — your best
bet is to use video or digital audio cables. Regular audio cables degrade the
sound at longer distances because they can't transmit the type of signal that
digital produces without affecting the quality of the sound. If you use audio
cables for longer distances, you lose some of the sound's definition. Some
people describe this sound as "grainy."

ADAT Lightpipe

The ADAT (Alesis Digital Audio Tape) Lightpipe format allows eight tracks
of digital audio to be sent at once. Developed by Alesis, ADAT Lightpipe
(or simply Lightpipe for short) has become a standard among digital audio
products. It consists of a fiber-optic cable that uses a special connector
developed by Alesis.

TDIF

TDIF (Teac Digital Interface Format) is Teac's return volley to the ADAT Lightpipe format. TDIF uses a standard computer cable with a 25-pin connector. Like the ADAT Lightpipe, TDIF cables can transmit eight channels of digital data at a time. TDIF isn't nearly as common as ADAT Lightpipe because Alesis made its Lightpipe technology available to other companies to use for free. Alesis encouraged these companies to adopt it as a "standard" because the Alesis ADAT recorders were so common.

USB

USB, which stands for Universal Serial Bus, is a common component in nearly all modern computers. In fact, your computer probably has more than one USB port. In case it's been a while since you've had to use your USB connection, take a look at Figure 2-8. As you can see, USB has the following different plugs that fit different jacks:

✦ **Rectangular connector:** This is called the "A" connector and is for any receiving device, such as your PC or a USB hub.

✦ **Square connector:** Called the "B" connector, this is used for a sending device, such as your USB audio interface or printer.

Figure 2-8: USB uses two types of connectors: the "A" connector (left) and the "B" connector (right).

Aside from having two different types of jacks and plugs, USB also has different standards, as follows:

✦ **USB 1.1:** This standard (the original) can handle a data rate of up to 12 Mbps (megabits per second).

✦ **USB 2.0:** Also called Hi-speed USB, this standard can handle 40 times the data flow of the earlier standard — 480 Mbps.

✦ **USB 3.0:** This is also referred to as SuperSpeed USB. This connection transfers data at an astounding 5 Gbps, tens times as fast as even USB 2.0.

You'll still find some USB 1.1 audio interfaces on the market, but most have migrated to the faster, 2.0 version. At the time of this writing there are no USB 3.0 audio interfaces out yet. Expect this to change soon (possibly by the time this revision is in your hands).

FireWire

Developed by Apple, FireWire (also known as IEEE 1394 or iLink) is a high-speed connection that is used by many audio interfaces, hard drives, digital cameras, and other devices. Even though FireWire was developed by Apple, you can find FireWire ports on devices from many manufacturers. FireWire cables, unlike USB cables (see the preceding section), have the same connector (see Figure 2-9) on both ends.

Like USB, FireWire comes in two flavors, which are described as follows:

✦ **FireWire 400:** This standard supports data-transfer speeds of up to 400 Mbps. Many audio interfaces currently use FireWire 400 as a way to connect with your computer. These interfaces can handle quite a few inputs and outputs.

✦ **FireWire 800:** Yep, you guessed it — this standard can handle data-transfer rates of 800 Mbps. A couple of FireWire 800 devices are available now, but you should see many more interfaces supported by FireWire 800 soon.

Thunderbolt

Thunderbolt is the fastest connectivity format to date, with speeds between 20 and 100 gigabits per second. Audio interface manufacturers are excited about this amazing speed, and many experts see Thunderbolt as the next format that the pros will embrace. But, like USB 3.0, Thunderbolt is too new for any products to be available. This may change soon, so keep your eyes open.

Figure 2-9:
FireWire
is a high-
speed data-
transfer
protocol.

The interface is essentially the same as the mini DV jack found on many of the Mac laptops. You can expect the first units to be relatively expensive, maybe not because of the cost of the technology, but because of the number of inputs and outputs that these units will likely have. For most home recordists, however, the existing connectivity options are sufficient for doing anything you want to do.

Working Efficiently in Your Studio

I hope you spend a great number of hours in your studio creating some great music (albeit possibly to the dismay of the rest of your family). Start by designing your studio layout for comfort and productivity. Then consider how to protect your equipment and also effectively place your audio monitors.

Setting up your studio for comfort and efficiency

One important thing to keep in mind is that you need to be comfortable. Start with a good chair. Then set up your workstation to be as easy to get around as possible. Figure 2-10 shows a classic L setup. Notice how everything that you need is within arm's reach.

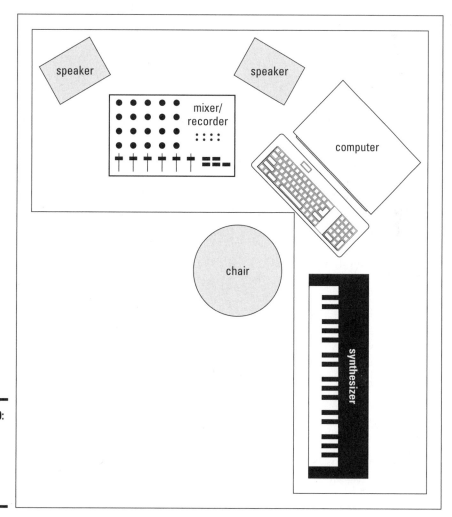

Figure 2-10:
A classic L setup: Everything is easy to reach.

If you have enough room, you may want to consider a U-shaped setup instead. You can see an example of that in Figure 2-11. If you don't have an external mixer/recorder, it's often best to put the computer in the middle position.

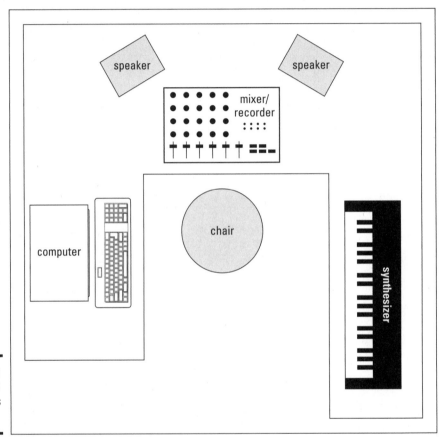

Figure 2-11:
A U-shaped setup works great.

If you use a lot of outboard gear — such as preamps or effects processors — and you think that you need to plug and unplug a lot, invest in a good patch bay so that you don't have to strain to get at your cords tucked away behind your mixer. A *patch bay* is a device that consists almost entirely of inputs and outputs, allowing you to route your gear in (and out) in an almost-infinite variety of ways. If you're going to do much plugging and unplugging, you'll quickly find out that a patch bay is truly indispensable.

Using a patch bay will not only save your back but will also save your cords because repeated plugging and unplugging wears them out quickly and produces buzzes that can be hard to locate.

Taming heat and dust

The number-one enemy of electronic equipment is heat. Dust is a close second. Try to set up your studio in a room that you can keep cool and fairly dust-free. Air conditioning is a must for most studios. Be careful with a window air conditioner, though, because it can make a lot of noise, requiring you to shut it off when you record. Depending on where you live, this could let your room heat up really fast. To deal with dust, try to cover up your equipment when you're not using it, especially your microphones. A plastic bag placed over the top of a mic on a stand works well.

You could also just put your mics away when you're not using them. However, if you use a particular mic a lot, you're best off leaving it on a stand rather than handling it because some types of mics are pretty fragile. (You can find more on caring for your mics in Book I, Chapter 5.)

Monitoring your monitors

If you have a set of *near-field monitors* — the kind that are designed to be placed close to you — they should be set up so they're equidistant from each other and from you, at a height that puts them level with your ears. Figure 2-12 illustrates the best placement for your monitors. Placing your monitors this way ensures that you hear the best possible sound from them and can accurately hear the stereo field. (For more on the stereo field, see Book VI, Chapter 1.)

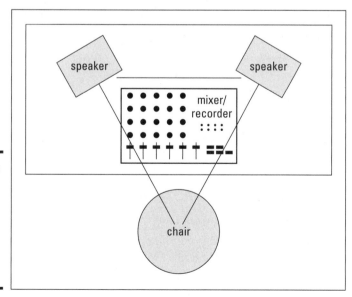

Figure 2-12:
Monitors sound best when equidistant from each other and you.

Optimizing Your Studio

Chances are that your studio occupies a corner in your living room, a spare bedroom, or a section of your basement or garage. All these spaces are less-than-ideal recording environments. Even if you intend to record mostly by plugging your instrument or sound module directly into the mixer, how your room sounds will have a big effect on how good your music will turn out to be.

Face it: As a home recordist, you're unlikely to have easy access to the resources that create a top-notch sound room. Commercial studios spend serious cash — up to seven figures — to make their rooms sound, well, professional. However, you don't need to spend near that amount of money (you mean you don't *want* to sell off the private jet . . .?) to get great sounding recordings. All it takes is a little understanding of how sound travels, some ingenuity, and a little bit of work.

Sound isolation

One of the concerns that you (and your neighbors) are probably going to have when you start recording in your home is the amount of sound that gets in and out of your room. Sound waves are nasty little buggers. They get through almost any surface, and there's not a lot you can do to stop it from happening.

You've probably noticed this phenomenon when somebody with a massive subwoofer in his car drives by blasting some obnoxious music. (Ever notice how someone else's music is obnoxious, whereas your music never is, no matter how loud you play it? Amazing . . .) Your windows rattle, your walls shake, and your favorite mug flies off the shelf and breaks into a thousand pieces. Well, this is one of the problems with sound: It's physical energy.

The best (and classic) way to isolate your studio room from everything around it is to build a room within a room.

I don't have the space to go into detail here, but you can find resources to get you started by doing a Google search with the keywords "sound isolation." Here are a couple of places to get you started:

✦ **Sound Isolation Company** (www.soundisolationcompany.com): Aside from selling products to help you keep the sound in (or out) of your studio, you'll find useful information here about the process of sound isolation.

✦ **Netwell** (www.esoundproof.com): Again, this company sells products to help control sound, but you'll also find good basic information here to get you started.

For the purposes of most home recordists who don't have the money or space to build a room within a room, the best thing you can do is to try to understand what noises are getting in and getting out — and deal with those. For example, if you live in a house or apartment with neighbors close by, don't record live drums at night. You could also consider using a drum machine or electronic drum set (plugged directly into the recorder) instead.

Another idea is to try to choose a room in your house or apartment that is farthest away from outside noise (an interior room, for instance). Basements also work well because they're underground and most of the sound gets absorbed by the ground. Installing a little fiberglass batting insulation in the ceiling — typical house insulation that you can find at your local home center — can isolate you pretty well from your neighbors' ears. Detached garages are generally farther away from other buildings, so sound has a chance to dissipate before it reaches your neighbors (or before your neighbors' noise reaches your garage).

Also keep these things in mind when trying to isolate your studio:

+ **Dead air and mass are your friends.** The whole concept of a room within a room is to create mass and still air space so that the invading or escaping sound gets trapped. When you work on isolating your room, try to design in some space that can trap air (creating *dead air*) — such as a suspended ceiling or big upholstered furniture — or use double layers of drywall on your walls (mass).

+ **Don't expect acoustical foam or carpet to reduce the noise.** Using these can help reduce the amount of sound that bounces around inside the room but won't do much to keep sound in (or out of) the room.

+ **Isolate the instrument instead of the room.** Isolating the sound of your guitar amp can be much less expensive than trying to soundproof your whole room. Most commercial studios have one or more *isolation booths* for recording vocals and other acoustic instruments. You can use that concept to create your own mini isolation booths.

One idea for a truly mini isolation booth is to make an insulated box for your guitar (or bass) amp. If you just have to crank your amp to get the sound you want, you can place it inside an insulated box to reduce the amount of noise that escapes to the outside world. Check out Figure 2-13 to see what I mean.

You can also create an isolated space in a closet by insulating it and closing the door when you record, or you can put your guitar amp (or drums) in another room and run a long cord from there to your recorder. If you do this, remember that for long cord runs, you need to use balanced cords. Otherwise you may get a bunch of noise, and your signal may be too low-level to record very well.

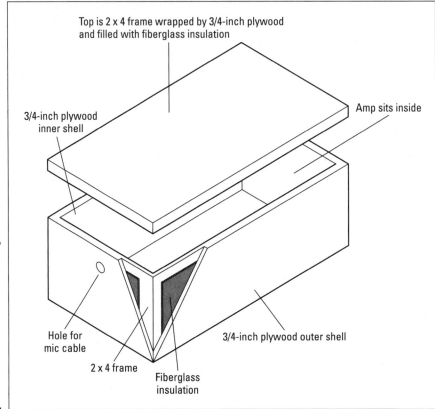

Top is 2 x 4 frame wrapped by 3/4-inch plywood
and filled with fiberglass insulation

3/4-inch plywood
inner shell

Amp sits inside

Figure 2-13:
An amp-
isolator box
reduces the
amount of
noise you
hear from
your amp,
even when
it's cranked.

Hole for
mic cable

3/4-inch plywood outer shell

2 x 4 frame

Fiberglass
insulation

Sound control

After you create a room that's as isolated from the outside world as possible, you need to deal with how sound acts within your room.

Sound travels through the air in the form of waves. These waves bounce
around the room and cause *reflections* (reverberations or echoes). One
problem with most home studios is that they're small. Compounding this,
sound travels very fast — 1,130 feet per second, to be exact. When you sit
at your monitors and listen, inevitably you hear the reflected sound as well
as the original sound that comes from your speakers. In a big room, you can
hear the original sound and reflections as separate sounds, meaning that the
reflections themselves become less of a problem. For a good home studio,
you have to tame these reflections so they don't interfere with your ability
to hear clearly what's coming from the speakers.

How all these reflections bounce around your room can get pretty complicated. Read up on *acoustics* (how sound behaves) to discover more about different room modes: *axial* (one dimension), *tangential* (two dimensions), and *oblique* (three dimensions). Each relates to how sound waves interact while they bounce around a room. Knowing your room's modes can help you come up with an acoustical treatment strategy, but there are very complicated formulas for figuring out your room's modes, especially those dastardly tangential and oblique modes.

You can find out more on room modes, as well as discover some room mode calculators, on the Internet by using your favorite search engine and searching for "room modes." Go to the website matches, and you'll see quite a few places to start looking. I recommend that you research these modes; this topic alone could fill an entire book.

So, at the risk of offending the professional acoustical engineers in the world, I'm going to share some tricks that I've been using in my studios. My main goal has been to create a room with a sound I like and that gives me some measure of control over the reflections within the room. Because I both record and mix in one room (as do most home recordists), it's helpful to be able to make minor adjustments to the sound to accommodate what it is I'm trying to accomplish.

The single best source I've found for sound control and acoustics information is Ethan Winer's forum at Musicplayer.com. You can check it out at `http://forums.musicplayer.com/ubbthreads.php/ubb/postlist/Board/24/page/1`.

The two aspects of recording where sound control plays a major role — tracking and mixing — each require different approaches for you to get the best possible sound out of your recordings. I cover both these aspects in the following sections.

Sound control during tracking

Tracking is what you're doing when you're actually recording. Two things that can make a room a bad environment for tracking are

+ Not enough sound reflection
+ Too much sound reflection

The goal when tracking is to have a room that's not so dead (in terms of sound reflection) that it sucks the life out of your instrument — yet not so alive that it colors the sound too much. The determining factor in how much reflection you want in your room is based upon the instrument that you record and how it sounds in the room.

If your room is too *dead* (not enough sound reflection), you want to add some reflective surfaces to liven up things (the room, that is). On the other hand, if your room is too *live* (too much sound reflection), you need to add some absorptive materials to tame those reflections.

You could go out and buy a bunch of foam panels to catch the reflections, or maybe put in a wood floor or attach some paneling to the walls to add some life, but you'd be stuck with the room sounding only one way. It may end up sounding good for recording drums or acoustic guitar, but then it would probably be too live for getting a great vocal sound (which requires a deader space). One solution that I've found to work well is to get (or make) some portable panels that can either absorb or reflect the sound.

Figure 2-14 shows an absorber/reflector that I've used and have found to work quite well. One side has an absorptive material (dense fiberglass insulation), and the other side has a reflective surface (wood). They are put together in an attractive frame and designed to stack easily when you want them out of the way. Even with very little woodworking experience, you can crank out a set of them in a weekend for very little money (about $50 per panel). I guarantee that if you make them (or hire someone to make them for you), you'll find dozens of uses for them around your studio.

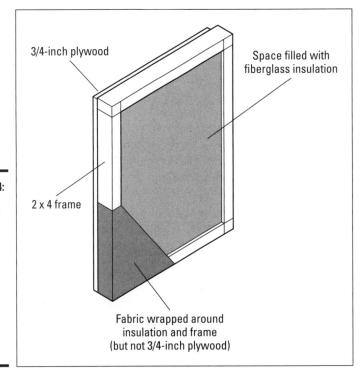

Figure 2-14:
Portable absorbers/ reflectors make changing the sound characteristics of your room quick and easy.

3/4-inch plywood

Space filled with fiberglass insulation

2 x 4 frame

Fabric wrapped around insulation and frame (but not 3/4-inch plywood)

Sound control during mixing

Your first step in getting control of the sound of your (probably less-than-perfect) room during mixing is to get a good pair of near-field monitors. Near-field monitors (as you can read about earlier in this chapter) are designed to be listened to up close (hence the "near" in their name) and will lessen the effects that the rest of the room has on your ability to hear them accurately and get a good mix.

The next step to mixing in an imperfect room is to mix at low volumes. I know: That takes the fun out of it, right? Well, as fun as it may be to mix at high volumes, it rarely translates into a great mix. Great mixing engineers often listen to their mixers at very low levels. Yes, they occasionally use high levels, but only after the mixing is pretty much done — and then only for very short periods of time. After all, if you damage your ears, you blow your career as a sound engineer. (Hey, that rhymes! Or is there an echo in here?) I don't want to sound like your mother, but try to resist the temptation to crank it up. Your ears last longer, and your mixes sound better.

Even with these two things (near-field monitors and low mixing levels), you still need to do something to your room to make it work better for you. The secret to a good mixing room is to tame the reflections of the sound coming out of your speakers.

Dealing with high and midrange frequencies is pretty easy — just put up some foam panels or the absorptive side of the panels shown in Figure 2-14. (See? I told you that you'd have a use for those panels.) Start by hanging two (or putting them on a stand or table) so they're level with your speakers on the wall behind you. Also, put one on each sidewall right where the speakers are pointed. (See Figure 2-15.) This positioning gets rid of the higher frequencies and eliminates much of the echo.

You may also need to put something on your ceiling right above your head, especially if you have a low (8 feet or less) or *textured* ceiling. (You know, one with that popcorny stuff sprayed on.) You may not want to mount one of the absorption panels over your head because they're fairly heavy. Wrapping up a couple of 2' x 4' panels made of dense fiberglass (the same ones used in the absorber/reflectors) in fabric would work just about perfectly (see Figure 2-16).

You can also place a set of these overhead panels in the corners of your room behind the speakers. Just hang them at the same height of your speakers so that they cut off the corner of the room. If there isn't enough room to fit the panels at an angle in the corner, you can eliminate the backing from the fiberglass and bend the fabric-covered panel to fit right in the corner. Either approach will absorb sound that may otherwise bounce around behind the speakers.

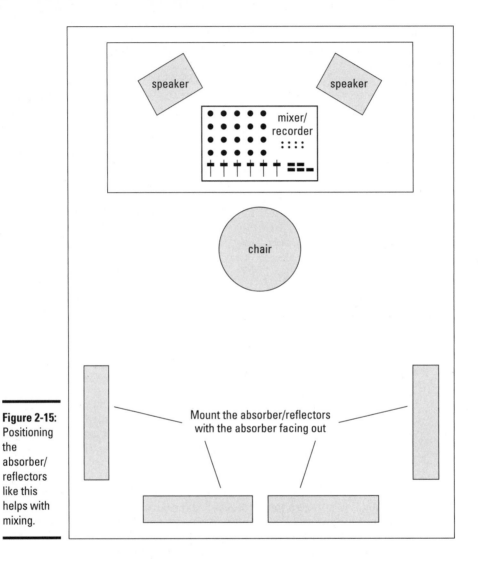

speaker

speaker

mixer/
recorder

chair

Figure 2-15:
Positioning
the
absorber/
reflectors
like this
helps with
mixing.

Mount the absorber/reflectors
with the absorber facing out

Another thing that you need to consider when you're mixing is *standing
waves,* which are created when bass tones begin reflecting around your
room and bounce into each other. Standing waves have a weird effect on mix
quality. They can either overemphasize the bass from your speakers (resulting in mixes that are short on bass) or cancel out some — or all — of the
bass coming out of your speakers (resulting in mixes with too much bass).
One of the problems with standing waves is that they can really mess up
your mixes, and you may not even be aware that they are there.

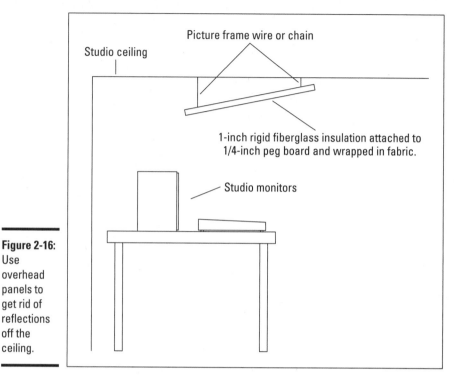

Picture frame wire or chain

Studio ceiling

1-inch rigid fiberglass insulation attached to
1/4-inch peg board and wrapped in fabric.

Studio monitors

Figure 2-16:
Use
overhead
panels to
get rid of
reflections
off the
ceiling.

To find out whether you have a problem with standing waves in your studio, sit in front of your monitors and put on one of your favorite CDs. Now listen carefully. Okay, now lean forward and backward a little bit. Does the amount of bass that you hear change as you move? Next, get up and walk around the room. Listen for places within the room where the bass seems to be louder or softer. You may find places where the bass drops out almost completely. If either inspection gives you a variable experience of the bass, you are the proud owner of standing waves. Don't worry, though. You can tame that standing-wave monster with a pair of bass traps.

Bass traps absorb the energy in the lower frequencies so they don't bounce all over your room and throw off your mixes. You can buy bass traps made of foam from some music stores, or (yep, you guessed it) you can make your own out of wood and insulation. Check out Figure 2-17 for a look at some homemade bass traps.

The most common placement for bass traps is in the corners behind you when you're sitting at your mixer (as shown in Figure 2-18). You may also find that putting a set in the other corners of the room helps even more.

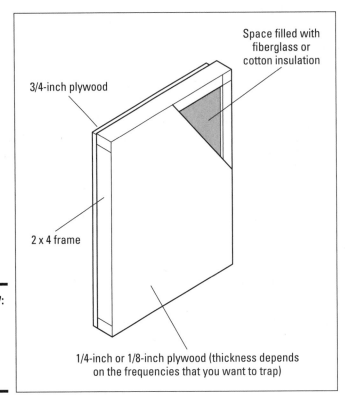

3/4-inch plywood

Space filled with fiberglass or cotton insulation

2 x 4 frame

1/4-inch or 1/8-inch plywood (thickness depends on the frequencies that you want to trap)

Figure 2-17: Use bass traps to get rid of standing waves.

After you place the bass traps, do the listening test again. If you notice some areas where the bass seems to get louder or softer, try moving the bass traps around a little. With some trial and error, you'll most likely find a place where they seem to work best.

Try not to get stressed out about the sound of your room. As important as your room's sound may be, it has a lot less effect on the quality of your recordings than good, solid engineering practices. I know, I keep saying this, but it's important to remember. Do what you can, and then work with what you've got.

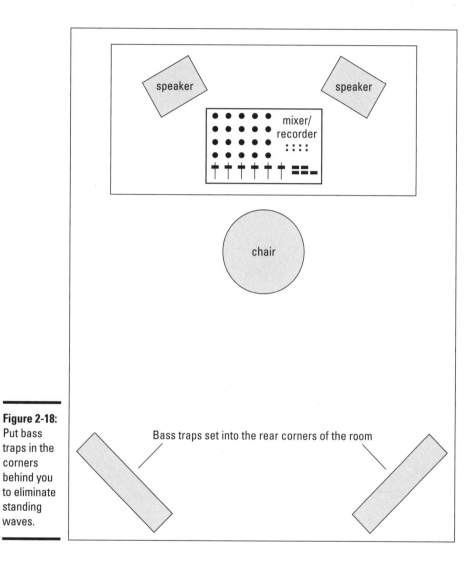

Figure 2-18:
Put bass
traps in the
corners
behind you
to eliminate
standing
waves.

Bass traps set into the rear corners of the room

Chapter 3: Meeting the Mixing Board

In This Chapter

✔ Understanding the mixer

✔ Deciphering channel strips

✔ Exploring routing and busing

*I*f you've ever been to a recording studio and watched a great recording engineer create a mix, you've probably been entranced by how he or she interacted with the mixing board: a dance around the mixer, a twist of a knob here, a push of a slider there. All this to the beat of the music. It's like watching a genius painter paint, or a great orchestra conductor conduct, or a brilliant surgeon surge . . . er, operate. I'll even bet that one of the reasons you got interested in home recording is so you could have a chance to play with those knobs yourself. Go ahead and admit it — you'll feel better.

Well, you get your chance in this chapter. Not only do you discover what each of those knobs does, you get a feel for all the functions that the mixer fulfills in the studio. You discover what makes up a channel strip and how it's used. You get a chance to see how routing works (and even discover what routing *is*). And you see how digital mixers use fader banks to provide numerous functions while taking up very little space.

Meeting the Many Mixer Types

Pro Tools has an integrated mixer as part of its software, with which you can effectively do anything that you could possibly want (and more) with your music. You can adjust equalizers (EQ), levels, panning, and routing (to name just a few) by either using keystrokes on your computer keyboard or administering a click of your mouse.

Even with all the power that the Pro Tools mixer has, some people (myself included) like to have some knobs to twiddle and some faders to slide while they work. If you're one of these people, the following sections help you decide which of the three hardware options would work best for you.

Analog mixer

An *analog mixer,* as shown in Figure 3-1, enables you to route the signals within the analog domain. Analog mixers tend to have many knobs, lights, and faders — a set for each channel. If you want to change from mixing inputs (your instruments) to mixing sounds recorded on the recorder, you need to plug and unplug cords, or you need to get a mixer with twice as many channels as your recorder.

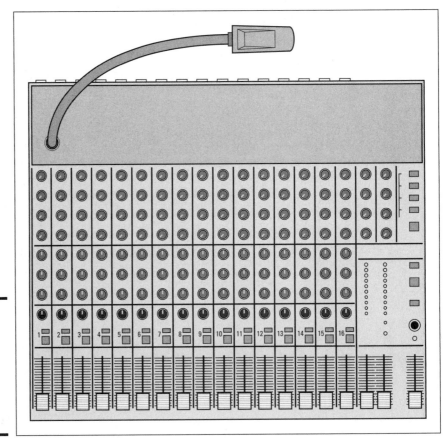

Figure 3-1:
An analog mixer has tons of knobs, lights, and faders to play with.

Many people prefer analog mixers because they believe they produce better sound than the mixer in Pro Tools software (not necessarily the case, at least to my ears), or they want to create elaborate mixes for a band to hear in their headphones while they record.

The main disadvantage to using an analog mixer with Pro Tools (or any other computer-based recording system) is that you need just as many analog inputs and outputs for your Digidesign/Avid hardware as you want channels to mix in your mixer. For example, if you want to mix a 16-track song, you need the equivalent of two Digi 002 Rack interfaces, assuming Digidesign/Avid would let you hook up two at once. At the time of this writing you are limited to just one. (For more on audio interfaces, check out Chapter 1 of this mini-book.) The other possible disadvantage is that each analog-to-digital-to-analog conversion degrades the sound of your music.

Digital mixer

A *digital mixer,* as shown in Figure 3-2, is a great option for Pro Tools users because it can perform the same functions as a conventional analog mixer in a lot less space, and you don't have to worry about having as many analog connections. Also, the whole issue of sound degradation from going back and forth to digital is moot because all your music stays in the digital domain.

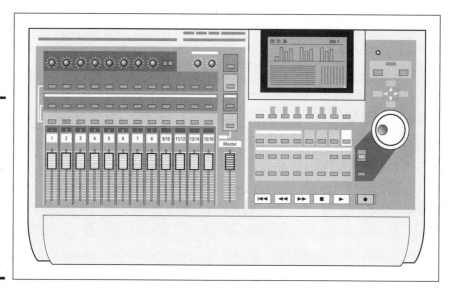

Figure 3-2:
A digital mixer performs the same functions but takes up less space than an analog mixer.

If you want to use a digital mixer with Pro Tools, make sure that it's compatible with the software — an easy task if you go to http://avid.force.com/pkb/articles/en_US/Compatibility/en353265 (Windows) http://avid.force.com/pkb/articles/en_US/Compatibility/en436391 (Mac) — and that you have enough channels of digital connection in your hardware. (Book II, Chapter 2 details each Avid hardware capability.)

Like in Pro Tools software, *routing* — sending your signals to various places within the mixer — becomes almost easy using a digital mixer. You can switch between input and track channels without having to change a single cord.

One of the great things about digital mixers is that any EQ or effects plug-ins that you use are powered by the processor in the mixer, not the processor in your computer. This can allow you to have many more effects on your mixes (not always a good thing) before your system bogs down.

The downside to this arrangement is that you're stuck with the EQ and effects that are part of your mixer. If they aren't that great to begin with, you may not want to use them.

The computer control surface

A *computer control surface* is a piece of hardware that interfaces with your computer to control the controls within the Pro Tools software. As far as I'm concerned, a computer control surface, like the one included with the Digi 003, is the way to go with Pro Tools — as long as you have a powerful-enough computer to handle the mix — because all your EQ and effects processing is still done in the computer, unlike what you'd get with a digital or analog mixer. (Chapter 1 of this mini-book has more on what constitutes a powerful-enough computer.) Quite a few control surfaces integrate smoothly with Pro Tools, including the cool-looking Command | 8 shown in Figure 3-3.

Before you buy a control surface from another manufacturer, check out the compatibility page at the Avid website at www.digidesign.com/compato to make sure that the one you want works with Pro Tools.

Figure 3-3:
A computer control surface acts like a digital mixer for a computer-based system.

These controllers send MIDI *messages* — coded with the Musical Instrument Digital Interface communications protocol — to the computer telling it which parameters to change. These controllers can easily be programmed to work like a separate digital mixer.

Understanding Mixer Basics

In spite of the many types of mixers out there (see the "Meeting the Many Mixer Types" section, earlier in this chapter), you'll discover that they all generally follow the same basic principles and have a number of elements in common. You'll also discover that regardless of the type of mixer you use, two mixing aspects — the channel strip and *busing* (routing) — are universal. The rest of this chapter concentrates pretty heavily on these two aspects.

Think of a mixing board as a sort of air-traffic controller for the audio world. Just like how the guys and gals in the towers near an airport communicate with all the planes in the air, making sure that collisions are avoided and that traffic moves quickly and efficiently, the mixer routes all the incoming and outgoing signals from the instruments, effects, and recording devices so they get to their desired destination without any problems.

Channel strip

The mixer is composed of numerous channels into which you process the signal of an instrument or microphone before it's sent to the recorder. This is the *channel strip.* (See upcoming Figure 3-6.) Even though the mixer may look confusing with all its knobs, lights, and sliders, you need to understand the basic makeup of just one channel to understand them all. The channel strip's job is to take the signal from an instrument or microphone and send it where you want it.

The channel strip also enables you to make adjustments to the level of the signal in a variety of ways: overall level, a certain frequency's level (different for each mixer), left or right stereo level, and effect levels.

The channel strip serves two functions:

+ To control the level of an input device (input channel)
+ To control the level of a recorded track (track channel)

Both functions of the channel strip operate the same way. In fact, you can use the same channel for either an input or a track signal. The only difference is which device (an instrument or the output from your recorder) is plugged in.

Input jack

An *input jack,* generally located on the back of the mixer (although it can also be on the upper part of the top of the mixer), is where you plug in your instrument (or microphone or the output from your recorder). Many professional mixers have both a quarter-inch and an XLR jack for each channel. (See Figure 3-4.) For the lowdown on jacks, read through Chapter 2 of this mini-book.

A ¼-inch jack is used for line-level sources, such as a synthesizer, a drum machine, or the cord from the Line Out of your guitar amp. An XLR jack is for the male end of the microphone cord. Most semi-pro and pro mixers also have phantom power available to a XLR jack. The *phantom power* feature sends a low level of current from the mixer to the microphone to get the microphone to produce a signal. Phantom power is necessary for professional condenser mics.

If you choose not to mic your guitar amp and instead want to plug your guitar directly into your mixer, you need to do one of three things:

✦ Plug your guitar into your amp and run a cord from the Line Output of the amp to the mixer's channel input.

✦ Plug your guitar into a *direct box* (a device that changes the impedance level of your guitar or bass; Book I, Chapter 1 has more on this) and plug the direct box into the channel input of your mixer.

✦ Plug your guitar directly into the hi-Z input (high impedance) of your mixer, if it has one. (You'll find this feature on many newer mixers.)

Most pro mixers allow you to use either a balanced or unbalanced cord. (For the scoop on balanced and unbalanced cords, see Book I, Chapter 2.) Read through the owner's manual for your mixer to find whether balanced connections are part of your mixer's specs. Balanced connections are important only if you have really long cords (longer than 25 feet, for instance) because they cut down on the noise that can result from long cord runs that use unbalanced cords.

Insert jack

Aside from quarter-inch and XLR input jacks, another jack — an *Insert jack* — is often found on the back of the mixer for each channel. Its purpose is to enable you to send the signal from the channel out to a processor, such as a compressor or an EQ, and to receive the signal after it's processed. Unlike the Effect Send (as described in the upcoming section on Auxiliary Send knobs), this jack won't let you mix in as much effect signal as you want — all of the signal is affected. Figure 3-4 shows a typical set of input jacks.

Insert and input jacks are different, serving two very different purposes. An Insert jack is a bit of a hybrid — it's an input jack as it acts as both an input and an output (which explains the cord that is used for it), but it still resides in the input section of a mixer, in this case below the XLR and Line input jacks.

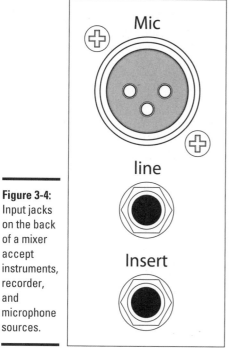

Figure 3-4:
Input jacks
on the back
of a mixer
accept
instruments,
recorder,
and
microphone
sources.

To use the Insert jack, you need a Y cable, as shown in Figure 3-5. You connect the plug at the base of the Y to the mixer Insert jack; the plugs on the two arms of the Y go into the input and output jacks of the processor.

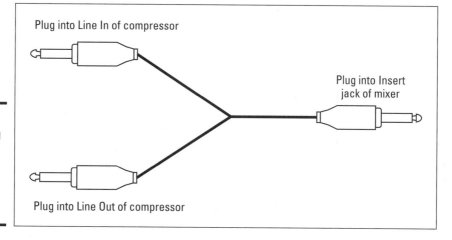

Figure 3-5:
Connecting
a signal
processor
to the
channel's
Insert jack.

Trim knob

The job of the *Trim knob* (labeled as *Gain* on your Avid interface) is to adjust the level of the input signal as it enters the mixer. (You usually find the Trim knob at the top of the front panel of the channel strip, as shown in Figure 3-6.) The amount that you adjust the Trim knob depends on the instrument that you plugged in to the channel strip; so be sure to listen as you make your adjustments.

✦ **If the Trim knob is set too high:** You get distortion.

If the Trim knob is set too low: You get too weak of a signal to record.

Most Trim knobs have a switch or markings for Line or Mic(rophone) signals. See these markings in Figure 3-6. Turn the knob all the way left for line sources — or slowly keep turning it right for microphone sources — until you get a nice, clean sound coming into the mixer. See Book III, Chapter 2 for more on setting your input levels.

If you choose to use an external preamp, check the owner's manual of your mixer to see whether you can bypass the internal preamp. Most professional mixers enable you to do this. Sometimes just having the Trim knob all the way down (to the Line marking) disengages the preamp from the circuit — and this is the case with the Avid preamps. You can also plug in to the line inputs if you want to keep your Avid preamps free for other mics or instruments.

Equalization

Semi-pro and pro mixers give you the opportunity to adjust the *equalization* (EQ) of your signal — that is, to boost or reduce specific ranges of sound frequency. Less expensive mixers have fewer equalizer settings (as few as two — one for high frequencies and one for low frequencies). Pro mixers have three or four; digital mixers and software mixers may have more.

Channel Auxiliary (Aux) Send knobs

You may want to add an effect such as reverb or delay to the signal coming into your mixer. With effects such as reverb, you don't want to use the Insert jack — like you would with a compressor — because you want to be able to control how much of the effect you actually hear. (Compressors affect the entire signal, not some portion of it. You can find more about compressors in Book VI, Chapter 4.)

This is where the *Auxiliary (Aux) Send* feature comes in. That's what the little knobs in the middle of the channel strip in Figure 3-6 are for. Adjust these knobs to send as much (or as little) of the signal as you want to go to the appropriate *auxiliary* component (Aux, get it?). Doing so specifies how much (or how little) of the effects processing shows up in your final sound. Turning the knob to the left produces less effect; turning it to the right gives you more effect.

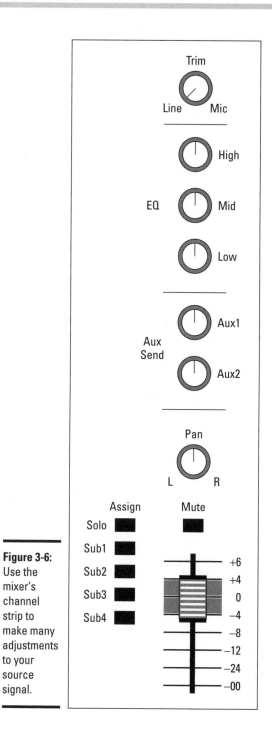

Figure 3-6:
Use the mixer's channel strip to make many adjustments to your source signal.

Not only can you set the Effect Send level at each channel (and you can send more than one channel's signal to each effect), you can also adjust the level of the affected signal that's brought back into the mixer and mixed with all the dry signals at the master bus. (See the "Routing/Busing Signals" section later in this chapter.) This is the *Aux Return,* which you can find out more about in the "Auxiliary (Aux) Return knobs" section, later in this chapter.

Pre/Post switch

The *Pre/Post switch* enables you to send the signal to the Aux bus (through the Aux Send knobs) either before (pre) it gets through the EQ and channel fader or after (post) it goes there. Use the Pre/Post switch to send an unequalized signal to the effect, and then to adjust the EQ of the *dry* (unaffected) signal without affecting what the effect sounds like. You can also use the Pre/Post switch to control the level of both the signal and the effect with the channel fader.

Having this option gives you more flexibility to control what the affected sound will sound like. For example, you can send the dry signal of a kick drum to a reverb (with the switch in the Pre position) and then boost the bass on the dry signal. Doing this gives you some reverb on the higher frequencies without adding it to the lower ones, which would create some mud in the final mix. The downside to this technique is that you can't use a fader to control the level of the signal being sent to the effect. (You bypassed the fader in the Pre position.) In this case, if you raise and lower the channel fader, the amount of effect that you hear in relation to the dry signal will change as well. For example, when you lower the fader, you hear more effect because less of the dry signal is mixed in. Comparatively, when you raise the fader, you hear less effect because the dry signal is louder and the effect level is the same.

Pan knob

Use the *Pan knob* to adjust where in the stereo field (how far left or right) your signal is heard. This knob is generally located toward the bottom of the channel strip and is an important part of mixing. Where you put something in the stereo field has an effect on how well it's heard among all the other instruments playing through the mixer. (Book VI, Chapter 1 has more details on panning and mixing.)

Mute switch

The *Mute switch,* located toward the bottom of the channel strip, enables you to silence (mute) the channel. This switch is commonly used during mixdown to help you work with the sound of a particular part in the mix. This switch allows you to quickly silence the parts you don't want to hear when you're mixing so you can concentrate on the sound of the instruments that you want to hear. For example, when you work in EQing and balancing the levels of the drum set, you can use the mute switch for all the other channels so you hear only the drumset tracks.

Solo switch

The *Solo switch,* when engaged, allows one channel to "sing solo" while muting all the rest. This switch (normally located near the Mute switch) is also commonly used during mixdown when you want to hear only one instrument. This saves you the hassle of having to press the Mute switch on all the rest of the channels. For example, when you work on EQing and are affecting the lead vocal, you can press the Solo switch to mute all the other instruments while you make your adjustments. Then, when you want to hear what your adjusted vocal sounds like with the rest of the instruments, all you have to do is disengage the Solo switch (press it again).

Assign switches

The *Assign switches* can be located just above the fader, at the top of the mixer, or right next to the fader. Use these switches to choose where to send the outgoing signal. You can send it to the Master bus or to any of the submix buses. (For more on *buses* — the electronic pathways along which signals are sent — see its upcoming section.) If your mixer doesn't have a separate Solo switch, one of the Assign switches can give you the option of soloing that channel.

Faders

A *fader,* usually a slider control located at the bottom of each channel strip, determines the overall level of the signal coming out of the channel strip before it makes its way to the recorder, the Master bus, or the Submix bus. (Check out the following section for more details.)

Routing/Busing Signals

After you have an instrument plugged in to the mixer channel strip, you want to send that signal somewhere. This is *routing* or *busing.* (The place where the signal ends up is, conveniently enough, a *bus.*) Most mixers offer numerous busing possibilities, including busing to the

+ **Master bus:** Send your mixed music to a two-track recorder.

+ **Submix bus:** Mix several tracks before they go to the Master bus.

✦ **Control Room bus:** Listen to the tracks through your monitors.

✦ **Auxiliary bus:** Add an effect to your signal.

In the following sections, I introduce you to some of the most used busing options and describe some ways to make this process easier.

The busing controls are generally located on the right side of the mixing console, as shown in upcoming Figure 3-7. Here you have faders for the Master and Submix (Sub) buses; dials for the Aux bus; and Solo and Mute buttons for the Master and Submix (Sub) buses. This area is often called the *master control section* of the mixer.

Master fader

A *Master fader,* located in the lower-right corner of Figure 3-7, controls the Master bus, where your mixed music goes out to the 2-track recorder or back into Pro Tools. When you have something plugged in to a channel input, it's automatically sent to the Master bus. Where you have your Pan knob set for each channel (how far to the left or right) dictates how much signal is sent to the left or right channels of the Master bus. Some mixers are designed with only one Master fader to control all channels, both left and right; on other mixers, you have one fader for each left and right channel.

Sub (submix) faders

Depending on the mixer you own, you may or may not have a group of Sub (submix) faders located to the left of the Master fader (refer to Figure 3-7). *Submix faders* control the Submix buses, which is where you can mix several of your tracks and group them independently of the rest of the tracks. You use the Assign switches for each channel to choose which (if any) Submix buses you want the signal sent to.

The submix can be sent out of the mixer as a unit. For example, you may want to record all the drums on one or two tracks instead of recording them individually. The submix is also routed to the Master bus as a unit. If you assign instruments to a submix, they get diverted from the Master bus and go to the Submix fader first. Then everything assigned to that Submix fader gets sent to the Master bus to be controlled by the Master fader. Most mixers also allow you to send the submix out without having to go through the Master bus first; often the Submix outputs are located on the back of the mixer.

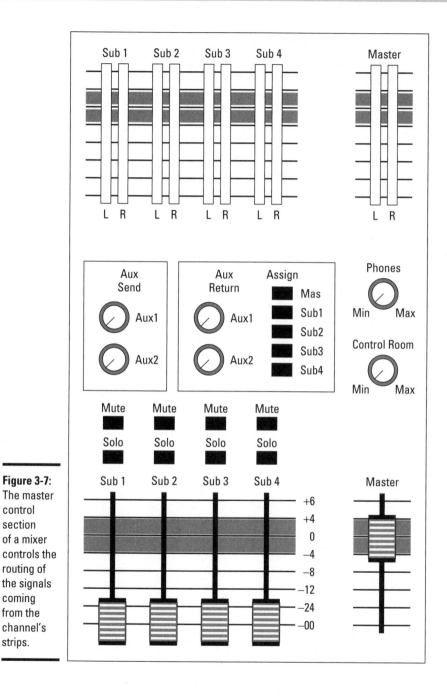

Figure 3-7:
The master
control
section
of a mixer
controls the
routing of
the signals
coming
from the
channel's
strips.

Solo/Mute switches

Above each Submix fader on your mixer, you'll most likely have *Mute* and *Solo switches,* as shown back in Figure 3-7. Use these switches to, well, solo or mute (that is, isolate or silence) the submix group. For example, you may want to hear only the submix of the drums or maybe background vocals. This switch allows a quick check of your submix.

Control Room level knob

The *Control Room level knob,* usually located above the Master fader (refer to Figure 3-7), controls the level of the signal going through the Control Room bus — the signal that's sent to your studio monitors. The Control Room level knob is fed by the Master bus and has the same mix that goes through the Master Output to your recorder. This allows you to monitor your mix at a different volume from that of the master level being sent out through the Master bus.

The Control Room level knob is especially useful when you're recording and sending a high level to the recorder but also want to listen to what's being recorded — at a more comfortable, lower volume — through the monitor speakers.

Phones knob

Like the Control Room level knob, the *Phones knob* (located above the Control Room level knob in Figure 3-7) enables you to adjust the level going to the headphones independently of the master level. The Phones knob is fed by the Master bus and has the same mix as the Master fader.

Auxiliary (Aux) Send knobs

The *Aux Send knobs,* also located in the master controls section of the mixer, allow you to send the entire mix from the Master bus to an effects processor, such as a reverb or delay. Looking back at Figure 3-7, you can see the Aux Send knobs above the Submix fader on the left.

Auxiliary (Aux) Return knobs

The *Aux Return knobs* control the overall level for each of the signals routed through an effects processor and sent back to the Master bus. You use these knobs to mix in the amount of *wet* (affected) signal that you want. The wet signal mixes with the *dry* (unaffected) signals from each of the channels.

Aux Assign

Some mixers can route a signal sent through an effects processor to any of the submix buses, where they can be controlled by the corresponding submix fader. This *Aux Assign* capability enables you to have (for instance) the reverb you want on the drums routed to the Submix fader that controls the overall drum level. You choose your bus by pressing in the corresponding Assign button.

Master Level meters

At the top of many mixers are the *Master Level meters,* which keep tabs on recording levels and warn you when you may be producing a signal that's too strong or too weak. Too strong of a signal can lead to distortion; too weak of a signal produces a sound that lacks fidelity (sounds *thin*). Master Level meters can come in the form of VU (volume unit) meters (the ones with needles that go back and forth) or as LED lights (where green is good, and red is bad).

Deciphering Output Jacks

Most mixers have a bunch of *output jacks* (where — you guessed it — the signal comes out) located at the left on the back of the mixer, as shown in Figure 3-8. You often find output jacks for the Master bus, headphones, monitors, and Direct Outs for each channel, as well as jacks for the Aux Returns.

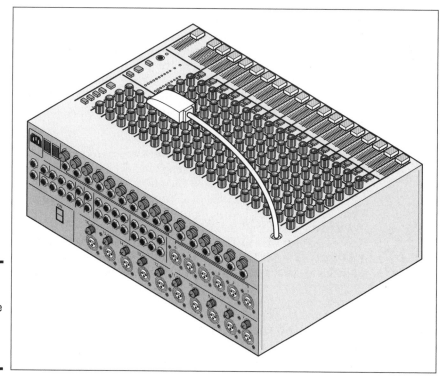

Figure 3-8:
Mixers usually have their output jacks in the back.

Master Out jack

The *Master Out jack* goes to the power amp for your speakers or to a mastering recorder (2-track). This jack is controlled by the Master fader and sends the signal that's routed through the Master bus.

Phones jack

The *Phones jack* is for your headphones and is fed by the Phones knob on the master console, which carries the same signal as the Master bus — only you get to control the volume separately.

Monitors jack

The *Monitors jack* is where you plug in your monitor speakers. Control this jack with the Monitor (or Control Room) knob on the mixer. It carries the signal from the Master bus to the speakers.

Direct Out jacks

You get *Direct Out jacks* on more full-featured mixers. These jacks are controlled by their corresponding channel fader (Channel 1 goes to Direct Out 1, Channel 2 to Direct Out 2, and so on). The signal goes directly out from each channel without going through the Master bus.

Most semi-pro and pro mixers won't actually have a Direct Out for each mixer channel. That's no big deal because Direct Out jacks are designed so you can send a signal directly out (hence the name) from the channel to a recorder. If you don't have Direct Outs on your mixer, you can just use the Insert jack to send your signal directly out of the mixer and into the recorder. The exact procedure for this connection depends on your mixer; check your owner's manual.

Direct Out jacks are really helpful when you're recording with *overdubs,* when you layer a track by recording one instrument at a time. For example, you could record the drums on Channels 1–4, the bass guitar on Channel 5, and the guitar part on Channel 6. You then send the signal via the Direct Outs from Channels 1–6 to the recorder's Tracks 1–6 and send those signals back to the mixer on Channels 9–14. You could then use Channel 7 to record the lead guitar part to Track 7 of the recorder while listening to Tracks 1–6 on Channels 9–14. This saves you from having to crawl behind your mixer and change cords when you want to hear the recorded track.

As you can see, the mixer setup can get complicated. Don't worry. After you get to know your mixer and get a chance to try some different routing configurations, this stuff will become second nature to you.

Aux Return jacks

Aux Return jacks are where you plug in the cord from the Line Out jack of your effects processor. This jack is fed to the Aux Return knob.

Making Life Easier with a Patch Bay

After you set up your mixer and plug it into the input devices, effects processors, and recorder, you're set to go. But what if you want to record a track and then listen to it right away to see whether you like what you hear? Well, for most home recordists, this can be a problem because you'll most likely have only enough channel strips in your mixer for either recording or for listening. If this is the case, you have to crawl behind the mixer and unplug your input device and then plug in the outputs from your recorder. Then, when you're done listening, you have to switch the cables back to record again. All this crawling and connecting can be time-consuming (and eventually hard on your cables).

The solution is to get a *patch bay* — a device that consists almost entirely of input and output jacks. You plug your gear into it so you can change the cord configuration without crawling around behind your big pile of technology. Check out Figure 3-9 for a look at a patch bay.

Figure 3-9:
Use a patch bay to avoid plugging and unplugging gear.

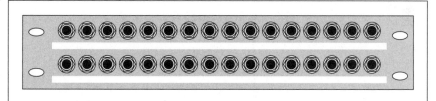

An essential tool for analog studios, a patch bay is also useful for the more complicated digital studios as well. Patch bays function by giving two series of jacks:

✦ One in the back where you plug in all your gear

✦ One in the front that you can use to *patch* — connect with cables — any one piece of gear into any other

For example, imagine that you want to plug in the output from your synthesizer into Channels 1 and 2, and you want to record your friend's guitar on Channel 3. At the same time, you want to monitor the bass guitar on Channel

4 and the drums on Channels 5–8. This is pretty straightforward, but what if you want to hear what you recorded on Channels 1–3? With a patch bay, all you have to do is change the cords going into mixer Channels 1–3 at the patch bay.

You still have to change cords when you use a patch bay, but at least everything is up front and accessible; without a patch bay, you're stuck having to crawl behind your mixer and recorder to change the cords.

Chapter 4: MIDI and Electronic Instruments

In This Chapter

✔ Understanding Musical Instrument Digital Interface (MIDI)

✔ Getting to know synthesizers, drum machines, and other electronic instruments

✔ Synchronizing MIDI devices

✔ Exploring sequencing

My first job in a recording studio was in 1985. I can still remember the first time I walked into that studio. The owner was sitting, arms crossed, in front of the mixing console (called a *console* in those days because the mixer was an actual piece of furniture that took up nearly the whole room). He looked at me and hit a key on the Macintosh computer sitting next to him. Then all of a sudden, a synthesizer started playing, then another, and yet another. "This is cool," I thought. But then I heard my nemesis — the drum machine.

Drum machines made me lose my recording gigs as a drummer and drove me to expand my career to that of a recording engineer as well. However, I eventually came to love that drum machine and the many others to follow (sigh). In fact, over the years, I became so captivated by the whole MIDI/drum machine thing that I assembled a whole series of electronic drumsets using drum machines and samplers — all controlled through MIDI.

In this chapter, you find out how MIDI enables synthesizers and computers to communicate with one another — a revolutionary thing for the musician. You get your hands dirty in the world of *sequencing* — recording MIDI performance information so you can play your performance automatically. You also peruse a variety of MIDI-capable instruments and explore the ins and outs of controlling your MIDI gear.

Like audio recording, MIDI can be a deep subject. You can go nuts trying to understand every little nuance of MIDI. (I know some guys who are not quite the same after plunging headfirst into this stuff.) The reality is that to use MIDI effectively, you don't need to know every little thing about it. In this chapter, I focus on what you need to know to get started.

Meeting MIDI

MIDI is a *protocol* (a set of agreed-upon standards) for musical instruments to communicate with one another through a cabled connection and a common digital language. This arrangement allows each one to understand the other, regardless of manufacturer or instrument. All that's required is an instrument equipped with MIDI ports (jacks).

MIDI data is different from an audio recording because it contains no sound as such; rather, it's limited to performance information. This includes information about various performance characteristics, which (for keyboards, at least) includes the following:

✦ **Note-on and note-off:** What note is played and when

✦ **Velocity:** How hard someone presses a key

✦ **After-touch:** Whether the key pressure changes after the initial press

✦ **Vibrato and pitch bend:** Whether the pitch changes while a key is pressed

This information allows the MIDI musician potentially to create a performance that is as rich in texture as those of the world's finest players.

Digital messages sent from one device to another across a cable (called the *MIDI cable,* of course) create MIDI data. The cable connects to MIDI ports on each device, and the messages are sent in the form of binary digits. Each instrument can understand and respond to these messages.

Perusing MIDI ports

The three types of MIDI ports are In, Out, and Thru.

✦ **In:** The In port receives incoming messages.

✦ **Out:** This port sends those messages.

✦ **Thru:** This port sends the messages that one device receives directly to the In port of another instrument. You use the Thru port when you create a *daisychain,* which means you connect more than two devices.

Figure 4-1 shows a daisychain setup.

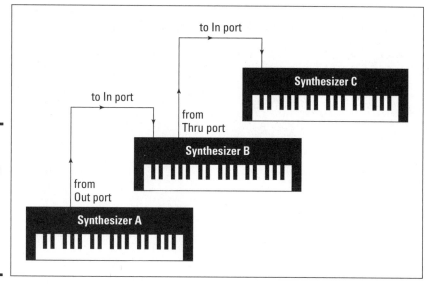

Figure 4-1:
MIDI
devices can
be chained
via the In,
Out, and
Thru ports
on each
instrument.

MIDI signals travel in only one direction. Data flows from the Out port of one device to an In port of another device — but not the other way around. Likewise, data going through the Thru port originates from the first device in the chain — not the device whose Thru port is being used. The particular way that data flows is what gives you flexibility in how you can connect different devices together. Here are some examples:

✦ **Example 1:** In Figure 4-1, three synthesizers are connected in a daisy-chain lineup. A cable connects device A's Out port to device B's In port. Another cable connects device B's Thru port to device C's In port. In this scenario, device A controls devices B and C. Devices B and C can't control any other device, because neither device B nor device C has a connection from its Out port.

✦ **Example 2:** Suppose you connect device B to device C by using device B's Out port instead of its Thru port. In this case, device A sends messages to device B but not to device C. Device B controls device C. Device C has no control over either A or B because neither one is connected to device C's Out port.

✦ **Example 3:** Now take a look at Figure 4-2. In this figure, two devices have MIDI cables running from the Out port of each to the In port of the other — which allows communication to go both ways. (The MIDI interface in this figure is necessary for making MIDI connections in a computer.) For example, a master synthesizer and a computer sequencer are frequently connected this way so you can send performance information from the synthesizer to the sequencer (when you're recording your part) and from the sequencer back to the synthesizer (when you want to play the part back again).

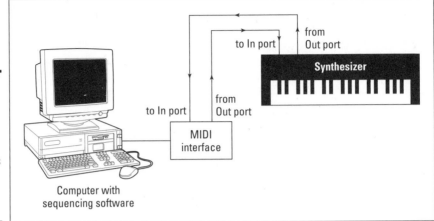

Figure 4-2:
Connecting
two devices
with cords
going both
ways allows
two-way
communi-
cation.

A connection to a MIDI device's In port or through a device's Thru port
doesn't allow the device to control another device. A MIDI device can control another device only if the cable is connected from its Out port to the
other device's In port.

Understanding MIDI channels

Okay, so you have a daisychain of MIDI instruments all hooked together, and
you want to control them from your master keyboard or sequencer program.
Now you want the drum machine to play the drum part and a sound module
to play the string part. This is where MIDI channels come in handy.

MIDI channels allow you to designate which messages go to a particular
machine. You can program each machine to receive messages on one or
more of the 16 MIDI channels. For instance, you can set your drum machine
to receive messages on Channel 10 (the default channel for drum sounds)
and set the sound module with the string sounds to receive data on Channel 1.
(You set the MIDI channels on your digital instrument by going into the
System Parameters menu. Check your owner's manual for specific procedures.) After you assign your channels, your master keyboard sends the
performance information for both MIDI signals — the drum machine and
the sound module playing the string sounds — across one MIDI cable. Each
receiving device responds only to the messages directed to the MIDI channel
that it's assigned to receive.

In this scenario, the sound module with the string sounds receives all the
data from the master keyboard, responds to the messages on Channel 1,
and simultaneously sends the data from the master keyboard onto the drum
machine (via the sound module's Thru port). The drum machine receives

the same messages from the master keyboard as the sound module but responds only to those sent for Channel 10.

Having 16 MIDI channels allows you to have up to 16 separate instruments playing different parts at the same time. You may use 16 different devices or 16 different parts from the same device if you have a multitimbral sound generator. (See the "Synthesizers" section later in this chapter for more on such sound generators.)

You'd think that each MIDI channel would be sent along its own wire in the MIDI cable. That's actually not the case. Inside the MIDI cable are three wires — two for data transmission, and one to serve as a shield. MIDI messages are sent across the two wires via a *channel code,* which tells the receiving device to what channel it should send the data following the code. Such a MIDI channel message, also called a *channel voice message,* precedes each performance command.

Appreciating MIDI messages

In order for MIDI instruments to communicate with one another, they need to have a vocabulary in common. This is where MIDI messages come in. MIDI messages contain an array of commands, including performance data, control changes, system-common messages, and system-exclusive messages (more about this shortly).

Not all MIDI devices recognize all MIDI commands. For example, a sound module generally can't send performance-data messages (such as aftertouch) because a sound module doesn't have triggering mechanisms that produce those commands.

Check your instrument's manual for a MIDI Implementation Chart. All MIDI instruments come with this chart. In it, you can find a list of all the MIDI commands that the device can send or receive. The chart also includes information on *polyphony* (how many notes the instrument can play at once and *multitimbrality* (how many different sounds the instrument can produce at the same time).

Performance data

Included in performance data are note-on and note-off messages, as well as specifications for velocity, after-touch, vibrato, and pitch bend.

MIDI performance-data messages each have 128 different values. For example, each note that you play on the keyboard has a number associated with it. Middle C is 60, for instance. Likewise, velocity is recorded and sent as a number between 0 and 127, 0 being the softest volume (no sound) and 127 the loudest that you can play.

Control-change messages

Control-change messages are a type of performance-data message. These messages contain data about expression, including modulation, volume, and pan.

System-common messages

System-common messages contain data about which channel the performance data is sent to and what sound in the sound library to play. System-common messages also include information about timing data, master volume, and effects settings.

System-exclusive messages

System-exclusive messages contain information that is exclusive to the system or device. These messages can include data transfers of new sound patches, among other things.

To use MIDI effectively, you don't need to know all (or even many) of the MIDI messages that a device can recognize. If you hook up your gear and play, your MIDI devices generate and respond to the messages for you.

Managing modes

Your synthesizer, drum machine, or other MIDI module has four operating modes, appropriately called Mode 1, Mode 2, Mode 3, and Mode 4. These modes dictate how your instrument responds to the MIDI messages it receives.

Mode 1: Omni On/Poly

In Omni On/Poly mode, your instrument responds to all the MIDI messages coming across the wires (well, except for the MIDI channel data). This means that your synthesizer (or whatever) tries to play the parts of all the instruments hooked up to your MIDI controller. In this mode, your device also plays *polyphonically* (more than one note at a time).

Some older MIDI devices default to Omni On/Poly mode (Mode 1) when you turn them on. In such a case, you have to reset your instrument if it's one of several in your MIDI setup. If you don't, the instrument responds to any MIDI message sent from the controller, not just the ones directed toward it.

Mode 2: Omni On/Mono

Omni On/Mono allows your device to receive messages from all MIDI channels but lets it play only one note at time *(monophonically).* This mode is rarely, if ever, used.

Mode 3: Omni Off/Poly

In the Omni Off/Poly mode, your device can play polyphonically but responds only to MIDI signals on the channels that it's set to. This is the mode you use most often when you're *sequencing* — recording or playing back MIDI data. (Book V, Chapter 2 covers this process in Pro Tools in greater detail.)

Mode 4: Omni Off/Mono

In the Omni Off/Mono mode, your instrument responds only to the messages sent on the MIDI channel that it's set to and ignores the rest. Rather than play polyphonically, like in Mode 3, your instrument plays only one note at a time. This can be advantageous if you're playing a MIDI controller from an instrument that can play only one note at a time, such as a flute or saxophone.

General MIDI

If you end up composing music for other people to play on their MIDI instruments — or if you want to use music from another composer — General MIDI is invaluable to you. General MIDI (GM) is a protocol that enables a MIDI instrument to provide a series of sounds and messages consistent with other MIDI instruments. With General MIDI, you can take a Standard MIDI File (SMF) of a song created on one sequencer program, transfer the file to another program, and use that other program to play the exact performance — sounds, timing, program changes, everything.

GM instruments contain numerous sound patches that the MIDI community has standardized. Not all these sounds are exactly the same as far as sound quality goes, but their sound type and location (acoustic grand piano on Patch #1, for instance) are the same on all GM-compatible machines.

Not all MIDI-capable instruments follow the GM standards. If this feature is important to you, be sure you find out before you buy whether the instrument that interests you is GM compatible.

GM standards dictate not only the particular sounds that a synthesizer has, but also which drum sounds are located on which keys, how many notes of polyphony the instrument has, and how many different channels the instrument can receive and send instructions on. The two levels of GM compatibility are Level 1 and Level 2.

GM Level 1 compatibility

Level 1 protocols were developed in 1991 and consist of a minimum of 128 instrument patches, 24 notes of polyphony, receiving and sending capability for all 16 MIDI channels, 16-part multitimbrality, and a host of controller and performance messages.

More is better

Roland and Yamaha both decided a while ago to raise the bar on the GM Level 1 standards by developing their own protocols. Called GS and XG, respectively, the machines conforming to either of these standards are synthesizers on steroids. For example, the Yamaha XG protocol calls for a minimum of 480 sounds, including at least 9 drumsets and 51 types of effects (reverb, chorus, and variations), among a host of control-change messages. The Roland GS standard, on the other hand, requires at least 226 different instrument patches and 20 different control-change messages, among other things.

If you use a GS or an XG synthesizer to compose your music, you may be disappointed if you play that composition back on a synthesizer that doesn't have the GS or XG enhancements because the sound won't be quite the same. You'll get the same instrument type (grand piano, for instance), but the sound of the instrument will be different. Also, if you use any of the additional MIDI messages contained in the GS and XG protocols (control change, for example), they won't be understood by the non-GS or -XG device.

GM Level 2 compatibility

Level 2 was implemented in 1999 and includes more sounds, polyphony, and features. A GM Level 2-compatible device has 32 notes of polyphony, 16-channel support, up to 16 simultaneous instrument sound patches, and a host of additional sounds (384, to be exact), including 2 channels of simultaneous percussion sounds. Also added to the GM2 standard are reverb and chorus effects.

Getting Started with MIDI

Enough with the technical aspects of MIDI — you want to know how to start using this great technology, right?

To get started, you first need to know just what you have to buy to do some MIDI-ing yourself. Well, I'm sorry to inform you that you can't do any of this cool MIDI stuff with your vintage Stratocaster guitar or your acoustic drumset (unless you do some fancy rigging to your gear — see the sidebar, "MIDI control this . . ."). What you do need is

+ **A sound generator:** This device, which enables you to hear the music, can be a synthesizer, drum machine, sound module, or sampler.

+ **A MIDI controller:** This device controls the MIDI instruments in your studio. You'll most likely use the MIDI functions in Pro Tools for this purpose. This may also be your keyboard, electronic drum pads, or other MIDI instruments (such as the Roland GK3).

✦ **A sequencer:** This device records and plays the MIDI performances that are programmed into it. The sequencer allows you to program your part into the synthesizer and have it play back automatically (much like the old-time player piano). Again, you'll most likely use Pro Tools software for this, but you can use a sequencer in your keyboard if you prefer.

✦ **A MIDI interface:** The MIDI interface is used to enable your computer to send and receive MIDI data. If you have an Mbox 2, an Mbox 2 Pro, an Eleven Rack, a Digi 003, a Digi 003 Rack, or one of the M-Audio interfaces with equipped MIDI ports, you already have what you need to get MIDI in and out of your system. (Sorry, Mbox2 Mini and non-MIDI M-Audio users: You have to buy a separate MIDI interface.)

I know this sounds like a lot of stuff, but most of this gear performs more than one function in the MIDI studio. For example, nearly all synthesizers come with drum sounds, and some synthesizers even include a sequencer. In this case, this one synthesizer can do the job of sound generator, drum machine, MIDI controller, and sequencer all in one.

In the following sections, I discuss the different types of sound generators. You may indeed find one piece of equipment that does everything you want. If that's not your situation, read on as I separate all the features that different equipment has. That way, you can understand the function of each feature and then decide how to configure your studio.

Sound generators

The sound generator is the core of the MIDI studio. This is what produces the sounds that you hear. Without it, you may as well skip the rest of the stuff because (of course) you won't hear any of your work.

Sound generators can come in many different shapes and sizes: a fully functional keyboard synthesizer, an independent drum machine, a standalone sound module, samplers, software synthesizers (soft-synths), and a computer sound card. Each of these devices has its strengths and weaknesses. (Read on for the details.)

In the following sections, I discuss the different types of sound generators. Although you may find one piece of equipment that does everything you want, in this section, I separate all the features that different equipment may have to help you understand the function of each feature and decide how to configure your studio.

Synthesizers

A synthesizer, like the one shown in Figure 4-3, consists of not only sounds but also a keyboard on which you can play these sounds. Synthesizers come in a variety of sizes and configurations. For example, some keyboards come with 61 keys (5 octaves), and others provide as many as 88 keys (the number on an acoustic piano keyboard).

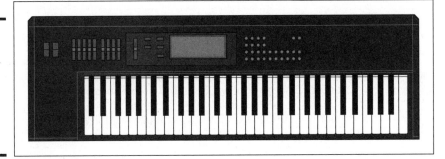

Figure 4-3:
A typical synthesizer contains a keyboard and a variety of sounds.

If you're in the market for a synthesizer, you need to consider several things:

✦ **Polyphony:** *Polyphony* is the number of notes that sound at one time. Most decent synthesizers nowadays have at least 16 notes of polyphony although models that can produce 32 notes at once are not uncommon.

Each manufacturer treats polyphony differently, and the GM standards allow some variations on the effective use of this parameter. For instance, a synth patch may use more than one digital sound to create the actual sound you hear. The synth patch that you love so much may, in fact, consist of four different sounds layered atop one another. In such a case, you just reduced your polyphony by three-fourths, just by using that one patch. If your synthesizer has 16-note polyphony, it's now down to 4-note polyphony because each of those 4 notes has four "sounds" associated with it. If you use this patch, you can play only 4 notes (a simple chord) at a time, not the 16 that you thought you had to work with.

Your best bet is to buy a synthesizer (or sound module) with the highest polyphony you can get, especially if you want to layer one sound on top of another or do multitimbral parts with your synth.

✦ **Multitimbrality:** Most decent keyboards allow you to play more than one sound patch at a time. This is *multitimbrality,* which basically allows you to have your keyboard divided into several groups of sounds. For example, a multitimbral synth can divide a song's chords, melody, bass part, and drum set sounds into different groups of sounds — and then play all those groups at once.

TIP

If you do any sequencing (recording or playing back MIDI data), a multitimbral synthesizer is a must-have. Otherwise, you would need a separate synthesizer for each type of sound that you want to play. Fortunately, with the GM standards, compatible synthesizers made in the last 15 years have the ability to play 16 sounds at once.

✦ **Keyboard feel:** Some keyboards have weighted keys and feel like real pianos, and other keyboards have a somewhat spongy action. If you're a trained piano player, a spongy keyboard may feel uncomfortable to you. On the other hand, if you have no training in piano and don't need weighted keys, you don't have to pay the extra money for that feature.

✦ **Sound quality:** This is a subjective thing. Choose the synthesizer that has the sounds you think you'll use. I know this seems kind of obvious, but buy the synthesizer whose sounds you like even if this means waiting and saving the money before you can buy. If you buy a synthesizer that was a good deal but don't love the sounds, you've wasted your money because you'll just end up buying the more expensive one later.

✦ **Built-in sequencer:** Many keyboards contain a built-in sequencer, which allows you to program and play back your performance. Units like these are usually called *keyboard workstations* or *MIDI workstations* because they contain everything you need to create a song. If you're considering one of these complete workstations, take a good, hard look at the sequencer and the user interface — make sure that you like the way those work for you. Each manufacturer treats the process of sequencing a little differently; you can probably find one that fits your style of working.

Drum machines

A *drum machine* contains the sounds of the drumset and other more exotic drums, as well as a sequencer to allow you to program rhythms. Figure 4-4 shows a typical drum machine.

Most drum machines contain hundreds of drum sounds, numerous preset rhythm patches, and the ability to program dozens of songs. All stand-alone drum machines have pads on which you can play the part. The more advanced drum machines can give your rhythms a more human feel. Effects, such as reverb and delay, are also fairly common on the more advanced drum machines.

Sound modules

A *sound module* is basically a stripped-down version of a synthesizer or drum machine. Sound modules don't contain triggering devices (such as the keys for the keyboard, pickups for the guitar, or pads for the drum machine). What they do contain are a variety of sounds (often hundreds) that a master controller or sequencer can trigger. The advantage to sound modules is they take up little space and cost considerably less than their fully endowed counterparts (the synthesizers and drum machines, that is).

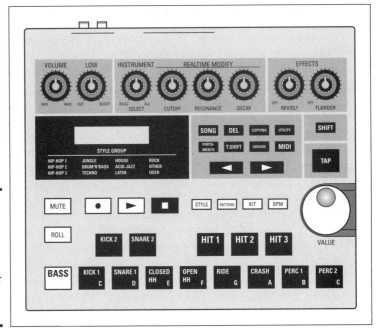

Figure 4-4:
A drum machine has drum sounds and a sequencer to program rhythms.

If you already have a master keyboard, you may find adding sound modules to be a cost- and space-effective way to add more sounds to your system.

Samplers

A *sampler* is a sound module that contains short audio samples of real instruments. Most samplers come with sound libraries containing hundreds of different types of sounds, from acoustic pianos to snare drums to sound effects. These sounds are often much more realistic than those that come in some synthesizers.

The real purpose of a sampler is to allow you to record your own sounds. For example, in the 1980s, it was cool to make a drumset from unusual percussive sounds. A snare drum can be the sound of a flushing toilet (don't laugh, I actually did this) or breaking glass. Tom-toms can be grunts set to certain pitches. You'd be amazed at the strange stuff that people have turned into music — all with the help of a sampler.

Another common use of a sampler is recording short sections of already recorded songs. This can be a melodic or rhythmic phrase, a vocal cue, or a single drum or synthesizer sound. Sampling other songs is common in electronic music, rap, and hip-hop (be careful of copyright issues before doing this, however). If you're into electronic music or hip-hop, you may find a sampler a necessary addition to your studio.

Soft-synths

Because you're using Pro Tools LE or Pro Tools M-Powered, your DAW (Digital Audio Workstation) software enables you to produce great sounds by using soft-synth plug-ins. *Soft-synths* are basically software equivalents of standalone synthesizers, sound modules, or samplers. As you can see in Figure 4-5, a soft-synth's GUI (its *graphical user interface,* the smiley face that the software shows the world) is often designed to look just like a piece of regular hardware, complete with "buttons" and "knobs."

Of course, soft-synths have their advantages and disadvantages:

✦ **Advantage:** Soft-synths cost less than standalone units because no hardware is involved.

✦ **Disadvantages:** Unlike regular synthesizers, soft-synths use up processor power. This can slow down your computer system and prevent you from recording as many audio tracks or applying as many effect patches as you'd like. Another downside (depending on whom you talk to) is that soft-synth programs may not sound quite as good as an external synthesizer.

Figure 4-5:
Computer-based DAW users can choose soft-synths to create synthesizer sounds.

Countless soft-synth plug-ins are available for Pro Tools. Check out the AvidAvid virtual synthesizers list for programs that will work with the software (www.avid.com/US/categories/Audio-Plug-ins/Virtual-Instruments).

MIDI control this . . .

MIDI controllers aren't just limited to those that you can find in your musical instrument store. In fact, a MIDI controller can be just about anything that you can imagine. Creative musicians have come up with interesting MIDI controllers, including body suits that allow you to tap on or move your body to trigger sounds.

You, too, can make your own MIDI controller. All you need is a little imagination and some basic building and electronics skills. For example, one of my first electronic drumsets consisted of kitchen pots and pans fitted with electric pickups routed to a Roland Octapad. This setup was easy to make. First, I attached a piezoelectric pickup (which cost about $1 from an electrical supply company) to the inside of a pan with silicon caulk. Then I connected the wires from the pickup to a cord with a quarter-inch TS plug on the end. I plugged the cord into the Octapad, and when I hit the bottom of the pan, the Octapad sent a MIDI message to my sampler. You can attach these simple $1 piezo-electric pickups to just about anything and trigger a sound source. (You may need a device, such as the Roland Octapad or other electronic drumset module, to convert the signal from the piezo pickup into MIDI messages.)

Sound cards

Most sound cards that you can put in your computer (or that come with a computer) have General MIDI sounds in them. Depending on the quality of your sound card, it may sound decent or border on unbearable.

To find out whether the GM sounds in your computer's sound card are any good, go ahead and play a MIDI file on your computer. First, do a search on the Internet for MIDI files (just type **MIDI** into your favorite search engine). Some sites require you to pay to download a song — especially for popular or familiar tunes — but you can find many sites that allow you to choose a song to listen to without downloading or paying a fee. Click a song, and it'll start playing automatically. You'll immediately know whether you like the sound of your sound card.

If you bought a new sound card for your computer to record audio with, you'll generally find that the sounds are pretty good. And (happily) with your audio program, you also have access to soft-synth patches.

MIDI controllers

A MIDI controller is essentially what its name describes: a device that can control another MIDI device. MIDI controllers come in many different formats. In fact, a MIDI controller can be anything from a synthesizer to a drum machine, or from a computer to a xylophone.

When MIDI first came out, your controller choice was limited to a keyboard, but now you can choose other options — keyboards, wind controllers (for saxophones or other wind instruments), guitars, or drums. So even if you don't play piano, you can find a controller that resembles an instrument you know how to play. Look around, and you may find one (or more) MIDI controllers that allow you to create music your way.

Sequencers

Although you can get standalone sequencers and sequencers integrated into a synthesizer, you probably want to just use the sequencer in Pro Tools for this. The reasons for this are many, but the overriding factor is that you can have your MIDI and audio tracks in one place, and Pro Tools offers you more powerful editing capabilities than a sequencer that's contained in a box and that uses a tiny LCD screen.

MIDI interfaces

The MIDI interface allows you to send and receive MIDI information from a computer. All Avid interfaces — with the exception of the Mbox — have a MIDI port. If you end up doing a lot of MIDI sequencing, though, and use more than one sound module or external controller — or if you have the Mbox 2 Mini — you need a separate MIDI interface, such as the one shown in Figure 4-6.

Figure 4-6:
A MIDI interface is necessary if you want to connect your instrument to a computer.

MIDI interfaces come in a staggering variety of configurations, so you have several things to consider when you buy a MIDI interface. Use the following questions to help you to determine your needs:

✦ **What type of computer do you own?** MIDI interfaces are configured to connect to a serial, parallel, or USB port. You determine which one to use by the type of port(s) you have in your computer. For example, new Macs have only a USB port although you can add a serial port if you remove the internal modem. A PC has either a parallel port or a USB port (sometimes both). PCs also have a joystick port, which accepts a special MIDI joystick cable; no MIDI interface is needed.

✦ **How many instruments do you intend to connect?** MIDI interfaces come with a variety of input and output configurations. There are models with two In and two Out, four In and four Out, and even eight In and eight Out. There are also "thru" boxes that have one or more inputs and several outputs. If you have only one or two instruments, you can get by with a smaller interface. In this case, a 2 x 2 interface — two In and two Out — would work great. If you have many instruments that you want to connect, you need a larger box.

Chapter 5: Understanding Microphones

In This Chapter

✔ **Looking at the various types of microphones**

✔ **Positioning microphones for the best sound**

✔ **Exploring a variety of preamps**

✔ **Taking care of your microphones**

A microphone's job is generally to try to capture, as closely as possible, the sound of an instrument. You can also use a microphone to infuse a specific sound characteristic into a performance. Likewise, a *preamp* — which boosts the signal of a microphone as it travels to the recorder — can be used to accurately represent a sound or to add texture and dimension to it. The fact is that microphones and preamps are the center of the sound engineer's palette. Just like a painter has his paints and brushes, you have your microphones and preamps. And just like a painter can create a stunning variety of visual textures with his tools, you, too, can make your creative statement with the judicious use of these two pieces of equipment.

In this chapter, you explore the two most versatile tools of your auditory craft. You look at the various types of microphones and preamps, and you gain an understanding of each one's role in capturing a performance. You also discover what types of mics and preamps work for particular situations. To top it off, this chapter guides you through purchasing and caring for your precious new friends (mics and preamps, that is). You can find out how to use your mics in Book III, Chapter 2, where I discuss specific mic placement options.

Meeting the Many Microphone Types

When you start looking at microphones, you'll find basically three different types of construction methods (condenser, dynamic, ribbon) and three basic polarity patterns (omnidirectional, figure-8, and cardioid). The following sections explore these various constructions and patterns and help you make sense of them.

Construction types

Whether a microphone is a $10 cheapie that has a cord permanently attached to it or a $15,000 pro model with gold-plated fittings, all microphones convert sound waves to electrical impulses that the preamp or mixer can read and the recorder can store. Each of the three main construction types captures this auditory signal in a different way, and as such, each adds certain characteristics to the sound. Here's how the different mics affect sound:

✦ **Condenser:** This type tends to have a well-rounded shape to its frequency response and a fast response, allowing it to often pick up high-transient material, such as the initial attack of drum, very well. These mics can sound more natural, but they can also be somewhat harsh if placed too close to a high-transient source.

✦ **Boundary:** Boundary mics are like condenser mics in that they can capture a broad range of frequencies accurately. Because these types of mics rely on the reflection of the sound source to a flat surface they are attached to, you need to make sure that this surface is large enough to reproduce the lowest frequency you want to capture. (Remember, sound waves get longer as the frequency gets lower.) Otherwise you lose the low frequencies.

✦ **Dynamic:** Dynamic mics tend to accentuate the middle of the frequency spectrum because the thick diaphragms (relatively speaking, compared to a condenser mic) take longer to respond.

✦ **Ribbon:** Because the ribbon mic is relatively slow to respond to an auditory signal, it tends to soften the transients (the initial attack of the sounds from an instrument) on instruments such as percussion and piano. The high end isn't as pronounced as with other construction types, so these mics tend to have a rounder, richer tone.

I detail these aspects in the following sections. In most cases, the type of construction dictates the general cost category in which the mics fit.

Condenser microphones

A condenser microphone is, without a doubt, the most popular style of microphone used in recording studios (home or commercial). Condenser mics are sensitive and accurate, but they can also be expensive. Recently, however, condenser mics have come down in cost, and you can buy a decent one for less than $100. Very good ones start at about $500.

Condenser microphones have an extremely thin metal (or metal-coated plastic or Mylar) *diaphragm* (the part that senses the signal). The diaphragm is suspended in front of a metal plate (a *backplate*). Polarizing voltage is applied to both the diaphragm and the backplate, creating a static charge in the space between them. When the diaphragm picks up a sound, it vibrates into the field between it and the backplate. This produces a small signal that can then be amplified. Figure 5-1 shows how a condenser mic is constructed.

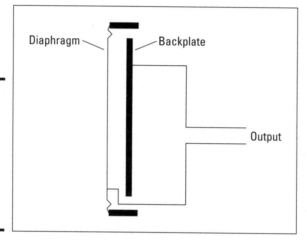

Figure 5-1:
A con-
denser mic
consists of
a very thin
diaphragm
suspended
parallel to a
backplate.

Condenser mics need a small amount of voltage (between 9 and 48 volts; V) to function. If you use a condenser mic, make sure that it has its own internal battery or that you have a preamp or mixer equipped with phantom power. (Not sure what "phantom power" means? You're in luck. The next section will enlighten you.)

Phantom power

Phantom power is the small amount of voltage applied to run a condenser microphone properly. In most cases, phantom power comes from your mixer or preamp and is sent to the microphone through one of the wires in an XLR cable. (I cover XLR cables in Chapter 3 of this mini-book.) Some condenser mics have an internal battery or separate power supply that provides this power.

A switch, which is usually located on the preamp or mixer, enables you to turn the phantom power off and on. Even though dynamic microphones don't use phantom power, this small amount of voltage doesn't damage them.

Tube or solid state

Condenser mics can be made with transistors (*solid-state* mics) or vacuum tubes (*tube* mics). Like with all gear that offers a choice between tube and solid state, base your decision on the sound characteristics that you prefer. For the most part, tube condenser mics have a softer high end (although not necessarily less high end) and a warmer overall tone. Solid-state mics, on the other hand, are often more *transparent:* They capture the sound with less coloration, sometimes with a bit greater clarity.

Large- or small-diaphragm

Condenser mics come in two broad categories: small diaphragm and large diaphragm (see Figure 5-2). Large-diaphragm condenser mics are more popular than their small-diaphragm counterparts; they offer a more pronounced bottom end (low frequencies). Large-diaphragm mics also make less *self noise,* which is electronic noise created by the microphone.

Before you go out and buy only large-diaphragm mics, consider this: Small-diaphragm condenser mics often have an even frequency response and can more accurately capture instruments with a pronounced high-frequency component (violins, for instance).

Figure 5-2: Condenser mics can have either small or large diaphragms.

Boundary microphones

A *boundary microphone* is essentially a small diaphragm condenser mic mounted in a housing that directs the diaphragm parallel to the surface on which it's mounted. You can see a diagram of a boundary mic's setup in Figure 5-3. The parallel setup allows the mic to pick up the sound that is reflected off the surface that it's mounted to, such as a wall or table.

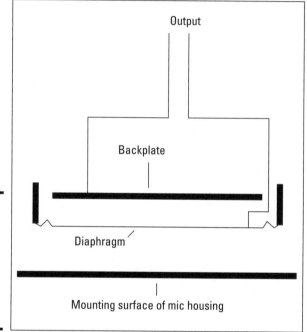

Figure 5-3:
Boundary mics are mounted on a flat surface to pick up the sound.

The advantage of a boundary mic is that it can pick up sounds accurately in reverberant rooms and can capture sounds from multiple sources. For example, if you were recording people talking in different parts of a room, one boundary mic could record everyone; you wouldn't need to use multiple mics.

Boundary mics are often mounted on the floor of a stage, a table in a conference room, or a lectern of a church or large hall. Because it's hard to find a surface large enough to vibrate to the lowest frequencies, it's more common to use these mics for vocals, pianos, and other instruments that don't have a super-low pitch. If you do record something like a kick drum with a boundary mic, you'll likely need to dial in some EQ on the lower frequencies. (Book VI, Chapter 3 has more on EQing your music.)

Boundary mics can be found in many of the same polarity patterns as condenser mics: omnidirectional and cardioid. These mics are fairly inexpensive and start under $100, though you can spend several hundred or more if you want.

The boundary microphone employs a condenser microphone diaphragm mounted parallel to the mounting surface to capture the reflections of the sounds off the surface to which the mic is mounted (see Figure 5-4). As the sound hits the surface that the mic is mounted to, it picks up the vibration, and the diaphragm creates an electrical charge that is sent to the preamp. These mics require phantom power to operate.

Figure 5-4:
Boundary
mics
place the
diaphragm
parallel to
the surface
on which it's
mounted.

Dynamic microphones

Chances are you've had a chance to use a dynamic mic. Two hugely popular Shure models characterize this type of mic — the SM57 and the SM58, which has a silvery ball of gridded wire at one end and an XLR connector at the other. Dynamic microphones have several qualities that make them unique. First, they can handle a lot of volume (technically known as *SPL,* or Sound Pressure Level), which makes them perfect for extremely loud signals, such as drums, amplifiers, and some rock vocals. Dynamic mics are not as *transparent* as condenser mics (they don't represent high frequencies as accurately), so they often impart a "dirty" or "gritty" sound to the signal.

The dynamic microphone uses a magnetic field to convert the sound impulse from the diaphragm into electrical energy (as illustrated in Figure 5-5). The diaphragm, often made of plastic or Mylar, is located in front of a coil of wire called a *voice coil.* The voice coil is suspended between two magnets. When the diaphragm moves (the result of a sound), the voice coil moves as well. The interaction between the voice coil's movement and the magnets creates the electrical signal.

The sound of a dynamic mic can be described as somewhat *boxy,* meaning that these mics don't represent the highest or lowest frequencies of your hearing spectrum accurately (not necessarily a bad thing). They are also durable. Rough treatment probably won't damage them much (aside from the diaphragm, which a tough metal screen protects). Dynamic mics are the type used most often for live shows. They tend to be inexpensive to buy and easy to maintain; you can get a good dynamic mic for around $100.

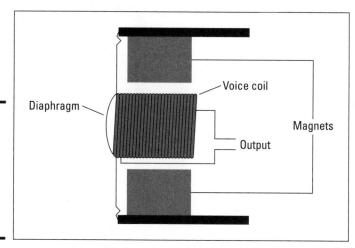

Figure 5-5:
Dynamic
mics pick
up a signal
by using a
magnetic
field and a
voice coil.

Ribbon microphones

A ribbon microphone produces its sound in much the same way as a dynamic mic. The diaphragm is suspended between two magnets. Ribbon mics use a thin ribbon of aluminum (see Figure 5-6) instead of the plastic or Mylar you'd find in a dynamic mic. Although ribbon mics were very popular from around the 1930s to the 1960s, they've mostly taken a backseat to condenser mics in today's studios. This is mainly because they are known to be fragile and expensive, and aren't as transparent as condenser mics. In fact, a gust of wind or a strong breath into the diaphragm is all it takes to break a ribbon mic.

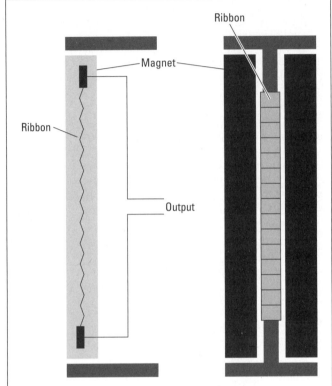

Figure 5-6:
Ribbon mics use a ribbon suspended between two magnets to create their signals.

Ribbon mics are experiencing a renaissance because a lot of recording engineers are searching for a vintage sound. Ribbon mics have a unique sound that is often described as silky or smooth. This essentially means that the high frequencies tend to *roll off* (gradually reduce) slightly, and the lower frequencies smear together a bit.

Until very recently, ribbon mics were fairly expensive. You'd have been hard pressed to find a new one for much less than $1,000. Nowadays, you can find some for just a few hundred dollars.

Polarity patterns

Microphones pick up sounds in different ways, which are known as *polarity patterns.* Here's how the various patterns work:

- ✦ **Omnidirectional mics** can capture sounds all around them.

- ✦ **Cardioid** (or directional) mics pick up sounds just in front of them.

- ✦ **Figure-8** (or bidirectional) mics pick up sounds from both the front and back.

Omnidirectional

An omnidirectional mic can pick up sounds coming from anywhere around it. Omnidirectional mics are useful for situations where you want to capture not only the source sound, but also the sound of the room it's coming from. You can find omnidirectional mics used in stereo pairs, suspended over drumsets to capture the whole sound of the kit, or used overhead to pick up groups of acoustic instruments (such as orchestras).

Omnidirectional mics are not generally used for close miking — placing the mic less than a foot from the sound source — because they tend to catch too much background noise. You can see the pick-up pattern of an omnidirectional mic in Figure 5-7. The round pattern shows that the mic picks up sound from all directions.

Understanding
Microphones

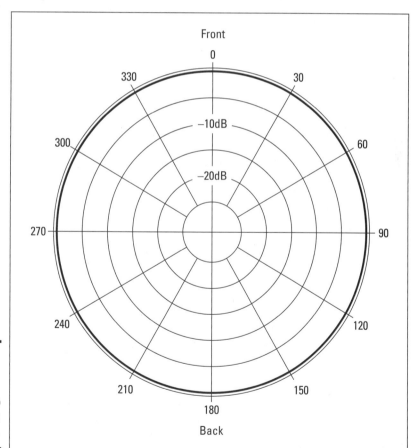

Figure 5-7:
An omnidirectional mic picks up sounds from all around it.

Cardioid

Cardioid microphones pick up the sound in front of them and reject any sounds that come from behind. Cardioid mics are the most common for live bands because you can control the sound that they pick up. If you have a cardioid mic on the tom-tom of a drumset, for example, the mic picks up only the sound of that drum and not the sound from the other instruments around it.

The three types of cardioid microphones are cardioid, super-cardioid, and hyper-cardioid. The differences among the types of cardioid patterns of each mic aren't that great. Check out the graphs in Figure 5-8 to see how the polarity patterns of cardioid microphones differ.

Generally, you don't need to think about the minor polarity-pattern differences among the types of cardioid mics when you buy or use a microphone. You won't notice the practical differences in the way these three types of mics work.

Figure 5-8: The three types of cardioid mics have similar polarity patterns.

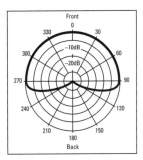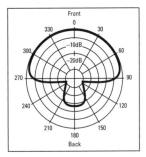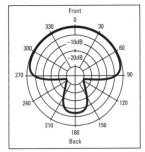

Figure-8

Figure-8 mics (also called *bidirectional*) pick up sound from both the front and back, but not all the way around. If you take a look at the graph in Figure 5-9, you can see that sound is not effectively picked up from areas on either side of the microphone.

Figure-8 mics are often used to record two instruments simultaneously. For example, you can place the microphone between two horn players with the side of the mic perpendicular to the players. This allows you to capture both instruments while eliminating any sound in front of the musicians.

Most figure-8 condenser mics have the same frequency response for both the front and back sides, but some ribbon mics produce very different responses that depend on whether the sound is coming from the front or the back. For instance, a Royer r121 ribbon mic picks up more high frequencies from behind the mic than from in front. You can use this to your advantage when recording an instrument. If the sound is too rich in low frequencies, just turn the mic around a little — or a lot, depending on how much of the high frequencies you want to add. (More on this in Book III, Chapter 2.)

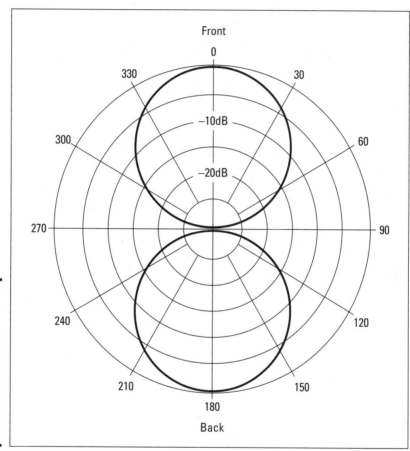

Figure 5-9:
Figure-8 micro-phones pick up sound from both front and back, but not the sides.

Multiple-pattern mics

Some condenser microphones can change their pick-up patterns. You can choose from cardioid, omni, or figure-8 (as in Figure 5-10). These mics (gen-erally, large diaphragm) can do this trick because they usually contain two sets of diaphragms and backplates, positioned back to back. You may want to have at least one multiple-pattern mic around to give you more variety in microphone positions.

The omni pattern in a multiple-pattern microphone works (and sounds) differently from a true omnidirectional mic. For critical applications (recording an orchestra, for instance), you may find that a multiple-pattern mic is not a fair substitute for an exclusively omnidirectional mic.

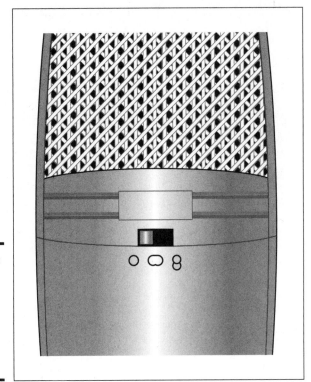

Figure 5-10:
Some mics have a switch that allows you to change polarity patterns.

Buying the Right Microphone for You

Buying microphones is, without a doubt, one of the most critical decisions that you'll make when setting up your home studio. Using the right microphone for the job can mean the difference between an okay track and a truly spectacular one.

A decade or so ago, your choice in microphones was between inexpensive dynamic mics (what most home recordists could afford) and expensive condenser or ribbon mics (what the pro studios had). But, as luck would have it, you've entered a time in home recording where your options are much more diverse. In fact, a whole line of project-studio mics has recently emerged.

This is a new market that manufacturers have found to be hugely profitable, so the choices are expanding almost daily. In some cases, a $400 project-studio mic can rival a $2,000-plus pro mic — at least for the home recordist's purposes.

So the question that you're inevitably going to ask is, "What microphones should I get for my home studio?" Good question. And the answer is, "Well, it depends on what you need." So before I go into detail about what mics may be best for you, try to spend a minute assessing your needs. These questions may help you figure out your needs:

✦ **What type of music will I record?** If you play rock or pop music, you probably want to start with dynamic mics because they're inexpensive and because their limitations in high or low frequencies don't matter as much as they would if you want to record your string quartet. In this case, a pair of condenser mics would do the trick.

✦ **What instruments will I record?** Loud amps, drums, and screaming singers beg to be recorded with dynamic mics, whereas light percussion, vocals, and stand-up basses shine through with large-diaphragm condenser mics.

✦ **How many mics will I use at once?** If you need to record your whole band at once, budget constraints may dictate your choice between dynamic and condenser mics or a condenser or ribbon mic for vocals. If you need only a couple of mics to record the occasional vocal or instrument, you can invest more in each mic.

How many, what kind

You will likely build your microphone collection over time rather than buying all your mics at once. This is the best way to buy mics because it gives you time to develop an understanding of what you can do with the microphone that you have before you plunk down your money for another. You're better off having a few mics that best fit your situation rather than a whole bunch of mics that just sorta work for you.

If you're like most people, your budget dictates how many mics you can buy and what kind they may be. In this section, I try to help you get the best mics for your recording needs and guide you through the process of slowly accumulating microphones.

Before you go out and buy a ton of mics, know this: Many digital systems have an effect called a *mic simulator* — a program that allows you to use a relatively inexpensive mic and get the sound of a much more expensive one. If your system has a mic simulator program (you can find out by searching through your system's effects patches), I recommend getting a basic dynamic mic first. You may find that you like how the mic simulator sounds and discover that you don't need as many mics as you thought.

Getting started

A basic mic setup consists of a couple of dynamic mics for drums, guitar amps, or other loud instruments; and a decent condenser mic for vocals or other acoustic instruments. You can buy a good, sturdy, all-around dynamic mic for under $100; a lower-end (but nice-sounding) condenser mic costs around $200.

For most home recordists, a large-diaphragm condenser mic is the first condenser mic. These are good all-around mics that can work well for a lot of applications.

Movin' on

After you have your basic mics, you can start to add a few more. If you intend to record your band, you need to at least mic the drumset. (Four mics will get you around the set.) In this case, you can add a couple more dynamic mics and start thinking about getting one or two that are designed for particular applications. For instance, you can find mics on the market that are made to work best on the kick drum of a drumset.

At this point, you can also get a second condenser mic — maybe a small-diaphragm condenser mic this time or a large-diaphragm tube condenser. You may want to choose one that sounds different from the one you already have — or, if you love the one you have, you can get a second one just like it so you have a stereo pair.

Going all out

As your mic collection grows, you'll probably start looking for a vocal mic that works best for your voice. In this case, you may consider large-diaphragm tube condenser mics or even a ribbon mic.

After this, your next step may be to buy a stereo pair of omnidirectional mics for drum *overheads* (mics placed over the drum set) or other multi-instrument applications.

Detailing applications

Certain mics work better than others for particular situations. In this section, I try to present some typical applications to give you an idea of what types of mics are traditionally used for various purposes. (You can find more ideas about mic usage in Book III, Chapter 2, where I discuss specific miking techniques.)

When you consider a mic, think about the frequency spectrum of the instrument(s) you're recording. If you use a dynamic mic for a symphonic orchestra performance, for example, you'll be disappointed by the results because it lacks an accurate high-frequency response. On the other hand, using a small-diaphragm condenser mic on the tom-toms of a drum set makes them sound thin and is a waste of money because you can get by with a much less expensive dynamic mic for this purpose.

Microphone choice is fairly subjective. The following list contains some basic suggestions, based on what's typically used in the recording industry. You may choose a different type of mic, especially if you try to create a certain effect. For instance, using a ribbon mic rather than a small-diaphragm condenser mic on a metallic shaker softens the highest frequencies of the instrument and gives it a mellower sound.

+ **Vocals:** Most people prefer the sound of a large-diaphragm condenser mic for vocals. If you have the budget, you may also want to audition some ribbon mics for your voice. A dynamic mic is best when you're going for a dirty or raw sound (excellent for some harder rock, blues, or punk music) or if your singer insists on screaming into the mic. A small-diaphragm condenser mic, rarely the first choice for most singers, isn't out of the question for some female vocalists if you don't mind a bright, *present* sound (reduced low-frequency content).

+ **Electric guitar amp:** A dynamic mic or a small-diaphragm condenser works well on an electric guitar amp. Some people use large-diaphragm condenser mics on guitar amps and like the added low frequencies that can result.

+ **Electric bass amp:** Your first choice when miking an amplified electric bass is either a large-diaphragm condenser mic or a dynamic mic. Either one can capture the frequency spectrum that the bass guitar encompasses. Small-diaphragm condenser mics aren't a good choice because of their inherent high-frequency focus.

+ **Acoustic guitar and other stringed instruments:** A large- or small-diaphragm condenser mic or a ribbon mic works well in most instances. A dynamic mic has too limited of a frequency response to create a natural sound but may create an effect that you like. Choose the large- or small-diaphragm based upon the overall frequency spectrum of the instrument. For example, if you want to capture the depth of a guitar's tone, choose a large-diaphragm mic. For an instrument with a higher register, such as a violin or mandolin, a small-diaphragm mic works great.

+ **Drumset:** Tom-toms, snare drums, and kick (bass) drums all sound good with dynamic mics because they don't put out any high frequencies. You can also use large-diaphragm condenser mics, but be careful where you place them because if your drummer hits them, they're toast.

+ **Cymbals:** For the cymbals of a drum set, a pair of small-diaphragm condenser mics works well although some people prefer to use large-diaphragm mics instead. Many old-timers are using ribbon mics on cymbals when they record digitally to give the cymbals a softer sound. A dynamic mic would lack the high-frequency response needed to make the cymbals shine through in a mix.

+ **Miscellaneous percussion:** Now, here's a broad category. By miscellaneous, I mean shakers, triangles, maracas, and other higher-pitched percussion toys. For these instruments, you'll find that either small- or large-diaphragm condenser mics work well. For a very quiet instrument, such as a small shaker, a large-diaphragm mic is preferable because of the higher self noise of the small-diaphragm mic.

If you intend to record loud instruments — drums, amplified guitars, or basses — look for a mic with a high SPL (a rating of how much volume, in decibels [dB], that the microphone can handle before distorting). A high SPL is more than 130 dB.

Some professional condenser mics have a pad switch that allows you to reduce the sensitivity of the mic, thereby increasing how well it can handle high sound-pressure levels.

Partnering with preamps

One of the most important relationships in your home studio is the one between your microphones and the *preamp* — the nice bit of hardware that boosts the mic's signal so it can be recorded. The greatest microphone in the world is wasted if it's run through a cheap preamp. By the same token, a cheap mic plugged in to a great preamp sounds only as good as the bad mic.

Your Digidesign hardware comes with at least two preamps. (Book II, Chapter 2 details each piece of hardware.) This may be enough for you, but you may want a separate preamp for a different (better) sound or if you need more inputs than your hardware provides.

For the most part, the preamps in the Digidesign hardware are more than adequate until your engineering skills are way up there. I recommend using them and spending your money on some decent mics first (unless, of course, you need more preamps than those that come with your hardware).

You can find three types of preamps in the marketplace — solid-state, vacuum tube, and hybrid — and each has its own characteristics. In the following sections, you get a chance to explore some preamp styles and discover how each relates to the sounds produced by the types of microphones I discuss earlier in the chapter. This can help you start considering the relationship between the microphone and preamp in your studio.

Solid-state

Solid-state preamps use transistors to boost the level of the microphone. Solid-state preamps can be designed to produce as clear and detailed (that is, *transparent*) of a sound as possible or can be designed to create a pleasing level of distortion (warmth) for your music. Solid-state preamps cost anywhere from a couple hundred to several thousand dollars.

A good clean, clear, solid-state preamp (such as those from Earthworks or George Massenburg Labs) is a great choice if you want as natural of a sound as possible on your recording of an instrument or if you're using a microphone that has a sound quality that you want to hear as clearly as possible. For example, I particularly like how a solid-state preamp works in conjunction with a tube condenser or ribbon mic. The warmth and smoothness of these types of microphones shines through clearly with a clean solid-state preamp.

On the other hand, a more *aggressive* (warm or pleasingly distorted) solid-state preamp, such as those modeled after the classic Neve designs, can add just a touch of "grit" to certain instruments. These types of preamps are great with dynamic, ribbon, or condenser mics, especially when recording drums, guitar, and some vocals.

Tube

Tube preamps use vacuum tubes to process and amplify the microphone's signal. This generally adds some coloration to the sound of your mic, although how much and what kind of coloration depends on the particular preamp. As you've undoubtedly discovered after reading any other chapter in this book, digital recording aficionados love the sound of tube gear, especially tube preamps. The advantage with a tube preamp is that it can add a nice warm sound to your mics. The disadvantage is that you often can't get rid of this colored sound. Professional recording engineers often have several tube preamps in their studios to give them different coloration options.

The preamps included in your mixer are solid state. If you find that you want the colored sound of a tube preamp, you have to buy an external one.

Tube preamps are great for imparting a subtle low-frequency addition to the sound of the microphone signal. Tube preamps also seem to soften the higher frequencies slightly. If you're like most people, you'll find the addition of a tube preamp to be welcome, especially if you intend to record rock, blues, or acoustic jazz music. The downside is that all-tube preamps are expensive, with the least expensive costing about $1,000 (the Peavey VMP-2: a nice-sounding preamp that you'll have to find on the used market) and most running several thousand dollars (for brands such as Manley Labs).

I prefer to use tube preamps with drums and any "woody" instrument (acoustic guitar, for instance). In this case, I often find myself reaching for a large-diaphragm condenser mic. And, in extreme cases, I may even use a large-diaphragm tube condenser mic with the tube preamp (for an extra dose of "tubiness").

Hybrid

A *hybrid preamp* contains both solid-state and tube components to boost the mic's signal. Most of the inexpensive (less than $1,000) tube preamps that you find in the marketplace are actually hybrids. An advantage to this design approach is that the preamp can often be adjusted to give you varying degrees of that warm tube sound. The disadvantage is that these relatively inexpensive tube preamps won't have as clear a sound as a great solid-state preamp, and they won't have quite the same pleasing character as an expensive all-tube preamp.

For most home recordists, this type of preamp offers a lot of flexibility and can allow you to get either a fairly clear, open sound of a solid-state preamp or a warm, colored sound characteristic of a classic tube preamp. If you can afford only one external preamp, you may find a great solution in one of these hybrid versions.

The countless hybrid preamps on the market vary widely. (In fact, most of the hybrid preamps are actually marketed as tube preamps.) Your best bet in choosing a hybrid (or any preamp, for that matter) is to do some research. Talk to people, read reviews, visit Internet forums, and then audition the two or three that stand out to you. Choose the one that you think sounds best for your needs.

Considering compressors

You use a compressor to alter the dynamic range of an instrument. Along with the microphone and preamp, a compressor is often added to the signal chain before it goes to the mixer. The advantage of using a compressor in the signal chain before it hits the mixer is that you can control the transients of an instrument so it doesn't overload your converters and create digital distortion.

The compressor plug-ins in Pro Tools are of no use to you if you want to control the transients of an instrument because they are located after the converters. If you don't want to use (or can't afford) an external compressor, keep your input level down a bit when you record. (Book III, Chapter 3 covers setting levels in detail.)

If you record a lot of vocals or real drums, consider using a decent external compressor. You can find some great-sounding compressors for as little as $200. (Check out my Web site at www.jeffstrong.com for some great bang-for-your-buck compressor finds.)

Preamp, compressor, and equalizer combos

As long as you're looking at preamps and compressors, take a look at *channel-strip devices* — combos that integrate preamp, compressor, and equalizer. For some people (maybe you), a channel-strip device is the way to go. Using just one unit cuts down on the number of cords, and it's designed to make the three parts function well together. Quite a few great-sounding channel-strip devices are available for less than $500.

Analyzing some microphone accessories

Along with your new mics, you're going to need a few accessories. These include mic cords, stands, and pop filters.

Microphone cords

Microphone cords can cost anywhere from about $10 to several hundred dollars. You're probably asking yourself, "Is there really a difference between a $10 or $20 mic cable and one that sells for hundreds of dollars?"

My answer is, "Supposedly, but chances are, you'll never hear it." Let me qualify this answer a little. Unless you have very good microphones, pre-amps, A/D (analog-to-digital) and D/A (digital-to-analog) converters, mixer, recorder, *and* monitors, you're wasting your money on expensive micro-phone cords. I know only one sound engineer (not me, though — I've spent too many years behind the drums) who claims that he can actually hear the difference between an average mic cord and one of the expensive ones. And he says that the difference is very subtle. (It would have to be; otherwise I'd hear the difference too.)

Don't waste your money on an expensive mic cord (or any cord) until you've got such kickin' equipment that the cord is the weakest link in your signal chain. By then, spending a couple hundred dollars on a cord will seem like pennies because you'll already have invested tens of thousands of dollars in top-quality gear.

Stands

A sturdy stand is essential if you intend to mic anything in your studio. Studio mics can get a bit cumbersome, and decent mic stands are relatively inexpensive, so try to resist the temptation to buy a flimsy stand. A good mic stand has a sturdy base and can securely hold your mics.

Good mic stands cost about $30 and have either a round, cast-iron base (great for getting into tight spaces) or a tripod base (superior stability). Either one works well. Check out Figure 5-11 to see these two types of stands.

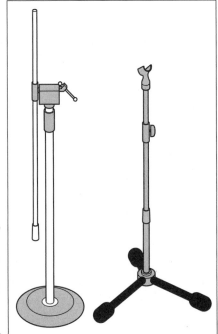

Figure 5-11:
A sturdy mic stand has either a cast iron or a tripod base.

Pop filters

A *pop filter* is a nylon screen that is used to eliminate the "pops" (technically called *plosives*) that singers make when they sing. Plosives are the result of sudden bursts of air projected into the mic (from singing words starting with Ps and Ts, for example). If you record vocals, a pop filter is a must-have.

Pop filters are relatively inexpensive, but if you want to make your own, you can with a pair of tights or pantyhose and a coat hanger. Bend the coat hanger into a circle and stretch the nylons or pantyhose over it. You can attach the coat hanger to the mic stand with duct tape. Adjust it so the pop filter is about four to six inches away from the microphone and have the singer sing through it. Check out Figure 5-12 for a look at a homemade pop filter.

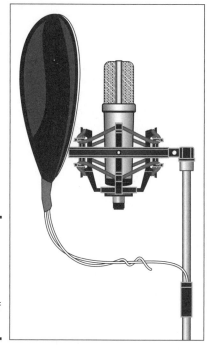

Figure 5-12:
You can
make a pop
filter from a
coat hanger
and a pair of
tights.

Caring for Your Microphones

After investing hundreds, if not thousands, of dollars in microphones, you probably want to know how to take care of them properly. Caring for or storing your microphones isn't rocket science. Just follow the general guidelines and ideas that follow, and you'll keep your mics in tip-top shape.

A good microphone lasts a lifetime. Take care of your mics, and they'll offer you years of service.

Daily care for your mics

Probably the most important thing to keep in mind when using your mics is to resist the temptation to blow into them. I know you've probably seen the doof on stage blow into a mic and yell, "Test! Is this thing on?" to see whether it's working. And some folks figure that's how the pros must check their mics. Well, it isn't. Blowing into a mic is one of the worst ways to test it — and for some sensitive models (like those expensive ribbon mics), it's a sure way to literally blow the diaphragm. If you want to check to see whether a mic is working, just speak into it in a normal voice.

Never blow or yell into any mic unless your singer's style is to yell into the mic and you're trying to set the input level. In this case, offer him your trusty dynamic mic and keep that expensive ribbon mic hidden.

Another thing to keep in mind when handling your mics is that they can be fragile. Condenser and ribbon mics don't survive rough handling well. In fact, if you drop a condenser or ribbon mic, you may just break it. (This is why you need a sturdy stand.) Dynamic mics, on the other hand, are more durable, which is why they are often used for live applications and on drums (where it's not uncommon for an overzealous drummer to whack them by accident — as a drummer, I know about this firsthand).

Keep your mics away from dust and high humidity. Dust is probably the number-one enemy of a microphone; it can settle on the diaphragm and lessen the sensitivity of the mic — even alter its frequency response. Always cover your mics or put them away when you're not using them.

Storing your mics

Most professionals have *mic lockers* where they can safely keep the mics that aren't in use. Mic lockers come in different forms. You can make a special locked box fitted with foam padding that has a cutout for each mic, or you can keep your mics in their pouches or cases (if they came with them) in a closet or cabinet.

Regardless of the type of storage cabinet you have, *try to handle your mics as little as possible.* In fact, if you have a mic that you use a lot, you're often better off leaving it on a secure stand between sessions instead of dragging it in and out of its case or storage cabinet.

If you do leave your mic out on its stand when it's not in use, cover it with a plastic bag and close the open end around the mic. (See Figure 5-13.) This keeps off the dust.

Humidity can also be a problem for microphones. If you live in a humid environment, store your mics with a bag of silica gel next to them. (*Silica gel* — the stuff that comes in the packaging of a lot electronic gear — absorbs moisture.) You can find silica gel listed as *desiccant packets* (Desi Pak) by the manufacturer. If you do an Internet search by typing **desiccant packet or dessiccant sacks/sachets** into your favorite search engine, you'll find a lot of options.

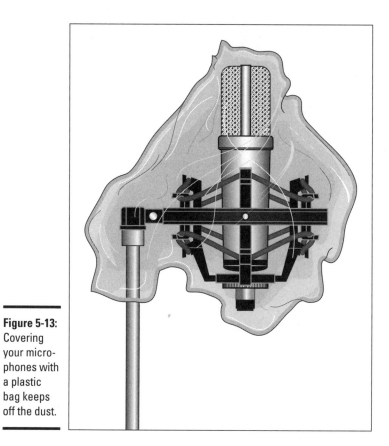

Figure 5-13:
Covering
your micro-
phones with
a plastic
bag keeps
off the dust.

Book II

Getting Started Using Pro Tools

Contents at a Glance

Chapter 1: Configuring Your Computer **117**

   Using Pro Tools on a Mac 117

   Using Pro Tools on a PC 122

   Keeping Bugs at Bay: Good Habits to Get Into 133

Chapter 2: Setting Up Your Hardware **135**

   Making Sense of the Mbox Series 137

   Exploring the Eleven Rack 148

   M-Audio Interfaces 152

Chapter 3: Examining Software Basics **155**

   Keeping Software Straight 155

   Getting Set Up 157

   Dealing with Sessions 165

   Getting to Know Audio and MIDI Files 171

Chapter 4: Understanding the Pro Tools Windows **173**

   Tackling the Transport Window 173

   Examining the Edit Window 181

   Managing the Mix Window 196

   Working with Window Configurations 207

Chapter 5: Importing and Exporting Files **215**

   Importing into a Session 215

   Exporting from a Session 228

   Managing Files 234

Chapter 1: Configuring Your Computer

In This Chapter

✔ **Choosing hardware**

✔ **Setting up a Mac**

✔ **Configuring a PC**

*P*ro Tools works well on both Macs and PCs, so no matter which type of computer you prefer, you can make good music without much hassle. However, you need to do a few things to your computer — and certain hardware requirements you need to observe — to run Pro Tools successfully.

This chapter gets you up to speed on these areas. I walk you through setting up and configuring your system and installing the software. As an added attraction, I include some advice on how to keep the bugs at bay. (You know, those nasty computer hiccups that can keep you from capturing your best guitar solo — or, worse yet, losing it after the fact.)

Using Pro Tools on a Mac

Getting up and going on a Mac is easy. After you have a computer with the right specs (which I cover in this section), it takes you less than 15 minutes to be ready to plug in your hardware (covered in Chapter 2 of this minibook) and start recording (covered in Book III). This section takes you step by step, turning your Mac into a lean, mean, audio-recording machine.

Understanding Mac system requirements

One of the great things about Macintosh computers is that there aren't a lot of variables. Almost any Mac can record audio with Pro Tools. (Well, as long as it meets the basic system requirements. See the following Remember icon.) Here are a few things, however, that you need to know to record well. These are covered in this section.

The best way to ensure that the computer you own or are considering buying will work with Pro Tools and the Avid hardware that you want is to go to the compatibility page on the Avid website at

    www.avid.com/US/products/Pro-Tools-Software/
    support#systemrequirements

Choose the hardware and operating system (OS) you use (or intend to use) to see whether it will work with Pro Tools.

Because the people at Avid can't test all possible hardware options, you may also want to check out the Avid User Conference (DUC) for any topics covering hardware issues. That web page is `http://duc.Avid.com`. Look for the section dedicated to Pro Tools for Macs.

Knowing which Mac to buy

For the most part, almost any Intel Mac will work, including Core 2 Duo and i3 and above. (The newest ones often take a few weeks for Avid to add to its list of compatible computers.)

Opting for a Mac operating system

You need at least Mac OS X version 10.6.7 (Snow Leopard) to run version 10 Pro Tools software. Some minor issues occurred with v. 10.7.1 when it first came out, so you definitely want to check out the Avid compatibility page (`http://avid.force.com/pkb/articles/en_US/Compatibility/en353265`) to see whether any issues are noted for the Mac OS you have.

I try to stay one version behind with all my software, especially the OS. I've learned the hard way to wait until the bugs are worked out before upgrading. One nice thing about Avid is that it constantly checks and approves the newest hardware and OS versions so you don't need to do it yourself.

Recognizing your RAM needs

Pro Tools requires at least 2GB of RAM for basic operation and at least 4GB of RAM if you run the DV Toolkit or Music Production Toolkit options, but I say go for broke here. Get as much RAM as you can afford or as your computer can handle. And don't buy the cheap stuff — get high-quality RAM. Its worth checking out `www.crucial.com` to find the best RAM for your system.

Getting a handle on hard drives

Pro Tools (and any other audio-recording software for that matter) likes to have more than one hard drive. In fact, I'll go as far as to say that Pro Tools *needs* more than one hard drive to run properly. My advice? Get two drives: one drive for all your system files and software, and the other for all your audio and MIDI files. Here's a look at how to organize them:

✦ **Drive 1:** This is the system drive. For your system drive, you can use the stock drive that came with your computer. If you have a choice, though, I recommend getting one with a spindle speed of 7,200 rpm. You'll be much happier, as will Pro Tools. And get a *big* one — hard drive, that is (at least 250GB).

Even if you have other programs on your computer (such as finance or word-processing software), you don't need to partition your drive. In fact, doing so may slow down your system.

✦ **Drive 2:** This is the audio drive. It used to be that you needed a good, high-speed SCSI drive to record and playback audio reliably, but this isn't the case anymore. You can use both IDE and FireWire drives for storing audio. Just make sure that you have a drive with the following (or better) specs:

• *Spindle speed:* Also called *rotational speed,* this is the rate at which the hard drive spins. For the most part, a 7,200-rpm drive works well for recording and playing back audio.

• *Seek time:* This is the amount of time that it takes the drive to find the data that's stored on it. You want an average seek time under 10 milliseconds (ms). Get as low as you can. (I prefer a seek time of 8 to 9 ms.)

• *Buffer size:* Often called a *cache buffer, buffers* are memory units that store data while it's being transferred. You want a buffer size of at least 2MB, but get one as big as you can. I recommend a drive with an 8MB buffer.

• *Chipset:* If you use a FireWire 800 drive, make sure that it comes with at least the Oxford 911 bridge chipset. This is necessary to get the most bandwidth from the drive and results in more tracks in your session.

A drive with these specs in a good size (1TB or so) will run you about $100, so you have no reason not to spring for the second drive.

Dealing with other software on your system

Not too long ago, installing any other software on the computer that you intended to record audio into was asking for trouble. This isn't a problem so much anymore, but you still need to be careful not to stress your system by putting too much junk on your computer. (Games come to mind.)

As an experiment, I had Pro Tools running while I had both my e-mail and Internet browser programs open and downloading files, as well as Photoshop and Microsoft Word running (talk about multitasking!) — and Pro Tools still ran fine. I wouldn't try to record or mix seriously with all this stuff going, but I was able to work without my system crashing.

With that said, if you're really serious about having a bulletproof system, try to keep any extra software (such as games, finance, publishing, graphics, and so on) off your audio computer. At the very least, keep all other applications closed while you work in Pro Tools.

Setting system settings

Before you install Pro Tools software, check to make sure that you have the latest version of OS X. (Also check the Avid compatibility web page at `http://avid.force.com/pkb/articles/en_US/Compatibility/en353265` to make sure this version is supported.) Then follow these steps to prepare your system for the software installation (these steps refer to version 10.6.8):

1. **Log on to your computer by using an administration account.**

Your OS X documentation will spell out this procedure for you.

2. **Choose ⌘➪System Preferences from the main menu, as shown in Figure 1-1.**

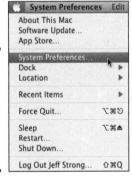

Figure 1-1: Find Systems Preferences under the Apple (⌘) menu.

3. **Under the Hardware Options, click the Energy Saver icon.**

A new window opens.

4. **On the Sleep tab, move the slider for Put the Computer to Sleep When It Is Inactive For option over to Never, as shown in Figure 1-2.**

This keeps your computer from shutting down because you haven't touched any keys if you're recording a long song and you (very sensibly) don't touch any keys while recording.

5. **Leave the Put the Hard Disk to Sleep When Possible option unchecked.**

   This keeps your computer from going to sleep during long sessions.

6. **Go back to the main Systems Preferences page by clicking the Show All button in the upper-left corner of the window.**

7. **Choose Software Update from the System options at the bottom of the page.**

8. **When the new window opens, deselect the Automatically Check for Updates When You Have a Network Connection option, as shown in Figure 1-3.**

   This keeps your system from dedicating resources to look for and download software updates when you're working.

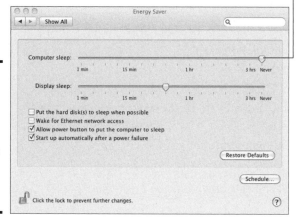

Figure 1-2:
Turn off the Sleep function for the computer in the Energy Saver window.

Figure 1-3:
Deselect the Automatic Software Update option from the Software Update window.

9. **Close the window by clicking the red button in the upper-left corner of the window.**

Installing the program

After you complete the system setup requirements in the previous section, you can install Pro Tools software by following these steps:

1. **Insert the Pro Tools software CD in your computer's CD drive or navigate to the download section of Avid's website to download the files and click the download icon. Pro Tools will download (it may take a while), and an installer will open.**

2. **In the new window that appears, double-click the Install Pro Tools icon.**

The OS X Administration window appears, asking you to enter your password.

3. **Enter your OS X Administration password and then click OK.**

The Pro Tools installer opens.

4. **Select the Startup hard drive as the destination drive.**

The installation path is set.

5. **Click Install.**

Pro Tools installs on your computer. This may take a few minutes, so sit back and contemplate the fun you're going to have after it finishes installing itself.

6. **Restart your computer.**

Wait to open the program until after you've attached your hardware. The complete details for this procedure are located in Chapter 2 of this mini-book.

Using Pro Tools on a PC

Getting set up with a PC is a little more complicated than it is with a Mac simply because you have a lot more hardware variables to deal with. As long as you keep the basic system requirements in mind, you can set yourself up with a very powerful system, often for less money than you'd shell out for a comparable Mac-based system. In this section, I cover some basic things to keep in mind when you're either purchasing or configuring a PC system for use with Pro Tools.

Understanding PC system requirements

Although the system requirements for PCs are similar to the basic ones for Macs, you do have to deal with a ton more variables. Of these variables, central processing units (CPUs), motherboards, and graphics cards are probably the most confusing to people starting out. These components — as well as the more basic stuff, such as hard drives and RAM — are covered in this section so you can get up and running on a PC in no time.

Again, the best source for the latest hardware compatibility information can be found online at the Avid website at

    http://avid.force.com/pkb/articles/en_US/Compatibility/
    en353265

or on the Avid User's Conference (DUC) web page at

    http://duc.avid.com

Picking a central processing unit (CPU)

A *CPU* is a small chip that's responsible for processing all the data in your computer. It's essentially the computer's brain. The two major CPU manufacturers in the PC world are Intel and AMD. Avid supports both, and each can work fine as the core of your Pro Tools host computer. For Intel systems, I recommend going with at least a Xeon or the Core i5; for AMD systems, go with a Phenom II X4 or X6 processor.

Because Pro Tools is a *host-based* system, it relies on the processing power of your computer's CPU instead of hardware-processing cards (as the more elaborate Pro Tools HD systems do). The number of plug-ins and amount of mix automation you can use in a session is directly related to how powerful (read: *fast*) your system is, so don't skimp on CPU speed. The good news is that the current higher-end processors can perform as well as, if not better than, the super-expensive Pro Tools HD systems.

Choosing a motherboard

A *motherboard* is the main circuit board in your computer, holding the CPU, memory, and other peripheral cards. The motherboard you choose depends on whether you run an Intel or AMD CPU. (See the previous section for more on both brands.) Each CPU type has its own motherboard requirements, and many choices are available for each, with new motherboards being released all the time. I have had good results over the years with Asus brand motherboards, but other brands can also work well.

When you select a motherboard for use with Pro Tools, your main concern is that it

✦ Supports the CPU you plan on using

✦ Has a compatible chipset

Be sure to check out the Avid compatibility site before you buy a motherboard.

Grabbing a graphics card

As of this writing only NVIDIA graphics cards are supported by Avid, and though Pro Tools doesn't make the same demands on your graphics card that modern game software does, you'd do best to stick with these. If you want to venture out, the main thing to consider is that the graphics card you use is compatible with your motherboard. In most cases, this isn't an issue — but check it out anyway as a hedge against Murphy's Law.

When purchasing a laptop, you have the option to choose to upgrade from an integrated graphics controller. Here how to find out whether your computer has an integrated graphics controller:

1. **Choose Start➪Control Panel➪System.**

2. **On the System Properties dialog box that opens, click the Hardware tab.**

3. **On the Hardware tab, click the Device Manager button.**

From the Device Manager window that opens, select Display Adapters from the tree (see Figure 1-4).

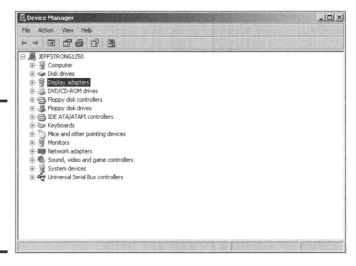

Figure 1-4:
Checking whether your computer has an integrated graphics controller.

Loading up on RAM

As far as RAM goes, Avid suggests using a minimum of 2GB unless you're using DV Toolkit or Music Production Toolkit options. In those cases, you need at least 4GB of RAM. As I mention in earlier chapters, get a lot more RAM — at least double the minimum amount. The other important thing to remember when buying RAM for your PC is that you get the proper type of RAM for your motherboard.

Don't buy cheap RAM because it can cause problems with your system. High-quality RAM is not much more expensive than the cheap stuff, so spend the extra few bucks. You'll thank me when your system doesn't freeze on you. As I mention in the earlier Mac section, I recommend checking out www.crucial.com to find the best RAM for your system.

Book II
Chapter 1

Configuring
Your Computer

Selecting hard drives

Hard drive requirements for a PC system are essentially the same as those for Macs. Check out the "Getting a handle on hard drives" section earlier in this chapter for the lowdown on buying hard drives for your system.

Opting for a Windows operating system

Windows 7 is required for Pro Tools 10 and all the compatible Avid hardware. This includes the Mbox, Eleven Rack, 002, and 003. At the risk of belaboring a point, check the Avid compatibility page to see what OSes are approved for your hardware and software version.

Preparing to install Pro Tools software

Before you can actually install your Pro Tools software, you need to get your system configured for it. This section describes the procedures and helps you make sure that your system will run trouble-free (at least as much as can be expected).

Windows settings

Although it's true for the most part that you can run Pro Tools just fine on a standard Windows 7 configuration, a few system adjustments will free up system resources, allowing more of your computer system's power available for use by Pro Tools. This is important because Pro Tools is a native DAW (Digital Audio Workstation) — one that relies solely on the host computer's processing power with no additional DSP (Digital Signal Processing) cards for support. And some of these adjustments — such as enabling DMA (Direct Memory Access) for all your IDE hard drives — are crucial for running Pro Tools successfully. The sections that follow lay out the basic system settings that I recommend.

Windows 7 Classic theme

You can accomplish the same basic housekeeping and setup tasks in Windows 7 in many ways. Because I don't know how your system is set up, I lead you through the process from the start. The first thing you want to do is set your system to the Windows Classic theme. Here's how:

1. **Click Start and then click Control Panel.**

The contents of the Control Panel folder appear onscreen.

2. **Click the Personalization icon.**

Or you can right-click an empty spot on the desktop and choose Personalize from the shortcut menu.

3. **In the Basic and High Contrast Themes section, choose Windows Classic (see Figure 1-5).**

Wait a few seconds as Windows 7 applies the theme to your computer.

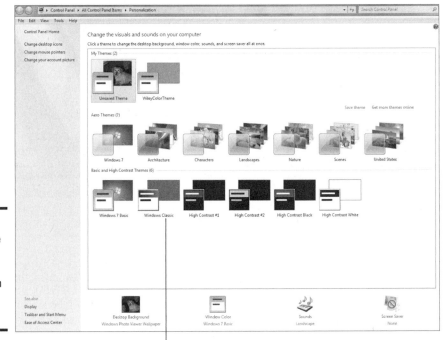

Figure 1-5: Choose the Windows Classic theme from the list of themes.

Select this option

This procedure disables the active desktop in Windows, which frees some valuable system resources.

Choosing Control Panel settings

Windows 7 is remarkably stable, but for those rare times when it (or a program running under Windows) crashes, it generates an error report and asks whether you want to send the report to Microsoft. This feature, called Error Reporting, takes system resources to run. Because I'm sure that you'd rather have those resources working hard to keep Pro Tools running smoothly, I recommend that you disable Error Reporting. Here's the drill:

1. **Click Start and click Control Panel.**

2. **Click the Action Center icon.**

3. **Click the down arrow next to the Maintenance section.**

4. **Click the Settings link under the Check for Solutions to Problem Reports option.**

5. **Select the Never Check For Solutions option.**

6. **Click OK.**

Standby power should be set to Always On for your Pro Tools system. To do this, follow these steps:

1. **Click Start and click Control Panel.**

2. **Click the Power Options icon.**

3. **On the Select a Power Plan screen, choose the High Performance option under the Preferred Plans section (see Figure 1-6).**

4. **Click the window to save the setting automatically.**

Figure 1-6:
Make sure to choose High Performance from the Preferred Plans section.

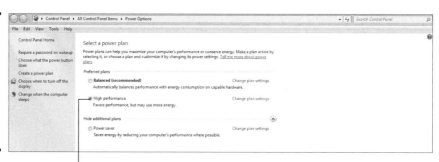

Select this option

You also want to make sure that your screen doesn't go to sleep and crash your session. These steps show you how to do this:

1. **Click Start and click Control Panel.**

2. **Click the Personalization icon on the screen that appears, and then click Screen Saver in the lower-right corner.**

3. **Choose None from the Screen Saver drop-down menu.**

4. **Click Apply and then click OK.**

5. **Click the Control Panel Home link in the upper-left corner of the screen.**

6. **Click the System icon.**

7. **Click the Advanced System Settings link in the upper-left corner of the screen.**

   The System Properties dialog box appears.

8. **Click the Advanced tab (if it isn't already selected) and then click the Settings button in the Performance section.**

   The Performance Options dialog box appears.

9. **Click the Visual Effects tab (if it isn't already selected).**

10. **Select the Custom option.**

    Make sure that none of the options listed in the dialog box are selected with a check mark (as you can see in Figure 1-7). If any are, simply click those pesky check marks so they disappear.

11. **Click OK.**

Your System Sounds need to be disabled to prevent potential problems with Pro Tools. To do this, follow these steps:

1. **Click Start and click Control Panel.**

2. **Click the Sound icon.**

3. **Click the Sounds tab.**

4. **From the Sound Scheme drop-down menu, choose No Sounds (see Figure 1-8).**

5. **Click Apply and then click OK.**

6. **Close the Control Panel.**

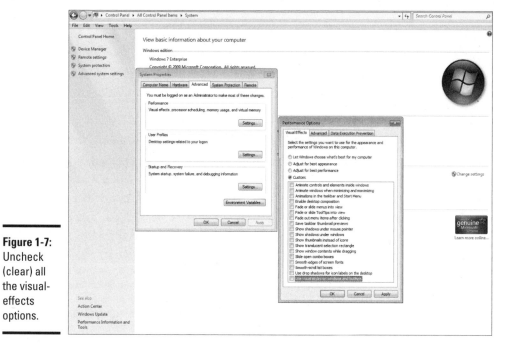

Figure 1-7:
Uncheck
(clear) all
the visual-
effects
options.

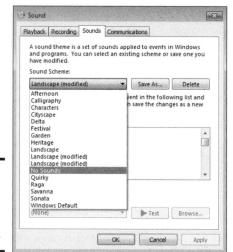

Figure 1-8:
Choose
No Sounds
on the
Sounds tab.

Congratulations! You just configured your system settings.

Enabling DMA

All IDE hard drives on your system *must* have DMA enabled before Pro Tools can effectively write and read data to and from your hard drives. To enable DMA, do the following:

1. **Click Start and click Control Panel.**

2. **Click the Device Manager icon.**

3. **In the Device Manager window, click IDE ATA/ATAPI Controllers.**

   The Device Manager tree expands to show the controllers associated with your system.

4. **From the listing, double-click the Primary IDE controller and then click the Advanced Settings tab (see Figure 1-9).**

   Check the box "Enable DMA" under the Device Properties section. If you have several disk drives on your system, you have to do the same for Device 0 and Device 1.

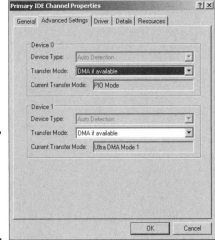

Figure 1-9:
Transfer
Mode menu
should be
set to DMA
If Available.

5. **Click OK and repeat Step 4 for the Secondary IDE controller.**

   The Secondary IDE controller is in Device Manager, directly below the Primary controller.

Disabling AutoPlay

AutoPlay is a feature of Windows 7 that automatically runs certain programs or plays music on a CD when you insert it into your computer's CD drive.

This is a handy feature in everyday life, but it can cause problems with the Pro Tools software. For the sake of Pro Tools, disable AutoPlay for all CD drives on your system. Here's the drill:

1. **Click Start and click Control Panel.**

2. **Click the AutoPlay icon.**

3. **If the Use AutoPlay For All Media check box in the upper-left corner of the screen (see Figure 1-10) is selected, click on it to deselect it.**

4. **Click Save and then close the Control Panel.**

Deselect this option

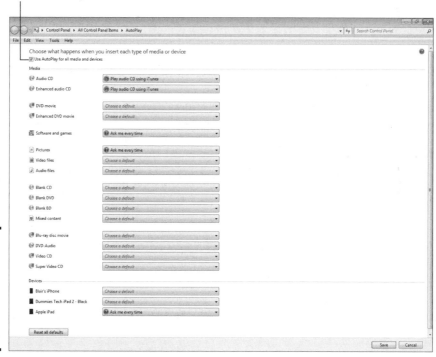

Figure 1-10: Select the Ask Me Every Time option from the drop-down menu.

Disabling virus protection

Virus protection is an important thing to have on any computer that connects to the Internet, but virus protection can also adversely affect Pro Tools performance. Ideally, your Pro Tools host computer would be dedicated to just running Pro Tools. However, many of you will be using an "all-purpose" computer that you will use for many tasks, such as surfing the Web for business, pleasure, and/or for helping with your children's homework.

In that case, you should turn off your virus protection and disconnect from the Internet whenever you run Pro Tools. Check with the documentation that came with your virus-protection software for the best way to do this. (And don't forget to re-enable virus protection before you log on to the Internet again.)

I hate to repeat myself, but I will: If you're really serious about having a bullet-proof system, try to keep any extra software (such as games, finance, publishing, graphics, and so on) off your audio computer. At the very least, keep all other applications closed while you work in Pro Tools.

After you make all these system adjustments listed earlier, you need to reboot your computer.

Connecting your hardware

After you have your system fine-tuned (as described in the previous sections), you can now connect your hardware. Shut down your computer and refer to Chapter 2 of this mini-book for the specifics on connecting your Avid hardware. Each piece of hardware has its own installation procedure; I cover each one, step by step, in that chapter. After you have the hardware connected, turn on your computer. Then, after the Windows desktop appears, turn on the power to your Avid hardware. (If you're using a product that doesn't have a power switch, you can ignore this step.)

On Windows PCs, wait to install the program until after you attach your hardware — and, if needed, power it on. The complete details for this procedure are located in Chapter 2 of this mini-book.

Installing the program

After you complete the Windows system-setup adjustments listed in the previous sections, you can install Pro Tools software by following these steps:

1. **Connect your Avid interface to your computer.**

   - *For a 002 or 002 Rack:* Connect the FireWire cable.

   - *For an Mbox:* Use the USB connection.

   - *For an 001:* Plug the PCI card into an open PCI slot and make the connection between the PCI card and the breakout box (the rest of the 001 system).

2. **Start Windows.**

   The Windows desktop appears.

3. **Turn on your Avid interface if it has a power switch.**

   If you're using a bus-powered device — such as the Mbox 2 interfaces — it'll already be powered on when you plug it in.

4. **Insert the Pro Tools software CD in your computer's CD drive.**

5. **Click the Computer icon on the Windows desktop.**

   The Computer window appears.

6. **In the Computer window, click the icon for your CD drive.**

   The contents of the CD are displayed in a new window.

7. **Open the Pro Tools Installer folder.**

8. **Click Setup.**

9. **After the Installer appears, click Next to continue.**

10. **Accept the Default paths for installation (they're fine, and it's less hassle) and then click Next.**

11. **Wait for the installation to complete.**

12. **Restart your computer.**

Avid has included additional drivers that aren't needed for use with Pro Tools, but are included in case you're using third-party programs and want your Avid hardware to interface with them. Frankly, I don't recommend installing these drivers unless you absolutely have to. Remember, it's best to keep a lean, mean DAW machine, and that means staying away from any unnecessary drivers and programs. If you have to install these drivers for use with a third-party audio program (such as Sonar or Cubase), refer to their manuals and the Avid documentation that came with your hardware for instructions.

Keeping Bugs at Bay: Good Habits to Get Into

One thing is certain with computers: Hiccups will happen. Just when you think everything is performing perfectly, something crashes your system. Because these things are inevitable, I recommend that you work on developing some good habits to keep these minor problems from becoming disasters. In this section, I list a bunch of things that can help give you as stress-free an experience recording on your computer as possible.

Back up your data often

There's an old saying about computer data — *If it doesn't exist in at LEAST two places, then it DOESN'T EXIST!* Your hard drive can be considered one such "location." There are several ways people usually back up their data:

✦ Get a second hard drive and back up to it every day. You can also use an automated backup program, such as Retrospect, to do this for you.

✦ Put your data on DVD +/-R discs or a USB thumb drive. Again, do this daily.

✦ Use a Cloud-storage solution such as Dropbox or Amazon Cloud Drive. This only works if your audio computer has an Internet connection, but with some services you can also mirror your system drive so if it does go down you can get back up and running quickly (see the next section for more on backing up your system drive).

Regardless of the method you choose, the important thing is *to back up your data.* Hard drives have become remarkably reliable, but as with anything else, failures can and do happen. If your hard drive should fail (or if you accidentally delete something that you shouldn't have), you'll be very happy you made copies of all your Pro Tools sessions to another storage device — and (if you didn't make copies) very sad to see your hard work disappear forever right before your eyes.

Back up your system drive

Because installing your OS, software applications, plug-ins, and so forth can take a considerable amount of time, I prefer to back up this information as well as my audio and session data. Some great programs are available that allow you to create an image of your system drive onto another hard drive or to removable media (such as DVD-Rs). In the event of a hard drive crash or other problem, you can restore your drive (or a new drive) to exactly the way you had it before the crash occurred. The best part is that this takes a lot less time than reinstalling everything from scratch.

I normally install my system software (Mas OS or Windows 7), then all my software, and then back it up. After that, I leave my system drive alone, and use my second drive exclusively for Pro Tools sessions and audio data, leaving the system drive for only the programs. Any time I add any new programs or plug-ins — or make any other significant changes to my system drive — I create a new Ghost backup before I install the new stuff. That way, if disaster does strike, my system can bounce back and be up and running with very little delay.

Two great options are

✦ **Norton Ghost,** `http://us.norton.com/ghost/`**:** This is for PCs only.

✦ **EMC Retrospect,** `http://www.retrospect.com/`**:** Versions are available for both Mac and PC.

A few minutes spent backing up your system drive and your Pro Tools sessions now can save you hours of work reloading all of your programs later — and can also save you from losing that session you spent so many hours perfecting. Get into the habit of backing up your data regularly.

Chapter 2: Setting Up Your Hardware

In This Chapter

✔ Setting up the Mbox series

✔ Checking out the Eleven Rack

✔ Getting to know M-Audio interfaces

*W*ith the release of Pro Tools 9 software, you no longer needed to have an Avid (actually, Digidesign because that was its name at the time) audio interface to use the program. This was a huge change for Pro Tools — and one that put it on par with all the other audio-recording programs out there. Avid also changed (pared down) its interface options, making it easier to choose one. I offer an overview of these interfaces in this chapter to help you understand which one best fits your needs.

All Avid and M-Audio interfaces work with either Macintosh- or Windows-based computers. Avid interfaces use Pro Tools 10 software, and M-Audio uses Pro Tools MP and SE software, but they all have essentially the same functions and almost-identical operation. Differences in the hardware include the number of inputs and outputs each interface provides, the sample rates each one supports, and the different ways that they connect to your computer. The differences in the Pro Tools Software versions are covered in Book II, Chapter 3.

In this chapter, you get the lowdown on Mbox models and the Eleven Rack. I also offer an overview of the M-Audio options to give you some insight into your choices. To help you choose the best interface for your needs, I tell you how many inputs and outputs you get, note the sample rates, and discuss connection requirements for each of these units. In this chapter, I also show you how to connect each interface so you can get your system up and running.

Throughout this chapter, I describe a lot of connector types. Some of these may be familiar to you, and others may seem a bit like rocket science. (What *is* an S/PDIF, anyway, and will it blow up if you plug it in?) If you start getting a little dizzy from all these new terms, check out Book I, Chapter 3, where I explain all types of analog and digital connectors in detail.

Despite the differences between the various Avid interfaces, they share many things, including

✦ **Preamps:** All Avid audio interfaces contain at least one preamp. *Preamps* boost the signal from microphones so that you can record them directly into Pro Tools. I discuss preamps in detail in Book I, Chapter 1.

✦ **Phantom power:** *Phantom power* is a small current (48 volts, written 48V) that's sent from your interface to your microphone (through the mic cable) and is necessary for your condenser microphone to work. Phantom power is available only on your preamp channels and can be toggled on and off.

✦ **Line-level inputs:** *Line-level inputs* are analog connections that you use to plug your guitar, keyboard, or other instruments into your interface without any gear between the instrument and the device. Getting your preamp inputs in the interface to accept line-level signals is easy; just click a button on the interface.

✦ **S/PDIF:** Use a Sony/Philips Digital Interface Format (S/PDIF) connector to plug an external converter into your interface, allowing you to bypass the analog-to-digital (A/D) or digital-to-analog (D/A) conversion process. Some people prefer this if they have separate converters whose sound they prefer over the ones contained in the interface. All Avid interfaces contain S/PDIF inputs and outputs except for the Mbox Mini.

✦ **ADAT Lightpipe:** The ADAT Lightpipe connectors, also known as *ADAT optical,* allow up to eight channels of digital information coming and going through your device. As with S/PDIF, this allows you to bypass the conversion process in your interface. ADAT Lightpipe is useful if you have an external digital mixer and you want to mix with that. The Digi 003 and Digi 003 Rack have ADAT Lightpipe inputs and outputs.

✦ **BNC wordclock:** This is a special type of connector for sending and receiving wordclock signals. (*BNC* stands for Bayonet Neil-Concelman, for the dude who created it. It's essentially a cable connector. A *word-clock* is the digital clock used to calculate the sample rate for your audio.) Use this connector to send and receive wordclock data to synchronize your digital hardware, which is necessary only if you have a bunch of digital devices connected. For example, if you have separate A/D or D/A converters connected to your Avid interface, you may want to connect them via the BNC wordclock to ensure that they all operate from the same digital clock to help optimize the sound of each unit.

You can also send and receive wordclock data via the S/PDIF connection, but this limits your optical jack input and output options to S/PDIF. In the case of the 003, ADAT optical is disengaged, and you lose the eight inputs and outputs that would be available through them.

Making Sense of the Mbox Series

Mbox (pronounced *em*-box) products are the least-expensive Avid interfaces. These Pro Tools hardware interfaces are perfect for people with limited input and output needs (and maybe limited cash flow), such as solo artists and singer/songwriters who need to record only a few tracks at a time (instead of, say, the Flatbush Philharmonic), and those who need something small and portable.

The three Mbox options each have a user in mind: Mbox Mini, Mbox, and Mbox Pro. The following sections detail these interfaces.

Mbox Mini

This small interface has two analog inputs and outputs. The Mbox Mini connects via USB 1.1 and contains internal power, so you don't have to plug the unit into an outlet. This makes it useful for portable recording. This USB 1.1 connection, which limits your recording to 24 bits and up to 48 kHz, can introduce some *latency* (time delay while the digital information enters and exits your computer). This limitation is mitigated by the zero-latency monitoring option. (More on this in the upcoming "Mbox" section this chapter.) You can see the Mbox Mini in Figure 2-1.

Figure 2-1:
The Mbox
Mini is a
portable two
input/two
output USB
interface.

The Mbox Mini has the following input/output configurations:

✦ **Inputs:** You can have two simultaneous inputs, including one with a preamp and phantom power for microphones.

✦ **Outputs:** You have two outputs for your speakers.

✦ **Headphone jack:** There is a separate headphone jack.

Connecting an Mbox Mini to a Windows computer

Hooking up the Mbox Mini involves these steps:

1. **With your computer turned on, plug a cord into the USB port in the Mbox Mini and the other end of the cord into a USB port in your computer.**

    Don't use a USB hub: Connect directly into your computer. This keeps your signal from being interrupted by having too much data trying to get through one USB line.

    If the New Hardware Wizard opens, leave it alone. Don't click Next — just leave it open and untouched. If the wizard starts to install anything automatically, click Cancel.

2. **Install the software and restart your computer according to the procedure that I detail in Chapter 1 of this mini-book.**

    At this point, the green light should be lit, showing power to the Mbox Mini. If it's not — or if it's blinking — unplug it from your computer, wait ten seconds, and then plug it back in.

Be sure to complete all the system setup procedures listed in Chapter 1 of this mini-book. This ensures that your system runs smoothly.

Connecting an Mbox Mini to a Macintosh computer

To hook up the Mbox Mini to a Mac, simply follow these steps:

1. **Install the Pro Tools LE software that came with the Mbox Mini and restart your computer.**

    Chapter 1 of this mini-book has the details of this process.

2. **With your computer turned on, plug a cord into the USB port in the Mbox Mini and the other end of the cord into a USB port in your computer.**

    Don't use a USB hub: Connect directly into your computer. The Mbox Mini doesn't function well when other devices are using the same USB port in the computer.

The green light on the Mbox Mini should be steadily lit. If it's not — or if it's blinking — unplug it, wait ten seconds, and then plug it back in.

Be sure to complete all the system setup procedures listed in Chapter 1 of this mini-book to ensure that your system runs smoothly.

Getting sound in and out of an Mbox Mini

The Mbox Mini has the following connectors and dials:

Book II
Chapter 2

Setting Up Your
Hardware

✦ **Input 1:** This input allows you to connect a microphone or an instrument (such as a keyboard, guitar, or bass). This input is controlled by the Input 1 dial on the front of the Mbox Mini. On the back are these jacks:

- *Microphone:* Use the XLR plug to plug in your microphone. When you do so, also disengage the Mic/DI button to set the device for a microphone signal. If you're using a condenser microphone, you engage the button — marked 48V — on the back of the device. This turns on phantom power. (Go to Book I, Chapter 5 for more on condenser mics and phantom power.) You may also want to engage the Pad if your signal becomes too loud.

- *Instrument:* The ¼" jack lets you plug in an instrument, such as a keyboard or drum machine. When you use this jack, depress the Mic/DI button — and, depending on the level of your instrument, the Pad button to reduce the level entering the device.

- *Guitar or bass:* The ¼" jack also functions as a direct box, so you can plug your guitar or bass directly into the interface without needing a separate device. (Check out Book I, Chapter 1 for more about direct boxes.) Because guitars produce a lower-level signal than other instruments, you need to disengage the Pad button.

✦ **Input 2:** This input consists of a ¼" jack that accepts either an instrument or a guitar connection. You control this input from the Input 2 dial located on the front of the Mbox Mini. You plug your instrument or guitar in at the back by using these settings:

- *Instrument:* When you use this jack for your keyboard or synthesizer, you may need to depress the Pad button to reduce the level of the signal entering the device.

- *Guitar or bass:* Guitars produce a lower-level signal than other instruments, so you'll need to disengage the Pad button when you plug in this jack.

✦ **Mon Out:** Monitor Outputs (Mon Out) is where you connect cords to go to your speakers (monitors) or the amp supplying your speakers if yours are not powered. For more on monitors, check out Book I, Chapter 1. This output is controlled by the headphone/speaker dial on the front of the Mbox Mini.

✦ **Headphones:** The ¼" jack on the front of the Mbox Mini is where you plug in your headphones. This jack is controlled by the headphone/speaker dial to the right of the jack.

✦ **Mix:** The front panel also has a Mix knob, which you use to monitor your inputs while you record and also listen to the playback of any recorded tracks. Adjusting this knob allows you to mix — in your headphones — the balance between your input and recorded stuff. I offer a little more detail on this process in the "Mbox" section that follows.

After you have all your gear connected, all you need to do is open Pro Tools software and start working. Chapter 3 in this mini-book (the next chapter) gets you up to speed on the basics of the software.

Mbox

Mbox is the second-generation Mbox interface. This is a bus-powered USB 2.0 interface, so you don't need to plug it in to an outlet and it's fast enough that you don't have to worry about latency the way you do with the Mbox Mini. You can record in 24 bits, at a sample rate of up to 48 kHz. You can also connect a MIDI instrument. The Mbox (as shown in Figure 2-2) has the following input/output configurations:

✦ **Analog inputs:** You can have two simultaneous inputs.

✦ **Preamps:** Both analog inputs have preamps for connecting your mics directly into the interface. You also have phantom power for both channels.

✦ **Analog outputs:** You have two outputs for your speakers or monitors.

✦ **Headphone jack:** There is a separate headphone jack.

✦ **MIDI In and Out:** You can connect a MIDI device via the MIDI Input and Output jacks.

✦ **Digital inputs and outputs:** Use the S/PDIF coax (RCA) In and Out to send and receive digital signal from the Mbox. This is handy if you have external A/D and D/A converters that you prefer.

Connecting an Mbox to a Windows computer

Hooking up the Mbox involves these steps:

1. **With your computer turned on, plug a cord into the USB port in the Mbox and the other end of the cord into a USB port in your computer.**

Don't use a USB hub: Connect directly into your computer. This keeps your signal from being interrupted by having too much data trying to get through one USB line.

If the New Hardware Wizard opens, leave it alone. Don't click Next — just leave it open and untouched. If the wizard starts to install anything automatically, click Cancel.

2. **Install the software and restart your computer according to the procedure I explain in Chapter 1 of this mini-book.**

   At this point, the green light should be lit, showing power to the Mbox. If it's not — or if it's blinking — unplug it from your computer, wait ten seconds, and then plug it back in.

Be sure to complete all the system-setup procedures listed in Chapter 1 of this mini-book. This ensures that your system runs smoothly.

Figure 2-2:
The Mbox is a portable, two-input/ two-output USB interface with MIDI capabilities.

Connecting an Mbox to a Macintosh computer

To hook up an Mbox to a Mac, simply follow these steps:

1. **Install the Pro Tools LE software that comes with the Mbox and restart your computer.**

   See Chapter 1 of this mini-book for the details of this process.

2. **With your computer turned on, plug a cord into the USB port in the Mbox and the other end of the cord into a USB port in your computer.**

   Don't use a USB hub: Connect directly into your computer. The Mbox doesn't function well when other devices are using the same USB port in the computer.

   The green light on the Mbox should be steadily lit. If it's not — or if it's blinking — unplug it, wait ten seconds, and then plug it back in.

Be sure to complete all the system setup procedures listed in Chapter 1 of this mini-book to ensure that your system runs smoothly.

Getting sound in and out of an Mbox

The Mbox has the following connectors and dials:

✦ **Inputs 1 and 2:** These inputs allow you to connect a microphone, an instrument (such as keyboard), or a guitar or bass. The inputs are controlled by the Input dials on the front of the Mbox. The Input jack that is enabled is selected by using the Source button (it's unmarked) located above the DI and Mic lights in each Input section and next to the Pad button. In back are three jacks that you can use for each channel:

   • *Microphone:* Use the XLR jack to plug in your microphone. When you do so, press the Source button until the Mic light illuminates. If you're using a condenser microphone, you engage the button (marked 48V) just to the right of the Input 1 section. Phantom power is on when the light is illuminated. (Go to Book I, Chapter 5 for more on condenser mics and phantom power.) You may also want to engage the Pad button if your signal becomes too loud.

   • *DI:* The ¼" jack labeled *DI* functions as a direct box, so you can plug your guitar or bass directly into the interface without needing a separate device. (Check out Book I, Chapter 1 for more about direct boxes.)

   • *Line:* Use the ¼" jack marked line (TRS) to plug in an instrument, such as a keyboard or drum machine. When you use this jack, you need to depress the Source button until both the DI and Mic lights are off for the input channel. Depending on the level of your instrument, you may want to engage the Pad button to reduce the level of the signal entering the device.

✦ **Mon Out:** Monitor Outputs is where you connect cords to go to your speakers (monitors). (For more on monitors, check out Book I, Chapter 1.) Use the Monitor dial on the front to control this output.

✦ **S/PDIF:** Here you can connect your digital devices by using a coaxial cable (RCA). The S/PDIF connection is handy for connecting external converters or other digital components, such as Digital Audio Tape (DAT) machines. There are no controls you have to worry about on the front. A light at the upper-left on the front panel alerts you if you have anything connected to these jacks.

✦ **MIDI:** You can connect your MIDI keyboard, MIDI controller, or other device to these. The MIDI In is connected to the MIDI Out of your device, and the MIDI Out goes to the MIDI In of the other device. There are no controls to worry about on the front panel of the Mbox.

✦ **Headphones:** The ¼" jack on the front of the Mbox is where you plug in your headphones. This jack is controlled by the headphone dial to the right of the jack.

✦ **Mono:** The Mono button on the front of the Mbox allows you to hear your song in mono. This is a good idea when you're mixing to make sure that you don't have any funny sounds (a highly technical term) happening in your stereo mixes. Check out Book VI, Chapter 1 for more about checking your mixes in mono.

✦ **Mix:** Use the Mix knob to monitor your inputs while you record and also to hear the playback of any tracks. Adjusting this knob allows you to mix the balance between your input and recorded stuff in your headphones. This makes it easy to overdub without hearing a delay from the time it takes your instrument's signal to enter and exit the computer. Because the Mbox uses a USB connection and because USB transfer rates are pretty slow (for audio, anyway), the delay is significant. Using the Mix function in the Mbox allows you to have zero-latency monitoring. In other words, you won't experience delay in your headphones when you overdub tracks.

Book II
Chapter 2

Setting Up Your
Hardware

Of course, using zero-latency monitoring causes other problems. That is, your overdubbed tracks are exactly 147 samples behind (the amount of time it takes the signal to enter the computer) your recorded tracks. If you use the Mix knob when you overdub and you played in time with the tracks recorded in Pro Tools, you need to move them to a point earlier in the session (song) to align them. This isn't a big deal, and I give you step-by-step instructions on how to do this in Book III, Chapter 4.

With all your gear hooked up, you're ready to start recording. I cover the specifics of this in Book III, but if you haven't used Pro Tools before, I recommend going to the next chapter (Chapter 3 in this mini-book), well, next.

Mbox Pro

The Mbox Pro is a step up from the other Mbox models. Pro features many more input and output options, but the most significant improvement is its FireWire interface. This means that you input/output latency is significantly reduced — so much that you don't have to use zero-latency monitoring trickery to eliminate the delay in your headphones while you record your tracks. Figure 2-3 shows the Mbox Pro.

This feature alone makes this interface a lot better than the other Mbox offerings, in my opinion. And because it uses FireWire, your transfer speed is fast enough for you to record in higher sample rates. In this case, you can record up to 96 kHz. This is in line with the more expensive 003 interfaces. The only thing missing in the Mbox Pro is enough inputs and outputs to record the better part of a band (as with the Digi 003 options). In this case, you have the following input and outputs numbers:

✦ **Simultaneous analog inputs:** You'll find two inputs with preamps and phantom power for your microphones as well as two inputs that accept an instrument or a turntable.

✦ **Analog outputs:** Pro offers two main monitor Outs for your speakers and four Line Outs for additional speakers or to send your outputs to other gear.

✦ **RCA phono inputs:** These allow you to connect a tape player, a CD player, or even a turntable to your interface.

✦ **Two-channel, digital S/PDIF In and Out:** These allow you to send and receive digital signal from an Mbox Pro. This is handy if you have external A/D and D/A converters that you prefer or if you have a CD player with digital outputs.

✦ **Headphone jacks:** There are two separate headphone jacks, each with its own volume control.

✦ **MIDI In and Out:** You can connect a MIDI device via the MIDI Input and Output jacks.

✦ **BNC wordclock In and Out:** These allow you to send and receive word-clock data so you can synchronize your digital hardware. This is one of the other Pro features of this interface.

✦ **Footswitch input:** You can connect a footswitch to start and stop your Pro Tools sessions with your foot — handy if you record yourself because you can start and stop the session hands-free.

In addition to these inputs and outputs, Mbox Pro is also bus-powered (as long as you have a 6-pin cable and a FireWire port), making it a portable interface.

Figure 2-3:
The Mbox Pro is a portable FireWire interface with MIDI capabilities and a bunch of Pro features.

Connecting an Mbox Pro to a Windows computer

Follow these steps to hook up the Mbox Pro:

1. **With your computer turned on, plug a cord into the FireWire port in the Mbox Pro and the other end of the cord into a FireWire port in your computer.**

Don't use a FireWire hub: Connect directly into your computer. This keeps your signal from being interrupted by having too much data trying to get through one FireWire cord.

If the New Hardware Wizard opens, leave it alone. Don't click Next — just leave it open and untouched. If the wizard starts to install anything automatically, click Cancel.

2. **Install the software and restart your computer according to the procedure that I detail in Chapter 1 of this mini-book.**

At this point, the green light should be lit, showing power to the Mbox Pro. If it's not — or if it's blinking — unplug it from your computer, wait ten seconds, and then plug it back in.

Be sure to complete all the system setup procedures listed in Chapter 1 of this mini-book. This ensures that your system runs smoothly.

You can open your software when you're ready to record. The next chapter of this mini-book has the details.

Connecting an Mbox Pro to a Macintosh computer

To hook up the Mbox Pro to a Mac, simply follow these steps:

1. **Install the Pro Tools LE software that comes with the Mbox Pro and restart your computer.**

See Chapter 1 of this mini-book for the details of this process.

2. **With your computer turned on, plug a cord into the FireWire port in the Mbox Pro and the other end of the cord into a FireWire port in your computer.**

Don't use a FireWire hub: Connect directly into your computer. The Mbox Pro 2 doesn't function well when other devices are using the same FireWire port in the computer.

You're ready to open your software and get started. Check out the next chapter of this mini-book to get familiar with the Pro Tools LE.

To ensure that your system runs smoothly, be sure to complete all the system-setup procedures that I list in Chapter 1 of this mini-book.

Getting sound in and out of an Mbox Pro

The Mbox Pro is pretty flexible about getting connected. Here's a rundown of the ins and outs of it all:

✦ **Inputs 1 and 2:** Use these inputs to connect a microphone, an instrument (such as a keyboard, guitar, or bass). The inputs are controlled by the Input dials on the front of the unit. The Input jack that is enabled is selected using the Source button (it's unmarked) located above the DI and Mic lights in each Input section. In back are three jacks that you can use for each channel:

  • *Microphone:* Use the combo jack on the back to plug in your microphone. When you do so, press the Source button until the Mic light illuminates. If you're using a condenser microphone, you engage the button marked 48V, just to the right of the Input 1 section; this turns on phantom power and illuminates the light. (Go to Book I, Chapter 5 for more on condenser mics and phantom power.) You may also want to engage the Pad button if your signal becomes too loud.

  • *Line:* The combo jack on the back of the Mbox Pro also allows you to plug in an instrument, such as a keyboard or drum machine. When you use this jack, you need to depress the Source button until both the DI and Mic lights are off for the input channel. Depending on the level of your instrument, you may want to engage the Pad button to reduce the level of the signal entering the device.

  • *DI:* The ¼" jack located on the front of the unit functions as a direct box so you can plug your guitar or bass directly into the interface without needing a separate device. (Check out Book I, Chapter 1 for more about direct boxes.) Press the Source button until the DI light is illuminated.

✦ **Aux In:** The Aux (auxiliary) input is for an instrument or a turntable. You have two options:

  • *RCA jacks:* You use the RCA jacks if you want to plug in your turntable. This jack provides a preamp and is engaged when you press the Source button on the front next to the Aux dial until the Phono light is lit up.

  • *¼" TS jacks:* These jacks are for instruments. The two jacks are for your left and right signals. You can theoretically plug two different instruments in these, but you have only one Gain knob on the front to adjust the input volume. Whatever instruments you plug in to these inputs, you engage them by pressing the Source button for the Aux channel until no light is lit.

- ✦ **Mon Out:** Monitor Outputs are where you connect cords to go to your speakers (monitors). (For more on monitors, check out Book I, Chapter 1.) This output is controlled by the Monitor dial on the front.

- ✦ **Line Outs:** Four line outputs use ¼" TS jacks. These are for connecting to other gear or speakers. These outputs don't have a volume control. The signal level going to these outputs is controlled by the Master fader of your session. If you want to be able to adjust the volume to a set of speakers, you need a mixer or external volume controller.

- ✦ **S/PDIF:** Here you can connect your digital devices by using a coaxial cable (RCA). The S/PDIF connection is handy for connecting external converters or other digital components, such as DAT machines. There are no controls you have to worry about on the front. A light on the upper-left part of the front panel alerts you if you have anything connected to these jacks.

- ✦ **Line Out 5/6:** These ¼" jacks allow you to send two additional outputs to an external location. This can be handy if you want to create an alternate monitor mix (for a submix, for example). As with the Line Outs described earlier, there is no volume dial for these outputs.

- ✦ **Footswitch:** Labeled Foot SW, use this jack to connect a footswitch to the interface so you can start and stop your session without using your hands. You can find footswitches for this purpose at almost any music store. They generally cost around $20.

- ✦ **Wordclock:** Use these jacks, which look like typical coax-cable jacks, to connect an Mbox Pro to other digital gear that has wordclock capabilities. This is only necessary when you have more than one digital piece of equipment (such as external digital converters) and you want to synchronize their clocks.

- ✦ **MIDI:** You can connect your MIDI keyboard, MIDI controller, or other device to these. MIDI In is connected to the MIDI Out of your device, and MIDI Out goes to the MIDI In of the other device. There are no controls to worry about on the front panel of the Mbox Pro.

- ✦ **Headphones:** The ¼" jack on the front of unit is where you can plug in your headphones. This jack is controlled by the headphone dial to the right of the jack.

After you have all your gear connected, you can get started recording. I recommend that if you haven't used Pro Tools before, finish Book II first. This will give you a solid foundation so you can work efficiently.

Book II
Chapter 2

Setting Up Your Hardware

Exploring the Eleven Rack

Avid's Eleven Rack is built for guitarists. This interface has a limited number of inputs and outputs, but it makes up for this deficit by including serious power for guitar-amp modeling and effects. Designed as both a recording interface and standalone live unit, the Eleven Rack offers some pretty cool features (Figure 2-4). This section lays it all out for you.

You may want to stick with the standard rate for CD audio: 44.1 kHz.

Discovering the Eleven Rack input and outputs

The Eleven Rack has the following input and output configurations:

✦ **XLR analog input:** This input includes a preamp and phantom power for your microphone.

✦ **Analog inputs:** You get two ¼" analog inputs for your instruments.

✦ **Analog outputs:** There are two XLR outputs and two ¼" outputs for connecting to an amplifier.

✦ **FX Sends and Returns:** The Eleven Rack comes with two ¼" sends/returns to be able to connect an external effects unit.

✦ **Alt In:** These alternate input jacks are handy for connecting a CD player or tape deck and listening to it without having to turn on the software or listening to reference CDs from an external player while you mix.

✦ **Digital In and Out channels:** These channels comprise two channels of AES-EBU digital and two channels of S/PDIF coax (RCA), which you use to send and receive up to four simultaneous digital channels to and from the Eleven Rack. This is handy if you have external A/D and D/A converters.

Figure 2-4:
The Eleven Rack is USB interface designed for guitar players.

+ **Headphone jack:** You get one headphone jack.

+ **MIDI In and Out:** The Eleven Rack has one MIDI In port and one MIDI Out port.

+ **Footswitch input:** You can connect a footswitch to control the transport of Pro Tools, which can be handy when recording yourself — you can start and stop the session hands-free.

Connecting the Eleven Rack to a Windows computer

Follow these steps to hook up the Eleven Rack:

Book II
Chapter 2

1. **With your computer turned on, plug a cord into the USB port in the Eleven Rack and the other end of the cord into a USB port in your computer.**

Don't use USB hub: Connect directly into your computer. This keeps your signal from being interrupted by having too much data trying to get through one USB cord.

If the New Hardware Wizard opens, leave it alone. Don't click Next — just leave it open and untouched. If the wizard starts to install anything automatically, click Cancel.

2. **Install the software and restart your computer according to the procedures that I describe in Chapter 1 of this mini-book.**

Be sure to complete all the system setup procedures listed in Chapter 1 of this mini-book. This ensures that your system runs smoothly.

You can open your software when you're ready to record. Chapter 3 of this mini-book has the details.

Connecting the Eleven Rack to a Macintosh computer

To hook up the Eleven Rack to a Mac, simply follow these steps:

1. **Install the Pro Tools LE software that comes with the Eleven Rack and restart your computer.**

See Chapter 1 of this mini-book for the details of this process.

2. **With your computer turned on, plug a cord into the USB port in the Eleven Rack and the other end of the cord into a USB port in your computer.**

Don't use a USB hub: Connect directly into your computer. The Eleven Rack doesn't function well when other devices are using the same USB port in the computer.

Setting Up Your
Hardware

You're ready to open your software and get started. Check out Chapter 3 of this mini-book to get familiar with the Pro Tools 10.

Be sure to complete all the system setup procedures listed in Chapter 1 of this mini-book to ensure that your system runs smoothly.

Connecting your gear to an Eleven Rack

Connecting audio and MIDI gear is much the same process for the Eleven Rack as for the Mbox Pro, with just minor variations on inputs and outputs. Here's a rundown of them all:

✦ **Volume dial:** This dial controls the volume of both the headphone and main outputs for the Eleven Rack.

✦ **Power Switch:** As you may guess, this turns the Eleven Rack on and off. Expect it to take a few seconds to boot up after you hit the switch. Also, make sure that you have volume down or monitors off when you turn this puppy on, lest you hear a big pop.

✦ **Mic Input:** Use this input to connect a microphone or other instrument that utilizes an XLR connector. This input is controlled by the Gain dial on the front of the unit. With this input you have three parameters to adjust:

- *Gain:* This set the volume level of your input signal. You set this in conjunction with the level meter in Pro Tools software for the channel you have it routed to.

- *48v:* This switch turns phantom power on and off for your mic.

- *Pad:* Engaging this switch drops your input level by some unstated amount (10–20dB is typical but Avid doesn't say). This is handy for very hot (loud) microphone signals.

✦ **Guitar Input:** This is where you plug in your guitar. Avid calls this a "True Z" input because it has a variable-impedance circuit that accommodates a range of instruments such as electric and acoustic-pickup-appointed guitars, electric basses, and electric pianos. This circuit adjusts dynamically; all you need to do is plug in your instrument and start playing.

✦ **Footswitch:** Labeled Foot SW, use this jack to connect a footswitch or an expression pedal to control a host of parameters such as Wah, volume, and effects and patch settings.

✦ **USB:** This is where you connect your USB cable to go to your computer.

✦ **Main Outputs:** The mains out have a ¼" TRS jack (stereo) and XLR left and right jacks. These are for connecting to an amp or powered speakers. These outputs don't have a volume control. The channel faders of your session control the signal level going to these outputs. If you want to be able to adjust the volume to a set of speakers, you need a mixer or an external volume controller.

✦ **FX Loop:** The FX Loop is for you to connect external effect units. You can use a TRS insert cable or separate TS cables (the TRS cable connects to the left/stereo jacks). There is also a "grid" switch that lifts the ground to reduce hum if line noise is a problem.

✦ **AES/EBU:** Here you can connect your professional-level digital devices by using an AES/EBU connection. This jack can either pass two channels' data at a bit depth of up to 24 bits at 96 kHz.

✦ **S/PDIF:** Here you can connect your digital devices with a coaxial cable (RCA). This S/PDIF connection is enabled whenever you have cords connected to these jacks and when you don't have the Optical jacks assigned for S/PDIF signals. There are no controls you have to worry about in the front.

✦ **MIDI:** You can connect your MIDI keyboard, MIDI controller, or other device to these. MIDI In is connected to the MIDI Out of your device, and MIDI Out goes to the MIDI In of the other device. There are no controls to worry about on the front panel for MIDI.

✦ **Headphones:** The ¼" jack on the front of the unit is where you plug in your headphones.

After you have all your gear connected, you can get started recording. I recommend that you finish Book II first if you haven't used Pro Tools before. This will give you a solid foundation so you can work efficiently.

Examining Eleven Rack's guitar-processing features

The features that make the Eleven Rack special are amp modeling and effects processing. This section gives you an overview of the various buttons and dials that control this power. (I don't go into details about all the effects and modeling that are included. Check out the manual or noodle around to see all that you can do.)

✦ **Edit/Back Button:** Click this button to gain access to the setting for your guitar *rigs* (Avid's name for your saved settings for processing and modeling). When you're in the Rig view, you use this button to go back to a previous screen. You can also hold this button in for a few seconds to enter the user-options mode so you can tweak your settings at will. Here are the controls:

✦ **Save Button:** This saves your new settings.

✦ **SW1 and SW2 Buttons:** These buttons allow you to access a variety of menus and functions in the edit views. When a switch is active, it will be lit.

+ **Scroll:** The scroll wheel makes windows and the sections easy to scroll through in the edit views.

+ **Control Button:** These buttons (located above the Eleven Rack logo) toggle the associated effect on and off, and provide access to additional controls for the effect (simply push and hold).

+ **Tap Tempo/Tuner Button:** This button lets you set the tempo for an effect (just tap quarter notes) or access the internal guitar tuner (press and hold for a second).

+ **Control Dials:** You can use these knobs to access various controls for the amp and effects. You'll quickly notice that these dials glow in different colors, depending on their function:

  • *Unlit:* When a dial is unlit, it's not actively assigned to any setting. As you may have guessed, turning it does nothing.

  • *Amber:* This dial is currently assigned to an amp, cab, or FX-loop parameter.

  • *Green:* In this case, the dial controls an effects parameter.

  • *Red:* This tells you that the setting for this dial has changed from the saved setting. You can adjust it until it turns amber or green again to get back to the saved setting — or you can hit the Save button to save it. Once saved it will turn back to amber or green.

M-Audio Interfaces

A few years ago, the Avid parent company bought the audio-hardware maker M-Audio. Rather than absorb the M-Audio product line, it chose to add Pro Tools functionality to many of the M-Audio interfaces through a version of Pro Tools called Pro Tools MP. You can also get some M-Audio products bundled with an even more limited version of Pro Tools called Pro Tools SE. Both of these versions of Pro Tools work only with the M-Audio interface. These are great interfaces for beginners; most of them can be used with the more complete version of Pro Tools, PT10. So if your skills (or track counts) outgrow the limitations of the MP and SE versions of Pro Tools, you can upgrade your software without having to change hardware right away.

M-Audio makes quite a few interfaces (10 variants, to be exact), so rather than go into all the details of all these hardware options, this section offers an overview of the basic features of the interface, such as input and output configurations. Tables 2-1 and 2-2 break down many of the currently compatible M-Audio interfaces and show you their capabilities.

www.Avid.com/index.cfm?langid=151&navid=35&itemid=4901

Table 2-1	Pro Tools M-Powered–Compatible Hardware Basic Features				
Name	*Interface Type*	*Max Bit Depth*	*Max Bandwidth*	*Price*	*Other Features (Including Breakout Box, Controller, and Keyboard)*
Avid Recording Studio	USB 1.1	24	48	$120	Bundled with PT SE
Avid Key Studio	USB 1.1	16	44.1	$130	49-note keyboard, bundled with PT SE
Avid Vocal Studio	USB 1.1	16	48	$100	Mic, bundled with PT SE
Fast Track	USB 1.1	24	48	$150	Bundled with PT SE
Mobile Pre	USB 1.1	24	48	$180	Comes with PT SE, $400 bundled with PT MP
Fast Track C400	USB 2.0	24	96	$310	Comes with PT SE, $500 bundled with PT MP
Fast Track C600	USB 2.0	24	96	$500	Comes with PT SE, $700 bundled with PT MP
Fast Track Ultra 8R	USB 2.0	24	96	$630	Doesn't come with Pro Tools software. Rack-mount unit
ProFire 610	FW	24	192	$500	
ProFire 2626	FW	24	192	$900	Rack-mount unit

Table 2-2   **Pro Tools M-Powered–Compatible Hardware Inputs and Outputs**

Name	Preamps	MIDI	Analog Ins	Analog Outs	Digi Ins	Digi Outs	Headphone
Avid Recording Studio	1	No	2	2	2	2	1
Avid Key Studio	1	No	2	2	2	2	1
Avid Vocal Studio	N/A	No	1	2	1	2	1
Fast Track	1	No	2	2	2	2	1
Mobile Pre	2	No	2	2	2	2	1
Fast Track C400	2	Yes	2	4	4	6	1
Fast Track C600	4	Yes	4	6	6	8	2
Fast Track Ultra 8R	8	Yes	8	8	8	8	2
ProFire 610	2	Yes	6	10	6	10	2
ProFire 2626	2	Yes	8	8	26	26	2

Some M-Audio interfaces don't come with Pro Tools software, so you may need to buy the software separately (around $250). Factor this into the total cost before you buy.

Chapter 3: Examining Software Basics

In This Chapter

✔ Getting to know Pro Tools conventions

✔ Configuring system settings

✔ Understanding sessions

✔ Managing files

*P*ro Tools software is one of the simpler and easier-to-use audio programs available. However, as with any software, you need to know some basic conventions to get it to work efficiently. This chapter covers the basics so you can better understand your software as well as get your system configured properly. This chapter also shows you how to open, set up, and navigate sessions (which I talk about in the second half of the chapter), as well as how to manage file formats and file types.

Keeping Software Straight

Pro Tools comes in several versions: for example, HD and HDX, MP, and SE, Mac and PC. Although the versions sport only minor differences, knowing the differences can help you better understand your own system. Read on to find out the details.

Looking at Pro Tools versions

Avid, the maker of Pro Tools software, offers four basic types of systems: regular (simply called Pro Tools 10), MP, SE, and HD and HDX. Although this book focuses on Pro Tools 10, you may encounter the HD and HDX versions if you take your files to a commercial studio. In this section, I offer an overview of these types of systems.

You can see the differences between all the current Pro Tools versions here: www.avid.com/US/products/family/pro-tools/compare.

Pro Tools 10, MP, and SE

Pro Tools 10, MP, and SE versions are *host-based* systems. The Avid (the Mbox, for example) or M-Audio hardware (the FireWire 410, for example) acts as an interface between the analog-and-digital world and the software. Pro Tools software relies on the processing power of your computer's CPU to work: That is, all the recording, playback, mixing, editing, and other processing you do depends on the power of your computer. So: The more powerful your computer, the more you can do with your host-based Pro Tools system.

This section provides a short rundown on the differences between the three host-based Pro Tools systems (these differences can change, so check out www.avid.com/US/products/family/pro-tools/compare for the most up-to-date comparisons).

Prior to Pro Tools 9, you needed to use Avid, Digidesign, or M-Audio hardware to run the host-based Pro Tools system. Not all M-Audio, Digidesign, or Avid hardware works with all versions of Pro Tools, so if you have an older version of the software or hardware, check with Avid to see which hardware or software will work with what you have.

Pro Tools 10

Formerly called Pro Tools LE, Pro Tools 10 is the most powerful host-based version that also lets you use any brand of audio interface — you're no longer limited to just Avid hardware. This version also offers the most power with up to 96 simultaneous audio tracks (at 48 kHz resolution) and sample rates up to 192 kHz. In addition, this version allows you to record with 32-bit resolution (helpful if you do a lot of plug-in processing).

Pro Tools MP

Pro Tools MP (currently version 9) offers a limit of 48 active audio tracks and up to a 96 kHz sample rate. This is plenty for most musicians, but the main limitation you have with the MP version is that you must use an M-Audio interface to run Pro Tools software. For most people, this is fine; for the money, the bundled M-Audio interface and Pro Tools MP 9 offer a good value and decent sound.

Pro Tools SE

Pro Tools SE is an entry-level program that comes bundled with select M-Audio interfaces. This version of Pro Tools is much more limited as far as functionality goes than the other Pro Tools versions. For example, you can have a maximum of 16 tracks (recording up to two channels at a time) and can only record at 44.1 kHz or 48 kHz sample rates. This is still a 24-bit recording system, so it can offer great sound if you know what you're doing (this book offers everything you need to get great sound).

Pro Tools HD and HDX

Pro Tools HD and HDX are *processor-based* systems, providing special computer chips that go into the computer to handle all the processing needs of the software. This takes the load off the computer and guarantees certain levels of performance. Pro Tools TDM (the precursor to HD and HDX) has been the professional standard because Avid hardware (with its own built-in processors) offered a stable, reliable, and predictable level of performance. It follows that putting the same processors in your computer can give you the same performance. Your track limits are much higher with the HD and HDX systems compared with the host-based — up to 96 audio tracks for HD and 256 audio tracks for HDX — and these track counts are guaranteed by the Avid DSP (Digital Signal Processing) chips. The downside is that HD systems are much more expensive than the host-based versions (HDX is even more so).

As a way of offsetting the higher cost, Avid offers a few features to HD and HDX users that host-based users don't have, such as more (and better) plug-ins — as well as a few extra editing and mixing options. The good news is that any recordings you do in your LE or M-Powered system can be opened in a HD or HDX system (at a commercial studio, for instance) to mix or otherwise process your tracks. This is handy if you want to record at home and then take it to a pro to mix.

Differences between Macs and PCs

Aside from the obvious hardware and operating system (OS) differences between Apple- and Windows-based computers, Mac and PC versions of the Pro Tools software are nearly identical. The only significant difference you'll find between the two is the keyboard shortcuts used to perform certain tasks. Throughout the book, I give both versions of the shortcuts.

Getting Set Up

Before you can do any work in Pro Tools, you have to set up both your hardware and your Playback Engine settings. This section walks you through how to do this basic preparation.

Setting hardware settings

One of the first things you need to do before you start using Pro Tools in earnest is to configure your hardware settings within the software program. This is done via the Hardware Setup dialog box, as shown in Figure 3-1. (To get there, choose Setup➪Hardware Setup from the main menu.) From this dialog box, you can check out your peripherals as well as set the clock source, bit rate, and digital input. I give you a rundown of these options in the following sections.

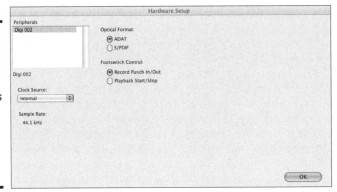

Figure 3-1:
The
Hardware
Setup
dialog box is
where you
configure
your
hardware
device.

Peripherals

Located in the upper-left portion of the Hardware Setup dialog box, the Peripherals pane shows what hardware is hooked up to your computer. In the case of Figure 3-1, it's the Digi 002. If you have an Eleven Rack or Mbox, you'll see either one of those listed in this pane.

Clock Source

From the Clock Source drop-down menu, you choose your source for the digital *master clock,* which controls the sample rate capture and playback. This makes sure that if you have more than one device (a separate analog-to-digital [A/D] converter connected to your Avid interface, for example), all devices are synchronized. If you just use the Avid interface, simply choose Internal from this menu. If you have other digital devices, such as a digital mixer or an external converter, choose the device that has the best clock as your clock source. In this case, you can choose from the following options:

✦ **Internal:** Uses the digital clock inside the Avid interface.

✦ **S/PDIF (RCA):** Synchronizes to a signal sent via the coaxial S/PDIF input.

✦ **Optical:** Synchronizes to a signal coming in the Optical input. The optical format that is used is based upon whether you select ADAT or S/PDIF in the upcoming "Optical Format" section.

For more on ADAT, S/PDIF, and Optical connections, check out Book I, Chapter 2.

Before you can use one of the digital connections as a clock source, you have to first connect the device to your Avid hardware — then you adjust the setting in the Hardware Setup dialog box. Otherwise the device won't show up in the dialog box.

If you have more than one digital device connected (such as a digital mixer connected to your Avid interface), do some experimenting by recording with different clock sources and then compare the chosen sources to see which one gives you the best sound. (Digital clocks vary in quality.) Also, if you have more than three digital devices connected to your system, consider using a specialized master clock and distribute this clock source to all your devices. This will likely give you a better sound because then all your devices follow the same clock timing.

Optical Format

From this area, choose how the digital inputs on your Avid hardware function. For example, with the Digi 002, you can use the Optical jacks (located on the back of the device — see Book II, Chapter 2 for more) to send and receive ADAT or S/PDIF signals. Your two options in this section of the dialog box are

Book II
Chapter 3

Examining Software Basics

✦ **ADAT:** Selecting this option means your RCA jacks are disabled (you can no longer send and receive ADAT signals), and the S/PDIF signals are sent through the Optical jacks instead.

✦ **S/PDIF:** Selecting this option means that your RCA jacks send and receive S/PDIF signals while the Optical jacks send and receive ADAT signals.

Footswitch Control

Here you can choose to have an optional footswitch operate one of two ways: to punch in and out, and to start or stop playback. Choose this option if you want to ignore this setting if you don't have a footswitch connected to your system. Footswitch inputs are available on the Avid Eleven Rack and Mbox Pro interfaces,

Sample Rate

From the Sample Rate drop-down menu, choose the sample rate in which to work. Depending on your hardware, you can choose 44.1, 48, 88.2, or 96 kHz. Check out the Book II, Chapter 2 to see which sample rates are supported by your Avid device. While you're at it, check out Book I, Chapter 1 for the nitty-gritty of sample rates.

The Sample Rate drop-down menu is editable only when you don't have a session open. If you have a session open (as is the case in Figure 3-1), this area shows the sample rate chosen when this session was created but won't allow you to make any changes. To choose a different sample rate, follow these steps:

1. **Close your open session.**

2. **Choose Setup⇨Hardware Setup from the main menu and make your choice.**

3. **Click OK and then open a new session.**

The new session is in the sample rate you just chose.

Playing with the Playback Engine settings

The Playback Engine dialog box is where you can tweak various options — hardware buffer size, CPU usage limit, and playback buffer size, for example — so your system runs at top efficiency. Getting there — where "there" looks a lot like Figure 3-2 — involves choosing Setup⇨Playback Engine from the main menu. As for what all these options actually mean, the following sections take care of that.

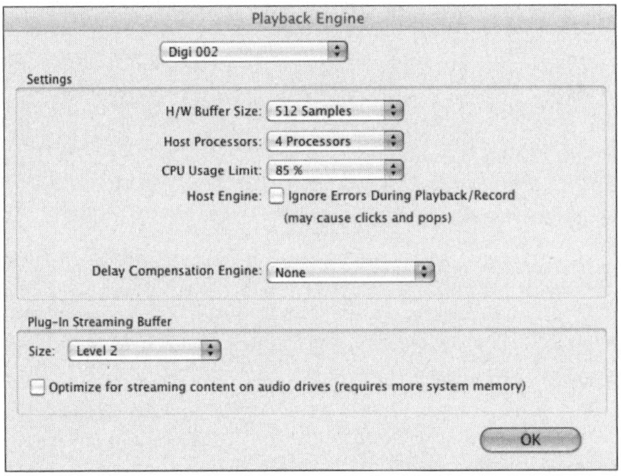

Figure 3-2:
Adjust your
system's
performance
from the
Playback
Engine
dialog box.

H/W Buffer Size

In this context, H/W here stands for *Hardware,* and the hardware buffer size controls the amount of memory used to handle the processing of audio (as well as plug-ins, such as reverb). The lower this setting, the lower the *latency* (time it takes to get sound into and back out of your system) that you hear when you record.

I suggest keeping this setting as low as possible while recording, especially when you do overdubs (I usually go with 32 or 64 samples). How low you can go depends on how many tracks you record at once — and on whether you want to use plug-ins reverb while recording. Using lots of tracks and lots of plug-ins requires lots of memory, which force you (rats!) to bump up the hardware buffer size. Higher buffer sizes mean higher latencies, which can make overdubbing tracks more difficult, so I reserve high buffer sizes until after I'm done recording all my tracks.

When you're ready to mix, go ahead and raise the buffer size. This puts less stress on your system and allows you to have more plug-ins running before you run into performance problems.

Host Processors

From the Host Processors drop-down menu, you can choose the number of available processors that Pro Tools will use. The number of processors you can choose depends on how many processors your computer has. My advice: Choose the highest number possible here.

CPU Usage Limit

From the CPU Usage Limit drop-down menu, set the amount of the computer's processing power (as a percentage) used to run the program. The default is 65%, but you can go much higher if you have only Pro Tools open when you work. The more programs you have open when working in Pro Tools, the lower the setting you want. Set it as high as you can without affecting the response of your screen redraws. A good setting to start with is around 75% to 85%.

Host Engine

The Host Engine check box allows you to avoid seeing an annoying error message if Pro Tools experiences any errors while you play back or record. Selecting this check box may result in clicks or pops in the audio if an error occurs. This is no big deal when you play back your session, but it can be a problem when you record because these clicks and pops will likely show up in your audio tracks. I recommend leaving this check box cleared whenever you record. The only time I select this check box is if I'm working on a rough mix and don't want any error messages to stop the flow of my creative process.

If you're getting a lot of error messages, reconsider how many plug-ins you're using — or maybe upgrade your computer so it can handle more.

Delay Compensation Engine

The Delay Compensation Engine allows you to choose a setting so any active plug ins (both insets and sends — check out Book 6, Chapter 2 for more on plug-ins) stay aligned phase- and time-wise. This is essential for any mixes you do where you have a bunch of plug-ins, like reverb delay, and even equalization. You have several levels of compensation to choose from including:

✦ **None:** This introduces no delay compensation. Choose this setting for tracking without plug-ins. If you have any plug-ins at all, choose one of the other settings.

✦ **Short:** This setting provides 1023 samples of delay compensation at 44.1 or 48 kHz (this amount doubles for 88.2 or 96 kHz to 2047 and doubles again for 197.4 or 192 kHz to 4094). This setting is usually a good choice for mixes with just a few plug-ins.

✦ **Long:** This setting offers 4095 (44.1 or 48 kHz), 8191 (882 or 96 kHz) and 16,382 (176.4 or 192 kHz) samples of delay for your plug-ins. This setting is best for sessions where you use a lot of plug-ins.

✦ **Maximum:** This setting adds a whopping 16,383, 32,767, or 65,534 samples, at the various sample rates of delay compensation, to your tracks. This setting should only be necessary if you have a ton of plug-ins or if you have a few power-hungry ones, such as a handful of convolution reverbs.

Applying delay compensation takes processing power from your computer. Choose the lowest setting necessary to keep your tracks sounding good to save the power for actually processing your tracks. You can always adjust the setting if you need to during a session (not while it's playing, though).

Plug-In Streaming Buffer

The Plug-In Streaming Buffer deals with the amount of memory the audio engine uses to manage the hard drive's buffers. Again, you want as low of a setting as you can get without sacrificing system performance. If the setting is too high, you experience a delay between when you use the Play command and when Pro Tools starts playing the recording. Using too low a setting, on the other hand, can create problems, such as *audio dropout* (the sound cuts off) when you record or play back tracks. Start with the default setting and make adjustments as needed.

The ins and outs of inputs and outputs

Pro Tools allows you to assign your Input, Output, Insert, and Bus routings as you want. You do this within the I/O Setup dialog box, as shown in Figure 3-3. Choose Setup➪I/O Setup to get there.

Input

From the Input tab of the I/O Setup dialog box, choose and change the name of the inputs coming from your Avid hardware. Simply clicking the Default button brings up the inputs of the hardware that you connected. To change the name of any of the inputs, double-click the current name, type in your new one, and then press Return/Enter. Whatever name you choose shows up in the Input section of the channel strip in the Mix and Edit windows.

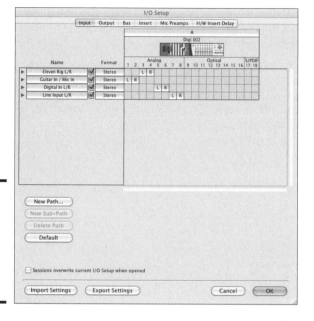

Figure 3-3:
Set your
system's
routings
from the
I/O Setup
dialog box.

Customizing the names of your inputs and outputs makes setting up sessions and remembering where everything is routed much easier. For example, if you use the S/PDIF inputs as your main microphone inputs (you'd have an external preamp and an A/D converter between your mic and the interface), you can name them mic 1 and mic 2 instead of S/PDIF.

Instead of choosing the default setup, you can start from scratch and set up your own Input routings by clicking the New Path or New Sub-Path buttons. You can also delete paths if you choose. Additionally, you can import or export routing settings by clicking the Import Settings or Export Settings buttons. This can save you time if you have custom settings that you want to use in all your sessions.

Output

Clicking the Default button on the Output tab of the I/O Setup dialog box displays the outputs of the hardware connected to your system. Like with the Input tab of the I/O Setup dialog box, you can change names for the outputs if you want. The Output tab, however, has three additional options, as shown in Figure 3-4. These options do the following:

✦ **Controller Meter Path:** This is the output assigned to the master meter in the Mix window. From this drop-down menu, you can assign any hardware or bus outputs as main outputs so you can know what the levels are.

✦ **Audition Paths:** This is the output where *audio regions* — the representations of the audio files in your tracks — play. (Book IV, Chapter 1 has more on audio regions.)

✦ **New Track Default Output:** Choosing your main output here automatically places this output in every track that you open in your session. Making your main output your default output means that you don't have to choose an Output setting in the Mix or Edit windows whenever you create a new track.

Figure 3-4:
The Output tab of the I/O Setup dialog box includes additional parameters.

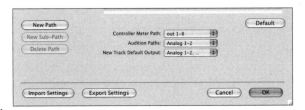

Insert

Use the Insert tab of the I/O Setup dialog box to set the routing for any of your insert effects, such as compressors and limiters. (See Book VI, Chapter 4 for more on insert effects.)

Bus

The Bus tab of the I/O Setup dialog box has the 32 available buses for your send/return effects, such as reverb. (Check out Book VI, Chapter 5 for more on send/return effects.)

Click the Default button for all the settings in the various tabs of the I/O Setup dialog box, and you'll be up and running quickly.

Mic Preamps

This tab allows you to assign PRE (Avid's Eight-channel microphone preamp) to your session. Unless you have a PRE connected this tab will not allow you to do anything.

H/W Insert Delay

This tab allows you to set the delay time for any external hardware effects units you have connected to your audio interface. Here you enter the delay time in the proper channel; when you have the Delay Compensation Engine running, Pro Tools will apply this delay amount to the tracks assigned to the appropriate input channel. This tab is only necessary if you have an external effects unit connected and routed to your Pro Tools session.

Dealing with Sessions

Before you can do any recording, editing, or mixing in Pro Tools, you have to set up a session in which to work. A *session* in Pro Tools is simply a song file that contains all the audio and MIDI tracks, plug-ins, and mixer settings for all your tracks. Session files don't actually contain the audio data; instead, they just have the audio files attached to them.

**Book II
Chapter 3**

Examining Software Basics

Creating a new session

To create a new session, choose File⇨New Session from the main menu or press ⌘+N (Mac) or Ctrl+N (PC). A dialog box appears, as shown in Figure 3-5, where you can choose the following.

✦ **Create a Session from Template:** Choosing this option opens a menu of saved templates. To get started I recommend choosing this and taking a look at your options — you may find one that fits your needs pretty well. When you choose a template, all the tracks and setting assigned to that template automatically show up in your session. This can be a real timesaver if you want to create a complicated session with lots of tracks and send routing. You still need to choose the session parameters listed below to create your session.

✦ **Create a blank session:** This opens a session with no tracks or routing assignments. This is the option to choose if you want to customize your session.

If you plan to create a lot of sessions with specific tracks and signal routing settings, I highly recommend that you save your empty session (without the audio tracks) as a template to save you time later.

Figure 3-5: The New Session dialog box is where you set up a new song file.

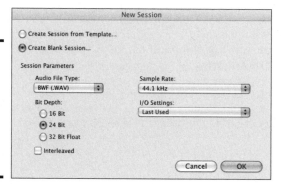

✦ **Audio File Type:** This drop-down menu lets you choose between BWF (Broadcast WAV File) or AIFF files. Choose the one that works best for you. (I always use BWF files because they're compatible with other software I use. Your needs may be different.) If you aren't transferring your files from one program to another, I suggest using the default BWF option.

✦ **Sample Rate:** Here you choose the sample rate of your session. Your options depend on the Avid hardware you have. For example, if you have an Mbox Mini, your choices are between 44.1 kHz and 48 kHz. If you have an Mbox, you can choose between 44.1 kHz, 48 kHz, 88.2 kHz, and 96 kHz. If you have an Mbox Pro, or Eleven Rack, you can choose from six options: 44.1 kHz, 48 kHz, 88.2 kHz, 96 kHz, 197.4 kHz, and 192 kHz.

✦ **Bit Depth:** Depending on your version of Pro Tools, you can choose between a 16-bit rate, a 24-bit rate, or a 32-bit float rate (the 32-bit rate is only available with Pro Tools 10, HD or HDX). For most sessions select the 24 Bit radio button.

✦ **I/O Settings:** From this drop-down menu, you can choose between the most recently used setting, a stereo-mix setting, or from a list of other saved settings.

When you click OK on your setting, you'll be asked what you want to name the file and where you want to save it in the Save dialog box. Choose your name and location and click Save.

The higher the sample rate you select in the New Session dialog box, the more work your computer processor has to do. You often have to balance your desire for the highest-resolution music possible against the capabilities of your system.

The sample rate you choose depends on your goals, intended final format (CD, for example), and the speed of your computer's processor. For example, if your session is going to have a ton of tracks and end up on a CD or be used for online distribution, your best bet is to choose 44.1 kHz because that's where you'll end up when you record to CD or this is the quality most online distributers want. Keep in mind, too, that using a whole slew of tracks means that your computer needs as much processing power as possible to handle mixing and processing tasks. In this case, recording at 96 kHz would likely put too much strain on your computer and deprive you of the power to do what you want during mixing.

On the other hand, if you suspect you won't use very many tracks and want the highest resolution possible — or if you have a very powerful computer and won't go crazy creating multiple tracks — 88.2 kHz or 96 kHz may better meet your goals.

I recommend getting to know your system before you record a lot of music with it. Experiment with different sample rates and track counts to see what your computer can handle. With this information, you can get a good sense of how hard you can push your system before you reach the limits of its performance.

Opening sessions

To open a session, choose File⇨Open Session from the main menu or press ⌘+O (Mac) or Ctrl+O (PC). The Open Session dialog box appears, as shown in Figure 3-6. Choose the file you want to open and then click Open.

Figure 3-6:
The Open
Session
dialog box.

If you have a session with more than 24 tracks and you want to keep those additional tracks, *don't* open it in a Pro Tools version earlier than 5.3 (or if you do, don't *save* it there) because any additional tracks will be lost when you click Save.

Saving sessions

You have three options for saving sessions in Pro Tools: Save Session, Save Session As, and Save Session Copy In. As well, you can always return to a previously saved version of your session with the Revert to Saved command. These options are detailed in the next sections.

Save Session

This is the same Save command that you find in any computer program. As usual, you choose File⇨Save to save your session. You can also initiate a save by pressing ⌘+S (Mac) or Ctrl+S (PC).

I highly recommend that you get used to saving from the keyboard often to prevent losing any data while you work. You can also turn on the Auto Save function and have Pro tools save your session automatically. Here's how:

1. **Choose Setup⇨Preferences to access the Preferences dialog box.**

2. **On the Operations tab, select the Enable Session File Auto Backup check box.**

Save Session As

Choose File⇨Save Session As to save your session with a new name and/or location. Figure 3-7 shows the Save Session As dialog box.

Use Save Session As to save a variation of a session that you've been working on. I do this a lot when I'm mixing because this way, I can have a bunch of different mixes to choose from. The good thing about this command is that it saves only the session data and not the audio or MIDI files, so the session won't take up much room on your hard drive.

Figure 3-7: Choose the session name and location here.

Save Session Copy In

If you want to transfer your files from one program to another (Pro Tools to Logic, for example), using the Save Session Copy In command can be useful. Choosing File⇨Save Session Copy In opens the dialog box you see in Figure 3-8. Here, you can change the filename, location, and file type, among other options:

✦ **Session Format:** From this drop-down menu, choose the Pro Tools version you want to save in. Your options include the current version as well as PT5.1–6.9, PT5, PT4 24bit, PT4 16bit, and PT 3.2.

Keep in mind that you may lose some data if you save this session in an earlier version.

✦ **Session Parameters:** Use this section of the dialog box to choose the audio file type, sample rate, and bit depth. You can choose from the same options that you had when you first opened the session. Here, you can also choose to force Mac/PC compatibility. If you want to share this session between a Mac and a PC, you need to select the Enforce Mac/PC Compatibility check box. Personally, I leave this check box enabled all the time just in case I want to transfer my sessions back and forth between a Mac and a PC.

✦ **Items to Copy:** The Items to Copy section includes options for audio files, plug-in settings, and movie or video files that may be part of the session. If you plan on taking this session to another computer, use Items to Copy function when you choose what you want to copy.

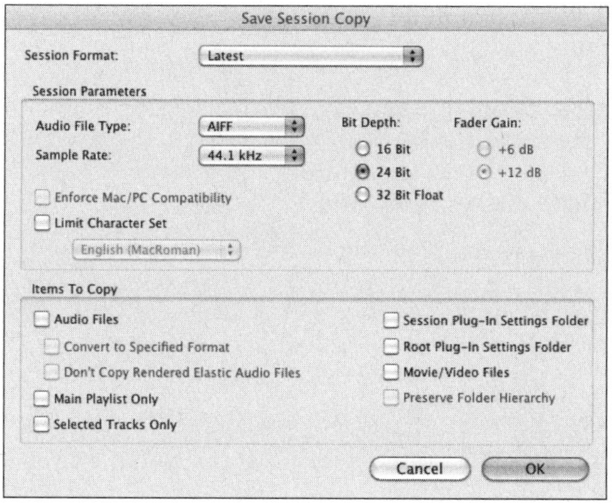

**Book II
Chapter 3**

Examining Software
Basics

Figure 3-8:
The Save Session Copy In dialog box allows you to change the type of file your session is formatted in.

Relying on Revert to Save

The Revert to Save command (choose File⇨Revert to Save) is a handy feature if you did a bunch of work since you last saved your session and want to undo it without having to use the Undo command (located under Edit menu) to backtrack through the steps and undo each one.

Personally, if I'm in the position of wanting to undo a bunch of stuff and haven't used the Save command since starting those changes, I choose to save the session with the Save As command. This way, I have those changes just in case I do decide to keep them. If I go that route, the changes will be sitting in a separate session file, safe and (ahem) sound.

Creating a session template

To make your life easier, you can create a session *template* with all the options you want already in place — track settings, window views, mixer settings, and so on — so all you have to do when you open a new session is open the template and save it with your new session name.

A variety of session templates comes with your Pro Tools software. To use them, choose the Pro Tools LE Session Templates folder from the Software CD-ROM and drag it onto your hard drive. Open the template session and rename it as your new session. You can use this folder for all your templates so that finding them again is easy. Choose File⇨Open session from the main menu, select the template folder from the Open Session dialog box, and scroll to the template you want to use.

To prepare a template, start by opening a new session and then creating your session as you want. After you set all the options to your liking, save the session file with a name that you'll remember (like *killer session template 1*) so you can find it easily.

To transform the session file you saved into a session template, use the following steps:

1. **Choose File⇨Save As Template.**

The Save Session Template dialog box opens (Figure 3-9).

Figure 3-9:
Use the
Save
Session
Template
to create
a template
for your
session.

> Save Session Template
>
> ⦿ Install template in system
>   Category: [Music   ▲▼]
>   Name: rhythm editing   [▲▼]
> ○ Select location for template...
> ☐ Include Media
>
>   (Cancel)   (OK)

2. **Select Install template in system or Select location for template.**

a. *If you choose to install your template in the system, you choose the category and assign a name; your template will go into the default template folder.*

b. *If you choose the select the location for your template, a navigation box appears when you click OK; then you can put the template anywhere you choose.*

3. **In the Include Media selector, you can chose to have certain media included in your session template. For example, you may want to use a series of rhythm-section audio files to use in multiple sessions. Check this box and each time you create a new session based on this template, the files will be there for you.**

   Your template is saved in the location that you chose when you opened the session.

Getting to Know Audio and MIDI Files

Every time you click the Record button with a track engaged (as I describe in Book III, Chapter 1, where you can find more on tracks) you create an audio or MIDI file. This section walks you through what these files are and how to deal with them.

Understanding audio files

An *audio file* is the data created from recording onto an audio track. Audio files in Pro Tools are *clips.* You can import, export, and edit these clips in a staggering variety of ways. (Book VI shows you many of the ways to edit audio.) Whenever you create a new audio file, this clip is added to the Clips list, where you can manage it (as shown in Figure 3-10). The Clips list is located on the right side of the Edit window. If the list isn't visible, click the double arrows at the bottom-right of the Edit window. This expands the Edit window to include the Clips list view.

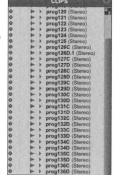

Figure 3-10: Audio files created by recording into an audio track show up in the Clips list.

Meeting MIDI files

MIDI files are created whenever (you guessed it) you record MIDI data into a MIDI track. MIDI tracks don't contain actual sounds; instead, they consist of the MIDI performance and system instructions used to control a

MIDI instrument. To have the MIDI data become sound, you have to record the *output* of your MIDI sound module (what it does in response to the MIDI file's instructions) onto an audio track. Then these sounds are contained in an audio file.

MIDI files show up in the Clips list (along with your session's audio files), where you can mange them. MIDI regions have a small circular MIDI jack-type icon to help you identify them. You can choose to see only the MIDI regions in the Clips list by choosing Show from the Clips drop-down menu and the selecting the MIDI option (or by clearing the Audio, Auto Generated, and Groups options).

Finding your session files

Whenever you open a session in Pro Tools, the program has to go out and find all the audio and MIDI files associated with that session before the session will actually open. If Pro Tools can't find the files — you moved them, for instance — the Missing Files dialog box opens. There you can choose to skip the file, let Pro Tools search for it automatically, or search for it manually. (See Figure 3-11 for a look at the Missing Files dialog box.) I always choose the automatic-search option — it finds the missing file nearly every time. The only time that hasn't worked for me is when I've moved a file to another hard drive. (Then I select the Manually Find & Relink radio button.)

Figure 3-11:
The Missing
Files dialog
box helps
you locate
truant files.

After your session opens, all the audio and MIDI files (regions) for that session are displayed in the Audio Regions list in the Edit window. Not only can you manage the files from these lists, but you can also import files that were originally recorded in another session — or even using another recording program (such as Logic or Nuendo).

Chapter 4: Understanding the Pro Tools Windows

In This Chapter

✔ Looking at the Transport window

✔ Examining the Mix window

✔ Discovering the Edit window

Recognizing that recording is a complex process, Pro Tools gives you three distinct windows in which to work: Transport, Mix, and Edit. Each window performs a certain set of functions and gives you control of a specific set of details. These are outlined in this chapter. These windows are the heart and soul of Pro Tools. The more comfortable you are navigating them, the easier life will be as you create your masterpieces.

Tackling the Transport Window

At its most basic level, the Transport window — see Figure 4-1 — acts like the transport mechanism of a tape deck that moves the tape past the record and playback heads: It controls the digital processes that correspond to recording, playing, stopping, rewinding, and so on. On a deeper level, however, it also offers a host of other functions. This section details all the Transport window's functions.

Figure 4-1:
The Transport window acts like tape-deck controls.

Adjusting the Transport window

Some people salivate at the thought of information overkill, while others live by the maxim, "Less is more." Pro Tools is smart enough to accommodate both schools of thought. In case you don't want all the information (and the accompanying clutter) present in the Transport window as shown in Figure 4-1, you can show or hide parts of it as you choose. You can find the commands for paring down the size of the Transport window under the View menu at the top of the main Pro Tools window. Just choose View➪Transport and then choose from the options listed — Counters, MIDI Controls, and Expanded — as shown in Figure 4-2.

Figure 4-2:
Adjust the
Transport
window
from the
View menu.

Basic controls

The upper-left portion of the Transport window is home to your basic, traditional transport controls. If you honed your recording skills on a tape deck, you'll be right at home. Taking a look at Figure 4-3, you'll find (going from left to right) the following:

Figure 4-3:
The Basic
controls.

✦ **Online:** Engaging this button allows you to control record and playback with an external device. Before you can use this feature, you need to connect your device and specify its synchronization settings in Pro Tools. (Check out the Synchronization section of the Pro Tools Reference guide that came with your software for details on how to do this.)

✦ **Return to Zero:** Clicking this button takes you back to the beginning of the session. You can also press Return/Enter if you prefer to use your keyboard instead of the mouse.

 ✦ **Rewind:** Clicking this button "rewinds" the session in one of two ways, providing a fine-tuned control that's really hard to get with the mechanics of a tape deck:

- *Click Rewind and hold down the mouse button.* The session rewinds until you release the mouse button. One cool thing about this way of rewinding is that when you release the Rewind button, a marker is placed in the song, and all you have to do to rewind back to that point is hit the Stop button. The session goes right back to that point. (This is great if you want to check the same spot several times — for example, to make sure that new guitar part comes in right on cue.)

- *Click the button.* Each click rewinds the session a prescribed amount, depending on the time-scale setting displayed in your main counter (more about that in the next section). For example, if you have your main counter set up to display bars (measures) and beats, clicking the Rewind button moves the session back one bar of music. If you have min:seconds or samples showing in the display, the session moves back in one-second increments.

 ✦ **Stop:** Clicking Stop simply stops the session. (You can get the same thing done much faster, though, by pressing the spacebar on your keyboard — no fumbling with the mouse required.)

 ✦ **Play:** Clicking the Play button starts the session. Simply clicking the Play button (or pressing the spacebar) starts playback; clicking the Record button first and then the Play button starts recording, as long as you have a track enabled to record. Book III, Chapter 3 covers this in detail.

 ✦ **Fast Forward:** To move quickly through the session, just use the Fast Forward button. You can use Fast Forward one of two ways:

- *Click Fast Forward and hold down the mouse button.* The session fast-forwards until you release the mouse button. Depending on whether you were playing the session when you press and hold the button or the session was stopped, releasing the Fast Forward button can either return you to play mode or stop the session at that point.

- *Click the button.* Each click forwards the session a prescribed amount based upon the time scale setting displayed in your main counter (see the next section). For example, if you have your main counter set up to display bars and beats, clicking the Fast Forward button moves the session forward one bar of music. If you have min:seconds or samples set in the display, the session moves forward by one-second increments.

✦ **Go to End:** Clicking this button takes you to the end of the session. If you don't want to use your mouse, you can also press Option+Return (Mac) or Ctrl+Enter (PC).

✦ **Record:** Clicking the Record button readies your session to record any enabled tracks. (Book III, Chapter 3 talks about this more.) You need to have at least one track enabled for this function to work. You'll be alerted if you don't. If you don't want to use the mouse, you can ready recording by pressing ⌘+spacebar (Mac) or Ctrl+spacebar (PC). To actually record, you need to click the Play button after clicking Record.

In addition to readying recording, you can toggle through the different Record modes by pressing the Control key while you click with your mouse (Mac) or right-click (PC). These Record modes are covered in detail in Book III, Chapter 4, but here is an overview:

- *Nondestructive:* This Record mode is indicated (rather subtly) by not showing an icon in the Record button; it doesn't delete any previous *takes* (a recorded performance) on that track.

- *Destructive:* This mode — indicated by a small *D* in the center of the Record button — records over the track, destroying any previous takes as it does so.

  Don't use this mode unless you absolutely don't want the previous take, because it's gone forever if you do so.

- *Loop:* This mode — indicated by a loop graphic inside the Record button — allows you to repeatedly record over a selected section of your track (called, curiously enough, a loop). It's a handy function if you have a section that may need more than one try to get right because when you're done recording a take, it returns you to the start of the looped section and begins recording over again. Each loop through the section is saved and added to your track's playlist where you can choose the best one later.

- *Quick-punch:* This mode is indicated by a *P* in the center of the Record button. Quick-punch allows you to automatically punch in and out of a section of a song. For example, if your bass player just laid down a killer part except for two lousy notes, you can *rerecord just those notes on* the fly by *punching in* (start recording) just before the notes and *punching out* (stop recording) right after them.

Counters

The Counters section of the Transport window tells you where you are in the session. This section contains only the main counter for your session.

If the Counters section isn't visible, choose View⊳Transport⊳Counter (to see the main counter) — or View⊳Transport⊳Expanded (to see the rest of the counters listed in this section). Figure 4-4 shows how the Transport window looks with both these options selected.

Figure 4-4:
The
Counters
and
Expanded
sections.

The Counters section of the Transport window is home to the main counter, which is located in the center of the window and shows where you are in the session. There is a drop-down menu located to the right of this counter where you can choose the format — bars:beats, min:seconds, samples — to be displayed. Simply click the white triangle and choose the format you desire.

Expanded

The Expanded section of the Transport window shows a secondary counter for your session as well as additional goodies to help you get around your session. These include pre- and post-roll setting; a transport master selector for synchronizing Pro Tools with other devices; and start, end, and length times for selections. These are all shown in Figure 4-4.

The Expanded section of the Transport window contains the following display extras:

✦ **Secondary counter:** Below the main counter is a secondary counter for your session. You can select the format displayed by opening the drop-down menu to the right of the counter. Again, your choices are bars:beats, min:seconds, and samples. This lets you have two different counters displayed at one time, which is handy if you want to see where you are in your session in two different formats, such as min:seconds and bars:beats.

✦ **Pre-roll:** Pre-roll allows you to choose an amount of time that the session plays before the timeline of your session begins or wherever you have the Start cursor. This is useful if you use a *click track* (the equivalent of an electronic metronome) or want to do some punch recording; whoever's playing can use it to get used to the tempo before you start to record. (See the "MIDI controls" section, later in this chapter, for more on using a click track. See Book III, Chapter 4 for more on punch recording.)

You choose the amount of your pre-roll by clicking in the value in the Pre-roll counter and then either typing a new value or (with the mouse button held down) scrolling up or down. Engage the Pre-roll function by clicking the Pre-roll button next to the counter.

✦ **Post-roll:** Post-roll is pretty much like Pre-roll except that in this case (surprise, surprise), you tack on a specified amount of time after the session ends (or wherever the timeline End point is set).

You choose the length of your post-roll by clicking in the value in the Post-roll counter and typing a new value — or, with your mouse held down, scrolling up or down. Engage the Post-roll function by clicking the Post-roll button next to the counter.

✦ **Transport Master:** The drop-down menu of the Transport Master box lets you choose a specific device to be the "master" of the main Transport functions (play, record, stop, and so on). You find two sub-menus here: Transport and Online. In the Transport sub-menu, you can choose the Transport Master from several options, including MMC (MIDI Machine Control), MIDI, and Machine. (Machine refers to the AvidAvid MachineControl software, which you have to buy from AvidAvid. This is used for post-production and film work.) From the Online sub-menu, you can choose to bring specific devices on- or off-line. The devices available will depend on the currently selected Transport Master.

If you want to get into synchronizing Pro Tools with other devices, check out the Avid reference manual for details on how to do this. If you have no other control devices synchronized to Pro Tools, then this box reads `Transport = Pro Tools`.

✦ **Start:** Use the Start counter to set the beginning of a range within which you can play or record. You choose this starting point by clicking in the counter window and then typing in the value, or clicking and holding with your mouse (scrolling up or down to get the value you want).

✦ **End:** The End counter shows you where the play or record range ends. You can choose this endpoint by clicking in the counter window and then typing in the value, or clicking and holding with your mouse (scrolling up or down to get the value you want).

✦ **Length:** The Length counter shows the length of the play range created with the Start and End counters. Like with the other counters, you can type in a value by clicking in the counter window first, or you can click and hold your mouse button while you scroll up or down.

Typing in a value other than what is shown after you set the Start and End counter changes the placement of the End counter.

MIDI controls

The MIDI controls section is located on the right side of the Transport window. (If it's not showing in your Transport window, choose View⇨ Transport⇨MIDI Controls.) The MIDI Controls section, as shown on the right side of Figure 4-5, includes the following.

Figure 4-5: The MIDI controls section of the Transport window.

Book II
Chapter 4

Understanding the Pro Tools Windows

+ **Wait for Note:** Clicking this button lets Pro Tools know it should wait to start recording until it receives a musical note from a MIDI device. This allows you to ensure that your first note is precisely at the beginning of the recorded section.

+ **Click:** Clicking this button turns on and off the metronome signal sent through the MIDI out of your MIDI interface.

  Double-clicking this button opens the Click/Countoff Options dialog box (see Figure 4-6) where you can choose various Click parameters, including when the click sounds, what note it transmits, and what MIDI port (output) it uses.

Figure 4-6: Choose click and countoff settings for your session.

✦ **Countoff:** Clicking this button turns on and off a specified count-off of the length chosen at the bottom of the Click/Countoff dialog box (see Figure 4-6). (Double-clicking the Countoff button opens this dialog box.) You can set the countoff to sound only during recording or during both recording and playback. You type in the length of this count-off in the Bars text box in the Click/Countoff Options dialog box. This number shows up in the Countoff button after the dialog box is closed.

 ✦ **MIDI Merge:** With this selector, you can either merge your recorded MIDI data with existing MIDI data on the record-enabled track or erase the existing data and replace it with the new stuff. Engaging the button lets you merge data.

 ✦ **Conductor:** Clicking this button turns on the tempo map defined in the Tempo line of the Edit window. (See "Examining the Edit Window," later in this chapter, for more on the Tempo line.) You create this map by double-clicking the Meter button (described next).

Alternatively, you can disable this button and choose a tempo by manually entering it (more about choosing the tempo in a minute).

 ✦ **Meter:** This button shows you the time signature for the present section of the session. Double-click the time signature, and a dialog box opens, allowing you to specify time signature (meter), tempo, and start point for these values. With this dialog box, you can set up a *tempo map,* which is a scheme describing tempo changes for your entire song, no matter how complex. (Book III, Chapter 3 details how to create a tempo map.)

✦ **Note:** When the Conductor button is not engaged, the Note icon tells you what value note the metronome is sounding. Click this icon, and a drop-down menu opens, letting you choose the value from whole notes to sixteenth notes.

✦ **Tempo:** With the Conductor button engaged, this box simply shows you what tempo the current section of the session is in. With the Conductor button disabled, you can manually enter any tempo you like. You can do this in two ways:

- *Type it in.* Click in the box where the tempo is displayed, type in a number (in beats per minute), and then press Return/Enter. The metronome and counters play at this tempo.

- *Slide it in.* Adjust the horizontal slider located under the Conductor, Meter, and Tempo buttons to choose your tempo. Slide to the right, and you get a faster tempo; slide left for a slower one.

- *Tap it in.* By pressing the T key on your keyboard to the tempo you want, you can set Pro Tools to a tempo without having to know exactly how many beats per minute you want. (This is a great feature for people who aren't comfortable with metronome numbers.)

Examining the Edit Window

The Edit window, as shown in Figure 4-7, is where you'll do most of your work. Here, everything is set up in a timeline so you can see what's happening in the session while it plays. This window contains a variety of tracking information, including inputs and outputs, sends, inserts, and automations data. The Edit window also has the tools you need to do audio and MIDI data editing, such as creating, arranging, and editing specific regions of an audio track.

Figure 4-7:
The Edit
window
shows a
timeline
of all your
session
data.

The list is almost endless. Don't fret though; everything you need to know to use this window effectively is in this section.

Taking a look at track controls

Each track, whether audio or MIDI, is shown in the Edit window. These run horizontally underneath the Timeline section of the window. Figure 4-8 gives you a close-up view of the track section of the Edit window.

Solo button

Track Name button | Mute button

Figure 4-8:
The track
section of
the Edit
window
shows
information
on each
track in the
session.

Record Enable button | Playlist selector

Track Height selector | Track Height selector

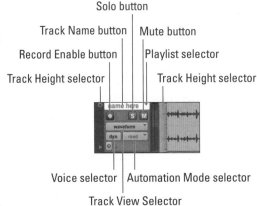

Voice selector | Automation Mode selector

Track View Selector

Figure 4-8: The track section of the Edit window shows information on each track in the session.

Basic controls

On the far left of the track section of the Edit window are some basic controls. These include the following:

✦ **Track Name:** Double-click this button (which shows the name of the track) to open a window where you can the track's name and also add some comments. (All comments show up in the Comments section of the expanded Edit window or in the Mix window.)

✦ **Playlist selector:** Click and hold this button to open a drop-down menu that allows you to choose from edit playlists. (See Book IV, Chapter 1 for more on editing playlists.)

✦ **Record Enable:** Click this button to enable the track for recording.

✦ **Solo:** Clicking this button *solos* a track — turns off the rest of the tracks — in a mix.

✦ **Mute:** Clicking this button turns off this track.

✦ **Track View selector:** Click and hold this button to open a menu that lets you choose different views in the Timeline section of the track in the session. Your options include Blocks, Waveform, Volume, Mute, and Pan.

✦ **Track Height selector:** Clicking this arrow opens a drop-down menu from which you choose the height of the track data display. You choices include Mini, Small, Medium, Large, Jumbo, Extreme, and Fit to Window. You can also click the ruler on the right side of the track control section to choose your track height. The options are the same.

✦ **Automation Mode selector:** Click and hold this button to open a menu that lets you choose from various automation modes, including Off, Read, Touch, Latch, and Write. Each of these display modes shows the waveform in the background and the setting for the automation data in the foreground. (Book VI, Chapter 6 has more on automation modes and how to use them.)

✦ **Voice selector:** Clicking this button turns the track on and off. Click and hold this button to choose between *Dyn* (the track is heard if it has data in it) and *Off* (the track doesn't sound, even if it has an audio or MIDI file attached to it). Because Pro Tools LE allows you to have only 32 active voices (24 on versions 5.3.1 and earlier), you can use this selector to keep a track from occupying one of those voices.

Optional windows in the track section

You can enhance your Edit window view by adding information from the Mix window for each track. Just choose View➪Edit Window➪All from the main menu, and you'll end up with something that looks like Figure 4-9. This is a handy feature if you have only one monitor and you want to be able to see the comments, inserts, sends, and I/O settings (or any combination) for each track without having to open the Mix window. (Not sure what inserts, sends, and I/O settings actually are? Don't worry. I detail those in the "Managing the Mix Window" section, later in this chapter.)

Figure 4-9:
The expanded view of the channel strip in the Edit menu.

One of the really cool things in this section of the expanded window is that you can actually open a channel strip for an individual track by clicking the small fader icon located to the right of the output selector in the I/O settings window. Click the icon again, and the channel strip disappears. Figure 4-10 shows the channel strip after it's called up from the Edit window. (This feature is so handy that I rarely use the Mix window anymore.)

Figure 4-10:
Click the
little fader
icon at the
bottom
of the I/O
settings
window,
and a
channel
strip
pops up.

Examining edit modes

Editing in Pro Tools is done on regions. *Regions* are representations of the audio or MIDI files stored on your hard drive. What makes editing this way so powerful is that when you change a region, you aren't actually changing the audio file itself. (There are some exclusions to this, which are covered in Book IV, Chapters 3 and 4; and Book V, Chapter 3.) Instead, you're changing only how Pro Tools plays it back.

When you want to move regions around in Pro Tools, you have four edit modes in which to work: Shuffle, Spot, Slip, and Grid, as shown in Figure 4-11. These are located in the upper-left corner of the Edit Window. The following list describes each of these modes.

Figure 4-11:
The four edit
modes in
Pro Tools.

✦ **Shuffle:** In this mode, you can shuffle a region and place it automatically at the end of the nearest region. For example, if you want to move the second bar of a four-bar phrase to the last bar, all you have to do is create a separate region for each bar, grab it by clicking it with the Grabber tool, and move it over to the end. (Book IV, Chapter 2 explains, in detail, how to do this.) The third bar moves over to replace the second; the original second bar snaps right to the end of the fourth bar. This mode is handy for shuffling regions while making sure that you don't have any overlap or dead space between them.

✦ **Spot:** You can use this mode to designate the exact timeline placement of a region you want to move. When you click a region with Spot mode active, a dialog box pops up, asking you to enter the start point. Do so and click OK; the selected region is placed right where you want it.

✦ **Slip:** Use this mode to move regions anywhere you want with your mouse by selecting them any of the ways described in Book IV, Chapter 2. You can have regions overlap or leave space between them, for instance.

✦ **Grid:** This mode enables you to move regions to a *time grid* — user-defined divisions of your session. You can set the time grid's scale by choosing Tools➪Grid Value in the main Edit window. You can choose from two types of grids: Absolute and Grid. I detail these in Book IV, Chapter 1.

For more detailed information on these edit modes, check out Book IV, Chapter 1.

Zeroing in on Zoom controls

The Zoom controls (see Figure 4-12) are located next to the Edit Mode selectors. Use these buttons to fit a good working view of your audio and MIDI regions into your screen by specifying horizontal and vertical zoom (as the following list makes clear).

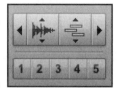

Figure 4-12:
The Zoom
controls.

✦ **Horizontal Zoom:** These outer two Zoom buttons control the horizontal zoom of the timeline as well as all audio and MIDI tracks and regions. Clicking the left button narrows the view; clicking the right button lengthens it.

✦ **Vertical Zoom:** These two center Zoom buttons control vertical zoom for audio and MIDI: The button for audio is at center-left, and the one for MIDI is at center-right. Clicking the arrow at the top of either button increases the height of the display; clicking the arrow at the bottom decreases the height.

✦ **Zoom Presets:** At the bottom of the Zoom Controls section are five easily programmable presets. On a Mac, you simply ⌘-click any one of the five buttons to assign your present setting to that button. On a PC, a Ctrl-click does the trick. The Zoom settings are saved, and you can recall them by clicking the assigned preset number.

Elucidating edit tools

Pro Tools has some powerful editing features, easily accessible from the Edit toolbar, found next to the Zoom controls at the top of the Edit window. Figure 4-13 shows you what the toolbar icons for these tools look like, and the following list tells you what the tools can do for you.

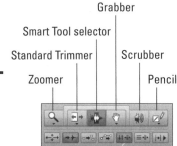

Grabber

Smart Tool selector

Standard Trimmer | Scrubber

Zoomer | Pencil

Figure 4-13:
Pro Tools
Edit tools
provide lots
of editing
power.

✦ **Zoomer:** The Zoomer tool does much the same thing as the Horizontal Zoom tool, with a handy editing advantage: It zooms right to the point that you click with your mouse or the area you click and drag across.

✦ **Standard Trimmer:** This tool lets you change the size of a region by clicking the beginning or end of the region and then sliding it to where you want it.

✦ **Selector:** Use the Selector tool to highlight a spot within a region so you can cut, paste, or do whatever you want with it. All you have to do is click and drag the mouse over the section you want to select.

✦ **Grabber:** In general terms, the Grabber tool lets you grab a region to move around your session. It has two options (which you can view if you click and hold the mouse button with the pointer over the tool): the Time and the Separation tools. (*Note:* Whichever tool you used last is the default tool until you select the other.)

  • *Time:* The Time Grabber tool lets you select an entire region and then move it anywhere within (that is, and between) tracks. You simply click the region with your mouse, hold down the button, and then drag the region to where you want it.

- *Separation:* The Separation Grabber tool lets you move a portion of a region within or between tracks. To select a portion to move, use the Selector tool described earlier in this list.

✦ **Scrubber:** Use the Scrubber tool to listen to a region without having to play the entire track. To use this tool, click the region and drag it forward to hear the audio play forward. Drag the mouse back along the region to hear the audio play backward. This tool is handy when you want to locate a specific note in the audio region.

✦ **Pencil:** Use the Pencil tool to redraw audio waveforms (great for drawing over clipped notes, for example); to do MIDI editing, such as inserting or deleting notes; or draw automation settings, among other things. (Book IV, Chapter 3 explains waveform editing in detail.) Clicking and holding this button opens a pop-up menu that offers seven Pencil types (as shown in Figure 4-14) as well as the Customize Note Duration option to use. (For more on custom note durations, see Book IV, Chapter 3.)

**Book II
Chapter 4**

Understanding the
Pro Tools Windows

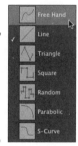

Figure 4-14:
The Pencil
tool has
five pencil-
shape
options.

✦ **Smart Tool:** This tool combines the functions of the Standard Trimmer, Selector, and Grabber tools. It changes how the cursor works according to where you are within a region, automatically becoming the appropriate tool for that section. This keeps you from having to constantly switch tools as you work. (Ah, progress.)

✦ **Zoom toggle:** This button lets you toggle between two zoom settings. To go to a saved zoom state, simply engage this button. If you don't like the setting, make a change to the horizontal or vertical zoom, and it will be saved if the zoom toggle button is engaged. Then to switch to the previous zoom state, disengage the toggle.

Looking at counter displays

The Edit window has two distinct counter displays; for each display, you have a choice among three different formats — bars and beats, minutes and seconds, and samples — for showing where you actually are in the session. You choose your format from a drop-down menu that you access by clicking the small arrow located to the right of the display, as shown in Figure 4-15. This is a handy feature for being able to see where you are in your session.

For example, I find that having my main counter set to bars and beats — and the secondary counter set to minutes and seconds — helps me keep track of where I am in the session and how that relates to the actual length of the tune. This is especially important if I have a tune that has to conform to a certain time limit (because I prefer to work in beats and bars).

Figure 4-15:
The counter displays can be set to show different formats.

Evaluating the Event Edit area

Next to the counter displays are the Event Edit displays. (See Figure 4-16.) These displays show the start point, end point, and length of a selected region in the same format as the main counter display. (See the previous section for more on counter displays.) If you choose a specific MIDI note to examine, another window opens that shows you the pitch, note velocity, and release velocity of that note.

Figure 4-16:
The Event Edit displays.

You can use the display to choose particular regions by clicking in the window and typing in the values you want. Press Return/Enter to activate the selection.

Instead of typing start points and end points into the Event Edit display, you can use the blue arrows in the Rulers section of the Edit window to choose your start point and end point, as shown in Figure 4-17. Click and drag each arrow to where you want it. You can also use the Selector tool and click and drag across the area you want to select. Book IV, Chapter 2 explains these options in detail.

Figure 4-17:
Select start
and end
points.

Additional Navigation Controls

Right beneath the edit tools are another variety of useful tools: navigation tools that get you around Pro Tools. The following list gives you the goods on what each tool can do for you:

✦ **Track View:** The track view settings can be accessed by clicking on the icon located at the upper-left corner above your tracks. Use the Track View tool to choose different view formats for the Track section (the leftmost column) of the Edit window. Clicking the down arrow calls up a drop-down menu from which you can choose Comments, Instrument, Inserts, Sends, I/O, Real-Time Properties, Track Color, All, or None.

✦ **Ruler View:** The Ruler View selector is located next to the Bars/Beats timeline title in the upper-left corner of the Timeline section of the Edit window. Use the Ruler View tool to choose different view formats for the Ruler section, which is the section running horizontally along the top of the Edit window. Clicking the down arrow calls up a drop-down menu, where you can choose to see Bars:Beats, Minutes:Seconds, Samples, Markers, Tempo, Meter, Key Signatures, All, or None. The selection(s) you make here appear in the Timebase ruler section of the Edit window. (Check out the "Rulers rule!" section later in this chapter for details on the Timebase ruler.)

✦ **Linearity Display Mode:** Click the Linearity Display Mode button, located above the first track listed in the Edit Window (to the right of the Track View selector) to choose how the Edit window shows your session timescale. You have two options:

  • *Linear Sample Display:* You see your session in samples.

  • *Linear Tick Display:* You see your session in bars and beats.

✦ **Tab to Transients:** The Tab to Transients button, when engaged, allows you to press the Tab key on your keyboard and move from transient to transient in the highlighted audio track. (A *transient,* by the way, is the loud initial attack that first attracts your attention to a sound.) You can find this button below the Edit tools in the upper section of the Edit window.

I love this feature for separating drum loops from a track. I simply engage this button, locate my cursor close to the start of my loop, and press the Tab key to go right at the start of the section I want to cut. Without this feature, I'd be messing around for quite a while, finding the exact start point of the part I want to separate.

✦ **Keyboard Focus:** Clicking the Command Keyboard Focus buttons toggle the Keyboard Focus option on and off. These buttons are located in the upper-right of the Groups, Clips and Track section of the Edit window.

What is the Keyboard Focus option, you ask? Well, here's the short answer: This option allows you to use your keyboard to perform shortcuts; for example, you can select regions from the MIDI or audio lists (see the "Looking at lists" section later in this chapter), perform an edit, or enable or disable groups. For the long answer — as in, *How do you actually use keyboard shortcuts?* — these shortcuts are interspersed throughout the book for each command as I describe them.

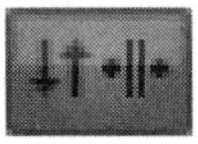

✦ **Link Timeline and Edit Selection:** By default, the Timeline and Edit selections are linked so that if you choose a section to edit, the Timeline start and end times coincide with the start and end times of this selection, as shown on the left in Figure 4-18. Sometimes you want to be able to have a Timeline setting remain unchanged as you select a different place to edit, as on the right in Figure 4-18. (In this case, click the Link Timeline and Edit Selection button once to turn linking off; click again to turn linking back on.)

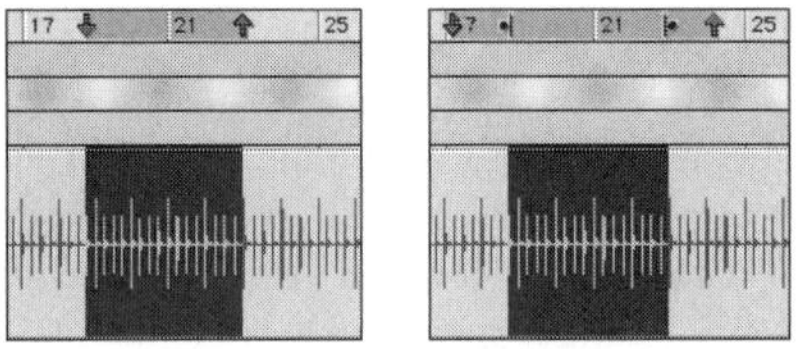

Figure 4-18:
The Link Timeline and Edit Selection button, turned on (left) and turned off (right).

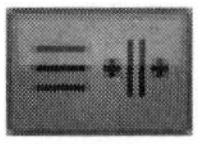

✦ **Link Track and Edit Selection:** When you have the Link Track and Edit Selection option engaged, making a selection in a track also highlights the track itself. This allows you to select several tracks and make adjustments to these tracks, such as adding them to a group or toggling the track view.

✦ **Mirrored MIDI Editing:** The Mirrored MIDI Editing function lets you globally edit all MIDI regions with the same name. This means that if you have a MIDI region that you use more than once per song and you want to change them all, clicking this button lets you make the change only once instead of for each time the region exists in your session.

✦ **Grid Value:** This display shows the value for the Edit window's *grid* — the boundary lines for your session. The grid boundary value appears in the same format as the main time scale — bars:beats, min: seconds, or samples — unless you choose otherwise from the drop-down menu, where you also choose the boundary resolution for the grid itself. This is a great function when you want to move regions around in a tune and have them align to certain locations. For example, if I move drum grooves, I can have them snap right to the beginning of a bar by setting the grid value to 1 measure and moving the region close to the start of the measure.

✦ **Nudge Value:** The Nudge Value display shows the setting for the distance that a region is moved with each press of the plus and minus keys on your keyboard. Clicking the down arrow calls up a drop-down menu, as shown in Figure 4-19, where you can choose this nudge value. Note that you can choose a number of different ways how your distances are to be measured — Bars:Beats, Min:Secs, Samples, or Regions/Markers.

Figure 4-19: Use the drop-down menu for the grid and Nudge Value display windows to assign your value.

✦ **Cursor:** The Cursor display tracks where your cursor is in the Timeline as well as the location of the sound wave in the selected track. (See Figure 4-20.) The cursor display is located below the time counter.

Figure 4-20:
The Cursor
display tells
you the
location of
the cursor in
the session.

Looking at lists

In the humdrum world, it's hard to get excited about laundry lists and shopping lists. In the world of Pro Tools, however, lists are something to crow about because they can help you keep track of your tracks, audio regions, MIDI regions, and groups.

The lists for your tracks, edit groups, audio files, and MIDI files are displayed on either side of the Edit window. To keep track of — and/or manipulate — any of these lists, you're going to want to familiarize yourself with one more list of features:

✦ **Show/Hide Tracks:** The Show/Hide Tracks list lets you choose which tracks get displayed in your Edit and Mix windows. As shown in Figure 4-21, you can choose to show all tracks, hide all tracks, or to show/hide only those tracks you already selected. This menu is opened by clicking and holding over the Tracks title at the left side of the Edit window. (Refer to Figure 4-7.) If the Show/Hide section of the window isn't visible, click the double arrows at the far lower left of the Edit window. The Show/Hide and Edit Groups (see the next bullet) section appear.

Figure 4-21:
Choose
which
tracks to
display in
the Edit and
the Mix
windows.

✦ **Edit Groups:** In Pro Tools, you can group selected tracks and perform an edit on them all at the same time. This is called working with an Edit

Group. These groups are displayed in the Edit Groups list; clicking the name of the group toggles the enabling of a group on and off. You can also create, delete, modify, or suspend groups by clicking and holding the Edit Groups title at the top of the groups list and then choosing an option from the drop-down menu that appears, as shown in Figure 4-22.

Figure 4-22: The Edit Groups list drop-down menu.

✦ **Clips:** The Clips list in Pro Tools contains representations of the audio and MIDI files associated with your session. The Clips list shows all the audio and MIDI regions that are part of your session. You can do a host of things to these clips, such as renaming, clearing, exporting, and compacting.

These functions are performed by opening the drop-down menu shown in Figure 4-23. To open this menu, click and hold the Clips title at the top of the Clips list. If the Clips list isn't open in your session, click the double arrow at the bottom-right corner of the Edit window to open it.

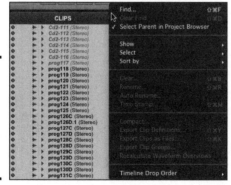

Figure 4-23: The Audio Regions list pop-up menu has many useful functions.

Rulers rule!

Lists hover discretely to the left or right of the Edit window. Rulers (as you might expect) lord it over the top of the Edit window and are masters of all they survey.

In Pro Tools-speak, rulers are actually referred to as *Timebase rulers;* they show you where you are within the session (see Figure 4-24). The Timebase Rulers section of the Edit window also lets you view the time, tempo, meter, and markers of a session. The following list gives details on the four timelines.

Figure 4-24:
The Timebase Rulers section shows where you are in the session.

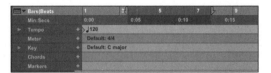

✦ **Time:** You have a choice between the now-familiar formats of Bars:Beats, Min:Secs, and Samples. By default, this timeline shows the same time format as the main counter, but it's easy to change to one of the other formats. Just choose View➪Rulers and then choose the format you want included in the Timebase Rulers section, as shown in Figure 4-25.

Figure 4-25:
View different rulers from the Rulers submenu.

✦ **Tempo:** The Tempo timeline shows you all the tempos and tempo changes in your section. But there's more! With the Tempo timeline, you can quickly change the tempos in the session by clicking the plus sign to the right of the Tempo title all the way to the right side of the figure.

Doing so opens the Tempo Meter Change dialog box, where you can enter a new tempo for the session. Book III, Chapter 3 goes into detail about creating Tempo changes in your session via the Tempo Editor.

If you don't plan on having any tempo changes and really don't want to see the Tempo timeline, you can hide it by choosing View⇨Rulers from the main menu and then deselecting the Tempo option.

✦ **Meter:** This timeline shows the *meters* (time signatures) contained in your session. To change the meter, click the plus icon to the right of the Meter title all the way to the right side of the figure. This opens the Tempo Meter Change dialog box.

If you prefer not to see this timeline, you can hide it by choosing View⇨Rulers from the main menu and then deselecting the Meter option.

Book II
Chapter 4

Understanding the
Pro Tools Windows

✦ **Key:** The Key timeline shows the musical key signature of the sections of your session. Here, you can change the key of your song. Clicking the + sign on the right of the key title opens the Key Change dialog box (seen in Figure 4-26). Here you can make any changes to the key signature of your session.

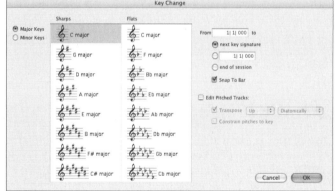

Figure 4-26:
You can change the key signature in your session from the Key Change dialog box.

If you prefer not to see this timeline, you can hide it by choosing View⇨Rulers⇨Key Signature from the main menu and then deselecting the Key Signature option.

✦ **Markers:** The Markers timeline shows the position of session markers. (For more on session markers, see Book IV, Chapter 2.) Clicking the plus icon to the right of the marker's name opens a dialog box where you can enter your marker information, as shown in Figure 4-27.

TIP

Markers are great for quickly locating sections of your tune. For example, placing a marker at the start of the verses and choruses can make moving between them a breeze. You can even use markers in Pro Tools to recall visual settings (such as track height and zoom settings) or record and playback options (such as pre- and post-roll times) as well as enabling grouped tracks for speedy editing.

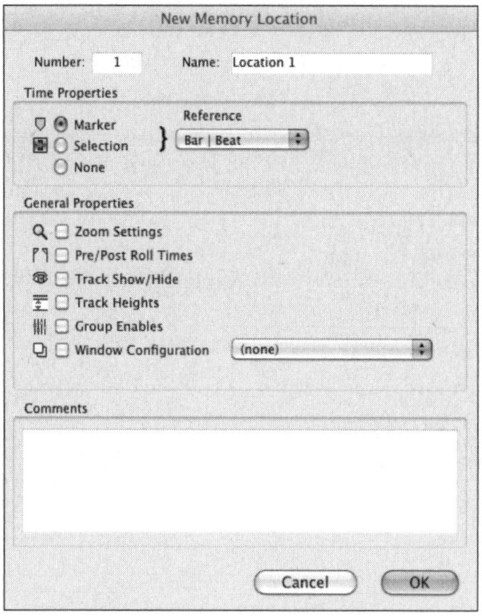

Figure 4-27:
The New Memory Location dialog box lets you set and define marker locations.

Managing the Mix Window

The Mix window is like a standard mixer, housing channel strips of each track type available in Pro Tools. Not only do these track types include audio, MIDI, auxiliary, and master tracks (as shown in Figure 4-28), but you can also choose various views of the channel strips, from a basic view to expanded views showing comments, inserts, and sends. Moreover, in addition to all your channel strips, the Mix window can list all the tracks in your session, along with any grouped tracks you may have created.

I know this sounds like a lot to keep track of (so to speak), but don't worry. The upcoming sections fill you in on all you need to know to keep things straight.

Figure 4-28:
The Mix
window
is like a
regular
hardware
mixer.

Book II
Chapter 4

Understanding the
Pro Tools Windows

Checking out channel strips

Each track in the Mix window has its own channel strip, and these channel
strips perform the same kinds of tasks you'd see channel strips doing in a
hardware mixer, such as volume control, panning, effects sends and inserts,
mute and solo switches, automation, input and output routing, and enabling
recording. The Mix window can handle pretty much any kind of track you
can imagine, including the track types covered in the next few sections.

Audio track

Your audio track is your basic meat-and-potatoes track, the main building
block in your sonic universe. Getting the audio track to do exactly what you
want takes a lot of work. Pro Tools is well aware of this fact, and therefore
provides you with a full-featured tool palette so you can take care of business.
More specifically, the audio track's channel strip contains the following tools
(as shown from top to bottom in Figure 4-29):

✦ **Input:** Clicking the Input button opens a drop-down menu where you can choose the sound source that feeds the track. It can either be a physical input from your hardware interface, or it can be a bus (an internal signal path; see Book I, Chapter 3 for more on buses). The hardware you use (Eleven Rack, Mbox, or whatever) determines the number of inputs you have to choose from.

✦ **Output:** This button controls the output of the track — where the sound goes when it leaves the track. Like the input selector button (see the preceding bullet), clicking it opens a menu that lets you choose from either the hardware outputs of your interface or any of 32 buses (internal signal paths) available in Pro Tools 10 (versions SE, MP, HD and HDX offer different numbers of buses).

✦ **Automation Mode:** In Pro Tools, *automation* means having certain mix parameters — such as volume, panning, mute, send level, and insert level — adjust dynamically throughout the session. Use this button to choose between the different automation modes, including Off, Read, Touch, Latch, or Write. (Book VI, Chapter 6 details these automation modes.)

✦ **Panning:** Use the dial to pan your track to the left or right in the *stereo field,* which is sort of the audio equivalent of a movie scene. (For more on panning, see Book VI, Chapter 1.)

✦ **Panning Display:** This display shows you your track's panning position — its place left, right or center, in the stereo field.

✦ **Solo and Mute:** Clicking these buttons either solo or mute the track. (For more on soloing/muting, see Book VI, Chapter 1.)

✦ **Record Enable:** Clicking the Record Enable button enables the track for recording. When enabled, this button flashes red.

✦ **Voice Dyn/Off:** This selector lets you choose between

   • *Dynamic:* The track plays if data is present.

   • *Off:* The track does not play.

✦ **Volume fader:** This is the control for setting the volume of the audio contained in this track.

✦ **Velocity meter:** This display, located to the right of the Volume fader, shows you the volume (*velocity,* in Pro Tools-speak) of the track while the music plays. Any notes above digital 0 show in red at the top of the display.

✦ **Group:** A little letter is present if this track is grouped with others. The letter itself tells you which group the track is a part of. If the letter is capitalized, the track belongs to more than one group. You can make changes to the group by clicking the icon to open a dialog box.

✦ **Track Type:** This icon shows you what type of track it is. In Figure 4-29, the small waveform lets you know that this is an audio track.

✦ **Numerical Volume:** This display shows you the volume of the track in decibels.

✦ **Track name:** This tells you the name of the track. You can change the name at any time by clicking the name and typing in a new one.

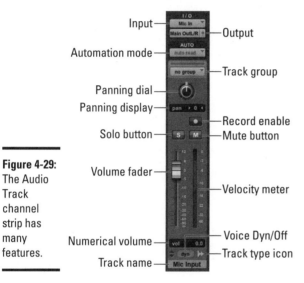

Input —
Output

Automation mode —

Track group

Panning dial —
Panning display —

Record enable

Solo button —
Mute button

Volume fader —

Velocity meter

Figure 4-29:
The Audio
Track
channel
strip has
many
features.

Numerical volume —
Voice Dyn/Off

Track type icon

Track name —

MIDI track

The MIDI track, as shown in Figure 4-30, shares many of the features of the audio track, but some important differences exist, as the following list makes clear:

✦ **Input:** The Input button lets you choose the MIDI input feeding this track. Clicking the button opens a drop-down menu from which you can choose the MIDI port and channel(s) that you want to receive MIDI data from.

✦ **Output:** The Output button lets you choose the physical MIDI output that you want to assign the track to — any of the 16 MIDI channels (or choose All).

✦ **Patch select:** This button (located below the channel fader) lets you change the sound that comes out of your MIDI hardware when a note is played. Clicking this button opens the MIDI Patch Select dialog box, in which you enter the program number or name of the sound to want the track to play. This lets you change sounds throughout the session.

✦ **Track type:** This MIDI track icon looks like a MIDI port.

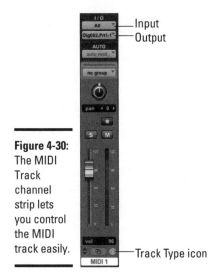

Input
Output

Figure 4-30:
The MIDI
Track
channel
strip lets
you control
the MIDI
track easily.

Track Type icon

MIDI 1

Instrument track

The instrument track, as shown in Figure 4-31, is a blend of the audio and MIDI tracks. Here's how it lays out:

✦ **Instruments Section:** You can open this section of the Instrument Track channel strip by choosing View⇨Mix⇨Instrument. This expands the top of the mix window to include controls for choosing your instrument source. You can see this at the top of Figure 4-31. You have the following options here:

• *MIDI Input selector:* Use this Input button to choose the MIDI input feeding this track. Clicking the button opens a drop-down menu from which you can choose the MIDI port and channel(s) from which you want to receive MIDI data.

• *MIDI Output selector:* Use this Output button to choose the MIDI output to which you want to assign the track — any of the 16 MIDI channels (or choose All).

• *MIDI volume:* Clicking this icon brings up the MIDI fader with which you can adjust the velocity traveling through the MIDI port.

• *MIDI Velocity meter:* This tiny meter shows you a visual representation of the velocity of the MIDI in the track.

• *MIDI Mute button:* This mutes the MIDI data from triggering your device.

• *MIDI Pan slider:* This pans your MIDI data left or right.

✦ **Inserts:** These function just like inserts for audio tracks except you can also choose an instrument from the drop-down menu to create the sound if you want to use a software synthesizer. (See Book I, Chapter 4 for more on software synthesizers.)

✦ **Sends:** Just like with audio tracks, you assign sends to the sounds coming from the track.

✦ **Input:** The Input button functions the same as an audio track where you select the hardware inputs for this track. This allows you to have a MIDI device connected through the Instruments section tools at the top of the channel strip while also having the audio outputs of the device, such as a synthesizer, input into this track.

✦ **Output:** Use the Output button to choose the physical audio output to which you want to assign the track: the same as with an audio track.

✦ **Patch select:** This button (located below the channel fader) lets you change the sound that comes out of your MIDI hardware (connected via the Instrument section listed above) when a note is played. Clicking this button opens the MIDI Patch Select dialog box, in which you enter the program number or name of the sound to want the track to play. This allows you to change sounds throughout the session.

✦ **Track type:** This instrument track icon looks like five notes of a music keyboard.

**Book II
Chapter 4**

**Understanding the
Pro Tools Windows**

Figure 4-31:
The instrument track is a blend of an audio and a MIDI track.

Auxiliary input track

An *auxiliary input track* is a track that you can use for grouped audio — or for MIDI tracks, effects sends, submixes, alternative mixes, monitor mixes, and so on. Auxiliary tracks are similar to audio tracks and have the same functions except that you don't have a Record Enable button because these tracks don't actually contain any audio. Instead, they are used only for routing other tracks through them. The Track Type icon is a blue down arrow. Figure 4-32 shows a typical auxiliary track's channel strip.

Figure 4-32: The Auxiliary Track channel strip is used for effects sends, submixes, and monitor mixes.

Master Fader track

The Master Fader track lets you control where your other tracks are sent. This track's channel strip is much simpler than the others; all it really does is add the other tracks. The features include just the outputs, automation modes, fader and velocity display, and the Groups button.

The Track Type icon for a Master Fader track is a sigma (Σ). Figure 4-33 shows a Master Fader Track's channel strip.

Figure 4-33:
The Master Track channel strip controls the master track functions.

Stereo and mono

Each of the tracks can either be in monaural or stereo. Stereo tracks differ from mono tracks: They have two panning dials and two velocity displays showing. Figure 4-34 shows a stereo track on the right next to a mono track (on the left).

Expanding the channel strips view

You can add three additional views to your channel strips by choosing View⇨Mix Window from the main menu and then choosing Comments, Inserts, and/or Sends. Figure 4-35 shows you what you can expect to see, and the next few sections tell you the particulars for each view.

Comments view

With this option, you can add comments to each track by just clicking the Comments box and typing your comments. This can be helpful for keeping track of info, such as microphones used, edits performed, or anything that can keep you organized while mixing.

Figure 4-34:
A stereo track's channel strip (on the left) looks very similar to a mono track (on the right).

—Inserts view

—Send view

Figure 4-35:
Channel strips can be expanded to include views for comments, inserts, and sends.

—Comments view

Inserts view

The Inserts view section of the channel strip displays any inserted DSPs (Digital Signal Processors) that you have for each track — usually effects such as compression or delay. Click the arrows in the window to open a drop-down menu where you can choose from the plug-ins in your system. Figure 4-36 shows a typical list of these inserts. (Book VI, Chapters 4 and 5 have more on inserted effects.)

Figure 4-36:
The Insert drop-down menu lets you choose your inserted effect.

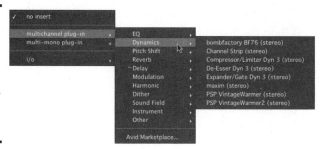

Sends view

The Sends View section of the channel strip lets you choose an effect bus to send your track's signal to. Clicking the arrows opens a pop-up menu (as shown in Figure 4-37) where you choose the bus or interface output to send your track's signal. (If you use outboard effects, see Book VI, Chapter 5 for more details.)

Looking at lists: The Mix Window variant

Plenty of lists appear in the "Examining the Edit Window" section (earlier in this chapter), but Pro Tools list-making capabilities crop up in the Mix window as well. Aside from containing all the channel strips for your project, the Mix window can also be set to list all the tracks in your session — as well list any groups you created with those tracks. These lists show up on the left side of the Mix window, as shown in Figure 4-38.

Show/Hide Tracks list

Going from top to bottom, the first list to the left of the Mix window is the Show/Hide Tracks list. Each track of your session is listed in this list. With this list, you can show or hide each track by simply selecting or deselecting it in the list window. When you hide a selected track, the channel strip disappears from the Mix window. This makes it easy to work with individual tracks or groups of tracks by keeping your Mix window uncluttered. To show a hidden track, click that track's name in the Tracks list and watch it reappear.

Figure 4-37:
Use the
Sends
window to
pick where
to send
your track's
signal for
effects
processing.

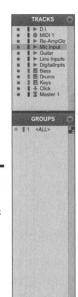

Figure 4-38:
The Show/
Hide Tracks
list and
Groups list
allow you
to organize
your tracks
in the Mix
window.

Groups list

The Groups list lets you create and manage grouped tracks — tracks that you assigned together so that you can edit them together. To create groups of tracks, hold down the Shift key down and then click the names of the tracks in each channel strip to highlight them. After they're highlighted, click and hold the Edit Groups title. When a drop-down menu appears, choose New Group; when a dialog box appears, enter a name for your new grouped track. After you create a few groups, you can show or hide them in any combination you want.

Working with Window Configurations

A *window configuration* is a saved setup of the various Pro Tools windows in the size order and arrangement you choose. You can have a window configuration for when you record new tracks, when you edit, when you mix, and when you master. In fact, in Pro Tools, you can create and save up to 99 different window configuration variations. This is handy for speeding up your work because you simply choose a configuration you want instead of having to open and close windows or resize them while you work.

As a long-time Logic user, this is one feature that I always missed when I worked in Pro Tools. Now that Pro Tools has added window configuration, I can move from window setup to window setup like I used to in that other program. This makes me happy, and I'm sure that after you get a few window configuration setups in your sessions, you'll be happy (and more productive) too. The following sections help you do this.

Creating window configurations

Creating a window configuration is easy. Here are the steps:

1. **Arrange the various windows in your session how you'd like to have them saved.**

This can include the Edit, Mix, Transport, plug-in, and any other window that Pro Tools lets you open and move around in your session.

2. **Choose Window➪Configurations➪New Configuration.**

The New Window Configuration dialog box opens, as shown in Figure 4-39. Choose the options you want within this dialog box. (See the following bulleted list for details about all the options in this dialog box.)

3. **Click OK or press Return/Enter.**

The New Window Configuration dialog box closes, and your settings are saved.

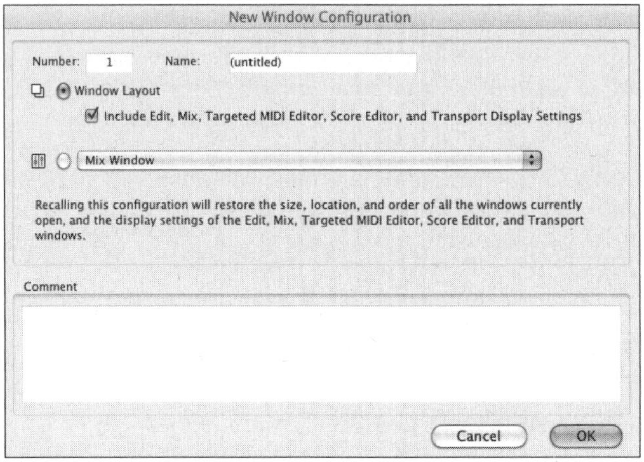

Figure 4-39:
Use the New Window Configuration dialog box to save your new window setup.

From the New Window Configuration dialog box, choose which properties of the windows you arranged in your session to save. These include the following:

+ **Number:** This is the number of your window configuration. By default, the next available number is entered into this box, but you can put any number that you like between 1 and 99.

+ **Name:** This is the name of your window configuration. Enter a descriptive name. I usually enter a name that represents the purpose of the configuration, such as *Audio editing* or *Tracking*.

+ **Window Layout:** Selecting this radio button stores the arrangement of all your open windows.

+ **Include Edit, Mix, and Transport Display Settings:** Selecting this check box saves all the display settings for each window, such as whether Inserts show in the Mix window.

If you choose to not select the Window Layout radio button, you can choose from the options in the Filter View drop-down menu. These include

+ **Edit Window Display Settings:** Choosing this option saves all window display settings for the Edit window. These include

  • *Rulers,* including the main ruler (which is always shown)

  • *Track list width and height*

  • *Groups list and Regions list width*

  • *Track columns that are shown,* such as Comments, Inserts, and Sends

  • *The Tempo Edit display*

  • *Transport controls*

✦ **Mix Window Display Settings:** Selecting this option stores the display settings for the Mix window, including

- *Track list width and height*

- *Groups list width*

- *Mixer view* (narrow or wide)

- *Track rows that are shown,* such as Sends, Inserts, and Comments

✦ **Transport Window Display Settings:** Choosing this option stores the display settings for the Transport window. These include

- Counters

- MIDI controls

- Expanded view

✦ **MIDI Editor Settings:** This option stores the display settings for the MIDI Editory window, both targeted and untargeted.

✦ **Score Editor Settings:** This option includes display settings for Score window displays.

✦ **Comment:** You can enter comments about your window configuration in this field, such as reminders or descriptions of your settings.

Recalling window configurations

After you have window configurations saved, you can recall them easily. My favorite way is to use keyboard shortcuts. Here's how:

1. **Press period (.) on the numeric keypad section of your keyboard.**

2. **Type the number of the window configuration you want to open.**

3. **Press the asterisk (*) in the numeric keypad section of your keyboard.**

Your desired window configuration opens.

You can also select a saved window configuration by choosing Window➪ Configurations➪*configuration name.*

Managing window configurations

You can easily manage your window configurations from the Window Configurations List window. You open the Window Configuration List window by choosing Window➪Configurations➪Window Configuration List. You can also open this window by pressing ⌘+Option+J (Mac) or Ctrl+Alt+J (PC).

The window shown in Figure 4-40 opens.

Figure 4-40:
Use the
Window
Config-
urations List
to manage
window
config-
urations.

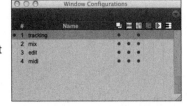

Window Configurations List window

The Window Configurations List window has many features that help you work with your window configurations to make the most of them. Here's a quick rundown of the window:

✦ **Name:** This is the name of your window configuration. You enter the name when you create a new window configuration. You can also change the name by double-clicking it to open the Edit Window Configuration dialog box (more on this in the next section, "Editing window configurations").

✦ **View filter icons:** Use these icons to filter the window configurations that you see in the list. The icons also help you see at a glance what windows are included in each configuration in the list. These icons are

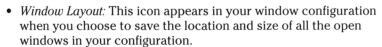
• *Window Layout:* This icon appears in your window configuration when you choose to save the location and size of all the open windows in your configuration.

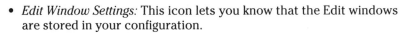
• *Edit Window Settings:* This icon lets you know that the Edit windows are stored in your configuration.

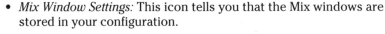
• *Mix Window Settings:* This icon tells you that the Mix windows are stored in your configuration.

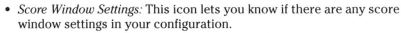
• *Score Window Settings:* This icon lets you know if there are any score window settings in your configuration.

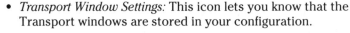
• *Transport Window Settings:* This icon lets you know that the Transport windows are stored in your configuration.

• *MIDI Window Settings.* This icon lists any MIDI window settings that are stored in a configuration.

You select these icons when you create or edit your window configurations. I detail this process in the next section.

✦ **Comments:** You can enter comments in this section to remind you of what is in the window configuration.

Window Configurations drop-down menu

You can easily manage your window configurations from the drop-down menu. Figure 4-41 shows this menu.

Figure 4-41:
Use the drop-down menu to manage your window config-urations.

Book II
Chapter 4

Understanding the
Pro Tools Windows

Here's a rundown of this menu and what it can do for you:

✦ **View Filter:** This menu lets you show or hide window configurations with the following settings:

- *Show Icons:* This shows or hides the icons in the Window Configurations List window.

- *View Configs with Window Layout:* This shows only those window configurations that were created with Window layout settings.

- *View Configs with Edit Window Settings:* This shows only those window configurations that were created with Edit window layout settings.

- *View Configs with Mix Window Settings:* This shows only those window configurations that were created with Mix window layout settings.

- *View Configs with Transport Window Settings:* This shows only those window configurations that were created with Transport window layout settings.

- *View All:* This shows all your window configurations.

✦ **Show Comments:** Select or deselect this option to show or hide, respectively, the comments section in the Window Configurations List window.

✦ **New Configuration:** Selecting this option opens the New Window Configuration dialog box, where you can create a new configuration.

✦ **Update "*Name*":** If you made any changes to the layout of your current configuration, choose this to save them in your existing setup.

+ **Edit "*Name*":** Selecting this option opens the Edit Window Configurations dialog box, where you can make changes to the options you chose when you created the configuration. The Edit Window Configuration dialog box is the same as the New Window Configuration dialog box (except for the title).

+ **Clear "*Name*":** Choosing this option clears the active window configuration without removing its slot in the list.

+ **Delete All:** Selecting this option deletes all your window configurations.

+ **Insert Slot before "*Name*":** Choosing this option inserts a slot before your current window configuration and changes the number of all the following configurations if necessary.

+ **Delete "*Name*" Slot:** Choosing this option deletes your current window configuration along with its slot, and renumbers all the following window configurations.

+ **Auto-Update Active Configuration:** Selecting this option automatically updates your current window configuration as you make changes to it.

Editing window configurations

You can edit window configurations by opening the Edit Window Configurations dialog box. Just follow these steps:

1. **If it isn't already open, open the Window Configurations List window by choosing Window➪Configurations➪Window Configurations List.**

2. **Click the window configuration that you want to edit in the Window Configurations List window.**

3. **Choose Edit "*Name*" from the Window Configurations List drop-down menu.**

   The Edit Window Configuration dialog box opens.

4. **Make the changes you want to make and then click OK or press Return/Enter.**

   The dialog box closes, and your edits are saved.

Updating window configurations

Many times, while I'm working, I find a better way to have my window configuration, so I want to update it. You can do this manually or automatically:

+ **Manually:** Make any changes to arrangement of your windows and then choose Window➪Configurations➪Update Active Configuration.

+ **Automatically:** Choose Window➪Configurations➪Auto-Update Active Configuration. Now, whenever you make a change, your active configuration is saved.

Deleting window configurations

Here's how to delete a window configuration:

1. **Open the Window Configuration List window by choosing Window⇨Configurations⇨Window Configuration List.**

2. **Select the configuration you want to delete by clicking it.**

3. **Choose Delete "*Name*" from the Window Configuration List drop-down menu.**

   Your configuration is deleted, and your remaining configurations are renumbered to fill the space occupied by the configuration you just deleted.

If you want to keep the slot occupied by the window configuration after you delete, simply choose Clear "*Name*" instead of Delete "*Name*" from the Window Configuration List drop-down menu. This is handy when you want to put a new window configuration in its place.

Chapter 5: Importing and Exporting Files

In This Chapter

✔ **Importing and exporting audio files**

✔ **Importing and exporting MIDI files**

✔ **Importing and exporting session data**

*O*ne of the most powerful aspects of Pro Tools is that it can import a variety of file types and formats into a session and then export them just as easily. You can record tracks in another session (or even another software program) and be able to edit, mix, and process them in Pro Tools.

For example, you can import and export audio files, MIDI files, and session tracks in formats from AIFF and BWF to Standard MIDI files (SMF) — and even import raw session data, the tracks, plug-in settings, and other session details. (Chapter 3 of this mini-book has more on Pro Tools sessions.) This chapter covers all these options. And if you have some files that use bit depths and sample rates different from the session you're working on, I show you how to import them, too.

Importing into a Session

If you want to fancy up your Pro Tools session, you can import audio and other data not only from other Pro Tools sessions but also from other recording programs, such as Logic. So prepare to get fancy.

Importing audio files

Before Pro Tools can import an audio file into your session, it has to find the file on your hard drive. Then you can add the file directly, copy it first and then plunk it down in your session, or convert it to a different format before you import it. The following sections take a look at the types of files you can import, as well as the steps that make it all possible.

Figuring out file types

You can import the following audio files types into a Pro Tools session without converting them:

✦ **WAV or BWF (Broadcast .WAV File):** This file type is the standard for older, PC-based Pro Tools systems. Currently, it's the most commonly used file type; for that matter, I normally work with it. BWFs are compatible with both Macs and PCs.

✦ **AIFF (Audio Interchange File Format):** This file format used to be native to Macs. You don't have to convert AIFF files to any other format before importing them into a Pro Tools session, even if it's on a PC.

The following files types can be imported into Pro Tools but first must be converted into either WAV or AIFF:

✦ **AAC (Advanced Audio Coding):** These files are the kind that iTunes sells. This file type, created by a group of companies, is said to offer a better sound than MP3s of the same size, and is playable on a wide range of devices.

✦ **ACID:** ACID files are Sony's file format for its ACID program. These are loop files that contain tempo and pitch information as well as the audio itself.

✦ **MPEG-1 Layer 3:** This type — yep, it's the famous *MP3* — is a great format for putting music on the Internet (say, a demo track for your band), as you'll find out when you check out Book VIII, Chapter 2.

✦ **MXF (Material eXchange Format) audio:** An MXF file is a container for audio data most commonly used in video recorders and contains timecode data.

✦ **QuickTime:** Pro Tools offers no built-in support for it (even though it shows up here). The QuickTime format is useful if you want to send the file via e-mail. You play QuickTime files using the Apple QuickTime player — a nice bit of software supported by many multimedia applications — but you have to purchase and install that program separately.

✦ **ReCycle (REX 1 and 2):** ReCycle (REX 1 and 2) is Propellerhead's proprietary file format, much Like Sony's ACID. These files, like Sony's, contain additional information about the audio.

✦ **SDI and SDII (Sound Designer I and II):** This was the native format for Pro Tools sessions on Macs many versions ago. However, this format isn't supported anymore.

✦ **Sound Resource (AIFL):** The only time to use this Mac-only format (in my opinion) is if you want to play the music in an application that doesn't support SDII or AIFF formats. If you end up with a file in this format, you can convert it easily via the Import Audio to Track command.

✦ **Windows Media (WMA):** This is a Windows-only format. As with other unsupported file formats, you can convert these files into something useable by accessing the Import Audio dialog box: Choose File⇨Import Audio to Track.

Importing audio

In the preceding section, I outline the different types of files Pro Tools can handle. In this section, I show how you can import those audio files into Pro Tools. The two most common ways of doing this are

✦ **From the keyboard:** Press Shift+⌘+I (Mac) or Shift+Ctrl+I (PC). This gets you to the same Import Audio dialog box.

✦ **From the File menu:** Choose File➪Import Audio to Track to access the Import Audio dialog box, where you can place the audio directly into a track in your session.

Whichever of these methods you choose, you end up with the Import Audio dialog box, where you choose the file you want to import. See Figure 5-1.

Book II
Chapter 5

Importing and
Exporting Files

Browser

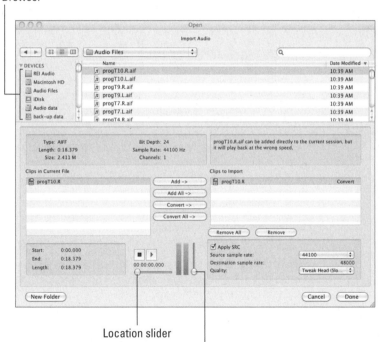

Figure 5-1: Use the Import Audio dialog box to choose and audition files to import into a session.

Location slider

Volume slider

The easiest way on a Mac to find the files you want to import is from the browser section, located under the From drop-down menu (located below the Enable drop down menu in the upper section of the window). You can use the scroll bar at the bottom to find the hard drive you want by moving it all the way to the left. From there, you can progress to the right by choosing the folders you want as you go until you get to the actual file you want to import.

You can limit the types of files that show up in the file browser by choosing to display only certain file types (WAV, for example) by selecting this file type in the Show drop-down menu.

To keep the Import process rolling along, follow these steps after the Import Audio dialog box opens:

1. **From the file browser section of the Import Audio dialog box, click the file you want to import.**

The properties of the selected file appear in the lower half of the dialog box.

Depending on the properties of the file you select — and the settings in your session — you have three options:

- *Add:* If the audio files are the same file type and bit depth as your session, you can add the files directly into your session. When you do so, you're telling Pro Tools to use the *original* file — *not a copy* — from its current place on your hard drive.

  If you do this, make sure that you don't alter this original file if it's also part of another session. Otherwise, it will be changed in that session, too.

  If you have to add files of different file types into your session, you can — SDII, AIFF, or WAV on a Mac; or, AIFF or WAV on a PC — but doing so slows down system performance.

- *Copy:* If your file is of the same type and bit depth as your session, you can make a copy of the file to put into your session. Doing this allows you to place the copy directly in the folder with the other files in your session. If you destructively alter the copy, you won't be altering how the original file plays in any other session.

  The only drawback to choosing Copy when importing an audio file is that you're adding more stuff that takes up space on your hard drive (not a big deal these days, given the low cost of huge hard drives).

  Convert: If the file you choose to import is of a different file type, bit depth, or sample rate than your session, you need to convert it first before importing it into your session if you want it to play correctly.

When you choose to convert a file, your set preferences automatically determine the quality of the conversion process. You set the conversion preferences from the Processing tab of the Preferences window, as shown in Figure 5-2. Access this by choosing Setup➪ Preferences. The drop-down menu that controls conversion quality is located on the right and under the Import section of the Processing tab the Preferences dialog box. Options range from TweakHead (highest quality/slowest conversion) to Low (lowest quality/fastest conversion).

If you want to use a conversion quality other than the one your preferences are set to, you can use the conversion quality section in the Import Audio window (located in the lower-right corner). This setting will only apply to the files you import during this import operation.

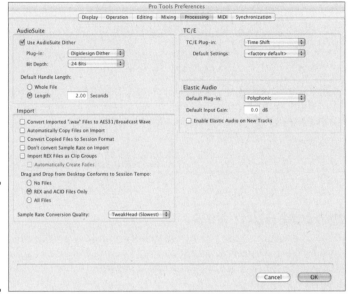

**Book II
Chapter 5**

**Importing and
Exporting Files**

Figure 5-2:
Select the quality of your file conversions here.

2. **Audition the selected file before importing it by clicking the Play and Stop buttons in the lower section of the Import Audio dialog box.**

   The vertical slider adjusts the volume of your audition; the horizontal slider adjusts your location in the auditioned file.

3. **Click the Add, Copy, or Convert button to place the file in the Clips to Import list.**

   You can select more than one file by Shift-clicking to highlight the files you want to include in the list. You can also click the Add All or Convert All button to include all the files in the current directory on the Clips to Import list.

4. **Click Done.**

   The Audio Import Options dialog box opens.

5. **Select the destination of the audio track(s). Your options are**

   ✦ *New Track:* The New Track option creates a new track in your session for each of the audio files you select. If you choose this option, you must select (from the drop-down menu) where you want the audio file to go in the new track. Your options are

- **Session Start:** This places your imported audio at the beginning of your session.

- **Song Start:** This places your imported audio at the Song Start Marker in your session. You can open the move Song Start window by choosing Event⇨Time⇨Move Song Start.

- **Selection:** Your audio will be placed in the specific location where your cursor is within your session.

- **Spot:** Choosing this option opens the Spot dialog box, where you want type where you want the audio to start.

✦ *Clips List:* The Clips List option simply puts your files in the Clips list on the right side of the Edit window where you can drag them into a track when you're ready to include them in your song.

6. Click OK.

Your audio file(s) are imported into your session. This may take a minute if your audio file(s) need to be converted.

Importing MIDI files

MIDI data contains all the performance information for your MIDI instruments, but it doesn't contain any actual sound. You need a sound source for that. Pro Tools lets you bring that data into a session where you can work with and add the sounds you want. This data is in the form of a Standard MIDI File. Standard MIDI files consist of data stored in a common format that can be read by nearly all MIDI devices. When you import a Standard MIDI file into Pro Tools, you get two choices:

✦ Import the file directly into a track.

✦ Import it into your session's MIDI Clips list.

The following sections detail the types of MIDI files supported by Pro Tools and how to import them.

Figuring out file types

Pro Tools allows you to import the following two types of Standard MIDI files:

✦ **Type 0:** Type 0 Standard MIDI files contain all MIDI data on one track. When you import this type of file into a session, Pro Tools sorts data appropriate for each stereo channel and places the data in separate Clips and tracks.

✦ **Type 1:** Type 1 MIDI files contain multiple tracks of MIDI data. When you import this type of file into Pro Tools, each track's data goes to a separate MIDI track or clip in Pro Tools.

Importing MIDI

You can import standard MIDI files into a Pro tools session one of two ways:

✦ **From the File menu:** Choose File⇨Import⇨MIDI to access the Choose a MIDI File navigation box (as shown in Figure 5-3).

✦ **From the keyboard:** Press Option+⌘+I (Mac) or Ctrl+Alt+I (PC).

Figure 5-3:
Select MIDI files to import into a session.

Whichever of these methods you choose, you end up at the Choose a MIDI File navigation box, where you choose the file you want to import.

The easiest way to find the files you want to import is from the browser section, located under the From drop-down menu located just beneath the Enable drop-down menu. To navigate this browser section, move the scroll bar at the bottom of the section all the way to the left to find the hard drive that contains your MIDI files. Click it to select it, and then click the folders you want from the boxes on the right until you get to the file you want to import.

Select the file using the browser and click Open. The MIDI Import Options dialog box opens (refer to Figure 5-3), where you can choose to place the MIDI file in a new track in your session or in the Clips list, where you can place it in a track later.

If you want to import your MIDI file into the Clips list, select the Clips List option in the Destination section and then click OK.

If you choose to import your MIDI file into a new track, you have some more decisions to make:

✦ **Location:** You can choose among three options from this drop-down menu:

- *Session Start:* Beginning of the session

- *Selection:* Where your cursor is currently located

- *Spot:* If you choose Spot, the Spot dialog box opens when you click OK to allow you to choose the exact spot in your session you want to MIDI file to begin.

✦ **Import Tempo Map from MIDI File:** If you want the tempo of the imported MIDI file to override the tempo of your present session, select this check box.

✦ **Import Key Signature from MIDI File:** As you can probably guess, selecting this check box imports the MIDI file's current key signature data to travel along with the MIDI performance data. Select this check box if you want this information in your session.

✦ **Remove Existing instrument Tracks:** Select this check box to choose to keep or discard any existing Instrument tracks or clips in your session. If you already have instrument tracks that you want to use in the session, be sure to choose to keep them; if not, go ahead and discard them.

✦ **Remove Existing MIDI Tracks:** Select this check box to choose to keep or discard any existing MIDI tracks or clips in your session. If you already have MIDI tracks that you want to use in the session, be sure to choose to keep them; if not, go ahead and discard them.

✦ **Remove Existing MIDI Clips:** Select this check box to choose to keep or discard any existing MIDI clips that you have in your session.

Your successfully imported MIDI file is placed in your session one of two ways:

✦ **If you imported by using the New Track option:** Your file is placed in a newly created MIDI track in your session. If this is the case, select the MIDI channel and instrument you want to specify for your MIDI track's output so that you can hear the performances when you play your session, as described in Chapter 4 of this mini-book.

✦ **If you imported by using the MIDI Clips option:** Your MIDI data is placed in the MIDI clips list. Click and drag the files from the MIDI clips list into an existing track to put them in your session.

Importing tracks

The Pro Tools Import Bag of Tricks isn't limited to just audio and MIDI files. In fact, you can import entire tracks from another session into your current session just by using the Import Tracks command. Choose File⇨Import⇨Session Data to call up the Import Session Data dialog box, and you're well on your way to getting that great track from last month's session embedded in your present project.

Understanding the Import Session Data dialog box

The Import Session Data dialog box is where you select the various properties of the tracks you want to import. If you're bringing in a track from a previous session, this is where you choose what aspects of your original track you want kept (say, keep the plug-in settings and lose the panning settings) when it gets imported into your present session.

As you can see in Figure 5-4, the Import Session Data dialog box gives you lots of properties to mull over. ("Do I import this? Don't I import that? What parts of this stuff do I or don't I import?" Ack. . . .) These properties include

✦ **Source Properties:** This includes the basics — session name, type, and start time; bit depth; sample rate — of the selected source file.

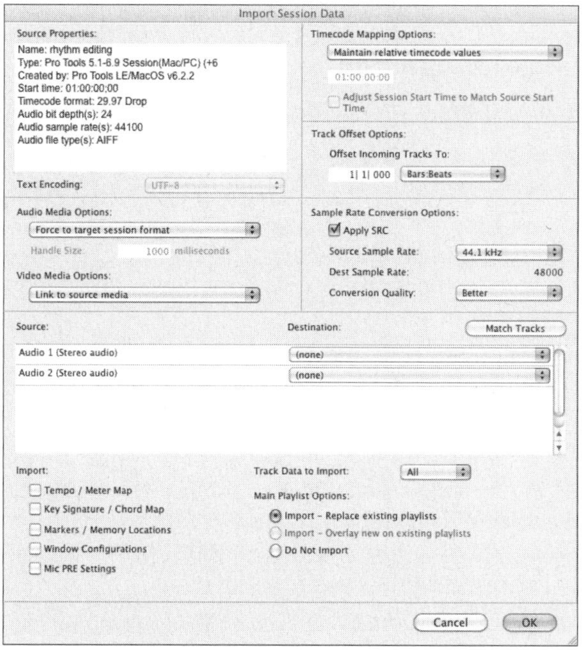

Figure 5-4:
Use the
Import
Session
Data dialog
box to set
parameters
for imported
tracks.

✦ **Audio Media Options:** From this drop-down menu, select how you copy and consolidate the source's audio files. Its options include

  • *Refer to Source Media (Where Possible):* Use this option if you want to avoid duplicating files — it refers to your original files whenever possible. The files are copied only if they don't reside on supported media (such as CD-ROM), or if they have a different sample rate or bit depth from the session you import into. This saves some space on your hard drives.

- *Copy from Source Media:* Choosing this option copies all the audio files, automatically converting any files that have bit depths or sample rates that differ from those of the target session. This uses up space on your hard drive, but with today's super-cheap drives, it's not as big a deal as it used to be (when drives were expensive).

- *Consolidate from Source Media:* This option copies and consolidates the audio in clips used in the source session, eliminating any unused audio from the parent files. When you choose this option, you also get to choose the *handle* length (the extra time before and after the clip start and end times). This keeps you from importing any unnecessary material if you're sure that you won't be using it in your session.

- *Force to Target Session Format:* This option copies — and converts — any files that don't have the same bit depth and sample rate as the target session; it points to (but doesn't copy) any files that do match these traits. Use this option if you don't want any extra stuff taking up room on your hard drives.

✦ **Video Media Options:** The drop-down menu here gives you two options when importing video data into a session: You can copy the stuff, or you can refer to the source material. Which option you choose depends on how much hard drive space you have and whether you think you need more than one copy of the original file. If you have tons of space and think you'll be editing the data, by all means copy it. However, if you know you won't be making any changes, there's no need to add to the clutter of your hard drive.

✦ **Time Code Mapping Options:** Every video file contains *time code* data (information that lets you know where you are in the video). You can choose from three ways to place imported material in the session:

- *Maintain Absolute Time Code Values:* This option puts your imported tracks at the same time location as the source session. This is a good choice if the session you import into uses the same start time as your source session and you want the imported session tracks to remain at the beginning of the session.

- *Maintain Relative Time Code Values:* This option places the imported material at the same time from the start of the session as their source session. This means that if you have tracks in a session that start 30 seconds from the beginning of the session, they will remain 30 seconds from the start of the session into which they're imported regardless of the actual start time of both sessions.

- *Map Start Time Code To:* This option lets you choose a new start time for your imported files. When you select this option, you also select the start time for your imported file in the Time Value field. This option is useful when you have a different start time on the session data you want to import, and you want to place the imported data at a specific point in the new session. This start point is entered into the Handle Size field.

✦ **Track Offset Options:** The options in this section allow you to place the tracks relative to their original start times. For example, if you want to import session data into a track and have it start four measures (bars) after the session starts, you can select Bars:Beats from the drop-down menu and enter **4** in the text field.

✦ **Sample Rate Conversion Options:** If your source and target sessions have different sample rates (you select the sample rate of a session when you create it), you're prompted to select whether sample rate conversion is applied and, if so, how it's done. This area of the Import Session Data dialog box lets you do that, using the following options:

  • *Apply SRC:* Select this check box to apply sample rate conversion to your imported session data. When you select this check box, you can choose from the following options:

  • *Source Sample Rate:* This option lets you choose the sample rate from which your source files begin the sample rate process.

  • *Destination Sample Rate:* This setting is always the same as that of your current session.

  • *Conversion Quality:* This drop-down menu lets you choose the sound quality you get from the sample-rate conversion process. You have a choice among Low (fastest), Good, Better, Best, and TweakHead (slowest).

✦ **Source Tracks:** This section of the Import Session Data dialog box shows you all the source tracks in the session containing the tracks you want to import. Each track has a drop-down menu that allows you to either select it for import or not.

✦ **Import:** This section enables you to determine whether to import tempo/meter, key signature, and other configuration settings:

  • *Tempo/Meter Map:* Select this check box to import tempo and meter maps (specified tempo and meter events throughout the session) from the source session. Select this option if your source session contains tempo and meter information that you want to use in the target session.

  • *Key Signature Map:* You can import existing key signature data into your session by selecting this check box.

  • *Markers/Memory Locations:* Selecting this check box includes markers and memory locations with your imported session data.

  • *Window Configurations:* You can import window configurations (size and locations of open windows) into your session by selecting this check box. You can find out more about window configurations in Chapter 4 of this mini-book.

  • *Mic PRE Settings:* You can include settings for any Pro Tools mic PRE links that may be present. Using this setting requires a Pro Tools PRE device.

**Book II
Chapter 5**

**Importing and
Exporting Files**

✦ **Data to Import:** This menu contains a list of all the track data in a session. The list includes these options:

- *All:* Selecting this parameter imports all of the source track's data listed below.

- *None:* Choosing this option only imports the main playlist and ignores the rest of the track data.

- *Alternate Playlists:* Checking this imports the alternate playlists from source track. These playlists appear in the playlist pop-up menu of the destination track.

- *Clips and Media:* This option imports the audio files from the source track and also places them in the Clip List.

- *Clips Gain:* This option imports the gain settings for any imported audio clips.

- *Volume Automation and Setting:* This option imports volume-fader settings and any automation data on the source track's volume-automation playlist, replacing the corresponding data on the destination track.

- *Pan Automation and Setting:* Selecting this imports panning dial and pan automation settings in a track. This replaces any data in the destination track.

- Mute Automation and Setting: This option imports any mute and mute-automation data settings and replaces any such data in the destination track.

- *Main Output Assignments:* Choosing this option imports any channel-output assignments from the source track, including any multiple output assignments, replacing any data in the destination track.

- *Send Output Assignments:* This imports send output assignments from the source track, replacing any in the destination track.

- *Plug-In Assignments:* This setting imports all plug-in assignments from the source track. Any plug-ins in the destination track are replaced.

  Note: If there is a plug-in from your source track that is not available in the destination system, the plug-in appears in the destination track but is listed as inactive.

- *Plug-In Settings and Automation:* Choosing this option imports the track's plug-in settings and any automation data associated with the plug-ins (if you choose the import the source track's plug-in assignments). If you choose not to import plug-in assignments, this option does nothing.

- *Elastic Audio Track State:* Selecting this option imports the Elastic Audio track state from the source track, replacing any in the destination track.

- *HW Insert Assignments:* This option, when selected, imports any hardware Insert assignments from the source track, replacing any such assignments in the destination track.

- *Voice Assignments:* This option imports the source track's voice assignment, replacing any voice assignments already in the destination track.

- *Input Assignments:* This option replaces the channel-input assignment of the destination track with that of the source track.

- *Side-Chain Assignments:* Selecting this option imports side-chain assignments associated with the plug-ins (as long as plug-in assignments are imported). If you choose not to include plug-in assignments, this option does nothing.

- *Track Active State:* This includes the active/inactive state of the source track.

- *Track Comments:* This setting imports any track comments associated with the source track, replacing any comment in the destination track.

- *Track Colors:* This imports the track color of the source track and replaces the destination track color.

- *Record Safe/Solo Safe Settings:* This setting imports the record-safe and solo-safe settings into your session, replacing any such settings in the destination track.

- *Track View Settings:* Includes the playlist view and track height of the track.

- *Mix/Edit Groups:* This imports groups from the session.

✦ **Main Playlist Options:** This menu lets you choose from the following options:

- *Import – Replace existing playlists:* This option replaces any existing playlists while importing the playlists from your source session.

- *Import – Overlay new on existing playlists:* This option also imports any playlist data, but instead of replacing items on an existing playlist, it adds to them.

- *Do Not Import:* This is self-explanatory. Choosing this option doesn't import any playlist options.

Importing tracks

After you have a chance to get comfortable with the Import Session Data dialog box, you can get some practical experience by using the following steps to import some actual tracks into a session:

1. **Choose File⇨New Session to create a new session or choose File⇨ Open Session to open an existing one.**

2. **Choose File⇨Import Session Data from the main menu.**

   A dialog box appears, prompting you to choose a file from which to import session data.

3. **Choose the Pro Tools file (.pts suffix) containing the track you want to import, and then click Open.**

   The Import Session Data dialog box opens. (Refer to Figure 5-4.)

4. **In the Import Session Data dialog box, go through the Source Tracks list and click the name of each track you want to import.**

   To select multiple noncontiguous tracks, press and hold ⌘ (Mac) or Ctrl (PC) while you click the track names. To select multiple contiguous tracks, press and hold Shift while you click the names.

5. **From the drop-down menus, choose your Audio Media, Video Media, Time Code Mapping, and Track Offset options.**

   See the previous section, "Understanding the Import Session Data dialog box," for more on how to use these options.

6. **(Session-dependent) If the sample rate of your new session is different from the sample rate of the session you're importing from, you need to first convert it to the target session's rate before you can import it. Do this by selecting the sample rate of the source session from the Source Sample Rate drop-down menu and then choosing an option from the Conversion Quality drop-down menu.**

   You find these drop-down menus in the Sample Rate Conversion Options section of the Import Session Data dialog box.

7. **(Optional) If you want to import meter/tempo maps, key signature maps, markers or memory locations, or window configurations from the source session, select the appropriate check box(es) in the Import section of the dialog box.**

   Importing these maps ensures that the target session has the same maps, locations, and/or window configurations as the source session.

8. **Click OK.**

9. **(Optional) If you chose to copy audio or video media — or consolidate data from them — select a location to place the media files.**

Exporting from a Session

Pro Tools lets you export audio, MIDI, and clip data from one session to another. This is handy if you want to take parts of a song and add them to parts of another song, as in the case of an R&B remix of a pop tune. This section describes the process.

Exporting audio

Pro Tools gives you several ways to export audio — as clips, as stereo-interleaved files, or as clip definitions, depending on what you want to do with it. Here's a rundown on these options (and what the heck these terms mean):

+ **Export Audio Clips as Files:** This lets you take a clip in your track and export it as its own audio file that you can then use in another session. This is great for making separate audio files of drum loops: for example, if you're ready to place them in your mix.

+ **Export as Stereo Interleaved Files:** This lets you take the Clips from a stereo track or two Clips from two mono tracks and save them as a single, stereo-interleaved file. (*Stereo-interleaved files* are the type that many other programs create when doing a stereo mix.)

+ **Export Clip Definitions:** This lets you export the information that defines the clip. Doing this keeps you from having to make a copy of the audio (which saves hard-drive space) — and you can still use the clip in a new session. (Pro Tools uses the original audio file so that you don't have two in your system.)

Exporting Clips

Because Clips are only portions of the audio in an audio file, Pro Tools lets you take this portion and make a separate file containing just this audio data. Exporting Clipsclips allows you to take a lovingly crafted musical element (a killer drum loop, for example) and use it in another session or application without having to re-create it from the parent audio file.

To export a clip as a new audio file, follow these steps:

1. **Select the clip(s) by one of two ways:**

- *From the Audio Clips list (located on the right side of the Edit window):* Select the clip(s) you want to export by clicking the clip's name. To select more than one clip, hold the Shift key while you click each clip's name. (If the list isn't visible, click the double arrows at the bottom left of the Edit window to call it up.)

- *From the Track playlist in the Edit window:* Click anywhere on the clip to select it. To select more than one clip, hold the Shift key while you make your selections.

2. **Choose Export Clips as Files from the Audio Clips drop-down menu (the menu you open by clicking and holding the Audio Clips name at the top of the Audio Clips list).**

The Export Selected dialog box opens, as shown in Figure 5-5.

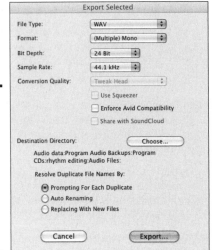

Figure 5-5:
Use the
Export
Selected
dialog box
to choose
export
settings for
your new
file.

3. **Choose the export settings you want for your new file.**

- *File Type:* Choose the file type of the session you want to use this file in. If you're not sure where you're going to use the file, choose BWF or AIFF. You can read about these file types earlier in this chapter.

- *Format:* Your choices here are (Multiple) Mono or Interealved (stereo). Choose the format appropriate for your file. If your drum loop, for example, is in stereo and has panning information, you'll want to select Interleaved.

- *Bit Depth:* You can choose bit depths of 8, 16, and 24 bits (plus 32-bit float if you're using Pro Tools 10, HD, or HDX). I recommend selecting the same bit depth as your current session.

- *Sample Rate:* You choices include 8, 11.025, 16, 22.050, 32, 44.1, 48, 88.2, 96, 177.4, and 192 kHz. Choose the sample rate of the session you want to put this file into. If you're not sure, select the same rate as your current session.

- *Conversion Quality:* If you choose a sample rate for your export that is different from the sample rate of the clip, you can select the quality of the conversion that will take place. These settings include Low (fastest), Good, Better, Best, and Tweakhead (Slowest). I always choose Tweakhead (I'm sure that says something about me).

- *Use Squeezer:* This option is available if you have the Squeezer plug-in. If you don't have this plug-in, this option will be grayed out.

- *Enforce Avid Compatibility:* Choosing this option includes frame accurate edits and limits your sample rate to either 44.1 or 48kHz. This ensures that your files are compatible with Avid video editing equipment. Unless you're dong music for film, skip this option.

- *Share with SoundCloud:* Enabling this option uploads your exported file automatically to your SoundCloud account, where you can share it with other SoundCloud users. This option is only available if you have a SoundCloud account and are connected to the Internet.

4. **Select a destination for the file in the Destination Directory field by clicking the Choose button and following the prompt.**

5. **Select from the Resolve Duplicate File Names By options:**

- *Prompting for Each Duplicate:* This stops the exporting process and lets you know when Pro Tools finds a duplicate filename. You can then choose to either replace the original or create a new name.

- *Auto Renaming:* You authorize Pro Tools to automatically create a new name for these files. This is the best option to choose if you don't want to have to answer a prompt for each duplicate filename and you want to make sure that your original files aren't replaced.

- *Replacing with New Files:* This option replaces any existing files containing the same name with your newly exported ones. This is the option to take if you're sure that you don't ever want the original files bearing the same name.

6. **Click Export.**

Your new file is created and saved to the destination you chose in the Destination Directory field of the Export Selected dialog box.

Exporting stereo-interleaved files

A *stereo-interleaved file* is a single audio file with all the stereo data contained in them. These types of stereo files are different than the ones used in Pro Tools, which consist of two separate audio files for stereo. One contains the left channel data, and the other contains the right channel data. Although Pro Tools doesn't support stereo-interleaved file types, you can export Clips from within your session as a single, stereo-interleaved file. This is an important feature because many other audio applications — such as mastering programs — use stereo-interleaved files instead of the separate ones that Pro Tools favors.

To export a clip as a stereo-interleaved file, do the following:

1. **Select either a stereo clip or two mono Clips one of two ways:**

- *From the Clips list (located on the right side of the Edit window):* Click the name of the clip to highlight it. To select two mono Clips, hold the Shift key while you click each clip's name.

- *From the track playlist in the Edit window:* Click anywhere on the clip within the track to highlight it. For more than one mono clip, hold the Shift key while you click each clip.

2. **Choose Export Selected as Files from the Clips list drop-down menu — the menu you open by clicking and holding the Audio Clips name at the top of the Audio Clips list.**

   The Export Selected dialog box opens. (Refer to Figure 5-5.)

3. **Choose Interleaved from the Format drop-down menu.**

4. **Choose the rest of your settings for this file.**

   Check out the previous section, "Exporting Clips," for tips on what settings to choose here.

5. **Click Export.**

   Your file is created and saved on your hard drive so you can use it in an application that supports stereo-interleaved files.

Exporting clip definitions

Clip definitions are the information that Pro Tools uses to define the location, start, and end times of a clip within the parent audio file. If you've come up with some Pro Tools Clips that you want to use in another session (or some other application that supports Pro Tools Clips data), you can export clip definitions from your session without having to copy the clip as an audio file. In effect, all you save using this command are the pointers that make up the clip definition: The definition points to the parent file and not to the audio itself.

If you actually want to use a clip definition in another session or application, make sure that the clip's parent audio file still exists on the hard drive. A definition that points to nothing is no help.

To export clip definitions, follow these steps:

1. **Select the Clips you want to export the clip definitions for:**

   - *From the Audio Clips list (located in the right side of the Edit window):* Select the clip(s) you want to export by clicking the clip's name. To select more than one clip, hold the Shift key while you click each clip's name. (If the list isn't visible, click the double arrows at the bottom left of the Edit window.)

- *From the Track playlist in the Edit window:* Click anywhere on the clip to select it. To select more than one clip, hold the Shift key while you make your selections.

2. **Choose Export Clip Definitions from the Audio Clips list drop-down menu — the menu you opened by clicking and holding the Audio Clips name at the top of the Audio Clips list.**

3. **Click Export.**

The pointing data for the selected Clips are exported.

Exporting MIDI

Ah, the miracle of MIDI — say you've laid down a kickin' "keyboard" part on guitar synth. How do you get it out of the current session? To export MIDI data to another device or application, you need to save your MIDI tracks and Clips as a Standard MIDI file. You can save them as Type 0 files (a single multichannel track) or as Type 1 files (multiple tracks).

To export MIDI tracks, follow these steps:

1. **(Optional) Mute any MIDI tracks you don't want to include in the Export MIDI procedure by clicking the Mute button for these tracks.**

Any muted tracks are excluded from the export function.

2. **Choose File⇨Export⇨MIDI from the main menu.**

The Export MIDI Settings dialog box appears, as shown on the top in Figure 5-6.

3. **From the MIDI File Format drop-down list, select the format of your heart's choosing:**

- *0 (Single track)*
- *1 (Multi-track)*

You must also select the Apply Real-Time Properties check box as you want.

4. **Click OK.**

The Save a MIDI File As dialog box appears, as shown in the bottom in Figure 5-6.

5. **Enter the name and location for this newly exported file in the Save As text field, and select a destination for the file from the Where drop-down menu.**

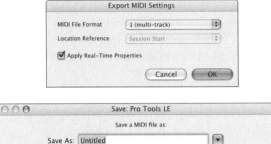

Figure 5-6:
Use these
dialog boxes
to choose
the settings,
name, and
location
for your
exported
MIDI file.

6. **Click Save.**

   Your new MIDI file is created from all the unmuted MIDI tracks in your session, in the location you designated. This file includes all notes; controller events; program changes; System Exclusive data (instructions exclusive to the device); and tempo, meter, and marker events. The Society of Motion Picture and Television Engineers (SMPTE) timecode start time is also included so that your MIDI files will start at their proper time when opened.

Managing Files

As soon as you start to record and edit your music, you start filling your hard drive with data. Properly managing your data helps you keep your system stable, lets you maximize your hard space, and protects you from the worst disaster of them all — lost data. This section details three important file-management tasks — compacting files, deleting files, and backing up data — you should routinely do to keep everything running smoothly.

Compacting files

Editing means cutting a snippet from here and taking the best chunk from there and putting it altogether to make a (hopefully coherent) whole. It also means that, after you extract that great 15-second bit from that 75-second clip, you're going to have a lot of stuff cluttering up the virtual cutting-room floor of your hard drive. What to do?

You can get rid of the clutter — the unused portions of the audio files in your session — by using the Audio Clips list Compact Selected command. This command deletes any audio from a file in your session where there are no Clips referencing the data. It helps conserve disk space.

Postpone using the Compact Selected command until *after* you finish all the editing in your session because it permanently deletes the unused audio data from the session. *Don't use this command until you're sure* that you don't want to use any of your data leftovers.

Compacting your audio files consists of three basic steps:

1. Select any unused clips in the session.

2. Clear these unused clips.

Steps 1 and 2 (ahem) clear the way to your final step:

3. Compact the files by removing the data for those cleared clips from the parent files.

Book II
Chapter 5

To compact an audio file, do the following:

**Importing and
Exporting Files**

1. **Choose Select⇨Unused Clips from the Audio Clips list drop-down menu (the menu opened by clicking and holding the Audio Clips name at the top of the Audio Clips list).**

Any clips not used in a track in the current session become highlighted in the Audio Clips list.

2. **Choose Clear Selected from the Audio Clips list (in the drop-down menu) to remove the unused clips.**

The Clear Audio dialog box appears.

3. **Click Remove.**

This removes the unused clips from your session.

4. **Select the clip(s) you want to compact from the Audio Clips list by clicking each clip's name.**

To select more than one clip, hold the Shift key while you click each clip's name.

5. **Choose Compact Selected from the Audio Clips list drop-down menu (the menu you open by clicking and holding the Audio Clips name at the top of the Audio Clips list).**

The Compact dialog box appears. This box contains a warning about the consequences of compacting a file (read the Warning icon earlier in this section) as a reminder that this is an irreversible process.

6. **(Optional) If you have crossfades in the selected clip(s), enter the amount of padding (in milliseconds) that you want to put around each selected clip.**

See Book IV, Chapter 4 for more on crossfades.

Padding adds space before and after your clips to account for any crossfades (see Book IV, Chapter 4). Choose a pad length equal to (at least) the longest crossfade length for your selected clips.

7. **Click the Compact button, located at the bottom of the Compact Audio dialog box.**

   Your file is compacted, and the session is saved.

Deleting unwanted files

As with any creative process, you end up with (in addition to your knockout musical creation) leftover junk that just takes up space. You can delete unwanted files in your session from your hard drive by using the Clear Selected command located under the Audio Clips list drop-down menu (opened by clicking and holding the Audio Clips name at the top of the Audio Clips list). Less unused data on your hard drive means more space for the good stuff.

To delete an audio file, do the following:

1. **Select the audio files you want to delete from the Audio Clips list.**

   The audio files are listed in bold letters in the Audio Clips list.

2. **From the Audio Clips list's drop-down menu (opened by clicking and holding the Audio Clips name at the top of the Audio Clips list), choose Clear Selected.**

   The Clear Audio dialog box appears. You have the options of Remove (which you use before compacting a file — see the previous section) and Delete. This is the one you want for this procedure.

3. **Click the Delete button in the Clear Audio dialog box.**

   Your file is permanently deleted from your hard drive.

The Clear Selected command is irreversible. After you click Delete, your data is gone *forever.* If you think you may want the data someday, choose Remove from the Clear Audio dialog box. Your file is removed from the session but not from your hard drive.

Backing up data

There's a saying in the computer world: *If the data doesn't exist in more than two places, it doesn't exist.* I know I said this elsewhere (Chapter 1 of this mini-book, to be precise), but I think it bears repeating. As someone who lost an entire project's worth of data because I "forgot" to back up my files, I strongly encourage you to make a habit of backing up your sessions.

Backing up your files to the same hard drive does you no good if your drive shuts down (a common occurrence). Always back-up to a *different* hard drive or to another medium, such as a USB flash drive, or a DVD-R. (Check out the manual for your DVD burner for steps on how to do this.) You can also pick up a copy of *CD & DVD Recording For Dummies,* 2nd Edition, by Mark Chambers (Wiley).

To back up your session files to another hard drive, do the following:

1. **Create a new folder on a different hard drive than your session and call it Back Ups.**

2. **Choose File⇨Save Copy In from the main menu.**

The Save dialog box appears.

3. **Use the file browser section of the dialog box to select the folder you created in Step 1 as the destination for your backup files.**

4. **Enter a name for your backup in the Save As field of the Save Session Copy In dialog box.**

Because this copy exists on a whole different hard drive, I can use the same name as that of my original session — and if it's an exact duplicate, I do. This is important because if the original files are lost, all you have to do is drag the backed-up files onto your audio drive and get to work. Using a different name means you have to rename or import all your files before you can use them.

5. **Under the Items to Copy box, select All Audio files as well as any other setting you want to save such as plug-in settings or movie/video files.**

6. **Click Save.**

The files you selected are backed up to the destination specified in Step 3.

You can also back up your files by clicking and dragging the folder containing your session and audio files from one hard drive to another on your computer's desktop.

Book III

Recording Audio

The 5th Wave   By Rich Tennant

©RICHTENNANT

"I ran this Bob Dylan CD through our voice recognition system, and he really is just saying, 'Manaamamanaabadhaaadbha...'"

Contents at a Glance

Chapter 1: Taking Care of Tracks 241

    Understanding Tracks in Pro Tools 241

    Setting Up Tracks 242

    Altering Your View of Tracks 245

    Grouping Tracks 250

    Soloing and Muting 255

    Managing Track Voices 256

Chapter 2: Miking: Getting a Great Source Sound 259

    Tracing Typical Microphone Techniques 259

    Taming Transients 266

    Setting Up Your Mics: Some Suggestions 270

Chapter 3: Preparing to Record 289

    Recognizing Record Modes 289

    Dealing with Disk Allocation 292

    Enabling Recording 294

    Setting Levels 297

    Setting a Record Range 299

    Monitoring Your Tracks 299

    Creating a Click Track 304

Chapter 4: Recording Audio 311

    Recording Tracks 311

    Playing Back Your Tracks 316

    Doing Additional Takes 320

    Getting Rid of Unwanted Takes 332

Chapter 1: Taking Care of Tracks

In This Chapter

✔ **Working with tracks**

✔ **Understanding track views**

✔ **Grouping tracks**

✔ **Managing track voices**

*B*efore you can do any recording in Pro Tools, you need to create and configure some *tracks* — specific places to put the vocals, instrumental parts, pterodactyl screeches, whatever. This involves setting up new tracks, naming the tracks, and assigning inputs and outputs to your newly created and named tracks.

But that's not all. When working with tracks in Pro Tools, you also need to know how to show and hide, activate and deactivate, solo, mute, and adjust your view of them, among other things. This chapter takes the mystery out of dealing with tracks and shows you how to work with them both efficiently and effectively.

Understanding Tracks in Pro Tools

Pro Tools has five types of tracks (Audio, Auxiliary Input, Master Fader, MIDI, and Instrument) as well as two track formats (mono and stereo). All possible permutations and combinations of these various types and formats are explained with subtlety and style in the following sections.

Track types

When you work with tracks in Pro Tools, you have to keep in mind that you're sure to end up dealing with five distinct flavors of tracks. They are

+ **Audio tracks:** An *audio track* contains audio files and can be mono or stereo.

+ **Auxiliary Input tracks:** These tracks are used as effects sends, for sub-mixes, or for other routing purposes.

+ **Master Fader tracks:** This track type contains the summed output for all the tracks routed to it. Master Fader tracks can be mono or stereo; stereo is most common.

✦ **MIDI tracks:** *MIDI tracks* contain MIDI *data* — instructions to MIDI devices on how to create specific digital sounds. (For more on MIDI, check out Book I, Chapter 4. For more on MIDI tracks, go to Book V.)

✦ **Instrument tracks:** *Instrument tracks* are blends of Audio and MIDI tracks that allow you to insert virtual instruments (such as software synthesizers) into your session. You can also route real instruments with their corresponding audio outputs into the same track. These tracks contain MIDI data while also allowing you some audio capabilities to make it easy to use both software and hardware instruments. Book V, Chapter 1 offers more about these hybrid tracks.

Track formats

Pro Tools offers a bit less variety when it comes to track formats. Unless you are using Pro Tools HD, HDX, or 10 with the optional Complete Production Kit, you get two — count 'em, two — choices:

✦ **Mono:** A *mono* (monaural) track consists of a single channel of audio or MIDI data. It uses, as its name implies, just one voice.

✦ **Stereo:** A *stereo* (stereophonic) track consists of two channels of audio and uses two voices. A MIDI track can't be stereo.

Setting Up Tracks

Setting up your recording project is a little like setting up a railroad: It'll take you somewhere only if you first put the tracks in place. Getting that done is what this section is about.

Creating new tracks

To create a new track, choose Track⇨New from the main menu or press ⌘+Shift+N (Mac) or Ctrl+Shift+N (PC). Either method opens the New Tracks dialog box (as shown in Figure 1-1), where you get to choose the following:

✦ **Number of new tracks:** The default here is 1, but you can pretty much create up to 128 mono audio tracks or Auxiliary Input tracks, 64 Master Fader tracks, 32 Instrument tracks, and 256 MIDI tracks. Just keep in mind that you can have only 32 voices of audio tracks playing at one time in your session.

✦ **Track format:** Here you choose stereo or mono.

✦ **Track type:** Clicking the arrows opens a drop-down menu that lets you choose between an Audio, an Auxiliary Input, a Master Fader, a MIDI, or an Instrument track.

✦ **Samples or ticks:** You can choose between samples or ticks (bars/beats) for your new tracks.

+ **Plus sign:** Clicking this adds another tracks selection row containing all the options listed in this section so that you can add more than one type of track without having to open the New Track window repeatedly.

Make your selections and then click Create to create your new track. This track then appears in the Edit and Mix windows and in the Show/Hide list located on the right side of the Edit window. If the Show/Hide list isn't visible, click the double arrow at the lower-left corner of the Edit window.

Figure 1-1:
Create a
new track
here.

Duplicating tracks

You can *duplicate* tracks — creating a new track that mirrors all the input, output, effects send settings, and insert settings of your original track — in two easy steps:

1. **Click the name of the track in the Mix or the Edit windows.**

    To select more than one track to duplicate, hold the Shift key while you click each track's name.

    The name is highlighted.

2. **Choose Track⇨Duplicate from the main menu.**

    The new track appears in the Mix and the Edit windows to the right of the track you're duplicating and just below the duplicated track in the Show/Hide list.

Naming tracks

When you open a new track (choose Track⇨New), Pro Tools creates a default name for the track — something really helpful, like Audio 1 — but you can change the name to anything you want. You do this by double-clicking the name of the track in either the Mix or the Edit windows. A dialog box similar to what you see in Figure 1-2 opens, from which you can use the fields to both change the name of the track and add any comments you want to include about the track. After you enter your track name and comments, click OK — you're set!

I highly recommend that you name your new tracks right away; give each a name that describes what you plan to record on it. Some examples include *Vox* (or *Vocals*), *Ld Gtr, Snare, Kick,* and so on. This will save you confusion later on when you start to mix.

Figure 1-2:
Choose a
track name
and add
comments
here.

Assigning inputs and outputs

To record with your new track, you need to assign an input to it so Pro Tools knows where your source sound is coming from. To hear the track play, you need to choose an output so Pro Tools can send the sound out to your monitors or to your headphone jack.

That makes sense, right? Now, to actually assign an input to your track, do the following:

1. **Choose View⇨Edit Window⇨I/O from the main menu to open the I/O section of the Edit window.**

    The I/O section shows the inputs and outputs for each track.

2. **Within the I/O section of your track in the Edit window, click and hold the Input selector (see Figure 1-3) until the Input contextual menu pops up.**

Figure 1-3:
Assign an
input or
output here.

3. **While still holding down your mouse button, move the mouse over the Input menu until it rests on the input listing you want.**

4. **Release the mouse button to select your choice from the Input contextual menu.**

    This menu closes, and the input you select appears in the Input selector.

Choosing your outputs requires pretty much the same procedure, although now you start things off by clicking the Output selector instead.

If you have an output you want to use for your session, such as Analog 1-2, you can set this as the default in the I/O Setup dialog box. To do this, follow these steps:

1. **Choose Setup⇨I/O to open the I/O Setup dialog box.**

2. **Click the Output tab.**

3. **Choose your output from the New Track Default Output drop-down menu.**

4. **Click OK.**

   The window closes, and all your new tracks automatically receive your chosen output upon creation.

Altering Your View of Tracks

Pro Tools gives you lots of options to change how tracks look in the Mix and the Edit windows. You can change a track's color, size, location, and even whether you can see it. The following sections get you up to speed on these options.

Showing and hiding tracks

Both the Edit and the Mix windows have the option of including an audio tracks list in the window view (see Figure 1-4). In this list, the Tracks list, you can show or hide selected tracks or groups of tracks. This list is located on the left side of either window. If it's not visible, click the double arrows at the bottom-left of either window to open the list in that window.

**Book III
Chapter 1**

**Taking Care
of Tracks**

Figure 1-4:
Use the list
to show,
hide, or sort
your tracks.

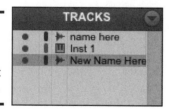

You can show and hide tracks in two ways:

✦ **Use the drop-down menu.** Click and hold the title bar of the Show/Hide Tracks list until a menu opens up, as shown in Figure 1-5. Then just choose the option you want.

Figure 1-5:
Use this menu to set how you want to see your tracks.

The Show Only Selected Tracks option and the Hide Selected Tracks option require that you first highlight your desired tracks in the main part of the Edit or the Mix windows. To select one track, just click the track's name. To select more than one track, hold down the Shift key while clicking each track you want. When you then use the Show Only Selected option, for example, all non-highlighted tracks are hidden.

✦ **Click the track name in the Show/Hide Tracks list.** Clicking directly on the track name located in the Show/Hide Tracks list toggles between hiding and showing the track. You can even move a track around by clicking and dragging it to where you want it in relation to the others.

If the Show/Hide Tracks list isn't showing, click the double arrow at the bottom-left corner of the window to open it (see Figure 1-6).

Figure 1-6:
To show the Show/Hide Tracks list, click the arrows in the lower left of the Edit or Mix windows.

Click here to show the Show/Hide Tracks list

You can also use the Show/Hide Tracks list drop-down menu to sort tracks by name, type, edit group, mix group, or voice, as shown in Figure 1-7. This menu is opened by clicking and holding the Show/Hide Tracks list title.

Figure 1-7:
You can sort your tracks in the Edit or Mix window.

Assigning track color

To make all your tracks easier to keep track of when you're working, you can assign color groups to the waveform display for each track in the Edit window. To do this, choose Setup⇨Preferences from the main menu and then click the Display tab in the Preferences dialog box. This opens the Preferences dialog box, as shown in Figure 1-8.

Figure 1-8:
Choose how to color-code your tracks.

On the right side of this dialog box is the Default Track Color Coding section. Here you can choose from several radio buttons:

✦ **None:** Makes the display for all the tracks the same color.

✦ **Tracks and MIDI channels:** Assigns colors to each waveform display based upon the audio track number and the MIDI channels assigned for each MIDI track.

✦ **Tracks and MIDI Devices:** Bases the colors for the waveform display on the audio track number and the MIDI device used.

✦ **Groups:** Colors the waveform display for your tracks according to a track's group membership.

✦ **Track Type:** Assigns colors according to the type of track in your session.

Changing track size

You can alter the viewed size of tracks in the Edit or the Mix windows. This can be a godsend, for example, when you have a ton of tracks in a session, and you want to see them all onscreen (pick a small size) or if you have a track that you want to edit (choose a giant-size one). Here are your options:

✦ **Edit window:** The Edit window allows you to choose from several different-size track views. Your options include Micro, Mini, Small, Medium, Large, Jumbo, Extreme, Fit to Window, and Expanded Track Display. You access these options by clicking the Track Height Selector (the little arrow to the left of the track name) or the ruler bar at the far-left side of the waveform display of the track, as shown in Figure 1-9.

If you're using Pro Tools version 7.3 and newer, you can simply drag your track larger or smaller by clicking and dragging your mouse up or down at the bottom of your track.

Height Selector

Figure 1-9:
Change
track height
here.

✦ **Mix window:** In the Mix window, you can toggle between Narrow and Regular channel strip views by choosing View↩Narrow Mix Window or View↩Regular Mix Window, respectively, as shown in Figure 1-10.

Pressing Option+⌘+M (Mac) or Shift+Ctrl+M (PC) also toggles between the two views.

Figure 1-10: Choose between Regular and Narrow channel strips in the Mix window.

Moving tracks around

You can move tracks around and arrange them in your Mix or Edit windows as you want them. This feature is handy if you have a group of tracks that you want to have next to each other, such as percussion and drums. I place any submixed tracks together to help me keep track (sorry, I couldn't help myself) of them all without having to move all over the Edit or Mix windows. The following steps show you one way to do this:

Book III
Chapter 1

Taking Care
of Tracks

1. **Locate the name of the track you'd like to move in the Tracks list, as shown in Figure 1-11.**

Figure 1-11: Click and drag to move tracks around.

2. **Click the track name and then drag the track up or down to where you want it.**

3. **Release the mouse button.**

   The track stays put where you dragged it.

Moving the track around in one window changes its location in the other.

Deleting tracks

To delete a track, follow these steps:

1. **Select the track by clicking its name in either the Edit or the Mix windows.**

2. **Choose Track⇨Delete from the main menu.**

3. **Click OK.**

Grouping Tracks

In Pro Tools, creating and managing groups of tracks is a snap. I strongly recommend taking advantage of Pro Tools grouping features because they let you perform lots of different tasks — edits, for example — on more than one track at a time.

Keeping track of grouped track parameters

When tracks are grouped, certain parameters become linked. These include

✦ Automation modes

✦ Editing functions

✦ Mutes

✦ Send mutes

✦ Send levels

✦ Solos

✦ Track view

✦ Track height

✦ Volume levels

That's a lot of parameters, but don't let this long list fool you into thinking that grouping links *everything* associated with your tracks. Some parameters are not linked when you use the grouping feature, including these:

✦ Creating plug-in instances

✦ Output assignments

✦ Panning

✦ Record enables

✦ Send panning

✦ Voice assignments

Having these parameters independent when tracks are grouped is nice because many times, these parameters vary from track to track. For example, you don't want the same plug-ins on all your drum tracks or the same panning setting on all backup vocal tracks. (Both of these are great candidates for grouping.)

Creating groups

You can create groups by following these steps:

1. **In either the Edit window or the Mix window, Shift-click the tracks you want in your group.**

   Which window you use as your starting point doesn't matter. Whatever groups are created in one window automatically get created in the other window.

2. **Choose Track⇨Group from the main menu, or New Group from the Group drop-down menu (the menu you open by clicking and holding the Group title in the Groups list section of the Edit or the Mix window).**

   The Create Group dialog box appears, as shown in Figure 1-12.

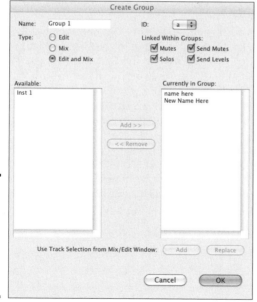

Figure 1-12:
The Create Group dialog box lets you create a new group.

3. **Enter a name for your group in the Name field.**

4. **Use the radio buttons in the Type section to choose which window(s) will show your new group.**

   Your choices here are

   - *Edit:* When you want the group listed just in the Edit window

   - *Mix:* When you want the group listed just in the Mix window

   - *Edit and Mix:* When you want your group listed in both windows

5. **Choose a group ID from the ID drop-down menu.**

   The group ID is a single letter that defines your group. This lets you see which group a track is in at a glance. (The group ID for a track is located beneath the track's level meters in the mix window.)

6. **Click OK.**

   The Create Group dialog box closes, and your new group appears in the Edit, the Mix, or both the Edit and the Mix windows (depending on your choice in Step 4).

If a track in a group is hidden in the Show/Hide Tracks list, that track won't be affected by edits done to that group. All mix operations — with the notable exception of Record Enable — do apply to hidden tracks, though.

Enabling groups

Before you can work with grouped tracks, you need to enable the group, which you do by clicking the group name in the Groups list. (You'll find the Edit Groups list in the lower-left side of the Edit window; the Mix Groups list is in the lower-left side of the Mix window. If they aren't visible, click the double arrow at the bottom-left corner of the Mix or the Edit window, respectively.) Highlighting in blue means the group is enabled. Click the group again to disable it. The blue highlight will disappear.

You can also enable and disable groups using a keystroke on your keyboard in the Mix window by simply pressing the key for the group ID. To do the same thing in the Edit window, you need to first make sure that the Keyboard Focus (A-Z) button to the right of the Edit Groups name is highlighted, as shown in Figure 1-13. (How will you know that it's highlighted? That's easy. In its highlighted state, a yellow border surrounds the box.)

Figure 1-13:
Highlight
the Edit
Group List
Keyboard
Focus.

Editing groups

After you set up some groups, you don't have to treat them as if they were set in stone. You can add — or subtract — group members, change the group name, or just delete the group altogether. These options are covered in the following sections.

Renaming a group

Follow these steps to rename a group:

1. Double-click the area to the left of the group name in the Groups list.

The Modify Groups dialog box appears.

The Edit Groups list is located in the lower-left side of the Edit window; the Mix Groups list is in the lower-left side of the Mix window. If they aren't visible, click the double arrow at the bottom-left corner of the Mix or the Edit window, respectively.

2. Type in your new name in the Name field.

3. Click OK.

Your group gets a spanking new name.

Adding a track to a group

You can add a track to an existing group by doing the following:

1. Double-click the area to the left of the group name in the Groups list.

The Modify Groups dialog box appears.

2. Select tracks from the Available window.

3. Click the Add button.

The selected tracks instantly appear in the Currently in Group window.

4. Click OK.

The selected tracks are added to the group selected in Step 1.

**Book III
Chapter 1**

Taking Care
of Tracks

Deleting groups

You can delete unwanted groups by doing the following:

1. **Click the name of the group in the Groups list.**

   Again, you find the Edit Groups list in the lower left of the Edit window, and the Mix Groups list in the lower left of the Mix window. If they aren't visible, click the double arrow at the bottom-left corner of the Mix or Edit the window, respectively.

2. **Click the Groups drop-down menu (opened by clicking and holding the Group title in the Groups list section of the Edit or Mix window) and choose Delete Active Group.**

   You'll be asked whether you're sure you want to do this because after you do, there's no changing your mind. Proceed if you're sure you don't ever want to use that group again.

   Your group is history.

Linking edit and mix groups

When you create a new group, you have the option of making that group an Edit group, a Mix group, or a combination Edit/Mix group. Regardless of which option you choose, by default, functions done in either the Edit or the Mix windows will affect groups in both. For example, if you have a drum group in your Mix window consisting of kick, snare, toms, and overheads, and you want to edit a bad note out of the snare drum in the Edit window, you end up editing not only the snare drum note but also the audio from the other members of the drum group you assigned in the Mix window.

This might be what you want most of the time, but maybe you don't want the default — where Edit or Mix functions affect entire groups. The way to get around this is to disable the Link Edit and Mix Groups option in the Preferences dialog box. Do so by following these steps:

1. **Choose Setup⇨Preferences from the main menu.**

   The Preferences dialog box appears.

2. **Click the Mixing tab in the Preferences dialog box and look under the heading Setup.**

   You see a screen that looks like Figure 1-14.

3. **Deselect the Link Mix/Edit Group Enables option.**

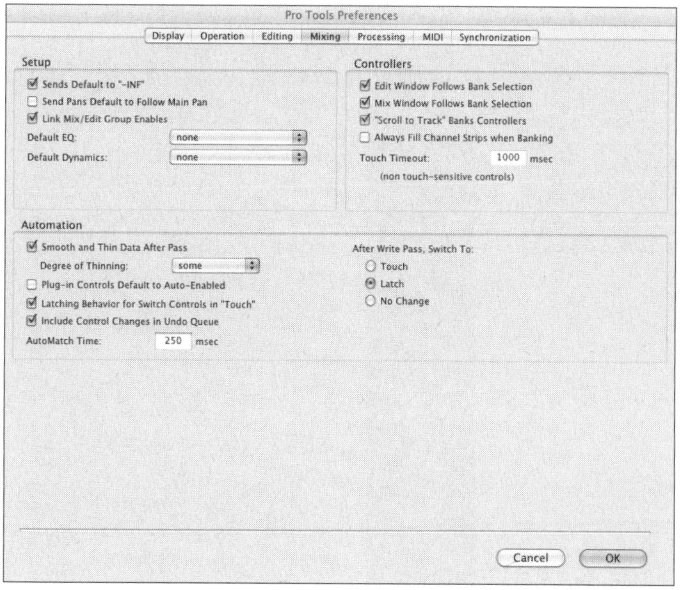

Figure 1-14:
The Link Mix /Edit Group Enables options.

Soloing and Muting

Soloing and muting tracks is a big part of the mix process. By being able to hear only those tracks you want to hear at a given time, you can find unwanted sounds lurking in your tracks by soloing the suspected track, or you can turn off the lead vocal when you tweak the backup vocals. You can solo and mute each track in the Edit window by clicking the Solo or the Mute button (respectively), located underneath the track name, as shown on the left side of Figure 1-15. You can do the same thing in the Mix window by clicking the Solo and Mute buttons located above the volume fader, as shown on the right side of Figure 1-15. Check out Book III, Chapter 4 for more on these windows and the location of the Solo and Mute buttons.

Soloing a track turns the mute function on for the rest of the tracks. You can solo and mute more than one track at a time. Choose the appropriate button for each track.

Solo   Solo

Mute   Mute

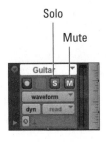

Figure 1-15:
The Solo
and Mute
buttons are
located on
each track
in the Edit
(left) and
Mix (right)
windows.

Managing Track Voices

Pro Tools offers a limited number of voices. The number of voices available to you depends on the version of Pro Tools you have. Here's a list of total voices available in the various Pro Tools systems:

✦ **Pro Tools SE:** 16 tracks at 44.1 or 48kHz.

✦ **Pro Tools MP:** 48 tracks at 44.1 or 48kHz or 32 tracks at 88.2 or 96kHz.

✦ **Pro Tools 10:** 96 tracks at 44.1 or 48kHz, 48 tracks at 88.2 or 96kHz or 24 tracks at 176.4 or 192kHz.

✦ **Pro Tools HD:** 256 tracks at 44.1 or 48kHz, 128 tracks at 88.2 or 96kHz or 64 tracks at 176.4 or 192kHz.

✦ **Pro Tools HDX:** 768 tracks at 44.1 or 48kHz, 384 tracks at 88.2 or 96kHz or 192 tracks at 176.4 or 192kHz.

Even though some of these track counts are really high, it's not unlikely that you'll have more than the number of available tracks in a session. Given this probability, Pro Tools offers you ways to manage your voices so you can hear all your tracks (or at least the important ones). This can be done one of two ways: setting voice assignments for each track, and setting voice priority. The next two sections give you the skinny on each method.

Assigning voices

In Pro Tools, the controls for each track let you choose between Off and Dyn for voice assignments. Figure 1-16 shows the Voice Assignment menu in the Edit (left) and the Mix (right) windows. With a tracks voice assignment set to Off, the track won't play. If you have the track's voice set to Dyn, Pro Tools automatically turns that track on and off according to how many voices are available for playback and where this particular track sits in the Voice Priority listing. (See the next section for more on voice priorities.)

Figure 1-16: You can choose the voice assignment for each track in the Edit (left) and Mix (right) windows.

For example, if you have a session containing more tracks than you can have, only your Pro Tools version's allotted amount will play at any one time. Now, if you have one track (rhythm guitar) that plays only during the verse and another track (lead guitar) that plays only during the chorus, you can get these two tracks to trade off so that only one at a time uses the available voice — and everybody's happy because every note recorded will get heard.

Imagine, though, that *both* guitar parts have to play in the bridge section of the song. In this game of musical chairs, one part won't find one of the available "slots" — and won't play. Which part ends up being silenced is determined by how high up the part sits in the list of tracks. You can choose how high by setting the voice priority of each track, something I cover in the next section.

Setting voice priority

Because Pro Tools lets you have more tracks in your session than the total number of voices available in your version of the software, you might need to do some finagling among the available voices if you want every track (or at least the most important ones) to be heard throughout the song. To pull off this trick, you have to set the *voice priority* of each track.

Voice priority is determined by the track's position in the tracks list in the Edit and the Mix windows: The higher its place in the list, the higher its priority for voice assignment. You can increase the voice priority of a track in the following ways:

+ **Using the Show/Hide Tracks List:** Click and hold with the pointer over the track you want, and drag that track up the list.

+ **Using the Edit Window:** Click and drag the name of the track up the list.

+ **Using the Mix Window:** Click and drag the name of the track to the left on the list.

The higher up the list a track is, the higher its priority and the stronger its claim on the available voices when you assign voices.

Freeing up a voice from a track

Because you can't make every track the highest priority, here are other ways to free up (or at least control) how your available voices get used. If you can identify a voice that's less crucial at a given moment, you can free that voice from a track by doing one of the following:

+ **Turn the voice assignment to Off.** From the Voice Assignment menu, choose (logically enough) Off. (See the "Assigning voices" section, earlier in this chapter, for more on the Voice Assignment menu.)

+ **Turn off any output or send assignments for that track.**

Chapter 2: Miking: Getting a Great Source Sound

In This Chapter

✔ **Exploring microphone techniques**

✔ **Miking drums**

✔ **Miking amplified instruments**

✔ **Miking acoustic instruments**

Y ou can do all the right things to get your Pro Tools software ready to record tracks (see Book III, Chapter 1 for more on that topic), but it won't mean diddly if you don't know how to set up your mics properly.

As you'll soon find out, the location of a microphone in relation to your instrument or a singer has a huge impact on the sound of your recording. In fact, just a movement of an inch or two or even a slight turn of the mic can bring out different characteristics in the sound. The art of placing mics is one that you will undoubtedly spend a lifetime discovering.

In this chapter, you discover the fundamentals of using microphones to get a good source sound. You explore tried-and-true miking methods along with some practical miking tips and tricks that you can use right away. You also examine the use of compression and mic placement to control and eliminate *transients* — the usual peaks in the instrument's sound.

Tracing Typical Microphone Techniques

Regardless of the style of microphone you use — or the type of instrument you record — you can use one or more of the following mic placement techniques to capture the sound you want:

✦ **Spot (or close) miking:** Put your microphone within a couple feet of the sound source. This includes instrument-mounted mics.

✦ **Distant miking:** Pull your mic back three to five feet from the sound.

✦ **Ambient miking:** Place your mic way back in a room.

✦ **Stereo miking:** Set up two mics at various distances from one another.

✦ **Combining miking strategies:** Use a combination of the four traditional placement strategies listed here.

This section introduces you to the four traditional mic placement strategies employed in recording. I cover the characteristics and purposes of each of these four methods and get a look at how each relates to a particular tonal or sound quality. I also discuss how you can combine these strategies.

Spot miking

Spot miking (also called *close miking*) involves placing your microphone within a couple of feet of the sound source. People with a home-recording setup use this technique most often because it adds little of the room (the reverb and delay) to the recorded sound. Figure 2-1 shows the spot miking placement.

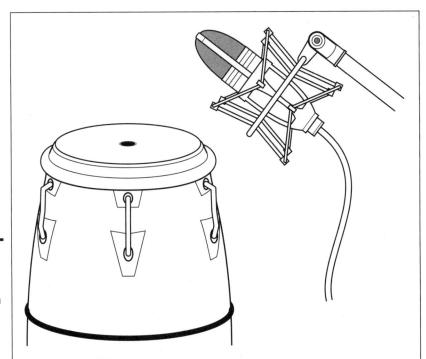

Figure 2-1: Spot miking places a mic within a few feet of the sound source.

With spot miking, where you place the mic is much more crucial than it is with any other technique. Because the mic is so close to the sound source, small adjustments to the mic's placement make a noticeable difference, and the mic might not capture the complete sound of the instrument. Finding the spot that sounds the best can take some trial and error.

Distant miking

When you use *distant miking*, you place mics about three or four feet away from the sound source. (See Figure 2-2.) Distant miking enables you to capture some of the sound of the room along with that of the instrument. An example of a distant miking technique is using an overhead drum mic, with which you can pick up the whole drumset to some extent. Coupled with a few select spot mics, you can record a natural sound.

Figure 2-2:
Distant miking places a microphone three or four feet from the sound source.

Ambient miking

Using *ambient miking* places the mic far enough away from the sound source so you capture more of the room sound (the reverb and delay) than the sound of the actual instrument. (See Figure 2-3.) You can place the mic a couple of feet away from the source but pointed in the opposite direction, or you can place it across the room. You can even put the mic in an adjacent room (although this is an unorthodox technique, I'll admit). The distance that you choose varies from instrument to instrument. For example, a flute would need a little closer mic than a double bass would.

Ambient mic placement works well in those places where the room adds to the sound of the instrument. Home recordists sometimes use stairwells, bathrooms, or rooms with wood paneling to liven up the sound. The sound you record is *ambient* (hence the name): steeped in the sonic qualities of the surroundings. If you mix this with a spot mic, you can end up with a natural reverb. If your room doesn't add to the sound of the instrument, you're better off not using any ambient mics. You can always add a room sound by using effects in the mixing process. (See Book VI, Chapter 5 for more on using effects.)

Figure 2-3:
Ambient miking involves placing the mic so it picks up more of the room's sound than the instrument's sound.

Stereo miking

Stereo miking involves using two mics to capture the stereo field of the instrument. You can use a variety of stereo miking techniques as well as some pretty complicated ways of using two mics to record. The three most common approaches, however, are X-Y (coincident) pairs, the Blumlein technique, and spaced pairs. You can also find stereo mics that do a good job on their own of capturing the stereo field of an instrument.

Stereo miking has the advantage of capturing a natural stereo image. When you listen to performances that were recorded with well-placed stereo miking, you can hear exactly where on the stage each instrument performed. Of course, there is an art to such wonderful stereo miking. You can't just randomly set up a couple of mics in a room and get a good stereo sound. Capturing a stereo image with two mics requires some careful planning.

X-Y pairs

X-Y (also called *coincident*) stereo miking uses two mics placed next to each other so that the diaphragms are at almost-right angles (anywhere from 90–135 degrees) as close together as possible without touching one another. X-Y stereo miking is the most common type of stereo mic setup and the one you'll probably use if you do any stereo miking. Figure 2-4 shows a basic X-Y setup. Notice how the mics in this figure are attached to a special mounting bracket. This bracket makes positioning the mics easy.

Figure 2-4:
The X-Y
stereo mic
approach
uses two
matched
microphones
placed close
together.

Blumlein technique

The Blumlein technique is named after Alan Dower Blumlein, who patented this approach in 1931. Blumlein stereo miking involves placing two figure-8 mics in much the same way as the X-Y pattern (at right angles to one another with the diaphragms as close together as possible). The two mics are mounted on separate stands, one above the other. The advantage with this technique is that the figure-8 mics pick up signals from both the front and back. This produces a very natural sound. You also don't have to contend with any *proximity effects* (enhanced bass response that comes from being close to the sound source) because figure-8 mics don't produce this effect. Figure 2-5 shows this technique. (For more on figure-8 mics, see Book I, Chapter 5.)

Spaced pairs

Spaced-pair stereo miking places two mics at a distance in front of the instrument(s) you want to record as well as at a distance from one another. This approach can work well if you record an ensemble that takes up a fairly large amount of room. Figure 2-6 shows a top view of a typical spaced stereo mic setup.

One of the most important things to consider when you use spaced pairs for stereo miking is that they can develop phase problems if you don't space the mics properly. For the most part, placing the mics three times farther apart than they are from the sound source takes care of phase problems. This is the *3:1 rule*. (For more on phase problems, see the "Problems with stereo miking" sidebar in this chapter.)

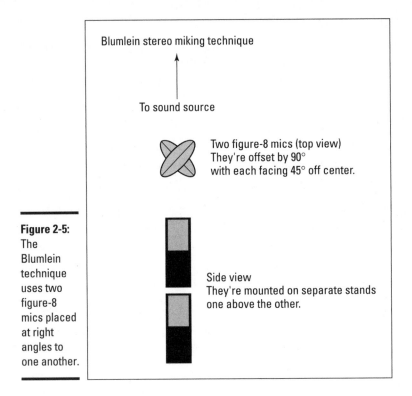

Blumlein stereo miking technique

To sound source

Two figure-8 mics (top view)
They're offset by 90°
with each facing 45° off center.

Side view
They're mounted on separate stands
one above the other.

Figure 2-5:
The Blumlein technique uses two figure-8 mics placed at right angles to one another.

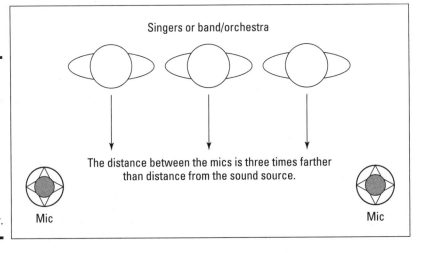

Singers or band/orchestra

The distance between the mics is three times farther
than distance from the sound source.

Mic

Mic

Figure 2-6:
To use the spaced-pair approach, place two mics away from the sound source and apart from one another.

Stereo microphones

If you want to record an instrument in stereo and don't want the hassle of fiddling with setting up stereo pairs, you can use a stereo mic. Stereo mics basically have two diaphragms in them and use a special cord that allows you to record the output from each diaphragm on a separate track. Take a look at an inexpensive stereo condenser mic in Figure 2-7.

Figure 2-7: A stereo microphone can do a good job of capturing a natural stereo image.

Mic combinations

Often you'll want to use more than one mic. The possible combinations are almost limitless: You can use several spot mics on one instrument, you can use a spot mic and an ambient mic, you can have a distant mic and a spot mic, or. . . . Well, you get my point. I don't go into detail in this section, but I do cover some great ideas (if I do say so myself) in the "Setting Up Your Mics: Some Suggestions" section, later in this chapter.

If you do end up using multiple mic combinations, listen for any phase problems. Do a couple of run-throughs to get level and balance, and try to correct phase troubles before you actually record the performance. Of course, because you're using Pro Tools, you can deal with some phase problems later. This is done one of two ways:

+ **Use the Invert command from the AudioSuites menu.** Choose AudioSuite⇨Invert from the main menu.

+ **Move your tracks around in your session to line up the waveforms.** This is *time aligning,* which I cover in Book IV, Chapter 3.

Taming Transients

The single most difficult part of getting a good sound with a microphone is dealing with sudden, extreme increases in the sound signal. These blips are *transients,* and they happen when a drum is first struck, when a vocalist sings certain syllables (for example, those that begin with *P*), and when a guitar player picks certain notes. In fact, because you can't always control the amount of force that you apply to an instrument, transients can happen any time — with any instrument — and without warning. (Highly-trained musicians produce fewer transients because they have a greater mastery over their muscular movements.)

Problems with stereo miking

When you use stereo miking, watch out for phase cancellation and poor stereo imaging.

Phase cancellation happens when the two microphones are placed in such a way that each one receives the sound at a slightly different time. When this occurs, you don't hear the bass as well: The low frequencies drop off. Improper mic placement — or two mics that are out of phase with one another — can cause phase cancellation.

Most digital recorders have a phase switch that allows you to reverse the phase of the signal. (Pro Tools lets you do this after it's recorded.) To test whether two mics are out of phase, just reverse the phase on one mic (don't do both) and listen whether the low frequencies become more apparent. If they do, you've corrected the problem and you're good to go. If this doesn't correct the problem, try changing cords on one of the mics because some mic cords are wired differently. If this doesn't work

either, you need to adjust the relationship between the two mics. Just move one around a little and listen for any changes in the bass response. When the missing bass appears, you know you've solved the problem.

You have a problem with *poor stereo imaging* if you can't tell clearly where the various instruments or vocals show up from left to right (or right to left, if that's how you think), or you can't hear a clear center point in the sound. Poor stereo imaging is a little more difficult to correct than phase cancellation, but you can fix it.

The solution depends on the stereo miking technique you use. If you use the X-Y technique, you probably placed your mics too close to the sound source. If you use the spaced-pairs technique, you probably placed the mics too close to one another in relation to their distance from the instruments. In either case, adjusting the placement of your mics should clear up the problem.

In digital recording, all it takes is one slight, unexpected note to cause clipping and distortion, ruining what might be a perfect musical performance. Believe me: Nothing is as heart-wrenching as listening to the perfect take and hearing the unmistakable sound of digital distortion. Although you can't eliminate transients completely (they are part of an instrument's character), you can tame the extreme transients that often cause digital *overs* (a thick signal at too high of a level, resulting in distortion). You can lash 'em down in three ways:

✦ **Set your levels properly so the transients don't overload the converters.**

✦ **Make sure you have proper mic placement.**

✦ **Run the signal through a compressor when recording.**

A *compressor* is a piece of hardware (not included in your Avid interface) that controls the dynamics of your signal to keep your levels from getting too high.

Setting your levels properly

Back in the days of 16-bit digital recording (in ancient times, oh, ten years or so ago), you wanted to record at as high a level as possible without going over the maximum of 0 decibels (dB). The idea was to ensure the highest-possible fidelity by using as many of the available 16 bits as possible. If you recorded at lower levels, you used fewer bits, resulting in lower fidelity and higher noise levels.

Now, in the advanced age of digital, your best bet is to record with 24-bit resolution. Those extra 8 bits gained since the olden days free you from having to record at the highest level possible. In fact, you can put your max levels down around –12 dB and still end up with great-sounding tracks. Giving yourself that kind of room (called, logically enough, *headroom*) allows an instrument's transients to be recorded without causing problems with your converters.

I highly recommend recording with peak levels no more than –12 dB or –10 dB unless you run the incoming signal through a compressor before it hits your converters. Sure, your tracks will be quieter, but you can deal with that during mixing (Book VI, Chapter 1) and mastering (Book VII, Chapter 1).

Placing mics properly

A microphone that's too close to a loud sound source (or pointed too directly at the point of attack) can easily pick up extreme transients. In most cases, all you have to do is to pull the mic away from the instrument a little or turn it ever so slightly so it avoids picking up too high a signal. (I cover mic setup thoroughly in the "Setting Up Your Mics: Some Suggestions" section.)

**Book III
Chapter 2**

**Miking: Getting a
Great Source Sound**

The main thing to keep in mind when placing your microphones is to experiment. Don't be afraid to spend time making small adjustments. After all, the track you save could be your own.

Compressing carefully

Compressors are processors that allow you to control the *dynamics* of a signal — extremes of loudness or softness — and boy, are they ever versatile. You can use them on the front end while *tracking* (recording) instruments to ward off any stray transients. You can use them to level off an erratic performance. And you can use them to raise the overall apparent level of a mixed song. In this section, you explore the first use of compression: the control of transients. (You can find out about the other ways to use compression in Book VI, Chapter 3 and in Book VII, Chapter 2.)

The compressor is an invaluable tool when you record digitally because it enables you to record at high levels without worrying as much about digital clipping. The only problem is that the careful use of compression is an art that normally takes a while to get the hang of. Don't worry, though. In this chapter, you get some guidelines for using compression. And in Book VI, Chapter 4, I offer quite a few conservative compression settings for a variety of instruments to get you started.

Pro Tools includes a compressor plug-in with the software program. You can use this built-in compression if you're tweaking a session you already recorded. For that matter, you can use this feature when you're recording your tracks, but that won't do you any good. Remember that the Pro Tools compression system is digital: It can't work with analog signals. Your signal has to go through the A/D converter (and get changed from analog to digital) on its way to being recorded. The A/D converter in your Avid interface — not the compression plug-in — is first in line after the preamp. All this defeats the purpose of using a compressor to control transients. (Bummer.) In fact, the A/D converter is usually where you often get your first dose of distortion. (Ditto.) If you're serious about using compression on the front end to tame those transients, consider using an external preamp that you can insert into the signal chain before the A/D converter: that is, before the signal gets to your Avid interface.

Compressors have a series of dials that allow you to adjust several parameters:

+ **Threshold:** This setting dictates the level at which the compressor starts to act on the signal, listed in decibels. For the most part, you want to set the threshold level so the compressor acts on only the highest peaks of the signal.

+ **Ratio:** This setting determines the amount that the compressor affects the signal. The ratio — such as 2:1, for instance — means that for every decibel that the signal goes over the threshold setting, it is reduced by two. In other words, if a signal goes 1 dB over the threshold setting, its output from the compressor will only be ½ dB louder. The ratio is the one parameter that varies considerably from instrument to instrument because the level of the transient varies.

✦ **Attack:** This knob controls how soon the compressor starts, well, compressing. The attack is defined in milliseconds (ms); the lower the number, the faster the attack. For the most part, you're trying to control transients, and they happen at the beginning of a note. Therefore, you want the attack set to act quickly.

✦ **Release:** This parameter controls how long the compressor continues to affect the note after it starts. Like the attack, the release is defined in milliseconds. Because transients don't last very long, your best bet is usually a short release time if you're using compression on the front end.

✦ **Gain:** Use this knob to adjust the level of the signal leaving the compressor. The setting is listed in decibels. Because adding compression generally reduces the overall level of the sound, you use this control to raise the level back up to where it was going in.

✦ **Hard knee or soft knee:** Most compressors give you the option of choosing one or the other of these odd-sounding settings (or they do it for you, based on the setting you've chosen). Both refer to how the compressor behaves as the input signal passes the threshold.

- A *hard knee* applies the compression at an even rate, regardless of how far over the threshold the level is. Thus, if you choose a compression setting of 4:1, the compressor applies this ratio for any signal over the threshold limit. Hard-knee compression is used for instruments such as drums, where you need to clamp down on any transients quickly.

- The *soft knee,* by contrast, applies the compression at a varying rate that depends on how far over the threshold setting the signal is. The compressor gradually increases the ratio of the compression as the signal crosses the threshold until the amount matches the level you set. Soft-knee compression is used on vocals and on instruments where the signal doesn't have fast peaks.

Using compression is an art form. There is no one way to get the sound you want. Although I go into detail on compression and offer some great compressor settings for a variety of applications in Book VI, Chapter 4, keep in mind a couple of things while you think about using compression on your tracks:

✦ **You can always add compression to a recorded track, but you can never take it away.** If you're not sure how much compression to apply to a particular situation, you're much better off erring on the side of too little because you can always run the sound through another compressor if you need to.

✦ **If you can hear a change in the sound of your signal, you most likely have it set too high.** The reason to use a compressor on the front end is to eliminate extreme transients, which you can't hear when you play anyway. If your compression setting changes the sound at all, you would want to turn it down slightly — unless, of course, you're going for that effect.

Setting Up Your Mics: Some Suggestions

When you start to record, you discover an almost infinite number of ways to set up your mics. I can't go into them all here (as if I really knew them all, anyway), but what I can do is share the miking approaches that I use and have found to work for me. Okay, they're not just *my* approaches; they're pretty common ways for miking a variety of instruments.

Telling you that a particular mic position will work for you is like telling you that you'll like a particular ice cream flavor. I don't know your tastes, goals, or specific recording conditions, so I can't truly know what will work for you beforehand. Think of the miking techniques in this chapter as a starting point — and don't be afraid to experiment until you find the sound *you* want. There's no absolute right or wrong when it comes to miking. There's only what works for you and what doesn't. (Book I, Chapter 5 talks more about microphone types and how they're used.)

Vocals

Regardless of the type of studio you have or the style of music that you record, you'll probably record vocals at some point. And unfortunately, vocals are one of the most challenging instruments to do well. First, you have to find the right mic for the person who's singing, and then you need to try different approaches in order to get the best sound out of him or her. Fortunately, you're in luck. In the next few sections, I lead you through the (sometimes complicated) process of getting good lead and backup vocal sounds.

The room and the vocals

To get the best recording of vocals possible, you need a *dead* room — a room with no reverberation. (Book I, Chapter 2 has some tips on how to deaden your room.) Recording vocals in a dead room gives a sense of "presence" and allows you to add compression to the vocals without making them sound distant. (That "distance" results because the compressor raises the level of the background noise, particularly the reverberation from a live room that bounces the sound around a lot.)

The easiest way to deaden your room for vocal recording is to hang curtains, carpet, or blankets around the room, or to use the absorbent side of the reflector/absorber panels that I discuss in Book I, Chapter 2. Try to cover the area in front — and to both sides — of the vocal with sound-absorbent materials. (If you use the reflector/absorber panels described in Book I, Chapter 2, you'd better use stands because the panels are only four feet tall.)

The mics and the vocals

You have a lot of options for miking vocals. The type of mic you use dictates where you place it. Here's the gist:

✦ **Dynamic mic:** Dynamic mics sound best when you place them close to the singer's mouth. The effect that you get is gritty. (Huh? Okay, by gritty, I mean *dirty*. That's no help either? Let me see. . . .)

Dynamic mics produce a *midrange-dominated* sound: The high frequencies aren't reproduced well. You'll find that when a singer sings with the mic right in front of his or her mouth, the sound lacks even more high frequencies because of the proximity effect. That is, close range enhances the low-frequency response. What you get is a deep, bass-heavy sound that's often described as gritty or dirty. This type of sound can be great for matching the mood of some styles of rock and blues music.

To set up a dynamic mic for this purpose, just put it on a stand so the singer can get his or her mouth right up against the windscreen. With this type of singing style, I recommend a compressor setting that *pumps and breathes* — that is, you can hear the compressor working. See my discussion of compression in Book VI, Chapter 4 for a recommended setting.

✦ **Large-diaphragm condenser mic:** Large-diaphragm condenser mics are those most commonly used for vocals. These mics can clearly reproduce the entire audible frequency spectrum, emphasizing the low mids slightly at the same time. What you get is a nice warm, full-bodied sound. (That sounds like I'm describing a wine.) The *proximity* effect (how close the singer is to the mic) determines how nice and warm-bodied the sound is. The closer the singer is, the deeper and richer the tone can be.

When you set up a large-diaphragm condenser mic for vocals, place the mic in such a way that the nasty *sibilants* (the sound from singing *S* and *Sh* sounds) and pesky *plosives* (pops from singing *P* and *T* syllables) don't mess up your recordings. To deal with plosives and sibilants, you can either use a pop filter (see Book I, Chapter 2) or have the singer sing past (instead of right into) the mic. If you want the singer to sing past the mic, you can

- Place the mic above the singer and set it at an angle pointing away from him or her. (See the left side of Figure 2-8.)

- Set up the mic below the singer and angle it away from him or her. (See the right side of Figure 2-8.)

- Put the mic off to the side and face it toward the singer (the center of Figure 2-8) but not squarely in the path of the vocal.

Figure 2-8:
Place the mic at different angles to control sibilance and plosives.

 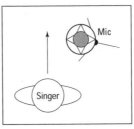 

✦ **Small-diaphragm condenser mic:** Small-diaphragm condenser mics create a much brighter, airier sound than their large-diaphragm cousins. You don't get the low-mid warmth of the large-diaphragm beast, so a small-diaphragm mic probably won't be your first choice as a vocal mic unless (for example) you're recording a female vocalist with a soprano voice and you want to catch the more ethereal quality of her higher frequencies.

You set up a small-diaphragm mic the same way you set up a large diaphragm mic.

✦ **Ribbon mic:** A ribbon mic is a good choice if you're looking for an intimate, crooner-type sound. (Think Frank Sinatra.) The ribbon mic is thought to add a silky sound to the singer's voice, produced by a slight dropoff in the high frequencies (not as severe as you'd get from a dynamic mic). To my drum-abused ears, ribbon mics have a kind of softness that large-diaphragm condenser mics don't have. The sound is more even, without the pronounced low-mid effect.

If you use a ribbon mic, you can set it up the same way you set up a condenser mic. You just need to be more careful about singing directly into a ribbon mic because the ribbon can break if you sing, speak, or breathe too hard into it.

Backup vocals

To record backup vocals, you can either track each part separately (using the same mic placement techniques that I describe earlier), or you can have all the backup singers sing at once into one or two mics. If you go for the latter method, you can use a stereo pair of mics, a figure-8 mic, or an omnidirectional mic.

If you use a stereo pair, I recommend setting them up in a coincident X-Y pattern. Have the vocalists stand next to each other, facing the mics at a distance of about three or four feet. Either large- or small-diaphragm mics work best for this setup. Check out Figure 2-9 for a neat top view of this arrangement.

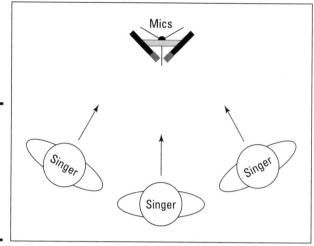

Figure 2-9:
The X-Y stereo miking pattern can work well for backup vocals.

If you choose to use a figure-8 mic, the singers can be placed at opposite sides of the mic (see Figure 2-10). The advantage of this setup is that the singers can look at each other while they sing, which helps keep the vocals tight.

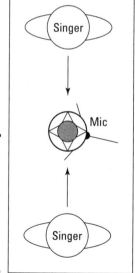

Figure 2-10:
Backup singers can stand on either side of a figure-8 mic and see each other.

An omnidirectional mic can also work well for backup vocals. In this case, the singers stand in a circle around the mic, as shown in Figure 2-11.

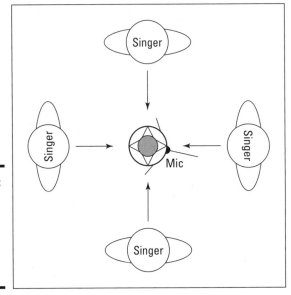

Figure 2-11:
Singers
stand in
a circle
around an
omnidirec-
tional mic.

Electric guitar

Miking your electric guitar is a personal thing. Every guitar player, it seems
to me (although I don't play guitar, so what do I know?), spends an awful lot
of time getting his or her "sound." If you're a *real* guitar player, you undoubtedly take great pride in getting your sound exactly right on tape — er, disc.
You likely spend countless hours tweaking your amp and adjusting the mic
to get it just right. On the other hand, if you're not a (harrumph) "real" guitar
player, you might just want to record the part and get it over with. Either
way, you can start looking for that perfect guitar sound by placing your mics
in one (or more) of the ways that I outline later in this chapter.

The room and the guitar

Whether you play through a small jazz chorus amp or power-chord your way
through a six-foot Marshall stack, the room that you play in has less impact
on your sound than it does if you play drums or sing. For the most part, look
for a room that is fairly dead — a room without natural reverberation. You
can always add effects later.

Guitar miking involves mostly spot mics, so your only consideration when
recording a guitar and using an amp is how your neighbors feel about the
noise, er, your most excellent guitar playing.

TIP

If you have finicky neighbors, you can put your guitar amp inside an amp-isolator box (see Book I, Chapter 2) to cut down on the noise. You can find the plans to build one on my website, www.jeffstrong.com. (Or, hey, you *could* try plugging the guitar directly into your Avid interface. You might like the sound you get. More about that in a minute.)

The mics and the guitar

The type of mic you choose depends largely on the type of sound you're looking for. For example, if you're looking for a distorted rock guitar sound with effects, you can get by just fine with a dynamic mic. If you favor a clean sound, a small-diaphragm condenser mic might work better for you. If you're going for a warm, full-bodied sound, try using a large-diaphragm condenser mic.

No matter which type of mic you use, you get the best sound from your amp speakers by putting the mic about 2–12 inches away from the cabinet, with the mic pointing directly at the cone of one of the amp speakers (specifically, the center of the speaker, which is that cone-shaped thing in the box). You can see this positioning in Figure 2-12.

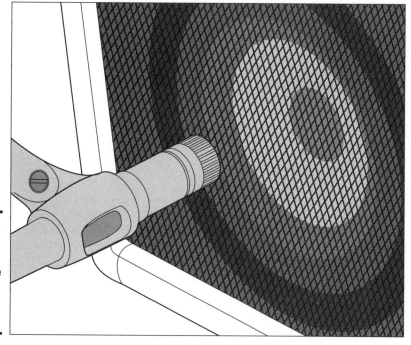

Figure 2-12:
Start by placing a mic near the cone of a speaker in your amp.

You might want to experiment with how far the mic is from the amp and the angle at which you point it. Sometimes just a slight movement in or out, left or right, can make all the difference in the world. You can even try pointing the mic at different speakers (if your amp has more than one) because each speaker has a slightly different sound.

For speaker cabinets that have more than one speaker, I know some engineers who actually disconnect all but one speaker to lower the overall volume without losing the intense, distorted sound. This can be especially beneficial if you have one of those amp stacks with a volume knob that goes to 11, and you just gotta crank the amp to get your "tone." (Come on, rockers, you know who you are.) This way you don't overload the mic (which creates the wrong kind of distortion) and can still get that nasty sound you're looking for.

If you can't quite get the sound that you want from your amp with the one mic pointed at the speaker cone, try adding a second mic about three or four feet away — also pointed directly at the speaker cone — to get a more ambient sound. This arrangement might also give your sound more life, especially if you have a room with natural reverberation. If you add a second mic, however, remember to watch for phase differences between the mics and make adjustments accordingly. (I discuss phase cancellation earlier in this chapter.)

Are you sick of the same old sound coming out of your amp? Wanna really shake things up (and I mean this literally)? Well, put your guitar amp in a tiled bathroom and crank it up. You can put a mic in the bathroom with your amp (a couple of feet away) and maybe another one just outside the door (experiment with how much you close or open the door). The effect is, well. . . . Try it and find out for yourself.

Electric bass

When you mic an electric bass, getting a good sound can be a real bear. Your two adversaries are *muddiness* (lack of definition) and *thinness* (a pronounced midrange tone). These seem almost polar-opposite characteristics, but they can both exist at the same time. I outline the best way to avoid these problems in the following sections.

Running your bass guitar directly into the board — via a direct box, your amp's Line Out jack, or a preamped input on your Avid interface — gives the guitar a punchier sound.

The room and the bass

The sound of an electric bass guitar can get muddy awfully fast. Your best bet is to choose a room that doesn't have a lot of reflective surfaces (such as paneled walls and wooden floors) that bounce the sound around. A dead room is easier to work with. Don't make your room too dead, however, or it just sucks the life out of your amp's tone. If you can get your amp to sound good in your room, placing the mic properly is easy.

Don't be afraid to be creative and to try recording your bass in different rooms. Look for a room with a warm sound to it. One thing, though: The bathroom amp trick doesn't work too well for a bass guitar, but it can be fun to try anyway.

The mics and the bass

Because the bass guitar produces low frequencies, a dynamic mic or a large-diaphragm condenser mic works well. I personally avoid using small-diaphragm condensers and ribbon mics for an electric bass, but try them if you want. Who knows? You might end up with an awesome bass track.

Mic placement for the electric bass is similar to the guitar; you place a single mic 2–12 inches away from one of the speakers. Sometimes, with bass, you can angle the mic and let the speaker's sound kind of drift past the diaphragm. Potentially, it's a great sound. For a bass, skip the distant mic (which generally just adds muddiness to the sound).

Acoustic guitars and such

At the risk of offending banjo, dobro, or ukulele players, I'm lumping all guitar-like (strummed or picked) acoustic string instruments together. I know, they all sound and play differently, but the microphone-placement techniques are similar for all these instruments. Allow me to explain.

Because all these instruments have a resonating chamber and are played with the instrument facing forward, you can pretty much use the same mic placement for any of them. You use different types of mics for different instruments, and I get to that in a minute.

The room and acoustic instruments

For recording acoustic instruments, the room plays a role in the sound that you end up recording. Unless you have a great-sounding room, you want to minimize its impact on your instrument's sound. You can do this in a couple of ways:

✦ **By recording with spot mics**

✦ **By placing absorber/reflectors in strategic places around your room**

  • *Absorberside-out* (toward the walls) if the room is too live

  • *Reflector-side-out* if the room is too dead

For example, if your studio is in a spare bedroom with carpeting and that awful popcorn stuff on the ceiling, you can put a couple of the reflector panels around your guitar player and the mic. This adds some reverberation to your guitar. Any unwanted reflections from the ceiling or walls are shielded from the mics because the absorber sides of the panels are facing the rest of the room.

The mics and the acoustic instruments

I prefer to use condenser mics when recording acoustic instruments. The type of condenser mic you use depends on the overall tonal quality that you want to capture or emphasize. For example, if a guitar has a nice, woody sound that you want to bring out in the recording, a large-diaphragm condenser mic is a good choice. On the other hand, if you're trying to capture the brightness of a banjo, a small-diaphragm mic is a better choice.

You can position your microphone in a variety of ways, and each accents certain aspects of the instrument's sound. Even a slight adjustment to the mic can have a significant impact on the sound. You might have to experiment quite a bit to figure out exactly where to put a mic.

To help with your experimentation, listen to the guitar carefully and move the mic around (closer in and farther out, to the left and right) until you find a spot that sounds particularly good. You need to get your ears close to the guitar to do this.

Here are some suggestions to get you started:

✦ Put the mic about 6–18 inches away from and 3–4 inches below the point where the neck meets the body of the guitar (or banjo, or whatever). Then make minor adjustments to the direction in which the mic points. Pointing it toward the sound hole(s) often gives you a richer, deeper tone. (This can translate to muddiness on some instruments.) Turning the mic more toward the neck brings out the instrument's brighter qualities. (See the image on the left in Figure 2-13.)

✦ Place a mic about three feet away from the instrument and point it directly at the sound hole. At this distance, you capture the rich sound from the sound hole and the attack of the strings. See the center image in Figure 2-13.

✦ Put a mic about six inches out from the bridge of the guitar. Try pointing the mic in different directions (slight movements of an inch or less can make a huge difference) until you find the spot that sounds best to you. See the image on the right in Figure 2-13.

✦ Try setting up a mic at about the same distance and angle from the instrument as the player's ears. Point the mic down toward the instrument so the mic is a couple of inches away from either side of the musician's head. This is an unorthodox approach that I like because I've found that guitar players adjust their playing style and intonation to correspond to what they're hearing when they play. With this technique, you're trying to capture exactly what the musician hears.

Drum set

If you're like most musicians, getting great-sounding drums seems like one of the world's great mysteries. (You know, along the lines of how the pyramids were built or how to cure cancer.) You can hear big, fat drums on great albums but when you try to record your drums, they always end up sounding more like cardboard boxes than drums. Fret not (hey, at least I didn't say that in the guitar section) because I have solutions for you.

First things first: Tuning your drums

The single most important part of getting killer drum sounds is to make sure your drums are tuned properly and that they have good heads on them. (Okay, that's two things.) Seriously, if you spend some time getting the drums to sound good in your room, you're already halfway to the drum sound of your dreams. There isn't space to go into detail here (especially if you play a large kit), but if you want specific drum-tuning guidance, you can do a search on the Internet or (ahem) check out a copy of my book, *Drums For Dummies* (Wiley).

You're looking for a clear, open tone on your drums. By and large, resist the temptation to apply duct tape or other dampeners to the drumheads. Drums that are deadened and don't ring clearly are *definitely* going to sound like cardboard boxes when you record them.

Figure 2-13:
Position the
mic like this
to produce
a good
acoustic
instrument
sound.

 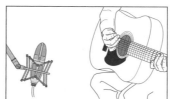 

What type of drum set?

If you want to buy a drum set for your studio, here are some guidelines that have worked for me:

- **Smaller drums can sound bigger.** At one point, I had two top-notch Gretsch drum sets in my studio. One was a rock kit that had a 24" kick; 13", 14", and 12" tom-toms; and a 6½" (deep) metal snare drum. The other was a small jazz kit, consisting of a 12" kick; 10" and 14" tom-toms; and a 5" (deep) wood snare. Guess what? Even for the hardest rock music, the small kit sounded much bigger. You tune the small drums down a bit, and they just sing!

- **Choose your heads wisely.** Not all heads are equal. Some sound great on stage, but others are better suited for the studio. Because the heads that come with a kit are (most likely) not the ones that sound the best on a recording, invest some money in testing different drumheads on your kit. I prefer either Remo pinstripes (great for rock and R&B) or coated ambassadors (great for jazz) on the top and either clear or coated ambassadors (either works, I just

choose what I like to look at) on the bottom of the drum.

- **Use cymbals with a fast decay.** Cymbals that sound great on stage are different from those that sound great in the studio. Stage cymbals often have long decays and slow attacks. This causes bleeding, especially through the tom-tom mics, and correcting the problem can be a headache. If you buy cymbals for your studio, choose those that have a very fast attack and a short decay.

- **More expensive isn't always better.** For recording, my favorite drum sets are used kits from the late 1960s and early 1970s. My all-time favorite recording set is a late 1960s Gretsch jazz drum set with a 12" kick drum, a 10" mounted tom-tom, and a 14" floor tom. For a snare, I love old 5" wooden snare drums (Gretsch, Ludwig, Slingerland, whatever). The last one of these sets I bought cost me $350, including all the mounting hardware and snare drum. It wasn't pretty, but boy, did it sound great.

After you get your drums tuned as well as you can, the next step is to take care of any rattles that might be coming from the stands or mounting hardware. Tighten up any loose hardware and move any stands that may be touching one another. You might need to make some small adjustments to the pitches of your drums if they're causing any hardware to rattle.

If you still have some ringing or unwanted overtones, you can deaden the drums slightly. Cotton gauze taped lightly on the edge of the head (away from the drummer) is often enough. If you want a really dry sound on your snare drum, you can use the wallet trick: Have the drummer place his or her wallet on the head. (Use the drummer's wallet — it'll probably be lighter because of all the money that isn't in it.)

When the tuning of your drums is perfect, you're ready to start placing some microphones. You can choose from an unlimited number of miking configurations, only a few of which I can cover here. (It would take a whole book to cover them all.)

The room and the drums

The room influences the drums' sound more than it influences that of the other instruments. If you're looking for a big drum sound, you need a fairly live room (one with lots of reflection).

I know you're thinking, "But all I have to work with is a bedroom for a studio, and it's carpeted." No worries; you can work with that. Remember, if you have a home studio, potentially you have your whole *home* to work with. Here are a couple of ideas to spark your imagination:

✦ Buy three or four 4' x 2' sheets of plywood and lean them up against the walls of your room. Also place one on the floor just in front of the kick drum. This adds some reflective surfaces to the room.

✦ Put the drums in your garage (or living room, or any other room with a reverberating sound) and run long mic cords to your mixer. If you have a laptop computer for your Pro Tools system, you can just throw it under your arm and move everything into your garage. Or, better yet, take all this stuff to a really great-sounding room and record.

✦ Set up your drums in a nice-sounding room and place an additional mic just outside the door to catch some additional ambient sound. You can then mix this with the other drum tracks to add a different quality of reverberation to the drums.

Kick (bass) drum considerations

The mic of choice for most recording engineers when recording a kick drum is a dynamic mic. In fact, you can find some large-diaphragm, dynamic mics specifically designed to record kick drums.

No matter where you place the mic, you can reduce the amount of boominess that you get from the drum by placing a pillow or blanket inside the drum. Some people choose to let the pillow or blanket touch the inside head. I prefer to keep it a couple of inches away from the inside head, but sometimes it's okay to let it touch the outside head.

That said, you can place your mic in several ways (all conveniently illustrated in Figure 2-14):

Book III
Chapter 2

Miking: Getting a
Great Source Sound

Figure 2-14:
You can place a mic in several places to get a good kick-drum sound.

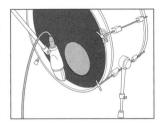

+ **Near the inside head:** If you take off the outside head or cut a hole in it, you can stick the mic inside the drum. Place the mic two to three inches away from the inside head and a couple of inches off center. This is the standard way to mic a kick drum if you have the outside head off or if a hole is cut in it. This placement gives you a sharp attack from the beater hitting the head.

+ **Halfway inside the drum:** You can modify the preceding miking technique by moving the mic back so it's about halfway inside the drum. In this case, place the mic right in the middle, pointing at where the beater strikes the drum. This placement gives you less of the attack of the beater striking the head and more of the body of the drum's sound.

+ **Near the outside head:** If you have both heads on the drum, you can place the mic a few inches from the outside head. If you want a more open, boomy sound (and you have the drum's pitch set fairly high), point the mic directly at the center of the head. If you want less boom, offset the mic a little and point it about two-thirds of the way toward the center.

If your drum sounds thin after trying these mic-placement approaches, you can try these two things:

+ **Tune the drum slightly higher.** In your quest for a deep bass tone, you might have tuned the drum too low. (This is especially common if you have a large bass drum.) In this case, the drum's fundamental tone might be too low to be heard clearly. Raising the pitch a bit usually solves the problem.

+ **Create a tunnel with acoustic panels.** Putting the mic in the tunnel often helps if you have a room that's too dead. Place two of the panels on their sides (reflective surfaces facing into the room) with one end of each panel near the outside of the drum. Angle the panels out so that where they are farthest from the drum set, the distance between them is just less than four feet. Then lay the other two panels (reflective surface facing down) across the side panels to create a tunnel. You can also place a piece of plywood on the floor under these panels to further increase the resonance. Place the mic halfway into the tunnel, facing the center of the drum.

Snare-drum considerations

A snare drum is probably the most important drum in popular music. The bass guitar can cover the kick drum's rhythm, and the rest of the drums aren't part of the main groove. A good, punchy snare drum can make a track, whereas a weak, thin one can eliminate the drive that most popular music needs.

Because the snare drum is located so close to the other drums (especially the hi-hats), a cardioid pattern mic is a must. The most common mic for a snare drum is the trusty Shure SM57. The mic is generally placed between the hi-hats and the small tom-tom about one or two inches from the snare drum head (see Figure 2-15). Point the diaphragm directly at the head. You might need to make some minor adjustments to eliminate any bleed from the hi-hats. This position gives you a nice, punchy sound.

If you want a crisper tone, you can add a second mic under the drum. Place this mic about an inch or two from the head with the diaphragm pointing at the snares. Make minor adjustments to minimize any leakage from the hi-hats.

If you have the available tracks, record each snare mic to a separate track and blend the two later during mixdown. If you don't have the available tracks, blend them until you have the sound that you want. You can also try reversing the phase of the bottom mic. (Some preamps have a phase switch for each channel, or you can reverse the phase by choosing AudioSuite⇨Other⇨Invert from the main menu.) Some people prefer the sound of the bottom mic this way.

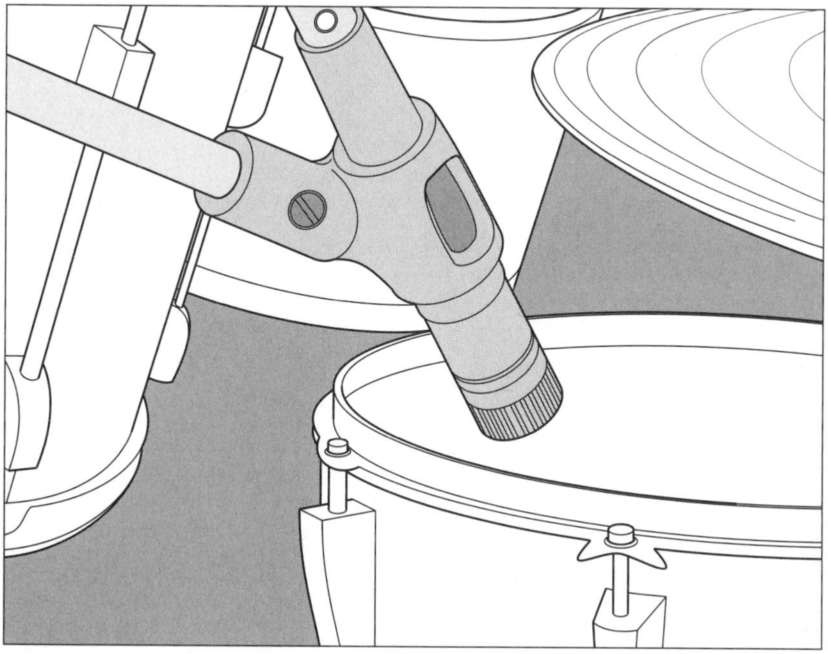

**Book III
Chapter 2**

**Miking: Getting a
Great Source Sound**

Figure 2-15:
The proper
placement
for a snare-
drum mic.

Tom-toms

Tom-toms sound best when you use a dynamic mic. For *mounted* toms (the ones above the kick drum), you can use one or two mics. If you use one mic, place it between the two drums about four to six inches away from the heads. (Figure 2-16 shows this placement option.) If you use two mics, place one above each drum about one to three inches above the head.

If you want a boomy sound with less attack, you can place a mic inside the shell with the bottom head off the drum.

Floor toms are miked the same way as mounted tom-toms:

+ Place a single mic a couple of inches away from the head near the rim.

+ If you have more than one floor tom, you can place one mic between them or mic them individually.

Hi-hats

Hi-hats are generally part of the main groove — as such, they're important enough that you want to spend some time getting a good sound. You'll probably have problems with a few other mics on the drum set picking up the hi-hats, particularly the snare drum mic and overhead mics. (Some people don't even bother miking the hi-hats for this reason.)

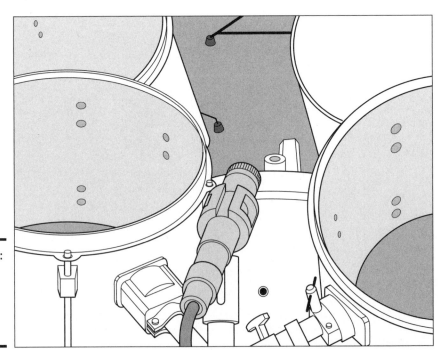

Figure 2-16: Miking mounted tom-toms with one mic.

I like to mic hi-hats because, to me, these cymbals often sound too trashy through the snare-drum mic. If you mic the hi-hats, make sure that the snare-drum mic is picking up as little of the hi-hats as possible by placing it properly.

You can use either a dynamic mic or, better yet, a small diaphragm condenser mic for the hi-hats. The dynamic mic gives you a trashier sound, and the small diaphragm condenser mic produces a bright sound. You can work with either by adjusting the EQ. I usually add just a little bit (4 dB or so) of a shelf equalizer set at 10 kHz to add just a little sheen to the hi-hats. Book VI, Chapter 3 covers EQ in detail.

Place the mic about three to four inches above the hi-hats and point it down. The exact placement of the mic is less important than the placement of the other instrument mics because of the hi-hats' tone. Just make sure your mic isn't so close that you hit it instead of the cymbal.

Cymbals

You want to know one secret to the huge drum sound of the Led Zeppelin drummer, John Bonham? Finesse. He understood (I'm guessing, because I never really talked to him about this) that the drums sound louder and bigger in a mix if the cymbals are quieter in comparison. So he played his cymbals softly and hit the drums pretty hard. This allowed the engineer to boost the levels of the drums without having the cymbals drown everything else out. Absolutely brilliant.

Because the drums bleeding into the overhead mics is inevitable and the overhead mics are responsible for providing much of the drums' presence in a mix, playing the cymbals softly allows you to get more of the drums in these mics. This helps the drums sound bigger.

 Ask (no, demand) that your drummer play the cymbals more quietly. Also use smaller cymbals with a fast attack and a short decay. Doing these things creates a better balance between the drums and cymbals and makes the drums stand out more in comparison.

Small-diaphragm condenser mics capture the cymbals' high frequencies well. You can mic the cymbals by placing mics about six inches above each cymbal or by using overhead mics set one to three feet above the cymbals. (See the next section for more on overhead mic placement.)

The whole kit

Most of the time, you want to have at least one (but preferably two) ambient mics on the drums, if for no other reason than to pick up the cymbals. These (assuming you use two mics) are *overhead mics,* and (as the name implies) you place them above the drum set (usually by means of a boom stand). The most common types of mics to use for overheads are large- and small-diaphragm condenser mics because they pick up the high frequencies in the cymbals and give the drum set's sound a nice sheen (brightness). You also might want to try a pair of ribbon mics to pick up a nice, sweet sound on the overheads.

Remember that ribbon mics can be fragile.

To mic the drum set with overhead mics, you can use either the X-Y coincident technique or spaced stereo pairs. Place them one to two feet above the cymbals, just forward of the drummer's head. Place X-Y mics in the center and set up spaced stereo pairs so they follow the 3:1 rule. (The mics should be set up three to six feet apart if they are one to two feet above the cymbals.) This counters any phase problems. Point the mic down toward the drums, and you're ready to record. Figure 2-17 shows both of these setups.

Hand drums

Hand drums can be anything from the familiar conga to unusual drums such as the North African tar, Middle Eastern doumbek, or Brazilian Pandeiro. Because you might encounter many types of hand drums, this section gives you some general guidelines when recording any hand drum.

Your selection in mics depends on the type of drum and its tonal characteristics. For example, conga drums occupy the middle of the frequency spectrum and produce a loud sound that a large diaphragm condenser mic can capture well. Or if you want a tighter, drier sound, you can use a dynamic mic. If you choose the dynamic mic, the mic colors the sound of your recording.

If you want to record any number of the smaller, higher-pitched hand drums, use either a large or small diaphragm condenser mic and skip the dynamic mic altogether.

Figure 2-17:
Overhead mics capture the cymbals and the drums.

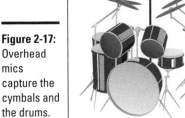

X-Y mics 1-2 feet above cymbals

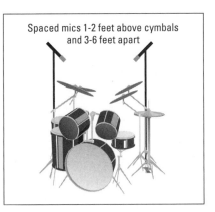

Spaced mics 1-2 feet above cymbals and 3-6 feet apart

Mic placement also varies considerably among the various hand drums. Listen to the sound of the drum and find a place where you like what you hear. For the most part, placing the mic anywhere from one to three feet from the drum creates the fullest sound. If you want a lot of attack, you can place the mic closer. You lose some of the drum's depth, however, when you place the mic closer than one foot.

Percussion

Miscellaneous percussion instruments, such as shakers and triangles, are nice additions to many styles of music. These instruments sound best with a good condenser mic. I choose a large or small diaphragm mic, depending on the characteristics that I want to pick up. For instance, a shaker can sound great with a large diaphragm mic because this mic brings out the lower frequencies of the instrument slightly and softens the overall sound a bit.

The room and the percussion

Most of the time, the room doesn't have a huge effect on percussion instruments because you mic them closely. If your room does get in the way, use the acoustic panels in much the same way that I suggest for vocals earlier in this chapter (partially surround the mic and musician with baffles).

The mics and the percussion

Both large and small diaphragm mics work well for percussion. The main thing to remember when recording percussion instruments is that they can have a high SPL (Sound Pressure Level, or just plain volume), so you might need to pad the mic.

As far as mic placement goes, I like to put a single mic anywhere from 6–18 inches away, depending on the size of the instrument. For example, because maracas are loud, I put the mic back a bit (18 inches), whereas with a triangle, I find that 6–8 inches sounds best.

Chapter 3: Preparing to Record

In This Chapter

✔ **Understanding record modes**

✔ **Allocating disk space**

✔ **Setting levels**

✔ **Monitoring track inputs**

✔ **Creating click tracks**

After you get your mics set up — see Chapter 2 of this mini-book for more on that — and before you actually start to record, you can still do a few things to make the process easier and to optimize the performance of your system. This chapter covers all you need to do before you actually start to record. For starters, this includes understanding and using Record modes and dealing with disk allocation.

This chapter also shows you how to enable your tracks to record, set your levels to give you the best sound possible, and manage your monitoring setup to perform at your best. To top it off, this chapter guides you through setting up a click track, song tempo, and meter map so when it comes time to edit your audio (not that your performances *need* editing), you'll be able to do it quicker and with less effort. If you're not sure what click tracks, tempo maps, and meter maps are, don't worry. By the time you finish this chapter, you'll be throwing these terms around like a seasoned sound engineer.

Recognizing Record Modes

Pro Tools offers the following four Record modes: Non-Destructive, Destructive, Loop, and QuickPunch. You can choose the mode you want by selecting the mode from the Options section of the main menu (choose Options➪QuickPunch) or by Control-clicking (Mac) or right-clicking (PC) the Record button in the Transport window. All this clicking cycles you through the four Record modes.

Each Record mode has its place, and knowing which one to use for a given situation can help you greatly in the efficiency department. These different modes are detailed in the following sections.

You can see which mode you're in by looking at the Record button in the Transport window. The modes are designated, as shown in Figure 3-1.

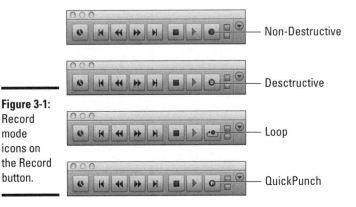

Figure 3-1:
Record
mode
icons on
the Record
button.

Non-Destructive

Desctructive

Loop

QuickPunch

Non-Destructive Record mode

Non-destructive recording is the default setting in Pro Tools. Whenever you record in this mode, a new audio file is created without erasing any previous files or clips. This new file gets added automatically to the Audio Clips list, where it resides with other recorded files. (This list is located on the right side of the Edit window. If it's not visible, click the double arrow at the bottom right of the Edit window.)

Destructive Record mode

Recording in *Destructive Record* mode erases any and all previously recorded audio clips found on that particular track, which basically mirrors the way traditional analog tape recorders work. This can be handy for keeping your hard drives from becoming full quickly, but you don't get a chance to use a previous take after you recorded over it. Because Non-Destructive Record mode is the default mode (see the preceding section), you need to select Destructive Record mode from either the Options menu (choose Options⇨Destructive from the main menu) or Control-click (Mac) or right-click (PC) the Record button in the Transport window until the D icon appears on the Record button, as shown in Figure 3-1.

Loop Record mode

Loop recording consists of choosing a start and end point on a track and having this section play over and over again while you record and rerecord. Each time the loop runs, it creates a new audio clip. That way, you can record a difficult section of a song as many times as you want and still have all the takes available for review later on. To enable Loop Record mode, chose Options⇨Loop Record or Control-click (Mac) or right-click (PC) the Record button in the Transport window until the Loop Record icon appears in the Record button. (Refer to Figure 3-1.)

To create a loop to record to, follow these steps:

1. **Enter the start point for your loop in the Start field of the Transport window.**

   The Transport window runs along the top of the Edit window. Its (many) features are discussed in detail in Book II, Chapter 4.

2. **Enter the end point for your loop in the End field in the Transport window.**

3. **(Optional) If you want a pre-roll, enter an amount of time for it to run, using the Pre-Roll field of the Transport window.**

   A *pre-roll,* by the way, is a section of your song before where you actually start recording that plays when you hit the Record button. A pre-roll happens only before the first time through the loop. After that, the loop runs the same way each time through: from start point to end point and then back to the start point.

To find out how to review a bunch of audio clips you recorded using loops, check out the section on auditioning takes in Chapter 4 of this mini-book.

QuickPunch Record mode

QuickPunch Record mode is great for manually adding a corrected musical phrase on the fly — *punching in* (starting to record) and *punching out* (stopping the recording process) onto record-enabled tracks while the song plays. Of course, you can punch in and out in Destructive and Non-Destructive modes (by selecting start and end points), but QuickPunch is designed for use on the fly: You can punch in and out up to 100 times during each pass of the song. To select QuickPunch Record mode, choose it from the Options menu (choose Options⇨QuickPunch from the main menu) or Control-click (Mac) or right-click (PC) the Record button in the Transport window until the QuickPunch icon (a little P; refer to Figure 3-1) appears on the Record button.

Using QuickPunch also ensures that you can constantly hear the audio while the punch in and punch out happen, seamlessly switching between monitoring the already-recorded track and monitoring the input source for the track being punched.

By default, Pro Tools switches automatically from the recorded material to the fresh input when the punch is enabled, and then back again when the punch is disabled. If you don't want this feature and prefer hearing your input source before and after the punch (as well as during the punch), choose Track⇨Input Only Monitoring from the main menu. (This is detailed in the "Monitoring Your Tracks" section, later in this chapter.)

Dealing with Disk Allocation

Recording and playing back audio tracks is a hard-drive-intensive process. To make this process as smooth as possible, set up your hard drive for the best possible *(optimized)* disk allocation to specify where your tracks get stored.

Basically, *optimizing* in this context means to limit how much hard-drive space is used for recording audio or to record to more than one hard drive. I cover both options in the following sections.

Allocating hard drive space

How fast you can write to or read from a hard drive depends on where the data is on the disk; if it's all over the place, the hard drive has to hunt for it, which means the data takes longer to read. To minimize any jumping around the hard drive has to do to find the data, you can tell Pro Tools to put your recorded audio on only a limited portion of the disk. This process — *disk allocation* — speeds up access time. (You'll find that certain types of hard-drive formats, such as HFS+ and NTFS, are especially prone to slow-pokiness and can benefit from this "marking off" of available disk space.)

To allocate your hard drive space, follow these steps:

1. **Choose Setup⇨Preferences from the main menu.**

   The Preferences dialog box duly appears.

2. **Click the Operation tab at the top of the Preferences dialog box.**

   The Preferences dialog box puts on its Operation face.

3. **In the Open Ended Record Allocation section, choose the Limit To radio button.**

4. **In the Limit To text field, type in a time slightly longer than the longest song you usually record.**

   This limits the maximum file size so that Pro Tools places it within certain boundaries on the hard drive, thus reducing the real estate that must be traveled for each file.

If you expect that you might end up with a really long song, select the Use All Available Space radio button, or choose a really high number (say, 60 minutes) for your limit. That way your recording won't stop before you want it to.

Using multiple hard drives for audio

One way to increase your ability to record and play back more tracks is to have more than one hard drive dedicated to audio. Yup, this means having *three* hard drives in your computer: one for the system files and applications, and two for audio.

To allocate a specific hard drive on which to record a track, choose Setup⇨Disk Allocation from the main menu to open the Disk Allocation dialog box (as shown in Figure 3-2). From this dialog box, you can manually choose the hard drive that each audio track is recorded to by clicking and holding the track name (a drop-down menu opens) and selecting one of the drives from the list. All the drives in your computer will show up in this list. Or you can select the Use Round Robin Allocation for New Tracks check box, in which case, Pro Tools distributes the tracks serially to more than one hard drive. All your files are placed in a folder created for the session by Pro Tools.

To designate a different folder to which to record your tracks, check the Custom Allocation Options check box and then click the Change button. Select the folder from the dialog box that appears.

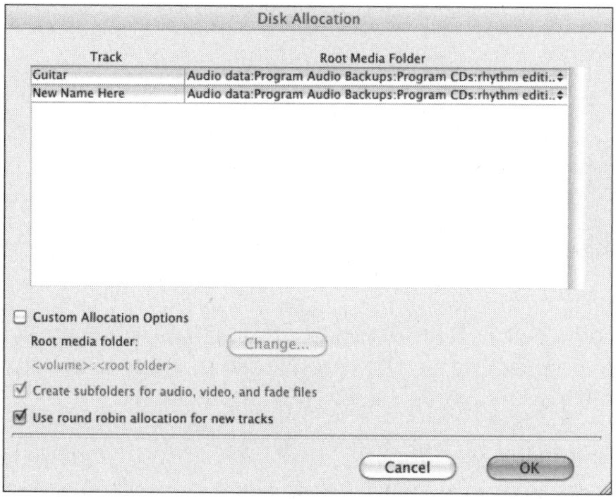

Figure 3-2:
The Disk Allocation dialog box lets you choose where your audio files record to.

	Disk Allocation
Track	Root Media Folder
Guitar	Audio data:Program Audio Backups:Program CDs:rhythm editi.. ⬦
New Name Here	Audio data:Program Audio Backups:Program CDs:rhythm editi.. ⬦

☐ Custom Allocation Options
Root media folder: (Change...)
<volume>:<root folder>
☑ Create subfolders for audio, video, and fade files
☑ Use round robin allocation for new tracks

(Cancel) (OK)

If you want to record audio to the system drive, bear in mind that audio takes up a big honkin' lot of space, which could compromise system performance. Choose the system drive to record only if you have no other options — say, if you have only one hard drive in your system or all your other drives are full.

Enabling Recording

When you enable recording for a track, you're ready to go. But before you click that ol' Record Enable button, check out what I have to say about the ins and outs of enabling recording, using Latch mode, and running Record Safe mode. Doing so might help you avoid some common pitfalls.

Record-enabling

Enabling a track for recording (the audio buzzwords are *record-enabling*) is easy: Just click the Record Enable button for that track in the Edit or the Mix window (see Figure 3-3). The track will stay in Record mode until you either click another track's Record Enable button or you toggle out of Record mode (by clicking the track's Record Enable button one more time).

Figure 3-3:
The Record Enable button in the Mix window (left) and the Edit window (right) arms the track for recording.

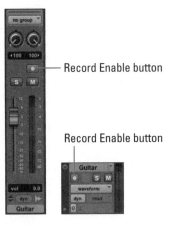

— Record Enable button

Record Enable button

You can keep a track in Record mode when you move on and enable other tracks. To do so, just engage the Latch mode (see the next section) or hold down the Shift key while you select your other track(s).

Aside from simply clicking the Record Enable button, you are free to use keyboard shortcuts to enable all tracks or selected tracks. These are done the following ways:

✦ **To record-enable all tracks:** Option-click (Mac) or Alt-click (PC) the Record Enable button of any track.

✦ **To record-enable selected tracks:** Shift-click each track to select multiple tracks and then Shift+Option-click (Mac) or Shift+Alt-click (PC) the Record Enable button on one of the selected tracks. You can select grouped tracks to enable by highlighting the group in the Edit Groups list (located in the lower left of the Edit window) and then Shift+Option-clicking (Mac) or Shift+Alt-clicking (PC) a Record Enable button on one of the tracks in the group.

This step is a timesaver only if you already have some tracks selected and you want to record-enable them. If your tracks aren't already selected, Shift-clicking the Record Enable button on each track is much faster.

After you have one or more tracks enabled for recording, you can click Record and then Play to start recording. (Chapter 4 of this mini-book has more on the intricacies of recording.)

Using Latch Record Enable mode

With Pro Tools, you have the option of latching — or unlatching — your Record Enable buttons. In Latch Record Enable mode, you basically "lock" down record-enabling so that when you enable recording on one track and then move to enable recording on another track, the first track stays in Record Enable mode. This allows you to consecutively enable more than one track.

With Latch Record Enable mode off, when you enable one track and then go to enable another track, the first track turns off and is no longer record-enabled.

Now that that's straight, here's how you actually turn Latch Record Enable mode on and off:

1. **Choose Setup⇨Preferences from the main menu.**

2. **From the Preferences dialog box that appears, click the Operation tab.**

The Operation view of the Preferences dialog box appears.

3. **Select the Latch Record Enable Buttons check box to turn it on.**

This check box is located in the upper right of the window, as shown in Figure 3-4.

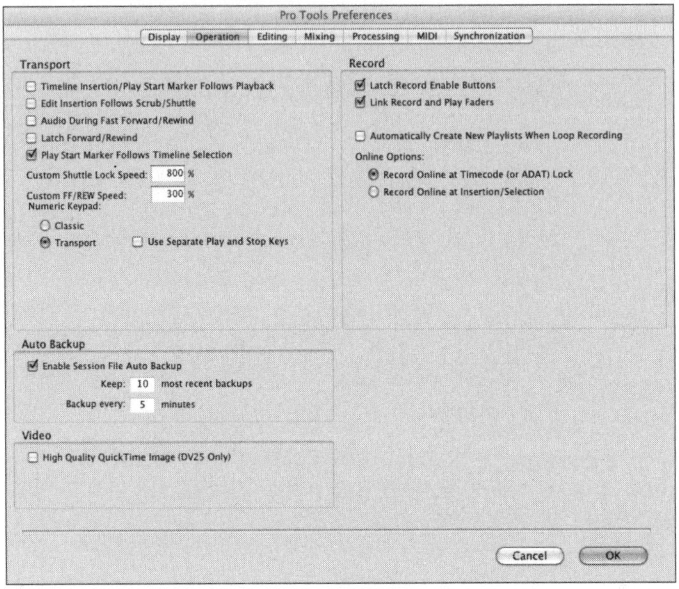

Pro Tools Preferences

Display | Operation | Editing | Mixing | Processing | MIDI | Synchronization

Transport

☐ Timeline Insertion/Play Start Marker Follows Playback
☐ Edit Insertion Follows Scrub/Shuttle
☐ Audio During Fast Forward/Rewind
☐ Latch Forward/Rewind
☑ Play Start Marker Follows Timeline Selection
Custom Shuttle Lock Speed: 800 %
Custom FF/REW Speed: 300 %
Numeric Keypad:
○ Classic
◉ Transport   ☐ Use Separate Play and Stop Keys

Record

☑ Latch Record Enable Buttons
☑ Link Record and Play Faders

☐ Automatically Create New Playlists When Loop Recording
Online Options:
◉ Record Online at Timecode (or ADAT) Lock
○ Record Online at Insertion/Selection

Auto Backup

☑ Enable Session File Auto Backup
    Keep: 10 most recent backups
    Backup every: 5 minutes

Video

☐ High Quality QuickTime Image (DV25 Only)

Cancel   OK

Figure 3-4:
Select the Latch Record Enable Buttons check box to choose more than one track to record-enable.

Running Record Safe mode

Record Safe mode does for your tracks what Write Protect features used to do for a floppy disk or a Zip disk in the olden days: namely, make it impossible for you to record-enable a track. This is a truly helpful feature that has saved me from accidentally recording over an already great track. To put a track into Record Safe mode, ⌘-click (Mac) or Ctrl-click (PC) the track's Record Enable button. (Remember: You can find the Record Enable button in the Edit window or the Mix window; refer to Figure 3-3.) If you clicked correctly, the Record Enable button will gray out, as shown in Figure 3-5. To reverse this procedure, ⌘-click (Mac) or Ctrl-click (PC) the button again.

Figure 3-5:
Using Record Safe mode disables the Record Enable button.

If you want, you can put more than one track at a time in Record Safe mode. Here's how:

+ **Placing selected tracks in Record Safe mode:** ⌘+Option+Shift-click (Mac) or Ctrl+Alt+Shift-click (PC) the Record Enable button for one of the selected tracks. This step assumes that you have tracks already selected; Shift-click the track names in the Edit or the Mix window to select them. If the tracks aren't already selected, ⌘-clicking (Mac) or Ctrl-clicking (PC) the track's Record Enable button for each track is much quicker.

+ **Placing all tracks in Record Safe mode:** ⌘+Option-click (Mac) or Ctrl+Alt-click (PC) the Record Enable button on any track.

To toggle either selection off, just repeat whatever click combination you used to get the multiple tracks selected in the first place.

Setting Levels

One of the most important parts of getting good recordings is to get your recording levels just right. Too low, and your instrument sounds thin or weak; too much level and you risk *clipping* (distorting) the signal.

In order to get a signal into Pro Tools, you need to

Book III
Chapter 3

Preparing to Record

+ Record-enable a track.
+ Have the Input selector set to the hardware input your instrument or microphone is plugged in to.

Book II, Chapter 3 has more on inputs in general and Input selectors in particular.

After you do this, you can set the recording level in Pro Tools by

+ **Using the preamp trim knob in your Avid audio interface:** The Digidesign 003, 003 Rack, 002, 002 Rack, and Avid Mbox Pro have four preamps, and the Avid Eleven Rack, Mbox and Mboxe Mini have two preamps. You can plug your microphone or your electric guitar or bass directly into the input and adjust the trim knob until you get a good signal showing in the track's level meter. (*Good* here means peaks that don't rise above the yellow. See the "What's a good level to record at?" sidebar.)

Condenser mics need phantom power to function. You can turn on phantom power to the channels with preamps by engaging the switch on the back panel of the interface.

✦ **Using the Line In inputs in your interface and adjusting the output level of your instrument via the instrument's volume control:** If you use Line In inputs, your instrument needs to be at line level. This means that you can plug your synthesizer directly into these inputs. However, if you want to use a microphone or an electric guitar or bass, you need to boost the signal beforehand.

For microphones, this involves using an external preamp and plugging your mic into the preamp and the preamp into your audio interface. For an electric guitar or bass, you need a *direct box* (or a preamp with a direct box connection). You place this device between your guitar's output and the audio input. Make adjustments to your signal level at this device, using the device's gain control.

The Volume fader for the track has no control over the Input level. It controls only the playback and monitoring level. If you want to adjust the Input level, you need to make the adjustments on your interface or preamp. (Check your owner's manual if you're not sure how to do this.)

Adjust the level of your input until you get a reading of the highest notes somewhere in the middle of the yellow range in the track's level meter.

What's a good level to record at?

Professional recording engineers debate as to what's the best level to record at in a digital recorder (such as Pro Tools). Some say you should get as high of a level as possible to take full advantage of the dynamic range that digital recording offers. Others say that it's better to record a little lower so you don't overload the summing bus of the software when it comes time to mix. According to this theory, doing so prevents unintentional clipping (distortion, in other words) from extreme transients (the initial attack of the instrument) when recording. So, which way should you go?

Well, because I record a lot of instruments with fast, extreme transients (such as drums), I fall into the "record lower to be safe" category. Typically I go for a level around –12 decibels (dB), with peaks no higher than –6 dB. (If you follow my lead here, your level meter should read in the low- to middle-yellow range.) This gives me a good signal that has plenty of dynamic range but still leaves some *headroom* (room for more signal before clipping) to work with. It also minimizes any possibility of extreme transients ruining the take.

I'm going to recommend, then, that you keep your maximum levels squarely in the low to middle of the yellow range in the track's level meter, regardless of the type of instrument you want to record. If you follow my advice, you'll definitely thank me when you start to mix all your tracks together. (Check out Book VI for more on mixing.)

Setting a Record Range

When you record in Pro Tools, you can start and stop your session while you record, or you can set a recording range so the Pro Tools starts and stops the recording process for you. This can be useful if you have your hands full with instruments and you don't want to take the chance that you'll miss your desired start or stop point by doing it by hand.

You can set the recording range by using one of these methods:

✦ **Type a start and end time into the Start and End fields of the Transport window.** For a detailed look at the Transport window, check out Book II, Chapter 4.

✦ **Select a range in the ruler or in a track's playlist.**

- *The ruler method:* Simply adjust the two blue arrows along the timeline until you have the Beginning arrow and the End arrow where you want them.

- *The track playlist method:* This is when you set beginning and end times by dragging across the record range with the Selector tool.

  Note: You must have the Link Timeline and Edit Selections turned on. This is done either by choosing Options⇨Link Timeline and Edit Selections from the main menu or by clicking the Link button in the Edit window. (The Link button, as shown here in the margin, is on the long, black toolbar right above the timeline in the Edit window. Book II, Chapter 4 tells you more about it.) To turn Link Timeline and Edit Selections off again, click the Link button again or choose Link Timeline and Edit Selections from the Options menu.

Of course, if you don't want to preset the recording range — letting the clips fall where they may, as it were — don't select either of these options and just let the playing start wherever it is and run to the end.

You can also set a pre-roll and post-roll time in the Transport window. You use pre-roll and post-roll settings to designate an amount of time for the song to play before (pre-roll) or after (post-roll) the actual recording happens. This can help you get into the groove of the song before you need to start worrying about how well you're playing.

Monitoring Your Tracks

To record effectively, you need to hear what you're doing. This is *monitoring*. Managing your input monitoring in Pro Tools involves setting up your monitor configuration and output and balancing between lowest *latency* (the delay between input and output of the sound) and system performance. These areas are detailed in this section.

Setting up monitoring

To set up your monitoring, you first need to choose the output of the tracks you want to monitor so they match the main outputs on your system. Do this by selecting the outputs in each track's Output selector, located above the Pan control in the Mix window. (Book II, Chapter 4 has more than you'd ever need to know about Output selectors and Mix windows.)

Choosing a monitor mode

Pro Tools has two monitor modes: Auto Input monitoring and Input Only Monitoring. (More on what these terms actually mean in a minute.) You can select between these two options by checking or unchecking Track⇨Input Only Monitoring from the main menu. (See Figure 3-6.)

Figure 3-6: You can choose to monitor input only from the Track menu.

Auto Input Monitoring mode

In Auto Input Monitoring mode, you hear your previously recorded audio (if any exists) on a record-enabled track right up until the point you start to record. After recording has begun, you hear the input source while it's being recorded. After the recording is done, Pro Tools switches you back to hearing the previously recorded stuff. This is useful for doing *punch recording,* where you start and stop recording while the session plays. This is the default setup for Pro Tools and is active when you don't have Input Only Monitoring checked in the Track menu.

Input Only Monitoring mode

In Input Only Monitoring mode, you hear only the input source through your monitors, regardless of whether other stuff is recorded on that track. When this mode is enabled, the Record button in the Transport window is green. When this mode is not enabled, the Record button is red. To enable this, choose Track⇨Input Only Monitoring.

Linking and unlinking Record and Playback faders

You have the option of "linking" the fader on your tracks when in Record Enable or Playback mode (meaning that moving the fader in one mode moves it the same distance in the other mode) or "unlinking" them (so you can maintain separate fader levels in each mode). If you opt for the unlinking option, Pro Tools remembers where your fader was set in both Record Enable mode and Playback mode and returns the fader to its position when you switch between these modes.

Unlinking your Record and Playback faders allows you to set the level differently for playback and record. This can be useful for punch recording because you can adjust both the recorded stuff and your input source independently and have the same relative levels between your previously recorded track and the input in the mix. Otherwise, your input source might be too loud or too soft in comparison.

To link Record and Playback faders, follow these steps:

1. **Choose Setup⇨Preferences from the main menu.**

2. **Click the Operation tab at the top of the Preferences dialog box that opens.**

The Preferences dialog box presents you with its Operation face.

3. **Select or clear the Link Record and Play Faders check box located in the column on the right, as shown in Figure 3-7, depending which way you want to work.**

Figure 3-7:
The Link Record and Play Fader check box.

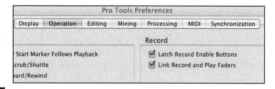

4. **Click OK.**

Adjusting monitoring latency

All digital systems have some *latency* — delay between the input of the audio and its output. Latency used to be a big deal in computer-based systems because to record more than a couple of tracks at once, you had to set your system — usually by using a high H/W (hardware) buffer size — resulting in painfully noticeable latency. This lag made it hard for many musicians to record because they heard a distracting delay in their headphones while they recorded.

Nowadays, latency isn't such a big deal because computers are often powerful enough to be able to handle a lower buffer size while recording. You can lower the buffer size in the Playback Engine dialog box, as shown in Figure 3-8. (To access the Playback Engine dialog box, just choose Setup⇨ Playback Engine from the main menu.) Depending on your Avid interface, you have the choice between 32, 64, 128, 256, 512, and 1024 samples. The lower the number, the lower the latency.

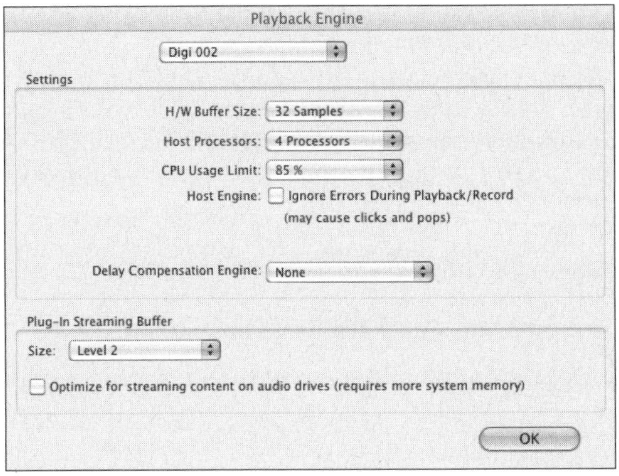

Figure 3-8:
Use H/W
Buffer Size
settings
to control
the latency
your system
produces.

Playback Engine	
Digi 002	
Settings	
H/W Buffer Size:	32 Samples
Host Processors:	4 Processors
CPU Usage Limit:	85 %
Host Engine:	☐ Ignore Errors During Playback/Record
	(may cause clicks and pops)
Delay Compensation Engine:	None
Plug-In Streaming Buffer	
Size:	Level 2
☐ Optimize for streaming content on audio drives (requires more system memory)	
	OK

For most recordings, you can get by with either 256-sample or 128-sample settings. When recording at 44.1 kHz, this represents only about a 3- and a 6-millisecond (ms) delay, respectively. This is equivalent to standing three or six feet away from your instrument/amp/speaker. As little as this is, you may find that high a buffer size distracting with headphones on — and may want to go lower when you record percussive instruments. Personally, I choose 32 whenever I can and will accept 64 if I get a lot of errors while recording. When mixing lots of tracks with a bunch of plug-ins, you want to adjust this to a higher setting — such as 512 or even 1024 — depending on the speed of your processor.

Using low-latency monitoring

If you want the least amount of latency possible and you don't mind not hearing reverb or other effects through your headphones, go for the low-latency monitoring option: Just choose Options⇨Low Latency Monitoring from the main menu. (See Figure 3-9.)

Options	Setup	Window	Marketplace
Destructive Record			
Loop Record			⌥L
✓ QuickPunch			⇧⌘P
Prepare DPE Tracks			
Transport Online			⌘J
Video Track Online			*⇧⌘J*
Video out FireWire			
Scrub in Video Window			
Pre/Post-Roll			⌘K
Loop Playback			⇧⌘L
Dynamic Transport			^⌘P
Edit Window Scrolling			▶
✓ Link Timeline and Edit Selection			
✓ Link Track and Edit Selection			
✓ Mirror MIDI Editing			
✓ Automation Follows Edit			
✓ Click			
✓ MIDI Thru			
Auto-Spot Clips			⌥⌘P
✓ Pre-Fader Metering			
Solo Mode			▶
Edit/Tool Mode Keyboard Lock			^⇧T
Delay Compensation			
Low Latency Monitoring			

Figure 3-9:
The Low Latency Monitoring option is located on the Options menu.

Low-latency monitoring bypasses the internal mixer in Pro Tools and sends the input's sound back out without processing it. This reduces latency, but it also limits what you can do. Here are some of the "strings attached" that come with low-latency monitoring:

✦ **Low-latency monitoring applies only to outputs 1 and 2 on your hardware.** Any tracks set to another output can't be monitored this way, so you must choose outputs 1 and 2 as your outputs for the track you want to monitor.

✦ **None of the plug-ins that you have routed to tracks 1 and 2 can be heard in this mode.**

✦ **Tracks set to record from an internal bus (a submix, for example) can't be monitored this way.** You can use this mode only for tracks that use a hardware input.

✦ **Tracks that you're recording to won't show up in the levels at the Master Fader channel.**

The Avid 2nd and 3rd Generation Mboxes offer a Zero-Latency Monitoring option that allows you to dial in your input monitoring to Pro Tools playback on the hardware. This works very well and eliminates the need for engaging the Low-Latency Monitoring function in the software.

Creating a Click Track

A *click track* is basically a metronome that you can listen to while recording to ensure that you stay in time with the session. Recording to a click track can have many advantages, including being able to match the song's sections to particular bars or beats within the session. It also makes finding edit points and performing certain edits much easier. I always spend a few minutes setting up a click track for my songs, and I recommend that you give it try, too. This is especially important of you want to use Beat Detective or Real Time Elastic Audio on these tracks later.

There are two ways to create a click track in Pro Tools: the easy way, and the potentially better-sounding way (assuming you have an external device that creates a nice sound, such as a drum machine). I cover both in case you can't stand the sound of the Click plug-in that's created in the easy way.

Getting a click track the easy way

Starting with Pro Tools version 7.3, you can create a click track in your session in just one step: Choose Track⇨Create Click Track. This places a track in your session with the click plug-in already inserted. Check out Figure 3-10.

The only other thing you may need to do to get this click going is to assign an output to this track if you haven't set your default output setting in the I/O Setup dialog box (Book III, Chapter 2 covers this). To assign your output, click and hold the Output selector for click track and drag to the physical output you want for your click. This is usually the main outputs for your session.

From here, you can follow the steps in the "Setting the tempo," "Choosing the meter," and "Enabling a click track" sections later in this chapter.

Figure 3-10:
Choosing
Track⇨Create
Click Track
creates a
track with
the click
inserted.

Getting a click track the hard way

If you have an external drum machine or synthesizer, you may want to perform a few extra steps so that the click you hear is something you want to hear (the click plug-in that comes with Pro Tools is hard for many people to tolerate). This involves several steps that are outlined in the following sections.

Configuring your external device

To play a click track using an external device in Pro Tools, you need to designate a device for creating the sound. This can be an external MIDI sound module (such as a drum machine or synthesizer).

To configure the click-track device, follow these steps:

1. **If you're using an external MIDI device for your click, connect the device to a MIDI port connected to your computer.**

Some Avid and M-Audio interfaces come with MIDI ports, but others don't. If your interface has MIDI ports, you're good to go. If it doesn't, however, you have to get a separate MIDI interface. (Book I, Chapter 4 can get you up to speed on this.) As well, if you use the Click plug-in, you don't need to use your MIDI ports.

2. **Double-click the Click button in the Transport window.**

Count Off

3. **In the Click/Countoff Options dialog box that appears (see Figure 3-11), open the Output drop-down menu to choose the device that will play your click.**

Be sure to choose the port and MIDI channel that your device is connected to.

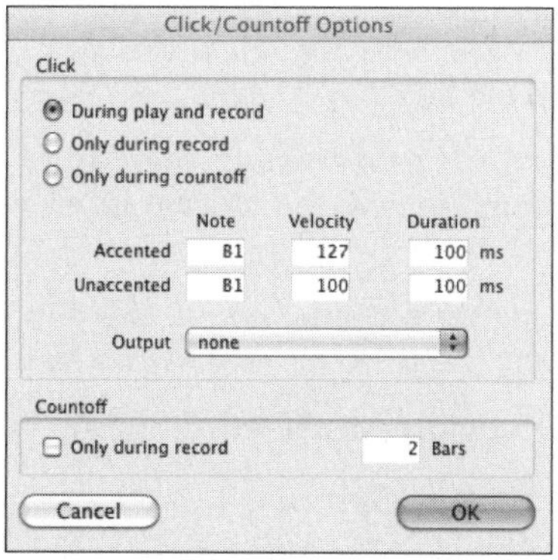

**Book III
Chapter 3**

Preparing to Record

Figure 3-11:
Use the
Click/
Countoff
Options
dialog box
to configure
your click
track
device.

Click/Countoff Options

Click
◉ During play and record
○ Only during record
○ Only during countoff

	Note	Velocity	Duration
Accented	B1	127	100 ms
Unaccented	B1	100	100 ms

Output [none   ▼]

Countoff
☐ Only during record   2 Bars

(Cancel)   (OK)

4. **Select when you want the click to be played by selecting one of the radio buttons at the top of the window.**

   You can select among During Play and Record, Only During Record, and Only During Countoff.

5. **Using the appropriate fields, enter the MIDI note, velocity, and duration for the accented and unaccented notes of the click.**

6. **(Optional) Select whether you want a countoff only during record and then enter the number of bars you want in the Bars field.**

   Selecting the Only During Record check box means that there will be no countoff when you play back the track. If you don't want any countoff at all, type in **0** in the Bars field.

Even with your device configured, you still won't get any sound out of your click track until you enable it in your session. The next section shows you how to do this.

Connecting an external device to sound a click

Follow these steps to connect your external MIDI device to sound the click:

1. **Connect the audio output of your external MIDI device to an audio input of your Avid hardware.**

2. **Create a new mono audio track by choosing Track⇨New from the main menu or by pressing ⌘+Shift+N (Mac) or Ctrl+Shift+N (PC).**

3. **When the New Track dialog box opens, use the drop-down menus to choose a single mono Audio track and then click Create.**

   Your track appears in the Edit and Mix windows and in the Audio Clips list located at the right side of the Edit window.

   Why mono? Well, it's annoying to hear the clicking in only one ear. Mono puts it in *both* ears, nice and clear.

4. **Using the Input selector for your new track in the Edit or the Mix windows, select the input that corresponds to the input your device is connected to.**

5. **Set the output to the main stereo outputs of your session, using the Output selector for your new track in the Edit or the Mix windows.**

6. **Record-enable the track by clicking the Record Enable button in the Edit or the Mix windows.**

   Your click track plays according to your choice in the Click/Countoff dialog box.

Setting the tempo

Whether you created your click track the hard or easy way, you still need to set your session tempo to get the click to pulse at the tempo you want to play to. Here's how you do this:

1. **Disengage the Tempo Ruler Enable button in the expanded Transport window (choose View⇨Transport⇨Expanded).**

   The little Conductor guy turns gray. If it's already gray, then leave it alone.

2. **Double-click in the tempo box in the expanded section of the Transport window (as shown in Figure 3-12).**

3. **Type the tempo number you want and click Return/Enter.**

   Your tempo is set.

Another way to change the tempo is to follow Step 1, and then click and drag the slider located below the tempo setting left or right to get to the tempo you want. Release your mouse button when you set the tempo.

Figure 3-12:
Use the Expanded Transport Window to choose the tempo of your session.

Choosing the meter

You also need to set the meter for the session. You do this using the Meter Change dialog box. You call up the dialog box by double-clicking the Meter button in the expanded Transport window (or choose View⇨Rulers⇨Meter then click on the plus (+) sign next to the meter ruler bar). The Meter Change dialog box appears, as shown in Figure 3-13. The Meter Change dialog box gives you the following parameters to adjust:

✦ **Snap to Bar:** Select this check box to align any meter events with the first beat in the nearest bar.

✦ **Location:** The number you enter in this field determines the beginning of the *meter* (time signature) event. For songs with only one time signature, you enter **1/1/000** (bars/beats/ticks).

+ **Meter:** In these fields, type the meter that you want to use (**4** in the top field and **4** in the bottom field for common time, for example).

+ **Click:** From this menu, you choose the note value for the clicks played in each measure. Choosing 1/4 note (a quarter note) gives you four clicks in a 4/4 measure.

Figure 3-13:
Use Meter Change view to designate the meter in your session.

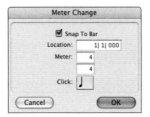

Enabling a click track

Even an electronic equivalent of a metronome has to be set in motion to do any good. After you set up your click track to do its job, you have to enable it so it will run while you're recording.

You can enable your click track by

+ **Choosing Options➪Click from the main menu.**

+ **Clicking the Click button in the MIDI section of the Transport window.**

When Click is engaged, this button is blue.

You can engage the countoff by clicking the Countoff button in the MIDI section of the Transport window. This button displays the number of bars that the countoff is set for, and shows as blue when it's engaged.

Setting up tempo and meter events

If your song has any tempo or meter changes, you can set up a map of these changes *(events)*. You might want to do this if you have complex songs with several different time signatures or tempos. This makes sure that your click track follows these changes so that you can stay in time, too. This section shows you how.

Creating new tempo or meter events

Tempo and *meter events* are changes to your tempo or meter throughout the song. You can make changes to the tempo or meter anywhere within the song, and the placement of these events throughout the session constitutes the tempo and meter maps. The easiest way to create new tempo or meter events is to type in the location of the change of tempo or meter in the Location field within the Tempo or Meter Change dialog boxes. You can also select your locations by doing the following:

1. **Click the Tempo or Meter ruler bar in the Edit window where you want your tempo or meter change to happen.**

   Book II, Chapter 4 gives you all the details on both the Tempo and Meter ruler bars.

2. **Open the Tempo or Meter Change dialog box by clicking the appropriate plus sign to the right of the label Tempo or Meter.**

3. **(Optional) In the Tempo or Meter Change dialog box, select the Snap to Bar check box if you want the tempo or meter event to start at the beginning of the nearest bar.**

4. **Type in the tempo or meter you want to use for that section.**

5. **Click OK.**

   A triangle icon (green for tempo and yellow for meter) appears at the location of this tempo or meter change.

You can use these steps to create more changes in tempo or meter (events) anywhere within the session. When you create these events, Pro Tools creates a map of them within your session with the little icons.

Editing tempo and meter events

When your tempo or meter events are in place, you can move, delete, copy, or paste them. The following list tells you how:

✦ **Moving a tempo or meter event:** You can move the location of tempo or meter events easily by dragging the corresponding triangle along the ruler to where you want it. Alternatively, you can double-click the triangle to open the Tempo/Meter Change dialog box, where you can use the Location field to set a specific location.

✦ **Deleting an event:** To delete an event, Option-click (Mac) or Alt-click (PC) over the triangle of the event you want to remove.

✦ **Copying an event:** To copy a tempo or meter event, follow these steps:

   a. *Set the Edit mode to Grid and the grid resolution to 1 bar.*

   Doing so ensures that you select the beginning of a bar. (Book IV, Chapter 1 details how to work with Edit modes and grid resolutions.)

TIP

    b. *Press ⌘ (Mac) or Ctrl (PC) and click and drag from the beginning to the end of the event you want to copy.*

       You can select more than one contiguous event by continuing to drag across the events you want to select.

    c. *Choose Edit⇨Copy from the main menu or press ⌘+C (Mac) or Ctrl+C (PC) to copy the events.*

  ✦ **Pasting an event:** To paste an event that you've already copied, follow these steps:

    a. *Click the place in the ruler bar where you want to paste the event(s).*

    b. *Choose Edit⇨Paste from the main menu or press ⌘+V (Mac) or Ctrl+V (PC).*

Chapter 4: Recording Audio

In This Chapter

✔ **Recording a track**

✔ **Recording multiple tracks**

✔ **Playing back audio**

✔ **Recording additional tracks**

Recording audio is what Pro Tools does best. (Well, that and editing it. See Book IV.) This chapter guides you through recording single and multiple tracks from analog and digital sources — as well as playing back all that stuff. In this chapter, you also discover the home recordist's best way to create full-blown songs: *overdubbing,* or adding tracks to those you already recorded. I guarantee that you'll use overdubbing a lot, so I spend a fair amount of time getting you up to speed on the best (and easiest) ways to overdub in Pro Tools.

Recording Tracks

Recording audio tracks in Pro Tools requires that you first choose your Record mode, create a track, set levels, enable recording, and turn on a click track (if you're using one). These steps are all covered in detail in the previous chapter in this mini-book, but you'll also find a basic overview of these topics in this section.

After you have all these steps taken care of, you're ready to record some audio. The following sections lead you through recording a single track or multiple tracks, undoing or canceling *takes* (recorded performances), recording additional takes, auditioning takes, and using playlists to organize and choose which takes to listen to.

Recording a single track

Most home recordists tend to record a single track at a time. (After all, most human beings can play only one instrument at a time.) Recording to a single track — whether mono or stereo — requires the following basic steps. (Steps 1–6 are explained in detail in Chapter 3 in this mini-book.)

1. **Open a session or create a new session.**

2. **Create a new audio track by choosing Track⇨New.**

3. **Assign an input and output to your new track from the Input and Output drop-down menus, found in the Controls section of the track.**

4. **Record-enable the track.**

5. **Set your recording level.**

Be sure that your monitor speakers are turned off or all the way down if you're recording in the same room as your monitors because the microphone might create *feedback* (an obnoxious hum or squeal) if it's too close to your speakers. My advice: When recording, use headphones to monitor your playing.

6. **Enable the click track and pre-roll (if you're using those features).**

7. **Click the Return to Zero button in the Basic Controls section of the Transport window, as shown in Figure 4-1.**

This ensures that you start recording at the beginning of the session.

Figure 4-1:
Use the
Basic
Controls to
record.

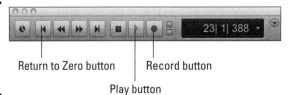

Return to Zero button   Record button

Play button

8. **Click the Record button in the Basic Controls section of the Transport window, as shown in Figure 4-1.**

The Record button blinks red.

Clicking Record doesn't actually start the recording process; it only gets Pro Tools ready for recording.

To record by using keyboard shortcuts for Step 8, you can use any of the following methods:

- *Press ⌘+spacebar (Mac) or Ctrl+spacebar (PC).*

- *Press the numberpad 3 key — that is, if you've set your system so your Numeric Keyboard mode is linked to Transport. (Linking your numeric keyboard to Transport is easy; just choose Setup⇨Preferences from the main menu to access the Preferences dialog box, click the Operation tab, and then select the Transport radio button in the Numeric Keypad section.)*

9. **Click the Play button in the Basic Controls section of the Transport window (refer to Figure 4-1).**

Only after you click Play does Pro Tools actually start recording; the Record button glows a nice red while recording (not that you'll be watching it as you play).

10. **When you're done recording, click the Stop button in the Basic Controls section of the Transport window or press the spacebar on your keyboard.**

This take appears in the Audio Clips list as a new clip.

The Audio Clips list is on the right side of the Edit window. If this list isn't showing, click the double arrow at the bottom-right corner of the Edit window.

Managing multiple tracks

Sometimes you want to record more than one track at a time — say, when you stereo-mic an instrument, when you record drums using several mics, or even when you want to record a few musicians at a time. Recording multiple tracks at one time follows much the same procedure as if you were recording a single track: The only difference is that you use one of the following methods to choose multiple tracks:

✦ **Select the Latch Record Enable Buttons option in the Operation tab of the Preferences dialog box, and then click each track's Record Enable button.** To call up the Preferences dialog box, choose Setup⇨Preferences from the main menu.

✦ **Record-enable noncontiguous tracks.** Press and hold the Shift key while you click each track's Record Enable button.

✦ **Select all the tracks in your session.** Option-click (Mac) or Alt-click (PC) the Record Enable button on any track.

✦ **Record-enable a selected track:** Option+Shift-click (Mac) or Shift+Alt-click (PC) the Record Enable button on the selected track.

Chapter 3 in this mini-book has more on these options.

Recording multiple tracks at once takes a toll on your system. A normal and common symptom of this load is a delay between the time you click the Play button and when the recording actually starts.

You can eliminate this delay by letting your system "warm up" first. This is done by following these steps:

1. **Click the Record button.**

2. **Press and hold Option (Mac) or Alt (PC) while you click the Play button.**

   The Record and Play buttons flash.

3. **Click the Play button when you're ready to record.**

   Pro Tools starts recording immediately, with no delay.

4. **When you're done recording, click the Stop button.**

Using pre- and post-rolls

A *pre-roll* or *post-roll* is a designated amount of time that the session plays before or after (respectively) the recording starts or stops. I'm a big fan of pre- and post-rolls (well, at least of pre-rolls). For example, setting a pre-roll for two or three bars lets me get into the groove of a song before the recording actually starts. You can set pre- and post-rolls several ways, as the following sections make abundantly clear.

Using the Pre-Roll and Post-Roll fields in the Transport window

To set the pre- and post-roll values in the Transport window, do the following:

1. **Choose View⇨Transport⇨Expanded from the main menu.**

   The Pre-Roll and Post-Roll fields appear beneath the basic transport controls.

2. **Click in the Pre-Roll Counter field in the Transport window and type in the length you want, as shown in Figure 4-2.**

   This field appears onscreen in the same format as the main counter. (In Figure 4-2, the format is bars and beats.)

3. **Press Return/Enter.**

Figure 4-2:
Clicking the Pre-Roll or Post-Roll field lets you enter a value for the pre/post roll.

4. **Click in the Post-Roll Counter field and type in your desired value.**

This value, too, displays in the format selected for the main counter.

5. **Press Return/Enter.**

6. **Click the Pre-Roll and/or Post-Roll button in the Transport window to enable it.**

The buttons are labeled Pre-Roll and Post-Roll and are to the left of the counter fields used in Steps 2 and 4.

All enabled buttons are highlighted.

Using the Pre-Roll and Post-Roll flags in the ruler bar of the Edit window

The Pre- and Post-Roll flags are located along the Timebase ruler in the Edit window (this is located above the track section). The flags are colored gray when they are disabled and green when they are enabled. Follow these steps to set the pre-roll and post-roll amounts using the flags in the ruler bar:

1. **Press ⌘+K (Mac) or Ctrl+K (PC) or choose Options➪Pre/Post-Roll from the main menu to enable Pre-Roll and Post-Roll flags on the ruler of the Edit window.**

The flags turn green to alert you that the pre- and post-roll functions are enabled.

Book III
Chapter 4

Recording Audio

2. **If you want the flag to snap to the grid, click the Grid button in the upper-left of the Edit window to select the Grid Edit mode. Otherwise use any other Edit mode.**

3. **Click and drag the Pre- and Post-Roll flags on the ruler to where you want them.**

If you want the same value for both the pre- and post-rolls, you can press Option (Mac) or Alt (PC) while you drag one of the flags. The other flag follows along while you move one.

Setting pre-rolls and post-rolls within a track's playlist

Playlists are the clips contained in a track and are located in the middle of the Edit window to the right of the track controls. Playlists most often display the waveform for the audio in the clips but can be set to display other things, such as automation views. In addition to all the other neat things you can do with a playlist, you can also enable and disable pre- and post-rolls. Just do the following:

1. **Choose Options⇨Link Timeline and Edit Selection from the main menu.**

2. **Click the Selector tool and drag along your track where you want the recording to start and stop.**

    This selects your record range.

3. **Option-click (Mac) or Alt-click (PC) the track's playlist where you want to put the pre-roll.**

    This both turns on the pre-roll and sets its location, as shown in Figure 4-3.

Figure 4-3:
Setting the
pre- or post-
roll flag.

4. **Option-click (Mac) or Alt-click (PC) the track's playlist where you want to put the post-roll.**

    This both turns on the post-roll and sets its location.

To turn off the pre-roll from within a track's playlist, Option-click (Mac) or Alt-click (PC) near the start point of the record range you selected. To turn off the post-roll, Option-click (Mac) or Alt-click (PC) near the end point of the record range you selected.

Playing Back Your Tracks

After you record a track, you'll most likely want to listen to it to make sure that it sounds the way you want. Pro Tools offers you many ways to play back a track. In the following sections, I guide you through a few of the many options for playing back audio clips.

Playing recorded tracks

After you record a track and click the Stop button, you can hear the track by turning off the Record Enable button (click it to make the light disappear, as shown at left in Figure 4-4) and then clicking the Play button (shown at right in Figure 4-4). You can adjust the volume by moving the channel's fader up and down.

Figure 4-4:
Disable
Record
Enable (left)
and then
click Play
(right) to
hear a track.

 If you use the Auto Input Monitoring option from the Track menu, you don't need to disable the Record Enable button. All you have to do is return to the beginning of the session (press the Return to Zero button in the Transport window) and then click the Play button in Basic Controls section of the Transport window. Pro Tools switches automatically to play back the recorded track. When you click Record and then click Play to record another take, Pro Tools switches your monitoring back to the input.

 Before you play back a track, make sure that the fader is turned down most of the way because too-high volume can ruin your ears or speakers. You can slowly bring it up as the session plays to get the volume you want.

 If you have Link Timeline and Edit Selection selected under the Options menu, you can play back your recorded track from anywhere in the session by clicking the Timebase ruler where you want to start — using the Selector tool in the Edit window — and then clicking Play. You can also use the Rewind and Fast Forward buttons to move through the session, but this tip makes getting around much faster and easier.

Setting scrolling options

Pro Tools lets you decide how you want the track material and Timebase ruler data to move (scroll) in Edit window as a session is playing or recording. You can choose between the following by choosing Options➪Scrolling, and then choosing an option, as shown in Figure 4-5.

+ **No Scrolling:** With this option selected, the Edit window remains where it is as the session plays. You can still move through the session by sliding the scroll bar at the bottom of the window while the session plays.

+ **After Playback:** Enabling the After Playback option keeps the Edit window static while the session plays and immediately takes you to the current location of the song after the session stops.

+ **Page:** Page scrolling during playback keeps the cursor visible at all times as the session plays. When the cursor moves from left to right, the window moves right.

✦ **Continuous:** This keeps the cursor in the middle of the Edit window, moving the Timeline across your screen.

This is the option I generally choose because I can easily keep track of where I am in the session at all times.

Figure 4-5: You can set the Edit window to scroll three different ways.

Listening to playback loops

If you want to hear a specific section of a session over and over — to find unidentifiable sounds, for example — you can create a playback loop. You set this up by choosing Options➪Loop Playback from the main menu, as shown in Figure 4-6. Or, you can press Shift+⌘+L or Control-click the Play button (Mac), or press Ctrl+Shift+L or right-click the Play button (PC).

Next, set the start and end points of the loop. You have several ways to designate the start and end points, including

✦ **Using the Start and End fields in the Expanded section of the Transport window:** Click in the Start and End fields and type in the Start and End points of your loop.

✦ **Selecting a range in the track's playlist or Timebase ruler (the timeline near the top of the Edit window):** Make sure that you have the Link Timeline and Edit Selection option selected in the Options menu. Then, using the Selector tool, choose the range you want to loop, either in a track or along the Timebase ruler, by dragging the Selector from the Start to End point.

✦ **Dragging the playback markers in the Timebase ruler (timeline):** With the Selector tool, click and drag the *playback markers* (also called Start and End Point markers). These are the blue arrows — or red if you have any tracks record-enabled — at the beginning and end points of your loop. You can move the markers either together or individually.

✦ **Using memory locators:** Memory locators are user-assigned markers in the song. (This option is covered in detail in Book IV, Chapter 3.)

Click the Play button in the Basic Controls section of the Transport window to listen to the loop.

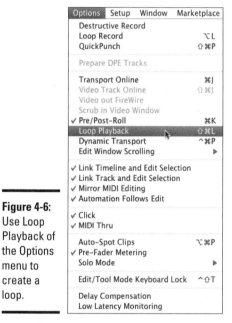

Figure 4-6:
Use Loop Playback of the Options menu to create a loop.

Using the Scrub feature

The Scrub feature in Pro Tools — located in the Edit window — works just like rocking the tape back and forth against the playback head of a reel-to-reel tape machine. (A *what?*) Um, okay. If you don't recall that bit of 20th-century technology, just trust me: *Scrubbing* was a way of listening to tiny snippets of a recorded track by moving the tape only a little. You can listen to a track by moving the cursor back and forth across the spot you want to hear. You can hear it forward or backward (in case you want to check the secret backward message . . . just kidding). This is useful when finding a specific note in the track — the hit of a snare drum, for instance. One of the great things about the Pro Tools Scrub feature (compared with other recording programs) is that you can scrub at any speed by simply moving the cursor at different speeds.

To scrub a track, follow these steps:

1. **Click the Scrubber button from the top of the Edit window, as shown in Figure 4-7.**

   The Scrubber button looks like a mini-speaker emitting sound.

2. **Click and drag over the waveform in a track to hear it played.**

You can scrub two adjacent tracks at once by dragging the Scrubber at the boundary between the two tracks.

Figure 4-7:
Use the
Scrubber
tool to listen
to a specific
point in a
track.

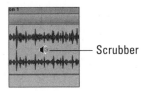

— Scrubber

Doing Additional Takes

Chances are that your first attempt at recording a track wasn't as good as you'd like. No problem. You can just do another take. This process is the same as recording your first one, but Pro Tools offers some options that can make it easy and fun to get the "perfect" performance. These include loop recording, punching in and out, and sometimes (if you're *really* on the fly) using the Pro Tools QuickPunch feature. Of course, you can always just record the whole thing over again if you want. All these options are covered in the following sections.

Starting over from scratch

Sometimes the best way to get it right is to start over. To record another take of the entire session, click the Return to Zero button in the Basic Controls section of the Transport window to return to the beginning of the session. Then follow the steps in the "Recording a single track" section, earlier in this chapter.

If you record in Destructive mode, any additional takes that you record onto a track will erase the previous one. So, if you want to make sure that you have a particular take for later, first make sure you're not using Destructive mode when you record over any existing takes on a track. Or you can create a new playlist for that track before you record your next take. (See the "Recording to playlists" section, later in this chapter, for more on how to do that.)

Punching in and out

If you like some of your initial take and want to record over only part of it, you can set points to start and stop this "recording over" within the session. This is *punching in and out.*

Punching in to or out of a track involves (first) setting a start point and an end point. You can do that in one of several ways, as I detail in the next few sections.

Before you create your start and end points for a punch, you need to decide where those points are going to be. To make this decision, you most likely need to play the track back so you can hear where you want to punch. If you're not sure how to do this, the "Playing Back Your Tracks" section earlier in this chapter gives you the details on this process.

Using the Start/End fields in the Transport

To set the start and end points in the Transport window, follow these steps:

1. Select the Expanded view option of the Transport window by choosing View⇨Transport⇨Expanded from the main menu.

2. Click in the Start field in the Basic Controls section of the Transport window and type in the beginning of the punch section you want.

This field appears in the same format as that of the main counter. (In Figure 4-8, it's bars and beats.)

3. Press Return/Enter.

4. Click in the End field and type in the end of the range.

This field, too, appears in the format selected for the main counter (as in Figure 4-8).

5. Press Return/Enter.

You're now ready to perform a punch. Check out the "Performing the punch" section, later in this chapter, for steps on how to actually perform the punch.

Figure 4-8:
Setting
your punch
range.

Selecting a section of a track's playlist

The playlist section of the Edit window contains all the clips for the track. You can make a selection within this playlist by following these steps:

1. **Choose Options⇨Link Timeline and Edit Selection from the main menu.**

This ensures that when you make your selection in a track's playlist, the Start and End Point markers in the Timebase ruler follow along.

2. **With the Selector tool, click and drag over the section in your track you want to record over, as shown in Figure 4-9.**

This highlights the selection and positions the start point at the beginning of your selection and the end point at the end.

Figure 4-9:
Selecting a track segment from a track's playlist is as simple as clicking and dragging it.

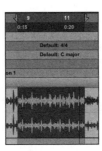

You're now ready to perform a punch. Go to the "Performing the punch" section later in this chapter for steps on how to actually perform the punch.

Dragging the Start and End Point markers along the ruler bar

The Start and End Point markers are located along the Timebase ruler in the Edit window and appear as up and down arrows — up for punch out, and down for punch in. The flags are colored blue when no tracks are record-enabled and red when one or more tracks are record-enabled. Setting Start and End Point markers in the Ruler bar consists of these steps:

1. **Choose Options⇨Link Timeline and Edit Selection from the main menu.**

This makes sure that when you drag the markers along the ruler bar, the corresponding section in the track's playlist is selected as well.

2. **If you want the markers to snap to the grid, click the Grid button in the upper-left of the Edit window to select the Grid Edit mode; otherwise use any other Edit mode.**

3. **With the Selector tool, click and drag the Start and End Point arrows to where you want them, as shown in Figure 4-10.**

Figure 4-10:
Drag the arrows to set your punch range.

You're now ready to perform a punch. The following section lays out steps on how to actually perform the punch.

If you want to select the entire length of the session, double-click one of the arrows.

Performing the punch

After you set the start and end points for your punch (whether in or out), you can record to that section by doing the following:

1. **Set and enable a pre-roll by clicking in the Pre-Roll field in the expanded Transport window (choose View⇨Transport ⇨Expanded to get there) and typing in the amount of pre-roll you want.**

   After you do this, you can hear the previously recorded track before the punch-in happens.

2. **Set and enable a post-roll by clicking in the Post-Roll field in the expanded Transport window (choose View⇨Transport⇨Expanded to get there) and typing in the amount you want for your post-roll.**

   Doing so lets you hear how your punch fits in with the previously recorded track.

3. **Choose Non-Destructive or Destructive Record mode.**

   • *Non-Destructive Record mode* is the default mode and is active if you have a Record button without any icon in it.

   • With *Destructive Record mode* selected, a small D is visible in the center of the Record button in the Transport window. Select Destructive Record mode by choosing Options⇨Destructive Record from the main menu.

   Use Destructive Record mode only if you're *really* sure you don't want to keep the previous take in the selected section.

4. **Click the Record Enable button for the track you want to record onto.**

   The button blinks red.

5. **Click the Record button.**

   The Record light flashes red.

6. **Click the Play button when you're ready to record.**

   The session starts at the pre-roll time, the Record button flashes red, and you hear the previously recorded track until the pre-roll is over. The monitoring switches to the input source, and the Record light stops flashing but remains red.

When you hit the end of the recording range, the session stops playing, or — if you have the post-roll enabled — stops recording. At that point, the Record button starts flashing again, and the monitoring switches back to the recorded clip until the end of the post-roll period. When the session reaches that point, it stops playing.

Loop recording

Loop recording lets you choose a section of the song to record repeatedly. This option makes it easy to try a bunch of takes without having to start and stop manually each time through the section. Loop recording can be done a bunch of ways. I describe one in Chapter 3 in this mini-book, but here's another:

1. **Choose Options⇨Link Timeline and Edit Selection from the main menu.**

   This ensures that when you make a selection in either the Timebase ruler or within a track's playlist, both are selected.

2. **Click the Selector tool at the top of the Edit window to select it.**

3. **With the Selector tool, click and drag across the section of the track that you want to record over.**

4. **Record-enable the track by clicking the Record Enable button in the Track Controls section of the Edit window.**

5. **Select the Loop record mode by choosing Options⇨Loop Record, pressing Option+L (Mac) or Alt+L (PC), or by Control-clicking (Mac) or right-clicking (PC) the Record button in the Basic Controls section of the Transport window until the Loop Record icon shows up.**

6. **Click the Record button in the Basic Controls section of the Transport window to prepare the session to record.**

7. **Click Play in the Basic Controls section of the Transport window to start recording.**

If you designated a pre-roll, it will happen only before the first time through the loop. After that, the loop goes from start point to end point, back to the start point, and so on.

Using QuickPunch

If you have sections that you want to replace in a track (say, a bunch of guitar counter points to support the lead vocal) and you want to record the new parts in just one pass of the session, you can use QuickPunch mode.

Setting up for QuickPunch requires these steps:

1. **Click the Return to Zero button in Basic Controls section of the Transport window to return to the beginning of the session.**

2. **Record-enable the track(s) you want to fix by clicking the Record Enable button for each track in the Track Controls section of the Edit window.**

3. **Set the Record mode to QuickPunch by choosing Options⇨QuickPunch, Control-clicking (Mac) or right-clicking (PC) the Record button, or pressing ⌘+Shift+P (Mac) or Ctrl+Shift+P (PC).**

   The QuickPunch (P) icon appears in the Record button.

4. **Click the Play button to start the session.**

   The Record button flashes while the session plays, and you hear the previously recorded track in the monitors.

5. **Click the Record button when you want to punch in.**

   The Record button stops flashing and recording starts immediately. Monitoring switches from what's recorded to what's coming in; you hear the input source.

6. **Click the Record button again to stop recording.**

   The button begins flashing again, and monitoring switches back to the recorded track.

You can repeat this procedure up to 100 times per session. (Probably enough to fix that pesky track, eh?)

Overdubbing: Recording additional tracks

Overdubbing is adding tracks to those already recorded. This process is the mainstay of the home recordist's recording repertoire because it allows you to play all (or as many as you want) of the instruments in your song. You can start with the drum tracks, add some bass guitar, then some rhythm guitar, and later the lead vocals, and so on.

Overdubbing is similar to recording your first track except that you have to be able to hear the other tracks and synchronize to them while you play. The main things to be concerned about when you overdub are

✦ **Creating a monitoring mix:** Take some time to create a mix of the previously recorded tracks that you can hear as you record so you have a blend that inspires you to perform your best. Depending on your system, you might not be able to add any effects to your mix, but getting the right balance between instruments can really help your recording. (Check out Book VI for more on mixing.)

✦ **Getting into the groove:** Make sure that you have the least amount of latency in your system when overdubbing; otherwise, it can really mess up the groove. Chapter 3 of this mini-book covers this in detail — and it's especially important for instruments with a fast attack and decay, such as drums and percussion, because they sound awful when they're slightly out of time.

With the Avid (and second-generation Digidesign) Mbox Mini and Mobox, you get a Zero-LatencyMonitoring setup that lets you monitor the input of the Mbox while hearing the output of your recorded tracks, which reduces the latency to, well, zero (almost). To set up your Mbox monitoring to record without hearing latency, follow these steps:

1. **Click the Mute button located in the Track Controls section of the Edit window to mute the track you're overdubbing onto.**

This keeps you from hearing the track as it comes back out of the system.

2. **Click the Mono switch on the Mbox.**

This allows both the input and the recorded tracks to play through both speakers. If this switch isn't depressed, you hear the input in one ear only.

3. **Adjust the Mix knob on the front of the Mbox to blend your input with the tracks playing in the session.**

You need to do this when the session is playing and you're playing your instrument at the same time so you can hear both the recorded tracks and your input. Try a test run-through to get a balance before you actually record.

Recording to playlists

Whenever you have material recorded to a track, it exists within the Edit window as a playlist. This playlist contains all the clips (representations of the actual audio on your hard drive) that are currently in a track. One of the nice things about Pro Tools is that you can create a bunch of separate playlists for a track and swap them in and out of the track. Whichever of a track's playlists is in the Timebase ruler section of the Edit window is the one that is heard when your session is playing back.

Playlists are handy for keeping all your takes organized, and they also let you record additional takes on a track even when you're using Destructive

Record mode. You can create a new playlist by clicking the little arrows next to the track's name in the Track Controls section of the Edit window. This opens a drop-down menu for a track, as shown in Figure 4-11.

To record to this playlist, follow the steps in the "Recording a single track" section, earlier in this chapter.

Figure 4-11: Use the playlist drop-down menu for a track to create a new playlist.

Auditioning takes

After you record a bunch of takes of a track, you can audition them to see which one you prefer: from the Audio Clips list, from the Take List drop-down menu, and from the track's playlist. You can also set preferences for viewing takes of a track, and you can audition takes from multiple tracks at once. All these options are covered in this section.

Auditioning from the Audio Clips list

You can take clips from the Audio Clips list, located at the right side of the Edit window (if this list isn't visible, click the double arrow at the bottom-right corner of the Edit window) and drag them directly into a track's playlist (the clips that represent the audio for a track), located to the right of the Track Controls section of the Edit window.

1. **Click the Grabber button in the Edit window to select the Grabber tool.**

2. **Click the current take in the track's playlist, as shown in Figure 4-12.**

    The playlist in a track consists of all the clips that you can see in the session.

Figure 4-12: Use the Grabber tool to select the take you want to replace.

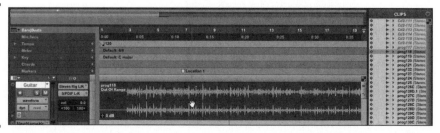

3. **Press ⌘ (Mac) or Ctrl (PC) and click another take in the Audio Clips list.**

    The Audio Clips list is located on the right side of the Edit window. If it's not visible, click the double arrow at the bottom-right corner of the window to expand the Edit window.

4. **Drag the track from the Audio Clips list onto the playlist, as shown in Figure 4-13.**

    The clip is placed in a track and is ready to play.

Clips list

Figure 4-13:
Click and drag the take you want from the Audio Clips list onto the track.

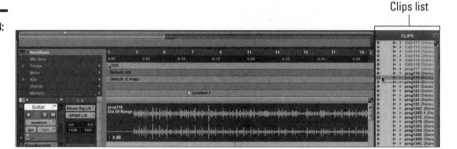

Auditioning from the Takes List drop-down menu

You can audition your takes by opening a drop-down menu that has a list of all the takes for a punch or loop recording session. This option lets you freely switch the takes while the session plays. This section outlines the procedures.

1. **Click the Selector button in the Edit window to choose the Selector tool.**

2. **Select a take within a track's playlist (the clips located to the right of the track name) and ⌘-click it (Mac) or Ctrl-click it (PC) to open the Takes List drop-down menu, as shown in Figure 4-14.**

    You can also click the precise Start point of the punch or loop range in the track's playlist or along the Timebase ruler without first selecting the track.

Figure 4-14:
The Takes List drop-down menu.

3. **Choose the take you want to hear from the Takes List drop-down menu.**

   This take replaces the previous one and is placed at its correct position in the session.

You can follow the steps for both of these approaches if you want to audition more takes.

From the Takes List drop-down menu, you can choose and change takes even while the session is playing.

The different takes are listed in the order they were recorded. If you start moving them around, though, you can identify them by the time stamp created when you recorded each take.

Choosing from a track's playlist

The track's playlist contains the clips located in a track. The playlist is located to the right of the Track Controls for each track and represents the audio data for the track. To audition tracks from a track's playlist, click in the little arrows next to the track's name in the Track Controls section of the Edit window to open the playlist drop-down menu and then choose the playlist to play, as shown in Figure 4-15. The name of the track changes to the name in the chosen playlist.

Figure 4-15:
Choose
a clip to
play from
the playlist
drop-down
menu.

Matching take criteria

You can use the "Alternates Match Criteria" in the Takes List dialog box (as shown in Figure 4-16 to choose which takes get listed in the Takes List drop-down menu to help you keep your various takes organized. This can be helpful if you're punching in a lot — and/or if you're punching in on multiple tracks at a time.

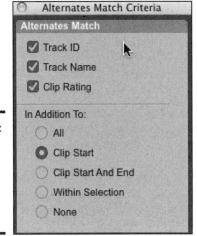

Figure 4-16:
The
Alternates
Match
Criteria
Takes List
options.

You can access this dialog box by choosing Alternates Match Criteria from the Takes list (follow the steps in the "Auditioning from the Takes List drop-down menu" section earlier in the chapter to get to this window).

The Alternates Match Criteria options include the following:

✦ **Track ID:** Takes recorded to the same track are considered matching.

✦ **Track Name:** This includes takes with the same track or name.

✦ **Clip Rating:** This option includes takes that have the same rating. This option only works, of course, if you've rated your takes. You can rate a take or clip by highlighting it (click it with the Selection tool) and choosing Clip⇨Rating⇨*rating#*. Your choices for a rating are None, 1, 2, 3, 4, 5.

✦ **In Addition To Match Options:** You can add other criteria to your match to narrow the field. These include.

• **All:** This option includes takes that include the current location of the cursor — as well as takes that fall either partly or entirely within the current time range of the selection in the Edit window.

• **Clip Start:** This option includes takes with the same start time as the clip that has the current cursor location or is presently selected.

• **Clip Start and End:** This option includes takes with the same start and end times.

• **Selection Range:** This includes takes that fit entirely within your selection range in the Edit window.

• **None:** This is the default and when you choose this no other criteria other than the main ones above (Track ID, Track Name, and/or Clip Rating) apply.

Auditioning takes from multiple tracks at one time

If you want to audition takes from multiple tracks at once — for example, when recording drums to several tracks at a time — follow these steps:

1. **Select both the Take Clip Name(s) That Match Track Names and the Take Clips Lengths That Match options in the "Matching Start Time" Takes List section of the Edit tab of the Preferences dialog box. (See the previous section.)**

2. **Click the Selector button in the Edit window to choose the Selector tool.**

3. **With the Selector tool, drag across all the tracks for the range you want to replace, as shown in Figure 4-17.**

4. **⌘-click (Mac) or Ctrl-click (PC) one of the tracks within that selected clip.**

The Takes List drop-down menu appears. Takes that match the preferences set in Step 1 show up in the list.

5. **Choose a clip (take) from the list.**

Figure 4-17: To select multiple tracks on which to audition takes, drag across the tracks you want.

Getting Rid of Unwanted Takes

If you have a take (recorded performance) that you don't like, you can get rid of it in one of several ways. You can cancel the take while you're recording, undo the take after you've recorded it, or clear the audio clip that contains the take from the Audio Clips list. All these options are detailed in the following sections.

Canceling your performance

Canceling a performance is handy when you're in the middle of recording and you *know* you're not going to keep the take. (For example, the mail arrived, causing the dog to go ballistic in the middle of your vocal.) To cancel a performance, simply press ⌘+. (period; Mac) or Alt+. (period; PC). This stops the session and clears the audio clip created for this take with one stroke.

You can't use this command if you record in Destructive Record mode.

Undoing your take

If you already stopped recording and you know that you don't want to keep your latest try, you can undo the take by choosing Edit⇨Undo Record from the main menu (as shown in Figure 4-18) or by pressing ⌘+Z (Mac) or Ctrl+Z (PC).

If you used QuickPunch mode, only the last punch will be undone. If you used Loop Record mode, on the other hand, *all* the looped passes will be undone. And if you used Destructive Record mode, your previous take will already have been erased when you recorded — so undoing the last take will leave you with nothing on that track.

Clearing the file from the Audio Clips list

After hearing a few of your takes, if you decide that you want to get rid of one or more of them, you can *clear* the take(s) from the Audio Clips list. The following steps show how:

1. **Click the clip you want to get rid of in the Audio Clips list to highlight it.**

   To select more than one clip to clear, press and hold the Shift key while you click each clip.

2. **Choose Audio Clips⇨Clear from the main menu (see Figure 4-19) or press Shift+⌘+B (Mac) or Ctrl+Shift+B (PC).**

   Your selected takes are deleted.

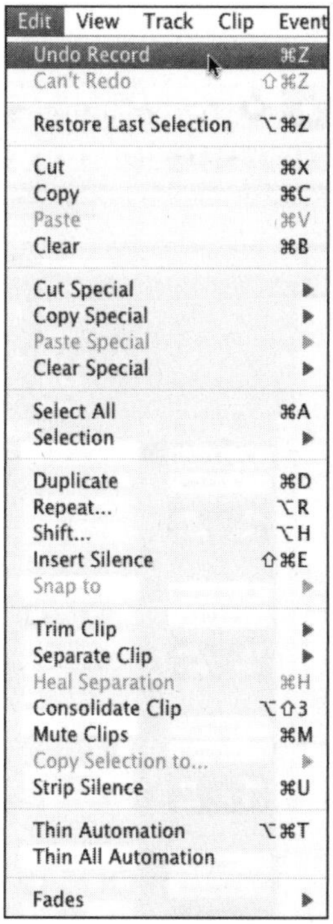

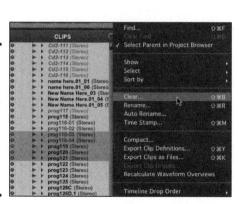

Figure 4-18:
Undo a take from the main menu.

Figure 4-19:
Choosing Audio Clips⇨Clear from the main menu gets rid of a selected take.

Book IV

Editing Audio

The 5th Wave   By Rich Tennant

INTENSE BUT UNINFORMED AUDIOPHILE BILLY WIGGINS ENJOYS HIS CUSTOM BURNED CD COLLECTION OF DIAL UP MODEM WARBLES

Contents at a Glance

Chapter 1: Audio Editing Basics 337

    Understanding Pro Tools Editing 337

    Getting to Know Clip Types...338

    Viewing Clips..340

    Understanding Edit Modes...347

    Working (Okay, Playing) with Playlists...................................350

    Using the Audio Clips List 352

    Managing Undos 355

Chapter 2: Selecting Material to Edit 359

    Selecting Track Material 359

    Making Changes to Your Selection...367

    Managing Memory Locations 371

    Playing Selected Material 383

Chapter 3: Getting into Editing 387

    Editing Clips 387

    Examining Edit Commands..409

Chapter 4: Adding to Your Editing Palette .413

    Signing On to the Smart Tool 413

    Perusing the Pencil Tool...418

    Silencing Selections 420

    Performing Fades and Crossfades...423

    Cleaning Up Your Session...433

Chapter 1: Audio Editing Basics

In This Chapter

✔ **Getting to know hard-drive editing**

✔ **Working with audio clips**

✔ **Using edit modes**

✔ **Editing playlists**

Hard drive recording — in general, and with Pro Tools specifically — makes editing audio fast and easy. In days of old, if you wanted to remove a bad note or shoddy drum hit, you had to break out a razor blade and some sticky tape, prepare the offending segment of magnetic tape for surgery, hold your breath, and apply a steady hand. Any changes to the recorded tracks got you into a messy, inexact, time-consuming process that many engineers weren't very good at. Even the steadiest hands couldn't come close to the accuracy and variety now available (to even the clumsiest of the bunch) through the editing functions of the new digital gear.

This chapter gets you started on the process of editing audio in Pro Tools. First, you get to know the basic ways that Pro Tools does editing — in particular, the role of *audio clips* (representations of your audio files in the Edit window). This chapter then guides you through finding and viewing clips so making edits is quick and easy. You also discover the joys of using playlists to work with these clips. And as if all that wasn't enough, this chapter also explains the four different edit modes available in Pro Tools.

Understanding Pro Tools Editing

Editing in Pro Tools on your computer is similar to working with any hard drive recorder — and often, it's much easier. Two things about editing in Pro Tools make it fast, easy, and (from the viewpoint of your creative work) safe:

✦ Unless you specify otherwise, it's *nondestructive:* That is, you can always undo your edit if you don't like it.

✦ You can perform most editing functions in Pro Tools while your session is playing back.

I detail both of these features in the following sections.

Nondestructive editing

Nondestructive editing does not change your original audio files when you edit an audio clip. Most editing functions in Pro Tools — clearing, cutting, pasting, separating, and trimming your audio clips, for example — are nondestructive. (All these operations are explained in Chapter 2 of this mini-book.)

Not all Pro Tool editing procedures are nondestructive. A few are destructive: Using them will permanently alter your source audio file. Whenever I describe one of these procedures, I'll warn you (look for a Warning icon) that after you perform the function, your source file will be changed.

Editing during playback

Most editing functions can be carried out while the session is playing. This feature makes editing much faster and easier because you can instantly hear (and see) what your changes have done. Some of these edits include

✦ Capturing, separating, and trimming clips

✦ Nudging, placing, rearranging, or spotting clips

✦ Creating fades or crossfades in and between clips (version 6.0 and later)

✦ Auditioning playlists

✦ Editing automation data

✦ Inserting RealTime plug-ins (version 6.0 and later)

✦ Processing audio using AudioSuite plug-ins

You can find out more about these functions throughout this chapter and the next three chapters (Chapters 2–4 in this mini-book).

Getting to Know Clip Types

When you record a track, a new audio clip is created in the track's *playlist* (the track displays you see next to the Track Controls section in the Edit window). This clip corresponds to an audio file of that performance, which resides on your hard drive. When you perform edits to your recorded performances, you do so by making changes to these clips.

Both edited and unedited clips appear on the *Audio Clips list,* the handy list you find to the right of the track playlist. (If the Audio Clips list isn't visible, click the double arrow at the far bottom-right of the Edit window to open it.) Several clip types show up in the list, indicating the entire audio file or a portion of it. These include

✦ **Whole-File:** *Whole-file audio clips* represent entire audio files recorded to your hard drive. Displayed in bold letters in the Audio Clips list, they're created when you do one of four things:

- First record an audio track.

- Import an audio file from outside the session.

- Consolidate existing clips.

- Nondestructively process audio by using an AudioSuite plug-in.

✦ **User-Defined:** *User-defined clips* are created when you do one of three things:

- Rename an existing clip.

- Capture, record, consolidate, or separate audio clips.

- Trim a whole-file clip.

✦ **Auto-Created:** These clips are created automatically when you edit a clip or punch-record over one. The more takes you record of your tracks — and the more edits you do — the more these clips add up. To keep your Audio Clips list from becoming cluttered, you can hide your Auto-Created clips easily, or you can convert them into full-fledged User-Defined clips by renaming them.

✦ **Offline:** These clips can't be linked to an audio file on your hard drive, usually because Pro Tools can't find the original file. In the Audio Clips list, the names of these clips are displayed in dimmed italics; in the track's playlist, they show up in blue italics. You can generally edit these clips just as you would any other clip except that you can't process them by using AudioSuite plug-ins.

✦ **Multichannel:** These audio clips are associated with stereo or surround files. If you click the triangle to the left of the clip name, you can see the included channels listed. These individual channels can be dragged onto separate tracks, if you choose.

✦ **Clip Groups:** You can group clips together and have them appear onscreen as a single clip in the Audio Clips list. These clips can exist on single or multiple tracks. Clicking the icon expands the group so you can see and move clips within the group.

✦ **Warped Clips:** *Warped clips* are those that have had Real Time Elastic Audio functions enabled. These clip types are identified by the Warp Indicator icon. Elastic Audio is a processing function where you can stretch or contract an audio file to fit the tempo of your session, among other cool things.

Book IV
Chapter 1

Audio Editing
Basics

Viewing Clips

You can customize how you view audio clips a number of ways in Pro Tools:
Select the track view, change the track height, assign name and time locations,
or zoom in and out. These options get a closer look in the following sections.

Selecting the track view

By default, audio tracks in the Edit window are set to Waveform view. This
view shows a visual representation of the sound produced by the audio
file associated with a particular clip. Pro Tools also gives you the option of
ditching the Waveform view and going with something different. You switch
between different views with the help of the Track View menu, as shown in
Figure 1-1, which you access by clicking and holding the Track View display
in the Track Controls section of the Edit window.

Figure 1-1:
Select a
view of a
clip in a
track from
the Track
View menu.

Your options are as follows:

✦ **Block:** *Block view* shows a blank box for each audio clip. This view
makes screen redraws much quicker, which is useful during mixing
when all the editing is done and you don't need to see the waveform.

✦ **Playlists:** *Playlists view* expands the track to show any additional playlists
for that track. These appear below the selected playlist for the track.

✦ **Waveform:** *Waveform view* is the default — a graphical representation
of the audio file, much like what you'd see if you ran a sound through
an oscilloscope. This is the best view to be in when you're editing clips
because you can easily find the start of a note. After a while, you'll probably be almost able to hear the track in your head just by looking at the
waveform.

Besides being able to see waveforms in their normal way — with both
positive and negative values — you can choose the Draw Waveforms
Rectified option, which displays the waveform as a summed value of
the positive and negative level. This can be useful when you want to

create volume automation to increase or reduce specific notes (such as, respectively, a weak or very loud drum hit). To get that rectified look, select the Draw Waveforms Rectified check box on the Display tab of the Preferences dialog box. (You know the drill: Choose Setup⇨Preferences from the main menu to get to the Preferences dialog box.)

✦ **Volume:** This view shows the volume level of the track. The volume level is displayed as a line superimposed over the waveform. In this view, the clip's name is hidden.

✦ **Mute:** This view shows whether the track is muted. When a track is muted, the line shows at the bottom of the view; when the track is unmuted, the line shows at the top. If a track uses automatic muting, a vertical line shows where the mute is turned on or off. This view also shows the waveform in the background.

✦ **Pan:** *Pan view* shows the apparent position of the track's output from left to right (pan) in the stereo sound. When the track is panned in the center, the line is centered in the view. Far-left panning shows up at the top; far-right is on the bottom. Settings in between these two extremes correspond to the pan value. In this view, you can also see a waveform display in the background.

You can toggle between Waveform and Volume views by highlighting the track and pressing Control+– (minus/dash; Mac) or Windows+– (minus/dash; PC).

Adjusting the track height

Pro Tools lets you adjust your track heights. You can either choose from various track heights (Micro, Mini, Small, Medium, Large, Jumbo, Extreme, and Fit to Window), or you can simply click and drag the lower boundary of your track with your mouse to the height that you want. These choices allow you to make tracks you're not editing small, while the tracks you want to edit can be made big enough so that you can really get in close to a wave-form when you edit. You choose your various track heights from the Track Height drop-down menu, which you can access from

✦ **The Track Height Selector button in the Track Controls section of the Edit window:** Click and hold with the mouse pointer over the button (it's a down-facing arrow immediately to the left of the track name) to make the Track Height drop-down menu appear, as shown in Figure 1-2. Choose the size you want.

✦ **The far-right edge of the Track Controls section:** Choose the track height you want by clicking and holding with the mouse pointer over the little ruler at the far side of the Track Controls section (as in Figure 1-3) and selecting an option from the Track Height drop-down menu that appears.

Figure 1-2:
Open the
Track Height
menu by
clicking
and holding
the Track
Height
Selector
button.

Figure 1-3:
Open the
Track Height
menu by
clicking the
far-right
edge of
the Track
Controls
section.

For stereo tracks, you can choose an expanded view that allows you to view each channel separately. If you edit the channels individually and they end up being different lengths, these stereo tracks become two mono tracks instead.

Assigning clip-name and time-location displays

Every audio clip has a clip name and time stamp attached to it. You can choose whether this information shows up on the clip displays in your tracks.

Displaying clip names

You can choose to show or hide the name of the clips in the track displays by choosing View⇨Clip⇨Name, as shown in Figure 1-4. (Choose View⇨Clip⇨Name again to uncheck the option.)

Choosing clip time stamps

You can choose any of several time stamp views by choosing View⇨Clip, and then selecting a time stamp view: Current Time, Original Time Stamp (as shown Figure 1-5), User Time Stamp, or No Time.

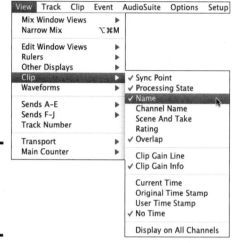

Figure 1-4:
Show the name in the Tracks Clip display.

Figure 1-5:
Choose time stamp views from the Clip option under the View menu.

Your options include

✦ **Current Time:** This choice shows the start and end times of each clip.

✦ **Original Time Stamp:** This option shows the time when the clip was created.

✦ **User Time Stamp:** This option displays a time stamp that you can define. By default, it shows the original time, but you can change it in the Time Stamp option under the Audio Clips list drop-down menu, which you can open by clicking the Audio Clips title bar at the top of the Audio Clips list. Selecting the Time Stamp option opens the User Time Stamp dialog box where you can enter the value you want, as shown in Figure 1-6.

✦ **No Time:** This option hides the time stamp.

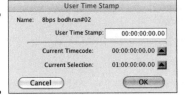

Figure 1-6:
The User
Time Stamp
dialog box.

Zooming in and out

You can zoom in and out of all tracks by using the Zoom buttons at the top of the Edit window (see Figure 1-7), or you can zoom in and out of a single track by using the Zoom tool (see upcoming Figure 1-8). You can also zoom in on the ruler and toggle the zoom back and forth between unzoomed and zoomed. Being able to zoom way into a clip lets you make precise edits to the waveform.

Zoom buttons

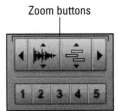

Figure 1-7:
Use Zoom
buttons to
zoom in
and out of
tracks.

Zooming in on all tracks with the Zoom buttons

The Zoom buttons section of the Edit window has buttons that allow you to zoom in and out both horizontally and vertically, as well as buttons for creating zoom presets for levels that you use frequently. The following list gives you the details on each feature:

✦ **Horizontal Zoom:** The outer two Zoom buttons control how wide of a portion of the timeline — and of all audio and MIDI tracks and clips — that you can see onscreen. Clicking the left button gives you a narrower view; clicking the right button gives you a wider view.

✦ **Vertical Zoom:** To zoom in vertically on audio (left Vertical Zoom button) or MIDI (right Vertical Zoom button) tracks, click the top or bottom part of the button with the waveform icon (at the left of the window). Clicking the top of the button increases the height of the display in the track's view; clicking the bottom decreases the height.

Increasing the vertical zoom might make the waveform too big to fit in the track display. If this is the case, you can increase the track's height as described in the "Adjusting the track height" section, earlier in this chapter.

✦ **Zoom Presets:** At the bottom of the Zoom buttons section are five presets that work like the presets on a car radio. To assign a setting to a Preset button, just get the Zoom setting you want — kind of like tuning a car radio to the station you want — and then ⌘-click (Mac) or Ctrl-click (PC) the Preset button. Then repeat the steps for the other four preset buttons.

You can select a preset by

- *Clicking the numbered Preset button you want in the Zoom buttons section of the Edit window*

- *Pressing the number of the Preset button you want on your keyboard while pressing Control (Mac) or Windows (PC)*

- *With Command Keyboard Focus (Commands Focus) enabled, pressing the number of the Preset number you want on the number pad of your keyboard*

Enable Command Keyboard Focus by clicking the Command Keyboard Focus button, as shown here in the margin.

Zooming in on a single track with the Zoom tool

Use the Zoom tool to select a specific spot in a track to zoom in and out of. The Zoom tool has two modes: Normal and Single Zoom.

✦ **Normal Zoom mode:** You can zoom in and out horizontally and vertically on the waveform when using this mode.

- *Zoom horizontally:* First click the Zoom tool button, as shown here in the margin, to select the Zoom tool. Then click and drag a section to select it, as shown in Figure 1-8. Pro Tools zooms to that section. To zoom in farther, click and drag again.

- *Zoom vertically and horizontally:* Press ⌘ (Mac) or Ctrl (PC) and then click and drag the section, as shown in Figure 1-9. Pro Tools zooms in. Repeat to zoom in farther.

  To zoom out again, press the Option (Mac) or Alt (PC) key while you click the zoomed area. Each click moves you out a little bit.

Book IV
Chapter 1

Audio Editing Basics

Figure 1-8:
Click and drag with the Zoom tool to zoom in horizontally.

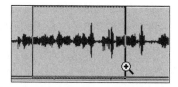

Figure 1-9:
Moving in
vertically
and
horizontally.

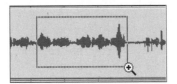

+ **Single Zoom mode:** If you're in Single Zoom mode when you finish zooming in on a spot, Pro Tools switches you back to the tool you were using. For example, if you want to scrub a section of a track and need to zoom in to get a more accurate start point, you can use the Single Zoom mode of the Zoom tool to zoom in. After you're zoomed in, you return automatically to the Scrub tool.

You can select Single Zoom mode by

- *Clicking and holding the Zoom tool button (as shown here in the margin) and selecting the Single Zoom option*

- *Clicking the Zoom tool button and pressing F5 on your keyboard to toggle back and forth between Zoom tool modes*

No matter which method you choose to select Single Zoom mode, after you're in this mode, the Zoom tool button changes its face to look like what you see here in the margin.

Zooming in on the ruler

If you have a spot in your session (the start of the chorus, for example) that you want to zoom into, you can use the ruler bar (where the location of your session is displayed) to select your zoom location. This is done by ⌘+Control-clicking (Mac) or Ctrl+Alt-clicking (PC) over a section of the ruler to zoom in one level. You can also drag over a section of the ruler while holding ⌘ and Control (Mac) or Ctrl and Alt (PC).

Zooming with the Zoom Toggle command

The *Zoom Toggle command* takes a selection, increases the track's height to Large, and fills the window. This command makes zooming quick: just one keystroke. This is a great function to use when you edit parts and need to get in really close to make an accurate edit, and then move out further to find the next spot to edit. To use the Zoom Toggle command, follow these steps:

1. **Choose the Selector tool by clicking it at the top of the Edit window.**

2. **With the Selector tool, select a portion of one or more tracks.**

3. **Press Control+E (Mac) or Windows+E (PC).**

   The track height changes to the Large setting (see the "Adjusting the track height" section, earlier in the chapter) and the selection fills the space.

4. **Repeat Step 3 to return to the previous view.**

If you want to change the default height for the Toggle Zoom to something other than Large, use the Zoom Toggle Track Height drop-down menu. (It's on the Editing tab of the Preferences dialog box, as shown in Figure 1-10.) Choose Setup➪Preferences from the main menu to call up the Preferences dialog box, from which you can select any of the possible Track Height options.

Figure 1-10:
Setting the default height for Toggle Zoom.

> Zoom Toggle
> Vertical MIDI Zoom: | selection |
> Horizontal Zoom: | selection |
> ☐ Remove Range Selection After Zooming In
> Track Height: | last used |
> Track View: | last used |
> ☐ Separate Grid Settings When Zoomed In
> ☐ Zoom Toggle Follows Edit Selection

Understanding Edit Modes

Pro Tools offers four basic edit modes; the mode you use depends on the task you want to perform. You get a chance to dig pretty deep into these edit modes in the next chapter, but here's a basic overview of each of them. Figure 1-11 shows all four edit mode buttons — Shuffle, Spot, Slip, and Grid — all nicely lined up on the toolbar — and coming right up is a list that gives you a taste of what each mode can do for you.

Figure 1-11:
Pro Tools offers four edit modes: Shuffle, Spot, Slip, and Grid.

✦ **Shuffle:** *Shuffle mode* allows you to move a clip around in an audio track, automatically placing it at the end of the nearest clip. This is a handy way to move clips around if you want to experiment with alternate arrangements of a song. For example, you can move the second bar of a four-bar phrase to the last bar by grabbing it and sliding it over to the end. The third bar moves to replace the second, and the second bar snaps right to the end of the fourth. Presto! New arrangement!

✦ **Spot:** In *Spot mode,* you can designate the exact timeline placement of a clip you want to move. Click to engage Spot mode, and then click a clip (which brings up the Spot dialog box, as shown in Figure 1-12). Enter the place you want to move the clip to in the appropriate field and then click OK.

Figure 1-12:
Use the
Spot dialog
box to
choose
where to
place a clip.

If you want to move the clip back to its original place, you can click the arrow to the right of the Original Time Stamp field in the Spot dialog box.

✦ **Slip:** Use *Slip mode* to move clips anywhere you want within the playlist. You can have clips overlap or leave space between them, for instance. To move a clip using Slip mode, click and hold over the clip and then drag it where you want.

✦ **Grid:** Moving a clip using *Grid mode* snaps the clip to the predefined time grid. Grid mode is useful if you want to quickly move a drum part over a beat, for example. Starting with version 6.0, Grid mode gives you two different options: Absolute and Relative. To choose one of these modes, click and hold the Grid button and then choose the one you want. Here's what they offer you:

• *Absolute Grid mode:* When using Absolute Grid mode, if you move a clip that doesn't begin where the grid resides — on the & of 1 when the grid is set to 1/4 notes, for example — the clip will snap to the resolution of the grid.

This isn't a good mode to use if you have a clip that starts on the & of 1 (1/8 note after the downbeat) with a 1/4-note grid and you want the clip to fit in the measure the same way after moving it. Your start point will move to a downbeat and all the rest of your notes will be off by an eighth note.

- *Relative Grid mode:* In Relative Grid mode, you move clips by the unit of the grid (1/4 notes, for example). So, in the example of a clip starting on the & of 1 with a grid resolution of 1/4 notes, the clip will move over by the grid value (1/4 notes), leaving the start time of the clip on the & of the beat.

Relative Grid mode is useful for moving a drum hit over and having it fit within the grid, even if its start point doesn't originally match the grid itself.

Setting grid resolution

Setting grid resolution is an outrageously handy tool for precision-tweaking the rhythms of your track. If you decide to go the Grid mode route, you can set the resolution of the grid that you work in by following these steps:

1. Click and hold on the Grid Value window, located under the Edit tools in the main Edit window, as shown in Figure 1-13.

The Grid Resolution menu appears, offering you choices for the resolution of your grid — 1/2 notes, 1/4 notes, 1/16 notes, whatever.

2. Drag to the resolution you want.

Within this menu, you can also choose the time scale you want the grid in as well as whether you want the grid to follow the main time scale.

Figure 1-13:
Click and hold on the Grid Value window to open the Grid Resolution menu.

Grid Value window

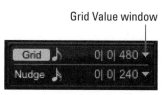

Displaying grid lines

Again, if you want to work in Grid mode, you might find the grid lines in the Edit window helpful. You can get them to appear onscreen by using one of two methods:

✦ **Click the Grid button (see Figure 1-14).**

✦ **With Grid Edit mode enabled, click the Timeline Ruler (Bars:Beats) button to toggle the grid on and off, as shown in Figure 1-15.**

Grid button

Figure 1-14:
Turn on the
Grid view
here.

Figure 1-15:
Click the
Timeline
Ruler button
to toggle the
grid on and
off in Grid
Edit mode.

Timeline Ruler button

Working (Okay, Playing) with Playlists

The Edit playlists within your tracks consist of various arrangements of the clips within a track. Each track can have one or more clips that you can arrange in any order that you want using the edit modes listed in the previous section. Edit playlists allow you to experiment with different arrangements of clips within a track — and you can still change them at will by switching to another playlist. This is handy if you want to try different arrangements of songs and easily compare them without having to create copies of entire sessions (as you would with some other programs).

You access your Edit playlists by clicking the Playlist selector in the Track section of the Edit window, as shown in Figure 1-16. From the menu called up by the Playlist selector, as shown in all its glory in Figure 1-17, you can choose from the various playlists as well as create, duplicate, or delete them.

Click here to open the Playlist
drop-down menu

Figure 1-16:
Find the
Playlist
selector in
the Track
Controls
section of
the Edit
window.

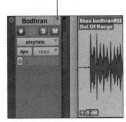

Figure 1-17:
Use the
Playlist
drop-down
menu to
manage
playlists for
each track.

Creating a new playlist

When you record or import audio into a track, you automatically create an empty playlist. With this new playlist, you can import audio clips, drag those clips in, or copy and paste them from other tracks. You can create additional playlists by opening the Playlist drop-down menu; just click the Playlist selector next to the track's name in the Track Controls section of the Edit window and choose New. (See Figure 1-17.)

Duplicating a playlist

Being able to duplicate a playlist makes creating different arrangements of a track or making edits to the clips in a playlist easy. Instead of creating a new blank playlist, you start from one you already created. To duplicate a playlist, click and hold with the mouse pointer over the Playlist selector and then choose Duplicate. You get the option of naming the new playlist or going with the default.

Deleting a playlist

Playlists take up no space on your hard drive, so you don't need to delete them to free up space. Still, if you want to delete a playlist from a session, follow these steps.

You can't undo this operation.

1. **Make sure that the playlist you want to delete isn't the active one in the track.**

2. **Open the track's playlist menu by clicking the Playlist selector (the arrows located next to the track's name in the Track Controls section of the Edit window).**

3. **Choose Delete Unused.**

   A dialog box opens, listing all playlists in the track (except the currently assigned playlist).

4. **Select the playlist that you want to delete from the list.**

   To delete more than one, press and hold the Shift key while you select the playlists.

5. **Click OK.**

   The selected playlist is deleted.

Renaming playlists

To rename the current playlist in a track, double-click the name of the track where the playlist resides and then type in a new name.

Choosing playlists

You can choose the playlist that appears in a track by clicking the Playlist selector (the arrows located next to the track's name in the Track Controls section of the Edit window) and dragging to the playlist you want. The name of the playlist then shows up as the track's name.

Using the Audio Clips List

All the audio clips in your session are displayed in the Audio Clips list, located on the right side of your Edit or Mix window, as shown in Figure 1-18. From this list you can

+ Drag a clip into a track.

+ Drag to rearrange clips in the list.

+ Audition any clip by Option-clicking (Mac) or Alt-clicking (PC) a clip in the list.

After you start recording, importing, and editing clips in your session, you can start accumulating clips in this list very quickly. Fortunately, Pro Tools helps you keep track of them by displaying clip types differently. The "distinguishing marks" are as follows:

+ Whole File clips are in bold.

+ Auto-Defined and User-Defined clips are in regular text.

+ Offline clips are in italics.

+ Stereo clips contain two mono clips that can be expanded by clicking the triangle to the left of the clip name.

Figure 1-18:
The Audio
Clips list
shows all
the clips in a
session.

Selecting clips

Here's how to select single or multiple clips from the Audio Clips list:

✦ **To select a single clip:** Click a single clip. It becomes highlighted. Then select the Clip List Selection Follows Track Selection check box on the Editing tab of the Preferences dialog box (the dialog box you get by choosing Setup⇨Preferences from the main menu). *Voilà!* The track containing this clip becomes highlighted to show it's selected.

✦ **To select a range of contiguous clips:** You have two choices:

   • *With the cursor on the left of the Audio Clips list (a marquee will appear), click and drag across the clips you want to select.*

   • *Shift-click to the left of the first and last clip names for a group of clips.* All the clips in between these two are selected.

✦ **To select multiple clips that aren't next to one another:** Your method depends on your platform:

   • *Mac:* With the cursor located over the name of the clip, ⌘-click each clip.

   • *PC:* Shift-click over the name of each clip.

Using the Audio Clips list drop-down menu

Audio clips can also be managed from the drop-down menu located at the top of the Audio Clips list, as shown in Figure 1-19. (The Audio Clips list is located at the right side of the Edit window. If it isn't visible, click the double arrow at the bottom-right corner of the Edit window to open it.) Open this menu by clicking and holding the Audio Clips title at the top of the Audio Clips list. Many of the functions in this menu are covered in this section.

**Book IV
Chapter 1**

**Audio Editing
Basics**

Figure 1-19:
Use the Audio Clips drop-down menu to manage your audio clips.

Sorting clips

After you start editing in earnest, the clips in the Audio Clips list start adding up. The only way to keep track of them is by being able to sort them. Pro Tools offers you several ways to sort, including by name, *time stamp* (when it was recorded), length, and a host of other parameters. To sort clips from the Audio Clips drop-down menu, choose Sort By from the menu and then choose one of the many options pictured in Figure 1-20.

Figure 1-20:
Sorting clips in many ways from the Audio Clips drop-down menu.

Finding clips

You can find clips in the list by choosing Find from the Audio Clips drop-down menu. When you do, a dialog box appears, as shown in Figure 1-21, where you can enter part of a word or a whole word for the clip you want to find.

Figure 1-21:
Type a word
or part of
a word of
the clip you
want to find.

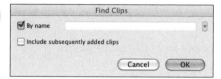

Displaying clip information

Besides displaying just the clip's name — the default for the Audio Clips list — you can have Pro Tools display some additional information about the clip in the playlist section of the track:

✦ **The complete path of the clip's location:** Choose the Show option from the Audio Clips list drop-down menu; then from this list, choose Full Path. Open this menu by clicking and holding the Audio Clips title at the top of the Audio Clips list located on the right side of the Edit window. (If this list isn't visible, click the double arrow at the bottom-right corner of the Edit window.)

✦ **The name of the file where the audio clip is located:** Choose Show from the Audio Clips list drop-down menu; then from that list, choose File Name.

✦ **The name of the hard drive where the file is located:** To see this information, choose Show from the Audio Clips list drop-down menu; then, from that list, choose Disk Name.

Managing Undos

Here's the realm where digital editing saves you vast quantities of time, hassle, and frustration: Pro Tools lets you undo operations that you perform in your sessions. This gives you vast flexibility and offers at least some safety net when you start messing around with your songs.

Setting levels of Undo

Prior to version 6.1, Pro Tools offered up to 16 levels of Undo. Versions 6.1 and later offer up to 32 levels of Undo. You don't have to use them all, though. In fact, if you have minimal memory on your computer, performing edit operations in Pro Tools will quickly fill it up and really slow things down. Or, if your memory is *really* low, you might not be able to perform an edit at all because all your previous edits are stored in RAM, right up to the number you specify in your preferences.

**Book IV
Chapter 1**

**Audio Editing
Basics**

Luckily, Pro Tools offers you the ability to choose the maximum levels of Undo that your session will have. You can set these levels on your session by doing the following:

1. **Choose Setup⇨Preferences from the main menu.**

   The Preferences dialog box duly appears.

2. **Click the Editing tab.**

3. **Type in the number of Undos you want in your session in the Levels of Undo field at the bottom of the window, as shown in Figure 1-22.**

4. **Click OK.**

Figure 1-22: Choose the levels of Undo in your session.

Levels of Undo: 32   Max: 32

Performing Undos

Performing Undos in Pro Tools is just like any other program: Choose Edit⇨Undo from the main menu. The Undo option also includes the name of the operation that you're undoing, as shown in Figure 1-23. This is helpful when you want to perform multiple Undos because you have to move back progressively through each operation that you performed. Keeping track of 32 operations can be tricky.

You can redo an Undo — but only the last one — by choosing Edit⇨Redo from the main menu.

Figure 1-23: When you're undoing an operation, the menu shows you what you're undoing.

Edit	View	Track	Clip	Event
Undo Clip Slide				⌘Z
Can't Redo				⇧⌘Z
Restore Last Selection				⌥⌘Z

Knowing when you can no longer Undo

Some operations result in clearing your Undo lineup. Whenever you perform the following operations, your previous operations can no longer be undone:

+ Importing track or session data.

+ Selecting Select Unused Clips or Select Unused Clips Except Whole Files from the Audio Clips list drop-down menu.

+ Deleting a track or clearing a clip from the Audio Clips list drop-down menu.

Pro Tools won't warn you before you perform these operations. But hey, sometimes we human beings actually *do* know what we're doing.

**Book IV
Chapter 1**

Audio Editing Basics

Chapter 2: Selecting Material to Edit

In This Chapter

✔ Selecting parts of clips

✔ Changing and extending selections

✔ Playing selections

*B*efore you can edit any audio clips, you have to make a selection. Pro Tools offers many ways to select material. You can select from a single track, grouped tracks, or the entire track list. You can select from a track's playlist or from the Timeline ruler. And you can make adjustments to the length and position of the selected material. All these options are covered in this chapter.

Selecting Track Material

When you select material to edit, the selection becomes highlighted. And, if you have the Edit and Timeline Selection Linked option chosen, you see little arrows in the Timeline ruler designating the Start and End points of the selection. Figure 2-1 shows a selection, whereas you can see the handy Link Timeline and Edit Selection button right here in the margin. The arrows are blue if no tracks are enabled for recording and red if tracks are enabled for recording.

If you haven't chosen the Link Timeline and Edit Selection option, Edit markers — instead of arrows — mark your selection, as shown in Figure 2-2.

Figure 2-1:
With Edit and Timeline selections linked, arrows in the Timeline ruler show where a selection starts and ends.

Figure 2-2:
When Edit and Timeline selections aren't linked, Edit markers do the same duty.

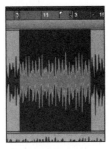

Selecting part of a clip

You can select material one of three ways:

+ **Drag within a track's playlist, as shown in Figure 2-3.** Do this by clicking and dragging your start and end points within the track's playlist.

Figure 2-3:
Drag within a track's playlist to select part of that clip.

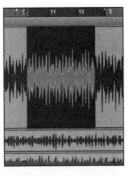

✦ **Drag along the Timeline ruler, as shown in Figure 2-4.** Do this by clicking and dragging your start and end points along the Timeline ruler or by moving the Start and End Point arrows to where you want them. Doing this selects all the unhidden tracks in the session.

Figure 2-4:
You can make selections in all tracks by dragging along the Timeline ruler.

✦ **Enter values in the Start and End fields of your Expanded section in the Transport window, as shown in Figure 2-5.** Do this by highlighting a track and typing in your start point in the Start field and then pressing Return/Enter. Type in your end point in the End field and press Return/Enter, or type in the length of the selection in the Length field and press Return/Enter.

Figure 2-5:
Enter Start and End values to select a section of a clip.

Start	12	2	102
End	15	3	550
Length	3	1	448

When you make a selection within a track that is part of a group, all tracks in the group — except those that are specifically hidden — are selected.

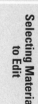

To create a selection that extends farther than the width of your computer screen, click the start point, scroll to the end point, and then Shift-click the point. You can toggle back and forth from the start and end points by pressing the left or right arrow keys, respectively.

Selecting across multiple tracks

You can select more than one track to edit in Pro Tools in several ways:

✦ **Drag across the tracks you want with the Selector tool.** (Click the Selector tool button at the top of the Edit window to, well, select it.) This only works if the tracks you want to include are adjacent to one another.

✦ **Group the tracks you want to select and click-drag on one of the tracks within that group.** Any hidden tracks in the group will not be selected. (For more on groups and grouping, see Book III, Chapter 4.)

✦ **Drag along the Timeline ruler to select all the tracks.**

✦ **To select all the tracks along with any conductor tracks (those dealing with Meter and Tempo changes), press Option (Mac) or Alt (PC) while dragging along the Timeline ruler.**

Selecting an entire clip

You can select an entire clip one of two ways:

✦ **Click in that clip with the Grabber tool.**

To enable it, click the Grabber tool button located at the top of the Edit window.

✦ **Double-click the clip with the Selector tool.**

To enable it, click the Selector Tool button located at the top of the Edit window.

Selecting two clips and any space between them

To select two or more clips and include any space that separates them, follow these steps:

1. **Select the Grabber tool by clicking the Grabber tool button at the top of the Edit window.**

2. **Click in the first clip with the Grabber tool.**

3. **Shift-click the next clip.**

To add more clips, Shift-click each one you want until you have them all chosen.

All clips selected become highlighted, along with any spaces that exist between them.

Selecting an entire track

You can select all the clips in a track one of two ways:

+ Triple-click one of the clips in the track.

+ Click in the track with the Selector tool and then choose Edit⇨Select All from the main menu or press ⌘+A (Mac) or Ctrl+A (PC).

Call up the Selector tool by clicking the Selector button located at the top of the Edit window.

Selecting all clips in all tracks

You can select all clips located in the tracks of your session (except the hidden ones) in any of four ways:

+ **Choose All from the Edit Groups list drop-down menu.** This menu is accessed by clicking and holding the Edit Groups title in the Edit Group List section of the Edit window. If the Edit Group List isn't visible, click the double arrow at the bottom-left corner of the Edit window.

+ **Triple-click any clip within a track in the playlist section of the Edit window.**

+ **Press Return and then ⌘+A (Mac) or press Enter and then Ctrl+A (PC) on your keyboard.**

+ **Double-click anywhere along the Timeline ruler (the session's timeline).**

If you want to include the *conductor events* in your selection (tempo or meter changes) of all clips in the tracks, make sure that you have the Edit and Timeline Selection Linked option chosen and then press Option (Mac) or Ctrl (PC) while you double-click the Timeline ruler.

Selecting on the fly

You can make selections while your session is playing by using the arrow keys. Follow these steps:

1. **Engage the Link Timeline and Edit Selection button or choose Options⇨Link Edit and Timeline Selection Linked from the main menu.**

Alternatively, you can engage the Link Timeline and Edit Selection button at the upper-right of the Edit window.

2. **Click the track somewhere before the place you want to start your selection.**

This is where the session will start playing back. If you want to select a point near the beginning of the session, you can skip this step and just start playing from the beginning.

3. Click Play in the Transport window or press the spacebar on your keyboard to start the session playing.

4. Press the down-arrow key (↓) on your keyboard when your playback reaches the point where you want the selection to begin.

5. Press the up-arrow key (↑) when your playback reaches the point where you want the selection to end.

6. Click Stop in the Transport window or press the spacebar on your keyboard to stop the session.

To scroll back to the selection start point, press the left-arrow key (←); to scroll to the selection end point, press the right-arrow key (→).

If you have either the Scroll After Playback or Page Scroll During Playback options selected under Scroll Options in the Operations menu, these options toggle off when you select on the fly. To reactivate one of them after you make your selection, you need to scroll down the Operations menu and check that option again (version 6.0 and later).

Selecting with the Selection Indicator fields

You can use the Selection Indicator fields to enter either the Start and End points or the length of a selection. The following sections describe how to do this.

Making a selection with the indicators

Here's how to make a selection by using the indicators:

1. With the Selector tool, click in the track you want to select.

Choose the Selector tool by clicking the Selector tool button at the top of the Edit window.

2. Click in the Start field, type in the start point that you want, and then press Return/Enter.

3. Click in the End field, type in the location of the end of the selection, and then press Return/Enter.

You can also enter the length of the selection after entering the start point. The end point is automatically entered in the End field.

Changing a selection using the indicators

Here's how to change the values in any of the indicator fields without typing in a value:

✦ Press the slash (/) key on your keyboard to move from one selection indicator to the next.

✦ Press the period (.) key or the left-arrow (←) and right-arrow (→) keys to move from one time field in an indicator to the next.

✦ Press the up-arrow key (↑) to increase the value in the field or the down-arrow key (↓) to decrease it.

Selecting objects using the Object Grabber tool

You can select individual clips within or across tracks by using the Object Grabber tool. This allows you to choose non-contiguous clips wherever they are in your session.

Selecting objects

Selecting non-contiguous clips in your session is really simple:

1. **Choose either Slip or Grid Edit mode from the Edit mode selector.**

This tool is not available within Spot or Shuffle modes.

2. **Engage the Object Grabber tool from the Grabber tool options (click-hold over the icon to see your options as shown in Figure 2-6).**

Figure 2-6:
The Object Grabber Tool lets you choose non-contiguous clips from within single or multiple tracks.

3. **Click the clip to select it.**

A black line appears around the edges to let you know it's been selected.

4. **Shift+click any other clips you want to include in your selection.**

If you want to remove a selected clip from the group, Shift+click it again to deselect it.

Selecting objects from within a time-based selection

You can select or deselect objects that are within a time-based selection. This is handy if you want to edit a lot of clips and only exclude a few. In this case, do the following:

1. **Choose the Selector tool and drag across the section you want to edit.**

You can choose the Selector tool by clicking the Selector tool button at the top of the Edit window.

2. **Double-click the Object Grabber tool.**

This tool must first be selected from the Grabber tool options. Also make sure you're in either Slip or Grid Edit mode otherwise the tool won't work.

3. **Shift+click to include any clips that were not initially selected (partially selected clips are excluded from the switch from time-based selection to object-based) or to exclude any clips that you may not want to edit.**

Making a selection with the Tab to Transients function

Transients are the initial attack in an instrument. In Pro Tools, you can move from one transient in a clip to another by using the Tab to Transients button and then pressing the Tab key. To use this function to choose Start and End points for a selection, do the following:

1. **Click the Tab to Transients button.**

The button here in the margin shows you what to look for.

2. **Make sure that you have the Edit and Timeline Selection Linked option enabled by selecting Options⇨Link Timeline and Edit Selection or by clicking the Link Timeline and Edit Selection button.**

3. **With the Selector tool, click in the audio track somewhere before the start point of the area you want to select.**

4. **Press the Tab key on your keyboard repeatedly to move from transient to transient until you get to the start point.**

If you go too far, you can back up by pressing Option (Mac) or Ctrl (PC) when you press Tab.

5. **Press the Shift key while you tab through the transients to the end point.**

Again, if you go too far, you can back up the end point by pressing Shift+Option+Tab (Mac) or Shift+Ctrl+Tab (PC).

Making Changes to Your Selection

Try as you might, after you make a selection on one of your tracks, you might find that your selection just doesn't cut it. Maybe you end up with too much or too little material at the beginning or end of the selection. Or you decide that you want to move the entire selection over in time to encompass different material. Perhaps you decide that you want to include other tracks in the selection. You also might want to change the track onto which you made your selection. Luckily, you don't have to start over selecting material to do this. You can make these adjustments to a selection quickly and easily in Pro Tools. This section describes these ways to change what you selected.

Changing a selection's length

After you make a selection, if you want to change its start or end point (say, skip the first two bars of your selection), you can do so by doing one of the following:

✦ With the Selector tool, Shift-click at the point you want outside the current selection.

✦ With the Selector tool, Shift-drag either the start or end point to where you want it.

✦ Drag the Playback marker (or Edit marker if the Edit and Timeline selections are unlinked) for the start or end point in the Timeline ruler (the section in the Edit window with the time markers located above the track playlists).

✦ Type in the new start or end point value in the Start or End field of the Expanded section of the Transport window and then press Return/Enter.

Nudging selections

Sometimes you want to move a selection very slightly forward or back in the Timeline to make sure you cover the exact material you want to edit. Pro Tools lets you use the Nudge function to move either your entire selection or just its start or end point so you can fine-tune your selections.

Nudging the entire selection

You can move a selection by the increments set up in your Nudge Value menu so that you can move across the material without actually moving that material itself. (The latter move is done after you finish making a selection; see Chapter 3 of this mini-book.) Follow these steps:

1. **Make your selection using one of the procedures listed earlier in this chapter.**

2. **Click and hold on the Nudge Value drop-down menu, located next to Nudge below the Counter section of the Edit window.**

The Nudge Value menu pops up.

3. **Select the desired value for your nudge in the drop-down menu, as shown in Figure 2-7.**

For more on using the Nudge feature, go to the next chapter (Chapter 3 of this mini-book).

4. **Press the Shift key along with either the + key or – key.**

Doing so "nudges" your selection to the right or left, respectively, by the designated nudge value.

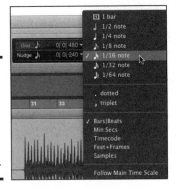

Figure 2-7:
Select
the nudge
value in
the Nudge
Value drop-
down menu.

 If you have the Commands Keyboard focus function enabled by depressing the Command Focus button, you can skip pressing the Shift key while you use the + or – keys.

Nudging the start point

Follow these steps to move the start point of a selection by the nudge value:

1. **Make your selection using one of the procedures listed earlier in this chapter.**

2. **Click and hold the Nudge Value drop-down menu, located next to Nudge below the Counter section of the Edit window.**

The Nudge Value menu pops up. (Refer to Figure 2-7.)

3. **Select the desired value for your nudge in the drop-down menu.**

For more on using the Nudge feature, check out Book IV, Chapter 3.

4. **Press Option+Shift (Mac) or Alt+Shift (PC), and then press the + or – key on your keyboard to "nudge" the Start point to the right or left, respectively, by the designated nudge value.**

Nudging the end point

To nudge the end point of a selection, follow these steps:

1. **Make your selection using one of the procedures listed earlier in this chapter.**

2. **Click and hold the Nudge Value drop-down menu, located next to Nudge below the Counter section of the Edit window.**

   The Nudge Value menu pops up. (Refer to Figure 2-7.)

3. **Select the desired value for your nudge in the drop-down menu.**

   For more on using the Nudge feature, go to Book IV, Chapter 3.

4. **Press ⌘+Shift (Mac) or Ctrl+Shift (PC) and press the + or – key on your keyboard to move the end point the designated nudge value to the right or left, respectively.**

Extending selection lengths

Sometimes, the best way to get all the material in your selection is to redefine its boundaries. Pro Tools offers you three ways to extend your selection: to the start or end point of the selected clip, to include an adjacent clip, or to markers (memory locations). These options are covered in the following sections.

Extending to the start or end point of a selected clip

Follow these steps to extend your selection to the start or end point of the clip:

1. **Select a portion of the clip by using the Selector tool, or simply click anywhere in that clip.**

   Choose the Selector tool by clicking the Selector button at the top of the Edit window.

2. **Press Shift+Tab to extend the selection to the end of the clip or press Shift+Option+Tab (Mac) or Shift+Ctrl+Tab (PC) to extend your selection to the start of the clip.**

Extending a selection to an adjacent clip

Use the following steps to extend a selection to include an adjacent clip:

**Book IV
Chapter 2**

Selecting Material to Edit

1. **With the Grabber tool, click the first clip to select it.**

2. **Press Shift+Control+Tab (Mac) or Shift+Windows+Tab (PC) to include the following clip. Or, press Shift+Control+Option+Tab (Mac) or Shift+Windows+Ctrl+Tab (PC) to include the previous clip.**

Extending a selection to a memory location (marker)

Memory locations (markers) are flags you can place within the session to make navigating your session faster. I usually make a habit of putting a marker at the beginning of each verse and chorus to help me find them quickly. To extend a selection to a marker or memory location, follow these steps:

1. **Click the start or end point in a track or make a selection in one of the ways listed earlier in this chapter.**

2. **Shift-click a marker in the Markers ruler (located above the track playlist section of the Edit window) or a memory location in the Memory Locations window.**

    The Memory Locations window is opened by clicking any of the markers in your session or by clicking the Marker icon at the left of the Markers ruler.

Moving and extending selections between tracks

You can take a selection on a track and extend it to include other tracks, or you can even move the selection to another track. For example, this is handy if you select the snare drum and then decide that you want to include the rest of the drum tracks in your edit. Another example is selecting one rhythm guitar track but deciding that you want to edit another rhythm guitar track instead. The following sections cover these options.

Moving a selection to another track

After you make a selection, if you decide that you'd rather edit a different track instead — while still using the same start and end points as the selection you already made — you can move the selection from one track to another. This process is done by following these steps:

1. **Click the Commands Focus button, as seen here in the margin, to enable the Commands Focus function.**

2. **Make a selection, using one of the procedures listed earlier in this chapter.**

3. **Press P to move the selection to the previous (above) track, or press ; (semicolon) to move the selection to the following (below) track.**

Extending a selection to an adjacent track

To include adjacent tracks in your selection — as in the case of adding drum tracks to a selection you made on the snare drum track — you can do this by following these steps:

1. **Click the Commands Focus button to enable the Commands Focus function.**

2. **Make a selection in a track in one of the ways listed earlier in this chapter.**

3. **Press Shift+P to include the previous (above) track, or press Shift+; (semicolon) to include the following (below) track.**

   Figure 2-8 shows what happens when you extend a selection to include an adjacent track.

If you got overzealous in extending your selection to adjacent tracks, you can remove the bottom track from this group by pressing Control+Option+; (semicolon; Mac) or Windows+Alt+; (semicolon; PC).

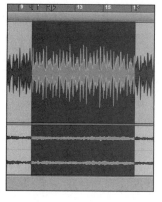

Figure 2-8:
Pressing Shift+; (semicolon) includes the adjacent track in a selection.

Managing Memory Locations

Memory locations let you quickly move from one position in a session to another with the click of a button. You can have up to 200 memory markers in each session.

Dealing with the New Memory Location dialog box

Whenever you create a memory location, a dialog box opens (as shown in Figure 2-9), where you choose the parameters of the marker. This box contains two sections: Time Properties and General Properties.

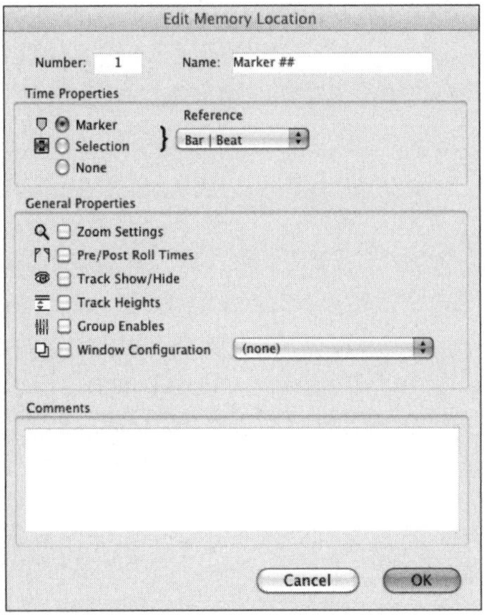

Edit Memory Location

Number: 1   Name: Marker ##

Time Properties

○ ● Marker
▣ ○ Selection   } Reference
   ○ None   Bar | Beat

General Properties

🔍 □ Zoom Settings
⌐ □ Pre/Post Roll Times
📼 □ Track Show/Hide
⚏ □ Track Heights
▥ □ Group Enables
🖥 □ Window Configuration   (none)

Comments

Cancel   OK

Figure 2-9:
The New
Memory
Location
dialog box
lets you
define the
location's
properties.

Setting time properties

In the Time Properties section of the New Memory Location dialog box, you
can choose from three options — Marker, Selection, and None — as well as
whether you want the reference in *bar/beat* (the location in your session
related to measures) or *absolute time* (the location in your session related to
the clock in minutes and seconds from the start of the session).

The following list fills you in on what each of the three options here means:

✦ **Marker:** This option marks a specific location and is designated by a
yellow icon in the *Markers ruler* — the ruler located at the top of the
playlist section of the Edit window. If you set the reference for the
location marker to Bar/Beat, the icon is a chevron (Figure 2-10, left). If
you set the reference to Absolute, it appears as a diamond (Figure 2-10,
right).

Figure 2-10:
Marker
memory
locations.

✦ **Selection:** Using this option marks a selected range within a track or
multiple tracks.

✦ **None:** This type of memory location is called a General Properties memory location. It actually doesn't contain any time-based information; rather, it memorizes just the selections from the General Properties section of the dialog box. (See the next section for more on the General Properties area.) This is a good option if you just want to remember a zoom or pre- and post-roll setting for part of the session.

Choosing general properties

In the General Properties section of the Memory Location dialog box (refer to Figure 2-9), you can set preferences for the information that you store with the memory location. These include

✦ **Number:** This is the marker number for your session. You can renumber any memory location by clicking in the field and typing the number you want for the location.

✦ **Name:** You can enter a name in this field to help you remember what the memory location is for.

✦ **Zoom Settings:** Use this option to store the horizontal and vertical zoom settings for the tracks.

✦ **Pre/Post Roll Times:** This option, which stores the pre- and post-roll times, is handy when using the Selection memory location for setting record ranges.

✦ **Track Show/Hide:** This setting allows you to store track layouts in your session (as far as them being shown or hidden, anyway).

✦ **Track Heights:** This option lets you store the height of tracks in your session.

✦ **Group Enables:** This setting stores both Edit and Mix groups for easy recall of them when mixing or editing.

✦ **Window Configuration:** This drop-down menu lets you choose one of your saved window configurations. You can find out more about configuring windows in Book II, Chapter 4.

✦ **Comments:** You can enter any comments or reminder in this section. This is handy for remembering what the marker is marking.

Creating memory locations

You create memory locations differently depending on the type — Marker, Selection, None — that you want. The following sections detail those ways.

Marker memory locations

Creating a Marker memory location requires these steps:

1. **Get all your Settings ducks in a row for your session so that the session is set up the way you want it to be.**

Settings here can include zoom settings, track heights, or any of the setting options listed in the previous section, "Dealing with the New Memory Location dialog box."

2. **Link your Edit and Timeline selections by clicking the Link Timeline and Edit Selection button, pressing Shift+/, or choosing Options⇨Link Timeline and Edit Selection from the main menu.**

   The Link Timeline and Edit Selection button is shown here in the margin.

3. **Open the Markers Ruler (if it's not already displayed) by choosing View⇨Ruler Markers from the main menu.**

   The Markers ruler appears just above the playlist section of the Edit window.

4. **Press Control (Mac) or Windows (PC) and position your cursor where you want the memory location in the Markers ruler. When the cursor changes to a Grabber tool with a +, go ahead and click.**

   or

   Choose the Selector tool by clicking the Selector button at the top of the Edit window.

5. **Click within any track where you want the memory location to go.**

6. **Click the Marker button located at the far left of the Memory Location ruler next to the Marker title.**

   The New Memory Location Dialog box opens. (Refer to Figure 2-8.)

7. **Select the Marker option and then use the Reference drop-down menu to choose whether you want the marker reference in bars/beats or absolute time, depending on whether you prefer to work referencing measures or the time from the start of the session.**

8. **Enter a name for the marker in the Name field and select the check boxes in the General Properties section that you want to include in the marker.**

9. **Click OK.**

   A Marker icon appears at the location you specify in Step 4.

Selection memory locations

If you have a section of the session that you think you want to go back to — such as with a drum edit — you can store that selection by creating a Selection memory location. To create a Selection memory location, follow these steps:

1. **Configure your session with the settings you want to save.**

2. **Select a section of a track or tracks that you want to memorize.**

   For more on how to select stuff, see the "Selecting Track Material" section, earlier in the chapter.

3. **Press Enter on the number pad section of your keyboard.**

   The New Memory Location dialog box opens. (Refer to Figure 2-9.)

4. **Choose the Selection option and then use the Reference drop-down menu to choose whether you want to use the bars/beats or absolute-time reference option.**

5. **Enter a name for the location and select any of the options in the General Properties section of the dialog box.**

6. **Click OK.**

   The memory location appears in the Memory Locations window (opened by choosing Window➪Memory Locations from the main menu). This window shows all the memory locations for your session.

To recall this memory location, simply click it in the Memory Locations window.

General Properties memory location

If you just want to store a zoom or pre-roll setting (or any other of the General Properties parameters) for your session, you can do so by creating a General Properties memory location. To create this type of memory location, follow these steps:

1. **Configure your session to the settings that you want to save.**

2. **Press Enter on the number pad section of your keyboard.**

   The New Memory Location dialog box opens. (Refer to Figure 2-8.)

3. **Select None.**

4. **Enter a name and select the parameters you want to save from the list in the General Properties section.**

5. **Click OK.**

   The location is stored and appears in the Memory Locations window. This window shows all the memory locations for your session and is opened by choosing Window➪Memory Locations from the main menu.

To recall this memory location, simply click it in the Memory Locations window.

Creating Marker memory locations on the fly

You can create memory locations while the session plays. You can create any type of memory location — Marker, Selection, or General Properties (none) — on the fly, but the most common are Marker memory locations. This "on-the-fly" business can be handy for marking the sections of your song or locations where you want to go back to make edits. Follow these steps to create Marker memory locations on the fly:

1. **Enable the Auto-Name Memory Locations When Playing option on the Editing tab of the Preferences dialog box.**

   Note: To get to the Preferences dialog box, choose Setup⇨Preferences from the main menu.

2. **Choose Window⇨Memory Locations from the main menu, as shown in Figure 2-11.**

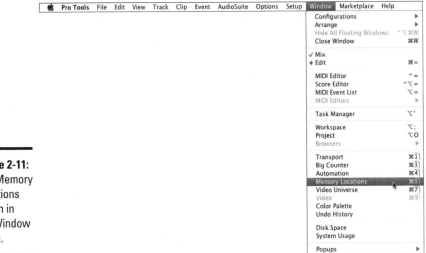

Figure 2-11:
The Memory
Locations
option in
the Window
menu.

The Memory Locations window appears. (See Figure 2-12.)

Note: You can also call up this window by pressing ⌘+5 (Mac) or Ctrl+5 (PC).

Click here to see the
window's drop-down menu

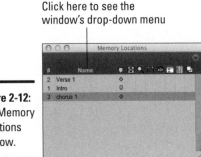

Figure 2-12:
The Memory
Locations
window.

3. **In the Memory Locations window, click the Name button and then choose the Default to Marker and the Auto-Name Memory Location options from the drop-down menu that appears.**

   If you don't choose this option, the new memory locations created on the fly are of the same type as the last one made.

4. **Set your session's time scale to bars:beats if you want the memory locations to reference bars/beats.**

   Use the arrow to the right of the Main Counter display located at the top of the Edit window to make this selection.

5. **Play your session by clicking Play in the Transport window or by pressing the spacebar on your keyboard.**

6. **Press Enter on the number pad of your keyboard when you want to place a marker.**

Getting to know the Memory Locations window

After you create a memory location, it appears in the Memory Locations window, as shown in Figure 2-12. (You access this window by choosing Window⇨Memory Locations from the main menu.) You can recall, view, name and edit your stored memory locations by using the window's drop-down menu, as shown in Figure 2-13. (You call up the window's drop-down menu by clicking the button next to the word Name in the Memory Locations window.)

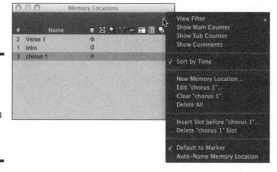

Figure 2-13: Click Name in Memory Locations to call up this menu.

Your choices on the drop-down menu for the Memory Locations window are as follows:

✦ **View Filter:** By selecting this option, a series of icons appears in the window, which lets you hide or show memory locations by their properties. The icons in this selection are (from left to right in Figure 2-14):

- Marker

- Selection Memory Location

- Zoom Settings

- Pre/Post-Roll

- Show/Hide Track

- Track Heights

- Group Enables

Descriptions of these properties can be found in the "Dealing with the New Memory Location dialog box" section, earlier in this chapter.

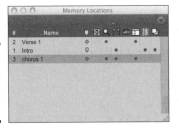

Figure 2-14:
Showing the
View Filter
icons.

✦ **Show Main Counter:** Selecting this option opens a column in the window that list the main time scale for Selection memory locations as well as the locations for Marker memory locations, as shown in Figure 2-14. General Properties memory locations have nothing listed in these columns.

✦ **Show Sub Counter:** Selecting this option opens two columns in the window that list the secondary (sub) time scales for Selection memory locations as well as the locations for Marker memory locations, as shown in Figure 2-15. General Properties memory locations have nothing listed in these columns.

✦ **Show Comments:** Here you can see any notes about the memory location that you entered when in the Comments section of the New Memory Locations dialog box. You can also add some comments by double-clicking the location in this dialog box. Double-clicking opens the New Memory Location dialog box, where you can make any changes you want.

✦ **Sort by Time:** By selecting this option, you sort your Marker memory locations by their Timeline positions in the session, followed by the Selection and General Properties locations in the order they were created. When this option isn't selected, memory locations are listed according to their assigned numbers (the order in which they were created).

Figure 2-15:
Enabling the
Show Main
Counter
option
expands
the Memory
Locations
window
to include
these
counters.

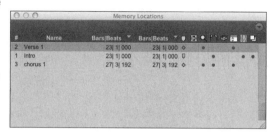

+ **New Memory Location:** Choose this option if you want to add a new location.

+ **Edit Memory Location:** Selecting this option opens the New Memory Location dialog box, where you can make changes to any of the settings.

+ **Clear Memory Location:** Choosing this option deletes the selected memory location from the list.

+ **Delete All:** This option removes all the memory locations in the session.

+ **Insert Slot:** This option creates a new memory location before this memory location in the list and renumbers all the following locations.

+ **Delete Slot:** This option deletes the selected memory location and moves the rest of the memory location in the list up and renumbers them.

+ **Default to Marker:** Choosing this option makes any memory locations that you create on the fly (see previous section) Marker memory locations.

+ **Auto-Name Memory Location:** Choosing this option automatically names memory locations created on the fly and keeps the New Memory Location dialog box from opening when you create on the fly. These names are consecutively numbered, but you can change the name later. To change the name, simply click the marker in the Markers ruler in the Edit window; when the New Memory Location dialog box opens, enter a new name in the Name field.

Recalling memory locations

You can recall memory locations from the Memory Locations window. Choose Window➪Memory Locations from the main menu to call the window up, or press ⌘+5 (Mac) or Ctrl+5 (PC). Marker memory locations can also be recalled by clicking the Marker icon in the Markers ruler located directly above the track playlist section of the Edit window.

**Book IV
Chapter 2**

**Selecting Material
to Edit**

Recalling from the Memory Locations window

Follow these steps to recall a memory location from the Memory Locations window:

1. **Open the Memory Locations window by choosing Window⇨Memory Locations from the main menu or by pressing ⌘+5 (Mac) or Ctrl+5 (PC).**

Refer to Figure 2-11 for a peek at what this window looks like.

2. **If your Link Timeline and Edit Selections option isn't enabled and you want to recall a Selection memory location, click the Link Timeline and Edit Selection button to enable the option.**

3. **Click the memory location you want in the Memory Locations window to recall it.**

or

Press the memory location number followed by a period (.) if you have the Numeric Keypad mode set to Classic mode. If your numeric keypad is set to Transport mode, press period (.) followed by the memory location number followed by another period (.).

To select your Numeric Keypad Mode options, first choose Setup⇨ Preferences from the main menu. After the Preferences dialog box appears, click the Operations tab and then select the appropriate mode check boxes.

Recalling markers from the Markers ruler

You can recall a Marker memory location in the Markers ruler by following these steps:

1. **Display the Markers ruler in the session by choosing View⇨Rulers⇨ Markers from the main menu.**

This ruler appears directly above the track playlist section of the Edit window.

2. **Click the marker.**

The General Properties settings stored in the marker are instantly recalled.

Editing memory locations

You can perform quite a few editing functions on your various memory locations including renaming them, deleting them, editing their properties, copying them, and pasting them. These functions are detailed in the following sections.

Renaming a memory location

To rename a memory location, follow these steps:

1. **Double-click the memory location in the Memory Locations window or Markers ruler.**

   The Edit Memory Location dialog box makes an appearance. (Refer to Figure 2-8.)

2. **Enter the new name in the Name field.**

3. **Click OK.**

Changing a memory location's properties

You can change the properties of a stored memory location a number of different ways, depending on the change you want to make. This section details changing general properties, location types, and selection ranges.

First off, you can redefine General Properties settings by using these steps:

1. **Set up your new General Properties settings (zoom, track height, and so on).**

2. **Open the Memory Location window by pressing ⌘+5 (Mac) or Ctrl+5 (PC) or by choosing Window⇨Memory Location from the main menu.**

3. **Control-click (Mac) or right-click (PC) the memory location in the Memory Location window.**

   You can also Control-click (Mac) or right-click (PC) the Marker icon in the Markers ruler if you want to redefine a Marker memory location.

   The Edit Memory Location dialog box opens.

4. **Enter the General Properties you want to include in this marker; optionally, enter a new name.**

   This only stores the settings you have in your session; it doesn't create them. You need to make sure that your screen is the way you want it before saving the settings.

5. **Click OK.**

You can change your memory location type — Marker, Selection, None — by doing the following:

1. **Open the Memory Location window by pressing ⌘+5 (Mac) or Ctrl+5 (PC) or by choosing Window⇨Memory Location from the main menu.**

2. **Double-click the name of the memory location (in the Memory Location window) or the Marker memory location (in the Markers ruler).**

   The Edit Memory Location dialog box opens.

3. **Select Marker, Selection, or None; optionally, enter a new name.**

4. **Click OK.**

You can change the selection range of a Selection location by following these steps:

1. **Open the Memory Locations window by choosing Window⇨Memory Locations from the main menu or by pressing ⌘+5 (Mac) or Ctrl+5 (PC).**

2. **Select a range of material within your session.**

   For more on how to select stuff, see the "Selecting Track Material" section, earlier in the chapter.

3. **Control-click (Mac) or right-click (PC) on the name of the Selection memory location you want to change in the Memory Locations window.**

   The Edit Memory Location dialog box opens.

4. **(Optional) Enter a new name for the Selection memory location in the Name field of the Memory Location dialog box.**

5. **Click OK.**

   Your new selection is saved with the Selection memory location.

You can move a Marker memory location one of these ways:

✦ **Drag a marker by grabbing the icon in the Markers ruler and dragging it to its new location.**

   The Markers ruler is located just above the track playlist section of the Edit window. If it's not visible, select View⇨Rulers⇨Markers from the main menu.

✦ **Align a marker by clicking with the Selector tool on the new location along the Timebase ruler or within a track's playlist and then Control-clicking (Mac) or right-clicking (PC) the name of the marker location in the Memory Locations window.**

✦ **Align the marker to the start of a clip by selecting the clip with the Grabber tool, and then Control-clicking (Mac) or right-clicking (PC) the name of the marker location in the Memory Locations window.**

Copying and pasting memory locations

You can copy single or multiple markers in a session by following these steps:

1. **Choose the Selector tool by clicking the Selector Tool button at the top of the Edit window.**

2. **Drag along the Markers ruler to select the portion of the session that contains the markers you want to copy. To select all the markers in the session, double-click anywhere in the Markers ruler.**

   If the beginning of your selection includes a marker, press ⌘ (Mac) or Ctrl (PC) for the Selector tool to appear because it will automatically disappear when your cursor is located directly over an existing marker.

3. **Choose Edit⇨Copy from the main menu or press ⌘+C (Mac) or Ctrl+C (PC) to copy the selection onto the Clipboard.**

If you want to paste the selection somewhere else in the session, follow these steps:

1. **Place your cursor along the Markers ruler where you want to paste the markers.**

2. **Press ⌘+V (Mac) or Ctrl+V (PC) or choose Edit⇨Paste from the main menu.**

Playing Selected Material

After you make a selection, you're free to give it a listen. The following sections cover a variety of ways of doing this.

Playing your selection

To play your selection, simply click the Play button in the Transport window or press the spacebar on your keyboard. All the tracks in the session will play during the selected range. If you want to hear only the track(s) in which you made your selection, you have one of two choices:

✦ Hide or mute the tracks you don't want to hear.

✦ Solo the track(s) you do want to hear.

Using pre- and post-rolls

You can set Pro Tools to play a designated length of time before and after your selection by using pre- and post-rolls. The following sections show you how to set your pre-rolls and post-rolls as well as how to audition them.

Setting and enabling pre- and post-rolls

To set pre- and post-rolls, do the following:

1. **Choose View⇨Transport⇨Expanded from the main menu.**

   The Pre- and Post-Roll fields appear in the window.

2. **Click in the Pre- or Post-Roll field in the Transport window, type in a number, and then press Return/Enter.**

3. **Press ⌘+K (Mac) or Ctrl+K (PC) or choose Options⇨Pre/Post-roll from the main menu to enable the Pre- and Post-Roll feature.**

Auditioning pre- and post-rolls

If you just want to hear the pre- or post-roll, you can audition them by doing the following:

✦ **To audition the pre-roll:** Press Option+← (Mac) or Alt+← (PC). The pre-roll plays to the start of the selection or to the position of the cursor in the selected clip.

✦ **To audition the post-roll:** Press ⌘+→ (Mac) or Ctrl+→ (PC). The post-roll plays from its beginning or from the current cursor location.

Auditioning start and end points

When you audition start and end points, you get to listen to just the beginning or end of a selection without having to listen to the whole thing. This kind of auditioning is done in the following ways.

Auditioning the start point

You can audition the start point of a selection either with or without listening to the pre-roll along with it. Both options are covered in this section.

✦ **To audition just the start point of a selection:** Press ⌘+← (Mac) or Ctrl+← (PC). The selection plays for the length of time designated in the Post-Roll field of the Transport window.

✦ **To audition the start point of a selection along with the pre-roll:** Press ⌘+Option+← (Mac) or Ctrl+Alt+← (PC). The pre-roll plays along with the length of the selection, as designated in the Post-Roll field of the Transport window as long as you have the Pre/Post-roll Playback function enabled. (Choose Options⇨Pre/Post-roll from the main menu.)

Auditioning the end point

Pro Tools lets you audition the end point of your selection, either with or without hearing the post-roll too. Here's how to use these options:

✦ **To audition just the end point of a selection:** Press Option+→ (Mac) or Alt+→ (PC). The selection starts at the point equal to the pre-roll amount from the end of the selection.

✦ **To audition the end point of a selection along with the post-roll:** Press
⌘+Option+→ (Mac) or Ctrl+Alt+→ (PC). The selection starts at the point
equal to the pre-roll amount from the end of the selection and continue
until the end of the post-roll.

Looping your selection's playback

If you have a section of the song that you want to listen to repeatedly (say,
if you're trying to find a chair-squeak to edit out), you can loop a selection
with the Loop command. This enables you to create looped sections and to
make sure that your start and end points play seamlessly. Follow these steps
to loop a selection:

1. **Engage the Link Timeline and Edit Selection option by choosing
   Options⇨Link Timeline and Edit Selection from the main menu or by
   clicking the Link Timeline and Edit Selection button.**

2. **Make a selection by using one of the techniques listed in the
   "Selecting Track Material" section, earlier in this chapter.**

3. **Choose Options⇨Loop Playback from the main menu, or Control-click
   (Mac) or right-click (PC) the Play button in the Transport window.**

4. **Click Play in the Transport window or press the spacebar on your
   keyboard.**

   If you have the pre-roll engaged, playback will begin with it; otherwise, it
   starts at the beginning of your selection. When the selection loops, the
   pre-and post-rolls won't play after the starting pre-roll (if you have the
   function engaged).

5. **Click Stop in the Transport window or press the spacebar on your
   keyboard to stop playback.**

Chapter 3: Getting into Editing

In This Chapter

✔ **Working with clips**

✔ **Using Edit commands**

✔ **Editing clips**

✔ **Working with looped material**

*P*ro Tools offers you many options for editing the audio files in your sessions, include cutting file segments, copying them, pasting them, clearing them, basting them, and marinating them. (Okay, maybe not the last two, but you get the point.) You can also edit by trimming segments, moving them, aligning them, locking them, and so on.

In this chapter, you discover the many Edit commands of Pro Tools and you begin to edit *clips* — the term for audio file segments — using the various Edit functions that Pro Tools is famous for. I also fill you in on creating loops you can use to build your song (if that's the way you want to work).

Editing Clips

Clips are the defined areas of the track in which you do your editing. Each audio file is represented in your session by a clip (or series of clips). A clip can be the entire file, or it can be bits and pieces of a file. When you edit in Pro Tools, you're not actually making any changes to the audio file. (Later in this chapter, I explain some exceptions to this.) Instead, you make changes to the way Pro Tools plays those files by editing the clips that represent the file.

For example, if you decide that a track really does sound better without that accordion solo and you cut that section of the clip containing that part, the section isn't really erased from your hard drive: It's simply not played back when you listen to your session. This allows you to make a stunning variety of edits without having to worry about ruining your original audio file.

Being able to create, capture, separate, trim, and heal clips is essential to being able to edit in Pro Tools. I explain these procedures in the following sections.

Creating clips

Whenever you record or import an audio file in Pro Tools, you create a clip of that entire file. You can edit that clip. However, after you cut, separate, paste, or perform any other edit to it, you're creating new clips from the original file. You have several ways to create new clips with which to work, including capturing selections, separating selections, and trimming to a selection. These are all covered in the following sections.

When you create a new clip, it appears in the track's *playlist* — the area next to the Track Controls section of the Edit window that contains the visual representations of the audio files (clips) — as well as in the Audio Clips list, located on the right side of the Edit and the Mix windows.

Using the Capture Clip command

Use the Capture Clip command to create a new clip within an existing one. The new clip is still part of the original clip, but it has its own name. If you want to create a clip that can be moved around separately from the original, use the Separate Clips command, as detailed in the next section. To use the Capture Clip command, follow these steps:

1. **Choose the Selector tool from the top of the Edit window.**

2. **Click and drag the track's clip in the playlist section of the Edit window where you want to create a new clip.**

3. **Choose Clip⇨Capture from the main menu or press ⌘+R (Mac) or Ctrl+R (PC).**

4. **In the Name Clip dialog box that appears, enter the name of this clip and then click OK.**

    The new clip is created, and the clip's name appears in the Audio Clips list menu in the track's playlist.

Employing the Separate Clips command

If you want to create a clip that can be moved around separately from the original, use the Separate Clips command. Here's how it's done:

1. **Choose the Selector tool from the top of the Edit window.**

2. **Click and drag on the track's clip in the track's playlist where you want to create a new clip.**

    To select more than one track, drag across the desired tracks.

3. **Choose Edit⇨Separate Clip from the main menu or press ⌘+E (Mac) or Ctrl+E (PC).**

    Here you have three options of where to create the clip:

- *At Selection:* Choose At Selection to create a new clip with boundaries at the selection start and end points.

- *On Grid:* Choose On Grid to create a clip according to the current grid resolution.

- *At Transients:* Chose At Transients to automatically create clip boundaries on detected transients within a selection. The program does this with the same method as when you employ the Tab to Transients feature.

4. **In the Name Clip dialog box that appears, enter the name of this clip and then click OK.**

    The new clip is created, and its name appears in the Audio Clips list menu. You can now move, copy, cut, or otherwise edit this clip.

If you don't want to have to type in a name for this new clip, you can use the Pro Tools Auto-Name feature, which automatically gives your new clips such exciting names as kick drum_02. To activate this feature, choose Setup⇨Preferences from the main menu, click the Editing tab in the Preferences dialog box when it appears, and then select the Auto-Name Separated Clips check box on that tab.

If you have a bunch of takes that you recorded in succession (when you loop-record, for example) and you want to separate them all at the same place, select the Separate Clip Operates on All Related Takes check box on the Editing tab of the Preferences dialog box. (Choose Setup⇨Preferences from the main menu to get to the Preference dialog box.) If you do this, make sure that both the Take Clip Names That Match Track Names and Take Clips Lengths That Match options are also selected on the second Editing tab of Preferences dialog box.

Using the Separation Grabber tool

If you want to separate and move a clip in one step, you can use the Separation Grabber tool, located in the Edit Tools section of the Edit window. You can toggle between the Grabber tool and the Separation Grabber tool by clicking and holding the Grabber button and choosing the Separation option from the pop-up menu that appears, as shown in Figure 3-1.

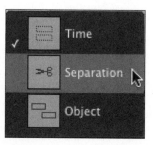

Figure 3-1:
Toggle the Grabber and Separation Grabber tools.

To use the Separation Grabber tool, follow these steps:

1. **With the Selector tool, drag over the part of the clip you want to separate in the playlist section of the Edit window.**

   This selection can be across multiple tracks or clips within a single track.

2. **Click and hold the Grabber tool and choose the Separation option from the pop-up menu that appears.**

3. **Click the selection you made in Step 1 and drag the selection to where you want.**

   Pro Tools automatically creates three new clips: the separated section as well as the parts before and after this section. These three sections all show up in the Audio Clips list menu.

If you want to leave the original clip as it is and grab a section from it to put somewhere else, press Option (Mac) or Alt (PC) when you drag the selection with the Separation Grabber tool. The original clip remains intact, and your selection is simply copied and moved.

Trying the Trim to Selection command

Use the Trim to Selection command to choose a section of a clip and remove the unselected parts of that clip. Follow these steps to trim unwanted parts from a selection:

1. **Choose the area you want to keep by selecting it in the track's playlist with the Selector tool.**

2. **Press ⌘+T (Mac) or Ctrl+T (PC) or choose Edit⇨Trim Clip⇨To Selection from the main menu, as shown in Figure 3-2.**

   The unselected parts of the clip disappear.

Healing clips

Use the Heal Separations command to recombine clips that you separated. Here are some restrictions to this process:

✦ You can't heal clips that come from different audio files.

✦ Your clips must be in the same places they were when you separated them.

Figure 3-2:
Use the Trim
to Selection
command
to get rid of
unselected
parts of a
clip.

To heal two clips, follow these steps:

1. **Using the Selector tool, select a portion of both clips along with the spot to be healed, as shown in Figure 3-3.**

2. **Choose Edit⇨Heal Separation from the main menu or press ⌘+H (Mac) or Ctrl+H (PC).**

   Your two clips become one again.

Figure 3-3:
Select the
area you
want to
heal.

If the selection doesn't heal (because one clip has been moved, for instance), you can use one of the following remedies:

✦ **Find what's hidden.** This procedure expands the clip to include hidden material. In this case, the hidden material is the stuff from the deleted clip.

    a. *Choose Slip Edit mode (from the Edit mode options at the top-left portion of the Edit window).*

    b. *Delete one of the two clips.*

    c. *With the Trimmer tool, expand the existing clip to its original size. (See the "Trimming clips" section, later in this chapter, for more on the Trimmer tool.)*

✦ **Delete both clips and drag the original clip into the track from the Audio Clips list.** Chapter 1 in this mini-book has more on this procedure.

Placing clips in tracks

All the clips for your session are located in the Audio Clips list; you can use this list to drag a clip (or clips) into any track.

Placing a clip in a track

Follow these steps to place a clip in a track:

1. **Select the clip you want to place in a track by highlighting it in the Audio Clips list.**

The Audio Clips list is located on the right side of the Edit and the Mix windows.

2. **Click the clip's name and drag it into the track where you want it.**

Depending on the Edit mode that you select (from the options located at the upper-left corner of the Edit window), your clip is placed in one of several possible ways:

✦ **In Shuffle mode:** Placing a clip while in Shuffle mode slides existing clips to make room for the one you're placing. This places clips end to end: They touch one another automatically.

✦ **In Spot mode:** Placing a clip while in Spot mode opens a dialog box where you can enter the position of the clip you're placing. This mode allows you to place a clip at a precise point.

✦ **In Slip mode:** Placing a clip while in Slip mode lets you drag the clip anywhere you want within the track's playlist, allowing you to overlap another clip or be separated from it.

✦ **In Grid mode:** Placing a clip in Grid mode places the clip to the nearest grid boundary. Pro Tools lets you temporarily disable the grid by pressing ⌘ (Mac) or Ctrl (PC) while you drag your selected clip into a track.

You can adjust the grid value for your session by opening the Grid Value drop-down menu, as shown in Figure 3-4. (To open this menu, click and hold the arrow to the right of the Grid title in the center of the Edit menu, right below the Edit tools.)

Figure 3-4: Use the Grid Value drop-down menu to choose the grid value of your session.

Placing a clip at the Edit Insert point

You can designate an Edit Insert point by clicking your cursor within a track in the playlist section of the Edit window; you can then place your clip right at this point. You can have either the clip's start or end point snap to the Edit Insert point.

To designate an Edit Insert point, start by locating your cursor at the place in the track where you want the clip placed, as shown in Figure 3-5. Then, depending on where you want your clip to end up, do one of the following:

✦ **To place the start of a clip at the Edit Insert point:** Press Control (Mac) or Windows (PC) while you drag the clip from the Audio Clips list to the track.

✦ **If the clip is already in the track and you want to move it:** Press Control (Mac) or Windows (PC) while dragging with the Grabber tool.

✦ **To place the end of a clip at the Edit Insert point:** Press ⌘+Control (Mac) or Ctrl+Windows (PC) while you drag the clip from the Audio Clips list to the track.

✦ **If the clip already resides in the track:** Press ⌘+Control (Mac) or Ctrl+Windows (PC) while dragging with the Grabber tool.

Figure 3-5:
Click a clip
to identify
the Edit
Insert point.

Using clip synch points

A *synch point* is a specific location in your session where you can have clips align. This lets you place a specific point in the clip (the *synch point*) precisely where you want without regard to the placements of start or end points of that clip. You can assign a clip synch point in Pro Tools anywhere within the session. This feature is helpful when you want to place a sound at a precise point in the session, like when you're *spotting* (positioning) sound effects for video. With a synch point, you first mark the location sound effect that you want to place (breaking glass, for instance) in the clip with this sound and then place that clip where you want the glass to start breaking in your session. This makes it easy to spot that sound even when the sound doesn't begin at the start point of a clip.

Creating a synch point

To define a clip's synch point, follow these steps:

1. **With the Selector tool, click within a track where you want your synch point to be.**

2. **Choose Clip⇨Identify Synch Point from the main menu, as shown in Figure 3-6, or press ⌘+, (comma; Mac) or Ctrl+, (comma; PC).**

   A small arrow appears at the bottom of the clip, as shown in Figure 3-7, to show you where you placed the synch point.

   You can remove the synch point by choosing Clip⇨Remove Synch Point from the main menu.

Each clip can have only one synch point at a time. To change the location of this synch point, simply select a new place in the clip and choose Clip⇨Identify Synch Point again from the main menu. The old synch point is removed, and a new one appears at the new location.

Figure 3-6:
Define a
synch point
from the Edit
menu.

Figure 3-7:
An arrow at
the bottom
shows
where
the synch
point is.

Placing a clip's synch point at an Edit Insert point

After you have a synch point defined, you can use it to place or align a clip within your track's playlist. To place the synch point of the clip to the Edit Insert point in the track's playlist, do the following:

1. **With the Selector tool, click a point in the target clip to define your Edit Insert point.**

2. **Press Shift+Control (Mac) or Shift+ Windows (PC) while dragging the clip you want to insert — the one containing the synch point you added, following the procedure outlined in the previous step list — from the Audio Clips list into the track.**

The clip's synch point snaps to the selected position in the track's playlist.

or

If the clip with the synch point already resides within the track, switch to the Grabber tool and then press Shift+Control (Mac) or Shift+Windows (PC) while clicking the clip.

The clip's synch point snaps to the selected position in the track's playlist.

Aligning clips

Pro Tools lets you align the start, end, or synch point of clips to the start point of another clip. This can be helpful for arranging clips in songs to get synchronized playback.

Aligning a start point of a clip with the start point of a clip on another track

To align a start point of a clip with the start point of a clip on another track, follow these steps:

1. **With the Grabber tool, click the clip in the playlist of the track you want to align to.**

2. **If the clip you want to move already exists in the playlist of the track from Step 1, press Control (Mac) or Windows (PC) and then click the clip you want to move.**

    The clip automatically moves into position.

    or

    If the clip you want to move resides in the Audio Clips list, press Control (Mac) or Windows (PC) and then click and drag the clip onto the track's playlist.

    Both start points are aligned.

Aligning the end point of a clip with the start point of a clip on a different track

To align the end point of a clip with the start point of a clip on a different track, follow these steps:

1. **With the Grabber tool, click the clip you want to align to in the track's playlist.**

2. **If the clip you want to move is located in the playlist of the track from Step 1, press ⌘+Control (Mac) or Ctrl+ Windows (PC) and then click the clip.**

   The clip automatically moves into position.

   or

   If this clip isn't already in the track's playlist, press ⌘+Control (Mac) or Ctrl+Windows (PC) and click and drag the clip you want to move from the Audio Clips list onto the playlist.

   The end point of the clip you moved is aligned to the start point of the first clip you chose.

Aligning a clip's synch point with the start point of another track's clip

To align the synch point of a clip with the start point of a clip on a different track, follow these steps:

1. **With the Grabber tool, click the clip you want to align to in the track's playlist.**

2. **If the clip you want to move is located in the playlist of the track from Step 1, press Shift+Control (Mac) or Shift+Windows (PC) while clicking with the Grabber tool on the clip.**

   The clip automatically moves into position.

   or

   If the clip doesn't already exist within the track's playlist, you can place and align a clip from the Audio Clips list by pressing Shift+Control (Mac) or Shift+Windows (PC) while clicking and dragging the clip from the Audio Clips list.

   The synch point of the second clip aligns to the start point of the first, as shown in Figure 3-8.

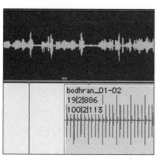

Figure 3-8:
You can align the synch point from one clip to the start point of another.

Book IV
Chapter 3

Getting into Editing

Trimming clips

You can trim clips by using the Trimmer tool, choosing Edit⇨Trim Clip from the main menu, or nudging the start or end point of a clip. The Trimmer tool, as shown here in the margin, consists of two options: the Standard Trimmer and the Time Trimmer. These trimming options are detailed in the following sections.

Using the Standard Trimmer tool

Use the Standard Trimmer tool to shorten or lengthen (to the maximum length of the parent audio file, anyway) a clip without altering the original file. Whenever you trim a clip, a new clip is created in the Audio Clips list.

To trim a clip with the Standard Trimmer tool, first call up the tool by clicking the Trimmer Tool button. Then do one of the following:

✦ **Place the cursor near the start or end point of a clip and drag the clip's start or end point to shorten or lengthen, as shown in Figure 3-9.**

Figure 3-9:
To trim or expand a clip, drag with the Trimmer tool.

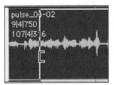

✦ **Place your cursor where you want to trim the clip and click with your mouse, as shown in Figure 3-10.**

Figure 3-10:
To trim a clip, click the Trim point with the Trimmer tool.

The clip is trimmed to the start point or the end point, depending on where you place the cursor. If the cursor is located closer to the start point, you trim the start point; conversely, if the cursor is closer to the end point, you trim the end point. You can reverse the default here by pressing Option (Mac) or Alt (PC) while you trim.

TIP

You can tell which way the trim is going to happen by the direction of the cursor. Figure 3-11 shows the cursor as it is set to trim the start point (left) and the end point (right).

Figure 3-11: Trimming the start point (left) or the end point (right).

REMEMBER

The Trimmer tools (both the Standard Trimmer and the Time Trimmer) behave differently depending on the Edit mode you're using. Here's a quick rundown of the differences:

✦ **Shuffle mode:** In this mode, any adjacent clips slide over while you expand or trim the clip.

✦ **Spot mode:** In this mode, the Spot dialog box appears, prompting you to type in the exact placement of the clip's start or end point.

✦ **Grid mode:** In this mode, any trimming or expanding that you do automatically snaps to the nearest grid boundary.

✦ **Slip mode:** In this mode, your clip moves to wherever you place it. Any other clips in the playlist remain where they are.

TIP

If you want to return the clip to its original size, you can

✦ Drag the original clip from the Audio Clips list to the track's playlist.

✦ Drag the start or end point of the clip with the Trimmer tool to its original length.

Tackling the Time Trimmer tool

Use the Time Trimmer tool, as shown here in the margin, to expand or compress a clip by using the Time Compression/Expansion (TC/E) plug-in to create a new audio file. Using the Time Trimmer is different from using the Standard Trimmer: Instead of cutting off part of the file when you trim, the Time Trimmer tool shortens how long the clip takes to play.

When you use the Time Trimmer tool to expand or compress a clip, it alters the speed at which the clip plays — and this alters how the material in the clip sounds. Compressing speeds up the clip; expanding slows it down.

To use the Time Trimmer tool, call it up by clicking and holding over the Trimmer tool button and then dragging down to select the Time Trimmer option. Then do one of the following:

+ **Place the cursor near the start or end point of a clip and drag the clip's start or end point to shorten or lengthen the clip. (Refer to Figure 3-9.)**

+ **Place your cursor where you want to expand or contract the clip and click with your mouse. (Refer to Figure 3-10.)**

  The start or end point of the clip moves out or in depending on which way the Time Trimmer Tool cursor is facing. (See upcoming Figure 3-12.)

The Edit mode you use determines how the Time Trimmer tool behaves and how the clips surrounding the trim react. Check out the previous section for a rundown of the different ways that the Edit modes work with the trim tools.

To return the clip to its original length, follow these steps:

+ Drag the original clip from the Audio Clips list to the track's playlist.

+ Choose Edit⟳Undo from the main menu (assuming this was the last operation you performed).

Taking advantage of the Trim command

You can trim clips using the Trim command located in the Edit menu. (Refer to Figure 3-2.) The menu gives you three options:

+ **Trim to Selection:** Using this command removes all the clip except the part you selected, as shown in Figure 3-12. To do this trim, select the part of the clip that you want to keep and then choose this command.

Figure 3-12:
Now you see it (left), now you don't (right): the Trim to Selection command.

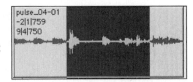
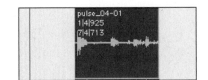

+ **Trim Start to Insertion:** This command trims the clip from the start point to the Edit Insert point designated by your cursor, as shown in Figure 3-13. To perform this trim, start by placing your cursor where you want to trim to and then choose this command.

Figure 3-13:
The Trim
Start to
Insertion
command.

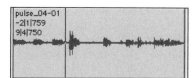 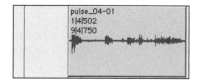

+ **Trim End to Insertion:** Using this command removes that part of the clip from the Edit Insert point to the end point of the clip, as shown in Figure 3-14. Doing this trim is as simple as placing your cursor at the desired place in the clip and then choosing the command from the Edit menu.

Figure 3-14:
The Trim
End to
Insertion
command.

Using the Nudge function to trim a clip

You can trim or expand the start or end points of a clip using the plus (+) and minus (–) keys on the number pad section of your keyboard. (To see how to set the Nudge value, go to the next section, "Moving clips.")

Here's how to trim the start point by using the Nudge function:

1. **With the Grabber tool, select a clip.**

2. **Press Option (Mac) or Alt (PC) along with the plus (+) key to trim or the minus (–) key to expand the start point.**

    Each time you press the key, you move the boundary of the clip by the Nudge value.

To trim the end point with the Nudge function:

1. **With the Grabber tool, select a clip.**

2. **Press ⌘ (Mac) or Ctrl (PC) along with the plus (+) key to expand or the minus (–) key to trim the end point.**

   Each time you press the key, you move the boundary of the clip by the Nudge value.

Moving clips

You can move (that is, slide) clips in a session either within a track or across tracks. You can nudge them, shift them, and — depending on the Edit mode you're using — move them to precisely where you want them. This section details the many ways you can move clips.

Before you do any moving, however, keep two things in mind:

+ **You can make a copy of a clip you want to slide by pressing Option (Mac) or Alt (PC) while you slide it.** This keeps the original in its place.

+ **When you move a clip from one track to another, you can keep its start point from changing by pressing Control (Mac) or Windows (PC) while you slide it.** This lets you move clips from track to track without losing (ahem) track of its position in the session.

Nudging

If you want to move a clip only a little bit, simply nudge it. With the Nudge function, you can set the Nudge value to be as fine or as coarse as you like.

To set the Nudge value, click and hold the arrow to the right of the Nudge title located just beneath the Counters in the Edit window to open the Nudge Value drop-down menu. Then select the scale and value you want, as shown in Figure 3-15. You can choose Bars:Beats, Min:Sec, or Samples for your Nudge scale. The values you choose depend on this scale. You can also choose to follow the main time scale for the session by selecting that option at the bottom of the dialog box.

Figure 3-15: Set the Nudge value from the Nudge drop-down menu.

To actually nudge a clip or multiple clips, do the following:

1. **With the Grabber tool, select the clip or clips that you want to move.**

Select the Grabber by clicking its icon in the upper part of the Edit window.

To select more than one clip, press the Shift key while you grab each clip.

2. **Press the plus (+) key or minus (–) key in the numerical section of your keyboard to move it right or left, respectively.**

Each press of the key moves the clip over by the Nudge value.

If you want to move the clip over faster and still use the Nudge function, you can have Pro Tools move the clip by the next higher Nudge value than the one you chose. For example, if you have the Nudge value set for quarter notes, you can nudge by half notes. Here's the drill:

1. **With the Grabber tool, select the clip(s) you want to nudge.**

2. **Press Control (Mac) or Windows (PC) as well as the slash key (/) to move the material forward (right) or the M key to nudge it back (left).**

You can skip using the Control (Mac) or Windows (PC) keys if you have the Commands Focus button enabled.

You can nudge the contents within a clip without moving its start or end points. This lets you keep the clip you have as well as its start and end points while changing which material from the clip's parent audio file is contained within the clip's boundaries.

1. **With the Grabber tool, select the clip you want to nudge.**

2. **Press Control (Mac) or Windows (PC) and the plus (+) key to move the clip's content to the right and minus (–) key to move the contents to the left.**

The clip stays put, and the audio from the original file moves within it, as shown in Figure 3-16.

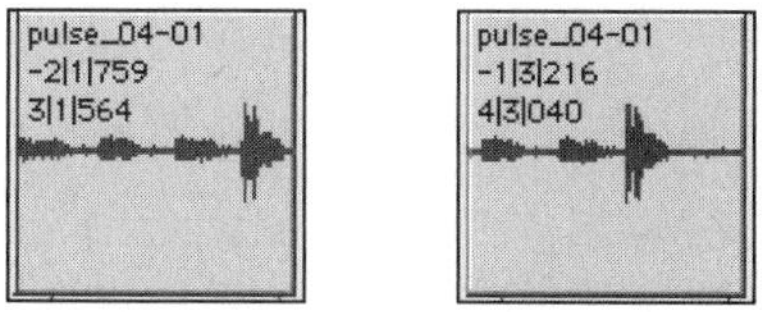

Book IV
Chapter 3

Getting into Editing

Figure 3-16:
Nudging a clip moves the audio file within the clip.

This process works only if audio information is located outside the current clip's boundaries.

Shifting clips

Use the Pro Tools Shift command to move clips by a specified amount. This is very handy when compensating for latency, such as with the Mbox or with some plug-ins.

To shift clips via the Shift command, follow these steps:

1. **Select a clip, using either the Grabber or the Selector tool.**

   You can select clips from more than one track. (Check out Book IV, Chapter 2 for details on how to do this.)

2. **Choose Edit⇨Shift from the main menu.**

   The Shift dialog box appears, as shown in Figure 3-17.

Figure 3-17:
Shift a clip by a specific amount.

3. **Enter the Shift value in the Shift dialog box as well as whether you want to shift the clip earlier or later.**

   This value can be in whatever time format you want: bars and beats, minutes and seconds, or samples.

4. **Click OK.**

   The clip shifts by the amount you specify in Step 3.

The Edit mode you're in has no effect on how the Shift command works. Your clip moves over by the specified amount regardless of whether any other clips are present on that spot.

Moving with Edit modes

When you move or slide clips around in sessions, each Edit mode treats the clips differently. In this section, I describe how these modes work. (You select your Edit mode by clicking the corresponding mode name in the upper-left side of the Edit window.)

✦ **Shuffle mode:** You can shuffle clips by selecting the Shuffle Edit mode. This mode lets you shuffle the clips in a track around, but they always snap to one another — start point to end point.

✦ **Slip mode:** In Slip Edit mode, you can move clips around at will. You can have space between them and have them overlap.

If you place a clip in a track using Slip mode and then switch to Shuffle mode, that clip stays where it is while you shuffle other clips in the track. These other clips might end up overlapping the slipped clip, or you might end up with empty space between them.

✦ **Spot mode:** In Spot mode, whenever you select a clip or part of a clip, the Spot dialog box opens, prompting you to enter your destination location.

✦ **Grid mode:** In Grid mode, your clips snap to the nearest grid boundary when you move them around. Grid mode offers you two options:

- *Absolute:* Whenever you move a clip in Absolute mode, the start point moves to the nearest grid boundary.

- *Relative:* When you move a clip in Relative mode, it moves by grid increments (the square units of the grid). This allows you to move a clip around while keeping its start point at the same position relative to a grid boundary.

For example, if you have a clip that starts on the last sixteenth note of a beat and your grid value is set for quarter notes, here's what the move looks like: Each time you move the clip by one grid increment, the clip moves by the value of one quarter note — but it *stays* at the last sixteenth note of the beat. This is handy for moving around drum rhythms.

You can change the grid resolution by opening the Grid drop-down menu — refer to Figure 3-4 — and choosing the grid scale and value. You open this menu by clicking and holding the arrow to the right of the Grid title situated under the Edit tools at the upper end of the Edit window.

You can show the grid in the Edit menu by clicking the Timebase ruler icon, located at the top of the Timebase ruler section of the Edit window. This grid is labeled with whatever time format you chose for your main counter. You can also select the Draw Grid in Edit Window option, on the Display tab of the Preferences dialog box, to show the grid. (Choose Setup➪Preferences from the main menu to call up the Preferences dialog box.)

Locking clips

You can lock clips in place after you put them where you want them. This keeps you from accidentally moving or deleting them when you work with other clips in the session. To lock a clip, do the following:

1. **With the Grabber tool, select one or more clips.**

   To select multiple clips on different tracks, press and hold the Shift key while you click each clip.

2. **Choose Clip⇨Lock/Unlock from the main menu.**

   A small closed-lock icon appears at the lower-left corner of the clip, as shown in Figure 3-18.

   To unlock a clip, select the clip and choose Clip⇨Lock/Unlock from the main menu.

Figure 3-18:
A small lock icon indicates a locked clip.

Lock icon

In effect, because they won't move, any clip after the locked clip is also locked when you're in Shuffle mode. Also, in this mode, you can't place a clip in front of the locked one if it's longer than the space available for it.

Quantizing clips

Quantizing clips in Pro Tools involves snapping a clip's start or synch point (if you have one defined) to the nearest grid boundary. It's a way to align clips, which is handy for working with drum and percussion parts because you can arrange them and then quantize them to make them fit the groove of the song. To quantize a clip, follow these steps:

1. **Set the grid value that you want in the Grid Value drop-down menu.**

   You open this menu by clicking and holding the arrow to the right of the Grid title, located just beneath the Edit tool sections at the top of the Edit window.

2. **With the Grabber tool, select the clip you want to quantize.**

   Selecting part of a clip quantizes the entire clip because this command moves the start point (and the rest of the clip with it).

3. **Choose Clip⇨Quantize to Grid from the main menu, as shown in Figure 3-19, or press ⌘+0 (zero; Mac) or Ctrl+0 (zero; PC).**

   The clip's start or synch point moves to the nearest grid boundary.

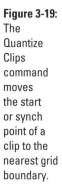

Figure 3-19:
The
Quantize
Clips
command
moves
the start
or synch
point of a
clip to the
nearest grid
boundary.

Muting/unmuting clips

You can mute clips or parts of clips. This gives you more flexibility than muting an entire track. To mute a clip, do the following:

1. **Select a clip or a portion of one.**

   • *To select the entire clip:* Use the Grabber tool and click anywhere on that clip within the track's playlist.

   • *To select a portion of a clip:* Use the Selector tool and drag across the clip in the track's playlist.

2. **Press ⌘+M (Mac) or Ctrl+M (PC) or choose Clip⇨Mute/Unmute from the main menu.**

   When muted, the clip appears dimmed in the playlist, as shown in Figure 3-20.

**Book IV
Chapter 3**

Getting into Editing

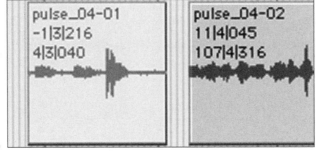

Figure 3-20:
Muted clips
are dimmed
in the
playlist.

To unmute a clip, follow these steps:

1. **With the Grabber tool, select the muted clip or portion of the clip.**

You select the Grabber tool by clicking the Grabber tool button at the
top of the Edit window.

2. **Choose Clip⇨Mute/Unmute from the main menu or press ⌘+M (Mac)
or Ctrl+M (PC).**

What was muted is now unmuted.

Splitting stereo tracks

When you work with stereo tracks, you usually work with both sides of the
stereo file at once. If you want to edit one or another of the stereo channels
independently, the first step toward doing so is splitting the stereo track
into two mono tracks.

You split a stereo track into two mono tracks by following these steps:

1. **Click the track in the Edit or Mix window with the Grabber tool to
select the track you want to split, as shown in the upper part of
Figure 3-21.**

If you want to split more than one track, Shift-click the rest of the tracks.

2. **Choose Track⇨Split into Mono from the main menu.**

The tracks are split and renamed automatically, as shown at the bottom
of Figure 3-21.

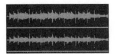

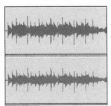

Figure 3-21:
A stereo track (top) can be split into two mono tracks (bottom).

Examining Edit Commands

If you've worked with any word processing program, you're probably familiar with Edit commands, such as cut, copy, clear, duplicate, and paste. Pro Tools, being the super-editor of audio it is, offers a few more: repeat and merge-paste. All these Edit commands are detailed in the following sections.

The view that you choose for a track affects the kinds of edits you can make using the commands in this section. If you have the Waveform view open, for example, any edit you do affects all the parameters for that track — including automation data. Comparatively, if you have one of the Automation Parameters views open, that parameter is the only one affected by the edit.

Each Edit mode treats the material in the tack differently when you use the Edit commands in this section. For instance, when you use Shuffle mode, clips slide over to make room for a pasted clip (or to close the gap left from a cut clip). Likewise, in Slip mode, existing clips stay put, no matter whether a space is left after cutting or if clips overlap from pasting.

Using the Cut command

Like in most programs that have a Cut command, any selection that you cut is removed from the track and placed in the Clipboard, from which you can paste it somewhere else. Here's how to cut a clip or selection:

1. **Click and hold the Track View selector (located in the Track Controls section of the Edit window) and drag down the list to choose the track view you want.**

   This determines what data is cut from the track. (See the Remember icon just under the "Examining Edit Commands" section heading.)

2. **Select the clip or part of the clip you want to cut.**

To select the entire clip, use the Grabber tool and click anywhere on that clip within the track's playlist. To select a portion of a clip, use the Selector tool and drag across the clip in the track's playlist.

3. Press ⌘+X (Mac) or Ctrl+X (PC) or choose Edit⇨Cut from the main menu.

The selection is placed on the Clipboard.

If you select only part of a clip to cut, Pro Tools creates new clips, basing them on the new clip arrangement for the track. For example, if you choose a part of a clip within the entire clip, you end up with three new clips listed in the Audio Clips list:

+ The portion to the left of the selection

+ The cut selection that no longer resides in the track's playlist and now sits on the Clipboard instead

+ The material to the right of the cut selection

Using the Copy command

The Copy command in Pro Tools functions just like it does in any computer software Copy function: The selected material is copied to the Clipboard. To copy a selection, follow these steps:

1. Click and hold the Track View selector (located in the Track Controls section of the Edit window) and drag down the list to choose the track view you want to edit.

This determines the data that is cut from the track. (See the Remember icon just under the "Examining Edit Commands" section heading.)

2. Select the clip or part of the clip you want to copy.

To select the entire clip, use the Grabber tool and click anywhere on that clip within the track's playlist. To select a portion of a clip, use the Selector tool and drag across the clip in the track's playlist.

3. Choose Edit⇨Copy from the main menu or press ⌘+C (Mac) or Ctrl+C (PC).

The selection is placed on the Clipboard. And, if you're not dealing with the entire clip, a new clip corresponding to your selection is created in the Audio Clips list.

Clearing selections

In Pro Tools, using the Clear command removes the selected material from a track without putting it in the Clipboard and without adding a clip to the Audio Clips list corresponding to the selection you cleared. To clear a selection, do the following:

1. **Choose the Waveform Track view if you want to clear all the data from the selection (or choose the Automation Parameters view if you only want to clear data from that parameter). To select a track view, click and hold the track view selector (located in the Track Controls section of the Edit window) and drag down the list.**

   This determines the data that is cut from the track. (See the Remember icon just under the "Examining Edit Commands" section heading.)

2. **Select the clip or part of the clip you want to copy.**

   To select the entire clip, use the Grabber tool and click anywhere on that clip within the track's playlist. To select a portion of a clip, use the Selector tool and drag across the clip in the track's playlist.

3. **Choose Edit⇨Clear from the main menu or press ⌘+B (Mac) or Ctrl+B (PC).**

   The selection is cleared from your session.

If you clear only part of the clip, Pro Tools creates new clips from the remaining material in the clip.

Performing a paste

When you paste a selection, the pasted material comes from the Clipboard, the result of a Copy or a Cut command. To paste a selection, do the following:

1. **With the Selector tool, place your cursor where you want to paste the material in the appropriate track.**

   If you want the selection to be right at the start or end point of a clip, you can move the cursor to the right or left to put it there:

   • Press Tab to move the cursor to the right.

   • Press Option+Tab (Mac) or Ctrl+Tab (PC) to move the cursor to the left.

2. **Press ⌘+V (Mac) or Ctrl+V (PC) or choose Edit⇨Paste from the main menu.**

   The material on the Clipboard is placed at the selection point.

If you paste a selection at an Edit Insert point (putting the cursor at a single point) in Shuffle mode, the material to the right of the cursor slides over to the end of the pasted section. If you paste into a selected section of the track, the pasted material replaces the selected material.

Using the Duplicate command

Using the Duplicate command in Pro Tools is essentially the same as copying and then pasting the start point of the selection right after the end point of the copied section. Duplicate makes quick work of creating loops. To duplicate a selection:

1. **Select the clip or part of the clip you want to duplicate.**

   To select the entire clip, use the Grabber tool and click anywhere on that clip within the track's playlist. To select a portion of a clip, use the Selector tool and drag across the clip in the track's playlist.

2. **Choose Edit⇨Duplicate from the main menu or press ⌘+D (Mac) or Ctrl+D (PC).**

   The selection is copied and pasted at the End point.

If you want to construct loops, make sure that you set the main time scale of your session to Bars:Beats. Also, use the Selector tool to drag your selection; or if you'd rather type in a specific value, type in the number of bars or beats in the start and end points in the Event Edit area. This ensures that your selection is duplicated and placed in the proper time location. Using the Grabber tool might result in the material moving by a few samples in one direction or another.

Performing a repeat

If you want to duplicate a selection more than once (when creating looped sections, for instance), you can use the Repeat command. The Repeat command works the same way as the Duplicate command except that when you choose Edit⇨Repeat from the main menu (or press Option+R, Mac or Alt+R, PC), the Repeat dialog box opens, as shown in Figure 3-22, where you can enter the number of times you want to repeat the Paste part of the procedure.

Each repeated selection is placed immediately after the previous one.

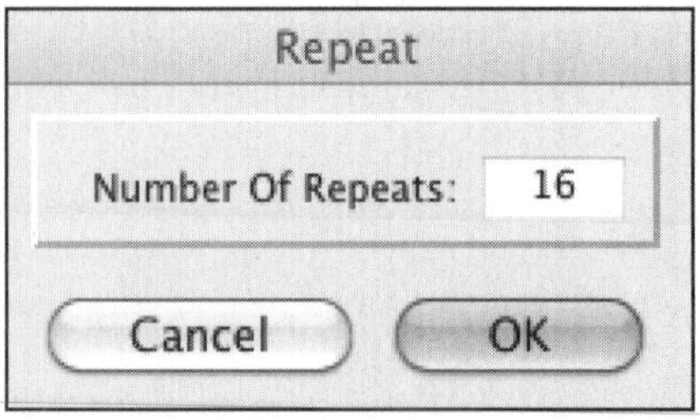

Figure 3-22:
Specify how many times you want the selection to repeat.

> **Repeat**
>
> Number Of Repeats: 16
>
> (Cancel)   (OK)

Chapter 4: Adding to Your Editing Palette

In This Chapter

✔ **Getting to know the Smart tool**

✔ **Fixing waveforms**

✔ **Silencing clips**

✔ **Using processing plug-ins**

✔ **Performing fades and crossfades**

A side from the basic editing methods — the ones I describe in the first three chapters of this mini-book — Pro Tools offers some extra goodies that can make the editing process easier. And what might I mean by *goodies?* In this particular case, I'm talking about the aptly named Smart tool, the Pencil tool, processing plug-ins, fades, and crossfades. This chapter lays out these tools and helps turn you into a Pro Tools editing pro (or at least an informed amateur).

Signing On to the Smart Tool

The Smart tool in Pro Tools is, well, smart. This tool consists of three tools I describe in Chapter 3 in this mini-book — the Trimmer, the Selector, and the Grabber. But the Smart Tool is more than just these three tools. The Smart tool actually changes how it works, depending on what you try to do with it. For example, if you place the cursor close to the start or end point of a clip, the Trimmer tool is activated. And if you place the cursor somewhere else within the clip, the Selector or the Grabber appears, depending on where you put the cursor.

To use the Smart tool, click the button located under the Selector tool in the Edit window, as shown in Figure 4-1.

Figure 4-1:
The Smart
tool: the
button
under the
Selector
tool.

Click here to enable the Smart tool

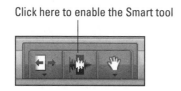

Using the Smart tool in Waveform view

When you're using the Smart tool with a track set to Waveform view, each Edit tool in the Smart tool set (Trimmer, Selector, Grabber) becomes active according to where you place the cursor in the clip. (See Book II, Chapter 4 for more on setting your view to Waveform view.) While you're in Waveform view, you can also perform fades and crossfades. This section details each of these editing tools and/or techniques.

Trimmer tool

To activate the Trimmer tool when you're in the Smart tool mode, position your cursor near the start or end point of the clip you want to work with. The Trimmer cursor appears, as shown in Figure 4-2. You can trim or extend a clip by clicking and dragging the start or end point to the left or right.

Figure 4-2:
Put the
cursor near
the start or
end point
to activate
the Trimmer
tool.

Trimmer cursor

Selector tool

You enable the Selector tool when you're in the Smart tool mode by positioning your cursor in the upper half of the clip, as shown in Figure 4-3. When you see the Selector cursor, you can drag across the clip to make a selection.

Figure 4-3:
Put the cursor in the upper half of the clip to enable the Selector.

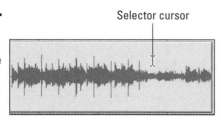

Selector cursor

Grabber tool

When you place the cursor in the lower half of a clip — but not near the start or end point — you enable the Grabber tool, as shown in Figure 4-4. To grab the clip, click it when the Grabber cursor appears. You can then drag the clip to another place.

Figure 4-4:
The Grabber appears when the cursor is in the lower half of a clip.

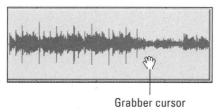

Grabber cursor

Fading in or out

Fade-ins and *fade-outs* are editing techniques by which you make the volume of the clip increase from silence or decrease to silence, respectively. These techniques are useful when you want to eliminate abrupt changes in sound, such as clicks, when a clip starts or ends. You can use the Smart tool to perform a fade-in or fade-out by placing the cursor in the upper corner of the clip near the start point (for a fade-in) or the end point (for a fade-out) and waiting until the Fade icon appears, as shown in Figure 4-5. Then you can select the Fade length by dragging your cursor to the right (to fade in) or left (to fade out). (For more on fade-ins and fade-outs, see the "Performing Fades and Crossfades" section, later in this chapter.)

**Book IV
Chapter 4**

**Adding to Your
Editing Palette**

Fade icon

Figure 4-5:
Getting the
Fade icon.

Creating crossfades

A *crossfade* occurs when the volume of the first of two adjacent clips
decreases to silence while the second of these two clips increases from
silence. This smoothes the transition from one clip to another. You can
create a crossfade between two adjacent clips by placing the cursor at the
bottom corner where the two clips adjoin and waiting until the Crossfade
icon appears, as shown in Figure 4-6. After the icon appears, you can drag
to the left or right to set the crossfade length. (The "Performing Fades and
Crossfades" section, later in this chapter, has more on crossfades.)

Figure 4-6:
To get the
Crossfade
icon, put the
cursor at
the bottom
where clips
adjoin.

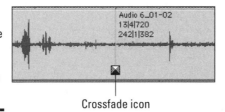

Crossfade icon

Using the Smart tool in Automation view

To add to the versatility of the Smart tools (outlined in the previous
sections), each tool in the set — Trimmer, Selector, and Grabber — performs
differently when you have a track set to one of the Automation views
(Volume, Panning, Mute, and Send Levels). (Book II, Chapter 4 has more on
track views; Book VI, Chapter 6 has more on automating a mix.)

Automating the Trimmer tool

To select a clip in one of the Automation views with the Smart version of
the Trimmer tool, position your cursor in the top 25 percent of the clip. The
Trimmer icon appears, as shown in Figure 4-7. You can move your cursor up
and down to change the automation value or to create *breakpoints* (places
where changes occur in the automation curves). If you want finer control of
the Trimmer tool and your work, press ⌘ (Mac) or Ctrl (PC) after you begin
trimming.

Figure 4-7:
To get the
Trimmer
tool, put the
cursor in the
upper 25%
of a clip.

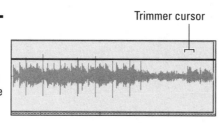

Trimmer cursor

Automating the Selector tool

To use the Selector tool in Smart mode when you have one of the Automation views set for a track, position your cursor in the lower 75 percent of the clip, as shown in Figure 4-8. You can then make your selection.

Figure 4-8:
To get the
Selector
tool, put
your cursor
in the lower
75% of a
clip.

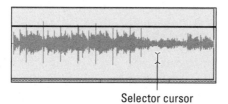

Selector cursor

Automating the Grabber tool

To use the Smart version of the Grabber tool in a track set to one of the Automation views, press ⌘ (Mac) or Ctrl (PC) with your cursor placed in the clip, as shown in Figure 4-9.

You can use the Grabber tool in several different ways when you have a track set to an Automation view. Here are two especially handy ways:

✦ **Editing existing breakpoints:** Just position the cursor near one of these points, and the Grabber magically appears. You can increase the resolution of your movements to fine control by pressing ⌘ (Mac) or Ctrl (PC) after you start moving the breakpoint.

✦ **Constraining the Grabber vertically:** To keep the Grabber from moving right or left, press Shift — or, if you set the tool to fine control, press ⌘+Shift (Mac) or Ctrl+Shift (PC).

**Book IV
Chapter 4**

Adding to Your
Editing Palette

Figure 4-9:
To get the
Grabber
tool, press
⌘ or Ctrl.

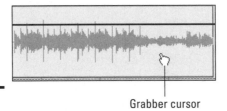

Grabber cursor

Perusing the Pencil Tool

In spite of all your effort to keep from creating any of the digital distortions known as *overs* — also referred to as *clipping* — you might have one pop through every now and then. No worries; use the Pencil tool to *redraw the waveform* and get rid of that nasty critter. (Is that cool, or what?) You can also use the Pencil tool to remove other unwanted pops or clicks that show up in your precious tracks.

The Pencil tool, as shown here in the margin, is active only when you zoom way into a waveform, as shown in Figure 4-10.

Figure 4-10:
You can
use the
Pencil tool
if you zoom
way in.

Using the Pencil tool to redraw a waveform is a destructive act; it changes your original audio file permanently. Before you redraw, make a copy of the original clip (using the Duplicate function under the AudioSuite menu) so you don't lose the good stuff in the original file. The next section tells you precisely how to do that.

Creating a copy of the original file

I strongly recommend making a copy of a clip before you edit it with the Pencil tool. (See the Warning icon in the previous section.) Here's how to do just that:

1. **Select the clip you want to work on.**

Perusing the Pencil Tool **419**

2. **Choose AudioSuite⇨Other⇨Duplicate from the main menu.**

   The Duplicate dialog box appears, as shown in Figure 4-11.

Figure 4-11: The Duplicate dialog box.

3. **Enable the Use in Playlist option on the right, and make sure that Playlist is chosen in the top-center field.**

4. **Click the Process button (lower right).**

   You now have a copy of the original clip that's put in the track in place of the original. (The original still resides in the Audio Clips list.)

Using the Pencil tool to redraw a waveform

To redraw a waveform (*after* you make a copy of it — see the previous section for why), follow these steps:

1. **Find the area in the clip that you want to edit.**

2. **With the Zoom tool, repeatedly click the spot you want to edit until you get into the sample level.**

   The waveform looks like a single wavy line. (Refer to Figure 4-10.)

3. **Select the Pencil tool.**

4. **Locate the exact spot to edit.**

   Your target, typically a moment of distorted sound, is usually easy to see because it looks like a sharp peak in the waveform. (See the left side of Figure 4-12.) If it isn't apparent, you might need to adjust the horizontal until you can see it clearly. (For more on adjusting the horizontal zoom, see Book II, Chapter 4.)

   If you have trouble seeing the problem, use the Scrub tool to listen to the audio.

5. **Draw over the waveform to round over the spot that was chopped off when the note got clipped. (See the right side of Figure 4-12.)**

   Take it easy when making changes to the waveform. All you want to do is smooth out the peak — not change the sound too much.

Book IV
Chapter 4

Adding to Your
Editing Palette

Figure 4-12:
The Pencil tool fixes a chopped-off peak (left) of a waveform (right).

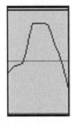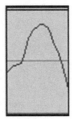

Silencing Selections

Pro Tools offers a couple of ways to manage silence in selections: You can strip silence from clips to reduce the size of your audio files, and you can insert silence into clips where you don't want any sound. I cover both of these options in the following sections.

Stripping silence

Using the Strip Silence command allows you to take a selection that meets a minimum sound level and silence it. This divides the clip that the silence was stripped from into smaller clips. This lets you isolate sound effects or musical passages so that you can quantize them or locate them at specific synch points within your session. (Check out Chapter 3 in this mini-book for more on synch points.) Stripping silence from clips also allows you to compact your audio file farther than you could if you didn't strip the low-volume parts to silence. (See the "Compacting a file" section, later in this chapter.) This technique saves hard-drive space by making your audio files smaller.

Understanding the Strip Silence window

Whenever you use the Strip Silence command (see the following section), a window opens (see Figure 4-13) where you can set the parameters under which the silence will be stripped from a clip. These parameters include

+ **Strip Threshold slider:** This setting determines the signal level below which the audio is silenced.

+ **Min(imum) Strip Duration slider:** This parameter makes sure that if you have a really small section that falls below the threshold, you don't end up with a ton of sections where silence was stripped and didn't need to be.

+ **Clip Start Pad slider:** This parameter adds a specified amount of time to the beginning of each clip created when you use the Strip Silence command.

+ **Clip End Pad slider:** This parameter is essentially the same as the previous one except that it adds time after the end of a clip stripped from silence.

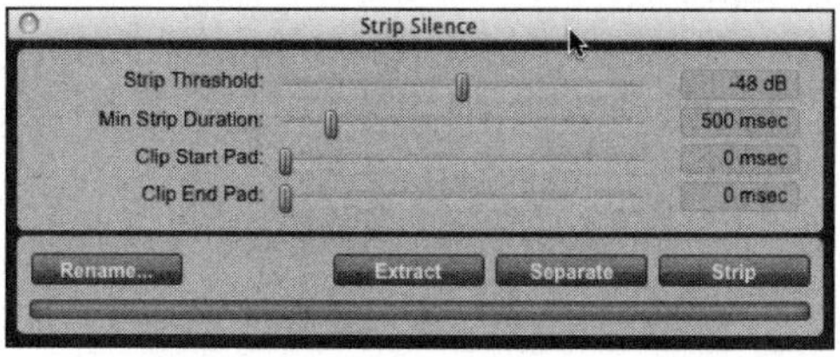

Figure 4-13:
Use the
Strip
Silence
window
to remove
silence.

+ **Strip button:** This performs the strip function and clears everything within the "silence" threshold determined by your settings in this window.

+ **Rename button:** Clicking this button opens the Rename Selected Clips dialog box (see Figure 4-14), where you choose how new clips are named after silence has been stripped.

+ **Extract button:** This parameter strips the audio specified in the strip silence settings and leaves the rest. This is the opposite effect of stripping the silence and leaving the audio. This is handy for keeping ambient noise so you can use it somewhere else. For example, if you want to replace a drum part, you can pre-record the drum and mix it in with the ambient noise to match the basic sound of the original track.

+ **Separate button:** This separates the clips created by the strip silence command. Each section of audio resides in its own clip.

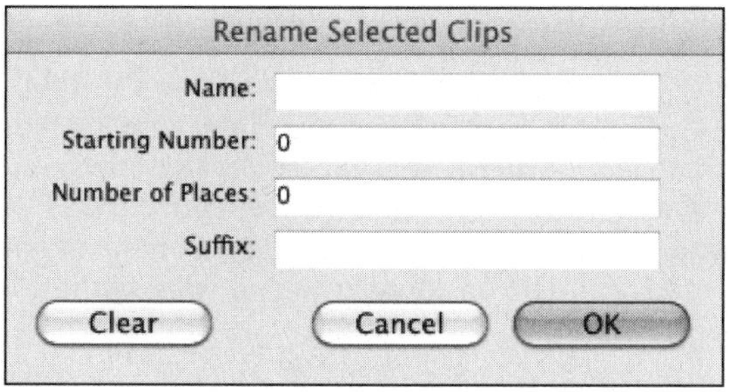

Figure 4-14:
Set the
name format
for each
new clip
created by
the Strip
Silence
command.

Using the Strip Silence command

To strip silence from audio clips, follow these steps:

1. **Select a clip or part of a clip.**

Chapter 2 in this mini-book has more on making selections.

2. **Choose Edit⇨Show Strip Silence from the main menu.**

The Strip Silence window opens. (Refer to Figure 4-13.)

3. **Click the Rename button to set your clip name preferences.**

4. **Adjust the parameter sliders until rectangles appear in the clip and any material you want to remove resides outside the rectangles, as shown in Figure 4-15.**

   This might take some time. If you want to increase the resolution of the sliders, press ⌘ (Mac) or Ctrl (PC) while you move them.

Figure 4-15:
Adjust the sliders to put unwanted stuff outside the rectangles.

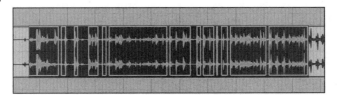

5. **When you have the rectangles where you want them, click the Strip button in the Strip Silence window.**

   Any part of the clip not in the rectangles is removed; each rectangled section then becomes a new clip, using the naming scheme that you choose in the Rename dialog box.

Inserting silence

If you're like most people, you keep the session rolling — even when you don't play anything during certain passages — to keep the feel happening throughout the tune. In this case, it's not uncommon to have passages where pretty much nothing is recorded (well, except for maybe a cough or a chair-squeak). Rather than cutting those sections from your track, you can insert silence into those sections instead. With the Insert Silence command, you can quickly and easily put silence anywhere you want within a track.

Inserting silence into tracks works differently for each Edit mode. This can often prove confusing, so to help you keep things straight, I not only show you how to insert silence, but also let you know what conditions apply when you use the different Edit modes.

Inserting an amount of silence

You insert silence into a track with the following steps:

1. **With the Selector tool, select the part of a clip that you want to silence; then click and drag across the section of the clip that you want to select.**

2. **Choose Edit⇨Insert Silence from the main menu or press Shift+⌘+E (Mac) or Shift+Ctrl+E (PC).**

   The selected section is silenced.

Understanding the results

When you're using the Insert Silence command, each Edit mode treats certain conditions differently. The difference depends on the mode in use at the time:

✦ **Shuffle mode:** If the track(s) you selected is set to Waveform view, all audio and automation data is cleared, and all subsequent clips are shuffled the amount of the silence.

✦ **Slip mode:** If the track(s) you selected is set to Waveform view, all audio and automation data is cleared. On the other hand, if your track is set to one of the Automation views, only the data from that view is removed.

✦ **Grid mode:** All audio and automation data is cleared. This is essentially the same as using the clear command; see Chapter 3 in this mini-book. All the clips stay where they are in the session when the silence is inserted.

Performing Fades and Crossfades

As I mention earlier in this chapter, you use fade-ins and fade-outs to make the volume of the clip increase from silence or decrease to silence, respectively. Both techniques are useful when you want to eliminate abrupt changes in sound, such as clicks, when a clip starts or ends. A *crossfade* combines a fade-out and a fade-in that happens at the junction of two adjacent clips to make a smooth transition between these two clips.

You can create fade-ins, fade-outs, and crossfades faster and easier than ever before in Pro Tools. You can use fades to bring clips in and out of a mix or to make a seamless transition from one adjoining clip to another. One of the key aspects of fades is creating a *curve* (how the fade happens) that fits the material you want to fade. Pro Tools gives you many options for shaping your curves.

Dealing with the Fades dialog box

Whatever kind of fade you create — fade-in, fade-out, or crossfade — you make the fade from the settings in the Fades dialog box. You access the Fades dialog box by choosing Edit⇨Fades⇨Create from the main menu. After you get the dialog box up on your computer screen (as shown in Figure 4-16), you can adjust the following parameters to meet your needs:

✦ **Audition:** Clicking this button plays the fade or crossfade so that you can hear what your settings will sound like.

✦ **View First Track:** Pro Tools lets you select more than one track to crossfade at one time. (The crossfade, however, takes place on each track and not across tracks.) The View First Track button allows you to view and audition the first of the tracks selected.

✦ **View Second Track:** In a selection that includes more than one track, this button shows you the second track. If you have more than two tracks selected, you can't view beyond the second.

✦ **View Both Tracks:** Clicking this button lets you view and audition both tracks selected for crossfading.

✦ **Fade Curves Only:** Enabling this button shows the fade curves but not the waveforms for the audio you want to fade or crossfade.

✦ **Fade Curves and Separate Waveforms:** This button lets you see both the fade curves and the waveforms for each track. The fade-out waveform shows up above the fade in waveform.

✦ **Fade Curves and Superimposed Waveforms:** This button superimposes the two waveforms one on top of the other and shows the fade curves.

✦ **Fade Curves and Summed Waveforms:** This button shows the fade curves and a single waveform depicting the sum of both original waveforms. Being able to see the sum of both waveforms makes it easier to see the overall volume of the audio.

✦ **Zoom In:** The Zoom In button increases the visual height of the waveforms. You can return to the default setting by ⌘-clicking (Mac) or Ctrl-clicking (PC).

✦ **Zoom Out:** Clicking the Zoom Out button decreases the visual height of the waveform. ⌘-clicking (Mac) or Ctrl-clicking (PC) returns the view to the default setting.

✦ **Out Shape settings:** Here, select the shape of the fade out curve. You have three options:

- *Standard:* This setting uses a basic fade-out shape that you can adjust by clicking the curve and then dragging the curve how you want it.

- *S-Curve:* This setting creates an S-shaped curve that you can adjust by clicking the curve and then dragging to the shape you want — well, as long as it's an S shape.

- *Presets:* Clicking here presents you with a drop-down menu containing seven preset curves for you to choose from, as shown in Figure 4-17. You can change a preset by clicking one of the end points and dragging it.

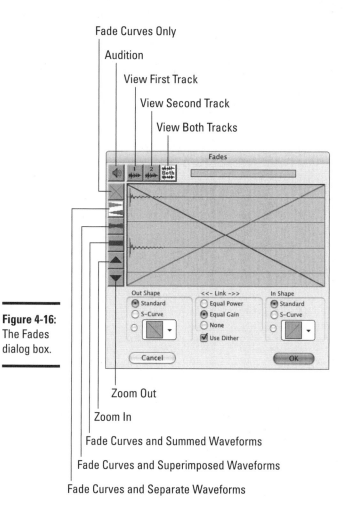

Fade Curves Only

Audition

View First Track

View Second Track

View Both Tracks

Figure 4-16:
The Fades
dialog box.

Zoom Out

Zoom In

Fade Curves and Summed Waveforms

Fade Curves and Superimposed Waveforms

Fade Curves and Separate Waveforms

Figure 4-17:
Choose
from seven
preset
curves to
make quick
work of
creating
fades or
crossfades.

**Book IV
Chapter 4**

**Adding to Your
Editing Palette**

✦ **Link settings:** You have the following three choices on how you want the fade-out and fade-in curves of your crossfades to relate to one another:

- *Equal Power:* This option keeps the relative volume of the Fade Out and Fade In clips the same. This selection is best for material that differs greatly in sound character, such as the fading out of one instrument and the fading in of another.

- *Equal Gain:* This setting keeps the Fade In and Fade Out selections from summing together and overloading the track, resulting in *clipping* (distortion). This setting is best used for selections that have the same relative volume and phase, such as one drum loop to another.

- *None:* This setting leaves the two fades independent of one another. This gives you more flexibility to create unique fades. If you want to edit the Fade In curve only, press Option (Mac) or Alt (PC) while you drag the curve. To adjust the Fade Out only, press ⌘ (Mac) or Ctrl (PC) while you drag the curve.

✦ **Use Dither:** Selecting this option applies *dither* — a way to improve the sound of very quiet material. (Book VII, Chapter 2 has more on dither.) You don't need this check box selected if you crossfade fairly loud material, but it's a good idea if the audio is quiet.

✦ **In Shape settings:** Here, select the shape of the Fade In curve. Like with Out Shape setting, you have these options:

- *Standard:* This setting uses a basic fade-in shape that you can adjust by clicking the curve and then dragging the curve how you want.

- *S-Curve:* This setting creates an S-shaped, fade-in curve that you can adjust by clicking the curve and then dragging it to the shape you want (as long as it's an S shape).

- *Presets:* As you might have guessed, you can choose from seven preset curves here, which are mirror images of the curves found in the Out Shape Presets menu. You can change them by clicking one of the end points and dragging it.

Creating crossfades

The three types of crossfades are centered, pre, and post. These different flavors — and the actual process of creating a crossfade — are covered in the following sections.

Creating a centered crossfade

A *centered crossfade,* the most common type of crossfade, is great for when the material in the two clips fits well together, such as with two different takes of a lead vocal part that end up being your final vocal track. Centered crossfades are fades where the crossfade happens evenly between the two clips, incorporating audio on both sides of two clips' *splice points* (where they meet). For this type of crossfade to work, you need audio data after the end point of the first clip and before the start point of the second clip.

To create a center crossfade, follow these steps:

1. **With the Selector tool, drag from the point where you want the crossfade to start (in the first clip) to where you want the crossfade to end (in the second clip), as shown in Figure 4-18.**

Figure 4-18:
Use the Selector tool to drag across where you want the crossfade.

2. **Choose Edit⇨Fades⇨Create from the main menu or press ⌘+F (Mac) or Ctrl+F (PC).**

   The Fades dialog box opens. (Refer to Figure 4-16.)

3. **Enter your crossfade preferences in the Fades dialog box as listed in the earlier section, "Dealing with the Fades dialog box."**

   Make adjustments to the view, the Fade In and Fade Out curves, and the Link option — auditioning the crossfade periodically as you go — until you have the crossfade you want.

4. **When you're happy with the sound of the crossfade, click OK.**

   Your crossfade is calculated. You can change the duration of the fade by trimming it; see the "Trimming a crossfade" section later in this chapter.

Creating a pre-crossfade

A *pre-crossfade* happens before the start point of the second clip, as shown in Figure 4-19. This is a good type of crossfade to use when you have an initial attack (a cymbal crash, for example) that happens right at the start point of the second clip. In this example, if the second clip isn't at full volume when the crash happens, you lose the impact of the cymbal. The pre-crossfade ensures that you get the full impact of the cymbal. For this crossfade to work, audio data has to be in place before the start point of the second clip.

Figure 4-19:
A pre-crossfade ends at the start point of the second clip.

Follow these steps to create a pre-crossfade:

1. **With the Selector tool, click in the clip at the point where you want the pre-crossfade to begin.**

2. **Shift-drag or press Shift+Tab to select to the end of the clip.**

3. **Choose Edit⇨Fades⇨Create from the main menu or press ⌘+F (Mac) or Ctrl+F (PC).**

   The Fades dialog box makes its appearance. (Refer to Figure 4-16.)

4. **Choose your Fade settings and audition them, adjusting the settings as you go until you have the fade that you want.**

5. **Click OK.**

   The fade is created.

Creating a post-crossfade

A post-crossfade happens after the end of the first clip, as shown in Figure 4-20. This type of crossfade is useful for when you have a sound that continues all the way up to the end of the first clip (to keep the drum theme going: a hi-hat note, for instance) and you want to make sure that the last hi-hat doesn't drop off in volume while it's being hit. This type of crossfade works only if the first clip contains audio data after its end point.

Figure 4-20:
A post-crossfade begins at the start of the second clip.

Follow these steps to create a post-crossfade:

1. **With the Selector tool, click in the clip at the point where you want the fade to end.**

2. **Shift-drag or press Shift+Option+Tab (Mac) or Shift+Alt+Tab (PC) to select back to the clip's start point.**

3. **Choose Edit⇨Fades⇨Create from the main menu or press ⌘+F (Mac) or Ctrl+F (PC) to open the Fades dialog box. (Refer to Figure 4-16.)**

4. **Choose your fade settings and audition them, adjusting the settings as you go until you have the fade you want.**

5. **Click OK.**

The fade is created.

Removing a crossfade

To remove a crossfade, select the crossfade with the Grabber tool and then press Delete (Mac) or Backspace (PC). You can also choose Edit⇨Fades⇨Delete from the main menu.

Trimming a crossfade

Here's how to change the boundaries of a crossfade:

1. **Select the crossfade by double-clicking with the Selector tool or by grabbing with the Grabber tool.**

2. **With the Trimmer tool, click and drag either side of the crossfade.**

Fading in and out

A *fade-in* happens when you make the volume of the clip increase from silence to smooth the transition into the clip. Comparatively, a *fade-out* is a decrease in volume that's useful when you want to smooth the transition leaving a clip. These types of fades are often used when you have accent parts that come and go in the song — keyboard or guitar licks that counterpoint the lead vocal, for instance — and you want them to seamlessly flow in and out of the song. Without a fade into or out of the clip, you might hear abrupt changes in the sound because of the background noise in those parts.

You can fade a single clip in or out via the Fades dialog box. Creating these fades saves you the trouble of performing automation curves to fade in or out. (Of course, you can still do that, but it does use more of your computer's processing power. I explain the process in Book VI, Chapter 6.)

Fading in to the beginning of a clip

To fade in to a single clip, follow these steps:

1. **With the Selector tool, select the beginning of the clip you want to fade into.**

   To make this process work, you have to begin your selection point before (or at) the start point — not after it.

2. **Choose Edit⇨Fades⇨Create from the main menu or press ⌘+F (Mac) or Ctrl+F (PC).**

   The Fades dialog box appears. (Refer to Figure 4-16.)

3. **Choose your parameters in the dialog box and audition the fade, making adjustments to the settings until you get the fade to sound how you want.**

4. **Click OK.**

   The fade is created, and the Fade curve appears in the selected clip.

You can also fade in without opening the Fades dialog box. When you do this, Pro Tools uses the setting you select in the Fades menu.

To fade in without using the Fades dialog box, follow these steps:

1. **Click an insertion point somewhere within the clip, as shown in Figure 4-21.**

2. **Press Control+D (Mac) or Windows+D (PC) or select Edit⇨Fades⇨Fade To Start from the main menu.**

   The Fade is created, and the curve appears in the selected clip.

Figure 4-21:
Creating a fade-in without opening the Fades dialog box.

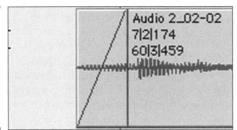

Fading out at the end of a clip

To fade out from a single clip, follow these steps:

1. **With the Selector tool, select the beginning of the clip you want to fade.**

Your selection point needs to stop after or at the end point — not before it — for this process to work.

2. **Choose Edit⇨Fades⇨Create from the main menu or press ⌘+F (Mac) or Ctrl+F (PC).**

   The Fades dialog box appears. (Refer to Figure 4-16.)

3. **Choose your parameters in the dialog box and audition the fade, making adjustments to the settings until you get the fade to sound how you want.**

4. **Click OK.**

   The fade is created, and the Fade curve appears in the selected clip.

You can also fade out without opening the Fades dialog box. When you do this, Pro Tools uses the setting you select in the Fades menu.

To fade out without using the Fades dialog box, follow these steps:

1. **Click an insertion point prior to the end of the clip, as shown in Figure 4-22.**

2. **Press Ctrl+G (Mac) or Windows+G (PC) or select Edit⇨Fades⇨Fade To End from the main menu.**

   The Fade is created, and the curve appears in the selected clip.

Figure 4-22:
Fading out without opening the Fades dialog box.

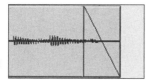

Creating batch fades

You can create more than one fade at a time by using the Batch Fades command and selecting multiple clips at a time.

Here's the way to create batch fades:

1. **With the Selector tool, choose the first clip you want to fade.**

2. **Click and drag across the clips you want to include in the batch.**

   Make sure that the entire last clip that you want to fade is selected, as shown in Figure 4-23.

Figure 4-23:
Select
across
multiple
clips to
perform
batch fades.

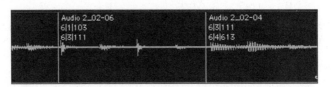

3. **Press ⌘+F (Mac) or Ctrl+F (PC) or choose Edit⇨Fades⇨Create from the main menu.**

   The Batch Fades dialog box appears, as shown in Figure 4-24.

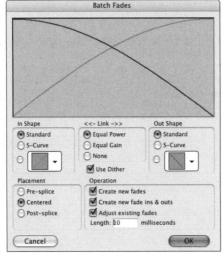

Figure 4-24:
Use the
Batch Fades
dialog box
to create
fades on
more than
one clip at a
time.

4. **In the Batch Fades dialog box, choose your In Shape and Out Shape, the Link option, fade Placement, the crossfade length (in milliseconds), and whether you want to create a new fade, create new fade-ins and fade-outs, or adjust existing fades.**

5. **Click OK.**

   The fades are calculated.

   You can trim or extend each of the fades later.

Cleaning Up Your Session

After you finish all your editing, you probably have a ton of clips in your Audio Clips list. Things can get cluttered up pretty quick, so before I start mixing the song, I like to clean up my session by consolidating clips, getting rid of any unused clips, and compacting the clips that I want to use. Doing these things makes it easier to deal with the clips in the session and frees up hard drive space. It can also make playing the tracks easier on your hard drive, depending on how many tracks you have in your session.

Consolidating selections

You can consolidate clips that make up a section of a song by using the Consolidate command. In effect, you take a bunch of clips — for instance, the various assembled takes of your guitar part that create the parts for a song's verse — and make them into one clip. This makes moving or copying this section easier and also makes for a less cluttered track playlist.

To consolidate selections, follow these steps:

1. **Select the clips you want to consolidate using either the Selector tool or the Grabber tool. Or, if you want to select all the clips in the track, triple-click anywhere in the track's playlist.**

2. **Choose Edit⇨Consolidate from the main menu or press Option+Shift+3 (Mac) or Alt+Shift+3 (PC).**

   The selected clips are replaced by a new clip, which contains all the audio from the selection, including any muted clips.

Automation data is not consolidated. If you have clips that you want to consolidate and you want to keep any automation data at all, your best bet is to do a bounce procedure for that selection. (I cover bounce procedures in Book VI, Chapter 7.)

Removing unused clips

You can easily get rid of any clips that are not being used in your session. Here's how:

1. **Open the Audio Clips drop-down menu by clicking and holding the Audio Clips title at the top of the Audio Clips list located on the right side of the Edit window.**

2. **Choose Select⇨Unused in the Audio Clips List drop-down menu or press Shift+⌘+U (Mac) or Shift+Ctrl+U (PC).**

   All clips in the list that aren't included in any tracks in the session are highlighted.

3. **Choose Clear from the Audio Clips list drop-down menu.**

   The Clear Clips dialog box appears, as shown in Figure 4-25, asking whether you want to remove the clips from the session or delete the audio files from your hard drive. Choose the option you prefer.

Figure 4-25: Get rid of any clips you aren't using in your session.

This operation clears selected clips.

REMOVE selected clips from this session, or permanently DELETE selected source files from disk?

Cancel   Delete   Remove

Removing the clips from your present session ensures that you have the clip to use in another session, but it won't reduce the amount of stuff on your hard drive. If you want to free up space and know that you won't use the clip in another session, delete it to save hard-drive space.

Compacting a file

You can *compact* an audio file (make it smaller) by using the Compact Selected command from the Audio Clips drop-down menu. Compacting an audio file in Pro Tools deletes any audio data that's not being used. This reduces the amount of space taken up in your hard drive, which makes backing up your data a quicker process.

Compacting an audio file is like taking all the pieces of tape that were cut from reels of recorded tape and — *gasp!* — throwing them away. (Well, okay, that's what it would have been like in the days before digital audio.) My point is that after you compact a file, you're committed to the results. This is one of the few editing tasks that you can do that you can't undo afterward.

You want to compact an audio file only after you do all your editing and you're sure you don't want any of the unused data. (You're sure. Right?)

To compact a clip, follow these steps:

1. **From the Audio Clips list, choose the clip(s) you want to compact.**

2. **Open the Audio Clips drop-down menu by clicking and holding the Audio Clips title at the top of the Audio Clips list and then choosing Compact.**

   The Compact Selected dialog box appears, as shown in Figure 4-26.

3. **In the Padding field, enter the amount of padding you want on your clips.**

Padding is how much data on either side of the clip's start and end points might contain fade information. If you have fades in the clip, set your padding amount to the length of the fade to ensure that your fades still work.

4. Click the Compact button.

Pro Tools deletes all the data outside the clip and its padding.

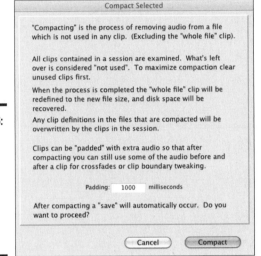

Figure 4-26:
Remove extra data from your clips, increasing available hard drive space.

Compact Selected

"Compacting" is the process of removing audio from a file which is not used in any clip. (Excluding the "whole file" clip).

All clips contained in a session are examined. What's left over is considered "not used". To maximize compaction clear unused clips first.

When the process is completed the "whole file" clip will be redefined to the new file size, and disk space will be recovered.

Any clip definitions in the files that are compacted will be overwritten by the clips in the session.

Clips can be "padded" with extra audio so that after compacting you can still use some of the audio before and after a clip for crossfades or clip boundary tweaking.

Padding: 1000   milliseconds

After compacting a "save" will automatically occur. Do you want to proceed?

Cancel   Compact

Book V

Managing MIDI

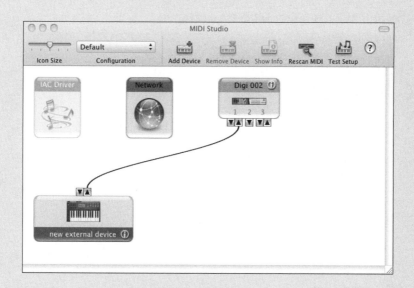

Contents at a Glance

Chapter 1: Preparing to Record MIDI 439

Setting Up Your MIDI Devices 439
Getting Ready to Record.. 448

Chapter 2: Recording MIDI 455

Recording MIDI Performances 455
Playing Back Your Tracks.. 458
Getting Rid of Unwanted Takes 461
Overdubbing MIDI Performances 463
Recording System-Exclusive Data 469

Chapter 3: Editing MIDI Data 473

Working with MIDI and Instrument Tracks 473
Dealing with Note Chasing 479
Editing MIDI in the Edit Window 479
Exploring MIDI Events 492

Chapter 4: Performing MIDI Operations 501

Getting Used to the MIDI Operations Window.. 501
Performing MIDI Event Operations 502
Recognizing MIDI Real-Time Properties 518

Chapter 1: Preparing to Record MIDI

In This Chapter

✔ Configuring MIDI devices

✔ Creating MIDI and instrument tracks

✔ Setting inputs and outputs

✔ Creating a click track

A s you can read in Book I, Chapter 4, working with Musical Instrument Digital Interface (MIDI) lets you record performance data and add the sounds later. This gives you some advantages over recording audio. First, your MIDI tracks take up less room on your hard drive (not a big deal in today's world, but worth mentioning). Secondly — and the most compelling reason for working with MIDI data — you can wait to choose the exact sound you want from your performance. This lets you tweak the sound as well as your performance. Of course, the drawback is that you can easily spend more time than you need when trying different options.

The MIDI capabilities in Pro Tools are not as sophisticated as those of some other programs, such as Sonar or Logic. This has its advantages for all but the most discerning MIDI power-user because you can get started creating music without a lot of fuss.

In this chapter, I walk you through setting up your system and session to record MIDI in Pro Tools. Along the way, you discover how to set up your devices, create MIDI tracks, and enable them for recording. You also get a chance to create a click track to play along with, which makes editing MIDI faster and easier.

Setting Up Your MIDI Devices

Setting up your MIDI device varies according to whether you use a Mac or a PC. Either way, though, setting up a MIDI device takes only a couple of minutes. Enabling MIDI devices is as easy as adding a printer to your system. The following sections walk you through what you need for each platform.

Enabling MIDI devices in Mac OS X

Before you can record MIDI in Mac OS X, you need to complete three overall procedures, in this order:

1. Set up your MIDI devices in OS X.

2. Enable the MIDI channels.

   This lets you choose the MIDI channels on which each device receives and sends data.

3. Enable the input devices in Pro Tools.

   That way, you can actually use those devices in Pro Tools.

To configure your MIDI devices in OS X, follow these steps:

1. **With your MIDI cables, connect the devices you want to use with Pro Tools to either the Avid hardware or to a separate MIDI interface.**

2. **Click the Audio MIDI Setup icon (as shown in the margin) on the Dock.**

   If this icon isn't showing, go to Applications⇨Utilities⇨Audio MIDI Setup.

   The Audio MIDI Setup window opens. If this MIDI Studio window isn't open, choose Window⇨Show MIDI Window.

3. **Click the MIDI Devices tab of the Audio MIDI Setup window.**

   A message appears that tells you your system is being scanned. After the scan is complete, your MIDI interface should appear in the tab's window, along with any devices connected to it, as shown in Figure 1-1.

Figure 1-1:
The Audio MIDI Setup window shows the MIDI devices connected to your MIDI interface.

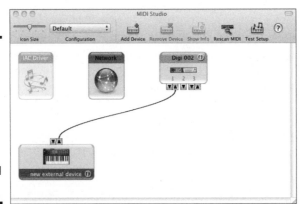

If one or more of your devices don't appear . . .

a. *Double-check your cables for proper connection.*

b. *Click the Rescan MIDI icon.*

If your device still doesn't appear . . .

a. *Click the Add Device icon.*

b. *In the dialog box that appears, enter the name, manufacturer, and model number of the device. Then click OK.*

4. **After your devices appear in the MIDI Devices tab of the Audio MIDI Setup window, close the window by choosing Audio MIDI Setup⇨Quit Audio MIDI Setup from the main menu (or press ⌘+Q).**

   You can also close this window by clicking the red X in the upper-left corner of the window.

To enable MIDI channels in your devices, follow these steps:

1. **Click the Audio MIDI Setup icon (as shown in the margin) on the Dock.**

   The Audio MIDI Setup window opens. (Refer to Figure 1-1.)

2. **Click the MIDI Devices tab of the Audio MIDI Setup window.**

   All MIDI devices connected to your MIDI interface should appear in the tab's window.

3. **Double-click the device for which you want to activate MIDI channels.**

   The Device window appears.

4. **Click the More Properties tab to expand the window.**

   The window expands to include Basic and Expert tabs containing settings you can make to your device.

5. **Click the Basic tab.**

6. **In the Transmits and Receives section of the Basics tab, click the channel number(s) through which you want to transmit and receive data.**

   Blue highlighted channels are active.

7. **Click OK to close the Device window.**

8. **Close the Audio MIDI Setup window by clicking the red X in the upper-left of the window or by pressing ⌘+Q.**

You can receive MIDI data from other software programs through the Pro Tools inputs. This is useful if you want to use a separate MIDI sequencer (such as Logic) to record and edit your MIDI performances before you bring them into Pro Tools. If you want to do more intensive MIDI editing than Pro Tools offers, this option can be very handy. (For more on using inputs, see Chapter 2 in this mini-book.)

If you use any control surfaces (such as a Mackie Control) or if you want to sync your system to another using MMC (MIDI machine control), you must enable the devices for these tasks in the MIDI Input Enable dialog box, along with your other MIDI devices.

To enable input devices in Pro Tools, follow these steps:

1. Choose Setup➪MIDI➪Input Devices from the main menu.

The MIDI Input Enable dialog box opens, displaying all the MIDI ports in your system, as shown in Figure 1-2.

Figure 1-2:
Use the MIDI Input Enable dialog box to select your MIDI devices.

2. Select the check boxes for the devices you want to use.

3. Click OK.

Enabling MIDI devices in Windows 7

This section details how to set up your MIDI devices in Windows 7.

Here's how to configure MIDI devices in Windows 7:

1. Install the drivers for your MIDI device as described in the device's manual.

If you use the MIDI ports in your Avid interface, this step was done when you installed the software, as I describe in Book II, Chapter 1.

2. With your MIDI cables, connect the devices you want to use with Pro Tools to either the Avid hardware or to a separate MIDI interface.

3. Turn on the power for the device.

Your device should show up in your MIDI tracks' Input and Output selector drop-down menus. If not, restart your computer. If this still doesn't work, you may need to go into the Device Driver menu and manually move the driver for your device into the Device Driver folder.

To enable input devices in Pro Tools, the steps are just like those you'd use for a Mac:

1. **Choose Setup➪MIDI➪Input Devices from the main menu.**

   The MIDI Input Enable dialog box opens, showing the MIDI ports in your system.

2. **Select the check boxes for the devices you want to use.**

3. **Click OK.**

Running MIDI Thru

MIDI Thru allows you to hear what your MIDI instrument is playing while the track it's assigned to is record-enabled. Pro Tools also lets you set up a default MIDI Thru instrument, so you don't have to choose a device each time you enable a MIDI track. Pro Tools uses the designated MIDI Thru instrument automatically.

To enable MIDI Thru, all you have to do is choose Options➪MIDI Thru from the main menu.

When you enable MIDI Thru, you also need to disable Local Control in each of your devices to keep them from receiving double messages and creating *stuck notes* (notes that continue playing indefinitely). This is done within each of your MIDI devices. Consult your device's manual for details on how to do this.

If you do end up with some stuck notes, choose Event➪All MIDI Notes Off from the main menu or press ⌘+Shift+. (period; Mac) or Ctrl+Shift+. (period; PC).

Here's how to set the default MIDI Thru instrument:

1. **Choose Setup➪Preferences from the main menu.**

   The Preferences dialog box opens.

2. **Click the MIDI tab.**

3. **Choose the MIDI device — as well as the channel you want to use to play the MIDI data — from the Default Thru Instrument drop-down menu, as shown in Figure 1-3.**

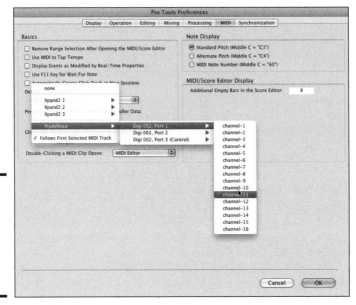

Figure 1-3:
Choose
the default
MIDI Thru
instrument
for your
session.

4. **Click OK.**

Managing the MIDI Input filter

Use the MIDI Input filter to ignore certain MIDI data while recording. For example, you can have Pro Tools ignore *after-touch* (extra pressure you place on the keyboard keys to change the sound that's playing) or *pitch bend* (raising or lowering the pitch as the note plays) messages when you record a drum part using your keyboard. This can be handy if you want to avoid recording *system-exclusive data* — that is, messages pertain only to the device and not related to performance information — when recording a MIDI performance.

To set the MIDI Input Filter parameters, follow these steps:

1. **Choose Setup⇨MIDI⇨Input Filter from the main menu.**

The MIDI Input Filter dialog box opens, as shown in Figure 1-4.

2. **Select the Record options:**

- *All:* Selecting All means that Pro Tools will record all the MIDI messages received.

- *Only:* Selecting Only means that only the parameters that you select in the upcoming Step 3 are recorded.

- *All Except:* Selecting All Except sets your system to record all the MIDI data it receives except for the check boxes that you select in the upcoming Step 3.

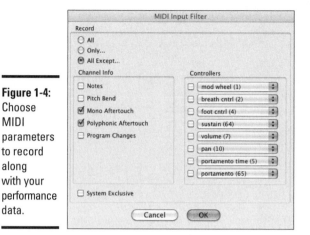

Figure 1-4:
Choose
MIDI
parameters
to record
along
with your
performance
data.

3. Depending on the mode you chose (see Step 2), select the check boxes in the Channel Info and Controllers sections that correspond to what you want to include or exclude from the recording process.

4. Depending on the choice you made in Step 2 and whether you want to include any system-exclusive data in your recording, select or clear the System Exclusive check box.

- *If you choose All in Step 2:* Selecting or clearing this check box doesn't matter because system-exclusive data is recorded either way.

- *If you choose Only in Step 2:* Selecting this check box means that system exclusive data is recorded.

- *If you choose All Except in Step 2:* Selecting this check box means that system-exclusive data is not recorded.

5. Click OK.

Quantizing your inputs

You can have Pro Tools automatically *quantize* your performance — that is, adjust the position of each note's timing so that it fits within a specified time frame. This can be useful if you want the timing of your performance to fit a selected grid exactly.

Be careful with quantizing. Stop short of doing too much because sucking the life out of a performance is very easy.

To quantize your input, follow these steps:

1. Choose Event➪Event Operations➪Input Quantize from the main menu.

The Input Quantize dialog box opens, as shown in Figure 1-5.

Figure 1-5:
Here you
can adjust
the timing
of your
performance
auto-
matically
while it's
being
recorded.

2. **Select the Enable Input Quantize check box to quantize and enter the rest of the options/parameters in the dialog box.**

   Here's a rundown on what each of these parameters means:

   From the What to Quantize section, choose the part of the note to quantize:

   - *Attacks:* This check box sets the quantization to the start of the selected notes.

     With Attacks selected, using the Preserve Note Duration option keeps the end of the note intact.

   - *Releases:* Selecting this check box quantizes the ends of the notes.

     With Releases selected, the start of the note is left intact.

     If both Attacks and Releases are selected, the Preserve Note Duration option is dimmed.

   - *Preserve Note Duration:* Selecting this check box produces different results depending on whether you choose Attacks or Releases.

   The Quantize Grid section is where you choose the resolution of the quantize grid, from whole notes to 64th notes.

   - *Note Selector:* From this drop-down menu, choose the note value of your quantize grid. Click the note to select it.

   - *Tuplet:* Select this check box to select odd note groupings, such as triplets. When you enable this option, you need to fill in the tuplet value. For example, to create a regular eighth-note triplet, choose 3 in Time 1; for a quarter-note triplet, choose 3 in Time 2.

- *Offset Grid By:* This field lets you move the quantize grid forward or backward by the selected number of ticks. This is helpful for creating grooves that lie slightly ahead or behind the beat.

- *Randomize:* This option adds a level of randomness to the quantizing of your selection. This can further help with keeping your rhythm from being too rigid. You can select values from 0–100%. Lower values place the randomized notes closer to the grid.

In the Options section, you can include other options with your quantize operation, including

- *Swing:* Select this check box to create a *swing* (a dotted quarter-eighth note triplet) feel. Use the slider to specify a percentage (from 0 to 300), with 100% being a triplet feel.

- *Include Within:* Selecting this check box only quantizes the notes that fall within the boundaries created with this setting. Your setting ranges are from 0–100%, with the smaller number affecting the narrower range of notes.

- *Exclude Within:* Selecting Exclude Within allows you to exclude any notes within the boundaries set in this field. Like with Include Within, you can set your boundaries from 0–100%.

- *Strength:* This is, in my opinion, the most useful function in the Pro Tool's quantize operation. Enabling this check box allows you to move your quantized notes by a percentage rather than just snapping them right to the grid. Your setting range runs from 0–100%, with the higher numbers keeping more strictly to the grid than lower values.

3. **Press Return/Enter to close the window.**

Offsetting MIDI tracks

Pro Tools lets you offset your MIDI tracks to be a specified amount of time in your session. This can be especially handy if you record your MIDI track while listening to your sound device through the Avid interface; you may notice some delay (also called *latency*) in the sound. This delay is the result of the time it takes the sound to travel through the interface, into the computer, and then back out the interface to your speakers. Depending on the Buffer setting you have in your session, this latency may be large enough to bother you. (Book II, Chapter 3 has more on Buffer settings.)

The way around this problem is to offset your MIDI tracks by moving them to a point earlier in your session by the amount of the delay. This makes Pro Tools play the MIDI track(s) earlier so you can hear them on time.

To offset all your MIDI tracks, follow these steps:

1. **Choose Setup⇨Preferences from the main menu.**

   The Preferences dialog box opens.

2. **Click the MIDI tab.**

   Refer to Figure 1-3 to see the MIDI tab of the Preferences dialog box.

3. **Enter a negative number equal to your H/W buffer setting in the Global MIDI Playback Offset field.**

   This offset amount uses *samples* (the individual snapshots of the audio in your session) as the unit of measure.

4. **Click OK.**

   Your specified offset will compensate for the latency.

To offset a single track, follow these steps:

1. **Choose Event⇨MIDI Track Offsets from the main menu.**

   The MIDI Track Offsets window opens.

2. **On the row for the track you want to offset, double-click the Sample Offset column.**

   The field is highlighted.

3. **Enter the offset value in the Sample Offset column.**

   A negative number moves the track to an earlier point in the session; a positive number moves it later. Enter a value equal to the H/W buffer setting (as described in Book II, Chapter 3).

4. **Press Return/Enter to save the value and close the window.**

Getting Ready to Record

Setting up MIDI and instrument tracks involves first creating the tracks for your session and then setting the inputs, outputs, and MIDI channels for the tracks you created. This section spells out how to do all these tasks.

Creating MIDI and instrument tracks

Of course, before you can manipulate a MIDI track, you have to have one. To create a new MIDI track, follow these steps:

1. **Choose Track⇨New from the main menu.**

   The New Tracks dialog box appears, as shown in Figure 1-6.

Figure 1-6:
Use the
New Tracks
dialog
box to
create new
MIDI and
instrument
tracks.

2. **Enter the number of tracks you want to create.**

3. **Select MIDI Track or Instrument Track from the drop-down menu.**

4. **If you select an instrument track, you also need to choose between Mono or Stereo.**

   If the plug-in you plan on using is a multichannel plug-in or if you intend to have any stereo information on it, I suggest choosing Stereo.

5. **Click Create.**

   Your new track(s) appear in both the Edit and the Mix windows.

When you create a new track, a default name is used — something not entirely useful (like MIDI 1 or Inst 1). You can rename this track by following these steps:

1. **Double-click the track name in the Edit window.**

   The track's dialog box appears.

2. **Type in the new name and add any comments about the track in the appropriate fields.**

3. **Click OK to close the window.**

   Your track gets a (hopefully more helpful) new name.

Setting inputs, outputs, and MIDI channels

For MIDI and instrument tracks, like with audio tracks, you need to select the input and output sources for your MIDI data to be able to record and play back your tracks. Where MIDI tracks differ from audio tracks is that you also need to set the MIDI channel(s) through which the MIDI data for each track travels. You can set the inputs and outputs for your MIDI tracks in either the Edit or the Mix window. If you want to set these in the Edit window, make sure that you set up the window so that it displays the Input and Output sections.

To view the Input and Output sections on a MIDI track, choose View⇨Mix Window⇨I/O View. To see the MIDI Input and Output section for instruments tracks, choose View⇨Mix Window⇨Instruments.

To set the input on a MIDI or instrument track, follow these steps:

1. Click the MIDI Input Selector drop-down menu.

You find the selector in the Track Controls section of the Edit window and above the track's fader in the Mix window for MIDI tracks. In instrument tracks, you can find the MIDI input/output selector controls at the top of the track's channel strip in the Mix window. In the Edit window, it will be to the right of the main track selection controls.

2. Drag through the menu to the MIDI device and channel you want.

3. Release your mouse button.

To set the output for your MIDI track, follow these steps:

1. Click the MIDI Output Selector drop-down menu.

You find the selector in the Track Controls section of the Edit window and above the track's fader in the Mix window.

2. Drag through the menu to the MIDI device and channel you want.

3. Release your mouse button.

With instrument tracks, you also need to choose a physical output to route the audio signal created by your instrument track's plug-in. Here's how:

1. Click the Audio Output Selector drop-down menu.

You find the selector in the Track Controls section of the Edit window and above the track's fader in the Mix window.

2. Drag through the menu to the output device (bus or hardware) and channel you want.

3. Release your mouse button.

You can assign multiple destinations for your MIDI tracks by pressing Control (Mac) or Windows (PC) when you select your input and output assignments.

Any devices and MIDI channels that are already assigned to another track are listed in bold letters. This makes it easy to keep from accidentally assigning two tracks to the same device and channels (although you can if you want).

Creating a click track

Click tracks (a metronome to play to) are useful for making sure that your performance data lines up with the bars and beats of your session. Having your MIDI line up allows you to do a variety of editing tasks much faster and more accurately.

To create a click track, you need to set a tempo and a meter and then enable the click in the Transport window. I cover the steps for these procedures in the following sections.

Setting the tempo

To set the tempo and meter of your session, or a section within your session, do the following:

1. **Disengage the Tempo Ruler Enable button in the expanded Transport window. If the Tempo Ruler Enable button isn't showing in the Transport window, choose View⇨Transport⇨Expanded.**

   The little Conductor guy turns gray. If it's already gray, leave it alone.

2. **Double-click in the Tempo box in the expanded section of the Transport window (see Figure 1-7).**

Figure 1-7:
Change the tempo here.

3. **Type the tempo number you want and then press Return/Enter. You can also click-drag the number with your mouse and release when you get to the number you want.**

   Your tempo is set.

Choosing the meter

You can set the meter for the session by doing the following:

1. **Double-click the Meter button in the expanded Transport window or choose Window⇨Show Tempo/Meter from the main menu.**

   Check out Book II, Chapter 4 for more on expanding the Transport window.

   The Tempo/Meter Change dialog box appears.

2. Choose Meter Change from the drop-down menu.

The Meter Change dialog box appears, as shown in Figure 1-8. It has the following four parameters to adjust:

- *Snap to Bar:* Select this check box to have any meter events align to the first beat in the nearest bar. (See the section on setting up tempo and meter events in Book III, Chapter 3.)

- *Location:* The number you enter in this field determines the beginning of the *meter* (time signature) event. For songs with only one time signature, you enter **1/1/000**.

- *Meter:* Use these fields to type in the meter that you want to use.

- *Click:* From this menu, choose the note value for the clicks that are played in each measure. Choosing a quarter note means you'll hear four clicks in a 4/4 measure.

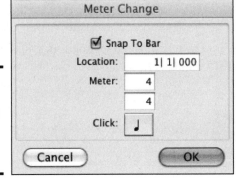

Figure 1-8:
Designate
the meter in
the Meter
Change
dialog box.

Configuring your device

Of course, to play a click track in Pro Tools, you need a device to create the sound (details, details). This can be an external MIDI sound module (such as a drum machine or keyboard) or the DigiRack Click plug-in.

Follow these steps to configure the click-track device:

1. Choose Setup⇨Click/Countoff Options from the main menu or double-click the Click or the Countoff button in the Transport window.

The Click/Countoff Options dialog box appears, as shown in Figure 1-9.

2. Use the Output drop-down menu to choose the device to play your click.

If you're using an external device, choose the port and MIDI channel that your device is connected to. If you're using the Click plug-in, choose None.

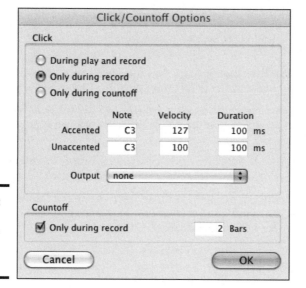

Figure 1-9:
Configure
your click-
track
device.

3. **Choose when you want the click to be played by selecting from the options at the top of the window.**

   You can select During Play and Record, Only During Record, or Only During Countoff.

4. **Enter the MIDI note, velocity, and duration for the accented and unaccented notes of the click in the appropriate fields.**

5. **Select whether you want a countoff as well as the number of bars you want.**

   Selecting Only During Record means that there's no countoff when you play back the track. If you select one of the other options and decide that you still don't want any countoff, type **0** bars in the Bars field.

The next order of business is to enable your click track, which you can do in one of two ways:

✦ **Choose Options⇨Click from the main menu.**

✦ **Click the Click button in the MIDI section of the Transport window. When Click is engaged, this button is blue.**

   You can engage the countoff by clicking the Countoff button in the MIDI section of the Transport window. This button displays the number of bars that the countoff is set for. This button is blue when it's engaged.

If you want to use the Click plug-in — rather than an external device — to play the click, do the following:

If you haven't completed Steps 1–5 in the preceding list and you want to use the internal click-track plug-in, you can simply choose Track➪Create Click Track. Then you're all set to go.

1. **Create a new instrument track by choosing Track➪New from the main menu or pressing Shift+⌘+N (Mac) or Shift+Ctrl+N (PC).**

2. **Use the Output selector to set the output of the track to the main outputs (the outputs you use for your monitors, which are usually 1 and 2).**

3. **Make sure that the Inserts option is chosen under the Mix Window Shows menu. (Choose View➪Mix Window to check.)**

4. **Choose Click from the Inserts drop-down menu (click and hold over the arrow, and then choose Plug-In➪Instrument➪Click) for the track you just created, as shown in Figure 1-10.**

   Your chosen click plays according to your choice in the Click/Countoff Options dialog box.

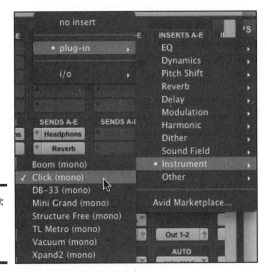

Figure 1-10: Choose the Click plug-in.

My usual device for creating a click track is a drum machine or other decent drum sound from an external device. The Click plug-in, as handy as it is, doesn't have the most pleasing sound.

Chapter 2: Recording MIDI

In This Chapter

✔ **Recording MIDI performances**

✔ **Playing back tracks**

✔ **Understanding overdubbing**

✔ **Recording system-exclusive data**

Recording MIDI in Pro Tools is much like recording audio. The advantage with MIDI is that you record only the performance data and not the sound itself. This allows you flexibility when choosing the sound that you ultimately want for your song.

In this chapter, you discover how to record MIDI in Pro Tools. You walk through enabling your tracks and recording your MIDI data. You also get a chance to overdub by using punch and loop recording.

Instrument tracks can be used the same way as MIDI tracks by recording MIDI information and passing it along to an instrument (in this case, by inserting an instrument into the track), which plays the notes and creates the sound.

Recording MIDI Performances

If you already read through Book III, Chapter 4, you pretty much know the basics of recording MIDI performances because the process is very similar to recording audio tracks. The only significant difference is that you can set your system to wait until it receives MIDI data before starting to record. (This keeps you from having to click the Record button in the Transport window.) The following sections detail how to record single or multiple MIDI and instrument tracks.

Enabling recording for MIDI and instrument tracks

You can record-enable your MIDI and instrument tracks the same way you enable recording for audio tracks. Let me count the ways:

✦ **To record-enable a single track:** Click the Record Enable button, which you can find in either the track's channel strip (in the Mix window) or the track menu (in the Edit window). The Record Enable button blinks red to let you know it's engaged.

+ **To record-enable all tracks:** Option-click (Mac) or Alt-click (PC) the Record Enable button on any track.

+ **To record-enable selected tracks:** Shift-click to select the tracks you want in the playlist and then Shift+Option-click (Mac) or Shift+Alt-click (PC) the Record Enable button of one of the selected tracks.

Setting the Wait for Note option

One of the nice things about recording MIDI in Pro Tools is that you can set your session to start recording only after it starts receiving MIDI data. This feature — Wait for Note — allows you to make sure that your first note is timed exactly where Record Start Time is set.

To enable the Wait for Note feature, do the following:

1. **Set your Transport window to display MIDI controls by choosing View⇨Transport⇨MIDI Controls from the main menu.**

The Transport window expands to include MIDI controls.

2. **Click the Wait for Note button to highlight it, as shown in Figure 2-1.**

Figure 2-1:
Engage
Wait for
Note to start
recording
the instant a
MIDI note is
received.

The Wait for Note button

Recording MIDI tracks in Pro Tools requires that you get a few tasks out of the way first — namely, choose the Record mode, create a track, set levels, enable recording, and turn on a click track (if you're using one). Those steps are all covered in detail in Book III, Chapter 3; when you've got 'em done, you're ready to record some MIDI.

The next sections give you a basic overview of what you can do at that point: Record a single track or multiple tracks, undo or cancel takes, record additional takes and audition takes, use playlists to organize the whole mess, or choose some takes to listen to.

Monitoring MIDI inputs

Even after you get your MIDI devices all hooked up and record-enabled, you still won't hear what you're playing unless you make some connection to the analog outputs of your MIDI device and route them to an audio track in Pro Tools.

To monitor your MIDI device through Pro Tools, do the following:

1. **Connect the analog output of your MIDI device to one of the analog inputs in your audio interface.**

2. **Choose Track⇨New from the main menu.**

   The New Tracks dialog box appears.

3. **Use the drop-down menus of the dialog box to enter the number of tracks you want (1), the type (Audio), and whether you want your track in mono or stereo. Click Create.**

4. **Using the new track's Input selector, select the analog input that your device is connected to in your audio interface.**

5. **Using the new track's Output selector, select the main outputs for your session.**

6. **Record-enable this track by clicking the Record Enable button in either the track's channel strip (Mix window) or the track menu (Edit window).**

   You should hear the sound coming from your MIDI device while you play your MIDI performance.

Hearing instrument tracks

Instrument tracks, because they are a hybrid of MIDI and Auxiliary Input tracks, are easier to set up to hear what you're playing: All you need to do is set an output in the audio out section of the track. You do this in the following way:

1. **Choose View⇨Edit Window⇨I/O from the main menu to open the I/O section of the Edit window.**

   The I/O section shows the inputs and outputs for each track.

2. **Within the I/O section of your track in the Edit window, click and hold the Output selector until the Output drop-down menu appears.**

3. **While still holding down your mouse button, move the mouse over the Output menu until it rests on the output listing you want.**

4. **Release the mouse button to select your choice from the Output drop-down menu.**

   This menu closes, and the output you selected appears in the Output selector.

Recording MIDI and instrument tracks

After you record-enable your MIDI and instrument track(s) (see the "Enabling recording for MIDI and instrument tracks" section, earlier in this chapter), you can begin recording. Follow these steps to record one or more MIDI tracks:

1. **Click the Record Enable button located in either the track channel strip (Mix window) or track menu (Edit window) to record-enable the track(s).**

2. **Using the channel strips located in the Mix window, set the level of the instruments in your session using the fader for each audio track associated with your MIDI devices.**

   This is so you hear your music the way you want.

3. **Enable the click track and the pre-roll, if you're using them.**

4. **Click the Return to Zero button in the Transport section of the Transport window.**

   Doing so ensures that you start recording at the beginning of the session.

5. **Click the Record button in the Transport section of the Transport window.**

   This step gets you ready to record; it doesn't start the actual recording process.

6. **Click the Play button in the Transport section of the Transport window.**

   Pro Tools starts recording.

7. **When you're done recording, click the Stop button in the Transport section of the Transport window or press the spacebar on your keyboard.**

   The finished take appears in the MIDI Clips list as a new clip.

Playing Back Your Tracks

After you record a track, you'll most likely want to listen to it to make sure that it sounds how you want. Pro Tools offers you many ways to play back a track. In the following sections, I guide you through a few of the many options for playing back audio clips.

Playing recorded tracks

After you record a track and click the Stop button, you can immediately hear the track by toggling off the Record Enable button on your MIDI tracks — click it to make the red light disappear — and then clicking the Play button. Leave the audio tracks associated with the MIDI devices in record-enable mode so that you hear the playback of the MIDI device from the recorded MIDI data instead of the recorded audio that was recorded to that track when you recorded your performance. You can adjust the volume by moving the fader up and down in the channel strip for the audio track associated with your MIDI device.

Setting scrolling options

Pro Tools lets you decide how you want the Edit window to scroll when a session is playing or recording. Just choose Options➪Scrolling from the main menu to see the choices displayed in Figure 2-2. The following list gives you the scoop on each option:

- ✦ **No Scrolling:** When you choose this, the Edit window remains where it while as the session plays. You can still move through the session by manually sliding the scroll bar at the bottom of the window while the session plays.

- ✦ **After Playback:** Choosing this takes you to where the cursor is located after the session is stopped.

- ✦ **Page:** Page scrolling during playback keeps the cursor visible at all times while the session plays. The cursor moves from left to right, and the Edit window follows gamely along (just like Little Bo Peep's sheep).

- ✦ **Continuous:** With this option the cursor is also always visible, and the session data scrolls past the cursor, which stays in the middle of the screen. This option is handy if you want to most easily see what's coming and going.

  This is the option I generally choose because I can easily keep track of where I am in the session at all times.

Changing sounds

One of the great features of recording MIDI data is that you can change the sound that the recorded performance plays. This lets you decide what sound you use in your song after you have played the part.

MIDI tracks

You can change the playback sound of a recorded MIDI track in one of two ways:

- ✦ **Change the MIDI device or channel.** Click the Output selector for the MIDI track and scroll to a different MIDI channel or MIDI device.

✦ **Change the MIDI patch.** Open the Patch drop-down menu located in the Track Controls section of the Edit window, as shown in Figure 2-3. After the Patch dialog box opens, as shown in Figure 2-4, choose a patch from the list and then click Done to close the window.

Figure 2-2: You can set the Edit window to scroll in three different ways.

Figure 2-3: The MIDI Patch drop-down menu is located in the Track Control section of the Edit menu.

Click here to open the Patch drop-down menu

Figure 2-4:
Use the Patch dialog box to choose a different patch for your MIDI device.

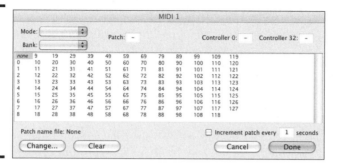

Instrument tracks

Because instrument tracks are a hybrid between a MIDI track and an Auxiliary input track, you make changes to the sound your track plays differently. Here's how to change the sound of an instrument track:

1. **Double-click the plug-in in the Insert section of either the Edit or Mix window.**

    This opens a window for the software instrument.

2. **Make any adjustments you want to the software instrument until you like the sound.**

3. **Close the software instrument's window.**

To change the software instrument connected to your instrument track, do the following:

1. **Click and hold the Insert selector for the inserted software instrument and drag to another instrument (assuming you have another one to choose).**

2. **Release the mouse button.**

    The window for your new software instrument opens.

3. **Choose the settings you want for your new instrument.**

4. **Close the window.**

Getting Rid of Unwanted Takes

If you have a *take* (a recorded performance) that you don't particularly like, you can get rid of it in several different ways. You can cancel the take while you're recording, you can undo the take after you record, or you can clear the audio clip from the Audio Clips list. All these options are detailed in the following sections.

Canceling your performance

Canceling a performance is handy when you're in the middle of recording and you know that you're not going to keep the take. To cancel a performance, simply press ⌘+. (period; Mac) or Ctrl+. (period; PC). This stops the session and clears the audio clip created for this take with two keystrokes.

Undoing your take

If you already stopped recording and you know you don't want to keep your latest try, you can undo the take by choosing Edit⇨Undo MIDI Recording from the main menu (as shown in Figure 2-5), or by pressing ⌘+Z (Mac) or Ctrl+Z (PC).

If you punch in more than once before you stopped the recording, only the last punch is undone. The rest of the punches remain. (Read more about this in the upcoming section, "Punching in and out.")

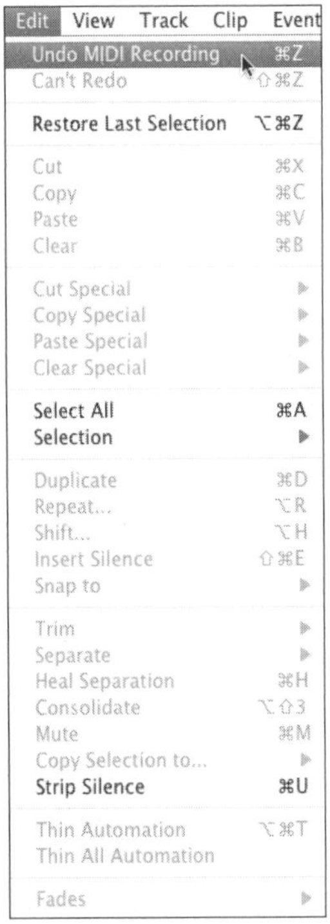

Edit	View	Track	Clip	Event
Undo MIDI Recording				⌘Z
Can't Redo				⇧⌘Z
Restore Last Selection				⌥⌘Z
Cut				⌘X
Copy				⌘C
Paste				⌘V
Clear				⌘B
Cut Special				▶
Copy Special				▶
Paste Special				▶
Clear Special				▶
Select All				⌘A
Selection				▶
Duplicate				⌘D
Repeat...				⌥R
Shift...				⌥H
Insert Silence				⇧⌘E
Snap to				▶
Trim				▶
Separate				▶
Heal Separation				⌘H
Consolidate				⌥⇧3
Mute				⌘M
Copy Selection to...				▶
Strip Silence				⌘U
Thin Automation				⌥⌘T
Thin All Automation				
Fades				▶

Figure 2-5:
You can undo a take by choosing Edit⇨Undo MIDI Recording.

When you use Loop record mode, all the takes from the loop sequence are undone.

Clearing the file from the Clips list

After hearing a few of your takes, maybe you want to get rid of one or more of them. Just clear the offending takes from the Clips list. Here's how to get that done:

1. **Highlight the clip you want to get rid of in the Clips list by clicking it.**

   The Clips list is located in the lower-right corner of the Edit window. If this section of the Edit window isn't visible, click the double arrow at the bottom-right corner of the Edit window to expand it.

2. **Click and hold the Clips list title at the top of the list to access the Clips drop-down menu and then choose Clear Selected (as shown in Figure 2-6), or press Shift+⌘+B (Mac) or Shift+Ctrl+B (PC).**

   To select more than one clip to clear, hold the Shift key while you click each clip.

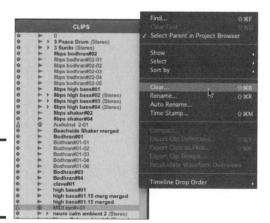

Figure 2-6:
Get rid of a selected MIDI clip.

Overdubbing MIDI Performances

After you have some MIDI performances recorded, you can add to or change them easily. The time-honored name for this kind of recording is *overdubbing,* but MIDI takes it to a whole new level. In Pro Tools, you can overdub MIDI in several ways: You can punch in or out, loop, and either *merge* (that is, add) new data or replace existing performance information. The following sections get you up to speed on these procedures.

Using MIDI Merge/Replace

When you overdub to a MIDI track, Pro Tools offers you the option to either replace existing material or add new data to it. Which option you use depends on the position of the MIDI Merge button located in the Transport window (as shown in Figure 2-7):

+ **When the button is engaged (MIDI Merge mode):** New material is merged with any existing MIDI data on the record-enabled track(s).

+ **When the button is disengaged (MIDI Replace mode):** New MIDI data replaces any existing information on record-enabled track(s).

Figure 2-7:
Engage the
MIDI Merge
button to
add new
performance
data.

The MIDI Merge button

To engage MIDI Merge, do the following:

1. **Open the MIDI controls section of the Transport window by choosing View⇨Transport⇨MIDI Controls from the main menu.**

    The Transport window expands to include the MIDI controls section.

2. **Click the MIDI Merge button.**

    The button becomes highlighted.

Punching in and out

If you like some of your initial take and want to record over only part of it, you can set points at which to start and stop recording within the session: that is, *punching in and out.* Punching in or out of a track involves first setting a start and an end point. This can be done in several ways; the next sections give you the details.

Using the Start/End fields in the Transport section of the Transport window

This method is pretty straightforward. To set your start and end points via the Transport section, do the following:

1. **Choose View⇨Transport⇨Expanded from the main menu to get a nice, big view of the window.**

2. **Click in the Start field in the Transport section of the Transport window, type in the beginning of the punch section you want, and then press Return/Enter.**

    This field displays in the same format as the main counter. In the case of Figure 2-8, the format is Bars and Beats.

3. **Click in the End field, type in the end of the range, and then press Return/Enter.**

   This field is displayed in the format selected for the main counter (like in Figure 2-8).

Figure 2-8:
Type the start and end points to set your punch range.

Start	23| 1| 000
End	23| 1| 000
Length	0| 0| 000

Selecting a section of a track's playlist

For those of you out there who are especially handy with a mouse, this method may have some appeal:

1. **Make sure that the Link Edit and Timeline Selection option is chosen under the Options menu.**

2. **Using the Selector tool, click and drag a recorded range in your track, as shown in Figure 2-9.**

   The section becomes highlighted, and the session start and end points are set to match the beginning and ending of this selection.

Figure 2-9:
Drag to select a recorded range from a track's playlist.

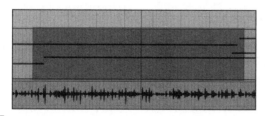

Dragging the start- and end-point markers along the ruler bar

The start- and end-point markers are displayed along the Timeline in the Edit window as up and down arrows — down for punch in and up for punch out. The arrows are blue when no tracks are record-enabled and red when one or more tracks are record-enabled. Setting start and end points in the Timeline consists of these steps:

1. **Make sure that the Link Edit and Timeline Selection option is chosen under the Options menu.**

2. **Select the Grid edit mode (click on the Grid mode selector in the upper-left of the Edit window) if you want the markers to snap to the grid. Otherwise, use any other Edit mode.**

3. **Click and drag the Start and End Point arrows to where you want them, as shown in Figure 2-10.**

Figure 2-10: Set a punch range by dragging the Start and End Point arrows.

Performing the punch

After you designate the start and end points of your punch-in-and-out range, you can record to that section by doing the following:

1. **Set and enable a pre-roll.**

   Doing so enables you to hear the previously recorded track before the punch-in happens. Here's the quick drill. (See Book III, Chapter 4 for details.)

   a. *Click the Pre-Roll field in the expanded version of the Transport window and type in a pre-roll time. (Choose View⇨Transport⇨Expanded if you need to expand the window.)*

   b. *Click the Pre-Roll button in the expanded version of the Transport window to enable the pre-roll function.*

2. **Set and enable a post-roll.**

   Doing so lets you hear how your punch fits in with your previously recorded track. Here's the quick drill. (See Book III, Chapter 4 for details.)

   a. *Click the Post-Roll field in the expanded version of the Transport window and type in a pre-roll time. (Choose View⇨Transport⇨Expanded if you need to expand the window.)*

   b. *Click the Post-Roll button in the expanded version of the Transport window to enable the post-roll function.*

3. **Choose the nondestructive record mode by making sure that destructive, loop, and quick-punch modes are disabled in the Options menu.**

4. **Choose either MIDI Merge or MIDI Replace mode.**

    See the "Using MIDI Merge/Replace" section, earlier in the chapter, for more on MIDI Merge/Replace.

5. **Click the Record Enable button in either the track's channel strip (Mix window) or the track menu (Edit window).**

    The track is record-enabled.

6. **Click the Record button in the Transport section of the Transport window.**

    The Record button flashes red.

7. **Click the Play button in the Transport section of the Transport window when you're ready to record.**

    The session starts at the pre-roll time, the Record button flashes red, and you hear the previously recorded track until the pre-roll is over. The monitoring then switches to the Input source, and the Record button stops flashing (but remains red). After you hit the end of the record range, the session stops playing, or (if you enabled a post-roll) the recording stops. If the recording stops to accommodate a post-roll, the Record button starts flashing again. The monitoring then switches back to the recorded clip until the end of the post-roll period. When the post-roll is done, the session stops playing.

Punching MIDI on the fly

With MIDI, you can punch in and out of a track while the session plays. This is *punching on the fly* and is especially effective if you have an interface with a footswitch input (such as the 003 or 003 Rack) *and* a footswitch connected to the footswitch input on your interface.

Here's how to punch on the fly:

1. **Choose the nondestructive record mode by making sure that destructive, loop, and quick-punch modes are disabled in the Options menu.**

2. **Select either MIDI Merge or MIDI Replace mode.**

    See the "Using MIDI Merge/Replace" section, earlier in the chapter, for more on MIDI Merge/Replace.

3. **Disable the Wait for Note and Countoff options in the Transport window.**

4. **Click the Record Enable button in either the track's channel strip (Mix window) or the track menu (Edit window).**

   The track is record-enabled.

5. **Click the Play button in the Transport section of the Transport window.**

   The session plays.

6. **When you reach the point where you want to start recording in the session, click the Record button or press the footswitch.**

   The punch begins.

7. **Play what you want.**

8. **When you reach the point that you want to stop recording, click the Record button or press the footswitch again.**

   Recording stops, but the session continues playing — and, with any luck, seamlessly.

Loop recording

Use *loop recording* to choose a section of the song to repeatedly record over. This makes it easy to try a bunch of takes without having to manually start and stop every time you go through the section. Loop recording can be done in a bunch of ways. I described two of 'em in the Audio Recording chapters (Book III, Chapters 3 and 4), but I prefer using MIDI Merge mode to loop-record MIDI. (Makes sense, doesn't it?)

To loop-record using MIDI Merge mode, do the following:

1. **Choose the nondestructive record mode by making sure that destructive, loop, and quick-punch modes are disabled in the Options menu.**

2. **Enable MIDI Merge mode.**

   The button becomes highlighted.

3. **Disable the Wait for Note and Countoff options in the Transport section of the Transport window.**

4. **Enable the Link Edit and Timeline Selection option in the Options menu.**

5. **Choose the Selector tool in the Edit window.**

6. **Click and drag across the section of the track that you want to record over.**

7. **(Optional) Click in the Pre-Roll field in the expanded Transport window and type in a pre-roll time. Click the Pre-Roll button in the Transport window to enable the pre-roll function.**

TIP

Choose View⇨Transport⇨Expanded if you need to expand the window.

If you don't want to hear a section of the session before the loop begins, skip this step.

8. **Click the Record Enable button located in either the track channel strip (Mix window) or track menu (Edit window) to record enable the track.**

9. **Select Loop Record mode.**

   You have three ways to make this selection:

   • *Check the Loop Record option under the Options menu.*

   • *Press Option+L (Mac) or Alt+L (PC).*

   • *Control-click (Mac) or right-click (PC) the Record button in the Transport window until the Loop Record icon shows up.*

10. **Click Play in the Transport section of the Transport window to start recording.**

    While the recording is under way, the new MIDI data appears in the track as a new clip (and in the MIDI Clips list) but doesn't replace the previously recorded material.

11. **Click Stop when you finish recording.**

REMEMBER

If you designated a pre-roll, it only happens before the *first time through the loop.* After that, the loop goes from start point to end point, back to the start point, and so on, as many times as needed.

TIP

If you loop-record using the Loop Record mode *without* engaging MIDI Merge, you create a new clip in the MIDI Clips list each time you go through the loop. This is in contrast to loop-recording audio tracks, in which all the takes are stored in one audio file.

Recording System-Exclusive Data

In Pro Tools, you can record *system-exclusive data* — data that is unique to your MIDI device — to a MIDI track. That means that you can record changes made to your *patches* (prepared sounds selected from a sound bank) to your configuration as well as any real-time changes in the system. For example, you can record patch changes so that your MIDI device changes its sound while the session plays (from, say, a Chainsaw patch to a Bagpipe patch). You can also store the parameter settings for a device and have Pro Tools automatically restore those settings to your device before your session plays.

To record system-exclusive data to a MIDI track in Pro Tools, do the following:

1. **Connect the MIDI Out of your device to one of the MIDI In ports configured in Pro Tools.**

2. **Choose Track⇨New from the main menu.**

   The New Track dialog box appears.

3. **Use the drop-down menus of the dialog box to enter the number of tracks you want (1), the type (MIDI), and whether you want your track in samples or ticks. Click Create.**

4. **Using the new track's Input selector, set the input of the track to the MIDI In port that's connected to your device.**

5. **Choose the non-destructive record mode by making sure that destructive, loop, and quick-punch modes are disabled in the Options menu.**

6. **Choose Setup⇨MIDI⇨Input Filter from the main menu.**

   The MIDI Input Filter dialog box appears.

7. **Enable system-exclusive recording by selecting the System Exclusive check box in the lower-left corner of the MIDI Input Filter dialog box (see Figure 2-11).**

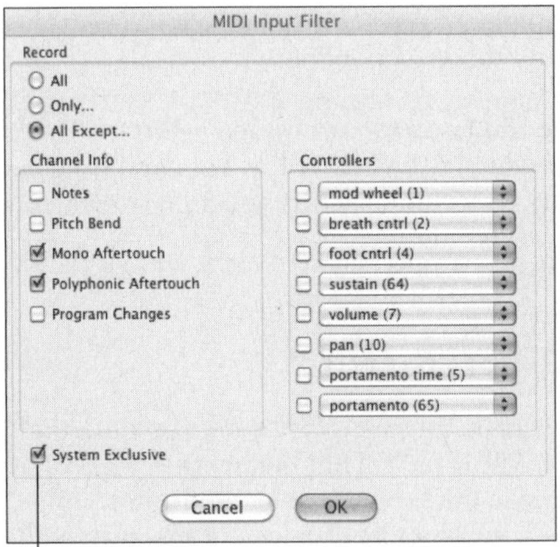

Figure 2-11:
Enable the
System
Exclusive
option on
the MIDI
Input Filter
dialog box.

MIDI Input Filter

Record
- ○ All
- ○ Only...
- ⦿ All Except...

Channel Info
- ☐ Notes
- ☐ Pitch Bend
- ☑ Mono Aftertouch
- ☑ Polyphonic Aftertouch
- ☐ Program Changes

Controllers
- ☐ mod wheel (1)
- ☐ breath cntrl (2)
- ☐ foot cntrl (4)
- ☐ sustain (64)
- ☐ volume (7)
- ☐ pan (10)
- ☐ portamento time (5)
- ☐ portamento (65)

☑ System Exclusive

[Cancel]   [OK]

Select this option

8. **Enable the Wait for Note function in the Transport window.**

9. **Click the Return to Zero button in the Transport window to return to the beginning of the session.**

10. **Click the Record Enable button in either the track's channel strip (Mix window) or the track menu (Edit window).**

The track is record-enabled.

11. **Click the Record button in the Transport section of the Transport window.**

The Record, Play, and Wait for Note buttons flash.

12. **Initiate the MIDI dump on your MIDI Device.**

Check your MIDI device's manual to figure out how this is done; it's different for every device.

The transfer begins.

13. **Click Stop when the transfer is finished.**

To send system-exclusive data back to your device, do the following:

1. **Make sure that the MIDI Out port of your MIDI interface is connected to the MIDI In port of your device.**

2. **Using the Output selector of the MIDI track that has the system-exclusive data, set the output to the MIDI port that's connected to your device.**

3. **Set your device to receive system-exclusive data.**

You might need to check your owner's manual for details on how to do this.

4. **Click the Return to Zero button in the Transport section of the Transport window to return the session to the beginning.**

5. **Click Play in the Transport window.**

The session plays, and the system-exclusive data is received.

6. **Click Stop when the transfer is complete.**

Chapter 3: Editing MIDI Data

In This Chapter

✔ **Understanding MIDI and instrument track views**

✔ **Selecting MIDI data**

✔ **Editing in the Edit window**

✔ **Understanding the MIDI Event window**

Although MIDI editing in Pro Tools isn't as elaborate as what you find in some programs (such as Logic or Sonar), it's plenty powerful enough to tweak your MIDI data quite a bit. If your overall MIDI needs are moderate, the relatively simple Pro Tools MIDI features can do what you need with minimum fuss.

In this chapter, you explore the MIDI-editing functions available to you in Pro Tools. You examine the many uses of the Pencil tool, discovering ways to edit MIDI notes, controller data, and system-exclusive messages.

Working with MIDI and Instrument Tracks

Working with MIDI and instrument tracks is almost the same as working with audio tracks. (The latter are covered in great detail in Book IV, Chapters 1 and 2.) The following sections explain track views, selecting MIDI data, understanding clips, and setting default program changes.

Taking a look at track views

You can adjust the track view for MIDI and Instrument tracks by clicking the Track View selector in the Track Controls section of the Edit window, as shown in Figure 3-1. The track views for MIDI and Instrument tracks include the following options:

✦ **Blocks:** In Blocks view, clips are displayed as blocks, each showing only the clip name. This view takes up the least amount of processing power to show and redraw, which makes this the best option after all your editing is done and you're ready to start mixing.

MIDI Track View selector

Figure 3-1:
Use the
MIDI
Track View
selector
to choose
between
track views.

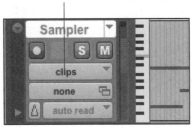

+ **Clips:** Clips view shows the clips in the track, also displaying notes in the track in the piano-roll fashion that you can see in Figure 3-2. The notes can't be edited, but the clips can be. This view is useful when you want to move or edit the clips in your track.

When you edit in Clips view on a MIDI or Instrument track, you edit continuous controller events (volume, pitch bend, after-touch — see Book V, Chapter 2) along with the clip because such events are connected to the clip and not to the track's playlist.

Figure 3-2:
The Clips
view shows
MIDI clips
for the
track.

+ **Notes:** Using Notes view displays the location, pitch, and duration of the notes in the track in piano-roll format (as shown in Figure 3-3). You can edit or insert MIDI notes in this view.

MIDI notes are shown as small rectangles. The horizontal range represents the location and duration of the note; the vertical placement shows the note's pitch.

Along the left side of the track's playlist is a representation of a keyboard with up and down arrows, which allow you to scroll through the octaves of the notes. This is necessary because not all the possible MIDI notes can be displayed in the track's playlist at one time. A single line at the top or bottom of the track display designates any notes that can't be displayed (because they're above or below the octave being displayed).

You can also scroll through the octaves in the playlist by using the Grabber tool and dragging the piano-roll display up and down.

Figure 3-3:
Notes view
is where
you edit
notes for
a MIDI or
Instrument
track.

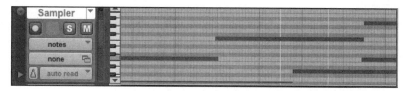

✦ **Velocity:** This view displays — and allows you to edit — *velocity* (note volume) settings for each note in the track. (You can still see the piano-roll data in the background.)

✦ **Volume:** Volume view shows automation volume curves with *breakpoints* — markers that show shifts in the automation level — displayed as dots along the line. Note data, in piano-roll format, is shown in the background. In this view, you can edit the volume data but not the underlying notes.

✦ **Pan:** This view displays and allows you to adjust panning automation data (far left at the top and far right at the bottom) with the piano-roll display in the background.

✦ **Mute:** This view shows mute automation settings for the track and allows you to mute or unmute the track. Note data, in piano-roll format, is shown in the background.

✦ **Pitch Bend:** Pitch Bend view shows any pitch bend data in the track as a line graph with editable breakpoints. The piano-roll data is shown in the background but can't be edited.

✦ **Mono After Touch:** This view shows *after-touch* data — the velocity of the note after the initial touch of the keyboard — as a line graph with editable breakpoints. The piano-roll data is shown in the background to help you know where you are in the session.

✦ **Program Change:** This view displays program-change information for the track with the piano-roll data in the background (uneditable, of course). Use this view to add or edit program-change events.

✦ **Sysex:** This view shows *system-exclusive data* — messages exclusive to the MIDI device — for the track.

✦ **Controllers:** This view shows continuous controller data, such as modulation wheel, breath controller, foot control, expression, and sustain with the piano-roll data in the background. Use this view to add or edit continuous controller data for your track.

You can toggle between the two most-used MIDI track views: Clips and Notes. Do this by pressing Control (Mac) or Windows (PC) while you press the minus key on the main section of the keyboard. Or simply press the minus key (from the main keyboard, not the number pad) after engaging the Command Keyboard Focus button. (See Book II, Chapter 4, for more on the Command Keyboard Focus feature.)

Selecting track material

You can select track material the same way you select material from audio tracks — well, okay, with a few variations. The following sections tell you about those variations; Book IV, Chapter 2 covers the selection stuff about audio tracks that's perfectly applicable to MIDI and Instrument tracks. (You may want to skim through Book IV, Chapter 2 to refresh your memory about selection basics.)

 MIDI notes are selected from Notes view; clips are selected from Clips view.

Selecting notes with the Pencil tool

 You select notes with the Pencil tool by clicking the notes. (No big deal, right?) To select more than one note, press the Shift key while you click each note. Selected notes become highlighted.

Using the Selector tool

 When you use the Selector tool to select notes, certain conditions apply. They're pretty straightforward:

✦ **Before a note can be included in a selection, its start point must be in the selection range.**

In Figure 3-4, for example, the note whose start point begins *before* the selection range is not selected. (You can tell it's not selected because it's not highlighted.)

✦ **Notes with end points outside the selection range are still selected.**

✦ **When you select notes with the Selector tool, you also select (automatically) all the underlying automation and controller data pertaining to the notes.**

Grabbing with the Grabber tool

When you select a series of notes with the Grabber tool, all notes partially or fully contained in the Grabber selection are selected, as shown in Figure 3-5. Notes selected with the Grabber tool don't include automation or controller data.

Figure 3-4:
The Selector tool selects notes only if the start time is included in the selection range.

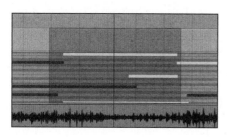

Figure 3-5:
The Grabber tool selects notes whenever any part of the note is in the selection.

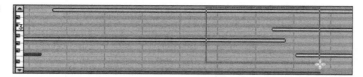

Selecting notes from the mini keyboard

You can select all the notes in a track that have the same pitch by clicking the represented MIDI note in the mini keyboard, which is located along the left side of the track's playlist display, as shown in Figure 3-6.

Figure 3-6:
Select notes of a desired pitch from the mini-keyboard.

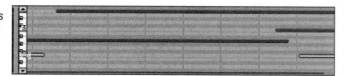

Recognizing clips

The procedures for working with MIDI clips are the same as those for audio clips. Book IV, Chapter 1 describes how to select and view clips in a track's playlist, as well as how to work with clips in the Clips list. The procedures for working with the MIDI Clips list are the same as those for working with the Clips list, so if you check out Book IV, Chapter 1, you're all set.

Setting MIDI patches on tracks

You can change the default program (sound patch) in use with your MIDI tracks so your MIDI device automatically resets to the program you want for your track. Here's how to make it happen:

1. **Click the Program button in the Track Controls section of the Edit window, as shown in Figure 3-7.**

The Patch Select dialog box opens.

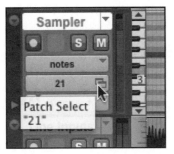

Figure 3-7:
The Program button is located in the Track Controls.

2. **Click the patch number or name that you want from the list in the main section of the dialog box.**

It becomes highlighted.

Depending on your MIDI device, you might need to specify a bank along with the patch number. The bank number is entered in one of the Controller fields at the top of the dialog box. Check the specification for your device to see what to enter in this field.

3. **Click Done.**

The Patch Select dialog box closes, and the patch number/name is displayed on the Program button of the Track Controls section.

You can have Pro Tools scroll automatically through the patches in your MIDI sound module by selecting the Incremental Patch option in the Patch Select dialog box and entering a value for the number of seconds that each patch sounds as your session plays.

Dealing with Note Chasing

Note chasing makes sure that when you start your session in the middle of a long MIDI note, the note is played. This is useful when you want to start and stop the session from anywhere and still be able to hear the notes that are recorded.

The Note Chasing feature is turned on by default, but you might want to turn it off on any tracks that play loops to ensure that the loop doesn't get out of sync when you start and stop the session in the middle of its sequence.

To turn on and off Note Chasing, do the following:

1. **Click the track's Playlist selector, located in the Track Controls section of the Edit window.**

   The selector is the arrow to the right of the name of the track.

   The Track Playlist drop-down menu opens with an option for engaging note chasing in the track.

2. **Choose Note Chasing from the Track Playlist menu.**

   You deselect (uncheck) to turn the Note Chasing feature off and select (check) to turn it on.

Editing MIDI in the Edit Window

Like with audio, you do most of your MIDI editing from the Edit window. The process, again, is very similar to editing audio (described in Book IV, Chapters 1–3). The following sections offer some tips and tricks tailored to inserting, deleting, and editing MIDI data. For the most part, though, I discuss the amazing Pencil tool, the Smart tool, and the Grabber tool.

If your MIDI clip exists in only one location (that is, it's not shared with other tracks or sessions), any changes you make to the data in that clip *change it permanently.* To ensure that you don't lose important data while editing (or if you want to be able to return to the original), make a copy of the playlist and work from there. (I explain playlists in detail in Book IV, Chapter 1.)

Perusing the Pencil tools

Pro Tools offers seven Pencil tools — Free Hand, Line, Triangle, Square, Random, Parabolic, and S-Curve — that you can use to create and edit MIDI data easily with your mouse. You select these tools by clicking and holding the Pencil Tool icon and then choosing from the drop-down menu that appears, as shown in Figure 3-8. Each tool can be used to add notes and draw velocity and controller data, but each one works a little differently, as the following sections make clear.

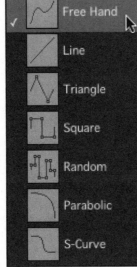

Figure 3-8:
Pencil tools in seven shapes for creating and editing MIDI data.

Free Hand

When you insert notes, here's what happens:

✦ **You can place them anywhere you want and drag your mouse to specify the duration you want the note to be.**

✦ **If you simply click with the Free Hand Pencil tool to insert a note, the note duration is equal to the grid value for your session.** (Grid values are boundaries you can set for your session and are set in the Grid Value drop-down menu, located just below the Pencil Tool button in the Edit window.)

✦ **Note velocity is determined by the setting you have in the MIDI tab of the Preferences dialog box.** Choose Setup⇨Preferences to access the Preferences dialog box.

When you draw velocity or continuous controller data, here's what happens:

✦ **You can draw any shape you want with your mouse.**

✦ **The resolution of the lines is determined by the settings you've chosen for controller data in the MIDI tab of the Preferences dialog box.** Choose Setup⇨Preferences to access the Preferences dialog box.

Line

When you insert notes, here's what you get:

✦ **You can place as many notes as you want as a single pitch.**

The note duration is equal to the current grid value in your session.

+ **The note velocity is determined by the setting you have on the MIDI tab of the Preferences dialog box.**

When you draw velocity or continuous controller data, these conditions apply:

+ **The line is straight from the initial mouse click through the drag and release.**

+ **The resolution of the lines is determined by the settings you choose for controller data on the MIDI tab of the Preferences dialog box.**

Triangle

When you insert notes, three conditions apply:

+ **You can place as many notes as you want as a single pitch.**

   The note duration is equal to the current grid value in your session.

+ **The note velocity oscillates between the setting you have for Note on Velocity on the MIDI tab of the Preferences dialog box and 127 (the maximum level).**

When you draw velocity or continuous controller data, here's what you see:

+ **The line is a triangular pattern, which changes direction according to the current grid value in your session.**

+ **The resolution of the lines is determined by the settings for controller data you chose on the MIDI tab of the Preferences dialog box.**

Square

When you insert notes, here's the skinny:

+ **You can place as many notes as you want as a single pitch.**

   The note duration is equal to the current grid value in your session.

+ **The note velocity alternates between the setting you have for Note on Velocity on the MIDI tab of the Preferences dialog box and 127 (the maximum level).**

When you draw velocity or continuous controller data, it works this way:

+ **The line is a square pattern, which repeats according to the current grid value in your session.**

+ **The resolution of the lines is determined by the settings you chose for controller data on the MIDI tab of the Preferences dialog box.**

Random

When you insert notes, here's what you get:

✦ **You can place as many notes as you want as a single pitch.**

The note duration is equal to the current grid value in your session.

✦ **The note velocity changes randomly between the setting you have for Note on Velocity on the MIDI tab of the Preferences dialog box and 127 (the maximum level).**

When you draw velocity or continuous controller data, the line is a random pattern, which changes value according to the current grid value in your session.

Custom note duration

 When you insert a note by using one of the Pencil tools and you want a different value than the grid setting in your session, you can choose the Custom Note Duration option, which is located at the bottom of the Pencil tool drop-down menu. Enabling this option adds the Notes button shown here in the margin beneath the Pencil Tool icon on the Edit Window toolbar.

The Custom Note Duration option lets you specify a note duration other than your current grid setting.

To choose a custom note duration when you're inserting a MIDI note, do the following:

1. **Click and hold the Pencil icon in the Edit window toolbar.**

The Pencil tool drop-down menu appears.

2. **Choose Custom Note Duration from the Pencil tool drop-down menu.**

The Notes button appears beneath the Pencil icon on the Edit Window toolbar.

3. **Choose which Pencil tool you want to use from the drop-down menu.**

4. **Using the Notes button beneath the Pencil Tool button, choose a note duration.**

5. **Using the Pencil tool you select in Step 3, insert the note in your track.**

Adding MIDI events

You can add MIDI notes or controller data (collectively called *MIDI events*) to a MIDI or Instrument track by using the Pencil tool. (See the preceding section for more about the Pencil tools.)

Inserting notes

To use the Pencil tool to insert a note, do the following:

1. **From the Track View drop-down menu in the Track Controls section of the Edit Window, set the track view to Notes.**

2. **Click and hold the Pencil icon and then choose the Pencil tool you want to use from the Pencil Tool drop-down menu that appears.**

3. **Locate the place you want to add your MIDI note in the track's playlist area.**

4. **With the Pencil tool you select in Step 2, click in the playlist to insert a note with a duration equal to the grid value.**

When you use the Free Hand tool, you can set the note to whatever duration you want. Do so by clicking the start point of the note in the track's playlist, dragging to the end point you want, and then releasing the mouse button.

If you want to hear the MIDI note while you insert it, first make sure that you have the Play MIDI Notes When Editing preference chosen on the MIDI tab of the Preferences dialog box. (Choose Setup➪Preferences to access this dialog box.)

If you have Grid mode enabled as your editing mode, the inserted note is snapped to the nearest grid boundary. To disable this function, press ⌘ (Mac) or Ctrl (PC) when you insert the note. (Book IV, Chapter 1 has more on editing modes.)

Drawing velocity or continuous controller data

To draw velocity or continuous controller data in a track's playlist, do the following:

1. **From the Track View drop-down menu in the Track Controls section of the Edit Window, set the track to Velocity or Controller view.**

2. **Click and hold the Pencil icon and then choose the Pencil tool you want to use from the menu that appears.**

3. **Locate where you want to enter your MIDI data in the track's playlist.**

4. **With the Pencil tool you choose in Step 2, click and drag in the track's playlist to sketch in the velocity or the controller level you want to draw.**

5. **Release the mouse button when you reach the end point of your edit.**

Inserting program changes

To insert MIDI program changes, do the following:

1. **From the Track View drop-down menu, set the track to Program Change view.**

2. **Click and hold the Pencil icon and then choose the Pencil tool you want to use from the menu that appears.**

3. **Click in the track's playlist where you want the change to occur.**

   The Patch Select dialog box opens.

4. **Click the patch number or name in the main section of the dialog box to select it.**

5. **Click Done.**

   The program change is inserted, as shown in Figure 3-9.

Figure 3-9:
A program-change event appears in the track's playlist in Program Change view.

Deleting MIDI data

You can delete MIDI notes and other data several ways. The following sections detail the process.

Deleting a MIDI note

To delete a MIDI note, do the following:

1. **From the Track View drop-down menu, set the track view to Notes.**

2. **With either the Grabber tool or the Selector tool, select the note in the playlist you want to delete.**

3. **Press Delete/Backspace on your keyboard or choose Edit⇨Clear from the main menu.**

Instead of using Steps 2 and 3 in the preceding list, start out with the Pencil tool. Then press Option (Mac) or Alt (PC) to change the pencil into an eraser, and then click the note to delete it.

If you use the Selector tool to select the note, all automation and controller data is deleted along with the note.

Deleting a program change

To delete a program change, do the following:

1. **From the Track View drop-down menu, set the track view to Program Change.**

2. **Select the program change you want to delete.**

- *With the Grabber tool,* click the event or drag across it to select it.

    If you drag, you can include other MIDI events in your selection to delete them as well.

- *With the Pencil tool,* press Option (Mac) or Alt (PC) while you click the event. You won't need to perform Step 3 using this procedure because the event is automatically deleted.

3. **Press Delete/Backspace on your keyboard or choose Edit⇨Clear from the main menu.**

    The event is deleted.

Changing MIDI events

In the Edit window, you can edit MIDI notes in a variety of ways including changing pitch, duration, velocity, and time location.

When you edit or move notes, you can make a copy of the note to move by pressing Option (Mac) or Ctrl (PC) while you drag the note.

Changing a note's pitch

To change a note's pitch, do the following:

1. **From the Track View drop-down menu, set your track to Notes view.**

2. **Select the Pencil or the Grabber tool.**

3. **Press Shift to keep the note's start point from changing while you move it.**

4. **Click the note and drag it up (higher pitch) or down (lower pitch) in the playlist.**

5. **Release the mouse button when the note is where you want it.**

Changing a note's duration

To change a note's duration — its Start or End points — do the following:

1. **From the Track View drop-down menu, set your track to Notes view.**

2. **Select the Pencil tool.**

3. **With the Pencil tool, click the note you want to change.**

    Press Shift while you click to select more than one note.

4. **Click the Start or End point of the note and drag it left or right.**

    - *If your edit mode is set to Grid,* the note is moved along the grid boundary.

    - *If you're using the Spot edit mode,* the Spot dialog box appears; there, you can type in a location for the note and then click Done.

5. **Release the mouse button when the note is where you want it.**

Changing a note's velocity

In the MIDI world, *velocity* means *volume.* To change a note's velocity, do the following:

1. **From the Track View drop-down menu, set your track to Velocity view.**

2. **Select the Grabber tool.**

3. **Click the diamond-shaped icon at the top of the *velocity stalk* — the vertical line with a diamond at the top representing the velocity level — in the track's playlist and then drag it up or down.**

4. **Release the mouse button when the velocity is where you want it.**

You can also use one of the Pencil tools to draw various velocity shapes. Select the desired Pencil tool and then draw a line in the track's playlist where you want the velocities to be. (See "Perusing the Pencil tools" section, earlier in this chapter, for more on drawing velocity settings.)

You can scale the velocities of several notes by using the Selector to select the notes and then the Trimmer to drag them up or down as a unit. This lets you keep the relationship between the velocities the same as you change the overall levels.

Changing time locations

Time locations define where the Start points of your notes are placed within your session. To change a note's time location, do the following:

1. **From the Track View drop-down menu, set your track to Notes view.**

2. **Select the Pencil or the Grabber tool.**

3. **Press Shift to keep the note's pitch from changing while you move it.**

4. **Click the note and drag it left or right.**

   - *If your edit mode is set to Grid,* the note is moved along the grid boundary.

   - *If you're using Spot edit mode,* the Spot dialog box appears; there, you can type in a location for the note and then click Done.

5. **Release the mouse button when the note is where you want it.**

Moving notes freely

To move a note freely in the track, do the following:

1. **From the Track View drop-down menu, set your track to Notes view.**

2. **Select the Pencil or the Grabber tool.**

3. **Click the note and drag it left or right, up or down.**

4. **Release the mouse button when the note is where you want it.**

Editing note attributes

To edit a note by changing note attributes as displayed in the MIDI Event List, do the following:

1. **From the Track View drop-down menu, set your track to Notes view.**

2. **Click the note by using the Pencil or the Grabber tool.**

   The note's attributes show up in the MIDI Event List window with a blue highlight (as shown in Figure 3-10).

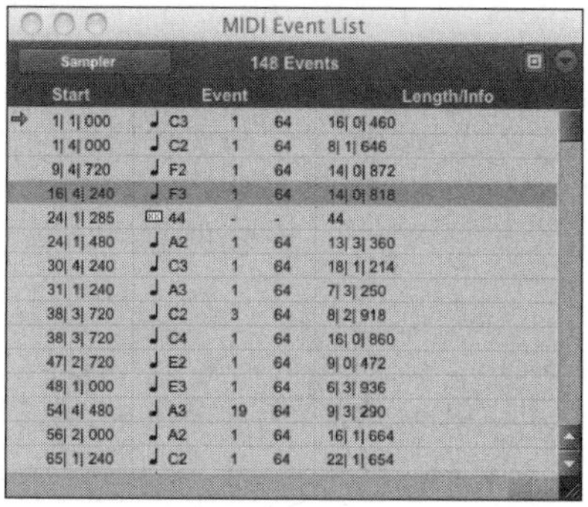

Figure 3-10: The MIDI Event List window shows the values for the selected note.

3. **Click in the Attribute field(s) you want to change:**

- *Start:* This field indicates the start point of the selected note. This is displayed in the main time scale setting for the session.

- *End:* This field controls the end point of the note, which is displayed in the main time-scale format. If this field isn't visible, click the Options button at the top of the MIDI Event List dialog box and choose Show Note End Time from the menu that appears.

- *Length/Info:* This field displays the duration of the note (shown in the session's main time scale). Changing the start or end times also changes this value. Changing this field alters the end point but leaves the start point untouched. MIDI events without length data (such as program changes or controller events) show data associated with that data, such as the program number or controller event type. If this field isn't visible, click the Options button at the top of the MIDI Event List dialog box and choose Show Note Length from the menu that appears.

- *Pitch:* This field displays the pitch of the note.

- *Attack Velocity:* This field shows the velocity of the start of the note as a MIDI value between 0 and 127.

- *Release Velocity:* This field displays the release velocity of the note as a MIDI value between 0 and 127.

4. **Enter in the new value in the field corresponding to the attribute you want to change.**

5. **Press Return/Enter.**

The note changes to match the new attributes.

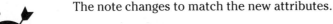

If you want to change more than one field, press / (the front-slash key) to move between fields.

Editing program data

Because MIDI contains no sound in itself, you can create program change events to change the sound patches of your MIDI sound modules throughout the session. This can keep your computer processing resources optimized as well as keep you from using more tracks than absolutely necessary for your session, which is a good thing because Pro Tools allows you to have no more than 32 active tracks playing in a session.

Changing program patches

Program patches are the sounds available in your MIDI device. Here's how to change program patches:

1. **From the Track View drop-down menu, set the track to Program Change view.**

2. **With the Grabber tool, double-click the program change event you want to change.**

The Patch Select dialog box appears.

3. **In the Patch Select dialog box, select the new patch name/number. (If the patch resides on a different bank as the current patch, select the new bank as well.)**

4. **Click Done.**

The Patch Select dialog box closes, and the new program is sounded when you play your session.

Moving program change markers

Program change markers are helpful little tools because they tell Pro Tools when to change the sound of your MIDI device while your session plays. To move a program change marker, follow these steps:

1. **From the Track View drop-down menu, set the track to Program Change view.**

2. **Select the Grabber or the Pencil tool.**

3. **Click and drag the Program Change Marker left or right.**

- *If you have Grid mode enabled,* the program change event moves to the closest grid boundary.

- *If you have Spot mode selected,* the Spot dialog box opens; there, you can enter a new location for the marker and then click Done.

Changing continuous controller data

When you deal with *continuous controller data,* you are dealing with Volume, Pan, Pitch Bend, Mono Aftertouch, and MIDI controllers. All this data is represented as a line graph punctuated by a series of breakpoints. You have a choice when you want to make changes: you can edit the line itself using the Pencil tool; or you can edit the breakpoints by using the Grabber, the Pencil, or the Smart tool.

Editing lines with the Pencil tool

To edit the line graph with a Pencil tool, do the following:

1. **From the Track View drop-down menu, select the track view that corresponds to the parameter you want to edit (Volume, Pan, Pitch Bend, Mono Aftertouch, MIDI Controller).**

2. **Click and hold the Pencil icon, and then select the Pencil tool you want to use from the menu that appears.**

3. **Click in the playlist where you want to start drawing and then drag your mouse to draw the new values.**

   The line is drawn, and breakpoints are inserted according to the resolution you set for the Pencil Tool Resolution When Drawing Controller Data option on the MIDI tab of the Preferences dialog box. (Choose Setup➪Preferences from the main menu to access the Preferences dialog box.)

4. **Release the mouse button when you reach the end of your edit.**

Editing breakpoints

If you're not adept at drawing lines, you might want to work with breakpoints instead. Here's how:

1. **From the Track View drop-down menu, select the track view that corresponds to the parameter you want to edit (Volume, Pan, Pitch Bend, Mono Aftertouch, MIDI Controller).**

2. **Select the Grabber tool.**

3. **Click and drag the breakpoint.**

4. **Release the mouse button.**

Scaling breakpoints

When you *scale breakpoints,* you move a group of breakpoints while retaining the relationship between them. You can use the Trimmer tool to scale breakpoints, as in the following step list:

1. **From the Track View drop-down menu, select the track view that corresponds to the parameter you want to edit (Volume, Pan, Pitch Bend, Mono Aftertouch, MIDI Controller).**

2. **Select the Selector tool.**

3. **With your mouse, click and drag across the breakpoints you want to scale.**

   The selection becomes highlighted.

4. **Select the Trimmer tool.**

5. **Click and drag the breakpoints up or down.**

   The breakpoints move as a unit, but they don't all move the same amount. Rather, they move differently to keep the relationship between the breakpoints intact.

6. **Release your mouse button.**

There are other ways to edit continuous controller data in Pro Tools. Check out Book VI, Chapter 6 to find out more.

Using the Smart tool

The Smart tool puts a new spin on three older tools: namely, the Trimmer, Selector, and Grabber tools. Basically, the Smart tool changes how it works depending on what you try to do with it. The following sections detail how this tool behaves when you work with MIDI data.

To use the Smart tool, press the button located under the Selector tool in the Edit window, as shown in Figure 3-11.

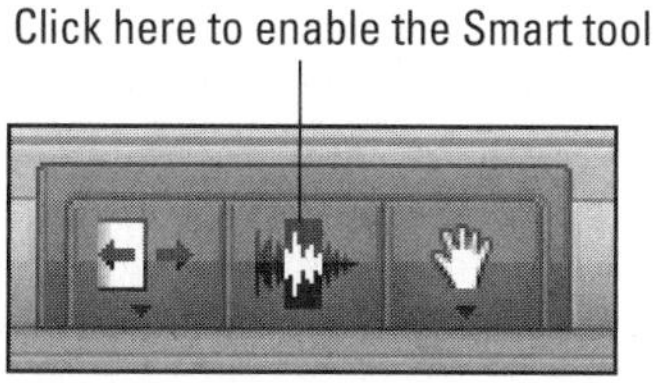

Figure 3-11: Enable the Smart tool by clicking the button under the Selector tool.

Click here to enable the Smart tool

Check out Book IV, Chapter 4 for more details about the Smart tool.

Using the Smart tool in Notes view

When you use the Smart tool with your Track view set to Notes, the tool behaves the following way:

✦ Placing the cursor so that it doesn't touch any notes or pressing ⌘ (Mac) or Ctrl (PC) enables the Selector face of the Smart tool. You can then click and drag to make a selection.

✦ Positioning the cursor near the middle of a note enables the Grabber face of the Smart tool.

✦ Placing the cursor over the start or end point of a note enables the Trimmer face of the Smart tool.

✦ To turn the Smart tool into an eraser, make sure the cursor isn't touching any notes (the Selector appears) and then press Control+Option (Mac) or Windows+Alt (PC).

Using the Smart tool in an Automation or in Controller views

When you use the Smart tool in an Automation view (Volume, Mute, or Pan) or in Controller view, the tool acts the following ways:

✦ **Trimmer:** To enable the Trimmer tool, position your cursor in the top quarter of the clip. The Trimmer icon appears. You can move your cursor up and down to change the value or to create breakpoints. If you want finer control of the Trimmer tool while you work, press ⌘ (Mac) or Ctrl (PC) after you begin trimming.

✦ **Selector:** To enable the Selector tool, position your cursor in the lower three-quarters of the clip. You can then drag your selection.

✦ **Grabber:** To enable the Grabber tool, press ⌘ (Mac) or Ctrl (PC). You can do several things with the Grabber tool with a track set to an automation view:

   • *Edit existing breakpoints:* Position the cursor near one of these points, and the Grabber appears. You can increase the resolution of your movements to fine-control by pressing ⌘ (Mac) or Ctrl (PC) after you start moving the breakpoint.

   • *Constrain the Grabber vertically:* To keep the Grabber from moving right or left, press Shift — or, if you set the tool to fine control, press ⌘+Shift (Mac) or Ctrl+Shift (PC).

Exploring MIDI Events

The MIDI Event List consists of all the MIDI data in your track. This list displays the location, pitch, velocity, and duration of every note as well as all other parameters for the track. The MIDI Event List window lets you edit all your track's MIDI data in one place, which makes it one extremely helpful tool in the Pro Tools toolbox. The following sections explain the ways to best use this window to edit your track.

Exploring the MIDI Event List window

The MIDI Event List window, as shown in Figure 3-12, displays MIDI data for a selected track. You can open the window in several different ways:

✦ **Choose Event↪MIDI Event List from the main menu.**

✦ **Press Control (Mac) or Windows (PC) while you double-click the MIDI track name in the Edit or Mix window.**

✦ **Press Option+= (equal sign; Mac) or Alt+= (equal sign; PC).** Pressing this combination again toggles you back to the Edit window.

If you have a selection made within a MIDI track and you open the MIDI Event List window, the selected note or range of notes is highlighted.

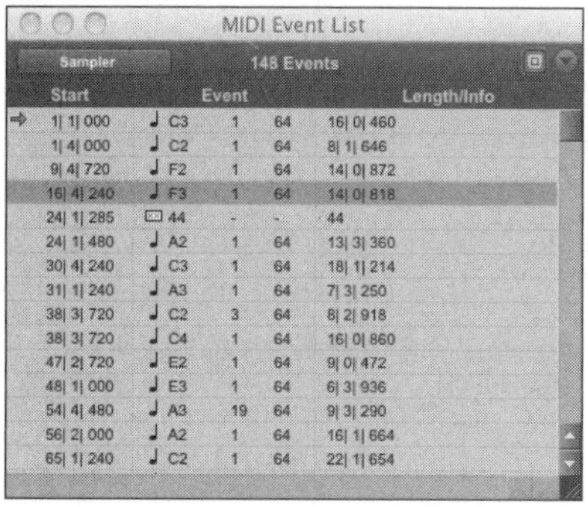

Figure 3-12:
Choose
Window➪
Show MIDI
Event List
to open the
MIDI Event
List window.

The cursor location is marked with an arrow in the MIDI Event List.

Examining MIDI Event menus

The MIDI Event List contains three menus at the top of the window: Track
Selector, Options, and Insert. The following list gives you the details on the
various menu options:

✦ **Track Selector:** This menu shows the track that's listed in the window
and lets you choose a different track to display.

✦ **Options:** This menu consists of the following options, as shown in
Figure 3-13:

• *Show Sub Counter:* This option displays the event times in the sub-
counter value. (Book II, Chapter 4 has more on how to use counters.)

• *Go To:* Choosing this option opens a dialog box in which you enter
the location in the session you want to go to.

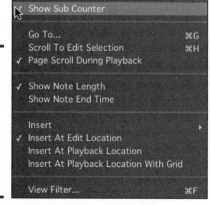

Figure 3-13:
Use the
Options
menu to
control
various
areas of
display and
operation.

- *Scroll to Edit Selection:* This automatically moves the MIDI Event List to the Edit Start or Insertion point for the session.

- *Page Scroll During Playback:* This option scrolls the MIDI Event List while your session plays.

- *Scroll During Edit Selection:* This option automatically scrolls the MIDI Event List while you move your edit point in the Edit window.

- *Show Note Length:* Selecting this option displays the length of the MIDI notes in the MIDI Event List.

- *Show Note End Time:* This option lets you display the end time of the MIDI notes in the Event List instead of the note length. (Sorry, but you can't have both.)

- *Insert at Edit Location:* This option lets you designate that any inserted event is placed at the Edit Start or Insertion point.

- *Insert at Playback Location:* This option lets you insert notes on the fly while the session plays back.

- *Insert at Playback Location with Grid:* This option snaps any inserted notes placed on the fly (see the previous bullet) to the nearest grid boundary.

- *View Filter:* This option opens the MIDI Event List View Filter dialog box, as shown in Figure 3-14. You use this dialog box to specify which fields appear in the MIDI Event List dialog box. This, in turn, affects which events are edited when you use Cut, Copy, and Paste. Any fields that are not displayed in the MIDI Event List aren't affected by Cut, Copy, and Paste commands. (For more about this dialog box, see Chapter 4 in this mini-book.)

Figure 3-14: The View Filter dialog box lets you choose what fields are displayed in the MIDI Event List.

✦ **Insert:** The Insert menu consists of the types of events you can insert into the track using the MIDI Event List. This menu is covered in greater detail in the "Inserting MIDI events" section, later in this chapter.

Although it isn't actually a menu option, the number of Events in your current track is displayed to the right of the three menus listed in this section.

Eyeing the rest of the MIDI Event List

Below the MIDI Event menus (see the preceding section) lies the whole range of possible MIDI events for the track. (Refer to Figure 3-12.) These events are listed in order from the beginning of the session to the end and are listed in three columns. (The "Inserting MIDI events" section, later in this chapter, explores these columns further.)

✦ **Start:** This column displays the location of the event's Start point in either the main or sub-counter time format, depending on whether you have the Show Sub Counter option selected in the Options menu. (See the "Examining MIDI Event menus" section, earlier in this chapter.)

If more than one event is located at the same place in the session (like with chords, for example), the location for all but the first event is dimmed. This makes it easier to see these multiple events.

To the left of the Start point is an arrow indicating the location of the cursor in the session.

✦ **Event:** This column shows the event type (indicated by the icon at the left of the column) as well as its associated values. In the case of notes, you see the note letter and octave as well as its attack and release velocities.

✦ **Length/Info:** This column shows the length or end point of the MIDI notes, depending on whether you have the Show Note Length or Show Note End Time option selected under the Options menu. (See the preceding section.)

Getting around the MIDI Event List

Here are several ways to move quickly around the MIDI Event List:

✦ Double-clicking the event in the list highlights your selection.

✦ Pressing Tab or the down-arrow key (↓) moves you to the next event.

✦ Pressing Option+Tab (Mac) or Ctrl+Tab (PC) or the up-arrow key (↑) moves you to the previous event.

✦ Using the left (←) or right arrow (→) moves you laterally in the event list.

+ Pressing Shift while you double-click or pressing Tab/arrow adds events to your selection.

+ Choosing Go To from the Options drop-down menu takes you to a specific location in the event list.

+ Selecting the Scroll to Edit Selection option under the Options menu lets you go automatically to the beginning of the edit selection.

Editing in the MIDI Event List

Editing in the MIDI Event list isn't for everyone. Many people prefer the visual format offered by the Edit window, but editing in the MIDI Event List window can be faster and more accurate. This section describes the process of inserting, deleting, and editing MIDI data in the MIDI Events List.

Inserting MIDI events

From the Insert menu, as shown in Figure 3-15, you can insert the following MIDI events into your track:

+ **Note:** Selecting Note lets you enter the start time, pitch, attack velocity, release velocity, and either the end time or duration of the notes.

+ **Pitch Bend:** When you enter pitch-bend information in the Event entry window, you include the start time and the bend amount. Positive values raise the pitch; negative numbers lower it.

+ **Volume:** In the Volume Event entry window, enter the start time, controller number (set to 7 for volume), and the volume level (0–17). The controller name appears in the far-right column.

+ **Pan:** The Pan Event entry window contains fields for start time, controller number (in this case, set to 10), and pan value (negative numbers pan left of center, and positive numbers pan right of center). The controller name (pan) appears in the far-right column.

+ **Mono Aftertouch:** The Mono Aftertouch Event entry window offers fields for the start time and the after-touch level (0 and 127). *After-touch* is the velocity of the note after the initial attack.

+ **Poly Aftertouch:** The Poly (polyphonic) Aftertouch Event entry window offers fields for the start time, note name, and the after-touch level (0 and 127).

+ **Program Change:** The Program Change Event entry window has fields for the start time, program number, controller 0 value, and controller 32 value. (Controller 0 and controller 32 are for sending program bank change commands. Some MIDI devices use controller 0, others use controller 32, and still others use both. Consult the manual for your MIDI device to determine which controller value it uses.) The program name appears when you choose the program number.

✦ **Controller:** This option lets you designate which of the many controller events you want to enter. The event's entry window for this option includes the start time, controller number, and the controller value. The controller number that you choose determines the controller parameter you change, and this parameter name shows up in the farthest column to the right.

✦ **Another Note:** This option enters the data from the previous inserted event into fields.

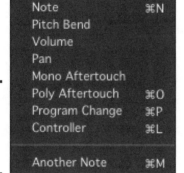

Figure 3-15:
Insert MIDI
events from
the Insert
menu.

To insert a MIDI note using the MIDI Event List, do the following:

1. In the MIDI Event List window, choose Note from the Insert menu.

The Note Event entry window opens at the top of the MIDI event list, as shown in Figure 3-16.

2. Enter the note in one of the following ways:

- Type its values in the appropriate fields.

- Play the note or operation on your MIDI keyboard.

- Scroll up or down in the fields.

3. Insert the note by performing one of these commands:

- Press Return/Enter to close the Event entry window when the event is accepted.

- Press Return/Enter to insert the event and keep the window open.

Figure 3-16:
The Note
Event entry
window.

○ ○ ○		MIDI Event List		
Sampler		148 Events		
Start		Event		Length/Info
1| 1| 000	1| 1| 000	♩ C3	120 64	0| 1| 000	0| 1| 000
1| 1| 000	1| 1| 000	♩ C3	1 64	16| 0| 460	16| 0| 460

To insert a controller event, do the following:

1. **In the MIDI Event List window, choose the controller event you want to insert from the Insert menu or choose Controller to specify the controller type later.**

The Controller event's entry window opens at the top of the MIDI event list, as shown in Figure 3-17. Unless you select the Controller option, the name for the event appears in the far-right column.

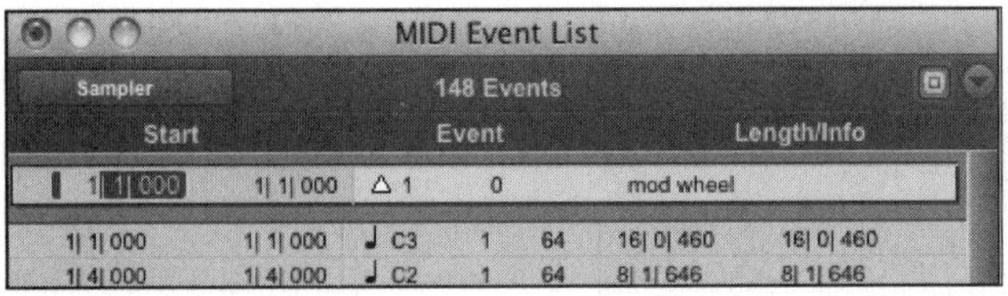

Figure 3-17:
The
Controller
Event entry
window.

2. **Enter the value in each of the fields in one of the following ways:**

- *Type the value into the fields.*

- *Press the ↑ or ↓ key to scroll the value.*

- *Drag up or down in the field by pressing ⌘ (Mac) or Ctrl (PC) while you drag.*

- *Play the controller event on your keyboard.*

3. **Insert the note by performing one of these commands:**

- *Press Return/Enter to close the Event entry window when the event is accepted.*

- *Press Return/Enter to insert the event and keep the window open.*

To insert a program change, do the following:

1. **In the MIDI Event List window, choose Program Change from the Insert menu.**

The Program Change Event entry window opens at the top of the MIDI event list, as shown in Figure 3-18.

2. **Enter the start time for the event.**

3. **Enter the program number or click the info column to open the Program Change window.**

4. **Insert the note by performing one of these commands:**

- *Press Return/Enter to close the Event entry window when the event is accepted.*

- *Press Return/Enter to insert the event and keep the window open.*

Figure 3-18:
The
Program
Change
event's
entry
window.

MIDI Event List			
Sampler	148 Events		
Start	Event		Length/Info
1| 1| 000	1| 1| 000	📷 -	-	-	none
1| 1| 000	1| 1| 000	♩ C3	1	64	16| 0| 460	16| 0| 460
1| 4| 000	1| 4| 000	♩ C2	1	64	8| 1| 646	8| 1| 646

Deleting events

You can delete MIDI events one of two ways:

✦ Press Option (Mac) or Alt (PC) while you click the event with one of the Edit tools located at the top of the Edit window.

✦ Select the event or events (hold the Shift key while you select more than one event) in the MIDI Event list with one of the Edit tools located at the top of the Edit window and then press Delete (Mac) or Backspace (PC) or choose Edit⇨Clear from the main menu.

Changing data

You can edit any MIDI event in the event list several ways, including using the familiar Cut, Copy, and Paste commands. These are covered in this section.

To select events to edit, do one of the following:

✦ **Click the event to highlight it.**

✦ **⌘-click (Mac) or Ctrl-click (PC) to select several noncontiguous events.**

✦ **Shift-click the beginning and end events of a group of contiguous events.**

✦ **Click and drag across multiple events.**

You can remove an event from a selection by pressing ⌘ (Mac) or Ctrl (PC) while clicking it.

To cut or copy events, do the following:

1. **Select your event as described in the preceding list.**

2. **Choose Edit⇨Cut or Edit⇨Copy from the main menu to place the event on the Clipboard.**

To paste events, do one of the following:

✦ Click within the track's playlist where you want the event to go and then press ⌘+V (Mac) or Ctrl+V (PC) or choose Edit⇨Paste from the main menu.

✦ Choose Go To from the Options menu in the MIDI Event List window, type in the location, and then click OK.

To manually edit an event, do the following:

1. Double-click in the field you want to edit of the event in the list.

Alternatively, press ⌘+Enter (in the numberpad section of the keyboard; Mac) or Ctrl+Enter (PC) when you have an event selected.

2. Enter the new value in the field you want to edit.

3. Insert the note by performing one of these commands:

- *Press Return/Enter to close the Event entry window when the event is accepted.*

- *Press Return/Enter to insert the event and keep the window open.*

Chapter 4: Performing MIDI Operations

In This Chapter

✔ Quantizing MIDI notes

✔ Flattening and restoring MIDI performances

✔ Changing note velocity and duration

✔ Transposing, selecting, and splitting MIDI notes

✔ Adjusting MIDI Real-Time Properties

*P*ro Tools offers a handful of MIDI operations (located under the MIDI section of the main menu) where you can transform a mediocre track into a stunning performance. (Well, almost, depending on how well you use these operations.) These operations allow you to make changes to the MIDI performance data on a track.

In this chapter, you get a chance to dig in to some of the most powerful MIDI editing operations in Pro Tools. With these operations in hand, you can do some really cool things, such as change the key of a song, alter the characteristics of a performance, or correct timing problems. This chapter also leads you through the MIDI Operations window and shows you how to perform each of the operations in the window.

Getting Used to the MIDI Operations Window

Logically enough, the MIDI Operations window is where you do all your MIDI operations. This window, as shown in Figure 4-1, is accessed by choosing any one of the Event operations listed under the Event section of the main menu, or by choosing Event⇨Event⇨Event Operations Window from the main menu.

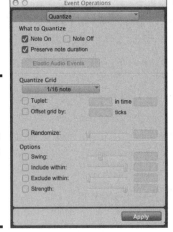

Figure 4-1:
The Event
Operations
window lets
you perform
many MIDI
operations
on selected
MIDI data.

After this window is open, you can select the operation you want to perform from the drop-down menu at the top of the window.

To close the window, press Return (Mac) or Enter in the alphanumeric section of the keyboard (PC) after you click the Apply button to apply the operation.

From the Event Operations window, you can use the following commands as a fast way to navigate and adjust parameters:

✦ Press Tab to move forward through the fields in the window; conversely, press Shift+Tab to move backward through the fields.

✦ Use the up-arrow (↑) and down-arrow (↓) keys to adjust values up and down in your selected field.

✦ In a highlighted field, press ⌘ (Mac) or Ctrl (PC) while you drag your mouse to adjust the value up or down in your selected field's text box.

✦ When adjusting the sliders, press ⌘ (Mac) or Ctrl (PC) to increase the resolution of the sliders while you use them to adjust the values in your selected field.

✦ Play a note on your MIDI controller to select a note in fields with pitch and velocity settings.

Performing MIDI Event Operations

MIDI Event operations are all done from the Event Operations window (see the previous section). The operations you can perform are listed in the drop-down menu at the top of the window. You have the following operations available to you (as shown in Figure 4-2):

✦ **Quantize:** Lets you adjust the timing of your selected notes and to the Quantize operation, except you use a groove template to create a grid to quantize to if you choose.

✦ **Change Velocity:** Use this to adjust the volume of the attack or the release of selected MIDI notes.

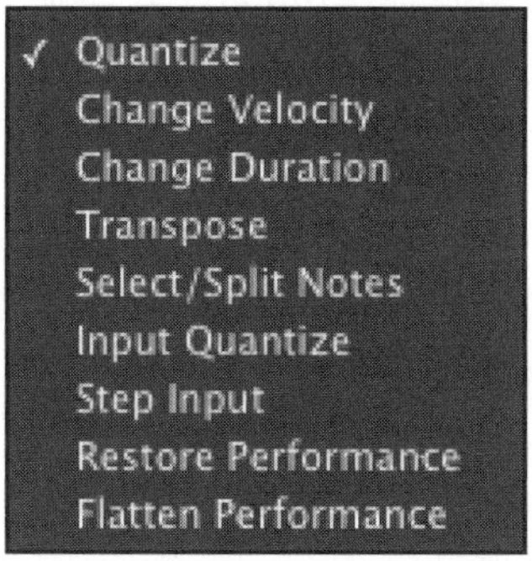

Figure 4-2:
The Event
Operations
window
includes
a pop-up
menu where
you can
select from
several
MIDI
Operations.

✓ Quantize
Change Velocity
Change Duration
Transpose
Select/Split Notes
Input Quantize
Step Input
Restore Performance
Flatten Performance

✦ **Change Duration:** User this to alter the length of recorded MIDI notes.

✦ **Transpose:** User this to change the pitch of selected notes.

✦ **Select/Split Notes:** Use this to choose specific MIDI notes or a range of notes in a selection, or copy or cut the selected notes.

✦ **Input Quantize:** Use this to set a Quantize value that your recorded performance is adjusted to automatically while you record it.

✦ **Step Input:** Use this option to input notes manually, one at a time. You can control the duration, velocity, and location of each note.

✦ **Restore Performance:** Use this option to return to saved performance settings.

✦ **Flatten Performance:** Use this option to tweak performance data and lock it in before you do any more tweaking.

Stay tuned: The following sections look at each of these MIDI operations in greater detail. If you want to perform any one of them, here's how:

1. **Select the note(s) you want to change.**

Book IV, Chapter 2 describes how to make these selections.

2. **Select the MIDI operation you want to perform from the Event section of the main menu. (Or, choose Event⇨MIDI⇨Operation Window from the main menu and choose the operation you want from the window's drop-down menu.)**

3. **Make the settings you want in the available fields.**

    Check out the section for each operation to see what to adjust.

4. **Apply the operation by clicking Apply or by using the keyboard:**

    - *To keep the MIDI Operations window open:* Press Enter in the number pad section of the keyboard.

    - *To close the MIDI Operations window:* Press Return (Mac) or Enter in the alphanumeric section of the keyboard (PC) to apply the operation and close the MIDI Operations window.

Grid/Groove Quantize

The Grid/Groove Quantize MIDI operation lets you adjust the timing of your selected notes. This is great when you want to conform the rhythmic placement of your MIDI notes to a grid or you have a problem with a really bad drummer and you want to fix his timing mistakes.

The Grid/Groove Quantize version of the MIDI Operations window, as shown in Figure 4-3, contains the following fields:

Figure 4-3: The Grid/ Groove Quantize options let you align your MIDI notes to a time grid.

✦ **What to Quantize:** From this section, choose which part of the note to quantize:

- *Attacks:* Selecting this check box sets the quantization to the start of the selected notes.

- *Releases:* Selecting this check box quantizes the ends of the notes.

- *Preserve Note Duration:* Selecting this check box produces different results depending on whether you choose Attacks or Releases.

With Attacks selected, Preserve Note Duration keeps the end of the note intact. With Releases selected, the start of the note is left intact. If both Attacks and Releases are selected, the Preserve Note Duration option is dimmed.

✦ **Quantize Grid:** Here is where you choose the resolution of the quantize grid, from whole notes to sixty-fourth notes. If you choose sixteenth notes, for example, your notes will move to the nearest sixteenth note when you quantize.

- *Note selector:* Choose the note value of your quantize grid from this drop-down menu. Click the note to select it.

- *Tuplet:* This check box allows you to select odd note groupings, such as triplets. When you select this option, you need to fill in the tuplet value. For example, to create a regular eighth-note triplet, enter 3 in Time 1; for a quarter-note triplet, enter 3 in Time 2.

- *Offset Grid By:* Use this option to move the Quantize grid forward or backward in time by the selected number of ticks. This is helpful for creating a groove that lies slightly ahead of — or behind — the beat.

- *Randomize:* Using this option adds a level of randomness to the quantizing of your selection — no, not to mess up the rhythm, but to keep it from being too rigid. You can select values between 0 and 100%. Lower values place the randomized notes closer to the grid.

✦ **Options:** Select these items to fine-tune your Grid/Groove Quantize operation by specifying which notes to quantize and by how much:

- *Swing:* This option and slider allows you create a *swing feel* (a dotted-quarter, eighth-note triplet). You specify a percentage (from 0 to 300%); selecting 100% provides a triplet feel.

- *Include Within:* Here you specify a range of notes to include. Selecting this option quantizes only selected notes that fall within the boundaries you set here (from 0 to 100%); the smaller the number, the narrower the range of notes affected.

- *Exclude Within:* Here you specify a range of notes to exclude from quantization. Any selected notes that fall within the boundaries you set here (between 0 and 100%) won't be quantized.

- *Strength:* This is, in my opinion, the most useful function in the Pro Tool Grid/Groove Quantize operation. You can use it to move your quantized notes *by a percentage* (from 0 to 100%) rather than just snapping them right to the grid. Higher numbers keep more strictly to the grid than do the lower values.

Using the options in these four sections well helps keep a natural feel in your performance.

The following list explains your options when you want to take the groove from a recorded performance and apply it to the MIDI sequence of your track. Just choose one of the templates from the Groove Clipboard in the Quantize Grid drop-down menu located in the Grid/Groove Quantize version of the MIDI Operations window (as shown in Figure 4-4).

Figure 4-4:
Select a groove template from the Quantize Grid drop-down menu.

When you select your groove template, the Grid/Groove Quantize menu options appear, as shown Figure 4-5.

Figure 4-5:
The Grid/Groove Quantize function lets you align your notes to a groove template.

One limitation of Pro Tools 10 is that you can't create your own groove templates. Instead, you either have to use what comes with Pro Tools (which aren't bad), buy one from Avid, or hunt one from a third-party maker. Of course, there's an off chance that you may find some downloadable ones on the Internet. To find out, I recommend checking out the Avid User Conference website at `http://duc.avid.com/` (do a search for *Digigroove template*).

The options in the Grid/Groove Quantize version of the MIDI Operations window include the following:

✦ **Groove template selector:** From this drop-down menu, choose a groove template to apply to your selection. (These templates are located in the Groove folder within the Pro Tools folder on your system's hard drive.)

After you choose your template, its content, meter, and tempo information show up in the Comments section in the middle of the window. To see these settings, simply click the Show Comments button.

✦ **Pre-Quantize:** When you have the timing field enabled (see the next section), selecting this check box applies the setting in the Quantize version of the MIDI Operations window to the template before you apply your selection using the Grid/Groove Quantize settings.

✦ **Randomize:** Selecting this check box adds a level of randomness to the quantizing of your selection — no, not to mess up the rhythm, but to keep it from being too rigid. Use the slider to select values between 0% and 100%. Lower values place the randomized notes closer to the grid.

✦ **Options:** Here's where you can tinker with your groove:

  • *Timing:* This option lets you adjust the timing of the quantization applied. A setting of 0% makes no change to the selection; a setting of 100% places the notes right at the groove template's grid settings. A setting of 200% moves the selected notes twice the distance from the template's grid locations.

  • *Duration:* This setting changes the duration of the notes to fit the groove template. A setting of 0% makes no change, a setting of 100% matches the notes to the groove template, and a setting beyond that increases or decreases the duration of the original notes according to their ratio to the notes in the groove template.

  • *Velocity:* This field changes the *velocity* — the volume — of the quantized notes. Like with the other fields (Timing and Duration), the lower the number, the less the velocity changes.

✦ **Slider Settings:** You can recall and save the slider settings of the options with a template.

  • *Recall with Template:* Selecting this check box resets all the option settings to those that are saved with the template.

  • *Save:* Click this button to save your current option settings. If you choose Save, you can add any comments about the template, and they show up in the Comments section of the Grid/Groove Quantize options of the MIDI Operations window.

Change Velocity

The Change Velocity version of the MIDI Operations window, as shown in Figure 4-6, allows you to adjust the volume (velocity in MIDI-speak) of the attack or release of selected MIDI notes.

This operation is a lifesaver for times when you have a drummer playing an electronic kit and *just one note* is weak — or when you need to tame overly aggressive cymbals.

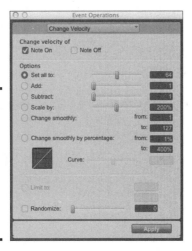

Figure 4-6: Use the Change Velocity options to adjust the volume of selected notes.

The Change Velocity options in the MIDI Operations window contain the following fields:

+ **Change Velocity Of:** Here you choose between the initial attack of the note (the Attacks check box) or the release value (the Releases check box).

+ **Set All To:** Selecting this radio button sets all the velocities of the selected notes to the value in the field. You can ether type the value in or move the slider to adjust the value up or down.

+ **Add:** Here you add a specified value to your existing one. You can either enter the value in the field or use the slider. Your selected notes will change velocity by the number you specify.

+ **Subtract:** Here you subtract a specified value to your existing one. You can either enter the value in the field or use the slider. Your selected notes will change velocity by the number you specify.

+ **Scale By:** Here you set a scale for how much the velocities of your selected notes are to change — a percentage between 1 and 400. (Again, you can use the slider or type in a number.)

✦ **Change Smoothly:** Use this option to change the velocity of selected notes gradually over time. This is useful for creating crescendos and decrescendos. Type in the beginning and end values in the From and To fields, respectively.

✦ **Change Smoothly by Percentage:** This option is similar to Change Smoothly (see the preceding bullet) except that you specify a percentage of change instead of typing in specific numbers. This field is also where you can use a curve graph to specify how much the notes' velocity must increase or decrease; choose a percentage value between –99 and +99. The curve graph then shows how your setting is implemented.

✦ **Limit To:** Select this option if you want to set a minimum and maximum range for your Change Velocity settings. You type those values into the fields. This field will be editable when you check the Randomize options (listed below).

✦ **Randomize:** Here, you create a random velocity change, specifying it as a percentage value between 0 and 100%. For example, if you choose a Set All To value of 60 and a Randomize setting of 40%, you end up with Change Velocity values from 48 to 72.

Be careful if you're changing groups of notes. Using Add or Subtract for that purpose can change the relationships between various notes. If you like the way the original notes sound together, try using the Scale option instead. This keeps the relationships between notes intact.

Change Duration

Use the Change Duration operation to alter the length of recorded MIDI notes. The Change Duration version of the MIDI Operations window, shown in Figure 4-7, contains the following fields:

✦ **Set All To/Add/Subtract/Scale option. This check box allows you to choose among several options:**

• *Set All To:* Select this radio button to set the duration of selected notes to the values in the accompanying fields.

• *Add:* Here, you add a specified value to your existing one.

• *Subtract:* Here you subtract a specified value to your existing one.

• *Scale By:* Here you set a scale for how much the velocities of your selected notes are to change — a percentage between 1 and 400.

✦ **Legato:** This option lets you lengthen your selected notes in one of two ways:

• *Gap:* Select this option to lengthen the notes to a point where a specified gap exists between your selected notes and the following ones.

- *Overlap:* Use this option if you want to extend the length of your select notes and have them overlap the following notes.

✦ **Remove Overlaps and Leave Gap:** This option lets you remove any overlaps between notes of the same pitch. You designate the amount of the gap in the field to the right.

✦ **Transform Sustain Pedal to Duration:** This option transforms sustain pedal data for a note and applies it to the duration of the note. Checking the Delete sustain events after transformation box removes the sustain data from the MIDI track.

✦ **Change Continuously:** This option gives you two different ways to change the duration of your selection over time. These are:

- *In Ticks:* Here you change the length of notes gradually over time, entering ticks in the From and To fields to specify beginning and end times for the change in duration. You can also enter a Curve value to modify the shape of the change. You can either drag the slider or enter a value in the field from –99 to +99.

- *By Percentage:* In this field, you apply the duration change smoothly (see the previous bullet) by a percentage rather than by entering quarter notes and ticks. You can also adjust the curve of the change, using values from –99 to +99.

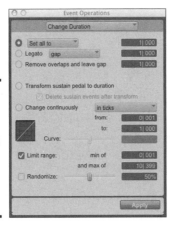

Figure 4-7:
The Change Duration function lets you adjust the length of selected notes.

✦ **Limit Range:** Use this setting to specify a minimum and maximum change duration for the settings you choose.

✦ **Randomize:** Use this field to create a random change in duration, based on the setting you choose in the fields described here.

The Change Duration operation is useful for changing the feel of the music by making your selection either more staccato or legato.

Transpose

Use the Transpose operation to change the pitch of selected notes. Checking out the Transpose version of the MIDI Operations window, as shown in Figure 4-8, you see that the Transpose operation offers these ways of changing pitch:

✦ **Transpose By:** Use this setting to transpose by octaves or semitones (one half-step). You can either type in the value or use the sliders to adjust the setting.

✦ **Transpose:** Here you type in the note and octave that you want to transpose from (in the From field) and to (in the To field). You can also use the slider to adjust the settings if you prefer.

✦ **Transpose All Notes To:** Selecting this option changes all your selected notes to the note you designate in the field.

✦ **Transpose in Key:** Here you can transpose your selected notes by scale steps.

Transposing using this MIDI operation makes it easy to change the pitch — in effect, the musical key — of the entire song or clip. This is especially helpful if you decide that the song needs to be in a different key for your singer to sing well.

Figure 4-8:
Use the Transpose function to change the pitch of a selection.

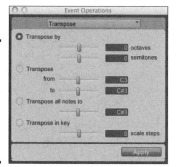

Select/Split Notes

The Select/Split Notes operation allows you to choose specific MIDI notes or a range of notes in a selection and to move them from the track or copy them to another track. Your options, as shown in the Select/Split Notes version of the MIDI Operations window you see in Figure 4-9, include the following:

Figure 4-9:
Use the
Select/
Split Notes
function
to select
specific
notes or
note ranges.

+ **All Notes:** Use this option to select all the notes in your selection.

+ **Notes Between:** Use this option to specify the range of notes to select. You can either use pitch references (C1, B1, and so on) or MIDI note numbers (0–127) for your selection.

+ **Top:** Using this option chooses the highest note or notes (depending on the number you enter) in each chord.

+ **Bottom:** Using this option selects the lowest note or notes (depending on the number you enter) in each chord.

You can also choose other criteria to include in your selection of notes, including

+ **Velocity Between:** Here you can select the minimum and maximum velocities to be included in your selection.

+ **Duration Between:** Use this option to designate minimum and maximum note durations.

+ **Position Between:** You can also control the location of your selected notes within certain beat and tick locations in each bar. Again, a minimum and maximum value determines the start and end points.

After you choose your selection parameters, you need to choose whether you want to select the notes or to split them. Selecting the Select Notes radio button simply selects them, but selecting the Split Notes option allows you to choose from two options:

+ **Copy:** This command copies your selected notes.

+ **Cut:** This command removes the selected notes from the original track.

The new location of your copied or cut notes is based upon your choice from the To drop-down menu:

+ **Clipboard:** Your notes are placed on the Clipboard.
+ **A New Track:** This places your selected notes into a new MIDI track.
+ **A New Track per Pitch:** This places each pitch in its own new track.

If you want to include all continuous MIDI data, select the Include All Continuous MIDI Data check box.

To select notes, do the following:

1. **Make a selection on a track or tracks that contain the notes you want to select.**

   Book IV, Chapter 2 has all you need to know about making selections.

2. **Choose Event➪MIDI➪Select/Split Notes from the main menu.**

   The Select/Split Notes version of the MIDI Operations window appears.

3. **Enter your note or note range in the window.**

   Again, your choices here are All Notes, Notes Between, Top, and Bottom.

4. **Choose the action for the selected notes (Select Notes or Split Notes).**

5. **Click Apply.**

The Select/Split Notes operation is handy for selecting the snare drum from a drum sequence before you change its note (pitch) or quantize it.

The Select/Split Notes operation is also handy for taking tom-toms from a drum sequence and moving them to their own track where you can edit, pan, and effect them separately from the rest of the drums. Another useful thing you can do with Select/Split Notes (keeping the drum-track theme going) is to make a copy of all the kick-drum notes and put them in another track where you can process them and add them to the original kick during mixdown. (Hey, why not get your kicks while you can? Sorry about that.)

To actually split notes from a MIDI track, do the following:

1. **Make a selection on a track or tracks that contain the notes you want to select.**

   Book IV, Chapter 2 has all you need to know about making selections.

2. **Choose Event➪MIDI➪Select/Split Notes from the main menu.**

   The Select/Split Notes version of the MIDI Operations window appears.

3. **Enter your note or note range in the window.**

   Again, your choices here are All Notes, Notes Between, Top, and Bottom.

4. **Choose the Split Notes action and then choose to copy or cut the selected notes from the track.**

5. **Select the location you want your split material to go: the Clipboard, a new track, or a new track per pitch.**

6. **Click Apply.**

To place the split notes that you placed on the Clipboard into another track, do the following:

1. **Position your cursor in the destination track at the same point as the start point of your Split Note operation.**

2. **Press ⌘+V (Mac) or Ctrl+V (PC) to place the copies or cut notes from your Clipboard into the track.**

Input Quantize

Use the Input Quantize operation to set a Quantize value that your recorded performance is adjusted to automatically as you record it. The fields you can adjust in the Input Quantize version of the Operations window (see Figure 4-10) are the same as with the Grid/Groove Quantize operation.

Unless your timing is really bad (or the person you record can't walk and chew gum at the same time), I suggest that you disable this function and quantize — if needed — *after* your performance is saved. Otherwise it's incredibly easy to overdo the quantizing and end up with a performance with absolutely no human feel to it.

Figure 4-10:
The Input Quantize function allows you to automatically adjust note timing while it's recorded.

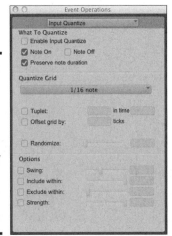

Step Input

Use the Step Input MIDI operation to add MIDI to a track manually. This can be handy if you want to "create" a performance that you're unable to play in real-time. This can be time-consuming, but it would likely be quicker than learning to play a really difficult part before recording it.

Figure 4-11 shows the Step Input options in the MIDI Operations window. Here's a run-down on the parameters you choose from:

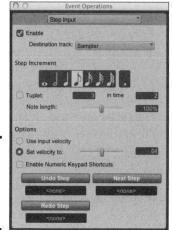

Figure 4-11: Use Step Input to add MIDI notes manually.

✦ **Enable:** This enables the Step Input function while also disabling any tracks that were record-enabled. If you have a default MIDI through instrument chosen (in the MIDI preference menu), it is also disabled.

✦ **Destination Track:** This is the track where your MIDI notes are added.

✦ **Step Increment:** In this section, choose the spacing and duration of your new MIDI notes. You can choose between whole, half, quarter, eighth, sixteenth, thirty-second, and sixty-fourth notes. As well, you can also choose

   • *Tuplet:* Use this to input triplets by dividing the step increment selected for Step Increment into the value chosen in the tuplet fields. For example, if you want to input triplets, select the quarter note in the Step Increment field, select the Tuplet check box, and then enter **3** and **2** in the fields to the right (so that is reads 3 in Time 2). This places three notes between quarter notes instead of two.

   • *Note Length:* Use this slider to choose a percentage of the note increment you select in the Step Increment section. For example, if you want a staccato pattern and you chose eighth notes as your step increment, you might want to select a 50% value. This will play the note for only half the total eighth-note duration.

You also have a few options that you choose from when step inputting notes:

- ✦ **Use Input Velocity:** Selecting this radio button assigns the velocity that you play on your instrument to the note.

- ✦ **Set Velocity To:** Use this slider to choose a velocity for this note so you don't have to worry about playing it at the right volume on your instrument.

- ✦ **Enable Numeric Keypad Shortcuts:** Selecting this check box allows you to enter your Step Input options via keyboard shortcuts.

- ✦ **Undo Step:** Clicking this button removes the last step input. If you have a note depressed on your MIDI instrument, clicking this changes the title to Decrement and removes the last step increment that you added to your track.

- ✦ **Next Step:** Clicking this button moves you to the next increment, adding a rest to your track. If you have a note depressed on your MIDI instrument, this button reads Increment and lengthens your note by the step increment value that you entered in the Step Increment section earlier.

- ✦ **Redo Step:** Clicking this button replaces the note that was removed by your previous Undo step operation.

Follow these steps to step input MIDI notes:

1. **Choose Event⇨MIDI⇨Step Input.**

   The Step Input options in the MIDI Operations window open.

2. **Select the Enable check box.**

   This enables the Step Input function.

3. **Choose the MIDI or Instrument track from the Destination Track drop-down menu.**

4. **Choose your note parameters (listed earlier in this section).**

5. **Play the note on your MIDI instrument.**

   Your note is placed in the designated track.

   Your cursor moves to the next step in your track. Repeat Steps 3–5 for each additional note you want to add.

Restore Performance

Restore Performance returns you to a saved performance settings. This operation is like having an Undo for all the other operations listed in this chapter. Your performance returns to one of two earlier states:

✦ The settings saved by using the Flatten Performance command (see the next section) if you used it.

✦ Its original settings (if you haven't saved any other settings).

Using the Restore Performance version of the MIDI Operations window, you can select from several areas to restore. (See Figure 4-12.)

Figure 4-12:
Use Restore
Performance
to revert
your
selection to
its original
state.

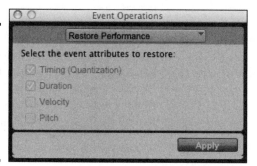

✦ **Timing (Quantization):** Selecting this check box restores the note's start time. If the Duration check box is cleared, the duration of the notes changes back to what it was originally.

✦ **Duration:** Selecting this check box restores the length of the note. If you don't have the Timing check box selected, the start times of your notes don't change but the end times may.

✦ **Velocity:** Selecting this check box restores the volume of the note.

✦ **Pitch:** Well, you know what this restores.

If you use the Grid/Groove Quantize operation when you recorded, you can remove it by using this operation. Choose the Timing (Quantization) option, and your original performance is resurrected in all its pristine beauty.

Flatten Performance

Flatten Performance is the operation you use when you want to save the performance data of a selection — timing, duration, velocity, and pitch — as the "original" setting that the Restore Performance operation (see the previous section) returns you to. The Flatten Performance version of the MIDI Operations window is shown in Figure 4-13.

Using this operation allows you to tweak performance data and lock it in before you do more tweaking. If you don't like the extra tweaking, you can just go back to these settings. It's a little added insurance when you're messing creatively with MIDI data.

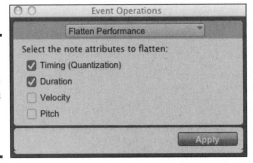

Figure 4-13:
The Flatten
Performance
function lets
you lock in
selected
notes.

Use the Flatten Performance operation to save the following data:

+ **Timing (Quantization):** The note's start time. If the Duration check box is cleared, the duration of the note changes back to what it was originally.

+ **Duration:** The length of the note.

+ **Velocity:** The volume of the note.

+ **Pitch:** Well, you know what that is.

Recognizing MIDI Real-Time Properties

Pro Tools allows you to adjust a variety of MIDI properties in real time while your song plays. This is done from the MIDI Real-Time Properties window. This feature is handy if you want to make adjustments to certain MIDI data, such as quantize, note duration, delay, velocity, and transpose, either across an entire track or a selected clip. This section details this process.

Access the Real-Time Properties window by selecting a MIDI or instrument track or clip and by choosing Event⇨MIDI Real-Time Properties from the main menu. The Real-Time Properties window opens, as shown in Figure 4-14. You can also see and edit real-time properties within the Edit window by choosing View⇨Edit Window⇨Real-Time Properties.

The Real-Time Properties window consists of the following parameters to adjust:

+ **Quantize:** This section is where you choose the resolution of the quantization. Your choices range from whole notes to sixty-fourth notes. If you choose sixteenth notes, for example, your notes will move to the nearest sixteenth note when you quantize.

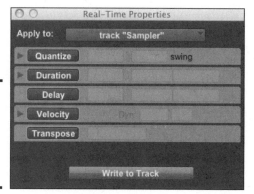

Figure 4-14:
Perform MIDI operations in real time here.

- *Note:* From this drop-down menu, choose the note value of your quantize grid. Open the drop-down menu by clicking the note. From here, you can drag to the note value you want as well as add either triplet or dotted note options. You can also select a groove template to quantize to.

    When you select a note for your grid value. The following options appear in the window:

- *Swing:* From this field, create a swing feel (dotted-quarter, eighth-note triplet). You specify a percentage (from 0 to 300%); selecting 100% provides a triplet feel.

- *Tuplet:* Select this check to select odd note groupings, such as triplets. When you select this option, you need to fill in the tuplet value. For example, to create a regular eighth-note triplet, choose 3 in Time 1; for a quarter-note triplet, choose 3 in Time 2.

- *Offset:* Selecting this option allows you to move the Quantize grid forward or backward in time by the selected number of ticks. This is helpful for creating a groove that lies slightly ahead of — or behind — the beat.

- *Strength:* This is, in my opinion, the most useful function in the Pro Tool Quantize operation. You can use it to move your *quantized notes by a percentage* (from 0 to 100%) rather than just snapping them right to the grid. Higher numbers keep more strictly to the grid than do the lower values. Checking this check box results in a text field appearing where you enter the percentage value for this operation.

- *Include:* Here you specify a range of notes to include. Selecting this option quantizes only selected notes that fall within the boundaries you set here (from 0 to 100%); the smaller the number, the narrower the range of notes affected.

- *Random:* Selecting this option adds a level of randomness to the quantizing of your selection — no, not to mess up the rhythm, but to keep it from being too rigid. You can select values between 0 and 100%. Lower values place the randomized notes closer to the grid.

✦ **Duration:** From this section, you can change the duration of your selected notes. You have several options to choose from a drop-down menu located next to the Duration properties option, including

  - *Set:* Select this option to set the duration of your selected notes to your desired duration, such as quarter notes or eighth notes. Or you can type in a specific number of ticks.

  - *Add:* Here you can add a specific amount to each selected note. You can choose between typing in a certain tick value or choosing one of the notes values that appear in the drop-down menu to the right of the data field.

  - *Subtract:* As with Add, selecting this option allows you to subtract your desired value from your selected notes. Again, you can choose between typing in a tick value or choosing a note value.

  - *Scale:* Select the scale option to adjust the duration of your selected notes by the percentage to designate in the data field. Your options range from 0% to 400%.

  - *Legato/Gap:* Selecting this option extends your selected notes to the next note, regardless of how far away it is.

  - *Legato/Overlap:* Select this option to extend your selected notes to the next note and beyond, creating an overlap (hence the name). Enter the amount of overlap you want in the data field to the right.

    You can narrow the effects of your real-time adjustments for note durations by setting a minimum note duration that will be changed by the settings you chose from the preceding above by selecting the Min and/or Max fields and then entering the value that you want.

✦ **Delay:** Use this property to move your selection a designated amount of time forward or backward in your session. This can be helpful when dealing with latencies or creating different feels, such as being "on top of" (just ahead of) or "behind" (just after) the beat. From the drop-down menu, choose to either delay or advance your selection. You enter the amount of this delay or advance in the field using either ticks or samples, which you choose from the drop-down menu to the right.

✦ **Velocity:** You've likely seen this option before. Use this to change to *velocity* (volume of the note strike) of your selection. Engaging this option opens the Real-Time Properties window to include the following parameters:

- *Dyn:* Use this parameter to select a percentage value for the velocity change you want to implement in your selection. You can choose percentages between 0 and 300%.

- *Absolute Value:* This unlabeled check box sits to the right of the Dyn option. Here, you can enter the amount of absolute change of velocity change you want to all selected notes. You can enter a value between −127 and +127.

- *Min:* Selecting this check box engages a minimum velocity that will be affected by the selections you make in previous options.

- *Max:* Selecting this check box engages a maximum velocity that will be affected by the selections you make in previous options.

  Selecting both affects only the selected notes that reside between the minimum and maximum values.

✦ **Transpose:** Use this option to change the pitch of your selected notes by the values you select; use one of the following options that exist in the drop-down menu located to the right of the Transpose title (it's now showing "In" key with the text box to the right):

- *By:* Selecting this transposes your selection by your chosen interval. Choosing this option from the drop-down menu opens two data fields in which you can enter octave (the left field) or semitones (the right field).

- *To:* Use this to transpose your selection to a specific pitch. Just select this option form the drop-down menu and enter the pitch in the data field that appears.

- *In:* Use this option to transpose in a specific key. Selecting this option from the drop-down menu adds a data field in which you can enter a value between −11 and +11. Each number represents a key step.

You can perform the Real-Time Properties functions by using these steps:

1. **Open the Real-Time Properties window by choosing Event➪MIDI Real-Time Properties or View➪Edit Window➪Real-Time Properties.**

The Real-Time Properties window opens. Figure 4-14 show the Real-Time Properties window that appears when you choose Event➪MIDI Real-Time Properties option.

2. **Select the track or clip(s) you want to make changes to, according to the following procedures:**

- *Track:* Click the track to select it.

  The name of the track will be highlighted, and that track will show up in the Apply To section of the Real-Time Properties window.

- *Clip:* Use the Grabber tool and click the clip to which you want to apply real-time changes.

  To select multiple clips, hold down the Shift key while grabbing.

3. **Engage the property you want to use by clicking the particular property (Quantize, Duration, Delay, Velocity, or Transpose) within the Real-Time Properties window.**

   The property becomes highlighted, and the window expands to include the controls for your chosen property.

4. **Select the parameters that you want for your MIDI property. You can do this while your session plays, or you can start your session after you make your selection.**

   You'll hear the effects that your settings have on your selection while your song plays.

5. **Make any adjustments you want until you get the effect or change that you're looking for.**

Book VI

Mixing In Pro Tools

Contents at a Glance

Chapter 1: Mixing Basics 525
Understanding Mixing 525
Managing Levels as You Work 526
Getting Started Mixing Your Song 527
Mixing In Pro Tools 528
Using the Stereo Field 531
Adjusting Levels: Enhancing the Emotion of the Song 534
Tuning Your Ears 536

Chapter 2: Setting Up Your Mix 541
Revisiting the Mix Window 541
Getting to Know Signal Flow 542
Rounding Out Your Routing 545
Accessing Output Windows 552
Playing with Plug-ins 555
Processing with External Effects 562

Chapter 3: Using Equalization 567
Exploring Equalization 567
Dialing In EQ 569
Equalizing Your Tracks 573

Chapter 4: Digging into Dynamics Processors 581
Connecting Dynamics Processors 581
Introducing Compressors 582
Looking into Limiters 589
Introducing Gates and Expanders 591
Detailing the De-Esser 594
Setting Up Side Chains 596

Chapter 5: Singling Out Signal Processors 599
Routing Your Effects 600
Rolling Out the Reverb 602
Detailing Delay 605
Creating Chorus Effects 607

Chapter 6: Automating Your Mix 609
Understanding Automation 609
Accessing Automation Modes 611
Setting Automation Preferences 612
Enabling Automation 614
Writing Automation 616
Viewing Automation 619
Drawing Automation 620
Thinning Automation 621
Editing Automation Data 622

Chapter 7: Making Your Mix 627
Submixing by Recording to Tracks 627
Mixing in-the-Box 629
Using an External Master Deck 632

Chapter 1: Mixing Basics

In This Chapter

✔ **Getting to know the mix process**

✔ **Managing levels**

✔ **Using control surfaces and external mixers**

✔ **Understanding the stereo field**

✔ **Using reference CDs**

Think about all the time it took for you to record all the tracks for your song. You spent countless hours setting up mics; getting good, *hot* (high, but not distorting) levels on your instruments; and making sure that each performance was as good as you could get it. You'd think, then, that most of your work would be done.

Well, on the one hand, it is — because you no longer have to set up and record each instrument. On the other hand, you still have to make all the parts that you recorded fit together. This process can take as long as it took you to record all the tracks in the first place. In fact, for many people, it takes even longer to mix the song than to record all its parts.

In this chapter, I introduce you to the process of mixing your music. You get a chance to see the basics of mixing using the Pro Tools Mix window. You also discover how to set up external mixing aids, such as MIDI control surfaces, digital mixers, and analog mixers. To top it all off, you discover how to reference your music to other people's recordings as well as how to train your ears so that your mix "translates" to different types of playback systems.

Mixing music is very subjective. You can relate one instrument to another in an almost infinite variety of ways. You might find that several mixes work equally well for your song. Allow yourself to experiment — and don't be afraid to record several different mixes.

Understanding Mixing

The goal of mixing is to make sure that each instrument can be heard in the *mix* — the recorded whole that results from blending all your recorded parts — without covering up something else or sounding out of place. You can pull this off in several ways:

✦ **Choose the parts that add to the emotional impact of the music and build intensity throughout the song.** By necessity, this also means choosing to not use unnecessary parts or those that clash with parts that have a greater effect.

✦ **Set the *level* (volume) of each instrument relative to the others.** That way, nothing is buried so far back in the mix that you can't hear it, and no instrument is so loud that it overpowers the other instruments.

✦ **Adjust the *equalization* (EQ, or frequency response) of each instrument.** This leaves room for all instruments in the mix. You get rid of any requencies of an instrument that clash with those of another, or emphasize certain frequencies that define the sound of an instrument so it can be heard clearly in the mix.

✦ **Take advantage of stereo *panning* (movement from left to right).** This puts each instrument in its proper place in the stereo field — toward the left or right — where it can either sound as natural as possible or produce a desired effect. Also, stereo panning allows you to make room for each instrument in the mix, especially those with similar frequency ranges.

✦ **Add effects (such as reverb or delay) to the instruments in the mix.** You place instruments in front or in back, relative to other instruments, or to create a desired sound.

During mixing, you can get really creative in crafting your song. The stress of capturing great performances is over: All that's left for you to do is to massage all the parts of your song into a cohesive whole. Don't be afraid to try new things. Experiment with different EQ, panning, and effect settings. Take your time and have fun. The great thing about mixing is that you can make as many versions as you want — and you can always go back and try again.

Managing Levels as You Work

When you mix all the tracks in your session, the *mix bus* (which, for its part, is controlled by the Master fader) is where they end up. There the signals are *summed* (added) and result in a *level* (volume) that's higher than that of the original tracks. One danger of mixing in-the-box (within Pro Tools) is that this level can get pretty high, and you might not recognize it unless you listen very carefully.

While you work, watch the level meter in the Master fader and make adjustments to the individual tracks to bring down the individual levels, rather than dropping the fader on the master.

Many people like to get the most volume out of a song when mixing, so they crank up the Master fader to where the levels peak right at 0decibels (dB) or maybe –0.1dB. This used to be considered okay, but more and more professional engineers are backing off on the mix bus by as much as 6dB. This is what I recommend as well. Keep your peak levels that go to the Master fader down to about –3dB to –6dB and make this up when you master (or have someone else master) your music. Sure, the volume will be lower than it is on the commercial CDs you own, but you can adjust that during the mastering process. (Book VII, Chapter 1 has more on mastering.)

The advantage to keeping down peak levels is that you get better levels going to the mix bus and reduce the chance that some *clipping* happens. (Clipping is also called *overs* in digital recording; it's distortion that results when the summed signals end up too hot and overload the mix bus.)

Getting Started Mixing Your Song

Before I start to mix a song, I do a few things to prepare myself for the process. My goal before I mix is to get in the headspace of mixing. This often means taking a step back from the song and approaching it as a listener rather than as the musician who recorded each track. Start the mixing process by following these steps:

1. **Determine the overall quality you want from the song.**

At this point, I don't mean *quality* in terms of, "Is it good or bad?" Rather, I define quality here as a musical style or a feeling. Do you want it to kick? Soothe? Scream? You probably don't need to think about this too hard if you had a definite sound in mind when you started recording. In fact, most composers hear a song in their heads before they even start recording.

2. **Listen to a song or two from a CD that has a sound or feel similar to the song you're trying to mix.**

Listen to the examples on your studio monitors if you can; try to get a sense of the tonal and textural quality of these songs. Listen to them at fairly low volume; be careful not to tire your ears. All you're trying to do at this point is get your ears familiar with the sound you're trying to produce in your music.

3. **Set up a rough mix, using no EQ or effects, and listen through a song once.**

For this listening session, don't think like a producer; rather, try to put yourself in the mindset of the average listener. Listen to the various parts you recorded — does anything stick out as particularly good or bad? You're not listening for production quality. You're trying to determine which instruments, musical phrases, licks, melodies, or harmonies grab you as a listener.

4. **Get a piece of paper and a pen to jot down ideas while you work.**

When you listen through the song, take notes on where certain instruments should be in the mix. For example, you might want the licks played on lead guitar throughout the song to be muted during the first verse. Or maybe you decide that the third rhythm guitar part you recorded would be best put way to the right side of the mix, while the other two rhythm guitar parts might be closer to the center. Write down these ideas so you can try them later. Chances are that you'll have a lot of ideas as you listen through the first few times.

Mixing In Pro Tools

Pro Tools comes with a powerful software mixer, and everything you might want to do can be done via your mouse and keyboard. Even so, many people — myself included — prefer to mix by using real faders, knobs, and buttons. This can be done several ways: using a computer control surface (such as the Digi 002 or 003 or a Mackie Control), a MIDI controller, a digital mixer, or an analog mixer. These alternative types of mixers are covered in more detail in Book I, Chapter 2; for now, I just want to cover the basic setups of these various options.

Using a control surface

If you have a computer control surface such as a Digi 002 or 003 (see Figure 1-1), your system is automatically integrated within Pro Tools software. With your system hooked up via a FireWire interface, all your faders, knobs, and buttons should work seamlessly with the software mixer. When you push a fader on the control surface, the corresponding track fader on the computer screen moves as well.

Check out the manual for the 002 or 003 to get familiar with the operation of its control options. Or you can just fiddle around a bit; the controller is set up very intuitively.

Using a MIDI controller

Quite a few MIDI control surfaces on the market work well with Pro Tools. (The Mackie Control is one that immediately comes to mind.) If you want to go the MIDI route, I highly recommend doing an Internet search for "Pro Tools compatible control surface" and see what comes up. You'll find a bunch of options and just as many opinions about each one.

Figure 1-1:
Mixing with
the 003's
control
surface lets
you use
your hands
to control
the mix.

Hooking up a MIDI control surface is the same as setting up any MIDI instrument, so go to Book V, Chapter 1 for details on configuring your system.

After you're hooked up and running, the control surface is basically the same as using a Digi 002 or 003. All your faders, knobs, and buttons on your control surface will adjust one of the parameters in the Pro Tools software. The manual for your MIDI control surface will spell out the function of each of the buttons. In the case of the Mackie Control, you can get a template that fits over the surface of the controller and shows you the appropriate functions in Pro Tools listed for easy reference.

Using a digital mixer

If you want to use a digital mixer with your Pro Tools system, you need to make sure that you have the proper number of digital inputs and outputs in your Avid interface to connect to your mixer.

With the 003 Rack, for example, you have ten outputs (eight ADAT and two S/PDIF) that you can use to send your tracks from your computer to your mixer. (Just make sure that your mixer can accept ADAT and S/PDIF signals — Book I, Chapter 2 has more on ADAT and S/PDIF — at the same time; otherwise you're down to eight.) This means you can send no more than ten tracks of material to your mixer to mix.

If you're equipped with one of the current Avid interfaces, such as a Mbox Pro, you don't have enough digital ins and outs to work successfully with a digital mixer. In this case, if you want to mix with faders you really need to go the computer controller route.

In this example, if you have a session with more than ten tracks, your digital mixer becomes somewhat useless unless you want to mix in stages (ten tracks at a time) or mix in the box (within Pro Tools) *and* from your mixer.

I don't recommend this half-in-the-box approach because you'll have a delay between the internal track and the tracks sent to your mixer. Any such delay will really mess with the feel of your music.

To connect your digital mixer to your Pro Tools system, simply run the appropriate cables (ADAT, for instance) from the output of your Avid interface to the input of your digital mixer. When you move a fader (or a button or a knob) in your mixer, the corresponding fader (or button or knob) track in the Pro Tools software you see onscreen won't be affected.

Using an analog mixer

Like with a digital mixer, your ability to mix in an analog mixer is limited by how many outputs your interface has. In this case, it all depends on the number of analog outputs you have. For example, the 002 Rack provides eight analog outputs, so this is the maximum number of tracks you can mix with an analog mixer at any one time.

Mixing a session with more than eight tracks is possible, but it's not worth the hassle (in my opinion) unless you have a really expensive analog mixer. Inexpensive analog mixers (those less than $10,000, for instance) won't sound any better than mixing within Pro Tools.

If you want to mix your session through an analog mixer, just connect each analog output from your Avid hardware to one of the inputs of your mixer. In the case of the 002 or 003 Rack, you need eight TS cables running from outputs 1 through 8 to the corresponding inputs of your mixer. (Book I, Chapter 2 has more on the various cables you meet in the recording world.) Again, if you have one of the new Avid interfaces you don't have enough analog ins and outs to mix anything other than simple songs (few tracks) using an analog mixer.

Using the Stereo Field

When you're at a live concert and you close your eyes, you can hear where each instrument is coming from on stage. You can hear that certain instruments are on the left side of the stage, others are on the right, and still others seem to come from the center. You can also generally discern whether an instrument is at the front or the back of the stage. Put all these sound-based impressions together, and you have a 3-D image made of sound — a *stereo field.*

What makes up the stereo field is the specific placement of sound sources from left to right and front to back. When you mix a song, you can set your instruments wherever you want them on the imaginary "stage" created by your listener's speakers. You can do this with *panning,* which sets your instruments from left to right. You can also use *effects* (such as reverb and delay) to provide the illusion of distance, placing your instruments toward the front or back in your mix. (See Chapter 4 of this mini-book for more on effects.) When you mix your song, try to visualize where on stage each of your instruments might be placed.

Some people choose to set the panning and depth of their instruments to sound as natural as possible, and others use these settings to create otherworldly sounds. There is no right or wrong when panning and adding effects to simulate depth — just what works for your goals. Don't be afraid to get creative and try unusual things.

Left or right

You adjust each instrument's position from left to right in a mix with the Panning control, located in the Pro Tools Mix window. (See Figure 1-2.) Panning for most songs is pretty straightforward, and I outline some settings in the following sections. Some mixing engineers like to keep their instruments toward the center of the mix; other engineers prefer spreading things way out with instruments on either end of the spectrum. There's no absolute right or wrong way to pan instruments. In fact, no one says you have to leave any of your instruments in the same place throughout the entire song. Just make sure that your panning choices contribute to the overall effect of the music. (Check out Chapter 5 of this mini-book for how to automate your panning in Pro Tools.)

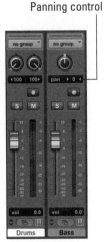

Panning control

Figure 1-2:
The Panning control in Pro Tools is located above the main fader in each track's channel strip. Left: a stereo track. Right: a mono track.

Lead vocals

Lead vocals are usually panned directly in the center. This is mainly because the vocals are the center of attention and panning them left or right takes the focus away from them. Some people will pan the vocals off center if there is more than one lead vocal (as in a duet), but this can get cheesy real fast unless you're very subtle about it. Of course, you're the artist and you may come up with a really cool effect moving the vocal around.

Backup vocals

Because backup vocals are often recorded in stereo, they are panned hard left and hard right. If you recorded only one track of backup vocals, you can make a duplicate of the track and pan one to each side, just like you can with stereo tracks. Then you can either nudge one forward or backward in time by a few milliseconds or adjust the pitch up or down a semi-tone to differentiate the two tracks.

In addition to tracks panned to each side, some mixing engineers also have a third backup vocal track panned in the center to add more depth. Your choice to do this depends on how you recorded your backup vocals as well as how many tracks are available for them.

Guitar parts

Lead guitar is often panned to the center, or just slightly off-center if the sound in the center of the stereo field is too cluttered. Rhythm guitar, on the other hand, is generally placed somewhere just off-center. Which side doesn't matter, but it's usually the opposite side from any other background instruments, such as an additional rhythm guitar, a synthesizer, an organ, or a piano.

Bass

Typically, bass guitar is panned in the center, but it's not uncommon for mixing engineers to create a second track for the bass: panning one to the far left and the other to the far right. This gives the bass a sense of spaciousness and allows more room for bass guitar and kick drum in the mix.

Drums

As a general rule, I (and most other people) pan the drums so that they appear in the stereo field much as they would on stage. (This doesn't mean that you have to, though.) Snare drums and kick drums are typically panned right up the center, with the tom-toms panned from slightly right to slightly left. Hi-hat cymbals often go just to the right of center; ride cymbals are just left of center; and crash cymbals sit from left to right, much like tom-toms.

Percussion

Percussion instruments tend to be panned just off to the left or right of center. If I have a shaker or triangle part that plays throughout the song, for instance, I'll pan it to the right an equal distance from center as the hi-hat is to the left. This way, you hear the hi-hat and percussion parts playing off one another in the mix.

Piano/synthesizers/organs

These instruments are usually placed just off-center. If your song has rhythm guitar parts, the piano or organ usually goes to the other side. Synthesizers can be panned all over the place. In fact, synths are often actively panned throughout the song: That is, they move from place to place.

Front or back

As you probably discovered when you were placing your mics to record an instrument, the quality of sound changes when you place a mic closer to — or farther away from — the instrument. The closer you place the mic, the less room ambience you pick up, which makes the instrument sound closer to you, or "in your face." By contrast, the farther from the instrument you place your mic, the more room sound you hear: The instrument sounds farther away.

Think of standing in a large room and talking to someone to see (well, hear, actually) how this relationship works. When someone stands close to you and talks, you can hear him clearly. You hear very little of the reflections of his voice from around the room. As he moves farther away from you, though, the room's reflections play an increasing role in the way that you hear him. By the time the other person is at the other side of the room, you hear not only his voice but also the room where you're at. In fact, if the room is large enough, the other person probably sounds as if he were a mile away from you, and all the reflections from his voice bouncing around the room may make it difficult to understand what he says.

You can easily simulate this effect by using your reverb or delay effects processors. In fact, this is often the purpose of reverb and delay in the mixing process. With them, you can effectively "place" your instruments almost anywhere that you want them, from front to back, in your mix.

The less reverb or delay you use with your instrument, the closer it appears on the recording; the more effect you add to an instrument, the farther away it seems.

The type of reverb or delay setting that you use has an effect on how close or far away a sound appears as well. For example, a longer reverb decay or delay sounds farther away than a shorter one.

In Chapter 4 of this mini-book, I go into detail about the various effects processors to help you understand how best to use them. I also present settings you can use to create natural-sounding reverb and delay on your tracks, as well as some unusual settings that you can use for special effects.

Adjusting Levels: Enhancing the Emotion of the Song

After you have a rough mix and get your EQ (described in Chapter 3 of this mini-book) and panning settings where you want them, your next step is to determine which parts of which tracks are used when — and sometimes whether a part or track is used at all. If you're like most musician/producers, you try to get all the wonderful instrumental and vocal parts you recorded as loud as possible in the mix so that each brilliant note can be heard clearly all the time. After all, you didn't go through all the time and effort to record all those great tracks just to hide them in the mix or (worse yet) mute them, right?

Well, I feel your pain. But when you get to the mixing point of a song, it's time to take off your musician's hat and put on the one that reads *Producer.* And a producer's job is to sort through all the parts of a song, choose those that add to its effect, and dump those that are superfluous or just add clutter. Your goal is to assemble the tracks that tell the story you want to tell and that carry the greatest emotional impact for the listener.

This can be the toughest part of mixing your own songs because you aren't likely to be totally objective when it comes to determining what to use and what not to use. Try not to get stressed out. You aren't erasing any of your tracks, so you can always do another mix if you just have to hear the part that you muted before.

One of the great joys when listening to music (for me, anyway) is hearing a song that carries me away and pulls me into the emotional journey that the songwriter had in mind. If the song is done well, I'm sucked right into the song; by the end, all I want to do is listen to it again.

What is it about certain songs that can draw you in and get you to feel the emotion of the performers? Well, aside from a good melody and some great performances, it's how the arrangement builds throughout the song to create tension, release that tension, and build it up again. A good song builds intensity so that the listener feels pulled into the emotions of the song.

Generally, a song starts out quiet, becomes a little louder during the first chorus, and then drops down in level for the second verse (not as quiet as the first, though). The second chorus is often louder and fuller than the first chorus, and is often followed by a bridge section that is even fuller yet (or at least differs in arrangement from the second chorus). The loud bridge section might be followed by a third verse where the volume drops a little. Then a superheated chorus generally follows the last verse and keeps building intensity until the song ends.

Book VI
Chapter 1

Mixing Basics

When you're crafting the mix for your song, you have two tools at your disposal to build and release intensity: dynamics and instrumental content (the arrangement).

Dynamics

Dynamics are simply how loud or soft something is — and whether the loudness is emotionally effective. Listen to a classic blues tune (or even some classical music), and you'll hear sections where the song is almost deafeningly silent, and other sections where you think the band is actually going to step out of the speakers and into your room. This is an effective and powerful use of dynamics. The problem is that this seems to be a lost art, at least in popular music.

It used to be that a song could have very quiet parts and really loud ones. Unfortunately, a lot of CDs nowadays have only one level — loud. This often isn't the fault of the musicians or even the band's producer. Radio stations and record company bean counters have fueled this trend, betting that if a band's music is as loud as (or louder than) other CDs on the market, it'll attract more attention and sell more copies. (You can read more about this trend in Book VII, Chapter 1.) But consider this: Whether you can hear the music is one thing; whether it's worth listening to is another.

Try recording a song with a lot of dynamic changes. I know this bucks the trend, but who knows? You might end up with a song that carries a ton of emotional impact. Also, while you mix your song, incorporate dynamic variation by dropping the levels of background instruments during the verses and bringing them up during the chorus and bridge sections of the song. You can always eliminate your dynamic variation (if you absolutely have to) by squashing your mix with compression during the mastering process.

The biggest mistake that most people make when they mix their own music is to try to get their song as loud as commercial CDs. This is the mastering engineer's job, however, and not yours, so don't worry about it. Get your song to sound good with a balance between high and low frequencies and loud and soft sections. Let the mastering engineer make your music as loud as it can be. He or she definitely has gear that is better designed to raise the volume of a recording without making it sound squashed or harsh.

The arrangement

Building intensity with the arrangement involves varying the amount of sound in each section. A verse with just lead vocal, drums, bass, and an instrument playing the basic chords of the song is going to have less intensity (not to mention volume) than a chorus awash with guitars, backup vocals, drums, percussion, organ, and so on. Most songs that build intensity effectively start with fewer instruments than they end with.

When you mix your song, think about how you can use the instruments to add to the emotional content of your lyrics. For example, if you have a guitar lick played at every break in the vocal line, think about using it less to leave space for lower levels at certain points in your song. If you do this, each lick will provide more impact for the listener and bring more to the song's emotion.

Tuning Your Ears

To create a mix that sounds good, the most critical tools you need are your ears because your capability to hear the music clearly and accurately is essential. To maximize this capability, you need a decent set of studio monitors and a good idea how other people's music sounds on your speakers. You also need to make sure that you don't mix when your ears are tired. The following sections explore these areas.

Listening critically

One of the best ways to learn how to mix music is to listen to music that you like — and listen, in particular, for how it's mixed. Put on a CD of something similar to your music (or music with sound that you like) and ask yourself the following questions:

✦ **What is the overall tonal quality or texture of the song?** Notice how the frequencies of all the instruments cover the hearing spectrum. Does the song sound smooth or harsh, full or thin? Try to determine what you like about the overall production.

✦ **How does the song's arrangement contribute to its overall feel?** Listen for licks or phrases that add to the arrangement. Notice whether the song seems to get fuller as it goes on.

✦ **Where are the instruments in the stereo field?** Notice where each instrument is, from left to right and front to back, in the mix. Listen to see whether they stay in one place throughout the song or move around.

✦ **What effects are being used on each instrument?** Listen for reverb and delay — in particular, how they affect decay lengths — as well as for the overall effect level compared to the dry (unaffected) signal.

✦ **What tonal quality does each instrument have?** Try to determine the frequencies from each instrument that seem dominant. Pay particular attention to how the drums sound, especially the snare drum. You'll notice a good mix lets all the instruments fit without fighting one another. Drums can take up a lot of room in the mix if you don't narrow them down to their essential frequencies.

Even if you're not mixing one of your songs, just sit down once in a while and *listen to music* on your monitors to get used to listening to music critically. Also, the more well-made music you hear on your monitors, the easier it is to know when your music sounds good on those same speakers.

A good mix should sound good on a variety of systems, not just through the speakers in your studio. Before you decide that a mix is done, copy it onto a CD and play it in your car, your friend's stereo, and a boom box. In fact, try to listen to your music on as many different kinds of systems as you can. As you listen, notice whether the bass disappears or becomes too loud or whether the treble becomes thin or harsh. Basically, you're trying to determine where you need to make adjustments in your mix so that it sounds good everywhere.

Unless you spent a lot of time and money getting your mixing room to sound world-class, you'll have to compensate when you mix to get your music to sound good on other people's systems. If your room or speakers enhance the bass in your song, the same tracks will sound thin on other people's systems. On the other hand, if your system lacks bass, your mixes will be boomy when you listen to them somewhere else.

Choosing reference CDs

A *reference CD* can be any music that you like or that helps you to hear your music more clearly. For the most part, choose reference CDs that have a good balance between high and low frequencies and that sound good to your ear. That said, some CDs are mixed really well, which can help you get to know your monitors and train your ears to hear the subtleties of a mix. I name a few in the following list. (***Disclaimer:*** I try to cover a variety of music styles in this list, but I can't cover them all without a list that's pages long.)

✦ Steely Dan, *Two Against Nature*

✦ Lyle Lovett, *Joshua Judges Ruth*

+ Norah Jones, *Come Away with Me*

+ Sting, *Brand New Day*

+ Ben Harper, *Burn to Shine*

+ Leonard Cohen, *Ten New Songs*

+ Beck, *Mutations*

+ Peter Gabriel, *So*

+ Sarah McLachlan, *Surfacing*

+ No Doubt, *Return of Saturn*

+ Los Lobos, *Kiko*

+ Marilyn Manson, *Mechanical Animals*

+ Depeche Mode, *Ultra*

+ Bonnie Raitt, *Fundamental*

+ Macy Gray, *On How Life Is*

+ Pearl Jam, *Yield*

+ Metallica, *S&M*

+ Dr. Dre, *2001*

All commercial CDs have been mastered. This is going to affect their sound a little: Most importantly, they'll be louder than your music in its premastered form. If you toggle between your mix and a reference CD, adjust the relative levels so that each one sounds equally loud coming through your speakers. The louder song always sounds "better." And whatever you do, don't try to match the volume of your mix to a reference CD.

Dealing with ear fatigue

If you've ever had a chance to mix a song, you might have found that you do a better mix early on in the process — and the longer you work on the song, the worse the mix gets. In most cases, this is because your ears get tired — and when they do, hearing accurately becomes harder. To tame ear fatigue, try the following:

+ **Don't mix at the end of the day, especially after doing any other recording.** Save your mixing for first thing in the morning when your ears have had a chance to rest.

+ **Keep the volume low.** I know you'll be tempted to crank the volume on your song while you work on it, but doing so only tires your ears prematurely and can cause damage, especially if you have monitors that can get really loud.

✦ **Take a break once in a while.** Just 10 or 15 minutes of silence can allow you to work for another hour or so. Also, don't be afraid to walk away from a mix for a day or more.

✦ **Try not to mix under a deadline.** This suggestion fits with the preceding one. If you're under a deadline, you can't give yourself the time you need to rest and reassess your mix before it goes to print.

Making several versions

One great thing about digital recording is that it costs you nothing to make several versions of a mix. All you need is a little (well, actually a lot of) hard-drive space. Because you can make as many variations on your song's mix as your hard drive allows, you can really experiment by trying new effects settings or trying active panning in your song and see whether you like it. You might end up with something exciting. At the very least, you end up learning more about your gear. That's always a good thing.

Print (that is, make a clear recording of) a mix early on. Most of the time, your best mixes happen early in the mixing process. Print (or save) the first good mix you make before you try making more "creative" ones. That way, if you get burned out or run out of time, you still have a decent mix to fall back on.

Chapter 2: Setting Up Your Mix

In This Chapter

✔ Understanding signal flow

✔ Routing inserts and sends

✔ Getting to know the Output windows

✔ Using plug-ins

✔ Processing external effects

*B*efore you can actually mix anything in Pro Tools, you have to get a few preliminaries out of the way first. More specifically, you need to become familiar with the Mix window, have a good grasp of how the signal flows through the system, know how to create auxiliary inputs and master faders, and get up to speed on inserts and sends. This chapter gives you the details on all these things.

Revisiting the Mix Window

When you mix in Pro Tools, you spend most of your time working in the Mix Window, as shown in Figure 2-1. The Mix window contains the channel strips for each track, routing information, and your master faders. Each part of the Mix window is covered in detail in Book II, Chapter 4.

To open the Mix window, choose Window⇨Mix from the main menu or press ⌘+= (equal sign; Mac) or Ctrl+= (equal sign; PC). You can then set up the display parameters of the window by choosing View⇨Mix Window from the main menu and choosing the options you want included in the view, as shown in Figure 2-2.

Figure 2-1:
The Mix window is where you do your mixing in Pro Tools.

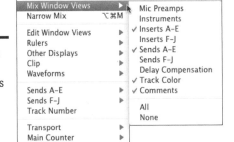

Figure 2-2:
Select parameters to view in the Mix window.

Getting to Know Signal Flow

Knowing how the tracks you record are routed through Pro Tools can help you make the best choices and keep your sound top-notch while you mix your song. Figure 2-3 shows how the signal (represented by the clip in your audio tracks) flows through the track channels in the Pro Tools mixer (shown in the Mix window).

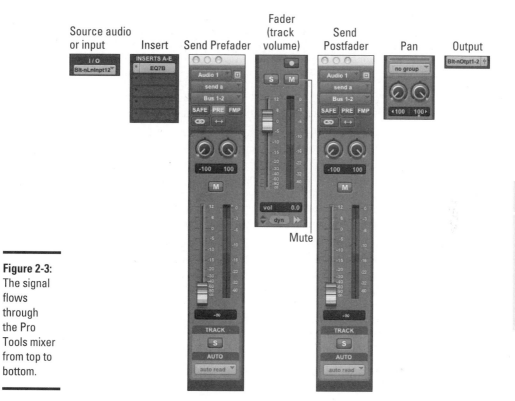

Figure 2-3:
The signal flows through the Pro Tools mixer from top to bottom.

The audio enters the mixer at the top of the diagram and flows downward. From top to bottom, here's how the signal flows through the channel strip:

✦ **Source audio or input:** This is the signal that's coming from your hardware input or that's recorded to your hard drive. The signal starts here and enters the track's channel strip.

✦ **Insert:** This function lets you insert effects into your track. This function is for effects, such as equalizers or dynamics processors, where you want to change the sound of the entire signal. Some SIAB systems, such as the Roland boxes, have separate EQ sections.

✦ **Send Prefader:** The Send function lets you route part of your signal out to an Aux bus, where you can then insert an effect such as reverb. With effects such as reverb, you don't want to use the Insert function — as you would with a compressor — because you want to be able to control how much of the effect you hear. (Compressors only enable you to affect the entire signal, not some portion of it.)

Adjust this slider or knob to *send* as much or as little of the signal to the appropriate *auxiliary* component (Aux, get it?) for effects processing, applying as much or as little of that effect to your final sound. Turning the knob to the left produces less effect, and turning it to the right gives you more effect.

Along with being able to set the Effect Send level at each channel (you can send more than one channel's signal to each effect), you can also adjust the level of the affected signal that's brought back into the mixer by using the Aux bus fader (which is described in the next section).

The Aux Send function can often be set to send the track's signal either prefader or postfader. Having this option gives you more flexibility to control the affected sound. For example, you can send the dry signal of a kick drum to a reverb (with the switch in the Pre position) and then boost the bass on the dry signal. Doing this gives you some reverb on the higher frequencies without adding it to the lower ones, which would create some mud in the final mix.

The downside to this technique is that you can't control the level of the signal being sent to the effect using the fader. (You bypassed the fader in the Pre position.) In this case, if you raise and lower the channel fader, the amount of effect that you hear in relation to the dry signal changes as well. For example, when you lower the fader, you hear more effect because less dry signal is mixed in — and when you raise the fader, you hear less effect because the dry signal is louder and the effect level is the same.

+ **Solo and Mute:** These buttons let you solo (silence all other tracks) and mute (silence) the output of the track.

+ **Fader:** This function lets you control the level (volume) of your signal leaving the track and going to the output(s) you have chosen in the Output section of the channel strip.

+ **Send Postfader:** When you have the Pre button disengaged, your Send signal is sent from your track after it passes through the track fader. Adjusting the volume of the track also adjusts the level going through your Send function.

+ **Pan:** This control lets you adjust the amount of your signal that goes to the left or right channel of your stereo output.

+ **Output:** This is where your signal goes as it leaves the track's channel strip. This can be the master bus.

To create a new track (audio, MIDI, auxiliary input, or Master fader), choose Track⟹New from the main menu to call up the New Track dialog box, where you can choose the type of track you want to create. (Book III, Chapter 1 covers this process in detail.)

Rounding Out Your Routing

When you start mixing in Pro Tools, it helps to have few routing setups under control. You need a Master fader so you can control the volume leaving Pro Tools, and you need to know how to use the Insert and Send portions of the channel strip so that you can insert effects into your tracks. The following sections outline these procedures.

If you're using version 6 or later, you can make a track inactive by ⌘+ Control-clicking (Mac) or Ctrl+Windows-clicking (PC) the Track Type indicator in the lower right of the track's channel strip (as shown in Figure 2-4). This frees up processing power, which I recommend for any tracks in your session that you don't want to play.

Figure 2-4:
Make
a track
inactive
to free
processing
power.

Click here to make a track inactive

Using a Master fader

You use a *Master fader* to control the level coming out of all the tracks routed to it. Here's a short list of a few of the things you can do with a Master fader:

✦ **Control the main level of your mix.** This is the standard use of this fader. All your tracks are routed to the Master fader, and you use it to control the overall level going to your monitors.

✦ **Control submix levels.** To control submix levels, route the tracks that you want to submix to one of your buses and assign the input of the Master fader to this bus. The output of this Master fader goes to your Master bus. You can set the individual levels of the submixed track at each track's fader and the combined level at this submix's Master fader.

✦ **Control effect-send levels.** You can route your *sends* — signals going through the Send section of your track — to a bus and designate that bus as the input of a Master fader. You can then insert your effect into this Master fader's input, setting the resulting output to go to your mix bus' Master fader.

✦ **Add effects to your entire mix.** You can add effects, such as compression or reverb, to the entire mix by placing it in the insert of the Master fader.

To create a Master fader, follow these steps:

1. **Choose Track⇨New from the main menu.**

The New Track dialog box appears.

2. **Use the drop-down menus to enter the number of tracks you want, the type (in this case, choose Master Fader) and whether you want your tracks(s) in stereo.**

3. **Click Create.**

The Master fader appears in your session.

4. **Click the Master fader's Output selector — the second of the three buttons in the middle of the channel strip — and set it to the output that you want it to control.**

If you want to make this the Master fader for your main mix bus, set this to the main outputs that all your tracks are routed to.

Adding auxiliary inputs

Auxiliary inputs are pretty much like audio tracks except that they receive a signal from within Pro Tools instead of from some external source (such as a microphone). Auxiliary inputs let you route internally and are great for some vital mixing tasks such as

✦ **Sending several tracks to a single effect processor:** This can reduce the stress on your system and can help you to make your tracks sound more cohesive — by blending their reverb sounds together, for example.

✦ **Controlling a submix with a single fader:** *Submixing* combines tracks before they are mixed by the Master bus. Chapter 7 in this mini-book details how to perform a submix in Pro Tools.

✦ **Inputting audio signals from your MIDI devices:** This lets you monitor the output from your MIDI devices when your MIDI tracks trigger them.

To create an auxiliary input track, follow these steps:

1. **Choose Track⇨New from the main menu.**

The New Track dialog box appears.

2. **Use the drop-down menus to enter the number of tracks you want, the type (in this case, choose Auxiliary Input), and whether you want your tracks(s) in stereo.**

3. **Click Create.**

   The auxiliary input appears in your session.

4. **Click the track's Input selector — the topmost of the three buttons in the I/O section of the channel strip — and choose the source for this track.**

   This can be an internal bus or a hardware input.

5. **Click the Output selector — the second of the three buttons in the middle of the channel strip — and set it to the output you want to send the signal.**

Inserting inserts

Inserts are effects that you can place into a track's signal to alter its sound. For example, inserting a compressor lets you control the dynamic range of your track, and inserting a delay can add an echo effect to your instrument. You can have up to five inserts in each track in Pro Tools. You can use either hardware or software (plug-in) effects in these inserts.

The signal passes through the effects in the order — from top to bottom — in which they appear in the Insert section of your track's channel strip. For example, in Figure 2-5, the signal goes through the compressor before it goes through the reverb. To change the order of your insert, simply click and drag it up or down the list.

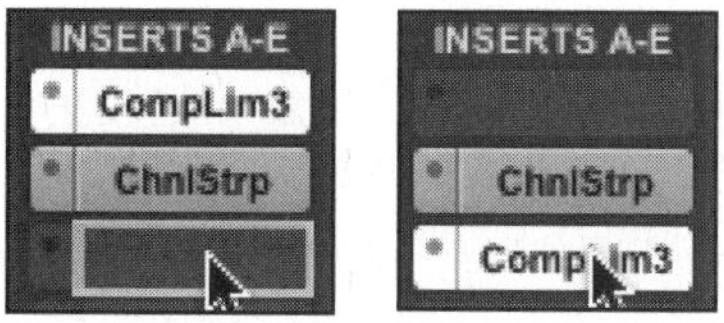

Figure 2-5:
Rearrange
inserted
effects by
dragging.

To insert an effect into a track's channel strip, follow these steps:

1. **Enable the Insert view in the Mix window by choosing View⇨Mix Window⇨Inserts from the main menu.**

   The Insert section of the Mix window appears at the top of your track's channel strip.

2. **Click an entry in the Insert section to open the drop-down menu.**

3. **Select a plug-in to insert (or the hardware output/input you want if you're using an external effect).**

If you choose a plug-in, the plug-in window opens. (See the "Playing with Plug-ins" section, later in this chapter, for more information.)

Turning off the effect in an insert

Here are the three ways to turn off the effect in an insert:

✦ **Remove the insert.** To remove the insert from the track, choose No Insert from the Insert drop-down menu. (Click and hold over the arrows located to the left of the Insert name to access the menu.) This removes the insert from the track and moves any inserts below it up the line.

✦ **Bypass the effect.** Do this by engaging the Bypass button in the plug-in window. To open this window, click the Insert name in the Insert section of the track's channel strip. This keeps the effect inline but turns it off. The effect still draws processing power even though you don't hear it.

✦ **Make the insert inactive.** Do this by pressing ⌘+Control (Mac) or Ctrl+Windows (PC) while you click the plug-in's name in the Insert section of the channel strip. Doing so removes the effect from the signal chain *but not from the Insert section.* This frees up processing resources and allows you to turn on the insert at any time. (You simply repeat the keystrokes-and-click you used to turn it off.)

Setting up sends

You can send the signal from your track to another bus for processing. Pro Tools lets you have up to five such sends per audio or auxiliary track. Sends are useful for two major purposes:

✦ **Applying effects to more than one track,** which you can do internally (using a plug-in) or externally (using a hardware device)

✦ **Creating submixes** that combine several tracks into one or two tracks

You can choose to send the signal pre-fader or post-fader, which means the signal going to the send is either sent before or after it travels through the track's fader. The Pre-Fader or Post-Fader options, along with the Send Level, Panning, and Mute options, are accessed through the Send window, as shown in Figure 2-6. You access this window by clicking the Send name in the Send section of the track's channel strip. If the Send section isn't visible in the track's channel strip, enable the Send view in the Mix window by choosing View⇨Mix Window⇨Sends from the main menu.

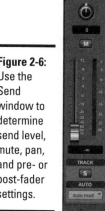

Figure 2-6:
Use the
Send
window to
determine
send level,
mute, pan,
and pre- or
post-fader
settings.

To assign a send, follow these steps:

1. **Enable the Send view in the Mix window by choosing View⇨Mix Window⇨Sends from the main menu.**

   The track channel strips expand to include the Sends section, located between the Inserts and I/O sections of the channel strip.

2. **Click one of the entries in the Send section to open the entry's drop-down menu.**

3. **Select the bus or hardware output/input to which you want to send the signal.**

   The Send window opens.

4. **In the Send window, select Pre-Fader or Post-Fader.**

   Selecting Pre-Fader sends the signal from your track before the fader control for that track and selecting Post-Fader sends the signal after it passes through the channel's fader.

5. **While still in the Send window, adjust your level, panning, and mute settings.**

To assign an effect to this sent signal, follow these steps:

1. **Choose Track⇨New from the main menu.**

The New Track dialog box appears.

2. **Use the drop-down menus to enter the number of tracks you want, the type (in this case, choose Auxiliary Input), and whether you want your tracks(s) in mono or stereo.**

3. **Click Create.**

The auxiliary input appears in your session.

4. **Assign the input for this auxiliary track to the bus that you chose for your send destination in the previous list.**

5. **Follow the steps for inserting an effect into a track.**

See the earlier section, "Inserting inserts."

Viewing sends

You can view your sends, send controls, and send assignments by opening the following windows in your session:

✦ **Send A-E Views:** You can see the controls for a send in the track's channel strip by choosing Views⇨Sends A-E from the main menu, where A-E represents a listing of the sends you have available to work with.

✦ **Send View Level Meters:** If you want to add to the basic Send view (see the previous bullet) to include level meters for the Send signal, select Show Meters in Sends View on the Display tab of the Preferences dialog box. (Choose Setup⇨Preferences from the main menu to access this dialog box.)

✦ **Send Assignments:** You can show Send assignments for your tracks by choosing View⇨Sends A-E (or F-J)⇨Assignments from the main menu. This lets you see the names of the sends assigned to a track.

✦ **Send Output Window:** You can open a window that contains all the Send settings in a large format by clicking the name of the Send in the Send section of the track's channel strip. This Send Output window is explained further in the upcoming section, "Accessing Output Windows."

✦ **Send Names:** As one more way to stay organized, you can name the destination buses for your sends. Do so by choosing Setup⇨I/O from the main menu and then clicking the Bus tab on the I/O Setup dialog box. On the Bus tab, double-click the name of one of the buses (to highlight it) and then type in its new name, as shown in Figure 2-7.

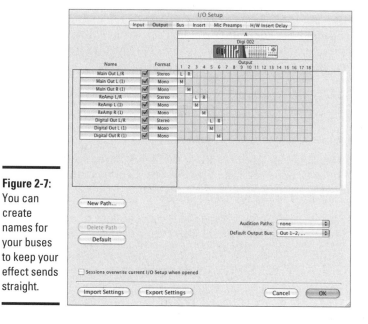

Figure 2-7:
You can create names for your buses to keep your effect sends straight.

Turning off the effect in a send

Here are three ways to turn off the effect in a send:

✦ **Remove the send.** To remove the send from the track, choose No Send from the Send drop-down menu. (Click and hold over one the arrows in the Send section of a track's channel strip to open the drop-down menu.) This removes the send from the track and moves any other sends below it up the line.

✦ **Bypass the effect.** Do this by engaging the Bypass button in the plug-in window. This keeps the effect inline but turns it off. The effect still draws processing power even though you don't hear it. To open the plug-in window, click the name of the plug-in in the track that this plug-in is inserted into. The Bypass button is located at the top of the window.

✦ **Make the send inactive.** Do this by pressing ⌘+Control (Mac) or Ctrl+Windows (PC) while you click the send bus' name in the Sends list. Doing so removes the effect from the signal chain but not from the Sends list. Making a send inactive frees processing resources, but you can still turn on the send at any time. (Simply repeat the keystrokes-and-click you used to turn it off.)

Using sends for groups

Controlling the send level and mute for sends across an entire group can be an enormous help because you can use one set of controls for all the tracks in a group. To control sends for a group, do the following:

1. **Choose Modify Groups from the Mix Groups drop-down menu.**

   You can find this in the lower left-hand corner of the Edit window.

   The Modify Groups dialog box appears.

2. **Check the Send Levels option and/or the Send Mutes option under the Linked Within Groups section of the Modify Groups dialog box.**

   This sets it up so that the following happens:

   • *If you select Enable Sends:* Any send level change you make on one track in the group affects all the tracks in a group.

   • *If you select Send Mutes:* Any send mutes that you create on one track in the group affect all the tracks in a group.

   For more on group sends, see Chapter 6 in this mini-book.

3. **Click OK.**

Accessing Output Windows

Output windows are floating sections of either the channel strip or the send settings. These windows allow you to adjust Output controls without having to search for them in the Mix window. This section details the Send and the Track Output windows.

Tackling Track Output windows

Track Output windows contain Fader, Pan, Automation, Output Selector, Solo, and Mute controls, as shown in Figure 2-8.

To open a Track Output window, just click the Output Window button in the track's channel strip in the Mix window, as shown in Figure 2-9.

The track output window includes the following controls:

✦ **Close:** Clicking this button closes the window.

✦ **Path Meter View Box:** When you click this button (the last button to the right at the top of the window), another window opens, showing the meters for the output path you selected in the Path Selector box. (See the upcoming Path Selector bullet.)

✦ **Track Selector:** This box lets you choose the track that shows in this window. You can choose from any track (audio, auxiliary input, or Master fader) in your session.

Track Selector

Target

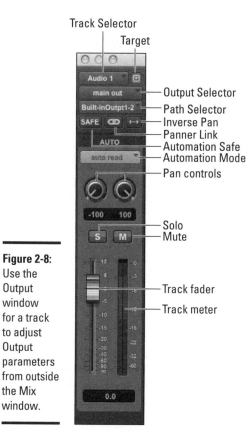

Output Selector

Path Selector

Inverse Pan

Panner Link

Automation Safe

Automation Mode

Pan controls

Solo

Mute

Track fader

Track meter

Figure 2-8:
Use the
Output
window
for a track
to adjust
Output
parameters
from outside
the Mix
window.

Output Window buttons

Figure 2-9:
Open a
Track
Output
window
by clicking
the Output
window
button in
the Mix
window.

✦ **Output Selector:** From this box, you can choose from among the outputs (whether track or send) in your system.

✦ **Path Selector:** This button lets you choose the output path for the current track.

✦ **Automation Safe:** Clicking this button puts the track in Automation Safe mode where no new automation data can be written. (Chapter 6 in this mini-book has more on automation data.)

✦ **Target:** Engaging this button keeps this track's window open if you click another Track or Send Output window. With the Target button disengaged (the button is red), whenever you open a send in the Output Selector box (see the earlier bullet) or another track's Output Window button, the current track is replaced by the new Track or Send Output window.

✦ **Inverse Pan:** For stereo tracks, this button ensures that when you move one of the pan controls (left or right), the other moves to exactly the opposite side. Make sure that the Panner Link button (see next bullet) is depressed so this function can work.

✦ **Panner Link button:** This button links the two pan controls on a stereo track. With this button engaged, moving one panning slider also moves the other to the same location; when the button is not engaged, you can move each panning control independently.

✦ **Pan controls:** These adjust the pan setting for the track.

✦ **Track fader:** This adjusts the volume of the track.

✦ **Track meter:** This display shows the level of the track as the session plays.

✦ **Mute:** Depressing this button mutes the track.

✦ **Solo:** Clicking this button solos the track.

✦ **Automation Mode:** From this drop-down menu, you choose the automation mode for your track.

Setting up the Send Output window

The Send Output window, as shown in Figure 2-10, shows the same basic information as the Track Output window (refer to Figure 2-8), with two exceptions:

✦ **Send Selector:** Instead of viewing and selecting the output for the track (Output Selector), you can choose any of the five sends for the track.

✦ **Pre/Post button:** This button controls whether the send is located before (pre) or after (post) the track's fader control. This is the button marked Pre, located just below the name of the track that feeds this send. Engaging this button sends the signal before the fader (pre-fader), and leaving the button untouched sends the signal after the fader (post-fader).

Send Selector

Pre/Post button

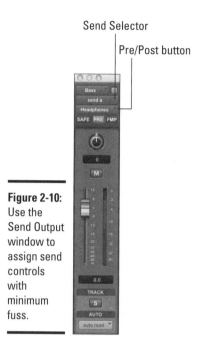

Figure 2-10:
Use the
Send Output
window to
assign send
controls
with
minimum
fuss.

To open a Send Output window, just click the Send name in the track's Send
list in the Mix window.

Playing with Plug-ins

Whenever you want to *process* tracks in Pro Tools — add EQ, effects, or
dynamics processors — you use a plug-in. *Plug-ins* are audio-processing
tools that change the sound of your original file. Some plug-ins permanently
alter the original file and work *offline* (that is, processing happens without
playing the session). This is the case with pitch-shifting, for example. Other
plug-ins — reverb, for example — affect the audio file without permanently
changing it, processing the audio in real time while the session plays.

These two types of audio processing — offline and real-time — are some of
the more powerful mixing tools available to you in Pro Tools. With them, you
can EQ your tracks and add compression, reverb, delay — and a myriad of
other enhancements — to your music. Your only limitations are the plug-ins
you have at your disposal and the processing power of your computer and
your pocket book. The following sections introduce you to the two types of
plug-ins — Real Time and AudioSuite — and then show you how to route
your system so you can use them effectively.

Real Time Plug-ins

Real Time plug-ins come in three types for Pro Tools systems: RTAS, AAX, and TDM. Here's a short description of each:

✦ **AAX (Avid Audio Extension):** This is Avid's new proprietary plug-in format. There aren't many plug-ins of this type available yet, but expect a lot more at time goes on. This type can be used with all Pro Tools systems.

✦ **RTAS (Real Time AudioSuite):** This plug-in format had been Pro Tools standard for a long time. Most of the plug-ins that you get with Pro Tools and find on the market from third-party plug-in creators are in RTAS format. All Pro Tools systems can use RTAS plug-ins.

✦ **TDM (Time-Division Multiplexing):** These are plug-ins created only for Pro Tools TDM systems (HD and HDX are the current TDM system types). You can't use TDM plug-ins in host-based Pro Tools systems.

Real time plug-ins process your audio while your session plays, allowing you to make adjustments on the fly and be able to hear these changes immediately. This is handy for adding compression, delay, and reverb, for example. The drawback to this is that anytime you process as your session plays, you're using up more of your computer's processing power — sometimes a lot more, as in the case of reverb. The following sections lay out the basics of using Real Time plug-ins; see Chapters 3–5 in this mini-book for more detailed information.

Routing your Real Time plug-ins

Real Time plug-ins are like the effects processors that you plug into your mixer. The sound from your tracks are sent to these effects and routed back through the mixer so you can hear the affected sound.

The two ways to place these effects in your mixer within Pro Tools are by using inserts or by using sends and returns. (Check out the earlier section, "Rounding Out Your Routing," for more on inserts and sends.)

✦ **Inserts:** Inserting a plug-in basically involves putting the effect inline with the audio as it travels through the channel strip in your mixer. This means all the sound from the audio file passes through the effect on its way out of the mixer (and to your ears).

When you insert a plug-in, you can choose from three formats:

- *Mono in/mono out:* One channel goes in and one comes out of the effect.

- *Mono in/stereo out:* One channel goes in, and two come out.

- *Stereo in/stereo out:* Two channels go in, and two channels come out.

✦ **Sends:** Using a send for your effects lets you route a portion of your track's signal that you can then control with the Send level. These sends are routed to an auxiliary track, into which the effect is inserted. Thus you can route more than one track to a single effect.

Understanding the Real Time Plug-In window

When you select a plug-in (or click its name in the Inserts section of a track's channel strip), a window opens, displaying all the controls for the plug-in, as shown in Figure 2-11. Most plug-ins usually have controls at the top of the window, similar to the ones described in the following list:

Figure 2-11: Most plug-in windows have some similar controls.

✦ **Track Selector:** This control lets you choose to view the plug-ins for any of the tracks in your session (except MIDI). Selecting a track without a plug-in shows no insert.

✦ **Insert Position Selector:** Use this to access any insert on the current track.

✦ **Plug-In Selector:** From this menu, choose from any Real Time plug-in that's located in your Plug-Ins folder (the one located within the Pro Tools folder on your hard drive).

✦ **Effect Bypass Button:** This button (surprise, surprise) bypasses the effect, allowing you to quickly and easily compare the affected and unaffected sounds. A bypassed effect shows as blue in the Mix and the Edit windows. If you bypass some (but not all) of a multi-mono effect, the effect shows as purple in the Mix and the Edit windows. This makes it easy for you to see whether one of your effects is bypassed without having to open all your Plug-In windows.

✦ **Settings menu:** Clicking and holding on the arrows at the left side of the plug-in window accesses the Settings drop-down menu, as shown in Figure 2-12, which lets you save, copy, paste, import, delete, and lock your plug-ins' settings, as well as set plug-in preferences (such as where to store these settings).

Figure 2-12:
Use the
Plug-Ins
Settings
menu
to save
settings,
among other
things.

✦ **Librarian menu:** From this drop-down menu, choose from plug-in settings you have stored. This menu is activated by clicking and holding the setting name (labeled Factory Default in Figure 2-11) next to the arrows for the Settings drop-down menu.

✦ **Previous (-) button:** Clicking this button moves to the previous saved plug-in preset in your preset list.

✦ **Next (+) button:** Clicking this button moves to the next saved plug-in preset in your preset list.

✦ **Preset list button:** Click this button to open the plug-in preset list, from which you can select the preset you want.

✦ **Compare button:** Click this button to toggle between your current and your previous setting.

✦ **Auto button:** Clicking this button opens the Plug-In Automation dialog box, from which you can set automation for your selected plug-in parameters. (Chapter 6 in this mini-book has more on automation.)

✦ **Automation Safe button:** Engaging this button keeps any written automation data from being overwritten.

✦ **Master Link button:** Enabling this button allows you to control all channels of a multi-mono plug-in at once. You can see the channels of your session in the gray box above this button. The small black square represents the channels. In Figure 2-11, you see two because this is a stereo session. The left square represents your left channel, and the right square represents your right channel.

✦ **Channel selector:** This button lets you choose the channel to adjust for the plug-in.

✦ **Target button:** Depressing this button keeps the current Plug-In window open when you open another plug-in. With this button off, clicking the plug-in name in a track's insert replaces the open window with a new window.

✦ **Phase Invert button:** This button (not available on all plug-ins) allows you to reverse the phase of the audio passing through the plug-in. This means flipping the waveform top to bottom. Book IV, Chapter 1 has more on waveforms.

Working with Real Time plug-ins

Chances are that you'll spend quite a bit of time using plug-ins. Unless you have a control surface, you'll probably end up spending more time than necessary just mouse-jockeying the controls. In the following list, I offer some shortcuts to make working with plug-ins quicker and easier:

✦ **To make fine adjustments with your mouse:** Press ⌘ (Mac) or Ctrl (PC) while you drag the plug-in control.

✦ **To return a control to its default setting:** Press Option (Mac) or Alt (PC) while you click that control.

✦ **To move through the controls in a plug-in:** Press the Tab key on your keyboard. To go backward, press Shift+Tab.

✦ **For plug-in parameters that offer kilohertz (kHz) values:** Press the K key after the number of kilohertz you want to enter. For example, to enter 10 kHz, type **10k**.

✦ **To increase the value of a parameter without using your mouse:** Press the up-arrow key (↑) on your keyboard; to decrease a value, press the down-arrow key (↓).

✦ **To enter a value via your keyboard:** Type in the value in the parameter box and then press Return/Enter.

Using AudioSuite offline plug-ins

Pro Tools comes with a variety of *offline* plug-ins — that is, effects that you can use to process your tracks so that you end up either altering the original audio file or creating a new one. These types of plug-ins are listed under AudioSuite in the main menu. Figure 2-13 shows the AudioSuite menu. Each item expands to include all plug-ins available for that plug-in type.

Figure 2-13:
Use
AudioSuite
plug-ins to
process
your tracks
offline.

When you select a plug-in from the AudioSuite menu, a window opens,
containing all the controls for the plug-in, as shown in Figure 2-14. You're
going to find the same kinds of controls for nearly all the plug-ins. They
include the following:

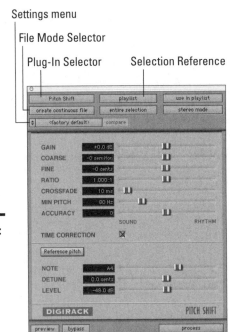

Figure 2-14:
AudioSuite
plug-in
windows
have some
similar
controls.

+ **Plug-in Selector:** From this menu, choose from any AudioSuite plug-in
listed in the AudioSuite menu.

+ **Selection Reference:** This menu lets you choose which clips are
processed. By default, when you select a clip in the track, the playlist, or
the Audio Clips list, all occurrences of the selected clip are processed.
You can limit the processing to the track/playlist or the Audio Clips list
by selecting from the drop-down menu. Your choices are

- *Playlist:* If you choose Playlist, only clips that are selected in tracks or playlists in the Edit window are processed.

- *Clip List:* If you choose this option, only clips selected in the Audio Clips list are processed.

✦ **Use in Playlist:** This button lets you choose whether your chosen processing happens to all instances of your selected clips throughout the session, or whether processing happens to only those you have selected. The settings are as follows:

- *Off:* When this button is disabled, your processed audio is added to the Audio Clips list but not put into the session.

- *On:* When this button is enabled, the processed audio is placed in the playlist according to the Selection reference you chose. (See the Selection Reference bullet.) If you have Clip List selected, all copies of the clip are replaced within the session. If you selected Playlist, only the clips that you selected in the tracks are replaced.

Book VI
Chapter 2

Setting Up Your Mix

✦ **File Mode Selector:** From this menu, choose how your audio is processed. You have three options:

- *Overwrite Files:* This option destructively overwrites your original file. Not all plug-ins have this option.

- *Create Individual Files:* This option creates a new audio file for each clip processed. These clips appear in the Audio Clips list.

- *Create Continuous File:* Choosing this option processes the selected clip as a single audio file. This option isn't available when you have Clip List chosen as your Selection reference. (See the earlier Selection Reference bullet.)

✦ **Process Mode Selector:** This menu appears if you have a selection that includes more than one clip. With it, you can select whether processing is done clip by clip or whether it affects the entire selection.

✦ **Settings menu:** This drop-down menu lets you save, copy, paste, import, delete, and lock your plug-ins settings as well as set plug-in preferences (such as where to store these settings). Figure 2-12 shows this menu.

✦ **Librarian menu:** From this drop-down menu, choose from plug-in settings that you have stored.

✦ **Compare button:** Click this button to compare the unprocessed sound with the processed sound.

✦ **Preview button:** Pressing this button lets you preview the audio before you commit to processing it.

✦ **Bypass button:** This button bypasses the effect, allowing you to quickly and easily compare the affected and unaffected sounds. (This button applies only to the Preview feature and doesn't change the processing of the file.)

✦ **Process:** Clicking this button processes the clip(s) you selected according to the rest of the settings in this window.

Using AudioSuite plug-ins to process an audio clip

You can use the AudioSuite plug-ins to process any part — or all — of an audio clip. If you choose part of a clip, that clip is split so the selected part becomes its own clip.

To use an AudioSuite plug-in, follow these steps:

1. **With the Selector tool, select the clip or clips (click and drag across them) in the Edit window you want to process.**

Book IV, Chapter 2 details this process.

When you process audio by using the Reverb or Delay plug-ins, make sure your selection includes extra room at the end of your material to include the actual reverb and delay; otherwise, the sound will be cut off.

2. **Choose the plug-in from the AudioSuite menu.**

The Plug-In window appears.

3. **Click Preview to hear your selected material.**

4. **Adjust the plug-in controls until you get the sound and processing settings you want.**

The previous section spells out what these settings are for.

5. **Click the Process button.**

Pro Tools processes your audio.

Be aware that the processing can take some time and always demands some computer resources.

Processing with External Effects

You can connect external effects devices (such as a reverb or compressor) to Pro Tools and easily route your sends or inserts to them. The advantage of using an external device (with its own dedicated source of processing power) is that you can reduce demand for your system's resources. The disadvantage is that going out and back into Pro Tools takes at least some time; you get a delay *(latency)* in the returned signal, especially if you're using the analog connection in your Avid interface. This latency isn't much of a problem with reverbs because a pre-delay on the effect is often desirable anyway, but it can be a real issue if you use an analog compressor. (Chapter 5 in this mini-book talks about pre-delay on reverb.)

The best way to eliminate the latency inherent in routing to an external analog device is to record your effect to a new track and then shift over the new clip in that track so that it synchronizes with the source track for that instrument. (Book IV, Chapter 3 explains the process of shifting clips.)

Using an external effects device requires three simple steps: creating a hardware insert, connecting the device to your interface, and assigning the insert in your track. How do you go about that? Glad you asked.

Creating a hardware insert

Before you can route your track's insert to an external device, you need to create a *hardware insert* — an insert in a track that routes your signal to one of the hardware inputs and outputs of your Avid interface. Follow these steps:

Book VI Chapter 2

Setting Up Your Mix

1. **Choose Setup⇨I/O Setup from the main menu.**

   The I/O Setup dialog box appears.

2. **Click the Insert tab on the I/O Setup dialog box.**

3. **Choose one of the insert paths listed (or choose Default if none are listed); double-click that path to create a new name for it.**

   The insert becomes highlighted.

4. **Type in a new name for the insert.**

5. **Select the proper format for the insert path (mono or stereo), and then click OK.**

Connecting your external device

You can connect an analog or a digital device as your hardware insert. The following sections describe connecting both devices.

Connecting an analog device

Nothing much to connecting an analog device, really. Just do the following:

1. **Select the output and input (or pairs for stereo) that correspond to the inserts I show you how to create in the earlier section, "Creating a hardware insert."**

2. **Connect the output of your Avid interface to the input of your external device.**

3. **Connect the output of your external device to the selected input in your Avid interface.**

Connecting a digital device

Whoa, here comes the high-tech stuff, right? Nah. Connecting a digital device is a bit more involved, but it's still not brain surgery:

1. **Connect your external device to your Avid interface by the digital connections on the back of your device.**

   Depending on your device, you either use an optical connection or a coaxial S/PDIF connection. (Book I, Chapter 2 has more about these types of connections.) Connect the output of your Avid interface to the input of your external device and the Output of your external device to the input of your Avid interface.

2. **Choose Setup⇨Hardware from the main menu.**

   The Hardware Setup dialog box opens.

3. **Click your Avid interface in the Peripheral section of the window to select your Avid interface.**

   If you have only one Avid interface connected to your computer, it's automatically highlighted.

4. **Perform one of the following in the Digital Input section of the Hardware Setup dialog box:**

   - *Connect through the optical ports.* Choose S/PDIF from the Optical Format drop-down menu.

   - *Connect through the coaxial (RCA) S/PDIF jack.*

5. **Choose your *clock source* — the digital clock that controls your system — from the Clock Source drop-down menu.**

   - *External:* If you want the effect device to be your clock source

   - *Internal:* If you want Pro Tools to be the clock source (or if you don't know what a clock source is)

   Check out the Pro Tools Reference manual or go to Book II, Chapter 2 for more on clock sources.

6. **Set your external device to the appropriate clock source: Internal if you select External in Pro Tools, and External if you select Internal in Pro Tools.**

   Your owner's manual should describe this process.

7. **Click OK.**

Routing your track

To route your track's insert to the hardware insert connected to your effects device, choose the hardware insert from the Insert drop-down menu, accessed by clicking and holding over one of the arrows in the Insert section of your track's channel strip.

You're now ready to dig in and use your external effect processor on your Pro Tools tracks.

TIP

The only disadvantage with using external effects in Pro Tools is that you can't save the effect settings with your Pro tools session like you can with an RTAS plug-in. In order to get around this deficit, I usually type the *effect patch* (setting number) I use for a track in the Comments section of the track. To enter this information, double-click the track's name in the Edit or the Mix window to call up the Name Track dialog box. Enter your effect patch and any other reminders you need in the Comments section, and then click OK to save your comments and close the window.

**Book VI
Chapter 2**

Setting Up Your Mix

Chapter 3: Using Equalization

In This Chapter

✔ **Understanding equalization (EQ)**

✔ **Inserting EQ in a track**

✔ **Getting to know the EQ options in Pro Tools**

✔ **Equalizing your tracks**

*E*qualization (EQ) comprises changing the frequency response of the data in the session's track to make the track sound how you want. The main goal when EQing during mixing is to get the instruments in your song to blend together smoothly (Book VI, Chapters 1 and 2 explore the process of mixing your tracks).

In this chapter, you discover the types of equalizers used in Pro Tools, and I walk you through applying EQ to your tracks. This chapter also offers some basic EQ settings for a variety of instruments to get you started EQing your songs.

Exploring Equalization

The most useful tool you have for mixing is equalization. You use equalizers to adjust the various frequencies of your instruments so that there's enough room for each of them in your stereo tracks. Pro Tools offers three types of equalizers — parametric, low-shelf/high-shelf, and low-pass/high-pass. I outline these types of EQ in the following sections.

Parametric

Using the *parametric equalizer* allows you to choose the frequency that you want to change as well as the range of frequencies around that frequency. With a parametric EQ, you dial-in the frequency that you want to change and then set the range itself (referred to as the *Q*) that you want to affect. This type of EQ is called a peak, or notch, EQ in Pro Tools; it's designated by the icon shown here in the margin.

Q is a number that signifies the range of frequencies that the EQ affects — usually between one-half and two octaves. Pro Tools offers settings from .33 to 12, with the lower numbers allowing larger ranges of frequencies to be EQed.

You choose your Q setting based on what you hear in the mix. Just as you can experiment with different frequencies to adjust in the mix, you can also try different Q settings to find the best possible frequency range to use.

The beauty of using a parametric EQ is that you can take a small *band* (range) of frequencies and then *boost* (increase) or *cut* (decrease) them. This capability enables you to get the various instruments in a mix to fit with one another. (This technique is *carving out frequencies.*) When you're mixing, the parametric EQ is the most useful equalizer because you can adjust the frequency response of each instrument so that the other instruments can be heard clearly in the mix. The only downside to using parametric EQs is that they need processing power to run. If you have a lot of EQing to do, you might end up stressing your system pretty hard. (Yet another reason to have a powerful computer.)

Low-shelf/high-shelf

A shelf equalizer affects a range of frequencies above *(high-shelf)* or below *(low-shelf)* the target frequency. Shelf EQs are generally used to roll off the top or bottom end of the frequency spectrum. For example, you can set a low-shelf EQ to roll off the frequencies below 250 hertz (Hz), which reduces the amount of rumble (low-frequency noise) in a recording. You generally use the shelf EQ to adjust the lowest and highest frequencies and the parametric EQ to adjust any in-between frequencies when you mix.

In Pro Tools, the low- and high-shelf EQs are designated with the icons seen here in the margin. The low-shelf is the left-facing fork, (top) and the high-shelf is the right-facing art in the margin (bottom).

Low-pass/high-pass

Believe it or not, sometimes your track just sounds better if you eliminate a few carefully chosen frequencies. You just need to know which ones to target. That's where a couple of Pro Tools capabilities can help with the needed audio acrobatics: *low-pass* (ducking the high frequencies you don't want) and *high-pass* (jumping over the low frequencies you don't want).

This type of EQ is actually called a *filter* because, um, it filters out frequencies either higher (low-pass) or lower (high-pass) than the target frequency. A low-pass filter is used for eliminating unwanted high frequencies, and a high-pass filter is useful for getting rid of unwanted low frequencies. In Pro Tools, the low- and high-pass filters are designated with the icons seen here in the margin. The low-pass filter is the downward slope (top) and the high-pass filter is the upward slope (bottom) art in the margin.

Dialing In EQ

Before you start EQing your tracks, you need to know how to insert the EQ plug-in in a track and how to actually make those adjustments with one of the EQ plug-ins in Pro Tools. The following sections detail these procedures.

Inserting an EQ plug-in in a track

To EQ a track, you first need to insert the Pro Tools AudioSuite plug-in in the track. To do so, follow these steps:

1. **Choose View⇨Mix Window⇨Inserts from the main menu to make sure that the Inserts section is showing in the Mix window.**

2. **Click the top arrow on the left side of the Inserts section of the track's channels strip.**

The Inserts drop-down menu appears, as shown in Figure 3-1.

3. **To fit the type of track you have, select the Multi-Channel Plug-In or the Multi-Mono Plug-In option.**

If your track is stereo, use Multi-Channel; if it's mono, use Multi-Mono.

4. **Select the 1-Band EQ3, 4-Band EQ-3, or 7-Band EQ 3 option.**

Your chosen EQ plug-in window opens. (The 1-Band EQ 3 option lets you set one EQ parameter, whereas the 4-Band EQ 3 option lets you work with four parameters. I bet you can guess how many parameters you work with in 7-Band EQ-3.) For more on which option would work best for you, check out the following section.

5. **Adjust the parameters that you want to EQ.**

You can find the particulars for each kind of EQ — parametric, low-shelf/high-shelf, and low-pass/high-pass — later in the chapter.

If you want to EQ a bunch of tracks at the same time and use the same settings (submixes, for example), you can do this the following way:

1. **Select one of the buses from the Output selector in each track that you want to submix.**

2. **Choose Track⇨New from the main menu.**

The New Track dialog box appears.

3. **Use the drop-down menus to enter the number of tracks that you want (choose 1), the type (choose Auxiliary Input), and whether you want your track in stereo or mono.**

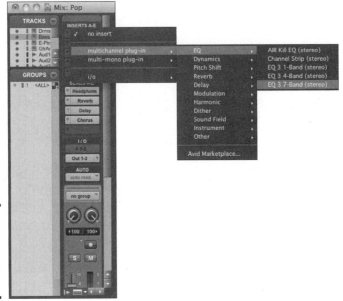

Figure 3-1:
Select the
EQ plug-in
to insert into
your track.

4. **Use your new track's Input selector to select the bus that you used for the output of the submix tracks as the input for this auxiliary track.**

5. **Insert one of the EQ plug-ins from the Insert drop-down menu in this auxiliary track.**

   The EQ plug-in window opens.

6. **Adjust the EQ settings to get the sound that you want.**

   You can find the particulars for each kind of EQ — parametric low-shelf/high-shelf, and low-pass/high-pass — later in the chapter.

Perusing Pro Tools EQ options

Using an EQ in Pro Tools comprises selecting one of the plug-ins, inserting it in the track that you want to affect, and setting your parameters. Pro Tools comes with three basic EQs: 1-band EQ, 4-band EQ, and 7-band EQ. They're part of the Real Time AudioSuite set of tools — RTAS — which is the plug-in format that Pro Tools uses.

You can also use any RTAS-type EQ plug-in, but these have to be purchased separately. If you do an Internet search with the keywords *RTAS plug-ins,* you're sure to find tons to choose from. The 1-band EQ plug-in for Pro Tools, as shown in Figure 3-2, lets you apply one EQ filter to a track. This EQ is useful if you just want to adjust one parameter. You can choose any of the types of EQs — parametric, low-shelf/high-shelf, and low-pass/high-pass — by clicking the appropriate button to engage your chosen EQ.

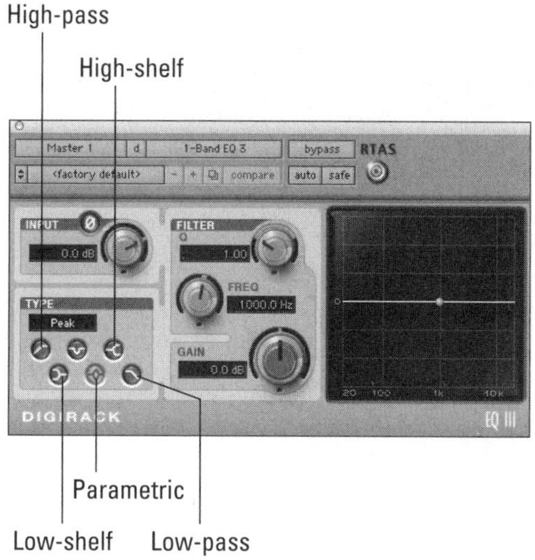

High-pass

High-shelf

Figure 3-2:
The 1-band
EQ plug-in
in Pro Tools
lets you
make one
EQ setting.

Parametric

Low-shelf   Low-pass

4-band and 7-band EQs

The 4-band and 7-band EQs in Pro Tools, as shown in Figure 3-3, let you
adjust up to four or seven (respectively) EQ filters to a track. This type of EQ
is useful when you have to do some major EQing to a track. Both EQs share
the same window. The difference is that with the 4-band EQ, you can select
only up to four of the seven possible bands of EQ. Comparatively, the 7-band
EQ lets you use them all.

Figure 3-3 shows all seven bands. These are

+ **HPF (High-Pass Filter):** Located to the left of the graphical display for
  the EQ, here you can choose the high-pass filter or the notch EQ setting.

+ **LPF (Low-Pass Filter):** Located just to the left of the graphical display for
  the EQ, here you can choose the low-pass filter or the notch EQ setting.

+ **LF (Low Frequency):** You can select between a peak or low-shelf EQ by
  clicking the appropriate icon next to the LF name.

+ **LMF (Lower-Middle Frequency):** Your only option is a peak EQ.

+ **MF (Middle Frequency):** Again, your only option is a peak EQ.

+ **HMF (High-Middle Frequency):** Here you can adjust a peak EQ.

+ **HF (High Frequency):** Like the LF option, this EQ can be a peak or shelf
  (this time a high-shield) EQ.

When you engage each band of EQ (by clicking the In button below the Q
knob), a dot shows up in the graphical section of the EQ window to show
you how your EQ is affecting the track the EQ is assigned to. You can check
this by looking for a blue illuminated "In" button. These dots are color-coded
to make it easy for you to see which band is where in the graph.

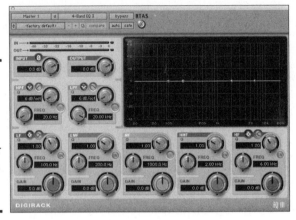

Figure 3-3:
Use the
4-band and
7-band EQs
in Pro Tools
to apply four
or seven EQ
filters to a
track.

Using parametric (peak and notch) EQ

To use the parametric EQ, click the Peak EQ button in whatever EQ plug-in window — 1-band or 4-band, for example — you have open. You have three settings to adjust:

+ **Q:** This is the range of frequencies that your EQ will affect. The higher the number, the narrower the range that gets EQed. You adjust this setting either by moving the knob or by clicking in the box and typing a value between .1 and 10.

+ **Freq:** This is the frequency that the EQ centers around. You select the range of frequencies above and below this point by using the Q setting (see the following bullet). You can type in the frequency on the box or use the knob to make your adjustment.

+ **Gain:** This is the amount of *boost* (increase) or *cut* (decrease) that you apply to the signal. You can either type in the amount in the box next to the Peak EQ button or use the knob to the right.

Using low-shelf/high-shelf EQ

To use low-shelf/high-shelf EQ, click the Low-Shelf and High-Shelf buttons in the EQ band you want to engage. When you use low-shelf/high-shelf EQ, you have three parameters to adjust:

+ **Q:** This is the range of frequencies that your EQ will affect. The higher the number, the narrower the range that gets EQed. You adjust this setting either by moving the knob or by clicking in the box and typing a value between .1 and 2.

+ **Freq:** This is the frequency that the shelf starts at. You can type in the frequency in the box or use the knob to make your adjustment.

✦ **Gain:** This is the amount of boost or cut that you apply to the signal. You can either type in the amount in the box next to the shelf button or use the knob to the right.

Using low-pass/high-pass EQ

Here's where you tell Pro Tools which frequencies to avoid in the course of adjusting the EQ. The low- and high-pass buttons appear next to the name of the EQ band. You have two parameters to adjust:

✦ **Q:** This is the range of frequencies that your EQ will affect. With these filters, you can select between 6, 12, 18, and 24 decibels (dB) per octave. The higher the number, the more severe the filter.

✦ **Freq:** This is the frequency that the filter starts at. You can type in the frequency in the box or use the knob to make your adjustment.

With all the EQ types, you can click and drag the color-coded dot in the graphical display section to set your EQ bands. Dragging left or right changes the frequency at which the EQ is set; by dragging up and down, you can change the gain.

Equalizing Your Tracks

Only so many frequencies are available for all the instruments in a mix. If more than one instrument occupies a particular frequency range, they can get in each other's way and muddy the mix. When you're EQing during the mixing process, your goal is to reduce the frequencies that add clutter — and/or to enhance the frequencies that define an instrument's sound. To do this, make a little space for each instrument within the same general frequency range, which you can accomplish by EQing the individual tracks as you mix. The first part of this chapter shows you how to get up to the point of doing some EQing. The rest of the chapter gets your hands dirty with some real EQing experience.

Here's a good trick to use when initially trying to decide which frequencies to boost or cut: First, solo the track(s) that you're working on and set your parametric EQ to a narrow Q setting (a high number). Next, turn the boost all the way up (move the Gain slider all the way to the right) and sweep the frequency setting as you listen (to sweep, just move the Freq slider to the left and right). Noticing the areas where the annoying or pleasing sounds are located can help you better understand the frequencies that your instrument produces. When you find a frequency to adjust, experiment with the Q setting to find the range that produces the best sound, and then adjust the amount of boost or cut until it has the effect that you want.

After you determine the frequencies that you want to work with, do your EQing to the individual track while the instrument is in the mix (not soloed). You want to make the instrument fit as well as possible with the rest of the instruments, and to do this you need to know how your instrument sounds in relation to all the music going on around it.

Your goal when making adjustments in EQ is to make all the tracks blend together as well as possible. In some instances, you may have to make some radical EQ moves. Don't be afraid to do whatever it takes to make your mix sound good — even if it means having cuts or boosts as great as 12dB.

General EQ guidelines

Although some instruments do call for specific EQ guidelines, you need to think about some general considerations when EQing, regardless of the instrument involved. When it comes to the audible frequency spectrum (about 20 Hz to 20 kHz), certain frequencies have special characteristics. Table 3-1 describes these frequencies.

Table 3-1	EQ Frequency Sound Characteristics
Frequency	*Sound Characteristic*
20–100 Hz	Warms an instrument or adds boominess to it.
100–200 Hz	Is muddy for some instruments but adds fullness to others.
350–450 Hz	Sounds boxy.
750–850 Hz	Adds depth or body.
1–2 kHz	Adds attack or punch to some instruments and creates a nasally sound in others.
2–5 kHz	Increases the presence of instruments.
5–8 kHz	Sounds harsh in some instruments.
8 kHz and above	Adds airiness or brightness to an instrument.

To adjust frequencies via Pro Tool EQ plug-ins, use the Frequency knob to choose the frequency you want to EQ and the Gain knob to control the amount of EQ that you boost (move the knob to the right) or cut (move the knob to the left) from your track.

You're generally better off cutting a frequency than boosting one. This belief goes back to the days of analog EQs, which often added noise when boosting a signal. This can still be a factor with some digital EQs, but the issue is much less. Out of habit, I still try to cut frequencies before I boost them, and I recommend that you do the same (not out of habit, of course, but because if a noise difference exists between cutting and boosting, you might as well avoid it).

The exact frequencies that you end up cutting or boosting depend on three factors: the sound you're after, the tonal characteristic of the instrument, and the relationship between all the instruments in the song. In the following sections, I list a variety of frequencies to cut or boost for each instrument (Table 3-2 shows an overview). If you don't want to follow all the suggestions, choose only the ones that fit with your goals.

The parametric EQ is the type of EQ you use most when trying to get your tracks to fit together. This EQ gives you the greatest control over the range of frequencies you can adjust. The other EQ types (high-shelf, low-shelf, high-pass, low-pass) can often be used successfully for the top or bottom frequencies listed in the sections that follow.

Table 3-2	EQ Recommendations per Instrument		
Instrument	*Frequency*	*Adjustment (dB)*	*Purpose*
Vocals	150 Hz	+2–3	Adds fullness
	200–250 Hz	−2–3	Reduces muddiness
	3 kHz	+2–4	Adds clarity
	5 kHz	+1–2	Adds presence
	7.5–10 kHz	−2–3	Cuts sibilance
	10 kHz	+2–3	Adds air or brightness
Electric guitar	100 Hz	−2–3	Reduces muddiness
	150–250 Hz	+2	Adds warmth
	2.5–4 kHz	+2–3	Adds attack or punch
	5 kHz	+2–3	Adds bite
Acoustic guitar	80 Hz	−3	Reduces muddiness
	150–250 Hz	+2–3	Adds warmth
	800–1000 Hz	−2–3	Reduces boxiness
	3–5 kHz	+2–3	Adds attack or punch
	7 kHz	+2–3	Adds brightness
Bass guitar	100–200 Hz	+1–2	Adds fullness
	200–300 Hz	−3–4	Reduces muddiness
	500–1000 Hz	+2–3	Adds punch
	2.5–5 kHz	+2–3	Adds attack
Kick drum	80–100 Hz	+1–2	Adds body or depth
	400–600 Hz	−3–4	Reduces boxiness

(continued)

Table 3-2 *(continued)*

Instrument	Frequency	Adjustment (dB)	Purpose
	2.5–5 kHz	+1–2	Adds attack
Snare drum	100–150 Hz	+1–2	Adds warmth
	250 Hz	+1–2	Adds depth or body
	800–1000 Hz	−2–3	Reduces boxiness
	3–5 kHz	+1–3	Adds attack
	8–10 kHz	+1–3	Adds crispness
Tom-toms	200–250 Hz	+1–2	Adds depth
	600–1000 Hz	−2–3	Reduces boxiness
	3–5 kHz	+1–2	Adds attack
	5–8 kHz	+1–2	Adds presence
Large tom-toms	40–125 Hz	+1–2	Adds richness
	400–800 Hz	−2–3	Reduces boxiness
	2.5–5 kHz	+2–3	Adds punch or attack
Hi-hats	10+ kHz	+3–4	Adds brightness or sheen
Cymbals	150–200 Hz	−1–2	Reduces rumbling
	1–2 kHz	−3–4	Reduces trashiness
	10+ kHz	+3–4	Adds brightness or sheen
Drum overheads	100–200 Hz	−2–3	Reduces muddiness
	400–1000 Hz	−2–3	Reduces boxiness
High percussion	500– Hz	−6–12	Cuts boxiness
	10+ kHz	+3–4	Adds brightness or sheen
Low percussion	250 Hz and below	−3–4	Reduces muddiness
	2.5–5 kHz	+2–3	Adds attack
	8–10 kHz	+2–3	Adds brightness
Piano	80–150 Hz	+2–3	Adds warmth
	200–400 Hz	−2–3	Reduces muddiness
	2.5–5 kHz	+2–3	Adds punch or attack
Horns	100–200 Hz	+1–2	Adds warmth
	200–800 Hz	−2–3	Reduces muddiness
	2.5–5 kHz	+2–3	Adds punch or attack
	7–9 kHz	+1–2	Adds breath

Equalizing vocals

For the majority of popular music, the vocals are the most important instrument in the song. You need to hear them clearly, and they should contain the character of the singer's voice and style. One of the most common mistakes in mixing vocals is to make them too loud. The next most common mistake is to make them too quiet. (The second mistake most often occurs when a shy or self-conscious vocalist is doing the mixing.) You want the lead vocals to shine through, but you don't want them to overpower the other instruments. The best way to do this is to EQ the vocal tracks so they can sit nicely in the mix and still be heard clearly. The following guidelines can help you do this.

Lead

The lead vocal can go a lot of ways, depending on the singer and the style of music. For the most part, I tend to cut a little around 200 Hz and add a couple dBs at 3 kHz and again at 10 kHz. In general, follow these guidelines:

- ✦ **To add fullness,** add a few dBs at 150 Hz.
- ✦ **To get rid of muddiness,** cut a few dBs at 200–250 Hz.
- ✦ **To add clarity,** boost a little at 3 kHz.
- ✦ **For more presence,** add at 5 kHz.
- ✦ **To add air or to brighten,** boost at 10 kHz.
- ✦ **To get rid of sibilance,** cut a little between 7.5 and 10 kHz.

Backup

To keep backup vocals from competing with lead vocals, cut the backup vocals a little in the low end (below 250 Hz) and at the 2.5–3.5 kHz range. To add clarity, boost a little around 10 kHz without letting it get in the way of the lead vocal.

Equalizing guitar

For the most part, you want to avoid getting a muddy guitar sound and make sure that the guitar attack comes through in the mix.

Electric

Electric guitars often need a little cutting below 100 Hz to get rid of muddiness. A boost between 120 and 250 Hz adds warmth. A boost in the 2.5–4 kHz range brings out the attack of the guitar, and a boost at 5 kHz can add some bite.

Acoustic

Acoustic guitars often do well with a little cut below 80 Hz and again around 800 Hz–1 kHz. If you want a warmer tone and more body, try boosting a little around 150–250 Hz. Also, try adding a few dBs around 3–5 kHz if you want more attack or punch. A few dBs added at 7 kHz can add a little more brightness to the instrument.

Equalizing bass

Bass instruments can get muddy pretty fast. The mud generally happens in the 200–300 Hz range, so I either leave that alone or cut just a little if the bass lacks definition. I rarely add any frequencies below 100 Hz. If the instrument sounds flat or thin, I boost some between 100–200 Hz. Adding a little between 500 Hz–1 kHz can increase the punch, and a boost between 2.5–5 kHz accentuates the attack, adding a little brightness to the bass.

One of the most important things to keep in mind with a bass guitar is to make sure that it and a kick drum can both be heard. You need to adjust the frequencies of these two instruments to make room for both. If you add a frequency to a kick drum, try cutting the same frequency from the bass.

Equalizing drums

The guidelines for EQing drums depend on whether you use live acoustic drums or a drum machine. (A drum machine probably requires less EQ because the sounds were already EQed when they were created.) The type and placement of your mic or mics also affect how you EQ the drums. (You can find out more about mic placement in Book III, Chapter 2.)

Kick

You want a kick drum to blend with the bass guitar. To do this, reduce the frequencies that a bass guitar takes up. For example, if I boost a few dB between 100 and 200 Hz for a bass guitar, I generally cut them in the kick drum (and maybe go as high as 250 Hz). To bring out the bottom end of a kick drum, I sometimes add a couple of dBs between 80 and 100 Hz. A kick drum can get boxy sounding (you know, like a cardboard box), so I often cut a little between 400 and 600 Hz to get rid of the boxiness. To bring out the click from the beater hitting the head, try adding a little between 2.5 and 5 kHz. This increases the attack of the drum and gives it more presence.

Snare

A snare drum drives the music, making it the most important drum in popular music. As such, it needs to really cut through the rest of the instruments. Although the adjustments that you make depend on the pitch and size of the drum and whether you use one mic or two during recording, you can usually boost a little at 100–150 Hz for added warmth. You can also try boosting at 250 Hz to add some depth. If the drum sounds too boxy, try cutting at 800 Hz–1 kHz. A little boost at around 3–5 kHz increases the attack, and an increase in the 8–10 kHz range can add crispness to the drum.

If you use two mics during recording, you might consider dropping a few dBs on the top mic in both the 800 Hz–1 kHz range and the 8–10 kHz range. Allow the bottom mic to create the crispness. I generally use a shelf EQ to roll off the bottom end of the bottom mic below, say, 250–300 Hz. Depending on the music (R&B and pop, for instance), I might use a shelf EQ to add a little sizzle to the bottom mic by boosting frequencies higher than 10 kHz.

For many recording engineers and producers, their snare drum sound is almost a signature. If you listen to different artists' songs from the same producer, you'll likely hear similarities in the snare drum. Don't be afraid to take your time getting the snare drum to sound just right. After all, if you become a famous producer, you'll want people to recognize your distinct sound. And you want it to sound good anyway.

Tom-toms

Tom-toms come in a large range of sizes and pitches. For mounted toms, you can boost a little around 200–250 Hz to add depth to the drum. A boost in the 3–5 kHz range can add more of the sticks' attack. For some additional presence, try adding a little in the 5–8 kHz range. If the drums sound too boxy, try cutting a little in the 600 Hz–1 kHz range.

For floor toms, you can try boosting the frequency range of 40–125 Hz if you want to add some richness and fullness. You might also find that cutting in the 400–800 Hz range can get rid of any boxy sound that the drum may have. To add more attack, boost the 2.5–5 kHz range.

Hi-hats

Most of the time, hi-hats are pretty well represented in the rest of the mics in the drum set. Depending on which mics are picking up the hi-hats, though, you can use a hi-hat mic to bring out their sheen or brightness. To do this, try boosting the frequencies higher than 10 kHz with a shelf EQ. You might also find that cutting frequencies lower than 200 Hz eliminates any rumble created by other drums that a hi-hat mic picks up.

Cymbals

With cymbals, I usually cut anything below 150–200 Hz with a shelf EQ to get rid of any rumbling that these mics pick up. I also drop a few dBs at 1–2 kHz if the cymbals sound kind of trashy or clanky. Adding a shelf EQ higher than 10 kHz can add a nice sheen to the mix.

Overhead mics

If you use overhead mics to pick up both the drums and the cymbals, be careful about cutting too much low end because doing so just sucks the life right out of your drums. Also, if the drums coming through the overhead mics sound boxy or muddy, work with the 100–200 Hz frequencies for the muddiness and 400 Hz–1 kHz frequencies for the boxiness. Depending on your mics, you may also find adding a little between 10kHz and 12kHz can add some sizzle.

Equalizing percussion

High-pitched percussion instruments (shakers, for example) sound good when the higher frequencies are boosted a little bit — say, higher than 10 kHz. This adds some brightness and softness to their sound. You can also roll off many of the lower frequencies, lower than 500 Hz, to eliminate any boxiness that might be present from miking too closely. (See Book III, Chapter 2 for more on mic placement.)

Lower-pitched percussion instruments, such as maracas, can also have the lower frequencies cut a little: Use 250 Hz and lower. Try boosting frequencies between 2.5 and 5 kHz to add more of the instruments' attack. To brighten them up, add a little bit in the 8–10 kHz range.

Equalizing piano

For pianos, you often want to make sure that the instrument has both a nice attack and a warm-bodied tone. You can add attack in the 2.5–5 kHz range, and warmth can be added in the 80–150 Hz range. If your piano sounds boomy or muddy, try cutting a little between 200 and 400 Hz.

Chapter 4: Digging into Dynamics Processors

In This Chapter

✔ Understanding and using effects in Pro Tools

✔ Getting to know compressors and limiters

✔ Introducing gates and expanders

✔ Examining side-chain processing

Dynamics processors allow you to control the dynamic range of a signal. *Dynamic range,* listed in decibels (dB), is the difference between the softest and loudest signals that a sound source produces. The larger the dynamic range, the more variation exists between the softest and loudest notes.

The four types of dynamics processors are compressors, limiters, gates, and expanders. This chapter gives you the lowdown on each type and how they can help you add punch to or smooth out an instrument's sound, even out an erratic performance, or eliminate noise from a track.

Connecting Dynamics Processors

Dynamics processors are Insert effects: When you insert them into a track, they become part of it, affecting the track's entire signal. To apply a dynamics processor in Pro Tools, follow these steps:

1. **Choose View⇨Mix Window⇨Inserts from the main menu.**

   This makes sure that the Inserts section is showing in the Mix window.

2. **Click the top arrow on the left side of the Inserts section of the track's channel strip.**

   The Inserts drop-down menu opens, as shown in Figure 4-1.

3. **Select either the Multi-Channel plug-in or the Multi-Mono plug-in option, depending on whether your track is a stereo (use multichannel) or a mono (use multimono) track.**

4. **Choose Bombfactory BF76, Compressor/Limiter Dyn 3, or Expander/ Gate Dyn 3 option from the Dynamics menu.**

   (I cover the three options in the sections that follow.) The chosen plug-in window opens.

Figure 4-1:
Choose the
Dynamics
processor
plug-in to
insert into
your track.

Introducing Compressors

A *compressor,* um, compresses (narrows) the dynamic range of the sound being affected. The compressor not only limits how loud a note can be but also reduces the difference between the loudest and softest note, thus reducing the dynamic range.

Compressors are used for three main purposes (although other purposes certainly exist as well):

✦ **Keeping *transients* — the initial attack of an instrument — from creating digital distortion during tracking.**

This is common with drums that have a very fast *attack* (initial signal) that can easily overload the recorder (or converters or preamps).

✦ **Evening any performance that shows signs of a high degree of unwanted dynamic variation.**

You do this during either the mixing or tracking stage. Some recorded passages are too loud, and others are too quiet.

✦ **Raising the overall apparent level of the music during mastering.**

For example, listen to a CD recorded before 1995 and then one from the last year or so. The newer CD sounds louder.

I cover the first purpose (the first bullet in the preceding list) in Book III, Chapter 2. Likewise, I explore the third purpose in Book VII, Chapter 2. So that leaves the second purpose to explore with sample settings later in this chapter.

Getting to know compressor parameters

Pro Tools comes with its own compressor plug-in, as I detail in the previous section. The compressor shown in Figure 4-2 is the Compressor/Limiter Dyn 3 plug-in. After you get this guy open, adjust the following parameters:

Figure 4-2:
Use the
Pro Tools
Compressor/
Limiter
plug-in
to adjust
several
parameters
to even out
your sound.

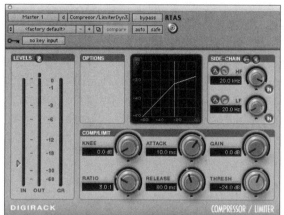

✦ **Knee:** Use the Knee knob to control how the compressor behaves while the input signal passes the threshold. The lower the setting, the more gradual the compressor acts while the signal passes the threshold.

✦ **Attack:** Use the Attack knob to control how soon the compressor kicks in. The attack is defined in milliseconds (ms); the lower the number, the faster the attack.

✦ **Gain:** Use the Gain knob to adjust the *level* (volume) of the signal going out of the compressor. This is listed in decibels (dB). Because adding compression generally reduces the overall level of the sound, you use this control to raise the level back up to where it was when it went in.

✦ **Ratio:** Watch the Ratio setting to see how much the compressor affects the signal. The ratio 2:1, for instance, means that for every decibel the signal goes above the threshold setting, it is reduced by two. In other words, if a signal goes 1dB over the threshold setting, its output from the compressor will be only 0.5 dB louder. With ratios above 10:1, your compressor starts to act like a limiter. (See the later section, "Looking into Limiters.")

✦ **Release:** Use the Release knob to control how long the compressor continues affecting the signal after it drops back below the Threshold setting. Like the attack, the release is defined in milliseconds (ms). The lower the number, the faster the release time.

✦ **Thresh:** The Threshold setting dictates the decibel level at which the compressor starts to act on the signal. This setting is often listed as dB below peak (0 dB). In other words, a setting of –6 dB means that the compressor starts to act when the signal is 6 dB below its calibrated 0 dB mark. In digital systems, 0 dB is the highest level that a signal can go before clipping (distortions due to going over the maximum level possible).

✦ **Levels:** The levels section of the Compressor/Limiter processor has four basic functions:

- **Phase Invert:** This button, located to the right of the Levels title, inverts the phase (reverses the sound wave) of your signal. Click this button to engage and disengage it. It illuminates blue when it's engaged.

- **Input:** This meter shows the level of your signal entering the effect.

- **Output:** This meter shows the level leaving your effect.

- **GR:** GR stands for Gain Reduction. This meter shows you the amount, in decibels, that your input level is attenuated.

Also note the Side-Chain adjustments next to the graphical section of the compressor/limiter window. I cover this in detail later in this chapter in the "Setting Up Side Chains" section.

Getting started using compression

A compressor is one of the most useful — and one of the most abused — pieces of gear in the recording studio. The most difficult part of using compression is that every instrument reacts differently to the same settings. In this section, I offer you some guidelines and ideas for using the compressor effectively.

The following steps show you one good way to get familiar with the compressor. First start by playing your track (hit the Spacebar or play button in the Transport window) and then follow these steps:

1. **Start with a high Ratio setting (between 8:1 and 10:1) and turn the Threshold knob all the way to the right.**

2. **Slowly turn the Threshold knob back to the left, watch the meters, and listen carefully.**

While you reduce the threshold, notice where the meters are when you start hearing a change in the sound of the track. Also notice what happens to the sound when you have the threshold really low and the meters are peaked. (The sound is very different from where you started.)

3. **Slowly turn the Threshold knob back to the right and notice how the sound changes back again.**

After you get used to how the sound changes from adjusting the Threshold setting, try using different Attack and Release settings and do this procedure again. The more you experiment and critically listen to the changes made by the different compressor settings, the better you'll understand how to get the sound that you want. The following guidelines can also help you achieve your desired sound:

✦ **Try to avoid using any compression on a stereo mix while you mix your music.** Compression is a job for the mastering phase of your project. If you compress your stereo tracks during mixdown, you limit what can be done to your music in the mastering stage. This is true even if you master it yourself and think you know what you want during mixdown.

✦ **If you hear noise when you use your compressor, you set it too high.** In effect, you're compressing the loud portions enough to make the level of the softest sections of the music (including any noise) much louder in comparison. To get rid of the noise, decrease the Ratio or the Threshold settings.

✦ **To increase the punch of a track, make sure that the Attack setting isn't too quick.** Otherwise you lose the initial transient and the punch of a track.

✦ **To smooth out a track, use a short Attack setting and a quick Release time.** This evens out the difference in level between the initial transient and the main body of the sound, and results in a smoother sound.

Book VI
Chapter 4

Digging into
Dynamics
Processors

REMEMBER

Less is more when using compression. Resist the temptation to turn those knobs too much to the right, which will just squash your music. On the other hand, if that's the effect you're going for, don't be afraid to experiment.

Using compression

When you first start experimenting with compressor settings, you most likely won't know where to start. To make this process easier for you, here I include some sample settings for a variety of instruments. Start with these and use the guidelines listed in the preceding section to fine-tune your settings.

Compressing vocals

Most recording engineers think that compression is a must for vocals to even out the often-erratic levels that a singer can produce and to tame transient jumps in level that can cause digital distortion. You can indeed use compression on vocals to even out the performance and to create an effect.

If you use a compressor to even out a vocal performance, you don't want to hear the compressor working (this can manifest as distortion or a pumping sound). Instead, you want to catch only the occasional extremely loud transient that would cause clipping.

A good compression setting has three elements:

✦ A fast attack to catch the stray transient.

✦ A quick release so that the compression doesn't color the sound of the singer.

✦ A low ratio so that when the compressor does go on, it smooths the vocals without squashing them.

A typical setting might look like this:

Threshold: –8 dB

Ratio: Between 1.5:1 and 2:1

Attack: <1 ms

Release: About 40 ms

Gain: Adjust so that the output level matches the input level. You don't need to add much gain.

If you want to use a compressor that *pumps* and *breathes* — that is, one that you can really hear working — or if you want to bring the vocals way up front in the mix, try using the following setting. This puts the vocals "in your face," as recording engineers say:

Threshold: –2 dB

Ratio: Between 4:1 and 6:1

Attack: <1 ms

Release: About 40 ms

Gain: Adjust so that the output level matches the input level. You need to add a fair amount of gain at this setting.

As you can see, the two parameters that you adjust most are Threshold and Ratio. Experiment with these settings and check their effects by toggling between the affected and unaffected sound. (Use the Bypass button in the plug-in window.) Watch the levels going to disk — make sure that they don't peak over –6 dB or –4 dB. This ensures a *hot* signal — one that is loud — and also leaves you some *headroom* (a few decibels below clipping) for when you mixdown. (Find more on this in Chapter 7 in this mini-book.)

Compressing electric guitars

Generally (these days, at least), the signal from an electric guitar gets run through a compressor and other external effects before it's even recorded. You don't need additional compression when you track the guitar unless you use a *clean* (undistorted) setting on your guitar. If you do want to use a little compression to bring the guitar forward and give it some punch, try these settings:

Threshold: –1 dB

Ratio: Between 2:1 and 3:1

Attack: 25 ms to 30 ms

Release: About 200 ms

Gain: Adjust so that the output level matches the input level. You don't need to add much gain.

The slow attack is what allows the guitar to have a bit of punch to it. If you want less punchiness, shorten the attack slightly. Be careful though because if you shorten it too much, you end up with a *mushy* sound. (Ahem . . . we're not talking romance here. I mean the guitar has no definition.)

Compressing electric basses

Another way to get a handle on the potential muddiness of the amplified bass guitar is to use a little compression. Compression can also help control any uneven levels that result from overzealous or inexperienced bass players. Try these settings for a start:

Threshold: –4 dB

Ratio: Between 2.5:1 and 3:1

Attack: Between 40 ms and 50 ms

Release: About 180 ms

Gain: Adjust so that the output level matches the input level. You don't need to add much gain.

Compressing acoustic instruments

You don't generally need a lot of compression on acoustic instruments, especially if you want a natural sound. You can use the compressor to even out the resonance of the instrument, which keeps the main character of the instrument from getting lost in a mix and also avoids a muddy sound. Here's a good setting for strummed or picked acoustic instruments:

Threshold: –6 dB

Ratio: Between 3:1 and 4:1

Attack: About 150 ms

Release: About 400 ms

Gain: Adjust so that the output level matches the input level. You don't need to add much gain.

Release is set very high because of the amount of sustain that these acoustic instruments can have. If you play an instrument with less sustain, such as a banjo, you may find that a shorter attack and release work just fine. In this case, you can try the following settings:

Threshold: –6 dB

Ratio: Between 2.5:1 and 3:1

Attack: Between 40 ms and 50 ms

Release: About 180 ms

Gain: Adjust so that the output level matches the input level. You don't need to add much gain, if any.

Compressing kick drums

A kick drum responds quite well to a compressor when tracking. For the most part, you can get by with settings that tame the boom a little and allow the initial attack to get through. A sample setting looks like this:

Threshold: –6 dB

Ratio: Between 4:1 and 6:1

Attack: Between 40 ms and 50 ms

Release: Between 200 ms and 300 ms

Gain: Adjust so that the output level matches the input level. You don't need to add much gain.

Compressing snare drums

Adding compression to the snare drum is crucial if you want a tight, punchy sound. You can go a lot of ways with the snare. The following settings are common and versatile:

Threshold: –4 dB

Ratio: Between 4:1 and 6:1

Attack: Between 5 ms and 10 ms

Release: Between 125 ms and 175 ms

Gain: Adjust so that the output level matches the input level. You don't need to add much gain.

Compressing percussion

Because percussion instruments have high sound levels and are prone to extreme transients, I like to use a little compression just to control the levels going to disk. Here's a good starting point:

Threshold: –10 dB

Ratio: Between 3:1 and 6:1

Attack: Between 10 ms and 20 ms

Release: About 50 ms

Gain: Adjust so that the output level matches the input level. You need to add a bit of gain.

Looking into Limiters

A *limiter* is basically a compressor on steroids. Rather than simply reducing a signal that crosses over the threshold setting, limiters put a ceiling on the highest level of a sound source. Any signal above the threshold is chopped off rather than just compressed. Using a limiter is great for raising the overall level of an instrument as well as for keeping transients from eating up all the *headroom* (maximum level) of a track.

Using the compressor/limiter in Pro Tools gives you more control than using a basic limiter in that you can adjust the ratio to be a little more subtle than just chopping off a signal.

Understanding limiter settings

Pro Tools comes with the Compressor/Limiter plug-in (that I cover earlier in this chapter) as well as the Bombfactory BF76 peak limiter, as shown in Figure 4-3. (You might have more plug-ins available if you own one of the bundle packs available from Avid.) You insert this plug-in into a track by following the procedures listed in the "Connecting Dynamics Processors" section at the beginning of this chapter.

Figure 4-3:
The Bombfactory BF76 peak limiter plug-in limits the maximum level of the signal passing through it.

The Bombfactory limiter contains the following parameters:

✦ **Input:** Use the Input dial to control the *threshold level* (when the limiter kicks in) as well as how much reduction the limiter applies to your signal. If you have the Gain Reduction (GR) option selected for the meter display (see its upcoming bullet), you can see how the dial relates to your gain reduction and make adjustments accordingly.

✦ **Output:** This is the same as Gain in most compressors. Use this dial to adjust the level (volume) of the signal going out of the compressor. You use this dial to raise the level back to where it was when it went in.

✦ **Attack:** Use the Attack dial to control how soon the limiter kicks in. With the Bombfactory peak limiter, the dial doesn't list your setting in milliseconds. This goes back to the inspiration for this plug-in (the classic 1176 compressor made in the 1970s), but the real-world numbers for this dial are from 0.4 ms to 5.7 ms, with the shorter attack when the dial is to the left, and the longer attack times as you turn the dial to the right.

✦ **Release:** Use the Release knob to control how long the limiter continues limiting the signal after it drops back below the threshold setting. Like with Attack, the Bombfactory BF76 uses arbitrary numbers on its Release dial. The real numbers for this setting range from 0.06 ms to 1.1 seconds. Faster release times are achieved when the dial is to the left; conversely, turning the dial to the right lengthens the release time.

✦ **Ratio:** Use the Ratio setting to show how much the compressor affects the signal. The ratio — 2:1, for instance — means that for every decibel the signal goes above the threshold setting, it is reduced by two. In other words, if a signal goes 1 dB higher than the threshold setting, its output from the compressor will be only 0.5 dB louder.

✦ **Meter:** You have the option to select how you want the meter to work. The Bombfactory peak limiter offers you four options (which you choose by clicking the appropriate button):

- *GR (Gain Reduction):* In this case, the meter shows you how many decibels your signal is being reduced when the limiter kicks in. This is the meter setting used most often.

- *–18:* This option shows you the level of your output signal, calibrated such that when the needle hits 0VU (Volume Units) your level is at –18 dB full-scale. Both this and the following option (–24) are used by people who want a certain amount of headroom (additional signal level higher than 0) on their meters or have other equipment that relies on either the –18 or –24 standard. The one you choose depends on how much headroom you want.

- *–24:* This option shows you the level of your output signal, calibrated such that when the needle hits 0VU (Volume Units) your level is actually at –24 dB full-scale.

- *Off:* This turns off the meter. This is a good option if you find yourself relying too much on "seeing" what your limiter is doing and too little on actually *listening* to your music as you make your adjustments.

Setting limits with the BF76 limiter

The Bombfactory BF76 peak limiter is essentially a compressor on steroids that's designed to impart a certain sound to your music. Using the default settings as a starting point gives you an idea of what this sound is supposed to be. Selecting an 8:1 ratio offers a good quick mix compression to give your songs a bit of life. Shortening the attack and/or release times adds more distortion to your signal. I caution from using too much of this limiter. When used judiciously, though, the BF76 can spice up your tracks a bit.

The BF76 plug-in is not the only limiter you might want to use on your music. In addition, some of the reasons for using it are different than for other limiters. When using any limiter, keep in mind these two tips to achieve the best results:

✦ **When using limiters to raise the volume of a track or mix, limit only 2 dB or 3 dB at a time.** This way, the limiter doesn't alter the sound of your signal but just reduces the highest peaks and raises the volume.

✦ **To add grunge (distortion) to a track, lower the Threshold setting so that you limit the signal 6 to 12 dB.** Tweak the Attack and Release parameters to get the sound you're after. This creates distortion that might work for a particular track, such as a snare drum.

Introducing Gates and Expanders

A *gate* is basically the opposite of a limiter: Rather than limiting how loud a note can get, a gate limits how soft a note can get. A gate filters out any sound below the threshold and allows any note above it to be passed through unaffected.

An expander is to a gate what a compressor is to a limiter. Instead of reducing the volume of notes below the set threshold by a specified amount, an *expander* reduces them by a ratio. In other words, with a gate, you set a certain decibel amount by which a signal is reduced. With an expander, you reduce the signal by setting a ratio. The ratio changes the signal gradually, making the affected signals sound more natural.

Use an expander when you want to subtly reduce noise from a track rather than just filtering it out completely. A classic example is when you deal with breath from a singer. If you use a gate, you get an unnatural-sounding track because the breaths are filtered out completely. With the expander, you can set it to reduce the breath just enough so that it's less noticeable, but you can leave a little of the sound in to make the singer sound normal. (I mean, everyone has to breathe, right?)

Gates, on the other hand, are useful for completely filtering any unwanted noise in a recording environment. A classic situation for using gates is when you record drums. You can set the gate to filter any sound (other drums, for instance) except for the sounds resulting from the hits to the particular drum that you miked.

Getting to know gate parameters

You can see the expander/gate plug-in that ships with Pro Tools in Figure 4-4. The various settings that you get to play with are similar to the ones for compressors and limiters, as the following list makes clear:

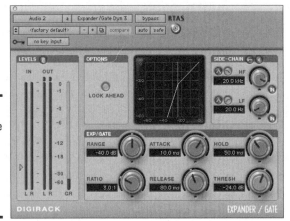

Figure 4-4:
Use the gate plug-in to filter noise below a certain level.

+ **Range:** The Range setting is similar to the Ratio setting on the compressor except that you choose the decibel amount by which the gate *attenuates* (reduces) the signal. For example, a setting of 40 dB drops any signal below the Threshold setting by 40 decibels.

+ **Attack:** Like with the compressor and limiter, use the Attack knob to set the rate at which the gate opens (in milliseconds). Fast attacks work well for instruments with, well, fast attacks, such as drums. Slow attacks are better suited for instruments with slow attacks, such as vocals.

+ **Hold:** Use the Hold setting to control how much time the gate stays open after the signal drops below the threshold. When the hold time is reached, the gate closes abruptly. This parameter is listed in milliseconds. The Hold parameter allows you to get the gated drum sound that was so popular in the 1980s. (Phil Collins, anyone?)

+ **Ratio:** The ratio dictates how much the signal is attenuated by the expander. When using a ratio of 2:1, for instance, the expander reduces any signal below the threshold by two times. In this case, a signal that is 10 dB below the threshold is reduced to 20 dB below it; likewise, a signal that's 2 dB below the threshold is reduced to 4 dB below it. Setting a ratio of 30:1 or greater turns the expander/gate effect to a gate. So, instead of lowering the levels of an effected signal, the signal is simply cut off.

✦ **Release:** Use the Release knob to control how long the gate is open after the signal drops back below the threshold setting. You can choose values between 5 ms and 4 seconds. Faster release times are achieved when the dial is to the left; conversely, turning the dial to the right lengthens the release time.

✦ **Thresh:** Use the Threshold knob to set the level (in decibels) at which the gate *opens* (stops filtering the signal). The gate allows all signals above the Threshold setting to pass through unaffected, whereas any signals below the Threshold setting are reduced by the amount set by the Range control.

✦ **Options: Look Ahead:** Enabling this button (click it to turn it blue) turns on the Look Ahead function for the Expander/Gate. This essentially means that the Expander/Gate will engage 2 ms before the sound actually crosses the threshold value. This keeps you from losing the initial transient of an instrument, such as for drums.

✦ **Levels:** The levels section of the Expander/Gate processor has four basic functions:

- **Phase Invert:** This button, located to the right of the Levels title, inverts the phase (reverses the sound wave) of your signal. Click this button to engage and disengage it. It illuminates blue when it's engaged.

- **Input:** This meter shows the level of your signal entering the effect.

- **Output:** This meter shows the level leaving your effect.

- **GR:** GR stands for Gain Reduction. This meter shows you the amount, in decibels, that your input level is attenuated.

✦ **Side Chain:** This section lets you insert a side-chain into the effect. I detail this in the "Setting Up Side Chains" section, later in this chapter.

Getting started using gates

Noise gates can be extremely useful for getting rid of unwanted noise. The most common use for a gate is to eliminate bleeding from drum mics. For example, you may get bleed from your snare drum into your tom-toms mics. When using noise gates, keep the following in mind:

✦ **When the threshold is reached, the gate allows the signal through.** If your background noise is high enough, when the gate opens, you still hear not only the intended sound but the background noise as well.

✦ **When gating drums, be sure to set the attack very fast.** Otherwise, the initial transient is lost, and you end up with mushy-sounding drums. You can also engage the look-ahead option to ensure that the transients are lost.

✦ **When setting the release time of the gate, adjust it until it sounds natural and doesn't clip off the end of your instrument's sound.**

✦ **Set the range just high enough to mask any unwanted noise.** If you set it too high, the sound becomes unnatural because the natural resonance of the instrument may be filtered out.

Getting started using an expander

Because the expander works much like a gate, you can use the same basic starting points. Choose between a gate and an expander based on the type of overall attenuation that you want of the signal. For example, the expander is a good choice if you have an instrument that contains sounds that are too loud but you don't want to get rid of them completely — you just want to reduce them a little.

Adjusting for a vocalist's breath is the perfect situation for using an expander rather than a gate. In this case, you can set the expander's threshold just below the singer's softest note and start with a low ratio (1.5:1 or 2:1, for instance). See whether the breathiness improves. If it doesn't, slowly move the Ratio knob until you get the effect that you want.

Be careful not to overdo it, though. If the breath is too quiet compared with the vocal, the vocal sounds unnatural.

Detailing the De-Esser

The De-Esser plug-in is handy for getting rid of the annoying *s* sounds in a vocal track (often referred to as *sibilance*). You can also use it to get rid of any high-frequency sounds, such as the whistles or the wind across a flute. You'll find the Pro Tools De-Esser (as shown in Figure 4-5) in the Dynamics listing with the plug-in menu.

Figure 4-5: Use the De-Esser plug to get rid of unwanted sibilance.

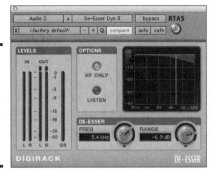

The De-Esser plug-in is simple to use, with only four basic parameters to adjust:

+ **Freq:** Use the Frequency parameter to select the frequency range affected by the De-Esser. You'll usually set this between around 4 kHz and 12 kHz.

+ **Range:** Use this knob to choose the frequency that the De-Esser is being applied to. Select a range that hits the highest note of the sibilance but not all the *s* sounds. You'll have to use your ears to assess what sounds natural.

+ **HF Only:** Engaging this parameter applies the De-Esser to the frequency you set with the Frequency dial. Not selecting it applies the De-Esser evenly across the frequency spectrum. For most De-Essing tasks, I choose to have this feature enabled.

+ **Listen:** Enabling this option lets you hear the effect that the De-Esser has on your audio signal. You want to use this to hear where the sibilance is and to help you fine-tune your settings. I generally enable this feature when I'm looking for the frequency of the sibilance.

+ **Graph:** The graph shows you where the De-Esser is working, including how much gain reduction you're getting and where this reduction fits in the frequency spectrum. Try to avoid putting too much weight on the graph and use your ears instead.

+ **Levels:** The levels section of the De-Esser processor has three basic functions:

  • **Input:** This meter shows the level of your signal entering the effect.

  • **Output:** This meter shows the level leaving your effect.

  • **GR:** GR stands for Gain Reduction. This meter shows you the amount, in decibels, that your input level is attenuated by the effect.

Book VI
Chapter 4

Digging into
Dynamics
Processors

Here's how to use the De-Esser:

1. **Insert De-Esser into your offending track after the compressor or limiter (if you're using one). Do this by clicking on the Insert drop-down menu for your track and choosing Plug-in⇨Dynamics⇨De-Esser for a mono track. For a stereo track, choose Multi-mono or Multi-channel plug-in⇨Dynamics⇨De-Esser.**

2. **Adjust the frequency to the point where the offending *s* sound is located.**

3. **Dial the range in until the *s* sound falls back far enough in the track to sound natural.**

You don't want to eliminate sibilance altogether, or your vocal will lack presence and begin to sound muddy (unclear).

Setting Up Side Chains

Using a *side chain* means that the signal from another track (through one of the buses) or from one of your interface inputs triggers your dynamics processor into action. The signal that you choose to do the triggering is the *key input.* Side chains are great for making tracks fit better in a dense mix or letting a kick drum be heard when it plays at the same time as the bass guitar. Not sure how to do this? Don't worry, I provide some examples in the following sections.

Setting up a side chain

Setting up a side chain in one of Pro Tool's dynamics processors is easy with the following steps:

1. **Click to open the Key Input drop-down menu, located next to the little key icon at the top of the plug-in window.**

2. **From the drop-down menu, choose the interface input or bus that has the signal that you want to use to trigger the dynamics processor.**

   This routes the signal from that input or bus to the processor.

3. **Click the External Key button to engage the side chain.**

   The External Key button is located in the Side Chain section on the right side of the various plug-in windows. (Refer to Figure 4-2.)

4. **Click the Key Listen button — located to the right of the External Key button — to hear the signal coming through your selected key input.**

5. **Play your session and adjust the processor's parameters until you get the sound that you want.**

The Side Chain section of Pro Tools Dynamics III plug-ins gives you the ability to use high-frequency (HF) and low-frequency (LF) filters within the plug-in. This can be handy for keying into certain frequencies, thus making the side chain more sensitive to certain frequencies. This section offers two options:

✦ **HF (High Frequency):** Turn on this filter by clicking the In button to the right of the top frequency dial in the Side Chain section of the plug-in. You can control the following parameters:

   • *Band-Pass Filter:* Engaging this filter (click it with your mouse; it will glow blue) is similar to using a parametric EQ. (Chapter 3 in this mini-book has more on parametric EQs.) Whatever frequency you select with the HF Frequency Control button (see the following bullet) is the center of the filter. Frequencies on either side of this drop off at a rate of 12 dB per octave.

- *Low-Pass Filter:* Engaging this filter is the same as using a low-pass filter in one of your EQs. (Chapter 3 in this mini-book has more on low-pass filters.) Your selected frequency is the beginning of the low-pass filter, and all frequencies above this number are attenuated (reduced) by 12 dB per octave.

- *HF Frequency Control:* Use this dial to choose from frequencies between 80 Hz and 20 kHz. Turning to the right increases the frequency, and turning to the left decreases it.

✦ **LF (Low Frequency):** Turn on this filter by clicking the In button, next to the bottom dial in the Side Chain section of the plug-in. You have three options to select from with this filter. These are:

- *Band-Pass Filter:* Engaging this filter (click it with your mouse; it will glow blue) is similar to using a parametric EQ. (Chapter 3 in this mini-book has more on parametric EQs.) Whatever frequency you select with the LF Frequency Control button (see the following bullet) is the center of the filter. Frequencies on either side of this drop off at a rate of 12 dB per octave.

- *High-Pass Filter:* Engaging this filter is the same as using a high-pass filter in one of your EQs. (Chapter 3 in this mini-book has more on high-pass filters.) Your selected frequency is the beginning of the high-pass filter, and all frequencies higher than this number are attenuated (reduced) by 12 dB per octave.

- *LF Frequency Control:* Use this dial to choose from frequencies between 25 Hz and 4 kHz. Turning to the right increases the frequency, and turning to the left decreases it.

Using a side chain

The uses for side chains are numerous, and only your creativity limits how you end up using a side chain. The most common use for a side chain is to create more room for your instruments in the mix. This is done by EQing the Key Input signal and then letting that EQed signal trigger a compressor or limiter.

To make room for a vocal in a dense mix, follow these steps:

1. **Route all your instruments in the mix (except the vocal) to bus 15 and 16.**

2. **Insert the compressor plug-in in this bus and set the Key Input to bus 14.**

3. **Make a copy of your vocal tracks and assign their outputs to bus 14.**

4. **Shift the copied vocal tracks ahead (to the right) a few milliseconds.**

5. **Adjust the settings on the compressor so that the volume of the instruments drops slightly whenever the vocals come in.**

   For a starting point, use the smooth vocal compressor setting that I mention in the "Compressing vocals" section, earlier in this chapter.

You can also use a special trick to make the bass guitar drop slightly in the mix whenever the kick drum is played. Follow these steps:

1. **Insert the compressor plug-in into the bass guitar track and set the Key Input to bus 16.**

2. **Make a copy of the kick drum track and set the output for the copied track to bus 16.**

   The kick signal triggers the compressor that's assigned to the bass guitar track.

3. **Use fast Attack and Release settings on the compressor.**

   You want the compressor to activate only when the initial strike of the kick drum happens. The bass guitar drops in volume when the kick drum plays. This means that the kick drum creates the attack, and the bass guitar produces the sustain.

This trick works really well for music that has a kick drum and bass guitar that play similar patterns.

Chapter 5: Singling Out Signal Processors

In This Chapter

✔ **Understanding and using effects in Pro Tools**

✔ **Getting to know reverb**

✔ **Introducing delays**

✔ **Examining offline effects processing**

*U*nless you record your songs using a live band in a perfect acoustic environment, your music will sound a little flat without the addition of some type of effects. Effects allow you to make your music sound like you recorded it in just about any environment possible. You can make your drums sound as if they were recorded in a cathedral or your vocals sound as if you were singing underwater. Effects can also make you sound "better" than the real you. For example, you can add harmony parts to your lead or backup vocals, or you can make your guitar sound like you played it through any number of great amplifiers.

In this chapter, you discover many of the most common effects processors used in recording studios. (*Signal processors* are the neat software plug-ins behind all the effects you can achieve in your Pro Tools studio.) You discern the difference between insert (that is, line) effects and send/return effects. You also get a chance to explore ways of using these processors, with recommendations for using reverb, delay, and chorus. To top it off, you get a glimpse into offline effects processing such as pitch-shifting.

The best way to learn how to use effects on your music is to experiment. The more you play around with the different settings, the more familiar you become with how each effect operates. Then you can get creative and come up with the best ways to use effects for your music.

The Effects Bypass button in the Pro Tools effects-processor plug-in window is your friend. With a click of the Bypass button, you can quickly turn off any effect in use with your signal. Use this button to check your effect settings against your original signal. Sometimes you'll like the original sound better.

Routing Your Effects

Effects processors can be used as either send/return or insert effects. In both cases, you can work with the *dry* (unaffected) signal and the *wet* (affected) signals separately. If you use the effect in a send/return routing, you can adjust the wet and dry signals with two track faders: Aux Send (opened by clicking the effect's name in the Send list) and Auxiliary. If you use the effect in a line configuration, the plug-in window displays a Mix parameter where you can adjust the wet/dry balance.

You choose whether to insert an effect in a track or to use the Send function based upon what you intend to do. For example, if you *insert* the effect into a track (as described in the next section), that effect only alters the signal that exists on the track it's inserted into. On the other hand, using an *effect send* for your effect allows you to route more than one track through that effect. (You can adjust the individual levels going to the send at each track so you still have control over how much effect is applied to each track going to the send.)

In addition, inserting an effect always puts the effect before the fader in the track (pre-fader); if you use a send, you can choose whether the effect does its magic before (pre-fader) or after (post-fader) signal enters the fader that controls the track's output. If you use a send to apply the effect to more than one track at a time, you also reduce the amount of processing power the effect has to use. (Inserting the same effect into each track you want to alter ends up using more processing power.)

Inserting effects

If you want to use an effect on only one specific track, you can insert it into the track by using the Insert function. To insert an effect in Pro Tools, follow these steps:

1. **Make sure that the Inserts section is showing in the Mix window by choosing View⇨Mix Window⇨Inserts from the main menu.**

2. **Click the top arrow on the left side of the Inserts section of the track's channel strip.**

   The Insert drop-down menu appears, as shown in Figure 5-1.

3. **If your track is a stereo track, select either the Multi-Channel Plug-In or Multi-Mono Plug-In option.**

   If your track is mono, you don't have a choice here. You're stuck using a mono plug-in.

4. **Choose your desired plug-in — D-Verb, Slap Delay, Long Delay, whatever — from the menu.**

The plug-in window opens. Here you can set your parameters. (My professional advice on what settings to actually tweak comes later in this chapter, when I cover the individual effects.)

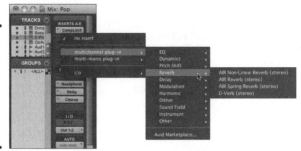

Figure 5-1:
The Insert menu opens when you click the Insert input selector.

Sending signals to effects

Sometimes you want to route a bunch of tracks to a single effect (in the case of reverbs, for instance). In this case, you follow these steps:

1. **Select one of the buses from the Send selector in each track that you want to route to the effect.**

The Send Output window appears, as shown in Figure 5-2. The window contains a handy channel strip for controlling the signal being sent to the selected bus.

Figure 5-2:
Use the Send Output window to control the signal going to the effect.

2. **Choose Track⇨New from the main menu.**

   The New Tracks dialog box appears.

3. **Use the drop-down menus to enter the number of tracks you want (1), the type (Auxiliary Input), and whether you want your track in mono or stereo.**

4. **From the Input selector drop-down menu, choose the bus you used for the send of the tracks in Step 1 as the input for this auxiliary track.**

5. **Choose one of the effects plug-ins from the Inserts drop-down menu and insert it into this auxiliary track.**

   The Effect plug-in window opens.

   The previous section, "Inserting effects," gives you the gory details on inserting effects.

6. **Adjust the effect settings to get the sound you want.**

Chapter 2 in this mini-book further details plug-ins and how to route signals through your system to them.

Rolling Out the Reverb

Reverb is undoubtedly the most commonly used effects processor. *Reverb,* the natural characteristic of any enclosed room, results from sound waves bouncing off walls, a floor, and a ceiling. A small room produces reflections that start quickly and end soon; in larger rooms, halls, or cathedrals, the sound has farther to travel, so you get slower start times and a longer-lasting reverberation.

This room effect enables you to place your track closer to the imaginary "front" or "back" of the mix. You do this by varying how much of the affected signal you include with the unaffected one. For example, mixing a lot of reverb with the dry (unaffected) signal gives the impression of being farther away, so your instrument sounds like it's farther back in the mix.

Seeing reverb settings

You can adjust several parameters when you use reverb, which gives you a lot of flexibility. Figure 5-3, which shows the Reverb plug-in that comes with Pro Tools, gives you a peek at the parameters you can play with.

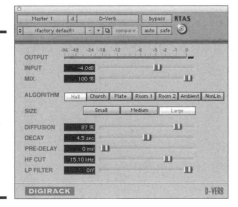

Figure 5-3:
Reverb
can add
ambience
to your
instrument,
giving it
a more
realistic
sound.

The following list explains how the parameters — most, but not all, visible in Figure 5-3 — affect the sound of the reverb:

✦ **Algorithm:** This setting lets you choose the type of room that the reverb sounds like. You have the option of a hall, church, *plate* (a type of reverb that uses a metal plate to create its sound), two different rooms, *ambient* (natural room sound), and *nonlinear* (less natural) sound. Each choice also sets the other parameters for the reverb, but you can adjust those as you like to give your reverb a distinct sound.

✦ **Size:** This option refers to the "room" choices you have in the Algorithm setting. You have three settings to choose from: Small, Medium, and Large. Clicking one of these options adjusts the rest of the parameters in the window, except for the Algorithm setting.

✦ **Diffusion:** Diffusion affects the density of the reflections in the "room" you chose. A higher diffusion setting results in a thicker sound. Think of the diffusion parameter as a way to simulate how reflective the room is. More reflective rooms produce a much higher diffusion. To simulate a less reflective room, use lower-diffusion settings.

✦ **Decay:** *Decay* is the length of time that the reverb lasts. Larger or more reflective rooms produce a longer decay.

✦ **Pre-delay:** A sound reaches your ears before the sound's reverb does, and *predelay* is the amount of time from the sound's beginning and the start of the reverb, which is described in milliseconds (ms). Because reverb is made up of reflections of sound within a room, the sound takes time to bounce around the room and reach your ears. By then, you've already heard the sound because it came directly to you. Predelay helps to define the initial sound signal by separating it from the reverb. This parameter is essential in making your reverb sound natural.

A small room has a shorter predelay than a large room.

+ **HF Cut:** This setting allows you to control the rate at which the high frequencies decay. Most of the time the high frequencies decay faster, so being able to control this effect can result in a more natural sounding reverb.

+ **LP Filter:** This filter controls the level of the high frequencies within the reverb. Setting this frequency gives the impression of a *darker* (lower-frequency setting) or *brighter* (higher-frequency setting) room.

Getting started using reverb

Reverb is like garlic: The more you use, the less you can taste it. Just as a new chef puts garlic in everything (and lots of it), many budding engineers make the same mistake with reverb. Go easy. Always remember that less is more.

Here are some other things to keep in mind:

+ **Mixes often sound better when you use reverb on only a few instruments instead of them all.** For example, it's not uncommon for just the snare drum of the drumset to have reverb on it. The rest of the drums and cymbals remain dry (unaffected).

+ **Try using reverb to "glue" instruments together.** Routing all your drum tracks to the same reverb, for instance, can make them sound like they were all recorded in the same room. When doing this, make sure that you adjust the Send level for each instrument so that the effect sounds natural. Also, use less reverb for all the instruments than you would for just one. This keeps the sound from becoming muddy from using too much reverb.

+ **Think about how you want each instrument to sit in the mix when you choose reverb.** Make sure that the type and amount of reverb fits the song and the rest of the instruments.

+ **Try putting the dry (unaffected) sound on one side of the stereo field and the reverb on the other.** For example, if you have a rhythm guitar part that you set at 30 degrees off to the right of the stereo field, set the reverb 30 degrees off to the left. This can be a nice effect.

+ **To keep the vocals up front in the mix, use a short reverb setting.** A vocal plate is a great choice because the decay is fast. This adds a fair amount of the reverb to the vocal without making it sit way back in the mix.

+ **Experiment with room types, sizes, and decay times.** Sometimes, a long decay on a small room reverb sounds better than a short decay on a large room or hall reverb.

Detailing Delay

Along with reverb, delay is a natural part of sound bouncing around a room. When you speak (or sing or play) into a room, you often hear not only reverb but also a distinct echo. This echo may be short or long, depending on the size of the room. The original sound may bounce back to you as a single echo or as multiple, progressively quieter delays.

Digging into delay settings

At your disposal are several types of delay effects, including a slap-back echo, tape delay, and multiple delays. Each is designed to add dimension to your instrument. To create these various effects, you adjust several parameters, as the following list and Figure 5-4 make clear. The Delay plug-ins that come with Pro Tools are pretty much the same. (Okay, the default setting for each is different, but that's a pretty minor thing.) The parameters that you can adjust include the following:

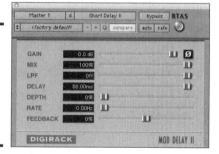

Figure 5-4:
A Delay plug-in allows you to create various echoes.

+ **Gain:** This lets you set the signal level going into the delay.

+ **Mix:** This parameter controls the output level of the effect. The higher you set this parameter, the louder the delayed signal is relative to the original signal.

+ **LPF:** The Low Pass filter (LPF) lets you filter some of the high frequencies from the delay.

+ **Delay:** This parameter controls the amount of time between the initial signal and the repeated sound. The time is listed in milliseconds and can be as short as a few milliseconds or as long as several seconds.

+ **Depth:** This parameter lets you add modulation to the delay so that you can create a chorus effect. (See the "Creating Chorus Effects" section, later in this chapter, for more on chorus and flange effects.) The higher the level on this setting, the greater the modulation.

✦ **Rate:** This setting lets you set the amount of time that the modulation takes to cycle.

✦ **Feedback:** The Feedback parameter controls how many times the echo repeats. A low setting makes the echo happen just once, and higher settings produce more echoes.

Some of the Delay plug-ins in Pro Tools also allow you to set the delay to the tempo of your song. The following list covers these settings:

✦ **Tempo Match:** This option allows you to set the delay to beat in time with the music. The Tempo Match feature is referenced to the tempo map that you set for the song. You can set this parameter to any note division, from sixteenth notes to whole notes, if you want the delays to keep time with your song. (Quarter- and eighth-note delays are the most commonly used note divisions.)

✦ **Meter:** This lets you set the meter of the song and the subdivision that you want the delay to follow. When you change this parameter, the Delay parameter moves, too.

✦ **Groove:** Use this parameter to adjust the rate of the delay in relation to the tempo and subdivision you chose. By changing this setting, you alter the delay (by percentages) away from the strict tempo and subdivision settings. This can be useful if you're adjusting the exact delay that you want. When you adjust this parameter, the Delay setting changes as well.

Getting started using delay

Delay is used a lot in contemporary music, and often you don't hear it unless you listen carefully. Other times, it's prominent in the mix (for example, the snare drum in some reggae music). Here are ways you can use delay in your music:

✦ **One of the most effective ways to use delay is as a slap-back echo on vocals.** A *slap-back echo* consists of one to three repeats spaced very closely together, which fattens the sound of the vocals. You generally want to set your time parameter between 90 and 120 ms. Set the level so you barely hear the first echo when your vocal is in the mix and adjust it from there until you like the sound. In pop music, a slap-back echo and a vocal plate reverb are commonly used on lead vocals. (It was *really* common in the 1950s, and shows up a lot — less subtly — in rockabilly.) The Slap Delay plug-in in Pro Tools is a good place to start, although the default setting has a longer delay time than I recommend.

✦ **Use the Tempo Match feature to have your delay echo in time with the music.** This can add some depth to the mix without creating a muddy or cluttered sound. Be careful because if you use this too much, it can make your music sound annoyingly repetitive.

Creating Chorus Effects

Chorus takes the original sound and creates a copy that is very slightly out of tune with the original and varies over time. This variance is *modulation,* and the result is an effect that can add interest and variety to an instrument. Chorus is used quite extensively to add fullness to an instrument, particularly guitars and vocals. Pro Tools doesn't come with a Chorus plug-in per se, but all Delay plug-ins can produce chorusing effects by adjusting the Depth and Rate parameters. (Check out the "Detailing Delay" section, earlier in this chapter, for more on delays.)

If reverb is like garlic, then chorus is like cayenne pepper. You may get away with a little too much garlic in your food without too much trouble, but if you add too much cayenne, you run the risk of making your food inedible. Such is the case with the chorus effect. Used sparingly, it can add a lot to your music; overdone, it can wreak havoc on a good song.

**Book VI
Chapter 5**

Singling Out Signal Processors

Try the following tips for making the best use of chorus effects:

+ To fill out a vocal track, try setting the rate at 2 Hz, the depth at about 20 to 30, and the delay at 10 to 20 ms. Keep the Feedback level low.

+ Use a chorus on backup vocals to make them much fuller and allow you to use fewer tracks.

+ Pan the chorus to one side of the mix and the dry (unaffected) signal to the other. This can be especially interesting on guitars and synthesizer patches.

Chapter 6: Automating Your Mix

In This Chapter

✔ **Understanding automation**

✔ **Writing automation**

✔ **Editing automation**

✔ **Playing automated tracks**

*Y*ou likely won't have a session without a single change in level, pan, EQ, or plug-in parameters somewhere in the song. Unless you have an external mixer or control surface, you're stuck making these changes with your mouse. The problem with all this mouse-intensive work is that you can't move more than one fader, panning knob, or plug-in setting at a time. To be honest, the only way you can really mix within Pro Tools is by using some kind of automation feature, which Pro Tools just happens to have in spades. In fact, Pro Tools has a quite powerful automation engine that allows you to control a variety of mix parameters.

Don't like how the guitar in the second verse sits in the mix? No problem. Just fix your automation data and mix it again. You can even save multiple versions of these settings so you can create as many mixes as you want. (Be careful here, though: When asked, most mix engineers say that they finish a mix only when they run out of time or money to keep trying things.)

This chapter gets you going on mixing the newfangled way: automatically. Well, not exactly *automatically* — you still need to program these mixing settings, but I show you how to do that. In this chapter, I lead you through automating the various aspects of your song — volume levels, mute and panning placement, EQ, and plug-in settings. In addition, you discover how to change your automation settings and also how to play the automation data back so you're ready to do your final mix.

Understanding Automation

You can automate a variety of parameters in Pro Tools. Each parameter has a playlist that contains its automation data. You can write this data one parameter (or more) at a time, and you can display and edit the data even while playing the session. This section describes the parameters you can automate in audio, auxiliary, Master fader, instrument, and MIDI tracks.

Audio tracks

You can automate the following parameters in your audio tracks:

+ **Volume:** Use this parameter to control the overall volume of the track.

+ **Pan:** Use this to set the left/right balance of the track in the stereo field.

+ **Mute:** This allows you to turn the track on and off.

+ **Send:** This parameter includes volume, mute, and panning settings for the *send,* which is the routing section that lets you send part of your track's signal to an effect.

+ **Plug-ins:** You adjust these parameters within the Plug-In window.

Automation data for each of these parameters resides in a playlist that's separate from the clips that contain your edits for that track. This allows you to move the clips in and out of the track's playlist without changing the automation data for that track.

Auxiliary input tracks

You can automate the following parameters when you're working with auxiliary input tracks:

+ **Volume:** Use this parameter to set the overall volume of your Aux track.

+ **Pan:** You can place your tracks anywhere from left to right in the stereo field.

+ **Mute:** Use this to turn the track on and off.

Instrument tracks

You can automate the following parameters when you're working with instrument tracks:

+ **Volume:** Use this parameter to set the overall volume of the track.

+ **Pan:** Use this to set the left/right balance of the track in the stereo field.

+ **Mute:** This allows you to turn the track on and off.

Master fader tracks

You can automate only Volume on Master fader tracks. It sets the overall volume of the MIDI data.

MIDI tracks

You can automate the following parameters when you're working with MIDI tracks:

+ **Volume:** Use this parameter to set the overall volume of the MIDI data.

+ **Pan:** You can place your tracks anywhere from left to right in the stereo field.

+ **Mute:** This allows you to turn the track on and off.

+ **Controller data:** This includes a number of MIDI settings, including options such as the modulation wheel, breath controller, and sustain.

Pro Tools stores the automation data for any MIDI track — with the exception of Mute settings — within the MIDI clip for that track. When you move a clip within a track's playlist, the automation data (except for any Mute settings) moves along with the clip.

Accessing Automation Modes

Pro Tools offers five automation modes: Auto Off, Auto Read, Auto Write, Auto Touch, and Auto Latch. You access these modes by clicking the Automation Mode selector in the channel strip of each track in the Mix window or in the Track Controls section of the Edit window, as shown in Figure 6-1. Each mode affects how Pro Tools writes or plays back automation data for a track — which I cover in this section.

Automation Mode selector

Figure 6-1:
Access
the five
Pro Tools
automation
modes here.

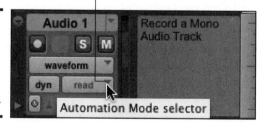

Now for the particulars. Here's what each mode actually does:

+ **Auto Off:** This mode turns off all automation data for the selected track.

+ **Auto Read:** This mode plays back the automation data for the selected track.

✦ **Auto Write:** This mode writes automation data for the selected parameter(s) while the session plays, thus overwriting any pre-existing automation data in the process. When you stop playback after writing automation in this mode, Pro Tools automatically switches the automation mode to Auto Touch (see the next bullet) so you don't accidentally erase this data next time you play back the session.

✦ **Auto Touch:** Auto Touch mode writes automation data only when you click a parameter with your mouse; it stops writing when you release the mouse button. (See the upcoming Remember icon for control-surface behavior in this mode.) At this point, your automated parameter returns to any previously automated position, according to the time that you set for AutoMatch on the Mixing tab of the Preferences dialog box. (See the "Setting Automation Preferences" section, later in this chapter, for more on the Preferences dialog box.) With Auto Touch, you can fix parts of your previously recorded automation data without erasing what you want to keep.

Auto Touch engages differently, depending on the control surface you use. If you have touch-sensitive faders (like those on the Digi 003), new automation data is written as soon as you touch a fader. If your control surface doesn't sport touch-sensitive faders, Auto Touch mode won't engage until you move a fader past the position it occupied in the previously written automation data (the *pass-through point*). After you hit that point, automation data is written until you stop moving the fader.

✦ **Auto Latch:** This mode works much like Auto Touch (see the previous bullet). After you touch or move a parameter, new automation data is written. The difference is that Auto Latch mode continues to write new automation data until you stop playback.

Setting Automation Preferences

Pro Tools writes and plays back automation data differently, depending on the preferences that you select. You set these preferences by opening the Preferences dialog box — choose Setup➪Preferences from the main menu to get there — and then clicking the Mixing tab (as shown in Figure 6-2).

The preferences in the Automation section are where you specify how automation behaves in Pro Tools:

✦ **Smooth and Thin Data After Pass:** Selecting this check box tells Pro Tools to automatically *smooth* (even out the rough spots) and thin automation data after you record your moves. (See the "Thinning Automation" section, later in this chapter, for more on thinning.) This can make your automation curves more manageable and also free memory for your automation data. (See the last bullet item in this section.)

✦ **Degree of Thinning:** From this drop-down menu, you determine the amount of thinning applied to automation data when you select the Smooth and Thin Data After Pass check box — or whenever you use the Thin Automation command. (See the "Thinning Automation" section, later in this chapter, for more about this command.)

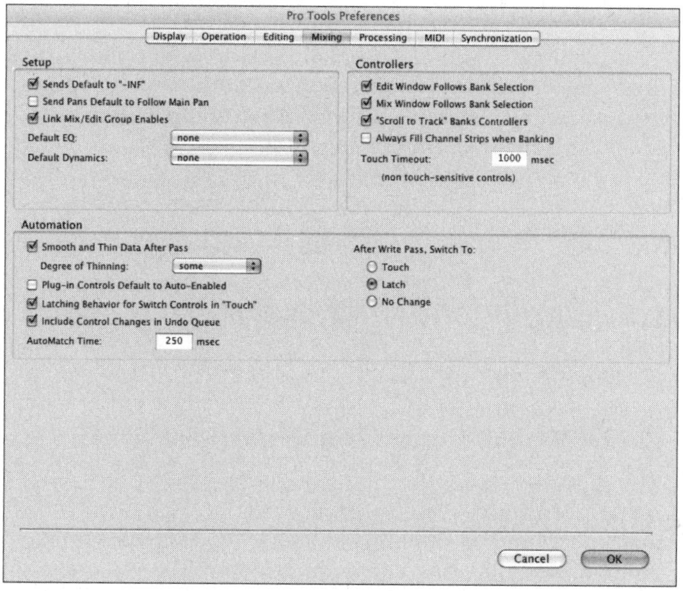

Figure 6-2:
Use the Mixing tab in the Preferences dialog box to determine how automation behaves in Pro Tools.

✦ **Plug-in Controls Default to Auto-Enabled:** Selecting this option puts all new plug-ins in Auto-Enabled mode when you choose to write automation data.

✦ **Latching Behavior for Switch Controls in "Touch":** Selecting this check box makes switched controls (such as mute or a plug-in bypass) latch to their existing state unless a breakpoint is encountered — in which case, the automation writing stops. If you stop your session while writing, the switch control automatically matches the underlying value.

✦ **Include Control Changes in Undo Queue:** With this check box selected, any changes to certain mixer controller data, such as a Fader level or Pan dial, are put in the Undo line-up along with any other operations to do. This means that if you choose to undo any prior operation, your control changes will be undone as well.

✦ **AutoMatch Time:** Use this setting to control the amount of time it takes for Pro Tools to return to written automation data when you stop recording new data in Auto Touch mode.

✦ **After Write Pass, Switch To:** Here, choose the automation mode that your session switches to after you record some automation data. You can choose between Touch, Latch, and No Change (maintaining the same mode you were in when you recorded your automation).

Enabling Automation

You can enable or suspend automation parameters on all tracks by using the Automation window (choose Window⇨Automation) or on individual or grouped tracks by using the automation drop-down menu (located in the Track Controls section of the Edit window). Here you can play with all the parameters for audio tracks that I list in the "Understanding Automation" section, earlier in this chapter, except for plug-ins, which are controlled in their respective windows.

Suspending or enabling automation across all tracks

To enable or suspend the writing of automation data across all the tracks in your session, do the following:

1. **Choose Window⇨Automation from the main menu.**

The Automation window appears, as shown in Figure 6-3. The default setting for this window is that all parameters are enabled: All parameters are highlighted. In the case of Figure 6-3, only the Volume parameter is enabled, meaning that when you set your track to one of the automation writing modes (Auto Write, Auto Latch, or Auto Touch), the only automation that is written is Volume data.

Figure 6-3:
The
Automation
window.

2. **To suspend automation across all tracks, perform one of the following:**

   • *To suspend a single control:* Click the name of an enabled parameter in the Automation window to deselect it. It's no longer highlighted.

   • *To suspend all the available parameters:* Click the Suspend button.

3. **To enable automation across all tracks, perform one of the following:**

   • *To enable a single control:* Click the name of the parameter in the Automation window. It becomes highlighted.

   • *To enable all the available parameters:* Press the Suspend button to deselect it.

Suspending automation for an individual track

You can suspend or enable reading or writing of automation without using the Automation window. In order to do this, though, you need to make sure that you haven't suspended automation via the Automation window. (See the preceding section.) You can suspend or enable automation for a single track or a group of tracks in a session by doing the following:

1. **Click and hold the Automation selector in the Track Controls section of the Edit window and then drag to the Automation parameter (Volume, Mute, Pan, Send Level, or Send Mute) that you want to suspend or enable.**

2. **Perform one of the following steps:**

   • *To suspend automation writing or reading for the control selected in the automation playlist:* ⌘-click (Mac) or Ctrl-click (PC) that control — Mute, Volume, Pan, whatever — in the Track View Selector in the Track control section of the Edit window.

   • *To suspend automation writing and reading of a singe control across all tracks:* ⌘+Option-click (Mac) or Ctrl+Alt-click (PC) or the control in one Track View Selector in the Track control section of the Edit window.

   • *To suspend automation writing and reading of all controls in a single track:* ⌘+Shift-click (Mac) or Ctrl+Shift-click (PC) or any control in the Track View Selector in the Track control section of the Edit window.

To enable these parameters, repeat the preceding steps to toggle between Suspend and Enable.

Writing Automation

Writing automation is easy — simply enable the parameter for which you want to write automation data, choose your automation mode, and then adjust the parameter as the session plays. The following sections detail this process.

While automation is being written, it appears in your track as breakpoints with lines (ramps) between these points. The breakpoints are placed in the track's *automation playlist:* that is, the playlist section of the track when you have the Tracks view set to one of the Automation views via the Track View drop-down menu. The number of breakpoints that appear is determined by the complexity of the changes to the automation levels and also by your setting in the Degree of Thinning drop-down menu on the Mixing tab of the Preferences dialog box. (Check out the "Setting Automation Preferences" section earlier in this chapter.)

When the Smooth and Thin Data After Pass check box is enabled, choosing None from the Degree of Thinning drop-down menu (refer to Figure 6-2) creates lots of breakpoints — you might not even notice any lines between them. Comparatively, selecting Most from the drop-down menu creates many fewer breakpoints, with longer, more pronounced lines between them. Pro Tools places lines between these breakpoints to connect them. These lines follow the level from one breakpoint to another, going up, down, or staying the same. The combination of breakpoints and connecting lines represent the automation curves for your track.

To keep from accidentally erasing or overwriting automation data, suspend the writing of automation for the parameter by using one of the methods of suspending automation listed in the preceding section.

Writing automation on a track

To write automation on a track, follow these steps:

1. **Choose Window⇨Automation from the main menu.**

   The Automation window appears. (Refer to Figure 6-3.)

2. **In the Automation window, click the buttons of the parameters you want to enable.**

3. **Select Auto Write in each track you want to write to (choose Auto Touch or Auto Latch for subsequent times) by clicking the Automation selector.**

   Find the Automation Mode selector in the Edit menu, as you can read in Book II, Chapter 4.

4. **Click Play in the Transport Window or press the spacebar to start your session.**

5. **Move the control for the parameters you want to automate.**

   For example, move the track's fader (located in the Channel strip of the Mix window) up and down to record changes in the volume level of your track.

6. **Click Stop in the Transport window or press the spacebar to stop the session.**

   Your automation shows up as a line with breakpoints (little dots) in the track's playlist — that is, as long as you have the automation view visible. If this view isn't visible, click the Track View selector in the Track Controls section of the Edit window to open the Track View drop-down menu and then select the automation parameter — Volume, Pan, Mute, Send Level, Send Mute — you want to view.

Book VI
Chapter 6

Automating Your Mix

If this was your first pass writing automation and you have Auto Write mode chosen, Pro Tools automatically switches the Automation mode to Touch when you're done.

To write over the first pass, start anywhere within the session by clicking within the track or along the Timeline where you want the automation data to start.

To overwrite switched controls (such as mute, solo, and plug-in bypasses), simply click and hold the button down while the session plays. Pro Tools writes new automation data as long as the switch is depressed, based upon the current state of the control (On or Off).

Writing plug-in automation

Here's how to write automation data for plug-in parameters:

1. **In the Mix window, click the name of the plug-in in the Insert section of the track's channel strip.**

   The particular Plug-In window appears.

2. **Click the Auto button in the upper-right of the Plug-In window.**

   The Plug-In Automation dialog box appears, as shown in Figure 6-4.

3. **Select the parameters you want to automate by clicking them in the column on the left and then clicking Add.**

   The selected parameters are added to the column on the right.

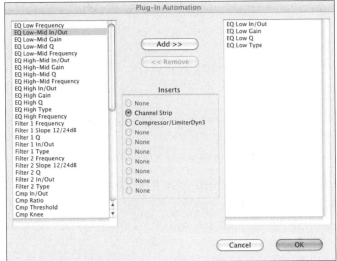

Figure 6-4:
Use the
Plug-In
Automation
dialog
box to
choose the
parameters
to automate.

4. **Click OK.**

The dialog box closes.

5. **Click Play in the Transport Window (or press the spacebar) to start your session.**

6. **Carefully move the control for the parameters you want to automate.**

7. **Click Stop in the Transport window (or press the spacebar) to stop the session.**

Your automation shows up as a line with breakpoints (little dots) in the track's playlist as long as you have the automation view visible. If it's not visible, click the Track View selector in the Track Controls section of the Edit window to open the Track View drop-down menu and select the automation parameter — Volume, Pan, Mute, Send Level, Send Mute — you want to view.

After you finish writing the automation for the plug-in, click the Safe button in the upper-right part of the Plug-In window to make sure that you don't accidentally record over the plug-in automation.

Writing send automation

To write automation data for Send Level, Mute, and Pan settings, follow these steps:

1. **Choose Window⊳Automation from the main menu.**

   The Automation window appears. (Refer to Figure 6-3.)

2. **In the Automation window, click the buttons of the Send parameters that you want to enable.**

3. **Choose View⊳Mix Window⊳Sends from the main menu.**

   Doing so displays the Send controls for the track(s) you want to automate.

4. **Select the Auto Write (choose Auto Touch or Auto Latch for subsequent times) in each track you want to write to by clicking the Automation selector.**

   You can find the Automation Mode selector in the Edit window. (See Book II, Chapter 4.)

5. **Click Play in the Transport Window (or press the spacebar) to start your session.**

6. **Carefully move the control for the parameters you want to automate.**

7. **Click Stop in the Transport window (or press the spacebar) to stop the session.**

   Your automation shows up as a line with breakpoints (little dots) in the track's playlist, as long as you have the automation view visible. If it's not visible, click the Track View selector in the Track Controls section of the Edit window to open the Track View drop-down menu and then select the automation parameter — Volume, Pan, Mute, Send Level, Send Mute — you want to view.

Viewing Automation

You can view automation data for a particular parameter by selecting the parameter name in the Track View selector in the Edit window, as shown in Figure 6-5.

Figure 6-5:
Select Track View for the automation parameter to display automation data in the track's playlist.

Select a parameter name here   Automation data

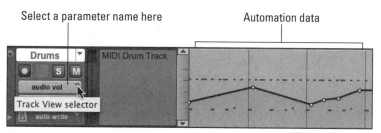

Drawing Automation

Aside from being able to record automation data by moving the parameter while your session plays (as I discuss in the chapter up to this point), you can manually draw automation with the Pencil tool. This can be handy for those visual people (you know who you are) who prefer to see what they're doing. **Note:** Just be sure you know what it's going to sound like: It *is* music, after all. Seriously, using the Pencil tool to draw automation can make creating fades or correcting automation data about as quick and easy as it gets.

You can draw your automation using the Pencil tool in the Edit window. The Pencil tool lets you draw seven different shapes, as shown in Figure 6-6. Access the various pencil shapes by clicking and holding the Pencil tool.

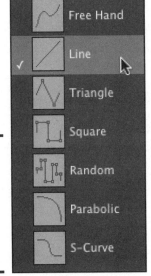

Figure 6-6:
The Pencil
Tool offers
shapes
to draw
automation
data by
hand.

✦ **Free Hand:** With this tool, you can freely draw *automation curves* — the changes to the settings for your automation data. If you're automating an audio track, the shape of the curve you draw determines the number of breakpoints (discrete levels) that Pro Tools creates. MIDI tracks follow the preferences you set on the MIDI tab of the Preferences dialog box.

Here's how you specify that MIDI setting:

a. *Choose Setup⇨Preferences from the main menu.*

b. *Click the MIDI tab.*

c. *Enter a value in the Pencil Tools Resolution When Drawing Controller Data text box.*

✦ **Line:** Using this tool draws a straight line. For audio tracks, you get two breakpoints: one at the beginning and one at the end. MIDI tracks create breakpoints based upon the resolution setting in the MIDI tab of the Preferences dialog box.

✦ **Triangle:** Using this tool creates a sawtooth pattern that follows the current grid value. Like with the Line tool, audio tracks contain two breakpoints (one at the beginning and one at the end of each line), and MIDI tracks are stepped according to the resolution you set on the MIDI tab of Preferences dialog box.

✦ **Square:** Using this tool draws a square pattern that repeats according to the current grid setting.

✦ **Random:** Using this tool creates random levels that change according to the grid value.

✦ **Parabolic:** This tool is not available for automation.

✦ **S-Curve:** Add text here. This tool is not available for automation.

So here's where automation gets visual and, well, kind of magical. To use the Pencil tool to draw automation, follow these steps:

1. **In the Edit window, click the Track View selector in the Track Controls section of the Edit window to access the Track View drop-down menu. Then select the automation parameter you want.**

The waveform fades in the track's playlist, and the automation line appears.

2. **Click and hold the Pencil Tool icon until the drop-down menu appears; then drag your mouse through the menu to choose the tool you want.**

3. **Click and drag within the automation line on the track's playlist where you want the data drawn.**

The new automation data replaces any existing data.

Thinning Automation

When you write, automation breakpoints are created at a maximum density. Depending on the shape of the curve, you might not need all these breakpoints to get an accurate playback of your moves. Because every breakpoint requires at least some computer memory, removing unnecessary breakpoints can be helpful. This is *thinning,* which can be done automatically or with the help of the Thin command.

Automatically thinning data

Pro Tools can automatically thin your automation data for you: namely, immediately after you write it. You can make it all happen from the Mixing tab of the Preferences dialog box, which you can open by choosing Setup⇨Preferences from the main menu and then clicking the Mixing tab.

From the Mixing tab, you enable automatic thinning by selecting the Smooth and Thin Data After Pass check box. Then, choose how much thinning you want by specifying an amount in the Degree of Thinning drop-down menu. (Refer to Figure 6-2.) The default setting is Some. (Is that sufficiently vague, or what?)

You can always thin your automation data further — at any time — by using the Thin command. To be safe, I always keep either Little or Some selected in the Degree of Thinning drop-down menu.

Using the Thin command

If the need for thinning doesn't become apparent until well into your creative process, you can use the Thin command to thin a selection at any time. To do so, follow these steps:

1. **Display the automation data you want to thin by using the Track View selector located in the Track Control's section of the Edit window.**

2. **With the Selector tool, select the section in the playlist that you want to thin.**

3. **Choose Edit⇨Thin Automation from the main menu.**

To thin all data for your selected parameter in a track, press ⌘+A (Mac) or Ctrl+A (PC) to select all the data. Then choose Edit⇨Thin Automation from the main menu.

You select the degree of thinning from the Degree of Thinning drop-down menu on the Mixing tab of the Preferences dialog box. (Choose Setup⇨ Preferences to access this dialog box.)

To check your thinning — basically to make sure that it still sounds good — play the thinned section. If you don't like what you hear, you can choose Edit⇨Undo from the main menu to undo the thinning.

Editing Automation Data

At your disposal are many ways to edit automation data after it's written. You can use one of the Edit tools (Grabber, Pencil, or Trimmer), you can cut/copy/paste, and (if you want to get drastic) you can delete your automation. These options are covered in the following sections.

Using editing commands

You can use standard Edit commands (such as Cut, Copy, Delete, and Paste) to edit your automation data. To edit using these commands, though, select the data first. Here's how:

1. **From the Track View selector in either the Edit or Mix window, display the automation parameter you want to edit.**

2. **With the Selector tool, highlight the section in the playlist you want to edit.**

If you're looking at the track in Waveform or Block view (for audio tracks) or in Block, Clip, or Notes view (for MIDI tracks), your edits affect all automation data for the selected section. To edit an individual parameter, display it in the Track View.

Grouped audio tracks are all edited (except when you're editing panning data) when you select data from one track in a group. To edit only the data on the selected track, press ⌘ (Mac) or Windows (PC) when you perform your edit.

Grouped MIDI tracks are edited individually (except for panning data) unless you press Control (Mac) or Windows (PC) while you perform your edit.

Panning data works in two opposite ways for groups of audio tracks and MIDI tracks. If you want to edit the panning data for a group of audio tracks, you have to press ⌘ (Mac) or Windows (PC) while you edit — which affects the entire group. Using this keystroke command (pressing ⌘ or Windows) on a group of MIDI tracks, however, edits panning data one track at a time.

Cut and Delete

You get rid of unwanted stuff when you cut and delete automation data, but the Cut and Delete commands treat unwanted stuff a bit differently:

✦ **Cut:** When you cut a selection of automation data, Pro Tools automatically adds two new breakpoints to your remaining data and places the cut material on the Clipboard. The two new breakpoints are placed at the beginning and end of the cut section. Any slope in automation curves that exists before and after the cut section remains, as shown in Figure 6-7.

In Pro Tools, cut by choosing Edit⇨Cut from the main menu or by pressing ⌘+X (Mac) or Ctrl+X (PC).

✦ **Delete:** When you delete selected automation data, the remaining automation data connects at the nearest breakpoints. Any curves between the breakpoints and the beginning or end of the deleted selection are removed, as shown in Figure 6-8.

Figure 6-7:
Before (left) and after (right) cutting automation data from a track.

In Pro Tools, delete by choosing Edit⇨Delete from the main menu or by pressing Delete (Mac) or Backspace (PC).

Figure 6-8:
Before (left) and after (right) deleting automation data from a track.

Copy

Choose Edit⇨Copy from the main menu to place copied data held on the Clipboard so you can paste it somewhere else.

Paste

When you choose Edit⇨Paste from the main menu to paste selected automation data in a new location, breakpoints are created at the beginning and end points of the selection. These breakpoints make sure that the automation levels and slope (change in level) that exist before the beginning and end points of the pasted material remain the same, as shown in Figure 6-9.

Figure 6-9:
Before
(left) and
after (right)
pasting
automation
data to a
track.

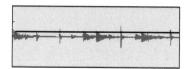

Editing with (surprise!) the edit tools

You can use the editing tools located in the Edit window to change automation data within a track. The three tools you can use are the Grabber tool, the Trimmer tool, and the Pencil tool. These are detailed in the following sections.

Grabber

 Use the Grabber tool to move, add, and delete breakpoints. To perform these operations, do the following:

✦ **Adding breakpoints:** To add a breakpoint with the Grabber tool, click in the automation line where you want the new breakpoint.

✦ **Deleting breakpoints:** To delete a breakpoint from an automation line, put the Grabber tool on it and then press Option (Mac) or Alt (PC) while you click.

✦ **Moving breakpoints:** To move a breakpoint, click and drag it to where you want it.

Pencil

You can add or delete breakpoints with the Pencil tool by doing the following:

✦ **Adding breakpoints:** To add a breakpoint with the Pencil tool, click in the automation line at the place where you want the new breakpoint.

✦ **Deleting breakpoints:** To delete a breakpoint, put the Pencil tool on it and then press Option (Mac) or Alt (PC) while you click.

Trimmer

Use the Trimmer tool to move selected breakpoints up or down by clicking and dragging them, as shown in Figure 6-10.

Figure 6-10:
Before (left) and after (right) adjusting automation levels using the Trimmer tool.

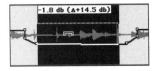 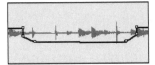

To move breakpoints left or right, select them with the Selector tool. Then, using the number pad on your keyboard, press the minus key (–) to move left or the plus key (+) to move right.

Chapter 7: Making Your Mix

In This Chapter

✔ **Submixing your tracks**

✔ **Mixing within Pro Tools**

✔ **Mixing to an external recorder**

The final step in mixing your music involves taking all your EQed, panned, processed, and automated tracks and recording them into a stereo pair of tracks. This is often called *bouncing* your mix. In the old analog days, bouncing meant sending all your tracks to two separate tracks on the same tape deck or to a different tape deck. Nowadays, with Pro Tools, you can create bounces several ways — all of which I cover in this chapter.

In this chapter, I lead you through making your mix either within Pro Tools *(in-the-box)* or by sending your tracks to a digital or an analog two-track machine — usually a Digital Audio Tape (DAT) or (yes, even today) a reel-to-reel tape deck.

Unless you have a seriously great analog deck and you want to add some of that sought-after "warmth-of-analog" tape sound to your final mix, your best bet is to go with the in-the-box approach — using the Pro Tools Bounce to Disk feature and keeping your music in your computer.

Submixing by Recording to Tracks

Submixing is mixing some of your tracks down to one or two additional tracks within your session. When you record to tracks, the submixed material automatically shows up in your session. You can then turn off the voices of the tracks that you submixed and control the resulting track(s) from one (or two) fader(s). This is handy if the following scenarios apply:

✦ **You have more tracks than your version of Pro Tools allows (Book 2 Chapter 3 describes the maximum track counts for each version of Pro Tools) in your song that you want to mix.** For example, you can reduce your track count by submixing your drums or backup vocals to two tracks and then using only those two for the final mix. Book II, Chapter 3 has more on available tracks.

✦ **You have MIDI tracks and want to record the audio output from your MIDI devices to audio tracks before doing your final mix.** Your MIDI tracks are just instrument-control data; they contain no recorded sound. At some point in the process of mixing, you need to record the actual audio output from your sound source to your audio tracks.

✦ **You want to record your final mix in real time and still be able to move the faders and other controls while your session plays.** Some recordists get antsy when Bounce to Disk mode (see the upcoming section, "Mixing in-the-Box") creates the bounce offline because it prevents them from adjusting any controls as the mix is created. (Hey, call it a control issue.)

To create a submix by recording to tracks, follow these steps:

1. **Set your effects, panning, and EQ settings for the tracks you want to submix.**

2. **Using the Output selector, assign the outputs for all tracks you want to submix (including any auxiliary tracks that your Send effects are routed to) to one of the stereo bus paths (buses 1 and 2, for instance).**

3. **Choose Track⇨New from the main menu.**

   The New Track dialog box appears.

4. **Use the drop-down menus in the New Track dialog box to enter the number of tracks you want (1), the type (Audio), and whether you want your track in mono or stereo.**

5. **If you created a stereo track to submix to, set the panning of the right track to hard right and that of the left track to hard left (see Book VI, Chapter 2).**

6. **Set the Input selector for the track you create in Step 4 to the same bus path that you chose for the tracks you want to submix (buses 1 and 2, in this case).**

7. **Using the new track's Output selector, select the main output for your session as the output path for the track.**

8. **Make sure that your Edit and Timeline selections are linked by choosing Options⇨Link Edit and Timeline Selections from the main menu.**

   Linking Edit and Timeline selections means the Timeline selection range follows the selection you make in a track's playlist.

 9. **With the Selector tool, select the section of the session that you want to submix.**

   If you want to record the entire session, be sure to put your cursor at the beginning of the session before you record it. If you want to record only part of the session, select the part you want. (Book IV, Chapter 2 details this process.)

10. **Click the Record Enable button on the new track.**

11. **Click Record in the Transport window.**

12. **Click Play in the Transport window.**

The submix process begins.

13. **Press Stop in the Transport window when you finish.**

If you selected part of the session to record, the session stops playing automatically when it reaches the end of your selection.

Be sure to let the session play until the last bit of reverb or other effect is finished playing to avoid cutting off the effect.

Mixing in-the-Box

Mixing in-the-box refers to using the Bounce to Disk feature in Pro Tools to create your final mix. The Bounce to Disk feature processes your audio tracks in real time (you can hear the session while it plays) but offline, meaning that you can't manipulate any controls when the bounce is happening.

Pro Tools creates a new file with the settings that you choose in the Bounce dialog box. What you get is a file that you can import back into your session; then you can play back your Bounced mix and evaluate how it sounds. The advantage of using the Bounce to Disk feature over recording to tracks (as described earlier in the "Submixing by Recording to Tracks" section) is that you don't need to have any extra voices available to receive the bounced files.

Examining bounce options

You access the Bounce dialog box, as shown in Figure 7-1, by choosing File⇨Bounce To Disk from the main menu.

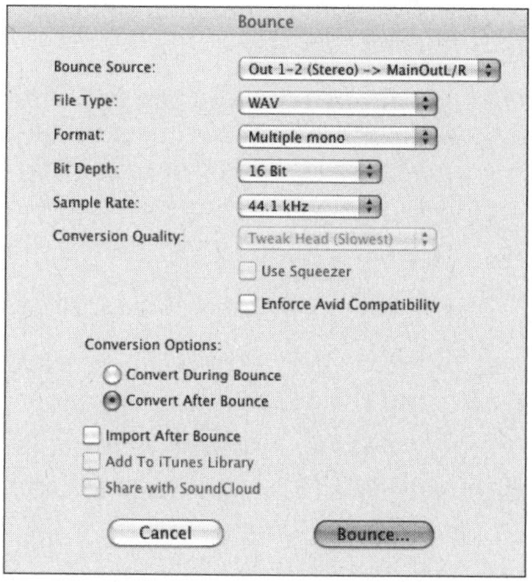

Figure 7-1:
Use the
Bounce
dialog box
to select
several
bounce
options.

Bounce

Bounce Source:	Out 1-2 (Stereo) -> MainOutL/R
File Type:	WAV
Format:	Multiple mono
Bit Depth:	16 Bit
Sample Rate:	44.1 kHz
Conversion Quality:	Tweak Head (Slowest)

☐ Use Squeezer
☐ Enforce Avid Compatibility

Conversion Options:
◯ Convert During Bounce
◉ Convert After Bounce

☐ Import After Bounce
☐ Add To iTunes Library
☐ Share with SoundCloud

(Cancel)   (Bounce...)

Here, you set the following options:

+ **Source:** Use the Bounce Source drop-down menu to select any output or bus path as your source for the bounce. (Figure 7-2 gives you a peek at some of the choices.)

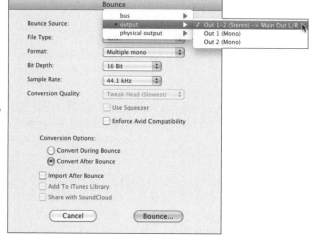

Figure 7-2:
The Bounce
Source
drop-down
menu shows
you your
choices.

+ **File Type:** Use this drop-down menu to set the file type for the bounced file. You have many choices — Book II, Chapter 5 details them all — but for your final mix, these common, Pro-Tools-supported file types are the ones to choose from:

  • *BWF (WAV):* This file type, which is the standard for older, PC-based Pro Tools systems, is currently the most commonly used file type. (One big reason is that BWF files are compatible with both Macs and PCs.) This is the type I generally choose.

  • *AIFF:* Audio Interchange File Format files used to be native to Macs. AIFF files can be imported without converting into any Pro Tools session — including those on a PC — but because BWF is becoming the standard, I skip this type. If you use a Mac and you plan to do your mastering on your Mac with Pro Tools, this file type is a fine choice.

+ **Format:** This drop-down menu determines whether your bounced file is in Mono, Multiple Mono, or Stereo Interleaved. These formats do have some differences that are good to know:

  • *Mono (Summed):* Choosing this option creates a single audio file that contains all the material without any panning information.

Because any stereo information is summed, getting too high of a combined signal is easy. This results in *clipping* (distortion). If you want to record in this format, make sure that you reduce your levels so that the left and right channels peak at no more than –3 db, although –6 dB is better. (Chapter 1 in this mini-book has more on setting levels.)

- *Multiple Mono:* This format puts the left and right channels of your stereo mix in separate files, labeling the files with the .L and .R filename extensions, respectively.

Multiple mono is the file format supported by Pro Tools, which makes it the one to use if you intend to master your music yourself within Pro Tools. If you plan to use a professional mastering engineer, call him to see what file format works with the mastering equipment (it will either be multiple mono or stereo-interleaved).

Book VI
Chapter 7

Making Your Mix

- *Stereo Interleaved:* This format contains all stereo information in a single stereo file. Panning information is retained. Any tracks set to even-numbered outputs end up on the right side of the stereo file; tracks set to odd-numbered outputs go to the left side of the stereo field.

✦ **Resolution:** Use this setting to choose one of three bit rates for your bounced files: 8, 16, or 24. (Book I, Chapter 1 has more on resolution.) For your final mix, choose 24 bit (maximum resolution). You can reduce it as needed later, either when you master your music yourself or when you have a professional do it for you.

✦ **Sample Rate:** You can save your file with any of several sample rates, but I recommend saving it with the same rate as the files in your session. Check out Book I, Chapter 2 for all the details about sample rates.

If you intend to have your music mastered by a professional, make sure to ask her what she prefers. Some mastering engineers want the files at the highest sample rate possible while others would rather have you not change the rate.

✦ **Conversion Quality:** If you choose a sample rate different from the files in your session — which I don't recommend — you're prompted to choose a level of quality for the conversion. Choose the highest quality possible for your mix material, but keep in mind that the higher the quality you choose, the longer it takes to do the conversion process.

Performing the bounce

To use the Bounce to Disk feature, first make sure that all your tracks are the way you want them. Check all routing, automation, effects, and EQ settings to make sure they're right. Then do the following:

1. **Choose File⇨Bounce to Disk from the main menu.**

   The Bounce dialog box appears. (Refer to Figure 7-1.)

2. **Set your Bounce options to the settings you want.**

3. **Click Bounce.**

   The Save Bounce As dialog box opens.

4. **In the Save As dialog box, choose a destination point for this file, enter the name of this mix, and then click Save.**

   The session plays while the bounce happens.

Using an External Master Deck

You can mix to an external device instead of mixing within Pro Tools. This section explains how to mix to both analog and digital recorders.

You can mix to an external digital device (such as a DAT deck) or, for you "classic technology" fans, to an analog device (such as a reel-to-reel tape recorder). Just follow these steps:

1. **Connect your device to your Avid interface.**

   For digital recorders, run a cable from the digital outputs of the interface to the digital inputs of your device. You'll need to use either an optical or a coaxial connection, depending on the interface.

   For analog recorders, run a cable from two of the analog outputs of the interface to the inputs of your device.

2. **(Optional) If you want to be able to monitor this device while it records, connect the device's outputs to your monitors (speakers) or plug your headphones into the headphone jack (if your device has one).**

3. **Using the Output selectors, set the output of your tracks, auxiliary inputs, and Master fader to the physical outputs of your interface.**

   These must correspond to the output you connected your device to.

4. **Enable recording in your external device.**

5. **Click Play in the Transport window of your Pro Tools session.**

6. **Adjust your input levels on your external device.**

7. **Rewind the session.**

8. **Start recording on the external device and immediately press the spacebar or click Play in the Transport window.**

The session plays, and you record it into your external device.

9. **Click Stop in the Transport window or press the spacebar when the music is done.**

You have a mix recorded into your external device (look out, world, here it comes . . .).

Book VII

Mastering with Pro Tools

The 5th Wave   By Rich Tennant

"Philip – come quick! David just used Pro Tools to connect the amp and speakers to his air-guitar."

Contents at a Glance

Chapter 1: Mastering Basics 637
Demystifying Mastering 637
Getting Ready to Master 639
Paying a Pro, or Doing It Yourself 640
Hiring a Professional Mastering Engineer 641

Chapter 2: Mastering Your Music 643
Considering General Guidelines 643
Setting Up a Mastering Session 644
Optimizing Dynamics 646
Perfecting Tonal Balance 648
Balancing Levels 650
Mastering Your Mix 651
Sequencing Your Songs 654

Chapter 1: Mastering Basics

In This Chapter

✔ Understanding mastering

✔ Knowing when to master your music yourself

✔ Knowing when to send your music to a mastering house

*Y*ou spent a lot of time getting all your tracks recorded and using the best mics you can afford — mics you carefully set up following the guidelines in Book III, Chapter 2, I hope! You adjusted your levels just right, EQed, panned, and added effects to each instrument with great care so they fit perfectly in the mix. Now you have awesome-sounding music. All that's left is to burn a CD, create cool cover artwork, and make some copies — then you're ready to go platinum, right?

Well, you could do that, but you'd miss one of the most important steps in getting your music to sound its very best: mastering. Mastering can turn your already-good music into a truly great CD. The problem is that most people have no idea what mastering is. It's been presented as some mysterious voodoo that only people who belong to some secret society and have access to a magical pile of gear can do.

This isn't the case, though. Mastering is, in fact, a pretty simple process, involving some plug-ins in Pro Tools that I show you how to use earlier in this book. Mastering does require specialized skills, but you don't need to go through any strange initiation rites to master (get it, *master?*) them. All it takes is an idea of what to do, decent ears (you have a couple of those, right?), and a dose of patience while you work your way through the process.

In this chapter, you get a chance to understand the "magic" that is mastering. You discover what's involved in mastering your music. You explore ways to make sure that your music is ready to master and discern when it might be best to find a professional to do the job for you.

Demystifying Mastering

Mastering involves preparing your music for duplication. Several steps are involved in taking your songs from individual, mixed tunes to part of a whole album. First, you need to optimize the dynamics and tonal balance of each song, and then process the songs so they match in volume with each other. These steps usually involve putting the songs through some EQing, compressing, limiting, and sometimes expanding.

You also need to *sequence* your music — put your songs in the best order possible, with an appropriate amount of time between songs if you intend to make your music available as an album as opposed to singles. Your last step is to put your mastered music into a format — and a medium — that enables you to duplicate and distribute (hey, even sell!) it. This format and medium can be a CD or it can be files ready for digital distribution. (I describe these processes in detail in Book VIII, Chapter 1 and Chapter 2.)

Processing

No matter how well you recorded and mixed your music, you still need to do some processing during the mastering stage. This usually consists of adjusting levels with compression, limiting, EQing, and (if needed) additional processing. Luckily, all this can be done right in Pro Tools, using the plug-ins that came with the software. The plug-ins that you use when mastering are covered in detail in Book VI, Chapters 3 and 4.

The purpose of the processing stage is to do the following:

✦ Balance the overall tonal characteristics of each song.

✦ Optimize the dynamics of each song so all the songs are at their best overall volume.

You can achieve these goals by using the following tools:

✦ **Compression:** Some music sounds best when it's smooth, and other music is much better when it has a punchy quality to it. Judicious use of a Pro Tools Compressor plug-in can produce either of these effects. A good mastering engineer knows when and how to make music punchy or smooth. (Sorry, you can't have both at the same time.)

✦ **Limiters:** If any instruments are too high in comparison with the rest of the mix, using a Pro Tools Limiter plug-in can tame them so you get the best overall difference between the songs' peak levels and average levels. This difference varies depending on the style of music, but it should never be less than 6 decibels (dB) and is usually between 12dB and 18dB. (For more on limiter plug-ins, see Book VI, Chapter 4.)

✦ **EQ:** Because you record and mix each of your songs over a period of time (often a long period of time), chances are that each song sounds a little different. Some might be brighter than others, and some might be heavier on bass, but one thing's for sure — each will have a different tonal quality.

Sequencing

Sequencing involves putting your songs in the order that you want and then setting the space between each song so that the CD flows well from one song to another. Because a CD is supposed to represent a cohesive body of work, this is one of the most important aspects of mastering.

Leveling

A crucial aspect of mastering a CD is *leveling* — getting the levels of all the songs the same. After all, you don't want your listener to adjust the volume of his stereo from one song to another. Having consistent levels from song to song helps with the cohesiveness and flow of a CD. This is done by using simple gain adjustments, compressors, and/or limiters. And by making those processes consistent, Pro Tools gives us mere mortals a crack at doing it right.

Getting Ready to Master

You can save yourself a ton of time and energy when mastering your music if you keep a few things in mind during the mixing stage. When wearing your Mixing Master hat, the following reminders can make the mastering process go a bit more smoothly:

✦ **Check your levels.** Listen to your mix quietly to tell whether one instrument sticks out too much in the mix. Also, burn a CD of your mixed song to test on other playback systems, such as your car, a boom box, or your friend's stereo system. Listen carefully. If the bass drum is even slightly too loud, it eats up headroom that the rest of the instruments need, so you can't get the overall volume of the song very high.

✦ **Check your EQ.** Even though the mastering engineer (you or a pro) EQs the entire song, the time you spent getting each instrument EQed in the mix is still a good investment. If you didn't get your EQ just right during the mixing process, and (for example) a muddy bass guitar sound has to be EQed during mastering, you lose some of the low end on *all* the instruments. This makes your mix sound thin. If your bass is EQed properly in the first place, you don't have to make that adjustment to the entire mix.

✦ **Test your mix in mono.** That is, turn off the stereo panning on your master bus. This helps you hear whether any instrument's volume or tonal characteristics are seriously out of balance with others. I never consider a mix to be finished until I monitor it in mono.

✦ **Apply compression on your mix before you record the two-track mix.** That way, you can hear what your music sounds like compressed.

Don't *record* the compression, though. Leave that for the mastering stage. By testing your mix with some compression, you might hear whether certain instruments are too loud in the mix; if so, they become more apparent when compressed.

✦ **Listen for phase holes.** *Phase holes* occur when you record an instrument (such as a piano or backup vocals) in stereo, and the left and right tracks are out of phase. (Book III, Chapter 2 has more in avoiding phase holes when you record.) To listen for phase holes, pay attention to how the instrument sounds in the stereo field. You have a phase hole if you hear sound coming only from the far right and far left and nothing coming from the center of the stereo field. If you have this problem, all you have to do is reverse the phase on one of the two channels for that instrument. You do this by inserting the One-Band EQ plug-in in one of the tracks (keep the Gain set to 0) and clicking the phase Invert button (this is the little 0 with a line through it next to the Input button).

Paying a Pro, or Doing It Yourself

Whether to master your music yourself or to hire a professional might be one of your toughest music-making decisions. If you master your music yourself, you can have complete control from start to finish and save yourself some bucks. On the other hand, if you hand your mixed music over to a skilled professional, you can have the added benefit of another person's ears and advice, and you can end up with a finished product that far exceeds your expectations.

So how do you choose?

Well, your first consideration is probably based upon economics. Do you have the money to spend on professional help (for your music, that is)? Mastering can cost anywhere from a few hundred to thousands of dollars. A midline mastering engineer often charges around $500 to master your CD (about ten songs). This might seem like a lot of money, but finding the right engineer for your music can make the difference between a decent CD and a truly world-class one.

Another consideration for hiring out your mastering is how well you know your equipment and how capable it is of performing the mastering procedure. To do mastering, you need at least one good (well, preferably great) multiband compressor, a limiter, and a great multiband parametric EQ. The plug-ins that come with Pro Tools can get you most of the way to a great-sounding master. If you really get into mastering in Pro Tools, you can add some third-party plug-ins (such as the Waves or PSPaudioware brands) that offer better sound and more flexibility. You also need to have a CD burner of some sort and the software to create a Red Book CD master. (Find more about CD burners and Red Book standards in Book VIII, Chapter 1.)

Before you decide, take a look at other benefits of hiring a skilled professional to do your mastering:

+ **A meticulously tuned room and top-notch monitors:** With this equipment, you can hear what your music actually sounds like.

+ **Equipment specifically designed to handle mastering:** EQs, compressors, and other gear that a mastering house uses can tweak your music to sound its best.

✦ **A fresh set of professional ears:** A pro with perspective might be able to hear things in your mix that need fixing. You might be so close to the project that you have a hard time hearing your mix objectively.

Hiring a Professional Mastering Engineer

If you do decide to use a professional mastering engineer, the following tips can help you choose one for your project:

✦ **Ask for referrals.** If you know local bands or musicians whose music you like and whose CDs sound great, ask them who mastered their music. Call local studios and find out whom they recommend for mastering in your area. Also, check out resources on the Internet. Two great Internet forums are

- ProSoundWeb.com (www.prosoundweb.com/forums)

- Recording.org's mastering forum (http://recording.org/home-studio-mastering/)

In a forum, search for the term *mastering* or post a new topic and ask your question. Try to get referrals from people who work with your type of music.

✦ **Listen to other recordings that the mastering house has done in a style of music similar to yours.** If you're entrusting your artistic vision to someone else, make sure that this person is the right person for the job. If you like what the prospective mastering engineer has done on other people's music, you'll probably like what he or she does with yours.

✦ **Clarify the fee for your project before you start working together.** Most mastering engineers charge by the hour and can give you a pretty good estimate of how many hours they'll need to do the job. You'll also be expected to pay for materials (reference CDs, for example).

✦ **If you don't like the way an engineer masters your music, you'll probably be charged at the hourly rate to redo it.** Some engineers will redo your project for free, but don't count on it. Be sure to discuss this possibility before you start the project to avoid unwanted surprises.

Many mastering engineers will do a demo for you, tooling up one or two songs so you can hear what kind of job they can do for your music before you hire them. Ask whether the mastering engineer you're interested in offers this service. This simple step can save both you and the engineer a lot of time and energy if he isn't right for the job. It can also help you determine whether your mixed music is ready for mastering. If you need to go back and make adjustments, now's the time to find out.

**Book VII
Chapter 1**

Mastering Basics

After you choose a mastering engineer who you think will work well for you and your music, you can make the process much easier and less stressful (for both you and the engineer) if you follow a few guidelines:

✦ **Discuss your expectations and desires.** This is the best way to ensure that your mastered music turns out how you want. People who are unhappy with the job that a mastering engineer does usually aren't clear about what they want or don't understand what is possible in the mastering process.

✦ **Take a few CDs whose sound you like with you to the mastering session.** Talk with the engineer about how you can get your music to sound similar. A skilled engineer can let you know right away whether the sound you want is possible.

✦ **Try to be present at the mastering session.** Many people send their music to a mastering engineer and expect him to do the job without their presence in the studio. Try to go to the studio. If you can't, be sure that the engineer clearly understands your desires and expectations.

If you're in the studio during the mastering process and things aren't going the way you want, talk with the engineer and try to get things on track again. If you're finding that you're unable to communicate with the engineer, stop the session, have him burn a *ref* (reference copy), pay for the time you used, and listen to the ref at home. If you don't like what you hear at home, you might be best off going somewhere else with your music.

Chapter 2: Mastering Your Music

In This Chapter

✔ Setting up a mastering session

✔ Converting your song files

✔ Processing your production

✔ Sequencing your songs

*Y*ou've done everything else yourself, so why not master your music, too? Well, I hear ya. Even though I'm a firm believer in the magic that a professional mastering engineer can bring to a production — check out the preceding chapter in this mini-book for my take on that — I'm also a do-it-yourself kinda guy. If you're like me, you at least need to give mastering a shot. After all, you have nothing to lose — except a little time — and everything to gain (or at least learn from).

This chapter walks you through how to master your music in Pro Tools. I offer some general guidelines that you can keep in mind while you work and help get you up to speed on mastering your music yourself. I also show you how to set up your mastering session in Pro Tools.

The Pro Tools mastering steps given here use the Bounce to Disk function. You don't necessarily have to go this route. If you want, you can also send your mastered tracks out to a digital device by following the steps in this chapter — and *then* use the steps that describe mixing to an external digital device (found in Book VI, Chapter 7).

Considering General Guidelines

In other chapters, I present some specific techniques and settings to get you started. Unfortunately, I can't do that when it comes to mastering because there are just too many variables. That also means too many ways to mess up your music when you're trying to master it. What I can do (and actually do) in the upcoming sections is walk you through the process of mastering and show you the tools to use for each step. When you're reading these sections, keep the following in mind:

✦ **Less is more when mastering.** Do as little as possible to your music. All you really *should* need to do when you're mastering is to optimize the dynamics and tonal balance of each song, get the levels between the songs even, and sequence your songs. If you find yourself doing more — having to make a lot of adjustments, for example — you might want to go back to the mixing process and try again.

✦ **Mastering is all about compromise.** Each adjustment you make to your mixed music affects all the instruments. If you use EQ to get rid of muddiness on the bass guitar, you affect not only the bass guitar, but also every other instrument in the mix.

✦ **Don't try to master a song right after you mix it.** Give yourself time and space away from that song before you do anything else to it. In fact, I recommend that you take a few days away from *any* of the songs on your album between the mixing and mastering stages. A little time to reflect and rest your ears can do wonders for your ability to hear what your music needs.

✦ **You can really master music effectively only if your monitors and monitoring environment are great.** Without a good reference for how your music sounds, trying to EQ or dynamically process your music does no good. The music might sound good through your speakers but if they aren't accurate, it probably doesn't sound good through other people's speakers. Before you master, make your room sound as good as you can and get to know the strengths and weaknesses of your monitoring environment by listening to a ton of commercial CDs that have a sound like the one you're trying to get.

Setting Up a Mastering Session

The first step in mastering your music in Pro Tools is to set up a mastering session. This involves creating a new Pro Tools session and importing the mixed tracks from each song you want on your CD. This section of the chapter details that process.

Start by creating a new session for mastering:

1. **Choose File⇨New Session from the main menu.**

The New Session dialog box appears, as shown in Figure 2-1.

2. **Type in the name of the file in the Save As field.**

I usually call the file `mastering` and include the name of the CD project that I'm working on.

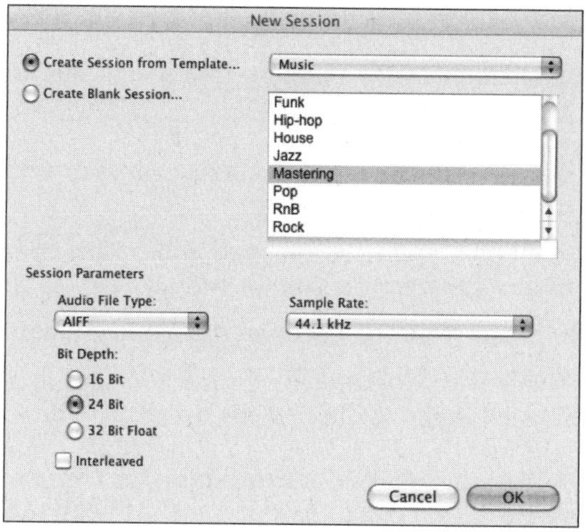

New Session

Create Session from Template...   Music

Create Blank Session...

Funk
Hip-hop
House
Jazz
Mastering
Pop
RnB
Rock

Session Parameters

Audio File Type: Sample Rate:

AIFF   44.1 kHz

Figure 2-1:
Create a
new session
to master
your songs.

Bit Depth:

○ 16 Bit
◉ 24 Bit
○ 32 Bit Float

☐ Interleaved

Cancel   OK

3. **In the Where field, choose the folder where you want to place the new session.**

    I usually create a new folder called `mastered mixes` so it's easy to find the files later when I burn them to CD. (Book VIII, Chapter 1 has the details on burning CDs.)

4. **Choose the session parameters that match the mixed files for your songs.**

    I'm talking audio file type, sample rate, I/O settings, and bit depth here. Book II, Chapter 3 has more on the basics of setting up a new session.

5. **Click Save.**

    Your new session opens.

The first time you create a mastering session, save it as a template before you add any audio files (just be sure to have your tracks and routing set up beforehand). This way the next time you're ready to master any of your music, you can simply choose this template to save some time.

The next step is to import your mixed songs into new tracks for this session:

1. **Choose File⇨Import⇨Audio from the main menu.**

    The Import Audio dialog box opens.

2. **Using the Look In field, navigate through your folder structure to find and select the song file you want to import.**

3. **Click Add.**

4. **Repeat Steps 2 and 3 for all the songs you want to master in this session.**

5. **Click Done.**

   A dialog box opens that allows you to choose whether the files enter a new track or appear in the Regions list.

6. **Choose the New Track option so that you audio files end up where you can use them right away in your session.**

7. **Choose Session Start from the Location drop-down menu.**

   Each song you selected appears in a new track in your session. You can also find them listed in the Audio Regions list.

You now have a session that contains all the songs for your project. Having them all in one session allows you to switch from one song to the next while you master your tunes and also makes it easy for you to check loudness levels and EQ balancing while you work. (See the "Perfecting Tonal Balance" and "Balancing Levels" sections, later in this chapter.)

Optimizing Dynamics

Okay, this is where the magic in mastering happens. This is where you can make your music shine or where you can royally mess it up. (How's that for adding a little pressure?) Before you get tense (okay, breathe), remember that you can always go back and try again. Oh, did I mention that you should make backup copies of your individual tracks and your final mix? Well, if you haven't already done the backing-up business, now would be a good time to do that. I'll wait.

You done? Okay, now to the job at hand — getting your music to be as loud as possible. (I'm just kidding; see the sidebar "Turn it up!" to see why.) Seriously, optimizing the dynamics of your songs doesn't mean getting it loud enough to level a city block, but rather getting it to have life and emotion. And, yes, this *also* means getting it to be loud enough to sound good.

The style of your music and the arrangements that you use determine how you optimize the dynamics of your music. For example, classical music has a much broader dynamic range than rock music, and the infamous "wall of sound" type of arrangement has a narrower dynamic range than a song with sparse verses and thicker choruses.

When you're optimizing the dynamics of your music, be sensitive to the song and try not to get sucked into the idea that you need to get the most volume out of your music. I know I'm beating this volume thing into the ground, but you'd be surprised how seductive the lure of Big Volume can be. ("C'mon, let's get just a *few* more dBs out of the song . . ." Trust me; you'll soon find out.)

You have two main types of tools to use when you work on the dynamics during mastering in Pro Tools — compressor plug-ins and limiter plug-ins — and each has its purpose. For the most part, if you're trying to add punch or smoothness to your music, using a compressor plug-in does the job nicely. On the other hand, if you're trying to squeeze a *little* more volume out of a song and you don't want to change the song's sound quality, using a limiter plug-in is your best choice.

Here are suggestions that might help you to use compression and limiting most effectively during mastering:

✦ **Use a mild compression ratio (between 1.1:1 and 2:1) to keep from overcompressing your music.**

✦ **Apply only 1 or 2 decibels (dB) of compression or limiting at one time.** If you need more than that, chain more than one compressor together by inserting more than one compressor plug-in in your track, and use these small amounts on each. If you compress or limit more than 1 or 2 dB at a time, you end up with *artifacts* (audible changes to your music caused by the compressor or limiter).

✦ **Work with your attack and release times.** An attack that's too short takes the punch out of your music by cutting off the initial transients. Likewise, a release time that's too long doesn't recover quickly enough, and the dynamics of the vocal disappear. In contrast, if the release time is too short, you hear distortion.

✦ **Set the threshold so that your compressor's meters *dance* (bounce) to the rhythm of the music.** The meter you want to watch in your Pro Tools Compressor plug-in is the one labeled *Reduction,* which is located below the input and output meters. Only the loudest notes (snare drum or lead vocal accents, for example) should trigger the meters — and then only by 1 or 2 dB.

✦ **Using a multiband compressor allows you to bring out individual instruments in the mix.** For example, if the bass drum seems to be getting lost, you can apply mild compression to the lower frequencies (around 80–100 Hz). This brings the instrument forward in the mix slightly.

Pro Tools 10 doesn't come with a multiband compressor plug-in. If you want to use one on your music, you need to get a third-party plug-in. Check out the Digidesign User Conference (DUC) at `http://duc.avid. com` for some options.

✦ **When you're not sure whether what you're doing sounds better, don't use the processor.** Any dynamics processing is going to affect the quality of your song's sound to some extent. If adding this processing doesn't improve the overall sound, you're better off not using it.

You can find out more about compression and limiting in Book VI, Chapter 4.

**Book VII
Chapter 2**

**Mastering Your
Music**

Turn it up!

Folks want their music to be as loud as possible. Louder sounds better. In fact, test after test has shown that when people listen to two versions of a song, they nearly always prefer the louder one (whether it actually sounds better or not).

Musicians, producers, and engineers seem to be in the middle of a competition to see who can make the loudest CD. If you compare a CD made before 1995 or so with one made this year, you'll notice that the newer one is much louder. Give them both a good listen, though. Does the louder one *really* sound better?

You can test this by setting them both to play at the same volume and then switching back and forth. (You need to turn the volume up a bit on the older CD to match the volume of the newer

one.) One way to do this is to record both songs into Pro Tools and set the levels of each so that they're the same. At the same volume, which song sounds better to you? I'm willing to bet that nine out of ten times, you'll prefer the older song because older recordings have more dynamic range than newer ones. The variety is pleasing to listen to, whereas the song with only a small dynamic range quickly becomes tiring.

Do yourself and your listeners a favor and resist the temptation to compress the dynamic variability out of your music. It will be much easier to listen to and have a lot more life and excitement. You can always turn the volume up on your stereo if it's not loud enough, but you can't add dynamic range after you squashed it out.

When you're testing compressor plug-in or limiter plug-in settings (by comparing the processed and unprocessed versions), be sure to have the volume of both versions exactly the same. Any difference in volume defeats the purpose of side-by-side comparison because people almost always prefer the louder version, regardless of whether it sounds better.

Perfecting Tonal Balance

Tonal balance of a song is how the various frequencies of the music relate to one another. You're not concerned with how each individual instrument sounds in the mix (that's the job for the mixing stage); instead, what you're looking for is an overall balance of frequencies within the hearing spectrum.

For the most part, a tonal balance consists of an even distribution of frequencies from 20–10 kHz with a slight drop-off (1 or 2 dB) from 10–20 kHz or higher. "That's great," you say, "but what does that sound like?" Well, listen to any number of great CDs, and you'll hear it.

When you master your music, you want to constantly compare what your song sounds like against other CDs whose sound you like. In Book VI, Chapter 1, I list a variety of excellent reference CDs for mixing. These CDs work just as well for mastering, so check them out.

When you work on adjusting the overall tonal balance of your songs, listen carefully for any frequencies that seem too loud or too soft. You can find these by listening to particular instruments in the mix or by using the parametric EQ plug-in and sweeping the frequency spectrum. To do this, set your Q fairly wide (0.6, for instance) and move the Gain slider all the way the right. Start with the lowest frequency and then slowly raise the frequency as the song plays by moving the Freq slider from left to right. Adjust any annoying frequencies by cutting them by a couple of dBs to see whether your overall mix improves.

As far as general EQ guidelines go, try these suggestions:

+ **If your mix sounds muddy:** Add high frequencies (higher than 10 kHz) or cut low ones (200–400 Hz).

+ **If your mix is too bright:** This is common with digital recording. As a remedy, try reducing the frequencies higher than 10 kHz by using a shelf EQ or a Baxandall curve.

To use a *Baxandall curve,* use a parametric EQ and set the threshold at 20 kHz with a Q setting around 1. This gradually cuts frequencies above around 10 kHz. You can adjust the Q to reach as far down as you want. Your EQ graph shows you what's happening.

Use the same EQ adjustments for both the right and left channels to keep the stereo balance intact and not alter the relative phase between the channels. For example, if you add some bass frequencies (100 Hz, for example) to the one channel but not the other, you might hear a wavering or a pulsating sound around this frequency go back and forth between the speakers.

+ **If you used a multiband compressor on any specific frequencies:** You might need to adjust the EQ for those frequencies; compression tends to mess with frequency response.

+ **If you need to adjust the EQ of certain instruments in the mix:** Suppose that the snare drum is buried. Be careful and notice the overall effect of your adjustments on the rest of the mix. If your adjustments aren't fixing the problem, go back to the mixing process and make your adjustments there. You'll be glad you took the time to do that.

Any adjustments you make to the EQ during mastering affect more than just those frequencies. Such adjustments alter the entire *frequency spectrum* — and the relationship between all the instruments. So listen carefully while you make adjustments and back off on the additional EQ if you don't like what you hear.

For more specific information on EQ and inserting EQ in your tracks, go to Book VI, Chapter 3.

Book VII Chapter 2

Mastering Your Music

Some people check the tonal balance of their songs against that of their favorite CDs. You do this by recording a song into your mastering program and taking a look at its frequency response by using a spectral analyzer. Pro Tools doesn't come with a spectral analyzer, but you can buy one as a third-party plug-in. Just look for an RTAS version to ensure that it works with Pro Tools. Then do an analysis of your song and compare it with the spectral analysis of a CD you like. This technique seems to work for many people (albeit not for me, because I like using my ears instead — alas, I'm old-fashioned).

Balancing Levels

For a truly professional-sounding CD, you want all your songs to be at nearly the same relative level so your listeners (I *hope* you have more than one) don't have to adjust the volume on their stereos from song to song.

Balancing the levels of your songs to one another is pretty easy. In fact, in most cases, you have very little to do after you EQ and optimize the dynamics of each song. You balance the levels from one song to the next in Pro Tools by putting each track's fader up to 0 dB — putting them at the level you mixed them — and then soloing Track 1 and comparing the level with Track 2 by soloing back and forth.

If you use a mouse to mix, getting to this balance can be kinda tricky because you can't press more than one button at a time. The best way I've found to deal with this situation is to follow these steps:

1. **In the Track Controls section of Track 1, click the Solo button to solo the track.**

   You hear only Track 1 in your monitors.

2. **In the Track Controls section of Track 1, click the Mute button so that both the Solo and Mute buttons for Track 1 are engaged.**

   Track 1 is silent.

3. **In the Track Controls section of Track 2, quickly click the Solo button.**

   You now hear Track 2.

4. **To switch back to hearing Track 1, click the Track 2 Solo button (disengage it). Then, as quickly as possible, click the Track 1 Mute button (disengaging the Mute button and engaging the Solo button).**

   You hear Track 1 again.

You get a short bit of silence when following this procedure, but you can still be able to hear the relative volumes of the two tracks.

Do this procedure for each of the tracks (Track 1 to Track 2, Track 2 to Track 3, and so on) until you check all the tracks in your mastering session.

If you miss one of the buttons while you're doing this quick-switch procedure, you might end up with both tracks playing at the same time. This will be very loud because the tracks are summed in the mix bus. To avoid damaging your speakers — or ears — keep your monitoring (speaker) volume down pretty low.

If you notice any differences, just raise (or better yet, *lower*) the levels until they are all roughly the same. Don't get too finicky. Some variation from song to song is okay. In fact, minor differences can help to make your CD more interesting to listen to. When you're balancing levels, just make sure that any differences aren't enough to make the listener run to his or her stereo or snatch up the remote to adjust the volume. If one or two songs seem much lower in volume than the rest, consider going back to the volume-optimizing stage and raising those songs a bit to make them more consistent with the rest of the songs on the CD. That way, you don't lower the volume of the entire CD because one or two songs are too quiet.

Mastering Your Mix

After you have all your songs dynamically optimized, EQed, and level-balanced (see the previous sections of this chapter), you're ready to record your final master. This process is essentially the same as making your final mix, so check out Book VI, Chapter 7 for the steps to do this. You need to do one more thing when mastering, however, which involves getting your songs to the CD format.

Most likely, your session's songs are recorded at 24 bits, using any number of possible sample rates (44.1, 48, 88.2, or 96 kHz), but your final master should be 16-bit at 44.1 kHz (this is the CD standard — anything else won't record as an audio CD and player in your CD player; also, most online distribution services prefer CD quality to work from). Making this change can reduce the sound quality of your music if it's not done right. The following sections detail how to change the sample rate and bit depth as you create a final master version of your music.

Making the most of your bits

Getting your music from 24-bit to 16-bit means either dithering or truncating your files. The following sections explain how these processes differ, giving you pointers on which one to use so your music sounds as good as possible.

Dithering

Dithering adds random noise to your music when 8 bits get cut from your pristine 24-bit files. This random noise helps keep the quiet sections of your song (fades-outs, for instance) from sounding grainy when those 8 bits are removed. Several types of dithering are available, each of which produces a slightly different result in a piece of music.

Pro Tools comes with two dithering plug-ins: Dither and POWr Dither. Each plug-in has different noise-shaping options, which use filters to move the random noise to inaudible frequencies. I'm confident that you'll find at least one of them works well for your music. Figure 2-2 shows these plug-ins.

Figure 2-2: Pro Tools comes with two dithering plug-ins: Dither (top) and POWr Dither (bottom).

To dither a song, simply insert one of the two dithering plug-ins into one of the inserts in your master fader, and then follow the steps (as detailed in Book VI, Chapter 7) for mixing your music. The dithering happens automatically while your song is mixed — or, in this case, mastered.

Truncation

Truncation simply cuts off the last 8 bits of information. This option works well for material that doesn't have quiet sections: for example, hard rock with punchy endings that don't fade out.

To master your music using truncation, follow the steps in Book VI, Chapter 7 for mixing your song and then choose 16-bit as your Bounce to Disk resolution — or use one of the digital outputs to send your signal out of Pro Tools. Either technique cuts off the last 8 bits without otherwise processing the signal. This is the difference from dithering.

To dither or not to dither (and which dithering option to use)? Those are the questions for which no universal answer exists. The only way to know which sounds better on your music is to try each of them. For the most part, songs with quiet passages and fade-outs often sound better if you dither 'em.

Mastering to 16 bits

When you master — regardless of whether you using the dithering approach — make sure you select the 16-bit option under the Resolution drop-down menu (located in the Bounce dialog box, as shown in Figure 2-3). If you have a dithering plug-in inserted into your Master fader, your music is dithered while it's being bounced; if you don't use a dithering plug-in, your music is truncated.

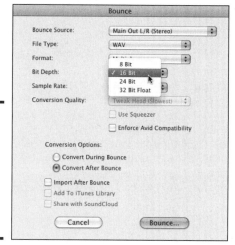

Figure 2-3: Choose 16 from the Resolution drop-down menu to bounce to 16 bits.

Settling on a sample rate

If you recorded at any sample rate other than 44.1 kHz, you need to do a *sample-rate conversion* (SRC) process. SRC can change the sound of your song (and not for the better). Your best bet when bouncing from one sample rate to another is to set the conversion quality as high as possible. The following steps show how:

1. **Choose 44.1kHz in the Sample Rate drop-down menu of the Bounce Menu.**

The Conversion Quality dialog box is enabled.

2. **From the menu, choose the TweakHead Setting.**

3. **From the Conversion Quality drop-down menu, (as shown in Figure 2-4), choose TweakHead if you want the highest quality possible.**

It takes a while to process (go get a cup of coffee or read your favorite gear magazine while you wait), but I think it's worth it.

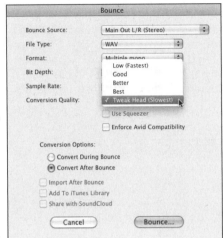

Figure 2-4:
Select the quality of your sample-rate conversion here.

You have several options for sample-rate conversion quality. Don't take my anal-retentive word for which works best for your music. Do some experimenting on your own. One of the lower-quality conversion settings might work just fine — and you won't have to wait so long while your song is being processed.

Sequencing Your Songs

Sequencing your songs is choosing the order of the songs on the CD as well as the amount of silence between songs. Chances are that when you recorded your songs, you had an idea about the order in which you wanted them to appear on your final CD. If you don't know how you want to arrange your songs, here are some things to consider:

+ **Consider each song's tempo in the sequencing equation.** Some CDs work well if songs with a similar tempo are grouped together, and others work best when contrasting songs follow one another.

+ **Think about a song's lyrics and how they relate to the lyrics from the other songs on your CD.** If you want to tell your listener a story, consider how the order of the songs can best tell that story.

+ **Think about the chords that you used in each song and how they relate to another song you might want to place before or after it in the sequence.** The ending chord of one song might conflict with the beginning chord of another — or lead right in.

For most of us, sequencing has more to do with the actual process of placing each song in its proper place on the CD than with trying to decide where that proper place might actually be.

Most of the sequencing process involves deciding how much time to place between the songs on your CD. No set amount of time has to be placed between songs. Choose what seems right for the two songs you're working with. Sometimes you might want just a second or two; other times, four or five seconds is more appropriate. For example, if you have a mellow ballad followed by an upbeat song, you might want to leave a little more time between these two songs so that the listener is prepared for the faster song. Try leaving a space that lasts about four to six beats at the slower song's tempo, for instance. On the other hand, if you want two tunes to flow together, you can leave less time between them. Use your ears, thinking about how you want your listener to respond when the music moves from one song to another.

You don't sequence your songs in Pro Tools; instead, this is done within the CD-burning program you use. After you bounce your mastered tracks in Pro Tools to 16-bit files with a 44.1 kHz sampling rate, you can then import them into your CD-burning software and arrange them the way you want. This includes arranging the order of the songs and setting the amount of silence between songs. Check out your CD-burning program for specifics on how it handles these operations.

**Book VII
Chapter 2**

**Mastering Your
Music**

Book VIII

Getting Your Music to the Masses

The 5th Wave   By Rich Tennant

"You know, a lot of symphony orchestras are putting their music online these days as a way to reach new audience members."

Contents at a Glance

Chapter 1: Putting Your Music on CD and Vinyl 659

Getting into CD Burning..659
Purchasing CD-Rs 660
Recording Your Music to CD-R 661
Making Multiple Copies 664
Pressing Vinyl 668
Promoting Your Music...669

Chapter 2: Getting Your Music on the Internet 673

Understanding Downloadable Music Files 673
Creating MP3 Files 677
Setting Up Your Own Music Website 680
Putting Your Music on a Music Host Site 682
Engaging in Social Media Networking 683
Offering Free Downloads 684
Selling Downloads 685
Streaming Audio 686
Podcasting..688
Selling Your CDs 689
Promoting Your Music...689
Connecting with an E-Mail Newsletter 690

Chapter 1: Putting Your Music on CD and Vinyl

In This Chapter

✔ **Understanding CD burning**

✔ **Finding the right CD-Rs**

✔ **Burning your first CD**

✔ **Preparing your CDs for duplication**

✔ **Finding a CD duplicator**

✔ **Pressing a vinyl record**

*O*ne of the coolest things about audio recording nowadays is that you can create music in your home and put it on the same medium that the biggest record companies use. When I started as a recording engineer, the best you could do was put your music on cassette for other people to listen to. Pressing vinyl was expensive. But now anyone with a computer, a CD burner, and a few inexpensive CD-Rs can put his or her music on the same format as all the best albums in the record store. You gotta love it!

In this chapter, you explore how to make CDs of your music. You discover the best CD-Rs to buy, and you get a chance to burn a CD. You also find out how to submit your mastered CD to a company that can mass-produce your music and make it ready to sell.

And because life tends to turn in a circle, you get a chance to explore vinyl records as a medium for your music. All that's left are some ideas for promoting your packaged product, which you can find in this chapter as well.

Getting into CD Burning

Because you're recording in your computer with Pro Tools, chances are you have a computer with a CD-R or CR-RW drive. If so, you also have software that you can use to burn your CDs. Most CD-burning software works fine for putting your mastered music onto CDs. If you don't already have a burner and want to add one to your existing computer, check the system requirements for the burner that interests you to make sure that your system can use it. For audio CDs, you can use just about any CD burner on the market (as long as it's compatible with your system, of course).

Recognizing Red Book CDs

Regardless of the CD burner you get, make sure that it can create a Red Book CD. I know that this sounds mysterious, but all *Red Book* means is that the CD is an audio CD, not a CD-ROM. Red Book is a standard for the data used to create an audio CD; a Red Book–capable burner follows that standard. This ensures that your CD can play on all audio CD players. Your CD burner clearly states whether it can burn audio, or Red Book, CDs.

Purchasing CD-Rs

A staggering variety of CD-R types are available. Available are green, blue, gold, and even black CDs; as well as data and music CDs. So which ones are best? Well, that depends.

Unless you have a consumer CD recorder from several years ago, you can record your CD onto any data CD-R. You can find these discs just about anywhere, and they can cost as little as five to ten cents apiece if you buy in quantity. If you have an older consumer CD recorder, you have to use music CD-Rs. These CD-Rs have a code in them that allows older consumer recorders to actually record. These CD-Rs cost a lot more not because they capture music any better, but because a royalty — about one dollar, which goes to the recording industry — is figured into the price of the CD. (Don't get me started.)

So, if you have a late-model CD-R recorder connected to your computer, or if you have a professional-grade CD burner (such as the Alesis Masterlink), you can get by just fine by using run-of-the-mill data CD-Rs.

As far as which of the countless CD-R brands to use, well, they're all pretty much the same as long as you go with a major manufacturer. Personally, I always go with Taiyo Yuden if I can find them. (Do a search on the Internet for some places that sell this brand.) Keep in mind, though, that some CD-Rs work better on some recorders, and the only way to find out is to try them and see. When you find a brand that works, try to stick with it.

Look for CD-Rs with a tough top surface. It's the scratches or pits in the top of the disc that cause it not to play over time, not the scratches or pits on the bottom.

Recording Your Music to CD-R

Burning a CD is easy. All you generally have to do is open your CD-burning software and follow the prompts. A few things, however, can be helpful to know to get the best sound and to create a CD that you can duplicate. Rundown coming right up.

Dealing with diversity: Using different CD recorders

If you're using a CD burner in your computer, burning a CD is as simple as opening your software and following the program's directions for making a CD. If you use a standalone CD recorder (burner), you have to connect it to your Avid interface (via a digital connection) and record to your CD recorder. These options are presented in the following subsections.

Computer-based systems

If you have a CD burner program (such as Toast, Jam, or CD Creator), burning your CD is easy. One advantage of using one of these programs to burn a CD is that you have quite a bit of flexibility to organize your songs and place space between them.

In general, all you have to do is click the Add Track button on the main screen and select the track you want to add. You're also prompted to choose any silence that you want to place before the track, as well as PQ subcode information. (A *PQ subcode* is "housekeeping" information added to the CD data; it includes instructions for start and stop times for each track.)

When you have all your tracks assembled, you can go ahead and burn your CD. Pretty simple, huh?

Standalone CD burners

A variety of standalone CD burners are available, and they all work differently. Some record the CD the same way a cassette player records tapes: You connect the digital input of the CD recorder to the digital output of your Avid interface and then press Record on the CD recorder while clicking Play in Pro Tools. The CD is then recorded in real time. Other standalone CD burners, such as an Alesis Masterlink (the CD-burning standard for many pro studios), work more like computer software programs than cassette recorders.

With the Masterlink, you first record the music from Pro Tools to the Masterlink hard drive (using the same procedures just listed). From there, you can edit, sequence, and even dynamically process each song before you burn all the songs to a CD-R. When you're happy with the order of the songs and the spacing between them, you can then burn your CD.

If you want to do any dynamic processing to your music in the Masterlink, be sure to send your files to the machine undithered and at 24 bit. You can dither in the Masterlink after you make your changes. This improves the sound of your final CD. If all you're doing is sequencing your songs, you can send the files dithered if you want. (For more on dithering, see Book VII, Chapter 2.)

Burning for mass production

If you intend to send your CD-R to a duplication or replication company to have it mass-produced, you have a few ducks to get in a row first. Here are a few things to keep in mind:

+ **Check for physical defects to the CD-R before you try to burn to it.** Scratches, fingerprints, smudges, and other imperfections on the mirror side (bottom) of the CD-R can cause errors in the data when burning the CD-R. Be sure to use a clean and unblemished CD-R for burning your master. After all, CD-Rs are cheap.

+ **Always write your master CD by using Disc at Once mode.** This allows the CD to be read as a Red Book audio CD. Your other option when recording a CD is Track at Once, which burns one song (track) at a time. Unfortunately, Track at Once produces more errors than Disc at Once, which burns the entire CD at one time. Because of the errors present on CDs burned when using Track at Once, a mass producer's equipment can't read — and therefore summarily rejects — CDs that people produce via this method. (In fact, many older CD players for homes and cars can't read these CDs, either.) So be sure that you use Disc at Once whenever you make a CD of your mastered music.

+ **If you can, use an error-detection software program to check for errors in your recorded CD or verify your disc when you burn it.** (This is an option you can generally choose within your CD-burning software; check your burner's manual for details.) If you don't have access to an error-detection program, put your CD into an audio CD player and listen all the way through, making sure it doesn't skip or stop. Also check the back of the CD for any blemishes (just as you did before recording onto it).

+ **Listen carefully to your entire CD after it's recorded.** Compare it with your original file and make sure that the CD is perfect. Also, spend time re-evaluating the order of the songs. Make sure that they flow well together (Book VII, Chapter 2 has more on sequencing your songs).

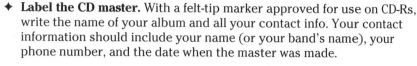

+ **Label the CD master.** With a felt-tip marker approved for use on CD-Rs, write the name of your album and all your contact info. Your contact information should include your name (or your band's name), your phone number, and the date when the master was made.

If the marker isn't specifically labeled as such, the ink might leak through the top surface of the disc over time, disrupting the data.

And don't use a ballpoint pen or an adhesive label (paper or plastic) to identify your master. A ballpoint pen can damage the surface of the CD. Adhesive labels can slow the rotation speed of the CD (causing errors in the duplication or replication process), and they've been known to come off inside a duplication machine, clogging up the works.

Write only on the top surface of the disc.

+ **Make three CD-Rs of your mastered music.** Keep one copy safe in your studio and send the other two to the duplication or replication company. Call it good insurance: If one of the two CDs that you send off for mass production has an error, you don't waste any time sending the company a replacement.

+ **Prepare a PQ subcode log.** PQ subcodes include additional information, written on the CD, that provides time-code information, such as track numbers and the start and stop times of the tracks. If your CD burner software doesn't support PQ subcodes, make a list of the start and stop time of each track (referenced from the start of the CD) on a separate piece of paper as well as the track number and length of each track; then send that info along with your CD masters. If your software program can generate a PQ subcode log, print it — and remember to send it with your CD master.

If you're burning a CD for a major record label, first of all, congratulations! Secondly, make sure you supply ISRC (International Standard Recording Code) codes with your CD. These codes contain information about the CD, such as the owner of the song, the country of origin, year of release, and serial number. (You can find more information and an application for obtaining ISRC codes for your music at https://usisrc.org/.)

You enter ISRC codes into a dialog box on most CD-burning programs, and the information is placed within the PQ subcodes.

Before you put your music out into the world, get it copyrighted. Getting a copyright on your music is easy and relatively inexpensive, so there's no reason not to do it. And it will protect you if there is ever a dispute about who wrote your music.

All you have to do is fill out an SR (sound recording) form and send it into the U.S. Copyright Office at the Library of Congress. You can find the form at www.copyright.gov/forms, or you can call the Copyright Office at 202-707-9100 to have it mailed to you. Choose (or ask for) Form SR with Instructions. The current cost for filing the form is $65, but double-check this fee before you send it in because it's been known to go up. (Hey, it's the government.) You can fill out one form for each CD, so the cost per song isn't very high. After you have your copyright, it's yours for life.

The form is pretty easy to fill out, but if you run into difficulty, you can call an information specialist to help you out. The number is 202-707-3000. Be prepared to wait on hold for a little while. (Hey, it's the government.)

Send your completed form, the fee, and a copy of your CD to the address listed on the form. You'll receive a certificate in the mail, but you can consider your music copyrighted as soon as you mail it in (as long as you sent it to the correct address). If you're especially protective of your music (paranoid? or is that paranoid *enough?*), you can wait until your check clears your bank. At this point, you can be almost certain that your form is being processed. If you can't sleep at night unless your music is copyrighted, you're best off waiting until your certificate arrives in the mail before you start selling or distributing your CD. (This is a good reason to file for your copyright early.)

Making Multiple Copies

When you have a CD that you want to copy, you can either make the copies yourself or hire someone to copy them for you. If you copy them yourself, you have to burn CDs one at a time, just like the first one. This can cost very little money but take a lot of time (as you undoubtedly found out when you burned your first CD).

Making copies yourself

Well, you've done everything else yourself, so why not add the copying process to the list? If you have more time than money and only need a few CDs, making them yourself might be a good option.

To make saleable CDs yourself, you need not only the CD burner, but also a graphics-design software program and a printer to print CD labels and cover material (CD sleeve and tray card). Even with this equipment, your package won't look as professional as the package that a CD duplication or replication company can create, but what you create is probably good enough for you to sell a few copies to friends, acquaintances, and maybe open-mic-night audiences.

A work of art

Cover artwork is an important part of your CD. Take the time to create a visually appealing CD cover and tray card. This is especially true if you intend to sell your CD through record stores or other retailers. Your package needs to look professional because it's going to be competing with the big boys (and girls) who have huge art budgets for their CDs.

If you can't create a professional package yourself (no shame there — not everybody can), hire someone to do it. Most CD replicators I discuss in this chapter provide design services. Sometimes these services are even included in the CD package price. I recommend that you take advantage of these services; sometimes you get best results by letting the pros do what they do.

Having someone else making copies

Depending on how many copies you want, you can either have them duplicated or replicated. Either process can provide you with a professional-quality product that you can sell alongside major releases. Your choice between duplication and replication depends on how many copies you plan to have made.

Duplication

Duplication involves making copies of your master CD-R the same way you made the CD-R in the first place. The only difference is that duplication companies use CD burners that enable them to make more than one copy at a time. Duplication is great if you want to make a small number of copies — anywhere from 50 to 300. Most CD-duplication companies include the actual discs (with printing on them), jewel cases with color-printed inserts, bar codes (see the "UPC bar codes" sidebar in this chapter), and shrink-wrap. You can expect to pay around $3 to $5 for each CD, depending on the quantity you order. You can also find other types of packaging, such as vinyl sleeves and one-color printing, for less per disc if $3 to $5 is too steep for you.

An advantage to having your CDs duplicated is that your CDs usually can be done quickly. Many duplication companies can provide you with a finished product in as little as a few days (although an average of seven days seems more common). The disadvantage is that you usually pay considerably more for each CD than you would if you did it yourself or went the replication route.

**Book VIII
Chapter 1**

Putting Your Music on CD and Vinyl

To have your CDs duplicated, you need to provide a CD-R *master* — that is, a CD-R recorded as a Red Book-compliant audio CD. If you want the duplication company to create retail-ready packages, you also have to provide artwork laid out to the company's specifications. (***Hint:*** Get 'em beforehand.)

If you're interested in going the duplication route, here are a few resources to get you started. You can also do a search on the Internet for more places by using the search term *CD duplication*.

- ✦ **CD Works,** 93 Park Street, Beverly, MA 01915; phone: 800-CDWORKS; website: www.cdworks.com.

- ✦ **DiscMakers,** Main office: 7905 N. Route 130, Pennsauken, NJ 08110; phone: 866-707-0012; website: www.discmakers.com/music.

- ✦ **Oasis CD Duplication,** 12625 Lee Hwy, P.O. Box 214, Sperryville, VA 22740; phone: 888-296-2747; website: www.oasiscd.com.

Most of the companies that I list in the following section also provide duplication services for smaller quantities.

Replication

Replication is the process used for making commercial CDs — lots and lots of them. Instead of making copies directly from your master CD-R, this process involves burning a *glass master* — the master disc from which all your CD copies will be made — from your master disc. The glass master is then used to transfer the data onto CD media. Replication is designed for larger runs: namely, 500 or more copies. Quantities of fewer than 300 aren't cost-effective because the glass master often costs between $100 and $200 to make, and the film needed for the printing of the CD and sleeve and tray card can cost several hundred more.

UPC bar codes

If you make a CD that you intend to sell through major retailers, such as record stores or Internet retailers, you need a UPC bar code. A *UPC bar code* is a string of numbers that identify your product. Every CD has its own unique bar code. You can go about a getting a bar code in one of two ways: You can register and pay $750 with the Universal Code Council (UCC), or you can pay anywhere from nothing to $50 to get one from a CD replicator or distributor.

Unless you intend to release more than 35 CDs, your best bet is to buy a bar code from a replicator or distributor, who can provide bar codes for a small (or no) fee with your CD order. Here are additional places where you can get a UPC bar code:

- ✔ **Disc Makers:** www.discmakers.com/music

- ✔ **Oasis Disc Manufacturing:** www.oasiscd.com

- ✔ **CD Baby:** www.cdbaby.com

CD replication usually comes with printing on the CD in one to four colors, and a tray card and sleeve often printed in four colors. Most CD-replication companies have retail-ready CD package deals that cover everything from layout of your artwork (some do, some don't, so be sure to ask first), printed CDs, jewel boxes, bar codes (see the "UPC bar codes" sidebar in this chapter), and shrink wrap. You can expect to pay between $1,000 and $1,500 for 500–1,000 retail-ready copies from most manufacturers.

If you're interested in going the replication route, you need to provide the replication company with a master audio CD, artwork set to its specifications, and a completed order form. Oh, and you'll probably have to pay half the money for the job up front before they start work on your project (bummer).

After people at the manufacturing company receive your order form, the CD, and the artwork, they make a *reference CD* (which shows you what the finished product will sound like) and proofs of your finished printed material. Be sure to look over the art proofs carefully: Listen to every second of the reference CD. Any mistakes you don't catch are your problem, so take your time and compare the reference CD very closely with the master recording. (You *did* make a copy of your master CD before you sent it out, right?) The master and the reference should be exactly the same.

Having your CD replicated is a stressful thing. You're spending a ton of money and getting quite a few copies; you'll need to be proud enough of them to go out in the world and *sell* them. Choosing a CD-replication company to work with is an important task. Quite a few companies are out there, so you should choose the place that makes you feel the most comfortable and makes a high-quality product.

Here is a list of the larger CD-replication companies. For more possibilities, do a search on your favorite search engine for *CD replication* or *CD duplication.*

+ **Disc Masters,** 2460 5N279 Wooley Road, Maple Park, IL 60151; phone: 888-430-DISC; website: www.discmasters.com.

+ **Oasis CD Duplication,** 12625 Lee Hwy, P.O. Box 214, Sperryville, VA 22740; phone: 888-296-2747; website: www.oasiscd.com.

+ **Groove House,** 5029 Serrania Ave., Woodland Hills, CA 91364; phone: 888-476-6838; website: www.groovehouse.com.

+ **DiscMakers,** main office: 7905 N. Route 130, Pennsauken, NJ 08110; phone: 866-468-9353; website: www.discmakers.com/music.

Many CD-replication companies can provide you with great resources, information, and even opportunities for promoting your work. Take advantage of these opportunities if you can, but don't choose a company based on its promotional promises. Choose a company because of its customer service, price, and the quality of its product.

**Book VIII
Chapter 1**

**Putting Your Music
on CD and Vinyl**

Be sure to ask for referrals (or at least a list of satisfied clients) before you go with a duplication or replication company. As always, your best bet when you're entrusting someone with your precious music to is to ask friends for recommendations. Also, take timing estimates with a grain of salt. I've had a couple of occasions when a company promised to finish my CDs by a certain date, and the discs didn't show up. So leave plenty of time between when you print your CDs and when you need them.

Pressing Vinyl

There is a trend for musicians to create compelling packaging to try to entice listeners into buying a physical product rather than just taking a free download. (Whether you offer a free download or not, chances are your music will be available for free somewhere through P2P sharing.) One of the ways artists are distinguishing themselves is to offer vinyl records.

This retro format is a viable option for breaking through the noise and getting your music heard (I cover more ways to "premiumize" your music to help with promotion in the next chapter). If you're interested in putting your music out on an old-fashioned record, here's what you need to know:

✦ **It takes a lot longer to make a vinyl record than a CD.** Expect to wait close to 8 weeks for your finished record.

✦ **Not everyone has a record player.** In fact, as attractive as it may be to put your music out on vinyl, the vast majority of your fans will not have the proper equipment to play it. So, when you print, keep this limited market in mind. The average independent artist only prints a few hundred records at a time.

✦ **A vinyl record doesn't hold a lot of music.** You may need to cut songs from your CD to fit the constraints of the vinyl. A 12-inch 33 ⅓ rpm record only holds about 18 minutes per side and a 7-inch 45 rpm record holds about 4 ½ minutes per side.

✦ **You may lose some fidelity.** If you're mixing your music with the modern style of having pretty heavy bass, you may need to dial that back to accommodate the limitations of the vinyl medium. You may also find that the high frequencies also drop as you move to vinyl. You can deal with this and make an excellent-sounding record if you have the special know-how. Here is an article on how to prepare your music for vinyl: `www.customrecords.com/prepare_music_for_vinyl_record.html`.

✦ **Most vinyl record pressing companies will include a download card** in your record's packaging so your listeners can download your music to a portable device. This allows you to offer the best of both worlds.

If a vinyl record interests you, check out these resources for the many options and prices:

✦ **Groove House,** 5029 Serrania Ave., Woodland Hills, CA 91364; phone: 888-476-6838; website: `www.groovehouse.com`.

✦ **Untied Record Pressing,** 453 Chestnut Street, Nashville, TN 37203; phone: 866-407-3165; website: `www.urpressing.com`.

✦ **Recordpressing.com,** 475 Haight Street, San Francisco, CA 94117; phone: 415-462-1992; website: `www.recordpressing.com/`.

✦ **Rainbo Records,** 8960 Eton Ave., Canoga Park, CA 91304; phone: 818-280-1100; website: `www.rainborecords.com/`.

Most CD duplicators and replicators also have recommendations for vinyl pressing companies that they work with regularly. So if you have a CD manufacturer that you like and you want a vinyl record, ask the manufacturer for a referral.

Promoting Your Music

Congratulations, you have a CD to sell. The hard — oops, I'm sorry, actually the *easy* — part is behind you. I'm sure you don't want to be stuck with boxes of expensive coasters, so now you have to work on getting people interested in buying your music. You've just gone from being a musician-composer-engineer-producer to being all those *plus* a record company-owner-business-person. (Exactly how hyphenated can a person get, anyway?)

Your friends and some acquaintances will probably buy a few copies, but after you've sold a CD to all of them, you need to get your music to the broader world. This can be tricky. After all, you're now competing with the big boys, and face it: You don't have nearly the resources that they do. Traditional channels of distribution and marketing are pretty much out of the question for you (and for most of us). So, to succeed in selling your music, you need to try some alternative approaches.

I'm no marketing guru, but I have managed to create a nice niche for myself and my music. So, trust me: You can do the same. All it takes is a little imagination and a lot of hard work. In the following list, I present a few ideas that have worked for me and other enterprising, independent artists:

✦ **Take yourself seriously.** No, don't go buy a limo. At least not yet. What I mean here is to take the job of promoting and selling your music seriously: Treat it as a business. Getting people to notice and buy your music is a lot of work, but it doesn't have to be a drag. (If it is, you're better off getting someone else to do it for you.)

✦ **Get organized.** Get your new business off on the right foot by developing a habit of keeping track of your sales and developing a contact list. One of the best investments that you can make is to get a contact-management database (ACT! is a good one) to keep track of promotion contacts (newspapers, radio stations, clubs), CD sales, and fans. Also, do yourself a big favor and keep meticulous records of your income and expenses; you'll be grateful you did that when tax time comes.

✦ **Create a mailing list.** This is one of the most cost-effective and powerful ways that you can start to develop a following. Make a sign-up sheet for your mailing list available at every public appearance. (Ask people to include both postal mail address and e-mail address.) Then enter those names into your database system. You can then either send out snail-mailings or e-mail notices whenever you play or do anything worth mentioning.

✦ **Get out and be seen.** This one is pretty straightforward. Get out in the world and let people know about your music. This can mean not only playing gigs but also talking about your music. I have a good friend who releases an album each year. He prints 1,000 copies, which he sells at his gigs, and every year he sells out. (Hey, that's an extra $10,000 a year after expenses. Not bad!) He also uses the CDs as his calling card in order to get more gigs.

✦ **Look beyond the music store.** Competing with the major labels in the music store is nearly impossible. Unless you live in a small town or know of a music shop that has a section devoted to local bands, ready and willing to sell your CDs, you need to think of other places to put your music. For example, another friend of mine has placed his CD at quite a few of the local businesses in his neighborhood around the holidays. Every place — from the local pack-and-ship to the video store — has a counter-top display with his CD. He creates a small poster that fits on the counter, describing him and his music. He sells quite a few CDs and gets a handful more gigs each year this way.

✦ **Capitalize on your style.** Some non-record-store venues just happen to fit what your music is saying. For example, another one of my friends composes folksy, new-age music, and he managed to get his CDs into a handful of new-age, gift-type shops. He often puts them in the stores on consignment and checks each store once weekly to refill the counter-top display and collect any money that the store took in (minus the store's cut, of course). Going into the stores every week helps him to develop a connection with the store owners, many of whom have arranged for him to do performances in their stores, which increases his exposure and sales.

✦ **Try something different.** Years ago, I teamed up with a local author and played at her book signings. (This is before I wrote any books myself.) She read a passage from her book, and then I played for a few minutes. I always ended up selling a few dozen CDs at these events.

✦ **Don't be stingy.** Give away your CD (within reason, of course). I usually count on giving away anywhere from 10–15 percent of the CDs I print. These can be for reviews, as a way to get gigs, or for any way to spread the word about the music. Giving out your CD as a promotional tool is an inexpensive way to let people know what you're doing.

Some of the bigger CD replication companies, such as Oasis and Disc Makers, offer independent artists (this would be you) promotional opportunities that can get you more distribution and exposure. I recommend looking at these distribution and promotion options when you consider a company to manufacture your CD. These opportunities can save you a lot of time and money, and they're often included in the replication price.

If you're interested in the possibilities for using the Internet to promote and sell your music, I discuss these in Chapter 2 of this mini-book.

I'm sure there are dozens more ways to promote and sell your music. Think outside the box and use your imagination. *Remember:* Don't be shy. Do whatever you can to get your music out into the world.

Chapter 2: Getting Your Music on the Internet

In This Chapter

✔ Understanding MP3 and AAC

✔ Finding a music host site

✔ Exploring streaming audio

✔ Formatting your music for the Internet

✔ Using the Internet to promote your music

*T*o make it as a musician, you have to get the word out that you and your music exist. Traditionally, you played gigs, sold your CDs at these gigs, and tried to get your music in local stores and on local radio. If you were lucky, you'd sell a few CDs at each gig, move a handful of others through local outlets, and maybe get some radio play on a college station. Forget getting any national exposure unless you had developed a following and had a busy touring schedule.

That's the way it used to play, but now the Internet makes it possible for any musician to get national — even international — exposure without going on the road (as much). All you have to do is get your music on the Internet and promote it well. You can then make money from your music while you sleep (or at least make your music available while you sleep).

So how do you do this? Well, that's the purpose of this chapter. Here, you explore how you can use the Internet to promote and sell your music. You discover how to put up music files so that your potential customers can either download your music or listen to it online. You find out about some of the best ways to get your music hosted online, and you take a look at promotional ideas to get you started.

Understanding Downloadable Music Files

I'm sure you've heard about MP3s or maybe AAC. In fact, I'm willing to bet that you've already downloaded a few MP3s or AAC files off the Internet and experienced firsthand the immediacy that these file types offer. You go to a website and choose a song to download. After just a short while, you have a copy on your hard drive that you can listen to any time you want. You can even put that song on a CD or portable player and take it with you.

What do you mean by near-CD quality?

You might have heard the term *near-CD quality* used in reference to MP3 sound. This "marketing" term means that it doesn't sound as good as a CD, but it sounds pretty darn close and maybe the buyer won't notice. If you sense a note of cynicism in my writing, you're right. Don't delude yourself into believing that the song you start with is going to sound quite the same after MP3 conversion.

The difference between a song on a CD and a song that's near-CD quality is like the difference between playing a CD in your car and then hearing the same song on the radio. You lose some high end, and the bass is thinner. You might even lose the stereo image, depending on the conversion mode you choose, and you'll probably lose some dynamic range. Overall, the song will have a little less life to it.

Although not a huge difference for most people, the difference is noticeable nonetheless. The good news is that most people don't seem to care (or are at least willing to accept it) — and that the song is now slim enough to zip through the Internet to potential customers.

With all this convenience and immediacy comes a downside: That MP3 song doesn't sound as good as one mastered to a CD. For most people, this is a small price to pay for the ability to download a song for free (well, okay, often for a buck a shot these days). After all, most people play their music on less-then-stellar-sounding stereos. (Can you say iPod?) But if you're one of the lucky few with a stellar (or more-than-stellar) stereo system, you're going to hear the difference, which prompts the following question: Why doesn't a song in MP3 or AAC format sound as good as one mastered to a CD? The answer: data compression.

MP3 is a process that compresses your music so that it takes up less hard-drive space. Data compression is necessary, or MP3s and AACs couldn't work over the Internet. Consider the numbers: A regular CD music file can take 30 MB to 40 MB (about 10 MB per minute). That same song can take only 3 MB to 4 MB in MP3 or AAC format. This is important because promoting music on the Internet is totally dependent upon speed. A 30 MB or 40 MB file is way too big to download or to stream on the web (even for people with broadband Internet connections).

Although compression causes your MP3 or AAC file to lose fidelity as well as megabytes, I think this loss of quality is an actual advantage. After all, it's normal that your MP3 won't sound as good as your mastered CD in its multimeg brilliance. It doesn't have to; you're giving listeners just a taste of your music. By giving people this taste, along with the opportunity to purchase a CD, you help them decide whether they want to buy the high-quality version.

Other file-compression formats being used, such as FLAC (Free Lossless Audio Coding) and AAC (Advanced Audio Coding), have improved the sound quality of MP3 and are being used by some delivery systems, such as AAC on iTunes, so you may find that encoding your music into one of the other file types works better for you. Some of the encoding software I mention later in this chapter can encode into these file types as well as MP3. You may want to try one of these on your music to see what you think works best — just make sure whatever file format you choose can be played by the people you want to hear your music.

Bit rate

Bit rate essentially determines the quality of your encoded music. When you encode your music, you have to choose what bit rate you want your file to be in, as shown in Figure 2-1. Bit rates range anywhere from 16 kilobaud per second (kBdps) to 320 kBdps. The higher the bit rate, the better the sound quality. The downside is that higher bit rates create larger files. When you convert your music to MP3, you're constantly balancing quality with file size.

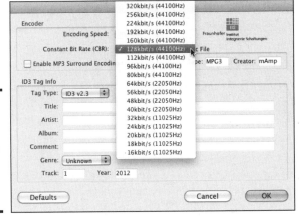

Figure 2-1: MP3 encoders allow you to choose the bit rate of your MP3.

Book VIII Chapter 2

Getting Your Music on the Internet

The bit rate that you ultimately choose depends on how you plan to use your MP3 or AAC file. For example, if you want to put your music on a downloadable music host site (an Internet site that makes people's MP3 or AAC music available for download), you most likely need to choose the 128-Kbps rate because this is what many host sites require for download. For Hi-Fi mode, you may choose 192 Kbps or even 256 Kbps, depending on the provider. On the other hand, if you want to stream audio on the web (and you want anyone, regardless of connection speed, to hear it), you're better off choosing a lower rate, such as 96 Kbps or even lower, depending on your host's requirements.

Variable bit rate (VBR) is an option that many encoders offer. VBR allows the encoder to change the bit rate while it compresses the file. The advantage to this approach is that the sections with fewer instruments — in effect, less data — can be compressed further than sections full of more critical information. The result is often a better-sounding MP3 that takes up less space. The only drawback — and it's a big one — is that few MP3 players can read a file created with VBR. So you're probably best off not using this approach for your web-based files.

If you're making MP3s to listen to through your own player and it supports VBR playback, using VBR keeps your files smaller. If you do choose VBR, you're prompted to choose an average bit rate or a minimum and maximum bit rate. Try them both and choose the one that sounds best to you.

Mode

Modes essentially refer to whether your file is in stereo or mono, only your choices include more than just plain stereo and mono. You can choose mono, stereo, joint stereo, or (sometimes) force stereo (also known as *dual mono*), as shown in Figure 2-2. Again, you choose the mode according to what your music needs to sound its best, and you balance quality against file size.

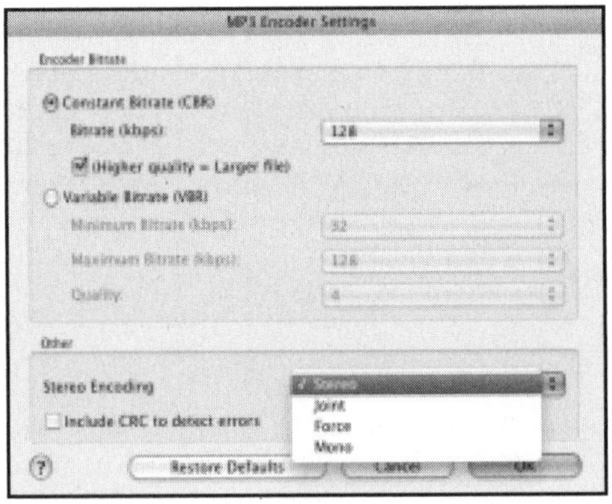

Figure 2-2: MP3 encoders have several modes to choose from.

Here's a look at the various modes and how they relate to quality and file size:

✦ **Mono:** Mono takes up little room because all the stereo data from your CD is contained on one track. The sound quality can be good, depending on the bit rate you choose, but you lose all stereo-imaging data. Choose the mono mode if the loss of the stereo image won't adversely affect your song, or if the overall sound quality is more important to you than the stereo information.

✦ **Stereo:** Stereo mode consists of two mono tracks. With stereo mode, you retain all your stereo information. The drawback is that your two tracks are at half the bit rate of a mono version using the same bit-rate setting, so they don't sound as good. For example, if you encode at 128 kBdps, each of your stereo tracks is actually only 64 kBdps. If you want each track to be at 128 kBdps, you have to encode at 256 kBdps. The resulting file is twice as large as the mono file at 128 kBdps, has no better sound quality, and takes longer to download.

Even so, it's your call. Stereo mode is a good choice if you have a song with complex stereo panning effects that you just can't live without, and you don't mind a sound quality that's slightly lower.

✦ **Joint Stereo:** This mode is a cross between mono and stereo: It creates one track of audio information and one track of information that tells the player to send certain sounds through one speaker or the other (a set of instructions called *steering data*). You get most of the stereo information with only a slightly larger file size than you'd get with the mono mode.

For most songs, the difference in stereo image between regular stereo and joint stereo is indistinguishable — and you end up with a higher-quality recording because the higher bit rate is used. You might find that this option works better for you than the regular stereo mode. Experiment and see whether you can hear a difference.

✦ **Force Stereo:** Also known as *dual mono,* this mode is essentially the same as the mono mode: One track of audio data is recorded, and the stereo panning information is lost. The only difference between mono and force stereo is that force stereo makes sure that the mono data is played through both speakers of the player. Choose Force Stereo mode if you don't mind your music being in mono but want to ensure that the player plays it through both speakers.

Creating MP3 Files

To create MP3 files, all you need (well, besides the computer) is MP3 encoding software and a CD or audio file of your music. To create an MP3 of your music, just choose the song to convert and let the encoder do the rest. Some variables can make your MP3s sound their best, such as which encoder to use and what parameters to choose. I cover these variables in the following sections.

Choosing encoding software

A bunch of MP3 encoders are available, but you're using Pro Tools, so I'm going to recommend trying the MP3 option for Pro Tools, which is included with the Pro Tools 10 software (I detail how to use this in the next section). You can demo it for 30 days to see whether you like it. If you do, pay $20 if you want to continue using it. (This small fee pays for the license that Avid must pay to use the MP3 algorithm from the creators.) If you try it and don't like using Pro Tools for your MP3 encoding, here are some other popular programs you can use:

✦ **iTunes (**www.apple.com/itunes**):** iTunes is free and can rip from CD into MP3 and AAC formats equally easily. It's simple to use and, if you have an iPod or if you buy music from the iTunes store, you already have it loaded onto your computer.

✦ **Switch Audio Converter Software (**www.nch.com.au/switch/index.html**):** You can download the basic version for free, which allows you to play, rip, record, and convert MP3s and audio CDs. This program works with Windows PCs and Macs. There is also a plus version available for more encoding options that cost $30.

✦ **Toast Titanium (**www.roxio.com**):** This is the most common Mac-based program. This program costs about $100 and allows you to not only create MP3s, but also record your mixes to CD — plus a lot more.

A lot of MP3 encoders are available, so if you're looking for a little more variety, I suggest doing a search for MP3-encoding software. You'll get a lot of options.

Encoding your music

The MP3 encoding process is pretty simple. To encode using the Pro Tools MP3 option, follow these steps:

1. **Select File⇨Bounce to Disk.**

The Bounce dialog box makes an appearance (Figure 2-3).

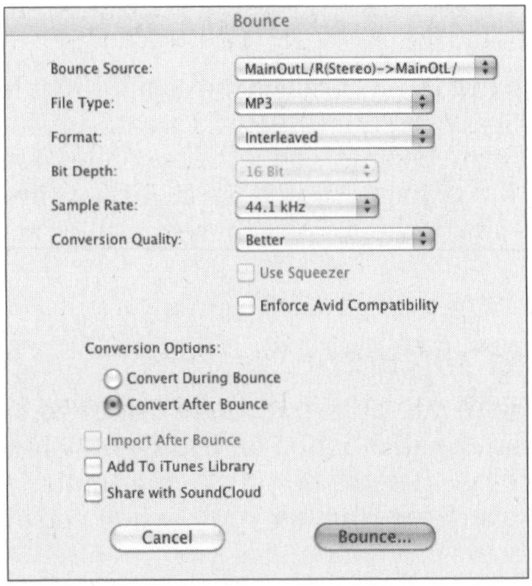

Figure 2-3:
The Bounce dialog box has an MP3 option.

2. **From the File Type drop-down menu, choose the MPEG-1 Layer 3 option.**

3. **From the other drop-down menus, choose the format, bounce source (these are the outputs you want to record your audio from), sample rate, and whether you want to convert during or after the bounce.**

4. **Click Bounce.**

   The MP3 window appears, as shown in Figure 2-4.

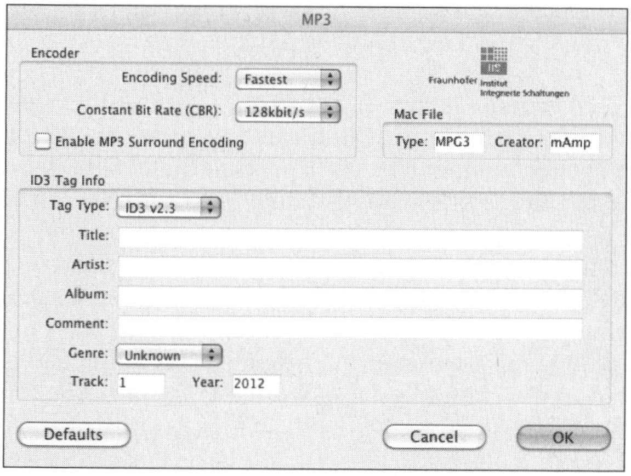

Figure 2-4:
Encode
MP3s within
Pro Tools
with the
MP3 option.

5. **Choose your encoding speed from the Encoding Speed drop-down menu.**

6. **Select the Constant Bit Rate (CBR) radio button and choose the quality of the MP3 from the drop-down menu.**

   For streaming audio, choose between 20 and 32 kBdps; for higher-quality downloads, choose between 96 and 128 kBdps.

7. **Enter the ID3 Tag Info in the dialog box.**

   This includes the name of the song, the artist's name, the album title, any comments you want to add, and the genre of your music.

8. **Click OK.**

   The Save Bounce As dialog box opens.

9. **Enter the name for your MP3 file in the Save As field.**

10. **From the Where drop-down menu, choose the location for your new MP3 file.**

11. **Click Save.**

Your file is bounced (this will take a few minutes), and the MP3 shows up in the location that you specify in Step 10. You can take that file and use it in your marketing efforts.

Setting Up Your Own Music Website

No matter what else you do, you need to have your own website. A website is your calling card — a place where you can showcase yourself and your music. With your own site, you can provide a lot more information for visitors to read. You can also offer more products that may make you more money than your CDs — T-shirts for instance.

Having your own website is not without challenges. For example, you have to design and maintain the site, which can take a lot of time. You also have to pay for things like hosting (that is, a service that will host your site files on its servers so that people who visit your web address can see your site). If you intend to sell products on your site, you need to provide online ordering, which you can do with simple options like adding a Checkout button via PayPal or Google (which charge a small fee for each sale) or, for large sales volumes, by setting up a merchant account with a credit card company. In all, having a website can be time-consuming and costs money, so be prepared to do a fair amount of work if you really plan on making money from your website.

Checking out musician-friendly hosting services

Some hosting services make it easy to create a website for you or your band and allow you to offer downloads or streams of your music, CDs, and other merchandise. All the following sites are geared toward musicians. The one you choose will likely depend on the fit for you or your band. Here are some options:

✦ **Bandvista** (www.bandvista.com). Bandvista's plans start at $15/ month, and it has hundreds of templates to start your design.

✦ **Bandzoogle** (http://bandzoogle.com). Bandzoogle has plans starting at $10/month, though if you want to create a design of your own (not from a basic template) it'll run $15/month.

✦ **HostBaby** (www.hostbaby.com). HostBaby has one plan ($20/month or $199/year — your unique domain name is another $12/year) and offers five free CD submissions to CD Baby, so it's pretty competitive with the other sites.

✦ **Rock Web** (http://rockwebhosting.com). Rock Web has hosting plans starting at $10/month and offers pretty much the same options as other sites for the money, but their templates are somewhat limited for a band or musician. Still, you can be creative and set up a site quick and cheap. And like all the other sites, you don't need to know HTML or any other web code.

Each of these sites offers slightly different features for the money. Take a close look at their plans and keep in mind that, while all offer free trials, you're unlikely to move from one host site to another, so choose the site that you feel best about and whose features most closely match your needs.

Designing your site

Your first step in getting a website up and running is designing it. When you design your website, keep the following points in mind:

+ **Make your site easy to navigate.** Make sure that your visitors know where they are on your site at all times. It's often a good idea to have a menu bar on each page so that they can at least return to the home page without having to search for it.

+ **Consider mobile devices in your design.** Smartphones and tablet computers are a growing segment of online users, and many of them don't support Flash technology. So I recommend skipping the fancy Flash intro and jumping right into the meat of your site.

+ **Make ordering your CD (or other stuff) easy.** Put a Buy My CD button or link on every page.

+ **Double-check all your links.** Nothing is worse for a web surfer than clicking on links that don't work. If you have links on your site, double-check that each one works. And if you have links to other people's sites, check the links occasionally to make sure that the page you're linking to still exists.

+ **Test your site.** Before you sign off on your site design, check it from a slow connection and multiple devices if you can (or have your web developer do this for you). You instantly get a sense of whether your site's download time is speedy. If it's slow to load or confusing to navigate, keep working on it until it works. You may also want to check your site using different Internet browsers and screen resolutions to make sure that your site still looks good.

+ **Make your site your browser's home page.** Years ago, before I knew better, I had a site down for weeks because I didn't have it set as my default site in my browser. I didn't find out until I got a call from a friend who told me it was down.

For more tips and tricks on creating a great website, check out *Web Sites Do-It-Yourself For Dummies,* 2nd Edition, by Janine Warner (John Wiley & Sons, Inc.).

When your site is live on the Internet, techniques such as search engine optimization (SEO), which makes your site appear higher in search results and social media networking can help your site and your work get noticed. SEO techniques are constantly evolving and beyond the scope of this book, but you can check out *Search Engine Optimization For Dummies* by Peter Kent (also from John Wiley & Sons, Inc.) to find out details. You find a brief introduction to social media networking later in this chapter.

Putting Your Music on a Music Host Site

An *Internet music host site* is a website that allows you to add your music to its list of available music downloads. Putting your MP3s on a host site can give you exposure that you wouldn't otherwise be able to get. You can direct people to the site to listen to your music and also benefit from traffic that the site itself, other musicians, and the site's fans generate. For some of the larger sites, that can be a lot of potential listeners. Although MP3 host sites are constantly changing, a few have managed to hang around for a while.

Internet music host sites are always coming and going. To find out what sites are currently available and what they offer, check out `www.indieguide.com/category/view/Music_Hosting_Sites` for a comprehensive list.

Be sure to read and understand the contracts (often called agreements) that each of these sites requires you to agree to. Make sure that you don't sign away your rights to your music. If you're not sure that you like a particular agreement, don't sign up for the service. You can find plenty of other places to put your music on the Internet.

AudioStreet.net

`www.audiostreet.net`

AudioStreet.net is a free music site, offering free music hosting and downloads. You can upload your songs, create a blog, and join the forum to connect with other musicians and your fans. Of course, beyond the basic free plan (which gives you up to 3 songs, 20 pictures, a calendar for you to list your upcoming gigs, and some other basic services), you can enroll in comprehensive plans that go from $10 to $20 per month.

iLike.com

`www.ilike.com`

iLike promotes itself as a "social music discovery service" (whatever that is) and allows you to create and maintain a presence on several social media outlets by managing one account on its site using its Universal Artist Dashboard. It's free so check it out and see if you like the concept.

Last.fm

www.last.fm

Last.fm is a streaming radio service with a dynamic community. You can put your music on the site plus offer links to your CDs and downloads. You can also sign up for a plan that pays you for the streaming, but it won't amount to much unless you have a ton of plays (check out the Terms and Conditions for details).

MySpace.com

www.myspace.com

MySpace.com used to be *the* place to be on the Internet for musicians. Originally just a place to hang out for a few lonely souls, it became a cultural phenomenon — and then became a cautionary tale for anyone wanting to promote themselves online (due to bad publicity surrounding privacy and safety for MySpace members). Not to mention that many MySpace users' "friends" were just other bands wanting as many "friends" as possible, who had no real interest in other people's music. Of course, with the pace of the Internet and the recent sale of MySpace to Specific Media, MySpace may experience a renaissance and become popular again (stranger things have happened). Regardless, tons of people still go to MySpace.com, so it's worth keeping an eye on this site to see if it turns around.

Engaging in Social Media Networking

People are atwitter (sorry, I couldn't help myself) about social networking as a way to promote themselves. I'm personally still a bit cool on the actual sales that can be made using Twitter, Facebook, and the other social networking sites, but I won't deny that these sites generate a lot of activity, and activity is always a good thing. So I'm not really going out on a limb to suggest that you join the social networking world, too. It can be a great way to connect with your fans (and possibly attract new ones).

Aside from the music hosting sites I list earlier in this chapter, there are some general social networking sites musicians are using. Here is a list of the most popular ones (as of mid-2011 anyway — chances are that this list will be out of date before too long):

+ **Facebook:** Facebook is the "new" MySpace (and has been for some time). That is, it's the largest, most active community on the Internet. With its size and reach it's not going away anytime soon. So if you're not already on Facebook, you really need to get to it. Because of its size, many of the other musician-centric sites, such as ReverbNation, have apps that allow you to connect your account to your Facebook page. This gives you the best of both worlds and makes it easier to manage your social networking.

+ **Twitter:** Twitter lets you share news and links in 140 characters. And for some reason this type of blogging (called *micro-blogging*) has become popular. I'm willing to bet you're already using Twitter, regardless of how many tweets you actually create or if you just follow others. If you're not, you should at least try it out and see if you like it.

+ **Google+:** Google+ allows you to connect with your social circle in a myriad of ways, most of it centered on sharing in new and unique ways. Given that this is Google's creation, there is a good chance it will become popular — and if it does become popular, you're probably going to want to engage in it in some way.

There have been a lot of complaints and concerns about privacy and content ownership with these social networks. If either of these are an issue to you, make sure you read and understand the user agreements that you are bound by when you sign up and use these sites. If you're unsure whether you have privacy or if you give up any rights to your music by posting it on these sites, you're better off erring on the side of caution and limiting what you share.

Offering Free Downloads

Offering a freebie can be a good way to get people interested in your music and a way to turn people into fans. Online promotion of your music almost requires you to make downloads available to your potential fans. You can talk about your music all you want, but what people want is to *hear* your music. The purpose of the free download is to get your listener excited enough about your music that he buys your CD or comes to see your show.

Turning a freebie listener into a buyer isn't that difficult. My company offers a variety of free download demos, and we have found that over 10 percent of the people who take a free demo end up buying a CD or program from us. This is an inexpensive way for us to get new customers and a very good return on investment. On top of that, by allowing our customers to try our recording first, we receive fewer requests for a refund (contrary to what most music creators do, we offer a money-back guarantee on all our CDs and programs).

So you won't be surprised to hear me suggest that you should offer free demos/downloads of your music. (I won't suggest a money-back guarantee unless you're doing something with a therapeutic purpose, as I am.)

Give people a taste of your music and sell an upgrade — other tracks, CDs, vinyl records, boxed sets, CD-and-T-shirt packages, tickets to a live concert stream — anything that turns a casual listener into a fan. There are some good models out there for monetizing your music if you look around.

I'm not a fan of making all your music free to download as a way of generating buzz. I see a freebie as a teaser. I believe that if you offer your fans something, they will buy it. Even if you're "not in it for the money," charging for your music says that you value what you do. And if you value it, your fans will too.

Selling Downloads

People are downloading music at a growing rate and feel comfortable purchasing their music in a digital format (don't let anyone tell you that people won't pay for it in digital form — just look at the success of iTunes, for example). When my company made our CDs available as downloaded files, it took less than five months for our download sales to overtake our physical CD sales. Now downloads account for almost 80 percent of our generalized recording revenues. And the best part is that we don't have to print or ship anything.

Tons of sites can host your music downloads, for free or at a cost to your fans. These sites include iTunes, Rhapsody, and Amazon.com. Depending on the online music provider, you may or may not be able to put up your music yourself. Here's a short list of the more popular online music sites:

- ✦ **iTunes** (www.itunes.com): iTunes is the most popular download-music site, so I recommend that you make your music available there. The problem is that unless you have 20 professionally manufactured albums with ISRC codes for each track, iTunes won't take your music. The good news is that iTunes will accept your music, even if it's just one CD, if you use an approved aggregator, such as CD Baby or TuneCore.

- ✦ **Amazon.com** (www.amazon.com): Yes, you can sell your music on Amazon.com. Boasting that it's the world's largest online retailer, Amazon.com offers two categories — Professional seller and Individual seller — so you will find a category that fits you. Go to www.amazon services.com for more information. To sell downloads on Amazon, your CDs need to be online, and you need to set up an artist page. If you don't have a physical CD on Amazon.com, you can still get your MP3s on the site by using one of the aggregators I list in this section.

+ **CD Baby (**http://members.cdbaby.com/whatwedo/default.aspx**):** CD Baby is an online music store that specializes in independent artists. Aside from allowing you to sell your physical CD, you can also sell your digital downloads. In fact, CD Baby not only enables you to sell CDs on its site easily, but as an aggregator, it can also help you sell your downloads on other sites (such as iTunes, Rhapsody, and Amazon.com). And CD Baby takes only 9 percent of your revenue for the trouble.

+ **TuneCore (**www.tunecore.com**):** TuneCore is an online music distributor and, as such, helps you make your music available in a lot of places. These include Amazon.com, iTunes, eMusic, Spotify, and others. TuneCore charges $50 per year for each CD/album you upload.

+ **Music Host Network (**www.musichostnetwork.com**):** Music Host Network is an online music distributor, like TuneCore, and offers pretty much the same service at the same price ($50 per year). You can try Music Host Network for free, although a free account has very limited digital distribution.

This is a very short list of online options. Look around for other places to sell your digitally formatted music. There are a ton of them — and more showing up every day.

Streaming Audio

Streaming audio is basically an audio file that begins playing without actually downloading to your listener's computer. The advantages are that it greatly reduces the amount of time your listener has to wait to hear your music, and it keeps your listener from being able to steal your music. The downside is that the quality of the audio can be lower.

You don't have to know any of this if you go with a website host that is set up for musicians, such as those I list in the "Setting Up Your Own Music Website" section at the beginning of this chapter. These hosts take care of creating the appropriate code for you.

You always want to make the process of navigating your site and listening to your music as fast as possible. This provides a much better experience than having to wait. The less time a person has to wait, the more likely he or she is to return. The more repeat visitors you get, the better the chance you have for selling CDs.

You can create streaming audio in a number of ways, but the most common is with an MP3 file. The process is the same with either method, except that your filenames are going to be different. Note that you need an encoder that can create a RealAudio file if you want to go that route.

The following steps walk you through the process of getting your MP3 file to stream on your site:

1. **Create an MP3 file, using a bit rate of 128 Kbps.**

2. **Save the MP3 file so that you can identify it.**

The easiest way to do this is to save your file as `songname128.mp3` (the 128 stands for 128 Kbps).

3. **Create a pointer file and name it** `songname64.m3u`**.**

A *pointer file* is a file that directs your visitor's audio player to the song so that it plays without waiting for the entire song to download. This file contains directions to your MP3 file. For example, your file would contain the following text:

`http://www.YourWebSiteAddress/songname128.mp3.`

You can also use the M3U file to create a playlist — that is, have more than one song play without making your visitor go to another page on your website. To do this, simply add another song on another line. Adding two more songs would then look like this:

```
www.YourWebSiteAddress/songname128.mp3
www.YourWebSiteAddress/anothersongname128.mp3
www.YourWebSiteAddress/yetanothersongname64.mp3
```

The M3U file plays the songs in the order they are listed in this file.

Keep in mind that if your visitor doesn't have an audio player, he or she can't listen to your music. It's a good idea to put a link on your site to another site where your listener can download an audio player.

4. **Create a hyperlink on your web page to the** `songname128.m3u` **file.**

For example, you can put the hyperlink in some text, like this: `Check out our new song, songname`; then link the text to the file. Or, you can place the hyperlink in a picture or graphic (or both).

5. **Upload your MP3 file, your pointer file, and the new page with your hyperlink to your website.**

6. **Go to your website and test how the streaming audio works.**

Make sure that your site-hosting service has its MIME types configured for MP3. Otherwise your streaming audio files won't work. (Don't worry. The people who work for your hosting service will know what you're talking about when you mention MIME types. That's their job.)

If all this sounds like too much work, you can just create a link to the streaming files on your MP3 host site. Then people can still hear your music, even if it isn't available on your site.

Podcasting

Podcasting is another way to offer audio online. Typically, podcasts are media feeds that your visitors can subscribe to and get updates automatically as they're published. If you regularly update your music or if you want to have an audio blog (or video blog) that your fans can listen to (or watch), this can be a great way to keep the fans involved in your music.

The process of creating a podcast starts with recording the content and then putting it in an MP3 format (if you're doing audio). You have this book, so you can create audio content easily. Just follow the steps outlined throughout the book to record and convert your music. Next, you need to host it or have a podcasting site host it for you. This process can get pretty complicated, so I recommend checking out *Podcasting For Dummies,* 2nd Edition, by Tee Morris, Chuck Tomasi, Evo Terra, and Kreg Steppe (John Wiley & Sons, Inc.). You can also check out these sites to learn more about podcasting:

+ **The Apple podcast page (**`www.apple.com/itunes/podcasts/specs.html`**):** This page on the Apple website contains tons of information on creating a podcast and publishing it. This is a good place to start.

+ **The Dummies.com podcasting series (**`http://etips.dummies.com/rss/podcastingfde.xml`**):** Here is a great podcast series describing how to podcast, brought to you by the authors of *Podcasting For Dummies.*

+ **Podcast.com (**`http://podcast.com`**):** Podcast.com has a ton of information about podcasting, both from a subscriber's and a creator's point of view. This is a good site to get you up to speed on what podcasting is and what you need to do to get started. The site doesn't offer the tools and steps to create your podcast, but after you have the content and your feed information, you can post your podcast on this site.

+ **Podcasting Tools (**`http://podcasting-tools.com`**):** As the URL suggests, this site has information, links, and tools for creating a podcast. This is a good place to find quality information.

If you're ready to get started podcasting, here are several sites worth looking into:

+ `www.hipcast.com`: Hipcast is an easy-to-use site that lets you create and publish your audio or video blogs. This site offers a 7-day free trial period, with plans starting at $5 per month. You don't find a lot of information on this site about podcasting, but if you're ready to give it a try, this is a good inexpensive option.

+ `http://podhoster.com`: podHoster, as the name states, hosts podcasts. With this service, you record your audio and podHoster hosts it. This is a good option for musicians who record their own music and know the ins and outs of the audio-creation process (that would be you after you've read this book). podHoster offers a 30-day free trial, with monthly plans starting at $5.

Selling Your CDs

Regardless of whether you have your own site, you can always sell your CDs on the Internet through other outlets. An advantage to selling your music through other online stores is that you can capitalize on the traffic that the store generates. A number of online retailers are out there, but the following list gives you the lowdown on some of the major players:

+ **CD Baby** (www.cdbaby.com): CD Baby puts your CD on its site for a small setup fee ($35). For this, you get a web page (which the people at CD Baby design) with pictures, bios, MP3s, and streaming audio. The site sells your CD for any price you set, takes $4 from the sale, and gives you the rest. You even receive an e-mail whenever someone buys one of your CDs. Signing up is easy; just direct your browser to www.cdbaby.com and click the Sell Your CD icon. The instructions are clear, and helpful articles on the site can help you to, well, sell your CD.

+ **Bandcamp** (www.bandcamp.com): Bandcamp is a way for you to sell, not only your CDs online, but also merchandise such as t-shirts, coffee mugs, and so on. Bandcamp doesn't charge a monthly fee but does take a cut — 15 percent or less, depending on how much you sell and the prices you set.

+ **Amazon.com** (www.amazon.com): If you want to sell your physical CD on Amazon.com, all you need is a "retail-ready" package (professional manufacturer and with a UPC code on it). To join, point your browser to www.amazonservices.com/ and follow the prompts.

Because the Internet is constantly changing and growing, you may find other sites that allow you to sell your music online. Use your favorite search engine to search for the phrase *sell your CD*. This gives you a ton of other places to consider when selling your CD online.

Promoting Your Music

The whole point of making CDs and putting MP3s of your music on the Internet is to promote and sell your music. To do this, you need exposure. As with any promotion technique, there are no hard-and-fast rules except to use your imagination. Experience will be your guide, but here are some ideas to get you started:

+ **Start an e-mail newsletter.** An e-mail newsletter is an inexpensive way to keep your music on people's minds. Try to be somewhat consistent in sending it out, but don't just send out the same message on a regular basis. Give your subscribers something. Provide new information in your e-mail, such as a press release about where you're playing next or a link to a new song that you've just uploaded. Check out the "Connecting with an E-Mail Newsletter" section later in this chapter.

✦ **Put your website address on everything.** People can't come to you if they don't know that you exist. So print your website address on all your promotional materials, including the CD itself. Also, include your website address on all e-mails and Internet correspondence that you do (as a signature on Internet forums if you belong to any, for example).

✦ **Network.** Check out as many independent-musician sites as you can. You not only learn a lot about marketing your music, but you'll also have an opportunity to spread the word about your music. Check out Getsigned.com (`www.getsigned.com`).

✦ **Stay up to date.** Keep track of where you put your music and check back often to make sure everything is working properly. Websites change and go out of business often. Unless you check the site occasionally, you might not know if your music suddenly disappears from there. Also, routinely search for new places to put your music.

✦ **Get linked.** Try to get folks to link from their sites to your own. Likewise, share the wealth and link to other sites that you like. Cross-promotion can be a good thing and allow you to pool your fan base with another band. This doesn't take away from your sales (after all, *you* listen to more than one band's CDs, right?). Visitors to your site will appreciate the link and will probably check back to see whether you added any new ones.

Connecting with an E-Mail Newsletter

An e-mail newsletter is an inexpensive way to keep your music on people's minds. Try to send newsletters to your subscribers somewhat consistently, but don't just send out the same message on a regular basis. Give your subscribers new information, such as a press release about where you're playing next or a link to a new song that you've just uploaded.

Don't send your newsletter to anyone who hasn't asked to receive it. This is called *spamming,* and it's illegal.

To build a subscriber list, encourage people to sign up for your mailing list at your gigs and on your website. Or offer them a free download when they sign up on your website, and put a subscription form on every page. (Check out my day-job website to see this in action at `www.stronginstitute.com`.) Always provide an easy way for users to unsubscribe from your list.

If you're serious about sending out an e-mail newsletter, an e-mail service provider (ESP) can collect and manage addresses and send out your messages. The advantages of using an e-mail service provider include ease of use, but the most important is that a good ESP will help your messages get to your subscriber. Sending e-mails directly from your e-mail account can get your messages blocked — and if the e-mail host (such as Gmail or Yahoo!) labels you as spam, they will ban your messages. The rules on this get pretty complicated, and trying to keep up with changes and be compliant is a fulltime job.

Your best solution to make sure your messages go through is to use an experienced ESP. Here are a few I recommend:

✦ **AWeber** (www.aweber.com). AWeber has been around a long time (I've used them for the last five years) and has the best customer service I've come across in this industry. You can actually get someone on the phone. In fact, they encourage it. Their plans start at $19/month (for up to 500 subscribers). You can try AWeber for a month for only a dollar, and they offer excellent e-mail marketing advice (through a newsletter, videos, and blogs).

✦ **Constant Contact** (www.constantcontact.com). This is a popular ESP that is easy to use and offers a 60-day free trial. Their basic (500-subscriber) plan is $15/month. Plans with more subscribers cost about the same as the other providers I list here. I haven't used Constant Contact, but I have friends who are very happy with this provider.

✦ **MailChimp** (www.mailchimp.com). I also use MailChimp, and what I like about this ESP is that it's super-easy to use and their data tracking (of clicks and whatnot) is very good. What I don't like is that they will not get on the phone with you if you have problems. You're stuck with instant chat or e-mail (not the worst thing but kind of annoying if you have a complicated problem). They have a free account option that allows you to try them out and see if you like them. Once you get to a couple thousand subscribers, their cost is about the same as everyone else in this list.

You can find a lot more by doing an Internet search using "E-mail Service Provider" or "e-mail marketing" as your search term.

If you choose a music-centric company to host your website (check out the "Setting Up Your Own Music Website" section earlier in this chapter), you may find that your blast e-mail needs are taken care of and you don't need to hire a separate ESP. However, if you end up with a lot of fans, you may find the features offered by a dedicated ESP useful.

Index

Numerics

0 (Single track) option, 233
¹/₄-inch plugs
  on Mbox Pro, 146
  mono/TS, 34–35
  overview, 34
  stereo/TRS, 35–36
1 (Multi-track) option, 233
3:1 rule, 263
4-band EQs, 571–572
7-band EQs, 571–572
16 bit mastering, 653
48v switch, 150

A

A connector, 40
A New Track option, 513
A New Track per Pitch option, 513
AAC (Advanced Audio Coding) format,
  32, 216
AAX (Avid Audio Extension) format, 556
Absolute Grid mode, 348
Absolute mode, 405
absolute time reference, 372
absorbers, 50, 52, 277
ACID files, 216
Acid program, 22
acoustic instruments
  compressing, 587–588
  equalizing, 575, 578
  miking, 105, 277–279
acoustical foam, 47
acoustics, 49
active monitors, 29
A/D converters, 18
ADAT Lightpipe connections, 39, 136
ADAT option, 159
Add option
  Change Velocity section, 508
  Import Audio dialog box, 218
Advanced Audio Coding (AAC) format,
  32, 216

Advanced Settings tab, 130
Advanced System Settings link, 128
AES/EBU connections, 38–39, 151
After Playback option, 317, 459
After Write Pass, Switch To setting, 614
after-touch feature, 76, 444
AIFF (Audio Interchange File Format)
  format, 31, 216, 630
Algorithm setting, 603
aligning clips, 396–397
All Except option, 444
All Notes option, 512
All option
  Alternates Match Criteria dialog box, 330
  Data to Import menu, 226
Alt In jacks, 148
Alternate Playlists check box, 226
Alternates Match options, 330
Amazon Cloud Drive service, 134
Amazon website, 685, 689
Amber dial, 152
ambient miking, 259, 261–262
analog connections
  ¹/₄-inch plugs, 34–36
  inputs on Eleven Rack, 148
  inputs on Mbox, 140
  inputs on Mbox Pro, 144
  overview, 33
  RCA connector, 37
  XLR connector, 36–37
analog devices, 563
analog mixers, 58–59, 530
analog-to-digital (A/D) converters, 18
Another Note option, 497
Apply Real-Time Properties check box, 233
Apply SRC check box, 225
arrangement levels, 536
assign switches, mixing boards, 67
At Selection option, 389
At Transients option, 389
Attack knob
  Bombfactory limiter, 590
  Compressor plug-in, 583
  compressors, 269
  expander/gate plug-in, 592

Attack Velocity field, 488
Attacks check box, 446, 504
attenuating sound, 26
audio. *See also* editing audio;
    recording audio
  exporting clip definitions, 232–233
  exporting clips, 229–231
  exporting stereo files, 231–232
  overview, 229
  streaming, 686–687
audio clips, defined, 337
Audio Clips list
  auditioning from, 327–328
  clearing files from, 332–333
  using, 352–353
audio drives, 119
audio dropout, defined, 162
Audio File Type drop-down menu, 166
audio files
  file types, 215–216
  importing, 217–220
  overview, 171, 215
Audio Interchange File Format (AIFF)
    format, 31, 216, 630
Audio Media Options drop-down menu, 223
audio regions, 164
audio tracks, 197–199, 241, 610
AudioStreet website, 682
AudioSuite offline plug-ins
  overview, 559–562
  using to process audio clips, 562
Audition button, 424
Audition Paths option, 164
auditioning
  from Audio Clips list, 327–328
  choosing from track playlists, 329
  end points, 384–385
  matching criteria, 329–330
  from multiple tracks, 331
  overview, 327
  start points, 384
  from Takes List drop-down menu, 328–329
Auto button, 558
Auto Input Monitoring mode, 300, 317
Auto Latch mode, 612
Auto Off mode, 611
Auto Read mode, 611

Auto Renaming option, 231
Auto Touch mode, 612
Auto Write mode, 612
Auto-Created clips, 339
AutoMatch Time setting, 613
Automatically Check for Updates When
    You Have a Network Connection
    check box, 121
automation
  audio tracks, 610
  auxiliary input tracks, 610
  drawing, 620–621
  editing data, 622–626
  enabling, 614–615
  Grabber tool, 417–418
  instrument tracks, 610
  master fader tracks, 610
  MIDI tracks, 611
  modes of, 611–612
  overview, 609
  Selector tool, 417
  setting preferences for, 612–614
  Smart tool, 492
  thinning, 621–622
  Trimmer tool, 416–417
  viewing, 619
  writing, 616–619
Automation Safe button, 554, 558
Auto-Name Memory Location option,
    377, 379
Auto-Name Memory Locations When
    Playing option, 376
AutoPlay feature, 130–131
auto-tuning, 28
Auto-Update Active Configuration
    option, 212
Aux Assign feature, 70–71
Aux Return jacks, 73
Auxiliary (Aux) Return knobs, 70
Auxiliary (Aux) Send knobs, 64–66, 70
Auxiliary bus, 68
auxiliary input tracks, 202, 241, 610
auxiliary inputs, 546–547
Avid Audio Extension (AAX) format, 556
Avid interfaces, 14, 153–154
AWeber website, 691
axial room mode, 49

B

B connector, 40
backing up files, 236–237
backplates, 92
backup vocals
  compressing, 585–586
  equalizing, 577
  miking, 272–274
  mixing, 532
balanced cords, 12, 36
balancing levels, 650–651
Bandcamp website, 689
Bandvista website, 680
Bandzoogle website, 680
bar/beat reference, 372
Basic and High Contrast Themes
    section, 126
bass drum. *See* kick drum
bass guitars
  compressing, 587
  connecting to Mbox Mini, 139
  EQ recommendations for, 575
  equalizing, 578
  mixing, 533
bass traps, 53–55
batch fades, 431–432
Baxandall curve, 649
Bayonet Neil-Concelman (BNC)
    connector, 136
BF76 peak limiter, 590–591
bidirectional microphones, 98
bit depth, 17–18
Bit Depth setting, 166, 230
bit rate, 675–676
bits
  16 Bits option, 653
  defined, 17
  dithering, 652
  overview, 651
  truncation, 652
Blocks view, 473
Blumlein technique, 263
BNC (Bayonet Neil-Concelman)
    connector, 136

BNC wordclock, 144
Bombfactory BF76 peak limiter, 589–591
Bottom option, 512
bouncing
  options for, 629–631
  overview, 627
  performing, 631–632
boundary microphones, 92, 94–96
breakpoints
  defined, 416, 475
  editing, 417, 490
  scaling, 490–491
Broadcast .WAV File (BWF), 216, 630
buffers, 20, 119
burning CDs, 659–662
Bus tab, 164
busing signals
  Aux Assign feature, 70–71
  Auxiliary (Aux) Return knobs, 70
  Auxiliary (Aux) Send knobs, 70
  Control Room level knob, 70
  Master fader, 68
  Master Level meters, 71
  overview, 67–68
  Phones knob, 70
  Solo/Mute switches, 70
  Sub faders, 68–69
BWF (Broadcast .WAV File), 216, 630
By Percentage field, 510
Bypass button, 561

C

cables
  for microphones, 109
  MIDI, 76
cache buffers, 20, 119
canceling performances, 462
Capture Clip command, 388
cardioid microphones, 98, 100
CD Baby website, 686, 689
CDs
  burners of, 661–662
  burning, 659–660
  CD-Rs, 660

CDs *(continued)*
  computer-based recorders, 661
  duplication, 665–666
  making copies of, 664–665
  mass production of, 662–664
  mastering with, 31
  replication, 666–668
  selling, 689
centered crossfades, 426–427
central processing unit (CPU), 19, 123
Change Continuously option, 510
Change Duration MIDI operation, 509–510
Change Duration option, 503
change markers, 489
Change Smoothly by Percentage option, 509
Change Smoothly option, 509
Change Velocity MIDI operation, 508–509
Change Velocity option, 503
channel auxiliary (Aux) send knobs, 64–66
channel code, 79
Channel selector button, 559
channel strips
  audio tracks, 197–199
  auxiliary input tracks, 202
  Comments view section, 203–204
  devices including, 109
  Inserts view section, 205–206
  instrument tracks, 200–201
  Master Fader tracks, 202–203
  MIDI tracks, 199–200
  overview, 61, 197
  stereo and mono, 203
channels, MIDI, 78–79, 449–450
Check for Solutions to Problem Reports
  option, 127
chipset, drives, 119
chorus effects, 27, 607
Clear Audio dialog box, 236
Clear Memory Location option, 379
Clear Selected command, 236
click tracks
  choosing meter, 307–308, 451–452
  configuring devices for, 452–454
  configuring external devices, 305–306
  connecting external devices to sound
    click, 306

  creating tempo or meter events, 308–309
  defined, 177
  editing tempo and meter events, 309–310
  enabling, 308
  overview, 304–305, 451
  setting tempo, 307, 451
Click/Countoff Options dialog box, 305
Clip End option, 330
Clip End Pad slider, 420
Clip List Selection Follows Track Selection
  check box, 353
Clip Rating check box, 330
Clip Start option, 330
Clip Start Pad slider, 420
Clipboard option, 513
clipping, 25, 297, 418
clips
  aligning, 396–397
  AudioSuite offline plug-ins, using to
    process, 562
  creating, 388–390
  defined, 171
  deleting, 433–434
  displaying information, 355
  fading in, 430
  fading out, 430–431
  finding, 354–355
  locking, 405–406
  MIDI, editing, 478
  moving, 402–405
  muting/unmuting, 407–408
  overview, 352–353
  placing in tracks, 392–394
  quantizing, 406–407
  selecting, 353, 360–362
  sorting, 354
  synch points, 394–396
  trimming, 398–402
  types of, 338–339
  viewing, 340–347
Clips and Media option, 226
Clips Gain option, 226
Clips list
  clearing files from, 463
  overview, 193
Clips view, 474

clock source setting, 158–159

Close button, 552

close miking. *See* spot miking

Cloud storage, 134

coincident stereo miking, 262

colors, assigning to tracks, 247–248

Command Keyboard Focus feature, 345, 368, 370–371

Comments field
   Memory Location dialog box, 373
   New Window Configuration dialog box, 209
   Window Configurations List window, 210

Comments view section, 203–204

Compact Selected command, 234–235

compacting files, 234–236, 434–435

Compare button
   AudioSuite menu, 561
   Real Time Plug-In window, 558

compressors
   acoustic instruments, 587–588
   electric basses, 587
   electric guitars, 586–587
   kick drums, 588
   mastering with, 638
   microphones, 108–109
   overview, 25–26, 582
   parameters for, 582–584
   percussion, 588
   plug-ins for, 108
   snare drums, 588
   transients, 268–270
   using, 584–585
   vocals, 585–586

computer control surfaces, 16, 60–61

computer mastering
   MIDI format, 31
   MP3 format, 31–32
   overview, 31
   WAV and AIFF formats, 31

computer recorders
   input and output, 21–22
   overview, 18–21
   software for, 22

computers. *See also* Mac computers; PC computers
   backing up data, 133–134
   CD burners, 661

overview, 117
Pro Tools requirements, 19

condenser microphones
   choosing, 104
   diaphragm sizes of, 94
   overview, 92
   phantom power, 93, 297
   recording vocals with, 271–272
   tube or solid state, 93–94

Conductor button, 180

conductor events, 363

connections, changing from unbalanced to balanced, 12. *See also* analog connections; digital connections

consoles, 75

Consolidate from Source Media option, 224

consolidating selections, 433

Constant Contact website, 691

continuous controller data
   drawing, 483
   editing breakpoints, 490
   editing lines with Pencil tool, 489–490
   overview, 489
   scaling breakpoints, 490–491

Control Panel settings, 127–129

Control Room level knob, 70

control surfaces, 528

control-change MIDI messages, 80

Controller Meter Path option, 163

Controller option, 497

Controller view, 475, 492

Conversion Quality setting, 631

Convert option, 218

Copy command
   overview, 410
   using for automation, 624

Copy from Source Media option, 224

counter displays, 187–188

Counters section, 176–177

Countoff button, 180

cover art, 665

CPU (central processing unit), 19, 123

CPU Usage Limit setting, 161

Create a blank session option, 165

Create a Session from Template option, 165

Create Click Track option, 304

Create Group dialog box, 251

crossfades
  centered, 426–427
  creating, 416
  deleting, 429
  Fades dialog box, 423–426
  overview, 426
  post-, 428–429
  pre-, 427–428
  removing, 429
  trimming, 429
Current Time option, 343
Cursor display, 191–192
Custom Allocation Options check box, 293
Cut command
  for automation, 623–624
  overview, 409–410
cymbals
  equalizing, 576, 579
  miking, 106, 285

D

D/A converters, 18
daisychain setups, 76–77
data
  automation, 622–626
  backing up, 133–134
Data to Import menu, 226
DAW (Digital Audio Workstation), 125
dead rooms, 47, 50, 270–271
Decay setting, 603
De-Esser plug-in, 594–596
Default to Marker option, 377, 379
Degree of Thinning drop-down menu, 613
delay
  compensation for, 162
  overview, 27, 605
  settings for, 605–606
  using, 606
Delay Compensation Engine setting,
    161–162
Delete All option
  Memory Locations window, 379
  Window Configurations drop-down
    menu, 212

Delete Unused option, 351
deleting
  automation, 623–624
  clips, 433–434
  crossfades, 429
  events, 499
  files, 236
  groups, 253
  MIDI notes, 484–485
  playlists, 351–352
  program changes, 485
  takes, 332–333, 461–463
  tracks, 250
Depth parameter, 605
desiccant packets, 112
designer cords, 35
Destination Sample Rate setting, 225
Destination Track drop-down menu, 515
Destructive Record mode
  canceling performances in, 332
  overview, 290
  performing punches in, 323
  using Record button in, 176
Device Manager button, 124
devices
  analog, external, 563
  digital, external, 564
devices, MIDI
  Input filter, 444–445
  offsetting tracks, 447–448
  overview, 439–448
  quantizing inputs, 445–447
  setting up in Mac OS X, 440–442
  setting up in Windows 7, 442–443
  Thru feature, 443–444
DI functions jack, 142
diaphragms, in microphones, 92–94, 104
Diffusion setting, 603
Digital Audio Workstation (DAW), 125
digital connections
  ADAT Lightpipe, 39
  AES/EBU, 38–39
  FireWire, 41
  MIDI, 38
  overview, 37–38
  S/PDIF, 39

TDIF, 40
Thunderbolt, 41–42
USB, 40–41
digital devices, 564
digital mixers, 59–60, 529–530
digital recorders
  A/D and D/A converters, 18
  bit depth, 17–18
  overview, 17
  sampling rate, 17
Digital Signal Processing (DSP) cards, 125
digital-to-analog (D/A) converters, 18
direct boxes, 10, 12, 298
Direct Out jacks, 72
directional microphones, 98
disk allocation
  hard drives, 292–293
  multiple hard drives, 293–294
  overview, 292
Display Adapters option, 124
distant miking, 259, 261
dithering, 426, 652
DMA feature, 125, 130
Do Not Import option, 227
downloadable music files
  bit rate, 675–676
  free, 684–685
  overview, 673–675
  selling, 685–686
  stereo and mono, 676–677
Draw Waveforms Rectified option, 340
drawing automation, 620–621
Dropbox service, 134
drum machines, 75, 85
drums
  compressing, 588
  cymbals, 285
  equalizing, 578–580
  hi-hats, 284–285
  kick (bass) drum, 281–282
  mics for recording, 105
  mixing, 285–286, 533
  overheads, using for, 104
  overview, 279
  rooms, 281
  snare-drums, 283

tom-toms, 284
tuning, 279–281
types of sets, 280
dry signals, 66
DSP (Digital Signal Processing) cards, 125
Duplicate command, 411–412
duplication of CDs, 665–666
Duration Between option, 512
Duration check box
  Flatten Performance operation, 518
  Restore Performance operation, 517
duration of notes, 486
dynamic microphones
  overview, 92, 96–97
  recording vocals with, 271
Dynamic option, 198
dynamic processors
  compressors, 25–26, 582–588
  connecting, 581–582
  De-Esser plug-in, 594–596
  expanders, 26, 591, 594
  gates, 26, 591–594
  limiters, 25–26, 589–591
  overview, 24–25, 581
  side chains, 596–598
dynamic range
  compressing, 25
  defined, 24
dynamics
  optimizing, 646–648
  overview, 535–536

E

ear fatigue, 538–539
Edit and Mix option, 252
Edit commands
  clearing selections with, 410–411
  Copy, 410
  Cut, 409–410
  Duplicate, 411–412
  overview, 409
  Paste, 411
  Repeat, 412
Edit groups, 192–193, 254–255

Edit Insert points
    placing clips at, 393–394
    placing sync points at, 395–396
Edit Memory Location option, 379, 381–382
Edit modes
    displaying grid lines, 349–350
    moving clips with, 404–405
    overview, 184–185, 347–349
    setting grid resolution, 349
Edit Selection button, 190
Edit window
    adding MIDI events, 482–485
    changing continuous controller data,
        489–491
    changing MIDI events, 485–488
    counter displays, 187–188
    custom note duration, 482
    deleting MIDI notes, 484–485
    deleting program changes, 485
    edit modes, 184–185
    edit tools, 186–187
    editing program data, 488–491
    Event Edit area, 188–189
    lists, 192–193
    navigation controls, 189–192
    overview, 181, 248, 479
    Pencil tools, 479–482
    Pre- and Post-Roll flags in, 315
    rulers, 193–196
    Smart tool, 491–492
    track controls, 181–184
    Zoom controls, 185–186
Edit Window Display Settings option, 208
Edit Window Settings icon, 210
editing audio
    aligning clips, 396–397
    clip synch points, 394–396
    clip types, 338–339
    clips, 352–355
    compacting files, 434–435
    consolidating selections, 433
    creating clips, 388–390
    crossfades, 423–429
    Edit commands, 409–412
    Edit modes, 347–350
    fades, 423–426, 429–432

healing clips, 390–392
locking clips, 405–406
memory locations, 371–383
moving clips, 402–405
muting/unmuting clips, 407–408
nondestructive editing, 338
Object Grabber tool, 365–366
overview, 337, 387
Pencil tool, 418–420
placing clips in tracks, 392–394
during playback, 338
playlists, 350–352
quantizing clips, 406–407
removing unused clips, 433–434
selecting all clips in tracks, 363
selecting clips across multiple tracks, 362
selecting entire clips, 362
selecting entire tracks, 363
selecting parts of clips, 360–362
selecting two clips, 362
Selection Indicator fields, 364–365
selections, 367–371, 383–385
silencing selections, 420–423
Smart tool, 413–418
splitting stereo tracks, 408–409
Tab to Transients function, 366
trimming clips, 398–402
Undo feature, 355–357
viewing clips, 340–347
editing memory locations
    changing properties of, 381–382
    copying and pasting, 382–383
    overview, 380
    renaming, 381
editing MIDI. *See also* Edit window
    clips, 478
    MIDI Event list, 492–500
    note chasing, 479
    overview, 473
    setting patches on tracks, 478
    tracks, 473–477
Effect Bypass button, 557
effects. *See also* external effects
    routing, 600–602
    turning off in inserts, 548
    turning off in sends, 551

effects processors
  chorus, 27
  delay, 27
  flanger, 27–28
  overview, 26–27
  pitch correction, 28
  reverb, 27
Elastic Audio Track State option, 226
electric basses
  compressing, 587
  mics for recording amps, 105
  miking, 276–277
electric guitars
  compressing, 586–587
  EQ recommendations for, 575
  equalizing, 577
  mics for recording amps, 105
  miking, 274–277
electronic instruments. *See* MIDI
Eleven Rack interfaces
  guitar-processing features, 151–152
  input and outputs, 148–151
  overview, 148
e-mail newsletters, 690–691
EMC Retrospect program, 134
Enable check box, 515
Enable DMA check box, 130
Enable Numeric Keypad Shortcuts check
    box, 516
Enable Session File Auto Backup check
    box, 168
encoding
  music, 678–680
  software, 677–678
End counter, 178
End field, 488
End Point markers, 322–323
end points
  aligning clips using, 396–397
  auditioning, 384–385
  dragging markers along ruler bar, 465–466
  nudging, 369
Energy Saver icon, 120
Enforce Avid Compatibility option, 231
Equal Gain option, 426
Equal Power option, 426

equalization (EQ)
  4-band and 7-band, 571–572
  bass, 578
  drums, 578–580
  guidelines for, 574–576
  guitars, 577
  inserting EQ plug-in in tracks, 569–570
  low-pass/high-pass, 568, 573
  low-shelf/high-shelf, 568, 572–573
  mastering with, 638
  mixing, 526
  mixing board controls for, 64
  overview, 567
  parametric, 567–568, 572
  percussion, 580
  piano, 580
  vocals, 577
equalizers
  graphic, 23
  overview, 23
  parametric, 24
  shelf, 24
Error Reporting feature, 127
Event column, 495
Event Edit area, 188–189
Event list
  changing data, 499–500
  deleting events, 499
  inserting MIDI events, 496–499
  menus, 493–495
  navigating, 495–496
  overview, 492–493
events, MIDI. *See* MIDI events
Expanded section, 177–178
expanders
  overview, 26, 591
  using, 594
Export as Stereo Interleaved Files
    option, 229
Export Audio Clips as Files option, 229
Export Clip Definitions option, 229
Export Selected dialog box, 230
exporting files from sessions
  audio, 229–233
  MIDI, 233–234
  overview, 228

external devices
  analog, 563
  configuring click tracks for, 305–306
  connecting to sound clicks, 306
  digital, 564
external effects
  connecting external analog devices to, 563
  connecting external digital devices to, 564
  hardware inserts, 563
  overview, 562–563
  routing tracks, 564–565
external hard drives, 21
external master decks, 632–633
external preamps, 14, 64
Extract button, 421

F

Facebook service, 684
Fade Curves buttons, 424
faders on mixing boards, 67
fades
  creating batch fades, 431–432
  Fades dialog box, 423–426
  fading in clips, 430
  fading out clips, 430–431
  overview, 429
  working in Waveform view, 415–416
Fades dialog box, 423–426
Fast Forward button, 175
Fast Track devices, 153–154
feedback, defined, 312
Feedback parameter, 606
figure-8 microphones, 98, 100–101
File Mode Selector menu, 561
File Type drop-down menu, 630
File Type setting, 230
files
  backing up, 236–237
  clearing from Audio Clips list, 332–333
  clearing from Clips list, 463
  compacting, 234–236, 434–435
  creating copies of, 418–419
  deleting, 236
  downloadable, 673–677
  exporting from sessions, 228–234

  importing into sessions, 215–228
  MIDI, 172
  MP3, 677–680
  overview, 215
FireWire connections, 41
FireWire ports, 21
FireWire standards, 41
flanger effect, 27–28
Flatten Performance MIDI operation, 517–518
Flatten Performance option, 503
footswitch controls, 159
Footswitch input
  on Eleven Rack, 149
  on Mbox Pro, 144, 147
Force Stereo mode, 677
Force to Target Session Format option, 224
Format drop-down menu, 630
formats
  for audio files, 31–32
  tracks, 242
4-band EQs, 571–572
48v switch, 150
Free Hand Pencil tool, 480
Free Hand tool, 620
Freq settings
  low-pass/high-pass EQ, 573
  low-shelf/high-shelf EQ, 572
  parametric EQ, 572
frequencies, 557–558
Frequency parameter, 595
FX Loop jack, 151

G

Gain setting
  Compressor plug-in, 269, 583
  delay settings, 605
  on Eleven Rack, 150
  low-shelf/high-shelf EQ settings, 573
  parametric EQ settings, 572
Gap option, 509
gates
  overview, 26, 591
  parameters for, 592–593
  using, 593–594

General Properties memory location, 375
GM Level 1 standards, 81–82
GM level 2 standards, 82
Go to End button, 176
Go To option, 493
Google+ service, 684
GR meter, 584
Grabber tool
  automating, 417–418
  automation, using for, 625
  overview, 415
  Smart tool, using with, 492
  tracks, using with, 476–477
graphic EQ, 23
graphical user interface (GUI), 87
graphics cards, 124
Grid button, 315
grid lines, 349–350
Grid mode
  moving clips in, 405
  placing clips in, 393
  Trimmer tool, using in, 399
grid resolution, 349
Grid Value option, 191
Grid/Groove Quantize MIDI operation,
  504–507
Groove parameter, 606
Groove template selector drop-down
  menu, 507
Group Enables setting, 373
groups
  adding tracks to, 253
  of clips, 339
  creating, 251–252
  deleting, 253
  edit and mix, linking, 254–255
  editing, 253–254
  enabling, 252–253
  overview, 250
  renaming, 253
  sends, using for, 552
  track parameters for, 250–251
Groups list, 207
GS standard, 82
GUI (graphical user interface), 87
Guitar Input jack, 150

guitars. *See also* bass guitars; electric
  guitars
  compressing, 586–587
  connecting to Mbox Mini, 139
  Eleven Rack interfaces for, 151–152
  equalizing, 577
  mics for recording, 105
  mixing, 532

H

hand drums, 286–287
hard drives
  backing up, 134
  disk allocation for, 292–294
  Mac computers, 118–119
  overview, 20
  PC computers, 125
  required for Pro Tools, 19
hard knee setting, 269
hardware inserts, 563
hardware settings
  clock source, 158–159
  footswitch control, 159
  optical format, 159
  overview, 157–158
  peripherals, 158
  sample rate, 159–160
Hardware Setup option, 157
headphone jack
  on Mbox, 140
  on Mbox Mini, 138
headphones
  connecting to Eleven Rack, 149, 151
  connecting to Mbox, 143
  connecting to Mbox Mini, 140
  connecting to Mbox Pro, 144, 147
  using as monitors, 28–29
headroom, defined, 267
heads
  choosing, 280
  placing mics near, 282
Heal Separations command, 390
healing clips, 390–392
Height selector, 248

HF (High Frequency) filter, 596–597
HF Cut setting, 604
HF Only parameter, 595
Hide Selected Tracks option, 246
hiding tracks, 245–247
high frequencies, 98
High Frequency (HF) filter, 596–597
High Performance option, 127
hi-hats
  EQ recommendations for, 576
  equalizing, 579
  miking, 284–285
Hipcast website, 688
Hi-speed USB, 41
Hold setting, 592
Horizontal Zoom buttons, 185, 344
horns, 576
Host Engine setting, 161
Host Processors setting, 161
host sites, 680–683
HostBaby website, 680
host-based systems, 123, 156
humidity, effect of on microphones, 112
H/W buffer size, 160–161
HW Insert Assignments option, 227
H/W Insert Delay tab, 164–165
hybrid microphones, 108
hybrid preamps, 14
hyper-cardioid microphones, 100

1

IDE ATA/ATAPI Controllers option, 130
Identify Synch Point option, 394
iLike website, 682
impedance level, 12
Import – Overlay new on existing playlists
  option, 227
Import – Replace existing playlists
  option, 227
Import Key Signature from MIDI File check
  box, 222
Import section, 225
Import Session Data dialog box,
  223–227, 228

Import Tempo Map from MIDI File check
  box, 222
importing files into sessions
  audio files, 215–220
  MIDI files, 220–222
  overview, 215
  tracks, 222–228
In Addition To Match options, 330
In port, 76
In Shape settings, 426
In Ticks field, 510
Include Control Changes in Undo Queue
  check box, 613
Include Edit, Mix, and Transport Display
  Settings check box, 208
Include Media selector, 171
indicators
  changing selections using, 364–365
  making selections with, 364
Input Assignments option, 227
Input button, 198, 199, 201
input devices
  instruments, 10
  microphones, 11
  overview, 9–10
  sound modules, 11–12
input jack, 62
Input meter
  Bombfactory limiter, 589
  Compressor plug-in, 584
Input Only Monitoring mode, 300
Input Quantize MIDI operation, 514
Input Quantize option, 503
Input tab, 162–163
inputs
  assigning to tracks, 244–245
  automating tracks, 610
  auxiliary, 546–547
  on Mbox Mini, 138
  MIDI, 449–450
  monitoring, 457
  quantizing, 445–447
Insert at Edit Location option, 494
Insert at Playback Location option, 494
Insert at Playback Location with Grid
  option, 494

Insert function, 543
insert jack, 62–63
Insert menu, 495
Insert Position Selector control, 557
Insert Slot option, 379
Insert tab, 164
inserting
  MIDI events, 496–499
  notes, 483
  routing effects, 600–601
inserts
  hardware, 563
  overview, 547–548
  plug-ins, using with, 556
  turning off effects in, 548
Inserts view section, 205–206
Install Pro Tools icon, 122
instrument cords, 34
instrument tracks
  automation of, 610
  enabling recording for, 455–456
  hearing, 457–458
  overview, 200–201, 242
  playing back, 461
  recording, 458
instruments. *See also specific instruments*
    by name
  connecting to Mbox Mini, 139
  as input devices, 10
Instruments section, 200
interfaces
  Eleven Rack, 148–152
  M-Audio, 152–153
  Mbox, 137–147
internal hard drives, 21
Internal option, 158
Internet
  creating MP3 files for, 677–680
  downloadable music files, 673–677
  e-mail newsletters, 690–691
  offering free downloads on, 684–685
  overview, 673
  podcasting on, 688
  promoting music on, 689–690
  putting music on music host sites, 682–683
  selling CDs on, 689
  selling downloads on, 685–686

setting up music websites on, 680–681
social media networking, 683–684
streaming audio on, 686–687
in-the-box mixing
  bounce options, 629–631
  overview, 629
  performing bounces, 631–632
Inverse Pan button, 554
Invert command, 266
I/O Settings drop-down menu, 166
isolation booths, 47
Items to Copy section, 169
iTunes program, 678, 685

J

Joint Stereo mode, 677

K

Key Signature Map check box, 225
Key Studio device, 153, 154
Key timeline, 195
Keyboard Focus option, 190
keyboard workstations, 85
kick (bass) drum
  compressing, 588
  equalizing, 575–576, 578
  miking, 281–282
Knee knob, 583

L

L setup, 43
large-diaphragm condenser
    microphones, 271
Last.fm website, 683
Latch Record Enable Buttons option, 313
Latch Record Enable mode, 295–296
Latching Behavior for Switch Controls in
    "Touch" check box, 613
latency
  adjusting, 301–302
  defined, 21, 137, 160
  low-latency monitoring, 302–303

lead vocals
    compressing, 585–586
    equalizing, 577
    mixing, 532
Legato option, 509–510
Length counter, 178
Length/Info column, 495
Length/Info field, 488
level for recording, 298
leveling, 639
levels
    of arrangement, 536
    balancing, 650–651
    dynamics, 535–536
    managing, 526–527
    overview, 534–535
Levels section
    Compressor plug-in, 584
    De-Esser plug-in, 595
    expander/gate plug-in, 593
LF (Low Frequency) filter, 597
Librarian menu
    AudioSuite menu, 561
    Real Time Plug-In window, 558
Limit Range setting, 510
Limit To option, 292, 509
limiters
    Bombfactory BF76 peak limiter, 590–591
    mastering with, 638
    overview, 25–26, 589
    settings for, 589–590
Line Pencil tool, 480–481, 621
Linear Sample Display option, 189
Linear Tick Display option, 189
Linearity Display Mode button, 189
line-level inputs, 136
lines
    editing with Pencil tool, 489–490
    unbalanced, 34
Link Record and Play Faders check
        box, 301
Link settings, 426
Link Timeline button, 190
Link Track and Edit Selection button, 190
Listen option, 595
listening, importance of, 536–537

lists
    Groups, 207
    overview, 192–193, 205
    Show/Hide Tracks, 205–206
live rooms, 50
Location drop-down menu, 221–222
Location field, 307, 452
Location slider, 217
locking clips, 405–406
Logic program, 22
Long option, 162
Loop Record mode, 176, 290–291, 324
loop recording, 324, 468–469
looping playback, 385
loud music, 648
Low Frequency (LF) filter, 597
low-latency monitoring, 302–303
low-pass/high-pass EQ, 568, 573
low-shelf/high-shelf EQ, 568, 572–573
low-Z cables, 37
LP filter, 604
LPF setting, 605

M

Mac computers
    differences with PC computers, 157
    installing Pro Tools on, 122
    overview, 117
    settings for, 120–122
    system requirements of, 117–120
MailChimp website, 691
Main Output Assignments option, 226
Main Outputs jack, 150–151
Main Playlist Options menu, 227
Maintain Absolute Time Code Values
        option, 224
Maintain Relative Time Code Values
        option, 224
Maintenance section, 127
Map Start Time Code To option, 224
Marker memory location, 373–374
Marker option, 372
Markers ruler, 380
Markers timeline, 195–196

Markers/Memory Locations check box, 225
Master bus, 67
master clock, 158
master control section, 68
master decks, external, 632–633
Master fader
  overview, 68
  routing with, 545–546
Master Fader tracks
  automation of, 610
  overview, 202–203, 241
Master Level meters, 71
Master Link button, 558
Master Out jack, 72
mastering
  balancing levels, 650–651
  bits, 651–653
  CDs, 31
  computer files, 31
  dynamics, 646–648
  leveling, 639
  overview, 30–31, 637–638, 643–644
  paying professionals for, 640–642
  preparing for, 639–640
  processing, 638
  sample rate, 653–654
  sequencing songs, 638, 654–655
  setting up sessions for, 644–646
  tonal balance, 648–650
Material eXchange Format (MXF)
    audio, 216
M-Audio interfaces, 152–153
Maximum option, 162
Mbox interfaces
  Mbox, 140–143
  Mbox Mini, 137–140
  Mbox Pro, 143–144
  overview, 137
memory
  overview, 19
  required for Pro Tools, 19–20
memory locations
  changing properties of, 381–382
  copying and pasting, 382–383

creating, 375–377
extending selections to, 370
General Properties, 375
Marker, 373–374
Memory Locations window, 377–379
New Memory Location dialog box,
    371–373
overview, 371
recalling, 379–380
renaming, 381
Selection, 374–375
Memory Locations window, 377–379, 380
memory locators, 319
Merge/Replace feature, 463–464
Meter button, 180
meter events
  choosing, 307–308
  creating, 308–309
  editing, 309–310
meters
  choosing, 451–452
  overview, 195
metronome, setting, 180
mic lockers, 112
Mic PRE settings, 225
Mic Preamps tab, 164
mic simulator program, 103–104
microphones. *See also* miking
  applications for, 104–106
  buying, 103–104
  compressors, 108–109
  connecting to Mbox Mini, 139
  cords for, 109
  daily care for, 111–112
  as input devices, 11
  overview, 91
  polarity patterns, 98–102
  pop filters, 110–111
  preamp, compressor, and equalizer
    combos, 109
  preamps, 106–108
  stands for, 109–110
  storing, 112–113
  types of, 92–98

MIDI. *See also* editing MIDI; operations, MIDI; recording MIDI
  cables for, 76
  connections, 38
  control-change messages, 80
  on Eleven Rack, 149, 151
  exporting files from sessions, 233–234
  file formats, 31, 171–172, 220
  GM level 1 compatibility, 81–82
  GM level 2 compatibility, 82
  importing files, 221–222
  interfaces for, 83, 89–90
  on Mbox, 142
  on Mbox Pro, 144, 147
  MIDI channels, 78–79
  modes of, 80–81
  overview, 75–76
  performance-data messages, 79
  ports for, 76–78
  samplers, 86–90
  sound generators, 83–86
  system-common messages, 80
  system-exclusive messages, 80
MIDI controllers
  building, 88
  devices, 82–83
  overview, 16, 88–89
  using during mixing, 528–529
MIDI controls section, 179–180
MIDI Event list. *See* Event list
MIDI events
  drawing velocity or continuous controller data, 483
  editing note attributes, 487–488
  inserting notes, 483
  inserting program changes, 484
  moving notes, 487
  note duration, 486
  note pitch, 485–486
  note velocity, 486
  overview, 482
  time locations, 486–487
MIDI Input filter, 444–445
MIDI Mute button, 200
MIDI Output selector, 200
MIDI Pan slider, 200

MIDI Thru feature, 443–444
MIDI tracks
  automation of, 611
  overview, 199–200
MIDI Velocity meter, 200
MIDI volume icon, 200
MIDI Window Settings icon, 210
MIDI workstations, 85
midrange-dominated sound, 271
miking
  ambient, 261–262
  backup vocals, 272–274
  distant, 261
  drum sets, 279–286
  electric basses, 276–277
  guitars, acoustic, 277–279
  guitars, electric, 274–277
  hand drums, 286–287
  overview, 259–260
  percussion, 287
  spot, 260
  stereo, 262–263
  transients, 266–270
  vocals, 270–272
Min Strip Duration slider, 420
mini keyboards, 477
Mirrored MIDI Editing function, 191
Missing Files dialog box, 172
mix groups, 254–255
Mix option
  Create Group dialog box, 252
  delay settings, 605
  Mbox, 143
  Mbox Mini, 140
Mix Window
  channel strips, 197–203
  lists, 205–207
  overview, 196–197, 541–542
Mix/Edit Groups option, 227
mixing. *See also* automation; in-the-box mixing
  adjusting levels, 534–536
  analog mixers, using, 530
  bouncing, 627
  control surfaces, using, 528
  digital mixers, using, 529–530

ear fatigue, 538–539
external effects, 562–565
external master decks, using, 632–633
importance of listening during, 536–537
making several versions during, 539
managing levels, 526–527
MIDI controllers, using, 528–529
Mix window, 541–542
Output windows, 552–555
overview, 525–526
plug-ins, 555–562
reference CDs, 537–538
routing, 545–552
signal flow, 542–544
sound control during, 51–55
stereo field feature, 531–534
submixing by recording to tracks, 627–629
mixing boards
   analog, 58–59
   assign switches, 67
   channel auxiliary (Aux) send knobs,
      64–66
   channel strip, 61
   computer control surfaces, 60–61
   digital, 59–60
   equalization, 64
   faders, 67
   input jack, 62
   insert jack, 62–63
   Mute switch, 66–67
   output jacks, 71–73
   overview, 14–16, 57
   Pan knob, 66
   patch bays, 73–74
   Pre/Post switch, 66
   routing/busing signals, 67–71
   Solo switch, 66–67
   Trim knob, 64
Mobile Pre device, 153, 154
modes. *See also specific modes by name
   or type*
   of automation, 611–612
   overview, 80–81
Modify Groups dialog box, 253
modulation, 607

Mon Out (Monitor Outputs), 139, 142
monitoring inputs, 457
monitoring tracks
   adjusting latency, 301–302
   Auto Input Monitoring mode, 300
   Input Only Monitoring mode, 300
   low-latency monitoring, 302–303
   overview, 299–300
   setting up, 300
monitors
   active, 29
   headphones, 28–29
   near-field, 29
   overview, 28
   passive, 29
   setting up, 45
   speakers, 29–30
Monitors jack, 72
mono
   downloadable music files in, 676–677
   tracks in, 242
Mono After Touch view, 475
Mono Aftertouch MIDI event, 496
Mono mode, 676
monophonically, defined, 80
mono/TS connector, 34–35
motherboards, 123–124
mounted toms, 284
moving clips
   with Edit modes, 404–405
   nudging, 402–404
   overview, 402
   shifting, 404
MP3 files
   choosing encoding software, 677–678
   encoding music, 678–680
   overview, 31–32, 677
muddiness, defined, 276
Multichannel audio clips, 339
Multiple Mono option, 631
multiple tracks, 313–314
multiple-pattern microphones, 101–102
multitimbrality
   defined, 79
   overview, 84–85

music
  host sites for, 682–683
  promoting, 689–690
  websites for, 680–681
Music Host Network website, 686
Musical Instrument Digital Interface (MIDI)
    controller, 12. *See also specific entries*
    beginning with MIDI
Mute Automation and Setting option, 226
Mute button
  on mixing boards, 66–67
  Track Output windows, 554
Mute view, 341, 475
muting
  clips, 407–408
  tracks, 255–256
MXF (Material eXchange Format) audio, 216
MySpace website, 683

N

Name field
  Memory Location dialog box, 373
  New Window Configuration dialog box, 208
  Window Configurations List window, 210
navigation controls, 189–192
near-CD quality, defined, 674
near-field monitors, 29, 45
Netwell website, 46
Never Check For Solutions option, 127
New Configuration option, 207, 211
New Hardware Wizard feature, 138
New Memory Location dialog box
  general properties, 373
  overview, 371–372
  time properties, 372–373
New Memory Location option, 379
New Session dialog box, 644–646
New Track Default Output option, 164
New Track option, 219–220, 222
New Tracks dialog box, 242
New Window Configuration dialog box, 208
Next Step button, 516
No Scrolling option, 317, 459
No Sounds option, 128

No Time option, 344
nondestructive editing, 338
Non-Destructive Record mode, 176, 290, 323
None option
  Alternates Match Criteria dialog box, 330
  New Memory Location dialog box, 373
Normal Zoom mode, 345
Norton Ghost program, 134
notch EQ, 572
Note button, 180
note chasing, 479
Note Length slider, 515
Note MIDI event, 496
Note Selector drop-down menu, 446
note-off MIDI feature, 76
note-on MIDI feature, 76
notes
  custom duration of, 482
  duration of, 486
  editing attributes of, 487–488
  MIDI, deleting, 484–485
  moving, 487
  pitch of, 485–486
  selecting from mini keyboards, 477
  selecting with Pencil tool, 476
  velocity of, 486
Notes Between option, 512
Notes view, 474, 491
Nudge function, 401–402
Nudge Value display, 191
nudging clips, 402–404
nudging selections
  end point, 369
  entire selection, 367–368
  overview, 367
  start point, 368–369
Numerical Volume display, 199

O

Object Grabber tool
  overview, 365
  selecting objects, 365
  time-based selection, 366
oblique room mode, 49

Off option, 198
Offline clips, 339
offline plug-ins
  overview, 559–562
  using to process audio clips, 562
Offset Grid By field, 447, 505
offsetting tracks, 447–448
Omni Off/Mono MIDI mode, 81
Omni Off/Poly MIDI mode, 81
Omni On/Mono MIDI mode, 80
Omni On/Poly MIDI mode, 80
omnidirectional microphones
  overview, 98–99
  recording vocals with, 273–274
On Grid option, 389
online backup service, 21
Online button, 174
Only During Record check box, 306
Open Ended Record Allocation
      section, 292
operating systems
  Mac computers, 118
  PC computers, 125
operations, MIDI
  Change Duration, 509–510
  Change Velocity, 508–509
  Flatten Performance, 517–518
  Grid/Groove Quantize, 504–507
  Input Quantize, 514
  MIDI Operations window, 501–502
  overview, 501
  Real-Time properties, 518–522
  Restore Performance, 516–517
  Select/Split Notes, 511–514
  Step Input, 515–516
  Transpose, 511
optical format setting, 159
Optical option, 158
optimizing hard-drive space, 292
Options: Look Ahead button, 593
Options menu, 493
organs, mixing, 533
Original Time Stamp option, 343
Out port, 76
Out Shape settings, 424
Output button, 198, 199, 201

output jacks
  Aux Return jacks, 73
  Direct Out jacks, 72
  Master Out jack, 72
  Monitors jack, 72
  overview, 71
  Phones jack, 72
Output Selector box, 554
Output windows, 552–555
outputs
  assigning to tracks, 244–245
  on Mbox Mini, 138
  MIDI, 449–450
overdubbing
  defined, 311
  loop recording, 468–469
  MIDI Merge/Replace feature, using,
      463–464
  overview, 325–326, 463
  punching in and out, 464–468
overdubs, defined, 72
overhead microphones, 104, 285–286, 580
overhead panels, 53
Overlap option, 510

p

padding, defined, 236, 435
Page Scroll During Playback option, 364, 494
Page scrolling option, 317, 459
Pan Automation and Setting check box, 226
Pan controls
  on channel strip, 544
  on mixing boards, 66
  Track Output windows, 554
Pan MIDI event, 496
Pan view, 341, 475
Panner Link button, 554
Parabolic tool, 621
parametric equalization, 24, 567–568, 572
passive monitors, 29
pasting
  automation, 624–625
  clips, 411
  memory locations, 382–383

patch bays, 44, 73–74
Patch select button, 199, 201
patches
  defined, 469
  program, 488–489
  setting on tracks, 478
Path Meter View Box button, 552
Path Selector button, 554
PC computers
  AutoPlay feature, disabling, 130–131
  connecting hardware on, 132
  Control Panel settings, 127–129
  differences with Mac computers, 157
  DMA feature, enabling, 130
  installing Pro Tools on, 132–133
  overview, 122
  settings, 125
  system requirements, 123–125
  virus protection, disabling, 131–132
  Windows 7 Classic theme, 126–127
PC Wizard tool, 19
PCI cards, 21
peak EQ, 572
peak limiters, 590–591
Pencil tool
  automation, using for, 625
  creating copies of original files, 418–419
  editing lines with, 489–490
  Free Hand tool, 480
  Line tool, 480–481
  overview, 187, 418, 479–480
  Random x tool, 482
  redrawing waveforms with, 419–420
  selecting notes with, 476
  Square tool, 481
  Triangle tool, 481
percussion
  compressing, 588
  equalizing, 576, 580
  miking, 106, 287
  mixing, 533
Performance Options dialog box, 128
performance-data MIDI messages, 79
peripherals setting, 158
Personalization icon, 126
phantom power feature, 93, 136

phase cancellation, 266
phase holes, 639–640
Phase Invert button, 559, 584
Phones jack, 72
Phones knob, 70
pianos
  equalizing, 576, 580
  mixing, 533
piezo-electric pickups, 88
pitch bend feature, 76, 444
Pitch Bend MIDI event, 496
Pitch Bend view, 475
Pitch check box
  Flatten Performance operation, 518
  Restore Performance operation, 517
pitch correction, 28
pitch of notes, 485–486
Play button, 175, 312–313
Playback Engine settings
  CPU Usage Limit, 161
  Delay Compensation Engine, 161–162
  Host Engine, 161
  Host Processors, 161
  H/W buffer size, 160–161
  overview, 160
  Plug-In Streaming Buffer, 162
playback loops, 318–319
playing tracks
  changing sounds, 459–461
  overview, 458–459
  scrolling options, 459
Playlist selector button, 182
playlists
  choosing from, 329, 352
  creating, 351
  defined, 338
  deleting, 351–352
  duplicating, 351
  overview, 350
  recording to, 326–327
  renaming, 352
  selecting sections of, 322
  setting pre- and post-rolls within, 315–316
  track, selecting sections of, 465
plosives, defined, 110, 271
Plug-In Assignments setting, 226

Plug-in Controls Default to Auto-Enabled check box, 613
Plug-in Selector menu
  AudioSuite menu, 560
  Real Time Plug-In window, 557
Plug-In Settings and Automation option, 226
Plug-In Streaming Buffer setting, 162
plug-ins. *See also* dynamic processors
  AudioSuite offline plug-ins, 559–562
  compressors, 268
  equalization, 569–570
  overview, 555
  Real Time plug-ins, 556–559
  writing automation for, 617–618
podcasting, 688
podHoster website, 688
polarity patterns
  cardioid, 100
  figure-8, 100–101
  multiple-pattern, 101–102
  omnidirectional, 99
  overview, 98
Poly Aftertouch MIDI event, 496
polyphony, 79, 80, 84
pop filters, 110–111
ports, MIDI, 76–78
Position Between option, 512
post-crossfades, 428–429
post-rolls, 177–178, 314–316, 383–384
Power Options icon, 127
preamp trim knob, 297
preamps
  hybrid, 14
  on Mbox, 140
  microphones, 106–108
  overview, 13, 136
  solid-state, 13
  tube, 13
pre-crossfades, 427–428
Pre-delay setting, 603–604
Preferred Plans section, 127
Pre/Post button, 554
Pre/Post Roll Times option, 373
Pre/Post switch, 66
Pre-Quantize check box, 507

pre-rolls, 177–179, 291, 314–316, 383–384
Preserve Note Duration check box, 446, 504
Preset list button, 558
Presets setting, 424, 426
pressing vinyl, 668–669
Preview button, 561
Previous button, 558
Pro Tools
  10 version, 156, 256
  HD and HDX versions, 157, 256
  installing on Mac computers, 122
  installing on PC computers, 132–133
  MP version, 22, 156, 256
  overview, 155
  SE version, 22, 156, 256
Process button, 562
Process Mode Selector menu, 561
processing, 638
processor-based systems, 157
processors, dynamics. *See* dynamic processors
processors, signal. *See* signal processors
ProFire 2626 device, 153, 154
ProFire 610 device, 153, 154
Program Change Event entry window, 496
Program Change view, 475
program data
  change markers, 489
  deleting, 485
  inserting changes to, 484
  overview, 488
  patches, 488–489
promoting music, 669–671, 689–690
Prompting for Each Duplicate option, 231
protocol, defined, 76
proximity effects, 263
punching in and out
  defined, 291
  overview, 321, 464
  performing, 323–324, 466–467
  "punching on the fly", 467–468
  selecting section of track playlists, 465
  selecting sections of track playlists, 322
  Start and End Point markers, 322–323, 465–466
  using Start/End fields, 321, 464–465

Put the Computer to Sleep When It Is
Inactive For option, 120
Put the Hard Disk to Sleep When Possible
check box, 121

Q

Q settings
low-pass/high-pass EQ settings, 573
low-shelf/high-shelf EQ settings, 572
parametric EQ settings, 572
Quantize Grid section, 446, 505
quantizing
clips, 406–407
inputs, 445–447
¼-inch plugs
on Mbox Pro, 146
mono/TS, 34–35
overview, 34
stereo/TRS, 35–36
QuickPunch mode, 325
QuickPunch Record mode, 176, 291–292
QuickTime files, 216

R

rack-mountable modules, 12
RAM (random-access memory)
Mac computers, 118
overview, 19–20
PC computers, 125
Random Pencil tool, 482, 621
Randomize option
Change Velocity section, 509
Grid/Groove Quantize MIDI operation, 505
quantizing inputs using, 447
Rate setting, 606
Ratio setting
Bombfactory limiter, 590
Compressor plug-in, 268–269, 583
expander/gate plug-in, 592
RCA connector
on Mbox Pro, 144, 146
overview, 37
Real Time AudioSuite (RTAS) plug-in
format, 556

Real Time plug-ins
overview, 556
properties of, 518–522
Real Time Plug-In window, 557–559
routing, 556–557
working with, 559
Recall with Template check box, 507
recalling memory locations
from Markers ruler, 380
from Memory Locations window, 380
overview, 379
Record button, 176, 312, 325
Record Enable button, 182, 294, 313
Record modes
Destructive, 290
Loop, 290–291
Non-Destructive, 290
overview, 176, 289–290
QuickPunch, 291–292
Record Safe mode, 227, 296–297
recorders
computer, 18–22
digital, 17–18
overview, 17
recording audio
auditioning takes, 327–331
click tracks, 304–310
deleting takes, 332–333
disk allocation, 292–294
enabling, 294–297
loop recording, 324
monitoring tracks, 299–303
multiple tracks, 313–314
overdubbing, 325–326
overview, 289, 311
playing back tracks, 316–320
pre- and post-rolls, 314–316
punching in and out, 321–324
QuickPunch mode, 325
Record modes, 289–292
recording to playlists, 326–327
setting levels for, 297–298
setting record range, 299
single tracks, 311–313
starting over, 320
recording CDs. *See* CDs

recording levels, 298
recording MIDI
  click tracks, 451–454
  creating tracks, 448–449
  deleting takes, 461–463
  enabling tracks for, 455–456
  hearing instrument tracks, 457–458
  monitoring inputs, 457
  overdubbing, 463–469
  overview, 439, 455
  playing back tracks, 458–461
  recording tracks, 458
  setting up MIDI devices for, 439–448
  settings for, 449–450
  system-exclusive data, 469–471
  Wait for Note option, 456
Recording Studio device, 153–154
recording to tracks, submixing by, 627–629
ReCycle file format, 216
Red Book CDs, 660
Redo Step button, 516
Refer to Source Media option, 223
reference CDs, 537–538
reflections, 48
reflectors, 50, 52, 277
regions, 184
Relative Grid mode, 349
Relative mode, 405
Release knob
  Bombfactory limiter, 590
  Compressor plug-in, 583
  expander/gate plug-in, 593
Release Velocity field, 488
Releases check box, 446, 504
Remove Existing instrument Tracks check box, 222
Remove Existing MIDI Clips check box, 222
Remove Existing MIDI Tracks check box, 222
Remove Overlaps and Leave Gap option, 510
Remove Synch Point option, 394
Rename button, 421
renaming groups, 253
Repeat command, 412
Repeat dialog box, 412
Replace feature, 463–464
Replacing with New Files option, 231

replication of CDs, 666–668
Resolution setting, 631
Resolve Duplicate File Names By options, 231
Restore Performance MIDI operation, 516–517
Restore Performance option, 503
Return to Zero button, 312, 317
reverb
  overview, 27, 602
  settings for, 602–604
  using, 604
Rewind button, 175
ribbon microphones
  overview, 92, 97–98
  recording vocals with, 272
Rock Web website, 680
Roland GS standard, 82
rotational speed, 20, 119
routing
  auxiliary inputs, 546–547
  defined, 59
  effects, 600–602
  inserts, 547–548
  Master fader, 545–546
  overview, 545
  Real Time plug-ins, 556–557
  sends, 548–552
  tracks, 564–565
routing signals. *See* busing signals
RTAS (Real Time AudioSuite) plug-in format, 556
ruler bar, 465–466
Ruler View selector, 189
rulers, 193–196
rumble noise, 24

S

sample rate, 159–160, 228, 653–654
Sample Rate Conversion options, 225, 228
Sample Rate setting
  Bounce dialog box, 631
  creating sessions, 166
  exporting from sessions, 230

samplers
    MIDI controllers, 88–89
    MIDI interfaces, 89–90
    overview, 86–87
    sequencers, 89
    soft-synths, 87–88
    sound cards, 88
sampling rate, 17
Save a MIDI File As dialog box, 233–234
Save As Template option, 170
saving sessions, 167–169
Scale By option, 508
scaling breakpoints, 490–491
Score Editor Settings option, 209
Score Window Settings icon, 210
Scroll After Playback option, 364
Scroll During Edit Selection option, 494
Scroll to Edit Selection option, 494
scrolling options, 317–318, 459
Scrub feature, 319–320
Scrubber tool, 187
scrubbing, defined, 319
S-Curve tool, 424, 426, 621
secondary counter feature, 177
seek time, 20, 119
Select a Power Plan screen, 127
Selection Indicator fields
    changing selections using indicators,
        364–365
    making selections with indicators, 364
    overview, 364
Selection memory locations, 374–375
Selection option
    Audio Import Options dialog box, 220
    MIDI Import Options dialog box, 222
    New Memory Location dialog box, 372
Selection Range option, 330
Selection Reference menu, 560–561
selections
    changing length of, 367
    changing using indicators, 364–365
    extending length of, 369–370
    extending to adjacent tracks, 371
    looping playback of, 385
    making with indicators, 364
    moving to other tracks, 370

nudging, 367–369
    overview, 367, 383
    playing, 383
    pre- and post-rolls, 383–384
    silencing, 420–423
    start and end points, 384–385
Selector tool
    automating, 417
    overview, 414–415, 476
    using Smart tool with, 492
Select/Split Notes MIDI operation, 511–514
selling CDs, 689
Send A-E Views window, 550
Send Assignments window, 550
Send Names window, 550
Send Output Assignments option, 226
Send Output window, 550, 554–555
Send Postfader function, 544
Send Prefader function, 543–544
Send selector, 554
Send View Level Meters window, 550
sends
    groups, using for, 552
    overview, 548–550
    plug-ins, using with, 557
    turning off effects in, 551
    viewing, 550–551
    writing automation for, 618–619
Sends area, 201
Separate button, 421
Separate Clips command, 388–389
Separation Grabber tool, 187, 389–390
sequencer devices, 83
sequencers, 89
sequencing
    defined, 75
    overview, 638
    songs, 654–655
Session Format drop-down menu, 168–169
Session Parameters section, 169
Session Start option, 220, 222
sessions
    compacting files, 434–435
    consolidating selections, 433
    creating, 165–167
    exporting files from, 228–234

files, 172
importing files into, 215–228
for mastering, 644–646
opening, 167
overview, 165
removing unused clips, 433–434
saving, 167–169
templates, creating for, 170–171
Set All To option, 508
Set Velocity To slider, 516
Settings menu
AudioSuite menu, 561
Real Time Plug-In window, 558
7-band EQs, 571–572
Share with SoundCloud option, 231
shelf EQ, 24
shifting clips, 404
Short option, 162
Show Icons option, 211
Show Main Counter option, 378
Show Note End Time option, 494
Show Note Length option, 494
Show Only Selected Tracks option, 246
Show option, 355
Show Sub Counter option, 378, 493
Show/Hide Tracks list, 192, 205–206, 246–247
Shuffle mode
Insert Silence command, using in, 423
moving clips in, 405
overview, 184–185, 348
placing clips in, 392
Trimmer tool, using in, 399
sibilants, 271
side chains
overview, 596
setting up, 596–597
using, 597–598
Side-Chain Assignments option, 227
signal flow, 542–544
signal processors
chorus effects, 607
delay, 605–606
dynamic processors, 24–26
effects processors, 26–28
equalizers, 23–24
overview, 23, 599

reverb, 602–604
routing effects, 600–602
silencing selections
inserting amounts of silence, 422–423
overview, 420
results of, 423
Strip Silence command, 421–422
Strip Silence window, 420–421
silica gel, 112
single tracks, 311–313
Single Zoom mode, 346
16 bit mastering, 653
Size option, 603
slap-back echo, 606
sleeve of connectors, 34
Slider Settings options, 507
Slip Edit mode, 392
Slip mode
Insert Silence command, using in, 423
moving clips in, 405
placing clips in, 392
Trimmer tool, using in, 399
small-diaphragm condenser
microphones, 272
Smart tool
in Automation view, 416–418, 492
in Controller view, 492
in Notes view, 491
overview, 187, 413–414, 491
in Waveform view, 414–416
Smooth and Thin Data After Pass check
box, 612
Snap to Bar check box, 307, 309, 452
snare drums
compressing, 588
equalizing, 576, 578–579
miking, 283
social media networking, 683–684
soft knee setting, 269
soft-synths, 87–88
software
audio files, 171
Bus tab, 164
for computer recorders, 22
differences between Mac and PC
computers, 157

software *(continued)*
  for encoding music, 677–678
  hardware settings, 157–160
  H/W Insert Delay tab, 164–165
  Input tab, 162–163
  Insert tab, 164
  on Mac computers, 119–120
  Mic Preamps tab, 164
  MIDI files, 171–172
  Output tab, 163–164
  overview, 155
  Playback Engine settings, 160–162
  Pro Tools versions, 155–157
  sessions, 165–171, 172
Software Update option, 121
solid-state microphones, 93–94, 107
solid-state preamps, 13
Solo button
  on channel strip, 198
  on mixing boards, 66–67, 70
  overview, 182
  Track Output windows, 554
Solo Safe setting, 227
soloing tracks, 255–256
Song Start option, 220
Sort by Time option, 378
sound cards, 88
Sound Designer file format, 216
sound generators
  drum machines, 85
  overview, 82–83
  sound modules, 85–86
  synthesizers, 84–85
sound isolation, 46–48
Sound Isolation Company website, 46
sound modules, 11–12, 85–86
Sound Pressure Level (SPL), 96
Sound Resource (AIFL), 216
sounds, MIDI
  instrument tracks, 461
  MIDI tracks, 459–461
  overview, 459
Source properties, 223
Source Sample Rate option, 225
Source Tracks section, 225
spaced pairs, 263–264

S/PDIF (RCA) option, 158
S/PDIF connections
  on Eleven Rack, 151
  on Mbox, 142
  on Mbox Mini, 140
  on Mbox Pro, 144, 147
  overview, 39, 136
speakers
  cabinets for, 276
  cords for, 35
  as monitors, 29–30
spindle speed, 20, 119
SPL (Sound Pressure Level), 96
splitting stereo tracks, 408–409
spot miking
  defined, 259
  overview, 260
Spot mode
  moving clips in, 405
  placing clips in, 392
  using Trimmer tool in, 399
Square Pencil tool, 481
Square tool, 621
Standard setting, 424, 426
Standard Trimmer tool, 186, 398–399
Standby power option, 127
standing waves, 52
stands for microphones, 109–110
Start markers
  dragging along ruler bar, 465–466
  overview, 322–323
start points
  aligning clips using, 396
  auditioning, 384
  nudging, 368–369
Start/End fields, using in Transport
    window, 321, 464–465
starved-plate preamps, 14
Step Increment section, 515
Step Input MIDI operation, 515–516
Step Input option, 503
stereo
  cords for, 35
  downloadable music files in, 676–677
  microphones for, 265–266

panning, 526
splitting tracks from, 408–409
tracks in, 242
stereo field feature
   backup vocals, 532
   bass, 533
   drums, 533
   front or back, 533–534
   guitar parts, 532
   lead vocals, 532
   overview, 531–532
   percussion, 533
   piano/synthesizers/organs, 533
Stereo Interleaved option, 631
stereo miking
   Blumlein technique, 263
   defined, 259
   overview, 262
   problems with, 266
   spaced pairs, 263–264
   stereo microphones, 265–266
   X-Y pairs, 262–263
Stereo mode, 677
stereo/TRS connector, 35–36
Stop button, 175
storage service, 21
streaming audio, 686–687
Strength setting, 447, 505
stringed instruments. *See* acoustic
   instruments
Strip button, 421
Strip Silence command, 421–422
Strip Silence window, 420–421
Strip Threshold slider, 420
stuck notes, 443
studio
   heat and dust, 45
   monitors, 45
   overview, 42–43
   setting up, 43–44
   sound control during mixing, 51–55
   sound control during tracking, 49–50
   sound isolation in, 46–48
Sub (submix) faders, 68–69
Submix bus, 67
Subtract option, 508

super-cardioid microphones, 100
SuperSpeed USB, 41
Swing check box, 447
Switch Audio Converter Software
   program, 678
synch points
   aligning clips using, 397
   creating, 394–395
   overview, 394
   placing at Edit Insert point, 395–396
synthesizers
   mixing, 533
   overview, 84–85
Sysex view, 475
system drive, 119
System Preferences option, 120
system-common MIDI messages, 80
system-exclusive data, 444, 469–471
system-exclusive MIDI messages, 80

T

Tab to Transients function, 189–190, 366
takes
   auditioning, 327–331
   defined, 311
   deleting, 332–333, 461–463
   loop recording, 324
   overdubbing, 325–326
   overview, 320
   punching in and out, 321–324
   QuickPunch mode, 325
   recording to playlists, 326–327
   starting over, 320
   undoing, 462
Takes List drop-down menu, 328–329
tangential room mode, 49
Tap Tempo/Tuner button, 152
Target button
   Real Time Plug-In window, 559
   Track Output window, 554
TDIF connections, 40
TDM (Time-Division Multiplexing) plug-in
   format, 556
templates, sessions, 170–171

tempo events
  in click tracks, setting, 307
  creating, 308–309
  editing, 309–310
  setting, 451
  timeline of, 194–195
Tempo Match feature, 606
Tempo/Meter Map check box, 225
Thin command, 622
thin sound, 71
thinness, defined, 276
thinning automation
  automatically, 622
  overview, 621
  Thin command, 622
3:1 rule, 263
threshold, defined, 26
Threshold setting, 268, 583
Thru port, 76
Thunderbolt connections, 41–42
time aligning, 266
time code data, defined, 224
Time Code Mapping options, 224
Time Grabber tool, 186
time grid, 185
time locations, 486–487
time rulers, 194
time signatures, 195
time stamps
  on clips, 342–344
  defined, 354
Time Trimmer tool, 399–400
Timebase rulers, 194
Time-Division Multiplexing (TDM) plug-in
    format, 556
Timeline Ruler button, 349–350
timelines, 194
Timing (Quantization) check box
  Flatten Performance operation, 518
  Restore Performance operation, 517
Timing option, 507
Toast Titanium program, 678
tom-toms
  equalizing, 576, 579
  miking, 284
tonal balance, 648–650

Top option, 512
Track Active State option, 227
Track Colors option, 227
Track Comments setting, 227
track controls
  functions of, 182–183
  optional windows in track sections,
      183–184
  overview, 181–182
Track Height Selector button, 182, 341–342
Track Heights option, 373
Track ID check box, 330
Track Name button, 182
Track name display, 199
Track Offset options, 225
Track Output window, 552–554
Track Selector control
  Real Time Plug-In window, 557
  Track Output windows, 552
Track Type icon, 199–202
Track View settings, 189, 227
tracks. *See also* equalization
  assigning inputs and outputs to, 244–245
  assigning voices to, 257
  automation of, 610–611
  click, 304–310, 451–454
  creating, 242–243, 448–449
  duplicating, 243
  enabling recording for, 455–456
  formats of, 242
  freeing up voices from, 258
  Grabber tool, using with, 476–477
  grouping, 250–255
  hearing, 457–458
  Import Session Data dialog box, 223–227
  importing, 227–228
  inserting EQ plug-in, 569–570
  monitoring, 299–303
  naming, 243–244
  notes, selecting with Pencil tool, 476
  notes from mini keyboards, selecting, 477
  offsetting, 447–448
  overview, 222, 239–241
  patches, setting on, 478
  placing clips in, 392–394
  playing back, 316–320, 458–461

recording, 311–316, 458
routing, 564–565
section of, selecting, 465
selecting, 362–363
Selector tool, 476
soloing and muting, 255–256
sound control during tracking, 49–50
sound of, 459–461
stereo, splitting, 408–409
submixing by recording to, 627–629
types of, 241–242
views for, 245–250, 473–476
voice priority, setting, 257–258
writing automation for, 616–617
Transform Sustain Pedal to Duration
    option, 510
transients
  compressing, 268–270
  defined, 189, 259
  overview, 266–267
  placing mics, 267–268
  setting levels, 267
transparent sound, 94, 107
Transport window
  adjusting, 174
  controls, 174–176
  Counters section, 176–177
  Expanded section, 177–178
  MIDI controls section, 179–180
  overview, 173
  pre-roll and post-roll fields, using in,
      314–315
  Start/End fields, using in, 321, 464–465
Transport Window Display Settings
    option, 209
Transport Window Settings icon, 210
Transpose MIDI operation, 511
Transpose option, 521
Triangle Pencil tool, 481, 621
Trim command, 64, 400–401
Trim Start to Insertion command, 401
Trim to Selection command, 390, 400
Trimmer tool
  automating, 416–417
  automation, using for, 626

overview, 414
Smart tool, using with, 492
trimming clips
  Nudge function, 401–402
  overview, 398
  Standard Trimmer tool, 398–399
  Time Trimmer tool, 399–400
  Trim command, 400–401
trimming crossfades, 429
truncation, 652
tube condenser microphones, 104
tube microphones, 93–94, 107–108
tube preamps, 13
TuneCore website, 686
tuning drum sets, 279–281
Tuplet check box
  Grid/Groove Quantize MIDI
      operation, 505
  Input Quantize dialog box, 446
  Step Input MIDI operation, 515
Twitter service, 684
Type 0 Standard MIDI files, 220
Type 1 MIDI files, 220

U

unbalanced connections, 12, 34
Undo feature
  limits of, 357
  overview, 355
  performing, 356
  setting levels of, 355–356
  undoing takes, 462
Undo Record option, 332
Undo Step button, 516
unmuting clips, 407–408
Unused Clips Except Whole Files
    option, 357
Unused Clips option, 235
UPC bar codes, 666
Update Active Configuration option, 212
USB connections, 21, 40–41, 90
USB standards, 41
Use All Available Space radio button, 293
Use AutoPlay For All Media check box, 131

Use Dither option, 426
Use in Playlist button, 561
Use Input Velocity option, 516
Use Round Robin Allocation for New
    Tracks check box, 293
Use Squeezer option, 230
User Time Stamp option, 343–344
User-defined clips, 339
U-shaped setup, 44

V

velocity
  drawing, 483
  of notes, 76, 486
Velocity Between option, 512
Velocity check box
  Flatten Performance operation, 518
  Restore Performance operation, 517
Velocity field, 507
Velocity option, 520–521
velocity stalk, 486
Velocity view, 475
versions, making, 539
Vertical Zoom buttons, 185, 344–345
vibrato feature, 76
Video Media Options drop-down menu, 224
View All option, 211
View Both Tracks button, 424
View Configs with Edit Window Settings
    option, 211
View Configs with Mix Window Settings
    option, 211
View Configs with Transport Window
    Settings option, 211
View Configs with Window Layout
    option, 211
View filter icons, 210
View Filter option, 377–378, 494
View First Track button, 424
View Second Track button, 424
views
  adjusting track height, 341–342
  assigning colors to, 247–248
  automation, 619

changing size of, 248–249
choosing clip time stamps, 342–344
deleting, 250
displaying clip names, 342
moving, 249
overview, 245, 340, 473–476
selecting track view, 340–341
showing and hiding, 245–247
zooming in on all tracks with Zoom
    buttons, 344–345
zooming in on ruler, 346
zooming in on single track with Zoom
    tool, 345–346
zooming with Zoom Toggle command,
    346–347
vinyl, pressing, 668–669
virus protection, disabling, 131–132
Visual Effects tab, 128
Vocal Studio device, 153, 154
vocals
  compressing, 585–586
  equalizing, 575, 577
  miking, 105, 270–272
  mixing, 532
Voice Assignments option, 227
voice coil, 97
Voice Dyn/Off selector, 198
Voice selector button, 183
voices
  assigning to tracks, 257
  freeing up, 258
  setting priority of, 257–258
Volume Automation and Setting option, 226
Volume MIDI event, 496
Volume slider, 217
Volume view, 341, 475

W

Wait for Note option, 179, 456
Warped clips, 339
WAV format, 31, 216
Waveform view
  creating crossfades, 416
  fade-ins and fade-outs, 415–416

Grabber tool, 415
   overview, 340, 414
   Selector tool, 414–415
   Trimmer tool, 414
waveforms, redrawing, 419–420
websites, for music, 680–681
What to Quantize section, 446, 504
Whole-file audio clips, 339
Window Configurations drop-down menu,
   211–212
Window Configurations List window, 210
windows
   configurations to, 207–213
   Edit, 181–196
   Mix, 196–207
   overview, 173
   Transport, 173–180
Windows 7 setup, 126–127, 442–443
Windows Classic option, 126
Windows key, 3
Windows Media (WMA) file format, 216
wordclock, defined, 136
writing automation
   overview, 616
   on plug-ins, 617–618
   on sends, 618–619
   on tracks, 616–617

X

XG protocol, 82
XLR connector, 36–37, 148
X-Y pairs, 262–263

Y

Y cords, 36, 63
Yamaha XG protocol, 82

Z

zero-latency monitoring, 143
Zoom Toggle Track Height drop-down
   menu, 347
zooming, 185–186, 187, 344–347, 424

Notes